Moving and Learning

THE ELEMENTARY SCHOOL
PHYSICAL EDUCATION EXPERIENCE

Moving and Learning

THE ELEMENTARY SCHOOL PHYSICAL EDUCATION EXPERIENCE

BEVERLY NICHOLS, Ph.D
Associate Professor,
University of Vermont,
Burlington, Vermont

TIMES MIRROR/MOSBY

ST. LOUIS   TORONTO   SANTA CLARA

1986

Editor: **Nancy K. Roberson**
Developmental Editor: **Michelle A. Turenne**
Manuscript Editors: **Lin A. Dempsey, Debra Ketterer, Mark Spann**
Book Designer: **Kay M. Kramer**
Cover Designer: **Diane M. Beasley**
Production: **Celeste Clingan**

Library of Congress Cataloging-in-Publication Data

Nichols, Beverly.
Moving and learning.

Bibliography: p.
Includes index.
1. Physical education for children—United States.
2. Movement education—United States—Curricula.
I. Title.
GV223.N53   1986   372.8′6   85-21743
ISBN 0-8016-3851-8

9 8 7 6 5 4 3 2 1   02/C/277

To
The Metcalf Girls

Ev, Jo, Edna and Do

PREFACE

Considerable changes have occurred in elementary school physical education in the past two decades. With the emergence of movement education, elementary school physical educators have added the teaching of the movement content to the teaching of motor skills and the development and maintenance of physical fitness.

Although there is recognition of the need for physical activity throughout life, studies continue to report a relatively inactive life-style for children and adolescents. A significant number of physicians involved in sports medicine are beginning to focus concern on the activity habits of children. Since activity habits are established early in life, physical education has an important role in teaching children about fitness and the effects of exercise on the human body as well as providing vigorous activity and teaching children motor skills for use outside of school. The development and maintenance of health-related physical fitness is an integral part of physical education as presented in this resource book. Activities that maximize participation for all children in vigorous activity to ensure the development of all aspects of health-related physical fitness are found throughout the book. Emphasis is given to developing fitness activities within each unit of instruction to help children learn how fitness may be developed and maintained in activities that are challenging and fun rather than through repetitive, boring exercises.

The elementary school years are important for motor skill development. During this time children master fundamental motor skills and are introduced to beginning dance and sports skills to encourage their continued participation. Activities to practice skills include not only those desired for improvement of technique but also those that lead to greater un-derstanding of how the body is used and how skills are adapted under varying conditions.

Knowledge about human movement is an important aspect of the physical education experience. Since one cannot be totally prepared in physical education for every possible movement activity in which one might participate in a lifetime, an understanding of one's movement potential and factors affecting movement is essential to future learning. Learning to use the body and space efficiently and to control force, balance, and time is important in moving effectively in any situation and essential to becoming physically educated.

Sport and dance are important elements in our culture. The movement curriculum developed in this book is unique in its approach to establishing the relationship between knowledge, motor skills, and movement activities. This is accomplished by first suggesting movement activities to develop an understanding of human movement, an essential aspect of beginning physical education experiences. This understanding is then applied to the learning of fundamental motor skills and later to the development of dance and sport skills for use in and out of school.

This teachers' resource blends the teaching of knowledge, motor skills, and fitness as well as the development of appropriate social skills throughout the book with the intent that greater understanding of human movement, movement efficiency, and the importance of physical activity to a healthy life-style might result.

WHO IS THE BOOK WRITTEN FOR?

This book is written as a resource for teachers. It is appropriate for both classroom teachers and physical education specialists in grades K-6. As an added feature, there is a listing of Essential Elements mandated by the State of Texas keyed to the book and to the companion Lesson Plans Manual. You will find these inside the front cover of this book.

The extensive coverage of the activity content for elementary school physical education offers teachers a wide variety of skills and activities with progressions appropriate for children in grades K-6.

SPECIAL CONTENT FEATURES

Several features set *Moving and Learning* apart from other elementary school physical education books:

Movement Curriculum

The content and development of *Moving and Learning* are consistent with an educational philosophy that recognizes the relationship between knowledge and skillful movement. Chapter 10 is devoted to activities to be used in introducing the movement concepts to children. In each activity chapter, movement concepts important for success are identified and activities to enhance development are suggested. Emphasis on increasing awareness of one's movement potential and the use of other movement concepts are stressed in all activities included in the book. Activities are used as the means for furthering understanding of human movement rather than as ends in themselves.

Developmental Approach and Levels

The developmental approach emphasizes progression in learning as a result of maturation and experience rather than age alone. Since the movement experiences of children differ considerably from one school setting to another, expectations for performance vary for children in any particular class and from school to school. This approach also recognizes the great variability within any one particular group of children. This approach assists the teacher in identifying the developmental needs of individuals rather than generalizing for the needs of the particular group. Throughout the book, selection of activities is based on four developmental levels rather than grade levels, which tend to overlook the individual needs of children. Each developmental level includes expectations for motor, cognitive, and social skill development.

Social Skills

Although most elementary school physical education texts cite social skills as an objective of physical education, few devote much space to its development. If appropriate social skills are to result, physical education experiences must be carefully planned and conducted. Children not only need skills to help them fully participate in the family and society but they also need those social skills important for successful participation in motor activities. Unique to *Moving and Learning,* Chapter 12 explores how to teach the skills necessary for cooperation and competition, which are an important part of physical education experiences at the elementary school level.

Health-related Physical Fitness

Chapter 13 is devoted to health-related physical fitness, which is introduced as an important objective of physical education in Chapter 1. It includes each of the components of fitness and their importance to health, as well as activities to assess and improve each component. Emphasis is placed on making fitness fun while enhancing the health-related physical fitness of children.

Variety of Activities

Moving and Learning includes a variety of activities for selection in developing program goals at all developmental levels in the elementary school. Numerous activities are included to introduce and apply movement concepts, and to practice motor skills. Additionally, a large selection of rhythmic activities, dance, games and team sport lead-ups, gymnastics, and other individual activities are provided to enhance development.

Teaching Styles

A variety of teaching styles are introduced in Chapter 6 with special emphasis placed on those that permit greater decision making on the part of the student. Throughout the text, examples of exploration, problem solving, and guided discovery are found in the movement challenges designed to enhance individual learning.

Evaluative Criteria and Teaching Points

A requirement for effective teaching of motor skills is the analysis of movement to determine individual needs. *Moving and Learning* develops evaluative criteria or teaching points for each of the locomotor and manipulative skills presented. These also serve as points of reference for children as they move and analyze their own performance.

Games Analysis

In selecting games for children, it is necessary to examine the motor skills and knowledge needed and the social interactions required for successful participation. Introduced in Chapter 21, the games analysis approach is designed to help teachers match games to the needs of the children in the class and to recognize the motor, social, and knowledge components for which they might be selected. This is accomplished through the use of games analysis charts in Chapters 22 through 28.

Safety

Chapter 7 helps establish the importance of a safe environment in physical education. In addition to concern for legal liability, the teacher strives to establish an environment in which children are encouraged to try new skills and to feel safe. Some activities require special considerations in planning to provide for the safety of all participants. Concerns for safety are identified in each of the activity chapters to help teachers in providing a safe movement environment.

ORGANIZATION

Moving and Learning is divided into eight parts. Part One is divided into two chapters. The first chapter discusses the importance of physical education as a part of the elementary school curriculum, its contributions to child development, and its goals and objectives. Chapter 2 traces child development over the elementary school years and the implications for physical education.

Part two discusses curriculum development. A historical perspective of where we have been and the emergence of the movement curriculum is developed in Chapter 3. The relationship between knowledge of human movement and motor skills is established as the basis for curriculum planning. The developmental approach is introduced and the progression in learning processes examined. Chapter 4 focuses on all aspects of elementary school physical education and provides a sequence for planning curriculum, the annual plan, and unit and daily planning.

Part Three provides suggestions for conducting physical education experiences. Learning principles are introduced in Chapter 5 and a variety of teaching styles, direct and indirect, are discussed with examples given in Chapter 6. Chapter 7 discusses safety and liability and offers a variety of strategies for effective classroom management. Chapter 8 identifies the need for effective communication, measures for class control, concerns in meeting special needs of children, and considerations for developing independent learners. Chapter 9 introduces evaluation techniques for assessing student needs, the effectiveness of teaching, and the success of the physical education program.

Part Four introduces the content for the four objectives of physical education. Chapter 10 includes teaching suggestions and activities to begin the study of human movement—body awareness, space, and qualities of movement. Chapter 11 presents the fundamental motor skills with a description and evaluative criteria for each, recognition of movement principles and other movement concepts, and activities to enhance their development. Chapter 12 introduces social skills, not to be left to chance, but rather to be taught in physical education classes, and includes skills of cooperation and competition. Chapter 13 establishes guidelines for the development and maintenance of health-related physical fitness with tools for assessment and activities to enhance each of the components.

Parts Five, Six, and Seven develop what might be referred to as the traditional content of physical education—gymnastics and other individual activities, dance, and games and team sports lead-ups. Skills are presented with evaluative criteria, suggestions for teaching, common errors, and activities to use for their development. Activities are presented in order of difficulty. In addition, in a presentation unique to *Moving and Learning*, the important movement concepts are identified and activities suggested to further their development within the context of the activity itself. Tables in Chapter 15 help the teacher select dances based on developmental level, dance steps, formations used and nationality. Games analyses in Chapter 22 through 28 help teachers match games to the developmental level of the children in the class.

Part Eight concludes the text with a discussion of extracurricular activities—intramurals, special events, open gym, and special interest groups. Although youth sports are not a part of the physical education program, many elementary school age children participate in these activities. Parents and teachers are often called on to help organize or conduct these activities. Guidelines for extracurricular and youth sports are included along with special concerns that must be addressed for developing activities designed to be in the best interests of children.

TEACHING AIDS IN THE BOOK

A number of teaching aids are included to assist the teacher and student in using the material contained in each chapter.

Part Openers

Each of the eight parts of the book begins with an overview about the material covered in that part, the relationship between its topics, and their importance to elementary school physical education.

Chapter Objectives

Objectives are listed at the beginning of each chapter to assist the teacher in identifying the chapter's key topics.

Second Color

Unique to *Moving and Learning,* a second color is used throughout to highlight and identify important aspects of each chapter and to facilitate teacher use.

Photographs

To enhance the presentation, numerous photographs are used throughout the text. Additionally, photographs are used to depict the movement sequence for many of the skills. These assist the teacher in analyzing movement and in helping children to develop the most efficient form.

Line Drawings

Drawn illustrations throughout the text demonstrate and clarify various concepts and activities and are also used to show movement sequences for a variety of skills.

Boxed Materials

Boxed materials including guidelines and examples aid the teacher in organizing information discussed in the chapters and provide practical tools for future reference.

Chapter Summaries

Summaries at the close of each chapter carefully reiterate its main points and reinforce the chapter objectives.

References

Each chapter provides the most complete and up-to-date references for further study of the material covered.

Additional Readings

Unique in this text, selected resources are provided with annotations to enhance the learning process.

Glossary

Important terms are defined in the comprehensive glossary and are printed in boldface italics throughout the text. Additionally, the glossary contains the page locations where terms first appear.

Appendixes

Equipment and other materials are needed to teach physical education. To aid schools in this selection process the following material is included:

1. Equipment for use in elementary school physical education with suggestions for care and storage
2. Vendors for elementary school physical education equipment including a list of records and record companies for dance and rhythmic activities
3. Plans for homemade equipment
4. Computer software for use in physical education
5. Screening devices, sources, and IEP forms for determining student needs
6. Video materials for use in physical education/ health programs
7. Classroom activities that identify activity content throughout the book that may be adapted for indoor classroom use

Lesson Plans Manual

The Lesson Plans Manual that accompanies the book has been prepared by Murray E. Banks, M.S., Elementary Physical Educator for the Bethel Public Schools, Bethel, Vermont, and professional fitness consultant. The manual is designed to give examples of lessons for elementary school children in a variety of activities and at varying developmental levels. Each lesson includes a statement of the day's objectives and the development of fitness, motor skills, and movement concept activities. Where appropriate, a culminating activity for the lesson is included to bring together the various parts of the lesson. Material is referenced to the pages in the book where the in-formation needed by the teacher may be found. While a variety of teaching strategies are suggested, each lesson maximizes the activity time for each child in the class. Selected lessons are provided for various stages of each activity, enabling the teacher to see a progression in learning for each developmental level. The manual is perforated and three-hole punched for convenience of use.

Beverly Nichols

CONTENTS

Part Seven   EDUCATIONAL GAMES AND TEAM SPORTS LEAD-UPS

Moving and Learning

THE ELEMENTARY SCHOOL
PHYSICAL EDUCATION EXPERIENCE

Coca-Cola
OLYMPICS
VOLUNTEER

OVERVIEW AND VALUE OF PHYSICAL EDUCATION

Physical education is an important part of the elementary school program. It contributes to the overall goals of the elementary school as well as making its unique contribution to the study of human movement and the development of motor skills. It is concerned with the total development of children: their physical, motor, cognitive, social, and emotional development.

Each child comes to the physical education experience with a unique genetic and experiential background. Teachers carefully examine the age characteristics of the individual children in their charge to plan and conduct meaningful movement experiences.

1 Physical Education in the Elementary School

2 The Elementary School Child

I

PHYSICAL EDUCATION IN THE ELEMENTARY SCHOOL

CHAPTER OBJECTIVES

1 To discuss the contributions of physical education to the goals of an elementary school

2 To describe the important role of the teacher in establishing an environment for learning and fostering positive attitudes toward active participation

3 To discuss the importance of physical activity in the development of children

4 To establish preparation for a lifetime of physical activity as the goal of physical education in the elementary school and to identify ways to meet this goal

The challenge of American education today is to provide the opportunity for each individual to achieve his or her potential. Since learning is a life-long process, the school strives to help each child learn how to learn and to develop the basic tools so that learning can take place in an ever-changing environment.

ELEMENTARY SCHOOL EDUCATION

Physical education is an important part of the school's instructional program. It is the only area of the curriculum in which motor skills and the study of human movement are presented and the opportunity to facilitate their development is provided. In addition, it contributes to the overall goals of an elementary school, an example of which can be found on p. 3.

All areas of the curriculum strive to enhance the development of positive feelings toward life-long learning by:

1. Helping children set realistic goals of achievement

2. Providing for the needs of children at varying levels of skill and social development through a series of progressively more challenging tasks

3. Encouraging each child's self-appraisal of accomplishments

4. Developing a variety of skills and knowledges that form the foundation for future learning

5. Supporting learning in one area of the curriculum in all other curriculum areas

6. Fostering creative thinking through the use of problem solving, analysis, and the seeking of solutions in a variety of settings

7. Teaching democratic ideals as children develop skills in working together; respecting, supporting, and listening to the contributions of others; and developing adequate communication skills

The results of research into the relationship between the opportunity for physical activity and academic achievement are as yet inconclusive. In a study of Texas children, Magill and Ash[12] found a significant positive relationship between participation in

ELEMENTARY SCHOOL GOALS

A. To help a student develop honesty with himself and others, and to develop within the student the desire for honest and consistent effort . . .

B. To help a student develop a self-image that is positive and realistic . . .

C. To help a student develop the skills that are needed in a rapid and changing society . . .

D. To provide for an equal learning opportunity for all students . . .

E. To develop the power of independent thought and creative expression . . .

F. To develop the awareness of the inseparability of freedom and responsibility . . .

G. To help each student to develop effective basic communication skills: literary skills of reading, writing, speaking, listening and computation . . .

H. To help each child develop a clarification and understanding of his values that will allow him to make a contribution to society . . .

I. To help each child respect the feelings and contributions of others . . .

J. To develop in each student a feeling for the challenge and importance of learning . . .

K. To diagnose the social-emotional, health and learning problems of the individual student . . .

From Superintendent's Office, South Burlington Vermont School District

children's sports and test scores in language arts and reading among third-grade children. However, because there was no consistent pattern evident over the other elementary school grades tested, they considered these results specious.

A positive physical education experience may, however, support learning in the classroom by enhancing individual attributes important to a favorable learning environment. In the Vannes experience in France,[1] in which nearly one third of the school day during the elementary school years was devoted to physical education, comparing the experimental group to the control group indicated favorable results for the experimental (physical education) group. Not only did those devoting one-third time to physical education do better academically, but also they were less susceptible to stress, were more independent, had good social skills, were more mature for their age, and had an outlet for controlling aggression. Students from the one-third time experience entering the secondary schools were academically comparable to other students, in better health, stronger, keener, and happier; tired less easily; had better attitudes about school; experienced fewer discipline problems; adapted to the new school more easily; and suffered less stress. As a result of this study the Ministries of Education and Youth and Sports in France concluded that physical education had positive effects on learning and should be regarded as an important part of the elementary and secondary school curriculum.

In many classrooms in the United States, where learning has traditionally taken place from a sitting position, we are beginning to see more movement. Classroom teachers, recognizing the children's activity needs, are beginning to incorporate movement activities in the teaching of many subjects. Cratty,[4,5] Gilbert,[8] Werner and Burton,[16] and others have written books offering suggestions to teachers regarding the use of movement to enhance academic abilities and promote learning in reading, math, science, and social studies. Movement in the classroom is not a substitute for physical education, but a well-planned and conducted program of physical education can contribute to learning in reading, math, science, and social studies as it strives to meet its own objectives.

The Physical Education Teacher In The Elementary School

The elementary school years are an important time in the development of attitudes toward active participation for life. While children enjoy moving and participate enthusiastically in physical education activities, these feelings may be enhanced or discouraged during the elementary school physical education experiences.

The teacher of physical education may be a classroom teacher or a *physical education specialist,* a

teacher specially trained and certified in physical education. The teacher is an important figure in the maintenance of positive feelings about moving. Positive attitudes are strengthened through the careful planning and conduct of the physical education activities. Positive attitudes result when children find success and the support of their classmates and teacher. Further discussion regarding the establishment of a positive learning environment is found in Chapter 8.

Not only is physical education an important part of the elementary school curriculum but also the physical education teacher is a vital part of the education team. All teachers share in the educational achievements of the children they serve. Teachers from all areas of the curriculum work together to provide the best possible learning environment for every child. Each teacher sees the child from a slightly different perspective. Yet all contribute essential pieces to the picture that describes every child's developmental status.

The teacher of physical education sees the children in a more informal setting than in the classroom. Since each child has the opportunity to interact with all other children more frequently, social behaviors such as sharing and working with others may be observed more easily in the gymnasium than in the classroom. The health status of children may also be readily observed. Problems of posture, the feet, obesity, low fitness level, and low level of motor ability may be first recognized during physical education activities.

When special needs are identified, physical education teachers must make every effort to communicate their observations to other school personnel. Children with special needs in the school environment rarely if ever experience problems in only one area of the curriculum. Physical education and classroom teachers must make a point of sharing their concerns regarding individual children with other school professionals such as the psychologist, nurse, or social worker. The planning together of all those involved is essential if children are to get the most from their school experience.

PHYSICAL EDUCATION AND THE DEVELOPING CHILD

The elementary school years are a time of continual change for the developing child. As a part of the elementary school curriculum, physical education contributes uniquely to human development in the areas of physical growth, fitness, and the development of motor skills. It also contributes to the social, affective, and cognitive components as well as playing an important role in the development of the *self-concept*.

Physical Growth

The relationship between human growth and physical activity is well documented. Physical exercise is an important component in the growth of healthy tissues, organs, and bones. Muscles increase in size and strength with use but atrophy with decreased activity; muscle atrophy occurs at an alarming rate with disuse during illness or injury.

Bones show evidence of increased mineralization as a result of activity. However, during long periods of inactivity, such as when broken bones are set in casts, decalcification of bone occurs; about one-half the calcium is lost from a bone in 1 week.[1] Houston concludes that activity throughout life is important in the maintenance of healthy bones.[1]

Since exercise requires an increased oxygen supply to working muscles, the acceleration of breathing and heart action to meet this demand results in an increased lung capacity, a better exchange of gases, and a more efficient heart muscle capable of pumping more blood. Unfortunately, this is not a permanent condition; cardiovascular efficiency is reduced when exercise levels are lowered.

The human body was built for movement. Vigorous physical activity is required for the development of a healthy body. With the increase in school busing and a more sedentary life-style, the only place where many children are encouraged to be physically active is in physical education classes. Although daily vigorous physical education is recommended, physical education classes may be available only two or three times per week in some schools. The physical education teacher must strive to teach the skills and knowledges important to active participation in an atmosphere that encourages their use in out-of-school play.

Health-related Physical Fitness

Health-related physical fitness is defined as the ability to perform strenuous activity without excessive fatigue and to show evidence of the traits and capacities that limit the risks of developing diseases or disorders that limit a person's functional capacity.[14] Components of health-related physical fitness are identified as *muscular strength and endurance, flexibility, cardiorespiratory endurance,* and *body composition*.

Physical education plays a vital role in the development and maintenance of fitness. Daily physical activity is a must. A program of progressively more demanding activities is provided until the desired level of fitness is achieved, at which time a maintenance program is incorporated. Fitness is considered to be important both in delaying cardiovascular problems in later life and in the recovery from heart attacks. Physical education programs in the elementary school should promote attitudes favorable to an active life through fun-filled vigorous activity.

An increasing body of evidence appears to link many adult health problems to inactivity during the childhood years. Autopsies of children show the beginnings of clogged blood vessels, a serious problem in adults with cardiovascular disease. Rose,[15] documenting the progress of arteriosclerosis in men, states that the first signs may appear as early as age 2 years. As the disease progresses, it becomes a serious health problem by the early 40s. High levels of cholesterol and triglycerides, two substances found in the blood, are commonly associated with risks of coronary heart disease. Blood levels of both have been shown to be reduced as a result of exercise.[3]

Childhood obesity, usually the result of poor nutrition and lack of activity, is another problem believed linked to adult health problems. The increase in childhood obesity in recent years is a cause of concern to pediatricians. Obese children are handicapped in physical education. Since the added weight tires these children more quickly and makes vigorous activity uncomfortable, they tend to be relatively inactive, which impedes normal physical development. Physical educators must be sensitive to the needs of overweight children in planning experiences that will be nonthreatening and will encourage them to move actively. They must help children to recognize their weight problems and help provide the support and guidance needed to overcome them.

Motor Skills

Many of the basic motor patterns, including locomotor and manipulative skills, are established before the child enters school. An instructional program early in the school experience, beginning preferably in kindergarten, is needed to ensure the refinement of these basic skills and the acquisition of more difficult locomotor and manipulative skills used in dance and sports activities.

The early motor experiences of children vary considerably. Some children begin their school years with a wealth of motor experiences behind them, including the opportunity to attempt many locomotor, climbing, and manipulative skills. For others motor experiences have been limited.

Opportunity for activity does not necessarily result in effectively and efficiently executed skills. Instruction early in life is essential. The longer children perform skills incorrectly, the more difficult it becomes to unlearn faulty patterns and to use more efficient movements. Physical education provides the opportunity for all children to learn and practice mo-

tor skills. The physical education classes broaden the child's repertoire of skills and the opportunities to use them. No other area of the curriculum concerns itself with the development of these important movement skills.

Cognitive Development

Physical education is a cognitive experience. Through physical education children develop an understanding of the body's potential for movement, mechanical principles and laws governing movement, and the application of these *movement concepts* in a variety of situations. It is more than a rote memorization of general rules and other knowledge about sports. Mastery of rules and knowledge is important for success in most games and sports, but as games and sports become more complex, the individual must also judge the conditions under which specific rules and knowledge apply.

Problem solving is an important part of the physical education experience. In the beginning years it is often used in helping children understand movement concepts. In later years it is used in the application of movement concepts to specific activities and in the analysis and subsequent strategy development of more advanced games.

Creative thinking is encouraged in the development of the movement concepts and in dance and gymnastics in which children learn to express their ideas in routines and original dances. Developing a flowing movement sequence and remembering it so that it may be repeated again and again is another outcome of dance and gymnastics.

Verbalization of ideas, a movement analysis, or a new strategy is as important to learning and sharing in physical education as it is in the classroom. Verbally identifying important elements leads to greater understanding. It also provides information essential to the teacher in determining individual needs. Although physical educators have a goal in planning to maximize the activity for all, they must also give children the opportunity to think, to develop their ideas, and to communicate these ideas to others.

Self-Concept

Maslow and Rogers state that each person controls the development of his or her own self-concept, that each of us has an inner drive for self-fulfillment.[17] Children enter school with a self-concept that has been developed over their short lives through the fulfillment of needs and feeling of worth derived from their relationship with their family. During childhood significant others will influence children's feelings about themselves as the environment expands. The school, teachers and peers, will play a part in development of the children's estimates of themselves.

Research into the relationship between self-concept and motor success is inconclusive. We do know children's self-concepts include feelings about their physical being. A pleasant physical appearance is valued in our society, as is physical skill. One might also observe that elementary school children with good physical skills are not only looked up to by their peers but also are often the children assuming leadership roles at an early age. Perhaps their valued skill level gives them the self-assurance or confidence needed to lead their less able classmates.

Physical education can play an important role in the development of a positive self-concept. The physical education class is conducted in an atmosphere in which the emphasis is on new learning rather than accentuating incompetencies and in which the progress of each child is valued. When children come to school, they create a social position for themselves. The physical education teacher must set the stage so the physical education experience is a positive one in which honest effort is valued by both peers and teachers, each child engaging in physical activitiy is successful, and children find physical education to be a pleasant, encouraging experience. Further discussion regarding the development of a positive self-concept may be found in Chapter 12.

Social Development

The social development of children undergoes dramatic changes during the elementary school years. During this 7-year period an egocentric 5-year-old will be transformed into a group-centered 12-year-old. It is a period for learning beginning social skills and the more advanced skills required for working cooperatively with others.

Social systems outside the school affect social development as well. The family, community recreation, and the media are important in this regard. Through the interaction with and the modeling of significant others, children will learn to accept certain behaviors for themselves. These may or may not be the behaviors the school wishes to encourage. For instance, the aggressive behavior of professional baseball players toward their opponents or the win-at-all costs attitude of some Little League coaches is not to be valued. The school can only affect those attributes that are reinforced inside the school setting. If the child encounters a difference of opinion outside, there will probably be little change.

Children come to the physical education experience with varied backgrounds in social development. Some have had little experience in playing with other children, whereas others have had much experience in playing with brothers, sisters, or other children in the neighborhood. Some have learned to share, to take turns, and to play with other children of similar ages, but for others this experience will be almost totally new.

The informality of physical education classes provides a natural environment for the development of social skills and emotional control. Group cooperation, leadership, followership, and group problem-solving skills are an important part of the physical education experience. Good sportsmanship and emotional control are valued outcomes of programs in which competition is carefully controlled and winning and losing are kept in perspective.

GOAL AND OBJECTIVES OF PHYSICAL EDUCATION

The primary goal of physical education in the schools is to assist each child in the development of the attitudes, skills, and knowledge of human movement that will result in a lifetime of participation in physical activity. This goal can be achieved only in an environment in which the natural enjoyment of moving is enhanced for all children, the poorly skilled and the "average" as well as the gifted. It is an atmosphere in which each child feels the thrill of achievement. These experiences enhance attitudes that value physical activity as an essential part of one's life-style.

Research evidence indicates that participation as a child is important in predicting adult involvement. This participation must be a quality experience geared to meet the needs of each child, not only the physical needs but the social and emotional needs as well. In the physical education class the developmental needs of children are met through a variety of experiences of progressively more challenging motor activities.

Regarding this goal, Bain[2] suggests:

1. Student enjoyment of movement participation is the central purpose of the physical education program.
2. Specific program decisions should be based on the contribution to student enjoyment of movement participation.
3. Programs should be evaluated by examining the degree to which they increase students' voluntary participation in movement activities.

Only when we have achieved this goal will the impact on the lives of those we serve be realized and the value of physical education in our schools be fully recognized.

Objectives Of Physical Education

Besides the contributions it makes to the overall school objectives, physical education has its unique contributions to the development of children. To meet our goal of a lifetime of activity, instruction in physical education must result in the following:

1. The development of understanding in the study of human movement
2. The development of an understanding of the importance of health-related physical fitness and the tools to assess, acquire, and maintain fitness throughout one's lifetime
3. The acquisition of fundamental motor skills and higher level sports and dance skills and provision for their use now and in the future in a variety of activities
4. The development of appropriate attitudes and social skills essential to successful participation

Study of human movement

Although we often think of physical education as being a movement experience, knowledge regarding human movement (the movement concepts) is an important outcome of the physical education program. Content areas to be considered include a knowledge of body parts and joint actions; space and time; mechanical principles of force, balance, and trajectory; and laws of motion.

Teaching these subjects does not imply that children are seated in a classroom. These concepts should be a part of the gymnasium experience taught at the appropriate time through activity. The Basic Stuff,[13] educational materials developed by the NASPE Council on Physical Education for Children of the AAHPERD is designed to help teachers teach the knowledge basic to our understanding of human movement and human behavior. Developing a better understanding of human movement and the movement potential of the body provides a sound basis for children to understand and learn to perform a variety of motor skills and to adapt them as the situation requires. Chapter 10 outlines the content for the study of human movement and offers suggestions for its instruction.

Health-related physical fitness

Children need to develop an understanding of their body's need for activity and fitness. Studying the effects of physical activity on the body including the muscular, cardiovascular, and respiratory systems is

an important part of the physical education movement experience. In an activity in which the children have been running hard and respiration is increased, the teacher might take a little time to talk about what's happening internally as children take a short rest. Dr. Norma Carr of Cortland State University in an address to the Vermont Association for Health, Physical Education, Recreation and Dance suggested it would be great, if in a science lesson in which children were studying the human body, the children could say, "We already learned that in physical education." Knowing what fitness is, why it is important to healthful living, what the relationship is between activity and diet, how the various components may be tested, what their own fitness assessment is, and how to improve and maintain an appropriate level of fitness are important to a healthy life. Chapter 13 further develops the components of health-related fitness and suggests activities for use in developing them.

Motor skills

The teaching of motor skills has been an important part of the physical education experience since its beginning. Elementary school children need exposure to many skills and a variety of situations in which to use them. Fundamental motor skills should be mastered first before a child is taught advanced skills. Many performers are limited by their own inadequacy in the fundamentals when they have moved too rapidly to higher level skills. The physical educator's role is to take the children where they are and to challenge them to greater accomplishments by individualizing the tasks to be accomplished.

In the learning of skills, children should be able to verbalize the key points to success and also to analyze their performance based on these key elements. To be successful one must be able to diagnose one's efforts. For example, children who are not able to get the ball into the target might recognize they are not following through in the direction of the target. Chapter 11 begins the development of the content in this area of study, including suggestions for providing a variety of experiences for practice and integrating skill learning with the study of human movement.

Social skills

Physical education is a laboratory for social interaction. In the early years, sharing equipment, taking turns, learning to listen to the ideas of others, following directions, developing independence in learning, and learning courtesy, cooperation, and responsibility are important in an environment in which individual skill development and movement exploration are achieved. In later years there are opportunities to interact in small and large groups in cooperative play. Group acceptance of everyone and group planning and decision making in increasingly complex social environments become important outcomes of the physical education experience. Controlled competitive activities in which opponents are equal in skill and emphasis is placed on performance rather than score should result in appropriate social behavior and favorable attitudes toward participation since success and failure are kept in balance.

In recent years, physical education has come under some attack regarding its claims of enhancing positive social attributes, since there is little research to back up these claims. Merely participating in an activity does not necessarily achieve positive social results. Too often the opposite may be the result. Sportsmanship and fair play are learned only through identification with and imitation of admired persons who demonstrate these behaviors. Havighurst[9] suggests that character values and attitudes are well defined by age 10 and change very little from this point on. If this is true, then early physical education experiences may have more of an impact on the development of favorable attitudes and resultant behaviors than upper elementary school years. Chapter 12 suggests strategies that encourage appropriate social behaviors.

SUMMARY

Physical education is an important part of the elementary school instructional program. Not only does it contribute to the overall goals of education but also it contributes uniquely in the study of human movement, the development and maintenance of fitness, and the development of motor skills and appropriate social behaviors. Goals and objectives are not necessarily the automatic outcomes of the program for which they have been stated. Careful planning is needed if objectives are to be realized. Physical activity is the medium in which learning takes place.

Although physical educators agree that children need a variety of movement experiences, one must keep in mind that any particular activity unit is the means to a greater end, which is to become movement educated. As a result activity participation can be changed as interests and maturation dictate throughout one's lifetime. In actuality it does not matter if everyone learns basketball, or any other specific activity. It is what we learn about movement and ourselves in the activity that counts. We must not lose sight of our goal and objectives in planning and conducting daily lessons.

REFERENCES

1. Bailey, D.: The growing child and the need for physical activity. In Albinson, J., and Andrews, G., editors: Child in sport and physical activity, Baltimore, 1976, University Park Press.

2. Bain, L.: Socialization into the role of participant: physical education's ultimate goal, JOPER **51**(7):48, September, 1980.

3. Bryant, J., and others: The effects of an exercise program on selected risk factors to coronary heart disease, J. Arkansas Medical Society **81**(1):69, June, 1984.

4. Cratty, B.: Active learning games to enhance academic learning, ed. 2, Englewood Cliffs, N.J., 1985, Prentice-Hall, Inc.

5. Cratty. B.: Intelligence in action, Englewood Cliffs, N.J., 1973, Prentice-Hall, Inc.

6. Dotson, C., and Ross, J.: Relationship between activity patterns and fitness, JOPERD **56**(1):86, January, 1985.

7. Getchell, B.: Physical fitness: a way of life, ed. 3, New York, 1983, John Wiley & Sons, Inc.

8. Gilbert, A.: Teaching the three r's through movement experiences, Minneapolis, 1977, Burgess Publishing Co.

9. Havighurst, R.: Developmental tasks and education, ed. 3, New York, 1979, Longman.

10. Johnson, M.: Physical education: fitness or fraud? A call for curriculum reform, JOPERD, **56** (1):33, January, 1985.

11. Katch, F., and McArdle, W.: Nutrition, weight control and exercise, ed. 2, Philadelphia, 1983, Lea & Febiger.

12. Magill, R., and Ash, M.: Academic, psycho-social and motor characteristics of participants and nonparticipants in children's sport, Research Quarterly **50**(2):230, May, 1979.

13. NASPE: Basic stuff, Reston, Va., 1981, AAHPERD.

14. Pate, R.: A new definition of youth fitness, The Physician and Sports Medicine **11**(4):80, April, 1983.

15. Rose, K.: To keep the people in health, JACHA **22**:80, 1973.

16. Werner, P., and Burton, E.: Learning through movement, St. Louis, 1979, The C.V. Mosby Co.

17. Zaichkowsky, L., and others: Growth and development: the child and physical activity, St. Louis, 1980, The C.V. Mosby Co.

ADDITIONAL READINGS

Misner, J.: Are we fit to educate about fitness? JOPERD **55**(9):28, October, 1984.

The important role of the physical educator as a leader in accomplishing fitness goals: considerations for the conduct and teaching of concepts essential for life-long fitness.

O'Brien, D.: Knowledge in physical education: a conversation between two frogs in the fog, JOPERD **56**(2):54, February, 1985.

A discussion of the importance of teaching knowledge in physical education.

Pate, R., and Corbin, C.: Implications for curriculum, JOPER **52**(1):36, January, 1981.

A look at a taxonomy of physical education objectives and the implications for planning and conducting physical education experiences that challenge school children at all levels.

Powell, K., and others: Objectives for the nation: assessing the role physical education must play, JOPERD **55**(6):18, August, 1984.

The importance of physical education and implications for programs to meet the surgeon general's objectives by 1990.

Ross, J., and others: Are kids getting appropriate activity? JOPERD **56**(1):82, January, 1985.

Report of the National Child and Youth Fitness Study to determine the degree to which children are participating in physical activity that will maintain functional cardiorespiratory fitness.

Struna, N.: Movement: our common goal, JOPER **48**(6):12, June, 1977.

Regardless of one's role in the profession of physical education (as dancer, diver, basketball player, and the like), the major purpose is to learn through the medium of movement.

2

THE ELEMENTARY SCHOOL CHILD

CHAPTER OBJECTIVES

1 To trace the physical growth, motor skill acquisition, and perceptual, cognitive, and social development of children during the elementary school years
2 To discuss the implications of age characteristics for the selection and conduct of activities in the elementary school physical education program

The elementary school years are an important time for human development. A time of steady physical growth ends in a growth spurt for most children. Motor skills become refined, and children begin to integrate skills into smooth, flowing movements. It is a time for active learning and cognitive development as children begin and complete up to one half of their formal education. It is also a time in which the social environment expands as children move out of the home and the dependence on family to an increased influence by teachers and peers.

The terms *growth* and *development* are often used interchangeably when discussing the changes in the human organism from birth to death. In this chapter we will refer to *growth* as a change in size and *development* as the process of maturation in which changes lead to more advanced use of particular mechanisms.

As one looks at the various aspects of human development and traces their emergence through the elementary school years, one recognizes that while all humans follow a similar sequential process, each is a unique individual. Not all children mature at the same rate. A great variation in individual development exists, and these individual differences increase with age and experience throughout the school years.

While the topics in this chapter may suggest to the reader separate components of human development, the child develops as a whole. A teacher who looks at children developmentally may find a child to be more mature in some areas than in others. For instance, individual children may have mature physical and motor development for their age and yet be functioning socially at a less advanced level. In planning experiences appropriate for children, the teacher must not make decisions based on only one aspect of human development but rather must look at the total child. In the past teachers have often used chronological age as the sole factor in selecting activities for children. A developmental approach will allow the teacher to better meet the needs of the children in the class through an examination of their developmental status rather than age alone.

PHYSICAL GROWTH

In tracing the growth changes in children during the elementary school years, one notes a variation in rate of growth of various parts and systems of the body over the years. At certain periods the growth rate is accelerated; at other times it is relatively steady.

Height and Weight

Rapid increases in height and weight occur during infancy and again at the onset of adolescence. As children enter school they are in a period of steady growth that continues to somewhere around 9 years of age for girls and approximately 11 years of age for

"

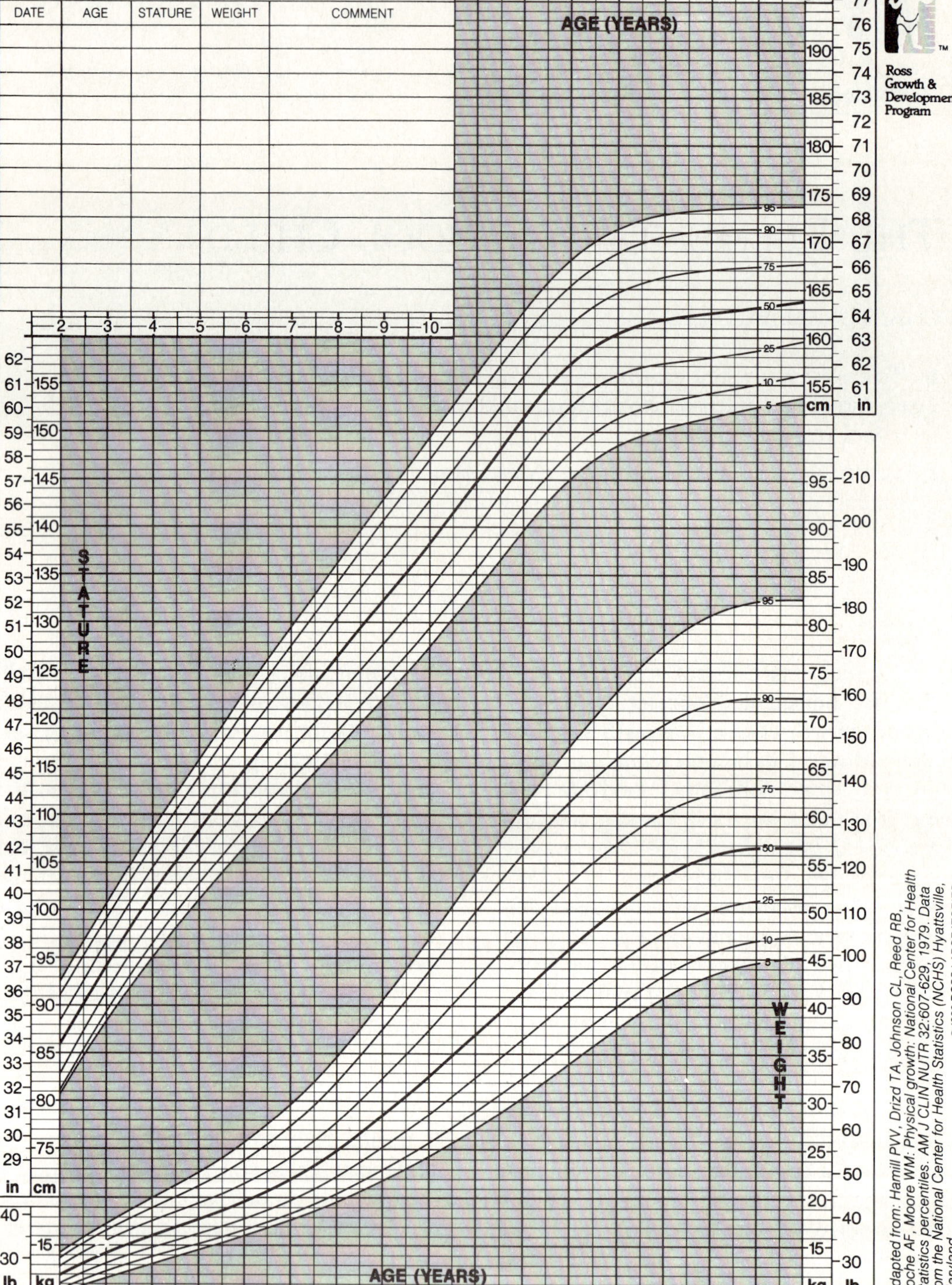

Figure 2-1

Percentiles for stature and age.

From National Center for Health Statistics: HRA 25, June 22, 1976, U.S. Department of Health, Education, and Welfare.

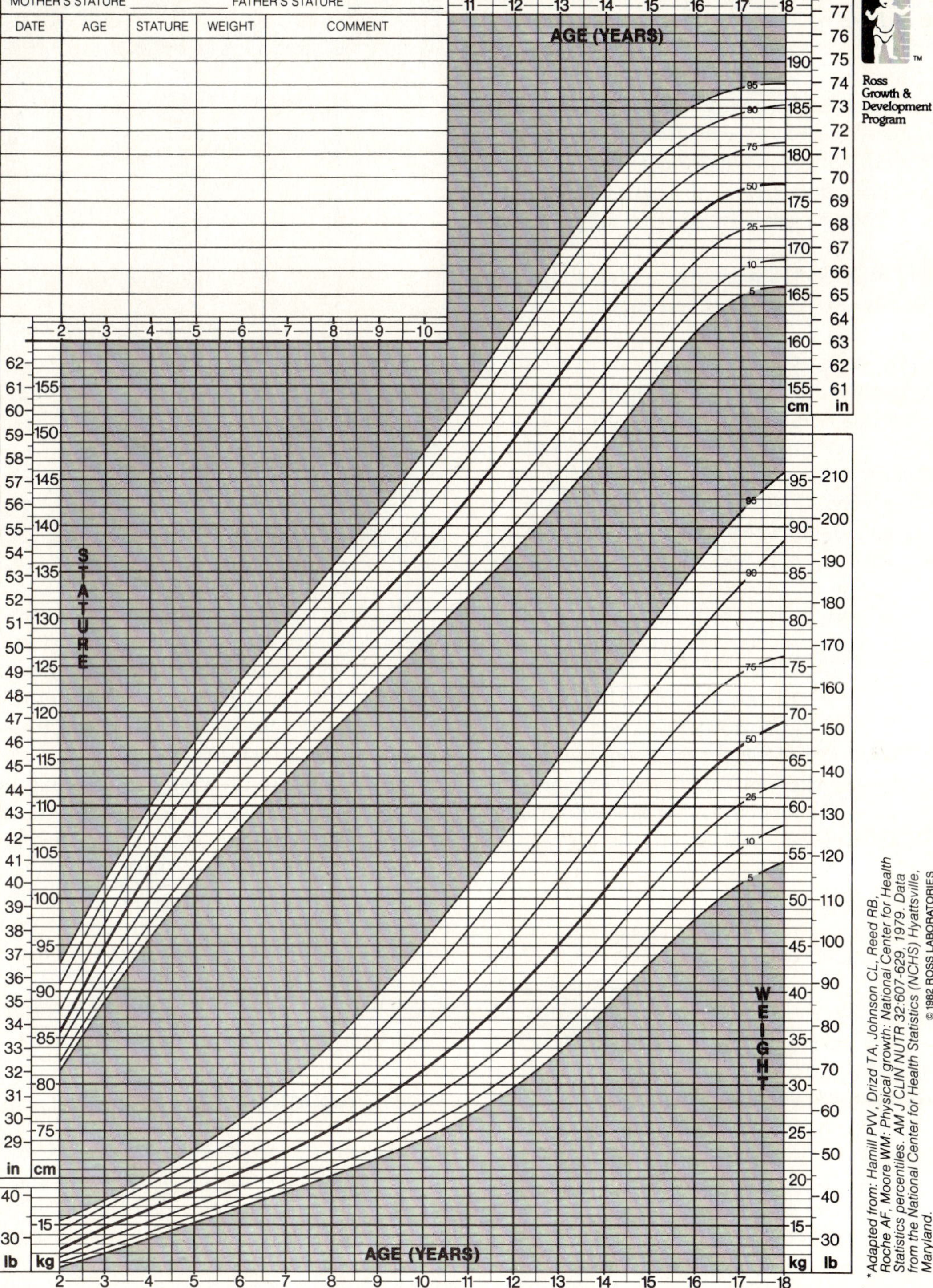

Figure 2-2

Percentiles for weight and age.

From National Center for Health Statistics: HRA 25, June 22, 1976, U.S. Department of Health, Education, and Welfare.

boys when the adolescent growth spurt begins. Figures 2-1 and 2-2 demonstrate the changes in height and weight over time. Considerable individual variation can be seen. Heredity and environmental influences interact to play a part in the individual differences observed. Even greater variation can be seen during periods of accelerated growth.

There is little difference in the height of boys and girls until about 11 years of age. At 12 girls are generally taller than boys. These differences in height continue until around 13 years of age, when the girls' growth rate begins to level off and the boys' accelerates.

Children will vary in age for the onset of the adolescent growth spurt. Girls may begin the accelerated growth period as early as age 9 or as late as 12 years, boys from age 11 to as late as 13 or 14 years. This growth spurt also may last a relatively short or long time. Children who begin the growth spurt early tend to complete their growth sooner than those who begin at a later age. The result is that late-maturing children tend to be taller, since they have had a longer period of growth than their earlier-maturing classmates.

There is relatively little difference in weight until about age 11, when the girls are often heavier. The girls' rate of weight gain shows a decrease at age 15 while the boys' rate of weight gain continues at an accelerated rate. After age 15 the boys again outweigh the girls. The variability in weight within each sex increases with age.

Skeletal Maturation

Bones begin as soft cartilaginous tissue and harden, or ossify, as the body matures. *Ossification* begins before birth and continues until late adolescence. At birth ossification has progressed to include the entire shaft of the long bones. At each end of the bone is a cartilaginous growth center called the *epiphysis.* Secondary ossification centers appear in the epiphyseal area. Between the secondary growth center and the shaft of the bone lies the epiphyseal plate, the growth plate, where the bone continues to grow until maturation. The appearance of the secondary ossification centers and the closure of the growth plate at maturation vary with the bone and sex. During these developing years girls are more advanced in bone maturation than boys.

Skeletal age, determined through x-rays of the bones of the wrists, is often used as an indicator of physical maturation. These x-rays show the stage of

ossification or progress toward maturity of the bones. Skeletal age may vary as much as 6 years in children of the same chronological age. For example, the skeletal age of 8-year-olds may vary from 5 to 11 years.

While vigorous activity is needed to stimulate normal bone growth, there is some concern about potential injury to growing bones during the developing years and especially to the epiphysis or growing part of the bones. There is some evidence that stress of overtraining may have some lasting effect on bone growth. Injury to mature children may result in little disturbance in the growth of bones, but epiphyseal injury to the young athlete may result in greater growth disturbance because the younger child has many more years of growth before maturity. This is discussed more fully in Chapter 29.

Body Proportions

During the period of physical growth from birth to maturity the proportions of body segments to total body size change dramatically. During this time the head, which at birth represents one quarter of the body length, doubles in size but makes up only about one eighth the body length at maturity. The legs increase five times their length at birth to represent about one half the body length at maturity. The arms increase in length four times their length at birth. The trunk triples in length. Body segments have accelerated growth rates of their own at various stages during the growing years. For example the 4- or 5-year-old's short stubby fingers will accelerate in growth, making object handling easier for the 6- and 7-year-old. Another example of varying growth rate may be seen at the onset of the adolescent spurt in growth, when the legs increase in length at a more rapid rate than other body segments.

Fat and Muscle Tissue

The rate at which fatty tissue is deposited in the body increases for a brief period from birth to the age of 6 months. It then decreases until 6 to 8 years of age; the decrease is more marked in boys. An increase in the rate of fat deposition occurs again just before the adolescent growth spurt. There is another decrease during the growth spurt for boys but not for girls. There are also sex differences and great variation within each sex in where fatty tissue is laid down in the body. This accounts for the differences in contours between boys and girls and the variability of shape within each sex.

During the growing years muscles increase in length, breadth, and width. The number of muscle fibers is determined by heredity and will not increase during life. Muscle weight increases about 40 times from birth to maturity. At birth muscle weight makes up from one fifth to one fourth the body weight; by early adolescence it constitutes one third the body weight, and it increases to two fifths the body weight by early maturity.

Muscle growth lags behind the changes in height, so it is not possible to determine children's strength by their size (Figure 2-3). Children grow taller and heavier before they grow stronger. There is little difference in the strength of girls and boys before puberty, although boys may be slightly stronger than girls. Both sexes increase in strength at the same rate before adolescence. Boys begin their spurt around age 14. The girls' spurt begins approximately 1 year before menarche and slows down once again about age 13. At age 13 boys have acquired about half of their adult strength, whereas girls have three quarters or more of adult strength, depending on the strength measurements used. At puberty the increase in the production of the male sex hormones influences muscle development. Early-maturing children are stronger than their later-maturing classmates.

During the early and middle elementary grades the similarity in strength puts girls and boys on an equal par in physical activity, when the difference in

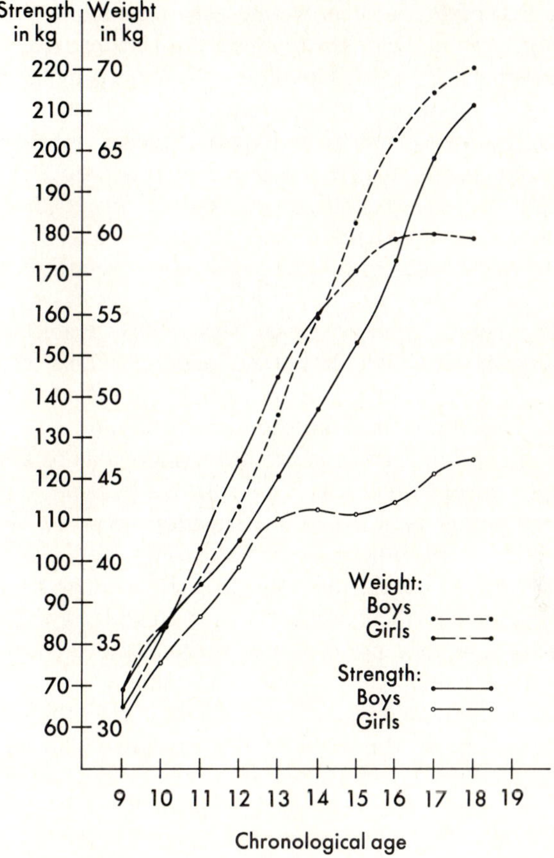

Figure 2-3

Weight and strength in school-age children.
From Tuddenham and Snyder.[10a]

size is considered. Girls often perceive themselves as less strong and boys see themselves as stronger than girls. It is up to the teacher to help children develop a realistic view of their own movement potential in order to develop to their fullest. Perceived sex differences not based on fact must be dispelled.

SENSORY PERCEPTION

Sensory *perception* refers to the ability to use input received through the sense organs in making judgments about one's environment. Most sensory-perceptual experts agree that there are three major developmental trends in sensory-perceptual maturation: (1) there is a shift in dominance of the sensory systems; (2) there is an increase in *intrasensory discrimination;* and (3) there is an improvement in *intersensory integration.*

As children respond to their environment, dominance in the use of sensory input shifts from tactile-kinesthetic to visual. This shift not only expands the sensory input beyond the child's reach but also utilizes a sensory system with greater facility for discrimination and increased speed in processing. At maturity there is greater dependence on vision than other sensory systems.

As the child matures, there is also a refinement in the sensory systems, which permits greater discrimination of sensory input. The child is capable of using more sensory data at any one time, can select the most relevant information, and can make more precise judgments about the input received.

In addition children are increasingly able to use the information received from several sensory systems simultaneously. In any situation they can use tactile, visual, auditory, or olfactory input in the perceptual process. In this way children have more information at their disposal to use in making decisions. The perception of movement is important to success in physical education. The ability to make accurate judgments and to respond to projectiles is dependent on this ability. This perceptual skill undergoes marked improvement during the elementary school years. It is not until the age of 11 or 12 that decisions about the movement of objects can be made quickly and accurately.[12]

Body awareness and kinesthetic perception of the position of body parts and the body's orientation in space undergo varying rates of development during the elementary school years. Young children develop a concept of the whole body before they are aware of its parts. Children entering school often have some difficulty in responding in activities calling for the movement of various body parts. At age 5 accuracy in describing body parts is about 55% correct, whereas a 12-year-old can accomplish the task with 100% accuracy.[12]

Physical education experiences that develop the children's understanding of their own body parts and their potential movement are essential because body awareness is so important in motor skill development. Teachers can also help children focus on particular sensory cues as they move.

MOTOR SKILL ACQUISITION

The elementary school child is capable of controlled purposeful movement. Many locomotor skills are well established by the time the child enters school. Walking, running, hopping, and jumping, which are executed in an even rhythm, may be done with perhaps only a few mechanical errors such as foot placement or use of the arms. Some children entering school may not have yet mastered skipping or galloping, which are more complex patterns of movement in which two locomotor movements are combined and performed in an uneven rhythm. Girls tend to skip earlier than boys, but boys may show greater ability in the gallop.

Throwing and striking skills show great variation during the elementary school years, with boys demonstrating somewhat more mature skills. In our culture the equipment and opportunities to develop these skills have generally been more accessible to boys than girls.

Sex differences before the onset of puberty are more a matter of opportunity and cultural expectations than a result of any physical differences between the sexes. Girls do better in skills that are expected of girls, and boys do better in skills considered to be more masculine. At adolescence the greater strength and size of boys gives them an advantage in the execution of many motor skills.

During the elementary school years three changes in motor development occur: mastery and refinement of fundamental motor patterns, adaptation of these skills under varying conditions, and the combining of motor skills with greater ease. In beginning physical education experiences, motor patterns are established for those who have not done so. These skills

are then refined during the period of steady growth. Once mastered, these skills undergo adaptation to new movement situations as children learn to execute skills with more or less force, with bigger or smaller equipment, alone or with others, and in a variety of movement activities. Finally the children's movement patterns become more fluid as they move through space while combining movements and changing level, direction, pathway, and speed.

In the upper elementary school grades there is great variability in motor skill performance for children of any one age and sex. Through the elementary school years girls tend to stay in their relative position in the group regarding skill development but boys do not. A boy who is outstanding at the elementary school level may or may not become a star at the high school level.[8]

COGNITIVE DEVELOPMENT

Language and communication skills, reasoning, memory, and attending skills are some of the cognitive skills developed during the elementary school years. All have meaning for the physical educator.

Attending behavior changes dramatically over the first 6 or 7 years of school. Kindergarten and first grade students have the ability to attend for only a short time, whereas upper grade children are able to stay with a task for much longer periods. Young children are easily distracted by other children or other environmental conditions, whereas older children can block out irrelevant stimuli as they work to accomplish their goals.

Elementary school children are intellectually curious, wanting to learn about themselves and the many activities that make up the physical education program. They have vivid imaginations and can be creative in solving movement challenges. The development of imagination and creativity appears to be decreased in later years, as the peer group gains in control over children's behavior.

The physical education experience should be one in which children are encouraged not only to move but also to think as they move. Problem solving and guided discovery stimulate their cognitive development. Young children in school are able to deal with limited bits of information at any one time, while upper grade children are able to handle more complicated rules and other knowledge. Therefore activities should be kept simple for young children and more complex for upper grade youngsters to challenge them intellectually. The physical education experience should also encourage verbal communication between the teacher and the students and should foster reasoning skills as new strategies are discovered.

SOCIAL DEVELOPMENT

Socialization, the process of learning behavior acceptable to life in society, is a lifelong process. Motor behavior provides some of the first socializing experiences as children reach out into their environment, interacting with parents and siblings and later others outside the home. During the elementary school years children move from the social context of the home to the school, peer group, and other social groups such as scouting or the church. In these settings they will learn to interact with others and grow to understand the behavior expected in each setting. During these developing years, children learn the specific roles of family member, student, friend, and activity participant. Much of the learning will be through the modeling of behavior of adults and other children.

During these years four major developmental trends appear:
1. Movement from egocentric to group behavior
2. Recognition of sex roles and preferences in play
3. Movement from dependence on the family and other adults to increasing dependence on the peer group as behavior models
4. Increased competitive behavior

These trends have far-reaching implications for education and physical education.

Kindergarten and first grade children tend to be egocentric in their behavior. They come to school with few group behavior skills. They work best alone or alongside other children. Some have not had the opportunity for much experience with a peer group, so they need to learn to share and to take turns. As they progress through the elementary school years, they begin to focus their attention on group activity. They learn to work together, to share in decision making, and to cooperate with teammates. By the fifth grade many prefer group activities to working alone. Sensitivity to the feelings of others begins to emerge in the later elementary school years.

Children learn sex role expectations early in life. Parents and family members model behavior expectations, so by the time children enter school they have some idea of appropriate behavior for each role. There is little place for stereotyping of behavior in today's society, and teachers must be careful not to reinforce these stereotypes. Often girls have the perception that physical activity is for boys only, or that they can never be as good as boys in motor skills performance. Children at all elementary school ages tend to select members of their own sex as partners. The teacher should encourage children to work with all children in the group. During the third or fourth grade some children may demonstrate some antagonism toward the opposite sex. They may avoid close contact or show aggressive behavior toward children of the opposite sex. Teachers need to deal with these behaviors by avoiding awkward social situations that intensify boy/girl relationships. Chapter 12 discusses strategies to use in dealing with these problems.

Dependence on adults decreases during the elementary school years. By the fifth or sixth grade most children are beginning to become more dependent on their peers for determining acceptable behavior. Conflicts between adult rules and children's desires are not uncommon. Even though the peer group is increasing in importance in the life of the child, upper elementary school children still look up to adults. Young children may seek approval openly, whereas older children are more subtle in their approach. All seek encouragement and recognition. Although children become group oriented, they often seek the help of adults to assist them in organizing their activities. Some sport sociologists believe there has been a decrease in spontaneous play of American children as the children become more involved in organized sports activities.

Children show an increase in competitive behavior during the elementary school years as well. This appears to be a cultural phenomenon, since children in some other cultures tend to develop more cooperative behaviors. While competition is important to our American society, teachers should strive to emphasize the cooperative aspects of play.

IMPLICATIONS FOR PHYSICAL EDUCATION

The characteristics and needs of children and the implications for physical education are summarized in Table 2-1.

Children require vigorous physical activity to stimulate normal growth and development. Since today many children do not have adequate opportunity for sustained vigorous activity, it is an important aspect of the elementary school physical education program. Maximum activity should be provided for all children to stimulate the development of the cardiorespiratory and neuromuscular systems. This is discussed further in Chapter 13.

The period of steady growth is an important time for the refinement of motor skills and the development of confidence in one's movement ability. The physical education program should provide a variety of activities to enhance the mastery of basic motor skills. As children approach adolescence, they are forced to cope with rapid changes in size and shape. These changes may result in a change in their perceptions of themselves as movers. Teachers must develop sensitivity to the needs of children adjusting to their new bodies. Since there is little difference in the size of boys and girls during the preadolescent period, there is no reason to separate boys and girls for physical education. The growth changes during the adolescent period suggest some special considerations, since the increased size and weight of the boys puts the girls at a physical disadvantage.

Young children have little awareness of the body and its function. Five- and 6-year-olds may be aware of most large body parts but few small ones. Seven- to 12-year-olds are capable of greater body awareness with increasing ability to analyze their own movements as they progress through the elementary school years. Perceptual mechanisms have progressed to the point that 11- and 12-year-olds can make accurate judgments about moving objects and can accurately move to intercept them.

Physical education activities should be designed to improve the children's perception of themselves and the use of body parts to perform a variety of motor movements. In presenting skills the teacher identifies how body parts are used and then helps the children to use this knowledge to analyze their own performance. The evaluative criteria included in the skills and activity chapters of this text describe the use of body parts in the performance of each skill. The elementary school years are important for the development of a variety of motor skills. In the early years the children concentrate on one skill at a time, whereas in the later elementary school years activities may require the combination of skills. It is important for the teacher to plan a variety of experiences in which the children will use each skill. These activities may vary in level of proficiency expected such as varying the distance to or the size of targets. Within the lesson children should be given some choice in activity based on their own perceived ability. When given these choices children usually choose activities just beyond the level of perceived competency since

Table 2-1

Age characteristics and the physical education program

		5-6 years	7-8 years	9-10 years	11 years
GROWTH					
Charac-teristics		Steady increases in height and weight ⟶		Growth spurt begins for girls	Girls generally taller and heavier than boys Growth spurt begins for boys
		Steady growth in strength for boys and girls ⟶		Increase in strength for girls ⟶	
		Flexibility good		Loss in flexibility ⟶	
The student needs		Vigorous physical activity to enhance fitness, growth and development ⟶			
				Flexibility activities ⟶	
		Equal expectations for strength of boys and girls ⟶			
The teacher provides		Running, climbing, support-ive activities ⟶			
		Equal strengthening activities for boys and girls ⟶			
				Stretching activities to en-hance increased under-standing of fitness ⟶	
AWARENESS OF BODY PARTS					
Charac-teristics		Aware of large body parts	Aware of all large and small body parts ⟶		
					Accurate judgments in intercepting moving objects
The student needs		Increased use of all body parts ⟶		Awareness and develop-ment of all body parts and systems ⟶	
The teacher provides		Movement challenges to ex-plore location and possible movements of body parts ⟶			
		Knowledge of how body parts are used to perform motor skills ⟶			
		Activities for total body de-velopment ⟶			
MOTOR SKILLS					
Charac-teristics		Gross motor skills improving →	Gross motor skills re-fined		
			Fine motor skills im-proving ⟶		
			Increasing variability in motor skill per-formance ⟶		
		Perform motor skills singly ⟶		Combine motor skills more fluidly ⟶	
				Balance improved	

Table 2-1

Age characteristics and the physical education program—cont'd

	5-6 years	7-8 years	9-10 years	11 years
The student needs	Opportunity to refine and use gross motor skills	To use gross motor skills in a variety of situations	————→	
		Opportunity to refine manipulative and other fine motor skills	————→	
	Opportunity to work with medium-sized objects	To work with equipment varying in size and weight	————→	
			To use motor skills in a variety of sports and dance activities ————→	
			To develop combinations of skills into movement sequences or routines ————→	
The teacher provides	A variety of experiences in using skills	A variety of experiences to challenge each child and requiring greater body and object control	————→	
	Experiences to explore the use of equipment such as ropes, hoops, balls, and wands	————→		
		Activities to further develop skills in ball handling	Activities requiring greater accuracy ————→	
			Activities combining motor skills and beginning sports and dance skills ————→	

ATTENTION SPAN

	5-6 years	7-8 years	9-10 years	11 years
Characteristics	Short attention span	Attention span short but increasing	Attention span increasing ————→	
	Very creative, imaginative ————→			
	Deals with small bits of information at a time ————→		Deals with increasing bits of information ————→	
The student needs	Short-duration activities ————→		Activities increasing in length of time and complexity ————→	
	Opportunity to develop own ideas ————→			
	Simple rules ————→		Rules increasing in complexity ————→	
The teacher provides	Movement into activity quickly ————→			
	Simple instructions ————→		More complex instructions ————→	
	Many different activities within the lesson ————→		Increasing time spent on activities in the lesson ————→	
	Activities with little information to remember (few game rules, simple dances) ————→		Activities increasing in complexity ————→	

Table 2-1
Age characteristics and the physical education program—cont'd

	5-6 years	7-8 years	9-10 years	11 years
	Work with one movement concept	Combinations of movement concepts increasing in difficulty ———→		
SOCIAL SKILLS				
Characteristics	Egocentric	Able to work where a little cooperation with partner or small group is needed	Interest in group activities increasing ———→	
	Aware of sex role expectations; prefers same sex partners ———→		Some sex antagonism	Sex antagonism decreasing
	Depends on adults for guidance ———→		Looking more to peers for direction ———→	
			Competitive, team spirit high ———→	
			Insensitve to others' feelings	Increasing sensitivity to others
The student needs	Activities to work alone or alongside others	Work with partners	Work with 3-5 persons in a group ———→	
	Opportunity to work with both sexes ———→			
	Direction from teacher on expectations for behavior	To assume increasing responsibility for own behavior ———→		
	To learn skills of sharing, taking turns ———→		Work on developing cooperation and joint decision making ———→	
	To recognize individual worth of all children ———→			
The teacher provides	Activities in which children work independently of others	Activities working with partners	Activities requiring group decisions ———→	
	Games with little cooperation needed			
	Some expectations of performance for each sex ———→			
			Activities organized to avoid physical contact of boys and girls	
			To expect boys and girls to work together in structured activities so cooperation is stressed ———→	
	Encouragement for supportive behavior ———→			
	To give opportunity for leadership as children are ready ———→		Opportunity to assume decision-making responsibilities as the group leader ———→	

they offer more of a challenge. These varied experiences provide opportunities for children not only to perfect their skills but to adapt them for use in new activities as well. This ability to successfully adapt learned skills to new situations is essential to using motor skills throughout one's lifetime.

Children begin elementary school with a relatively short attention span, which requires the teacher to plan a variety of activities of short duration for each lesson. Instruction should be short and to the point, with the children given small bits of information with which to work at any given time. Games are of short duration with few rules. Children are very creative and enjoy activities in which they can use their imagination. Children respond spontaneously to movement challenges that call for simple movement responses.

As the children progress through the elementary school grades, their lengthening attention span permits them to deal with increasing amounts of information and more complexity in movement challenges and other activities. With some teacher direction, they are able to deal with several movement concepts at one time and can understand some of the finer points of skill execution. The complexity of games increases with more rules, the designation of different responsibilities to participants, and more advanced use of skills. The activities increase in duration as they increase in complexity.

Physical education activities for young children tend to be individual or of a parallel play nature. Activities may require children to work independently or alongside other children but with little dependence on one another. The interaction of players in games may require a one-on-one confrontation, such as in a tag game in which each child, while moving in a group, is really interacting with the child who is "it." Although young children generally select a partner of the same sex, they are willing to work with all children in the group.

Group behavior emerges during the elementary school years. The physical education experiences gradually move to activities in which there is more demand for working with others. This begins with activities in which partners work together to accomplish a task; gradually the size of groups increases so by grades five and six there is some decision making in groups of four or five. The progression in games and team sports lead-ups demonstrates the increased social interaction and group dependency of children. The structure of folk and square dancing also depends on group cooperation. In the middle grades some children may be more adamant about having partners of the same sex. It may be advisable not to insist on holding hands while performing folk dances, but the physical educator should expect that each child will work with any other child in the group.

Children learn various group roles as well. Each should have the opportunity to be a leader and a follower. In the beginning squad leaders may begin as merely the first person in line or the one to distribute equipment to the group. As they are ready they should assume more responsibility. In later years the group leader may determine the rotation of players to various positions in the activity, help children in the group with skill execution, or determine when the group is ready to move on to the next activity.

As team spirit increases, so does the competitive behavior of children. In the early grades activities often have no declared winner, while in the upper grades there may be competition between teams resulting in a team score. The teacher must stress the cooperative efforts of teams rather than the winning score. Equalizing competition and avoiding emotionally charged activities such as relays will go a long way in minimizing the importance of winning. Children need to learn to compete in socially acceptable ways. Sportsmanship and strategies to aid its development are discussed in Chapter 12.

SUMMARY

During the elementary school years a number of growth and developmental changes take place that have implications for the physical education program. The steady growth in height and weight of the early years makes it an important time for skill refinement. This period of steady growth is followed by an adolescent growth spurt for girls at about 10 or 11 years of age and for boys 1 year later. Vigorous physical activity is important at all ages if normal growth and development is to occur.

The perceptual mechanisms mature during this time, with increased body awareness and the ability to use sensory input to make movement decisions. Increased body awareness aids the child in the refinement and adaptation of skills to new movement situations. As the neuromuscular system matures, children move more smoothly as they combine motor skills to accomplish the tasks required in a variety of individual and group activities.

Understanding of their own potential for movement is an important aspect of cognitive development in elementary school children. As children progress through the elementary school grades, they become increasingly more able to understand complex rules and strategies and to analyze movement situations.

Socially an egocentric kindergarten child is transformed into a group-centered participant by the fifth or sixth grade. Dependence on adults is replaced by a growing importance of the peer group for establishing patterns of behavior.

In planning and conducting physical education experiences the teacher must keep the whole child in mind. Children mature at different rates. They may not be at the same developmental level regarding their physical, perceptual, motor, cognitive, and social characteristics. In meeting the needs of children the teacher must plan experiences appropriate to the characteristics of the individuals in the group. Physical education will only be successful if the activities meet the total needs of the children.

REFERENCES

1. Albinson, J., and Andrew, G.: Child in sport and physical activity, Baltimore, 1976, University Park Press.
2. Branta, C.: Physical growth and motor performance, JOPERD **53**(5): 38, May 1982.
3. Corbin, C.: A textbook of motor development, ed. 2, Dubuque, 1980, William C. Brown Co.
4. Cratty, B.: Perceptual and motor development in infants and children, ed. 2, Englewood Cliffs, N.J., 1979, Prentice-Hall.
5. Gallahue, D.: Understanding motor development in children, preschool through the elementary grades, New York, 1982, John Wiley & Sons.
6. Lowrey, G.: Growth and development of children, ed. 7, Chicago, 1978, Year Book Medical Publishers.
7. Rarick G.: Motor development: its growing knowledge base, JOPER **51**(7):26, September 1980.
8. Rarick, G.: Physical activity: human growth and development, New York, 1973, Academic Press, Inc.
9. Ridenour, M., and others: Motor development: issues and applications, Princeton, 1978, Princeton Book Co. Pub.
10. Thomas, J.: Motor development during childhood and adolescence, Minneapolis, 1984, Burgess Publishing Co.
10a. Tuddenham, R., and Snyder, M.: Physical growth of California boys and girls from birth to eighteen, Berkley, 1954, University of California Press, p. 364 (2). Used with permission.
11. Wickstrom, R.: Fundamental motor patterns, ed. 3, Philadelphia, 1983, Lea & Febiger.
12. Williams, H.: Perceptual and motor development, Englewood Cliffs, N.J., 1983, Prentice-Hall, Inc.
13. Zaichkowsky, L., and others: Growth and development: the child and physical activity, St. Louis, 1980, The C.V. Mosby Co.

ADDITIONAL READINGS

Andres, F., and others: Actual and perceived strength differences, JOPERD **52**(5):20, May 1981.
Although they are physiologically similar in strength, preadolescent boys and girls perceive that there is a difference in favor of boys.

Chausow, S., and others: Metabolic and cardiovascular responses of children during prolonged physical activity, Research Quarterly for Exercise and Sport **55**(1):1, March 1984.
Evidence that children's response to prolonged exercise is much like that of adults but their short attention span results in dropping out of activity.

Erbaugh, S.: The relationship of stability performance and the physical growth characteristics of preschool children, Research Quarterly for Exercise and Sport **55**(1):8, March 1984.
The relationship between several anthropometric dimensions and stabilometer performance.

Roberton M., and Halverson, L.: Developing children: their changing movement, Philadelphia, 1984, Lea & Febiger.
A look at cognitive, perceptual, psychosocial and motor aspects of child development and implications for teaching. Changes that occur as motor patterns develop are shown with special suggestions to help children get the most out of their motor experiences.

Smith, H.: Implications for movement education experiences drawn from perceptual-motor research. In National Association for Sport and Physical Education: Echoes of influence, Washington, D.C., 1977, AAHPERD.
Vision, audition, tactile perception, balance, and proprioception and their implications for physical education.

Whiting, H.: Acquiring ball skill, Philadelphia, 1970, Lea & Febiger.
A systems analysis of perceptual-motor skill performance and discussion of factors that affect the development of ball skills, including information processing, judgment needed, reaction time, and visual factors.

Part Two

PLANNING THE PHYSICAL EDUCATION EXPERIENCE

The movement approach to physical education in the elementary school emphasizes the understanding of human movement and a child-centered approach to learning. A variety of activities are planned to help children develop motor skills and to increase their understanding of their own movement potential and human movement in general. A developmental approach enables teachers to identify cognitive, motor, and social and affective needs of children in selecting curriculum content and process for learning.

Adequate curriculum, annual, unit, and daily planning are the first steps to good teaching. The elementary school teacher of physical education must carefully set objectives and select the content and processes to challenge children cognitively as well as in the use of motor skills.

3

THE ELEMENTARY SCHOOL PHYSICAL EDUCATION PROGRAM

CHAPTER OBJECTIVES

1 To describe the evolution of the movement approach in elementary school physical education

2 To identify the content and processes used in the movement curriculum

3 To explain the differences between several curriculum implementation models

4 To describe the developmental approach to teaching in physical education

5 To identify instructional outcomes for each developmental level of the movement curriculum

Physical education in the schools should be considered a 13-year instructional program. The elementary school years mark the beginning of instruction and are considered the developmental period. Although the child has been engaged in many kinds of motor activities before coming to school, most children have little understanding of their body and its potential for movement. During the elementary school years children explore the use of body parts as they refine fundamental movement patterns and learn about mechanical principles; laws governing force; balance and time; and the use of space. Movement efficiency is an important outcome of their movement. As the children are ready, they are introduced to a variety of dance and sport skills for use now and later in school and recreational participation.

If the elementary school program is successful, children moving on to secondary school programs have the knowledge and skills to make decisions about their future movement activities. At the junior high or middle school level children need exposure to a variety of dance and sport activities to further develop the skills and knowledge they began to acquire at the elementary school level. At the high school level students should be given the opportunity to choose the activities they would like to pursue at a much higher level of skill.

Significant changes in school physical education programs have taken place in the United States in the twentieth century. One of the most significant is the evolution of the movement approach to learning.

HISTORICAL PERSPECTIVE

The change in elementary school physical education from a formal physical fitness program of calisthenics, gymnastics, and dance in the 1920s to a movement-centered program today has been a dramatic one. Although many consider the movement approach a relatively new development of the past two decades, Margaret H. Doubler proposed the study of basic movement as the foundation of all physical education in the 1930s. Movement fundamentals programs for women began to appear shortly thereafter on the campuses of colleges and universities, especially in the midwestern and western states. These programs were often required for all women students as a foundation for future physical education experiences.

In the years preceding World War II research in many areas of child growth had increased our understanding of the needs of children. Ruth Murray, Dorothy LaSalle, Gladys Andrews, and others suggested a new elementary physical education curriculum with greater concern for the individual child's needs, the enhancement of creativity, and the development of an understanding of movement.

Following World War II and the Korean conflict there were periods of concern for our nation's fitness. During the Eisenhower administration the President's Council on Physical Fitness was founded. In 1956 the AAHPER published its first motor fitness test of seven items with norms for boys and girls from 10 to 18 years old. Physical education programs reflected this concern. However, the emphasis on basic movement was never really lost.

Before World War II Rudolph Laban, an Austrian dancer, fled Nazi Germany and went to England. Although his theory of movement was known to the dance community throughout much of the world, it was new to physical education. Known as *movement education,* this theory of movement soon replaced the physical training syllabus as the basis for physical education in England.

Table 3-1
Movement

Aspects	Dimensions
Body (what body does)	Actions of the body
	Actions of body parts
	Activities of body
	Shapes of body
Effort (how body moves)	Time
	Weight
	Space
	Flow
Space (where body moves)	Areas
	Directions
	Levels
	Pathways
	Planes
	Extensions
Relationship (what relationships occur)	Body parts
	Individuals and groups
	Apparatus and equipment
	Other types

From Logsden, B., and others: Physical education for children: a focus on the teaching process, ed. 2, Philadelphia, 1984, Lea & Febiger.

In the late 1950s an enthusiastic group of Americans went to England for the First Anglo-American Workshop on Physical Education. At this conference and a second conference held in the 1960s, American physical educators were introduced to Laban's movement education approach.

The 1960s and 1970s saw the development of programs of movement education in the United States, where sometimes they replaced traditional programs of games and sports. Other programs included the movement content in their course of study. Federal grants were awarded for the development of movement education programs in several areas of the country. Plattsburgh, New York, was one site where Tillotsin and others developed a model elementary school physical education program.

Movement education has been defined by Tillotsin[12] as "that phase of the total education program which has as its contribution the development of effective, efficient and expressive movement responses in a thinking, feeling and sharing human being." The aim of movement education is to develop "an awareness of the self in the physical environment, the body and its capacities, and the components of movement which, in turn contribute to the understandings, knowledges and movement responses of each child in every class."[12] Table 3-1 is a basic framework of Laban's classification system as outlined by Logsdon and others.[7]

With the introduction of movement education came not only a change in physical education content but a significant change in the methodology of elementary school physical education experiences as well. Content shifted from the teaching of specific skills, games, and other activities to the development of a broader understanding of the body as a tool for initiating movement and an understanding of the environment in which movement takes place. The goal was the development of a process for understanding movement that an individual could apply to any motor activity. Methodology shifted from a direct approach to *problem solving* and *exploration*.

In both England and the United States the movement education theory has been readily applied to what has become known as educational dance and educational gymnastics. The integration with sport skills has been slow in coming. Some evidence of its application to games has been seen in recent years in higher education and athletics. Coaches, primarily in the field sports, have been developing small group games and practices in which an understanding of movement concepts, especially space, is developed.

Much has been written about movement education, and Laban's theory of movement has undergone many interpretations and modifications. However, the idea of a physical education program based on the development of an understanding of human movement is here to stay.

CURRICULUM IMPLEMENTATION MODELS

The content of elementary school physical education programs has been organized into several curriculum implementation models that depict the relationship of the important elements. For our discussion these models will be placed on a continuum (Figure 3-1).

Model I	Model II	Model III	Model IV
Traditional	Unit	Integrated	Movement

Figure 3-1

Curriculum models.

At one extreme we have the traditional physical education curriculum and at the other movement education. As we move along the continuum from model II to model IV, we see the inclusion in some form of the movement content. Models I and IV are the extremes; model I ignores the movement content, while model IV ignores traditional physical education activities. Table 3-2 shows an example of the arrangement of the content for each model.

The *traditional curriculum model* is an activity-centered curriculum composed of activities long associated with elementary school physical education: games and sports, dance, and individual activities. Relative emphasis in each area is based on age characteristics, with the greatest emphasis on individual activities throughout the early years and games and sports in the upper grades. Units of instruction are planned for each activity area included: educational games, folk dance, stunts and tumbling, etc. Each unit is viewed as a unique experience, and the relationships between activities are rarely taught. Although a variety of teaching strategies may be utilized in this curriculum, teacher-centered approaches tend to be used most often.

The *unit curriculum model* is similar to the traditional curriculum but the movement content is considered as one aspect of the physical education content. As in the traditional curriculum, many separate activity units are presented. The movement content represents one unit of instruction. The major disadvantage of this model is that the movement content is treated as a separate experience from games, dance, and individual activities. Therefore the children are not taught to see the relationship between the movement content and the other content areas.

The *integrated curriculum model* is perhaps the most appropriate model for elementary school physical education today. In this curriculum the study of human movement is begun with the development of an understanding of humans, their environment, and their movement in the early years. As the children's understanding of the movement content increases, they are taught to see the relationship between what they have learned about movement, motor skills, and performance in a variety of physical education activities. In the upper grades the teacher identifies the concepts most important to success at each particular level. The activity unit is then built around these concepts.

The movement model stresses the movement content as the only legitimate content of the physical education program for children in grades one

Table 3-2
Organization of content for curriculum models

Model I	Model II	Model III	Model IV
Traditional Level II (grade 3)	Unit Level II (grade 3)	Integrated* Level II (grade 3)	Movement Level II (grade 3)
FALL			
Running and tag games Basic skills Soccer lead-ups	Movement concepts Basic skills Soccer lead-ups	Running and tag games Basic skills Soccer lead-ups (space/ force)	Body awareness Space Qualities of movement (use of the body)
WINTER			
Creative dance Folk dance Rhythmic activities	Creative dance Folk dance Rhythmic activities	Creative dance Folk dance Rhythmic activities (time)	Body awareness Space Qualities of movement (with small equip- ment)
Stunts and tumbling Large apparatus	Stunts and tumbling Large apparatus	Stunts and tumbling Large apparatus (balance, body awareness)	
Net games	Net games	Net games (space/force)	
SPRING			
Running games Ball games	Running games Ball games	Running games Ball games (space/forcc)	Body awareness Space Qualities of movement (with large appara- tus)
Small equipment Track and field	Small equipment Track and field	Small equipment Track and field (force, body awareness)	

*All concepts integrated, special emphasis on concepts in parentheses.

through six. Emphasis is placed on the development of an understanding of the components of movement: body awareness, space, and movement qualities. The example included in Table 3-2 includes a repeat of the three content areas during the school year. In the beginning of the year the children work with the concepts using only body movements. They work later with balls, hoops, or other small equipment and finally with large apparatus to further their understanding of the movement content. Other approaches may also be used. Exploration, problem solving, and other child-centered teaching strategies are employed exclusively. In this model motor skill development is believed to occur as a result of the movement experiences. In some programs they are taught as a part of the movement experience; in others they happen only by chance. Traditional physical education activities, such as games, track and field, gymnastics, and folk dance, are usually not included.

THE MOVEMENT CURRICULUM

As the body of knowledge in all areas continues to increase at a rapid rate, education has shifted its emphasis in curriculum planning from the accumulation of facts to the development of learning skills that enable the individual to continue to learn throughout life. The movement curriculum combines the content of physical education with the development of a process that enhances lifelong learning. It provides children with the knowledge about their movement as they learn to move efficiently and effectively. These skills and knowledge are presented in a way that encourages thinking and self-discovery.

The goal of physical education is to provide movement experiences that enhance the involvement of individuals in physical activity throughout their lifetime. Many of the activities in which learning begins during the elementary school years will not be the activities in which future adults will participate. Therefore the activities of the elementary school physical education program are not only those to meet present needs but also those that are the means for learning in the future. The goal of physical education thus becomes one of providing experiences that will aid the individual in selecting and successfully participating in activities appropriate at various stages of life.

Movement Content

The content of the elementary school physical education curriculum in this text goes beyond Laban's movement theory. Figure 3-2 outlines the curriculum within the scope of this book. An attempt has been made to include experiences that broaden children's understanding of themselves as movers as well as develop an understanding of principles that apply to effective and efficient movement.

Body awareness

Body awareness activities enhance children's understanding of themselves as movers and help develop a sensitivity to their physical being. Learning begins with the identification of body parts and knowledge about the body's capacity for movement. Developing an understanding of how the human body moves includes becoming aware of how the body works, that is, muscles and joints, respiration, and the cardiovascular system. The importance of fitness and the means to its assessment are also studied. Awareness of body tension and the development of conscious relaxation techniques should begin at the elementary school level. Communication through the use of the body should be explored and should include purposeful and unintentional body language. As children develop motor skills, body awareness is encouraged as they learn to use body parts efficiently and effectively in performing motor tasks.

Space

An understanding of the space concepts is essential if children are to move effectively in any movement situation. In a program emphasizing individual movement and problem solving the understanding of *self* and *general space* is crucial. Children must first recognize their own space and the space of others if they are to move independently. This concept is also important for success in the classroom, where children must learn to share space with each other, whether at a table or sitting with a group in a reading lesson. Effective use of space also includes the ability to move in different *directions* and at all *levels:* high, medium, and low. *Pathways,* the line of movement in space, and *range,* the relationship of the body parts to each other or of the body to objects in space, are other concepts to explore.

Qualities of movement

The study of the *qualities of movement* enhances children's understanding of movement and the laws that apply to movement efficiency. One aspect of this content is the study of mechanical principles important in the use of the body to create, apply, and absorb force. Children also learn about gravity and the efficient use of the body in maintaining stability. The study of time and flow completes the content in this area.

Motor Skills

As children begin to understand the three areas of movement concepts, they are helped to apply them to other learning in physical education. One of the first applications is made in the development and use of fundamental motor skills, an important aspect of the elementary school physical education curriculum.

Since children have varied motor backgrounds, it is essential for the teacher to help individual children reach their movement potential through a carefully planned and conducted program of activities. A variety of interesting activities that encourage mastery of these important motor skills is presented. These skills become more meaningful to children as they gain understanding through the application of movement concepts. It is this link between knowledge and skill that enables children to plan and use their skills more effectively in solving movement challenges. This understanding of movement concepts and the ability to apply them to motor skills makes it possible for children to move on to the application of the movement concepts in dance, games, and individual activities.

Physical Education Activities

The application of movement concepts to the traditional activities of an elementary school program becomes increasingly important as children move through the elementary school years. As the activities increase in complexity, children's success depends on their ability to solve more advanced movement challenges. Activities become more complex in the nature and use of the skills required. Children learn to combine skills in interesting and functional ways in activities such as gymnastics and basketball. Children combine movements creatively in dance and rhythmic activities. The interaction of individuals requires children to relate to an increasingly larger group. Each participant plays a unique role in the activity, such as the positions and changing player relationships in a soccer game. These activities provide an exciting experience for children in the movement challenges they impose. It is not possible to teach each child all the skills and knowledge needed for a lifetime of motor activity. Exposure to a wide variety of skills and activities is needed. However, the key to future success may lie in the ability to apply old learning to new situations. A process for accomplishing this must begin during the elementary school physical education experience.

PROCESS FOR LEARNING

Much learning in physical education is through the imitation of skills presented by the teacher with little understanding of why the skills are executed in a particular way. The movement curriculum attempts to bring to a conscious level the understanding of efficient movement. If we are to emphasize understanding the environment, movement, and people as Allenbaugh[1] suggests, then the physical education program must reflect this thinking.

In the past the physical education curriculum has included a set of broad goals and a list of the activity content. Today the curriculum has a much broader scope that includes all the planning that takes place before teaching begins.[5] If we accept this broader definition, then the physical education curriculum must include not only the content but also the process involved in learning. In this conceptual framework, the physical educator becomes the facilitator in helping each child learn how to learn.

Physical education is concerned with the education of the "whole" person. Learning is focused not

Body awareness
Name and location of body parts
Body shape
Possible actions of body parts
Relationships of body parts in moving
Using body parts to accomplish movement tasks
Conscious relaxation and tension control
Body language
Understanding one's physical fitness

Space
Self space
General space
Direction
Pathway
Level
Range

Qualities of movement
Creating force
Absorbing force
Balance
Time
Flow

Application to movement skills
Locomotor skills
Nonlocomotor skills
Manipulative skills

Application to physical education activities
Dance
Creative rhythms
Singing games
Folk and square dance
Rhythmic activities with ball, ropes,
and other equipment

Games and sports
Educational games
Recreational games
Dual sports
Lead-ups to team sports

Individual activities
Stunts and tumbling
Hand apparatus
Large apparatus
Track and field

Figure 3-2

Movement content of the integrated curriculum.

only on the development of motor skills but also on the cognitive, social, and affective development of children. The new physical education gives closer attention to each learner. If physical education is to really educate the whole person, then the whole child must be involved. The study of the behavioral domains is helpful in our attempt to organize and analyze educational objectives in physical education.

The cognitive domain is concerned with the child's intellectual skills. In the 1950s Bloom and his associates[2] published a taxonomy of educational objectives for the cognitive domain. The major categories included were as follows:

1. Knowledge—the knowing of facts and other specifics
2. Comprehension—the ability to interpret, translate, and extrapolate
3. Application—the ability to apply what is known to a variety of situations
4. Analysis—the ability to identify key elements, to see relationships, etc.
5. Synthesis—the ability to arrange an entire structure
6. Evaluation—the ability to make judgments

Cognitive behaviors in physical education often stop with the knowledge of rules and terminology, which falls at the lower end of Bloom's taxonomy. Problem solving, creative endeavors, and decision-making abilities, which involve higher level processes, are more difficult to measure and are often neglected in the evaluation of the physical education curriculum. Corbin[3] suggests that the loss of interest in physical education as children progress through the educational system may well be the result of our unwillingness to move students beyond these lower level objectives.

Jewett and Mullan,[5] after studying the works of Bloom and others, formulated the taxonomy of movement process categories that follows.

Physical education experiences in the past have primarily dealt with the learning and refinement of a variety of motor skills with the assumption that students who have mastered them will automatically use them effectively as the circumstances demand. In the movement curriculum more attention is given to the process of perceiving by attending to the need for better self-awareness. Children's understanding not only includes the awareness of body parts and their potential movement but also the understanding and application of movement principles to their actions as they perform motor skills. Increasing awareness of the movement environment is also an im-

portant part of perceptual processing.

Once the task has been accurately perceived, attention is focused on the patterning of the movement. During this phase children learn to use body parts consistently to accomplish the task. Teacher assistance is important during this phase to help children learn the correct movement patterns. Mastery of the skill is not achieved at this level, but the skill should be easily recognizable.

The next two processes, adapting and refining, lead the performer to mastery and habituation of the motor responses. In adapting, the child learns to modify the newly learned skill to varying conditions, such as throwing and catching balls varying in size or kicking for varying distances. Refining denotes mastery of the skill into a smooth, flowing movement performed consistently and efficiently.

The creative movement categories are extremely important to the physical education experience. Emphasis is on individualizing the movements to meet the performer's purposes. Although adapting is the result of externally imposed conditions, such as the size of an object, varying is not. In varying there may be changes in the body parts used or in the tempo of the movement. The movement becomes unique to the individual.

Improvising is extemporaneous or spontaneous movement that is not preplanned. This is a valuable part of the movement exploration and problem solving associated with the development of the move-

MOVEMENT PROCESS CATEGORIES

A. *Generic Movement:* Those movement operations or processes which facilitate the development of characteristics and effective motor patterns. They are typically exploratory operations in which the learner receives or "takes in" data as he or she moves.
  1. Perceiving: Awareness of total body relationships and of self in motion. These awarenesses may be evidenced by body positions or motoric acts; they may be sensory in that the mover feels the equilibrium of body weight and the movement of limbs; or they may be evidenced cognitively through identification, recognition, or differentiation.
  2. Patterning: Arrangement and use of body parts in successive and harmonious ways to achieve a movement pattern or skill. This process is dependent on recall and performance of a movement previously demonstrated or experienced.

B. *Ordinative Movement:* The process of organizing, refining, and performing skillful movement. The processes involved are directed toward the organization of perceptual-motor abilities with a view to solving particular movement tasks or requirements.
  3. Adapting: Modification of a patterned movement to meet externally imposed task demands. This would include modification of a particular movement to perform it under different conditions.
  4. Refining: Acquisition of smooth, efficient control in performing a movement pattern or skill by mastery of spatial and temporal relations. This process deals with the achievement of precision in motor performance and habituation of performance under more complex conditions.

C. *Creative Movement:* Those motor performances which include the processes of inventing or creating movement which will serve the personal (individual) purposes of the learner. The processes employed are directed toward discovery, integration, abstraction, idealization, emotional objectification and composition.
  5. Varying: Invention or construction of personally unique options in motor performance. These options are limited to different ways of performing specific movement; they are of an immediate situational nature and lack any predetermined movement behavior which has been externally imposed on the mover.
  6. Improvising: Extemporaneous origination or initiation of personally novel movement or combination of movement. The processes involved may be stimulated by a situation externally structured, although conscious planning on the part of the performer is not usually required.
  7. Composing: Combination of learned movement into personally unique motor designs or the invention of movement patterns new to the performer. The performer creates a motor response in terms of personal interpretation of the movement situation.

From Jewett and Mullan.[5]

ment concepts. Creative dance and other experiences allow performers to create as they move. Composing is the highest order of movement processes. It is here that the performer puts together learned movement into a meaningful motor response. This is the level at which new skills evolve. For example, new moves in gymnastics are the product of composing. In addition, creative dance, rhythmic activities, and work with small equipment are activities in which elementary school children can be easily involved in composing. Providing children with the opportunity to develop new movements, which may be named for the child who created them, adds to the creative experience.

The affective domain formulated by Krathwohl and his associates[6] includes emotions, interests, attitudes, motivation, and values. An outline of the categories follows. Since the building of attitudes conducive to lifelong physical activity is an important outcome of the physical education program, attention to the affective domain is essential. Attitudes toward participation will most likely be the result of the conduct of the elementary school physical education program rather than the activities themselves. Elementary school children enjoy physical activity. College students interviewed about their likes and dislikes regarding their past participation in physical education most often cite class organization and other problems of conduct as their reasons for disliking physical education. Too often these problems may be traced to their early physical education experiences in the elementary school.

Behaviors of the affective domain are not concrete and therefore difficult to assess. Successful performance in motor activities may be the result of such behaviors, since interest and motivation affect a person's achievement. The values we hold for participation will also be reflected in our movement behavior. For instance, an individual who values physical fitness behaves in a way that improves or maintains an adequate fitness level.

Singer and Dick[11] formulated a social domain "associated with personal and social adjustment; both related to the socialization process." It is briefly outlined below. The physical education class provides more opportunity for social interaction than any other subject taught in the elementary school. It is a natural environment in which to develop social skills. However, acceptable social behaviors do not happen by chance. Physical educators must be careful to plan and conduct motor activities in such a way that appropriate social behaviors are the result. A program that promotes feelings of self-worth, acceptance of others in a helping atmosphere, fair play, and a cooperative spirit will do much to develop the social behaviors we prize highly.

Looking at behavior in terms of these domains does not assume that the child can be divided into parts. Each domain is strongly linked to the others. By looking at all domains teachers begin to develop objectives in physical education that go beyond the

THE AFFECTIVE DOMAIN

1. Receiving: willing to receive or attend to certain cues or situations.
2. Responding: motivated to actively attend; willingness.
3. Valuing: determining worth in a behavior, from accepting to commitment.
4. Organization: structuring values in a system.
5. Characterization: stabilization, consistency in value organization.[11]

development of motor skills. Examples of objectives are found later in this chapter.

Education is a process that changes the learner. Physical educators must ask themselves which changes they seek. Physical education is an active learning experience in which the learner uses motor skills in solving movement challenges while interacting with others. If our goal for the learner is to develop processing skills, then the physical education program must be process oriented. One who understands not only will move more efficiently but also will solve movement challenges more effectively.

DEVELOPMENTAL APPROACH TO CURRICULUM EMPHASIS

Since physical education may be scheduled from 1 to 5 days per week during the elementary school years, great variation exists in the level of achievement of children from program to program. A grade level approach to the organization of content assumes similar experiences for all children at a particular grade level. Since children's opportunities and achievements vary from school to school, a grade level approach is inappropriate in helping teachers select suitable experiences for the children in their classes.

The activity content in this text uses a developmental approach, which was first introduced by Schurr.[10] Four levels are identified: level I represents the beginning stages of learning, and level IV the most advanced level achieved during the elementary school years. Each level represents a distinct period in the development of the physically educated child.

THE SOCIAL DOMAIN

1. Conduct (sportsmanship, honesty, respect for authority)
2. Emotional stability (control, maturity)
3. Interpersonal relations (cooperation, competition)
4. Self-fulfillment (confidence, self-actualization, self-image)[11]

In this approach teachers select activities based on the behavioral needs of children—motor, cognitive, and affective/social. In selecting appropriate activities the teacher uses information about each child to determine the kind of experience needed. Depending on their movement background, children may be ready for experiences at one level in some activities and at another level in others.

Program objectives for the four developmental levels follow. Programs for levels III and IV may vary considerably from school to school depending on the equipment and facilities available. For this reason specific motor skills are not listed for levels III and IV. The program objectives listed may be met in experiences unique to each physical education setting. Children with daily instruction in physical education should achieve the objectives by the end of the following years: level I, first grade; level II, third grade; level III, fifth grade; and level IV, sixth grade. Obviously children with limited physical education will not reach the objectives for level IV by the sixth grade.

Level I

Level I comprises the first physical education experiences. It is a time for beginning the study of human movement and an important time for the development of fundamental skills. The majority of time in physical education should be devoted to these outcomes. In addition to these important areas children should be given the opportunity to use their skills and begin to apply the movement concepts in a va-riety of activities. It is a time for learning to share equipment, to take turns, and to play with others. It is also a time to establish values about the importance of physical activity in their life. Singing games, folk dances, and simple rhythmic activities with balls and other hand apparatus challenge the children to respond to an imposed rhythm. Creative dance, stunts and tumbling, and activities with large apparatus, beanbags, balls, wands, and other equipment provide an opportunity for the development of new uses of the body.

Level II

Level II is also an important time for the development of an understanding of human movement and fundamental motor skills. At this level the concepts should be well defined, and children are able to work with increasingly more complex movement challenges. In basic skills children work on control and accuracy. Games may require a little more group cooperation, and there may be some delegation of responsibilities in games. During this time simple dance steps may be introduced. Children's dances not only include a variety of steps but also are less imitative and use fewer nonlocomotor movements. Children use problem solving to apply what they know about movement and their ability to move in the many different activities in which they engage.

PROGRAM OBJECTIVES FOR
LEVEL I

MOTOR DOMAIN

The child:

- Performs the following locomotor skills: walk, run, hop, jump, skip, gallop, and slide
- Starts and stops efficiently
- Jumps and lands in a balanced position from a low bench
- Jumps over a series of low obstacles
- Jumps the long rope in rhythmical fashion beginning in the rope
- Moves on and off apparatus with control
- Moves in a variety of ways while the body is in various spacial orientations (for example, inverted)
- Rolls ball from side of body to partner
- Throws a medium-sized playground ball with a two-hand underhand throw
- Catches a rolling ball with two hands
- Catches an accurately thrown playground ball
- Throws small ball overhand for distance
- Bounces a medium-sized playground ball with either hand
- Kicks a stationary ball with inside of foot
- Controls force when executing locomotor or manipulative skills
- Absorbs force while stopping, jumping, hopping, and other locomotor skills
- Responds to signal to start/stop movement
- Moves within the boundaries or within the immediate area of a circle
- Overtakes and gently tags another child
- Avoids being tagged by changing direction, pathway, or speed
- Is able to assume a balanced position on one or more body parts
- Maintains balance while walking on a line or low balance beam
- Balances objects on various body parts
- Can adjust speed from very fast to very slow
- Moves to the underlying beat of the accompaniment
- Recognizes and responds to tempo changes
- Performs locomotor and nonlocomotor movements in time to music
- Performs simple singing games and dances
- Responds appropriately to movement stimuli such as stories, poems, and songs

PROGRAM OBJECTIVES FOR
LEVEL II

The child demonstrates the objectives of level I.

MOTOR DOMAIN

The child:

- Changes movements with little hesitation
- Dodges effectively
- Enters and exits the long jumping rope
- Performs simple stunts while jumping long rope
- Jumps the short rope rhythmically
- Performs beginning level running and field events in track and field
- Executes a two-hand underhand throw with increasing accuracy
- Executes a shoulder pass
- Dribbles a playground ball with either hand while moving
- Adjusts body position to receive a ball thrown to either side
- Dribbles ball with feet with some control
- Strikes ball with hand in underhand motion
- Hits a moving target with a ball with increasing accuracy
- Absorbs force with various body parts
- Absorbs force appropriately in ball skills
- Performs simple dance steps to musical accompaniment
- Moves to accompaniment in various meters: 2/4, 3/4, 4/4, 6/8
- Performs simple folk dances
- Performs simple ball rhythms
- Performs beginning skills on apparatus
- Performs simple combinations of stunts on the mat or on apparatus

COGNITIVE DOMAIN

The child:

Locates and names all body parts

Matches own body parts with those of others

Is aware of possible movements of body parts

Understands how body parts are used in the execution of basic skills

Knows the difference between tension and relaxation

Understands the importance of physical activity in maintaining physical fitness

Is aware of the dimensions of self space moves in a variety of ways in self space

Finds own space in general space

Is aware of the dimensions of general space

Moves in a variety of ways in general space

Moves in general space independently of others

Is aware of possible directions in space

Moves in a variety of ways in all directions

Is aware of levels in space

Executes a variety of movements in the high, medium, and low levels

Is aware of possible pathways in space

Moves in a variety of ways in different pathways

Is aware of range in space

Varies range

Understands how body parts are used to create and absorb force

Creates force with various body parts

Applies understanding of balance to simple movement problems

Solves simple movement problems on apparatus

Recognizes even and uneven rhythms

Responds to phrasing

AFFECTIVE/SOCIAL DOMAIN

The child:

Listens to the teacher and classmates

Follows simple directions

Shares equipment with other children

Takes turns

Plays cooperatively with children in small and large groups in simple group activities

Respects others' space by moving with control to avoid personal contact

Adheres to safety rules while at play

Takes care of equipment and helps to put it away

Willingly participates in all activities

Stays at the task at hand (for a short time)

COGNITIVE DOMAIN

The child:

Understands the use of body parts in the execution of skills

Assumes a variety of body shapes while moving through space with or without support

Has a beginning understanding of conscious relaxation

Has adequate body awareness to perform simple fitness activities

Relates performance in some activities to personal physical fitness

Is able to move to empty spaces without hesitation

Is able to put objects into empty spaces

Recognizes and moves to available pathways while moving in general space

Anticipates the pathway of other children and objects

Moves with partners using space wisely

Controls objects while moving in space

Adjusts movement as space increases or decreases

Moves in a variety of ways in one, two, or all three levels

Controls force in doing ball skills by selecting appropriate amount of force for task

Assumes a balanced position in more complex balance problems

Changes speed without hesitation as the task requires

Distinguishes changes in rhythm or tempo

AFFECTIVE/SOCIAL DOMAIN

The child:

Works independently of direct supervision

Willingly works with a partner designated by the teacher

Assumes responsibility for own actions

Begins to recognize the need to delegate responsibilities in games

Works with others to achieve game goals

PROGRAM OBJECTIVES FOR
LEVEL III

The child demonstrates the objectives of level II.

MOTOR DOMAIN

The child:

Throws balls varying in size with increasing accuracy to stationary and moving targets

Moves a ball through space with control by striking it with a body part or an implement

Receives objects varying in size with the hands, feet, other body parts, or an implement

Performs beginning skills required in the team sports progression

Uses game skills without hesitation

Combines movement skills efficiently

Performs simple square dance moves such as allemande right and left and grande right and left

Matches steps with those of a partner's so they move together in performing dances

Performs a movement sequence alone, with a partner, or with equipment

Performs more advanced skills on the mats and apparatus

Combines a number of skills in a logical progression and performs them smoothly

COGNITIVE DOMAIN

The child:

Uses space more effectively in game play

Selects the appropriate amount of force to control an object while working with objects of varying size, shape, and weight

Judges with accuracy the flight of an object

Maintains relationships with partners and others in the group while performing dances and other rhythmic activities in a variety of formations

Creates and repeats a movement sequence

AFFECTIVE/SOCIAL DOMAIN

The child:

Assumes responsibility for organizing activities in small groups

Works with others in small groups to solve more complex game goals

Shares in the decision making in developing simple strategy

Accepts the judgment and decisions of others

Recognizes the need for and follows game rules

Is helpful to children who are less skilled

Level III

Level III marks a transition in curriculum content. At this level movement concept education and skill development continue through traditional physical education activities. Children are now able to grasp the more complex relationships between what they know about movement and the new activities in which they are engaging. Motor skill development moves to the development of more advanced movement patterns. The children's ability to combine skills more easily is demonstrated as they move smoothly from one skill to the next. Lead-ups to team sports all but replace other forms of games. Learning in this area proceeds through a progression of increasingly more complex movement activities through levels III and IV. Dance activities include folk and square dance and rhythmic activites with not only balls but also ropes and other equipment. Individual activities require increasingly more advanced skills and application of the movement content.

PROGRAM OBJECTIVES FOR
LEVEL IV

The child demonstrates the objectives of level III.

MOTOR DOMAIN

The child:
- Is more accurate in the use of skills
- Combines skills as needed
- Creates and performs a movement sequence in a small group
- Performs a variety of folk and square dance movements
- Smoothly combines skills into a routine on the mats and apparatus

COGNITIVE DOMAIN

The child:
- Relates to an increasing number of individuals in games
- Understands the delegation of responsibilities for various positions in the game
- Selects and uses skills effectively during game play
- Participates in group problem solving in developing strategy for more advanced games
- Creates spaces for self, others, or objects
- Can close spaces to opponents or objects in games
- Varies the force used in performing skills
- Creates and repeats a movement sequence using a ball, rope, or other equipment alone or with others
- Creates gymnastics routines increasing in length and complexity

AFFECTIVE/SOCIAL DOMAIN

The child:
- Assumes more responsibility for the organization and conduct of group activities
- Assumes responsibility for leading a group in various capacities
- Officiates an activity impartially
- Supports each member of the group emotionally

Level IV

Level IV continues the study of human movement through traditional physical education activities. At this level lead-ups to team sports require the interaction of more persons, higher level sports skills, and more complex rules and strategy. Dance activities include folk and square dance in which more advanced dance steps are needed and more complex relationships of individuals within the group are required. Individual activities require more complex application of the movement content as children learn more advanced techniques.

SUMMARY

The movement approach to learning has become well established in the elementary school in the past two decades. It focuses on the process of learning in the study of human movement. Child-centered methods are used to help children develop skill in problem solving.

The elementary school curriculum has been organized into several different implementation models. The traditional model uses a unit approach that is activity centered and treats each unit as a separate entity. It does not include the movement content.

The unit approach is similar to the traditional arrangement but includes the movement content as one of the units of instruction. The movement model presents only the movement content throughout the school year.

The integrated approach focuses on the learning of the movement concepts as the basis for all learning with application to a wide variety of motor skills and activities. The curriculum includes the study of the body's potential for movement, the use of space, and the qualities that affect efficient movement, namely balance, force, time, and flow. These movement concepts are integrated into the learning of motor skills and sports and dance activities.

The movement curriculum takes in all aspects of human development. Taxonomies of cognitive, motor, affective, and social learning are considered in developing the curriculum content for elementary school age children. Physical education has received some criticism for its adherence to only low level objectives. The movement curriculum focuses its attention on moving the children to higher level objectives in the learning process, including analysis, synthesis, and creative movement as well as higher levels of interpersonal relations and self-fulfillment.

The developmental approach to selecting curriculum content enables teachers from varying educational settings to identify the motor, cognitive, and affective/social needs of the children in their classes. Teachers then select program objectives with these needs in mind.

REFERENCES

1. Allenbaugh, N.: Learning about movement. In Sweeney, R., editor: Selected readings in movement education, Reading, 1970, Addison-Wesley Publishing Co.
2. Bloom, B., and others: Taxonomy of educational objectives. Handbook I: cognitive domain, New York, 1977, McKay.
3. Corbin, C.: First things first, but don't stop there, JOPERD 52(6):12, June 1981.
4. Jewett, A., and Bain, L.: The curriculum process in physical education, Dubuque, 1985, William C. Brown Co.
5. Jewett, A., and Mullan, M.: Curriculum design: purposes and processes in physical education teaching-learning, Washington, D.C., 1977, AAHPER. Box on p. 33 reprinted by permission of the American Alliance for Health, Physical Education, Recreation, and Dance, 1900 Association Drive, Reston, Virginia 22091
6. Krathwohl, D., and others: Taxonomy of educational objectives. Handbook II: affective domain, New York, 1969, Longman.
7. Logsdon, B., and others: Physical education for children: a focus on the teaching process, ed. 2, Philadelphia, 1984, Lea & Febiger.
8. McIntosh, P.: The recent history of physical education in England with particular reference to the development of movement education. In Bennett, B., editor: The history of physical education and sport, Chicago, 1971, The Athletic Institute.
9. Melograno, V.: The balanced curriculum: where is it, what is it? JOPERD 55(6):21, August 1984.
10. Schurr, E.: Movement experiences for children, ed. 3, Englewood Cliffs, N.J., 1980, Prentice-Hall, Inc.
11. Singer, R., and Dick, W.: Teaching physical education, ed. 2, Boston, 1980, Houghton Mifflin Co.
12. Tillotsin, J.: A brief theory of movement education. In Sweeney, R., editor: Selected readings in movement education, Reading, 1970, Addison-Wesley Publishing Co.

ADDITIONAL READINGS

Broer, M.: Movement education: wherein the disagreement? Quest Monograph 2:19, April 1964.

A discussion of the meaning of "movement" and a look at the teaching of efficient movement as an aim of physical education.

Howard, S.: The movement education approach to teaching in English elementary schools, JOHPER 37(6):30, June 1967.

Observations of movement education in England and its effects on participants: proficiency in body management skills, interest and active participation, success for all, and a high level of physical fitness.

Ludwig, E.: Toward an understanding of basic movement education in the elementary schools, JOPER 38(3):26, March 1968.

Traces the history of basic movement education and the importance of this approach in enhancing creativity in children. A discussion of how the content blends into our present currciulum and the values of this approach.

Ross, J., and others: What are kids doing in school? JOPERD 56(1):73, January 1985.

Report of a study to describe the status of physical education programs in the schools, including days per week and class activities.

Siedentop, D.: Physical education: introductory analysis,. ed. 3, Dubuque, 1980, William C. Brown Co.

A look at the scope of physical education in the United States, its varied meanings, and physical education as play education.

Silverman, S., and others: Academic learning time in elementary school physical education (alt-pe) for student subgroups and instructional activity units, Research Quarterly for Exercise and Sport 55(4):365, December 1984.

A study of the time on task (alt-pe) in cognitive or motor activity, motor practice, and level of difficulty of practice in a movement education setting and a traditional setting. A variety of activity units and student characteristics such as sex, skill level, and special needs were studied.

Ward, D., and Werner, P.: Two curricular approaches: an analysis, JOPER 52(4):60, April 1981.

Developmental stages and movement analysis approaches to curriculum, including purpose, content, methodology, and evaluation.

4

PROGRAM PLANNING

CHAPTER OBJECTIVES

1 To discuss the relationship between all aspects of the elementary school physical education program
2 To identify factors affecting the elementary school physical education program
3 To list guiding principles in planning the instructional program
4 To outline the steps in curricular planning—program, unit, and daily lessons
5 To provide suggestions for effective unit and lesson planning

Successful implementation of the program begins with careful planning of all aspects of the elementary school physical education experience. Each school setting is unique because it is affected by the interaction of factors such as environment, budget, staffing, and the learners themselves. Regardless of these individual characteristics, each elementary school physical education program is developed on the following premises:

Physical education experiences are an integral part of the school curriculum.

All children shall have an equal opportunity for participation in physical education.

Physical education provides an opportunity for all children to develop their unique qualities.

The rights of the individual and the nature and needs of a democratic society are reflected in the physical education experiences.

Physical education promotes favorable attitudes about personal worth and activity for life.

THE ELEMENTARY SCHOOL PHYSICAL EDUCATION PROGRAM

The elementary school physical education program is the first step in physical education instruction, which may end formally at high school graduation but continue on a more informal basis throughout one's lifetime. It includes the teaching of motor activities in the physical education classes, the conduct of special classes in physical education for children whose needs cannot be met in the regular classes, and the extracurricular program of intramurals and special events.

The Physical Education Class

The study of human movement, instruction in health-related physical fitness, and the development of motor and social skills are the primary concerns of the physical education class. Classes at each developmental level are based on what we know about children, and each class reflects the specific needs of the children in the group. Activities are presented in a logical progression to enable each experience to move the student toward the next level of achievement. Evaluation is discussed in Chapter 9.

Special Classes

Some children may not be able to benefit fully from the physical education classes provided within the district. Often a temporary or permanently disabling condition limits the children's motor experiences to the point that they fall well behind the normal expectancies of physical fitness and motor skill development. These children need physical education that will improve their performance to the degree required for participation in the regular physical education class. Further discussion of these special needs is included in Chapter 8.

Intramurals and Special Events

Intramurals and special events are an outgrowth of physical education classes. These activities provide an opportunity for children to use their skills and knowledge in a recreational setting and to demonstrate what they have learned to others. The extracurricular program in the elementary school is for all children regardless of ability or physical condition. These activities are more fully discussed in Chapter 29.

CURRICULUM PLANNING

Curriculum planning is the first step in the improvement of instruction and a means to better teaching. It does not guarantee effective teaching, but it gives good teachers direction in the planning and carrying out of appropriate learning experiences for children.

Physical education curriculum planning is a district-wide responsibility. All teachers at all levels should share in the decision making for the kindergarten through twelfth grade program of study.

Curriculum planning is a long-range task as a sound curriculum is developed over time. Curriculum change is a continuous endeavor. Those responsible for the curriculum must be willing to make the necessary modifications to keep it viable as conditions in education and society change. In today's society curriculum must consider more than the activity content of physical education. The process for acquiring skills and knowledge about human movement must also be a concern if individuals are going to acquire the tools for continuous learning in the future.

The physical education curriculum must have as its foundation a common core of learning experiences beginning in the early years and commencing at high school graduation. This core content should be centered around the understanding of movement and body management skills. Each level of the curriculum should include appropriate learning activities geared to meet the developmental needs of children. A wide variety of activities are utilized to enable children to use their skills and understanding in many different situations. The physical education curriculum must provide maximum opportunity for youngsters' involvement in learning situations that require cognitive, social, and affective as well as motor responses and that result in favorable attitudes, skills, and knowledge.

The curriculum provides sequential, progressive learning experiences that allow not only for the acquisiton of skills and knowledge but also for the ability to process information in more sophisticated ways. The curriculum takes children beyond the accumulation of information and develops in them the ability to vary, improvise, and create as the movement situation requires.

Program planning involves an analysis of factors that affect the curriculum, the development of program goals, and the selection of content and processes as discussed in Chapter 3. Following this process the schedule of activities for the year, the annual plan, is devised. Final preparations include planning the units and daily lessons of activity with special consideration for each class of children. The needs of children in special classes and the intramural program are outgrowths of and important aspects of instructional planning.

Step 1: Analyzing Factors Affecting the Curriculum

Several factors must be considered in planning the curriculum. These are outlined in Figure 4-1.

Status of the learners

The needs, interests, and experiences of the learners are important considerations in curricular planning. Previous physical education experiences, as well as the informal play experiences of the children, are important. If children have long bus rides to and from school, their leisure time activities may be limited to activities they engage in after dark. Their attitudes about activity and their concept of physical education will reflect their previous experiences in physical education. The children's experience at home and in school also will affect their ability to be self-directed, and this has implications for curricular decisions.

The community

The value and importance parents and the school board place on physical education are reflected in the curriculum. The family influences children's attitudes

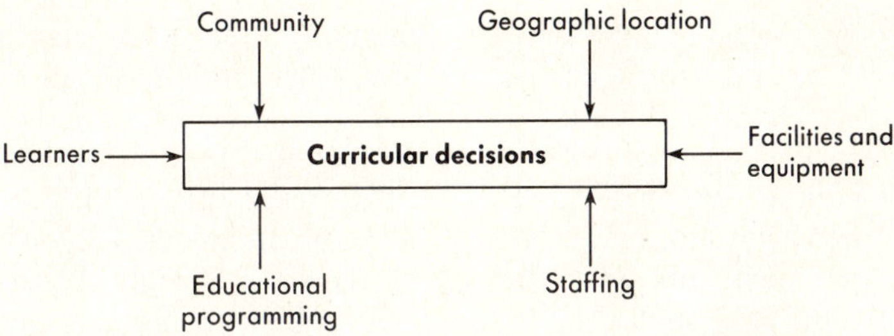

Figure 4-1

Factors affecting curriculum planning.

toward school in general and physical education in particular. Some communities may value a positive physical education experience for all children. Others may value only the successful high school athletic teams. Community interest in age group sports activities may influence expectations for physical education.

Geographic location

The location of the school system will affect the physical education curriculum. The climate, the length of seasons, and the natural surroundings are important factors in curricular decisions. Obviously the curriculum for a community in the Southwest will differ considerably from a physical education program in New England.

Facilities and equipment

The facilities and equipment available in the school may place some limitations on curricular options. However, resources in the community may be used to supplement those available at the school. The budget for equipment must be adequate to provide maximum activity for all children. Ball skills cannot be developed with one ball, just as reading cannot be taught with one book. Physical educators must set priorities regarding equipment purchases to provide the best possible learning environment for all. Often industrial art classes at the high school or interested parent groups can provide equipment for the playground and for physical education use at a minimal cost. There should be a plan for the maintenance, repair, and storage of equipment if each piece of equipment is to last as long as possible.

Educational programming

Educational programming in the school has several implications for physical education. Where possible physical education classes should be held daily for periods of approximately 30 minutes for young children and 40 to 45 minutes for children in the upper elementary school grades. Unfortunately, 2-and 3-day-a-week programs are more often the rule. Obviously much more can be gained from a program that meets every day than from one that meets only twice a week.

Another factor in educational programming is the organization of classrooms and children. In some elementary schools children of several ages may be grouped together in the class. This has serious implications for physical education classes, since the needs that resulted in the arrangement may not be the same needs to be considered for grouping in physical education.

Staffing

The teacher responsible for the physical education program may be a trained professional in physical

education or the classroom teacher. Professional physical educators may be hired to teach all the classes, or the physical education specialist may be responsible for the program development, with the classroom teachers carrying out the implementation. In other situations the physical educator may work with the children 1 or 2 days each week while the classroom teacher continues the program for the remaining days. When the responsibility for instruction is shared by physical educators and classroom teachers, much effort is required to coordinate the efforts of both. Inservice training for classroom and physical education teachers must be provided on a regular basis.

Step 2: Establishing Program Goals

The second step in curriculum planning is the establishment of the overall goals to be attained by each child who participates in the physical education program. These goals must be in tune with the overall goals of the educational system in which the physical education program is a part. Although these goals tend to be broad in nature, one must be careful that they are not so broad as to be meaningless. Each goal should be able to be translated into specific outcomes.

The whole person must be considered in determining these important goals. Physical education programs have traditionally included goals in physical development and fitness; the development of motor skills, social skills, and attitudes; and cognitive development. One should answer the following questions in determining program goals:

What motor skills should children be able to perform?

What knowledge should children have?

How should children behave as they work alone or with others?

These questions are all closely related as we establish our goals and later translate them into meaningful learning experiences for children.

The physical experience in physical education is unique to education. As participants in motor activities children not only enhance their physical development but also acquire the foundational motor patterns necessary for successful participation throughout life. Some programs of physical education choose to stress the development of motor skills, some physical fitness; others combine the two. With the introduction of movement education into American physical education more emphasis has been placed on the knowledge base in physical education. Understanding body awareness, space, and movement qualities and applying this information to a variety of activities has been added to our knowledge base. Physical educators now seek to impart knowledge beyond the rules, the execution of skills, and set strategies. Movement situations are designed to help children solve movement challenges that require varying skills, as well as improvising and creating new movements.

Social and affective goals are commonly included in the physical education curriculum. However, these are not automatic outcomes of a physical education program. Experiences must be carefully planned and conducted if appropriate behaviors are to be realized.

Step 3: Determining Content and Process

The third step in curriculum planning is the determination of content and the processes through which children will become movement educated. We must now answer the question "What are the kinds of experiences children should have to meet the stated goals?" To respond to this question we must consider the activities in which the children will engage and the nature of the experiences that will facilitate the understanding and application of what we know about human movement while they also enhance the social skills and attitudes for which we strive. The selection of content may go beyond the scope of this text. Physical educators may choose additional activities characteristic of the leisure interests of their geographical location, such as cross country skiing and aquatics. Including activities popular in the area is important in preparing students for lifetime participation.

Guiding principles for selecting content

The following statements serve as guiding principles in selecting content for the elementary school physical education program.

The movement content is the core of the physical education program. Physical education has as a primary responsibility the study of human movement, including the understanding of the human body's movement potential and the external factors that affect the efficiency and effectiveness of the movement in which we engage. The concepts of body awareness, space, and the qualities of movement enrich the children's understanding of movement. The application of such knowledge now and in future movement experiences increases the movement possibilitiies and enhances success as children and adults engage in motor activities new to them.

Activities should be selected on the basis of their contribution to the goals of the physical education program. Activities that contribute to more of the educational goals should have priority over those that contribute to fewer goals. Some activities contribute to all or most of the goals of physical education. Other activities only contribute to a few. For instance, softball and volleyball do not contribute to fitness goals. They do, however, contribute to other goals by providing group activity and involving striking skills. Gymnastics provides unique experiences in body awareness and folk dance the necessity to move to an imposed rhythm. In settings in which time is limited for physical education, planners must make careful choices in the selection of content to ensure the goals will be met.

The program should include a variety of activities. Sometimes the physical education program is limited to the activities that the teacher chooses to teach rather than a variety of activities that will meet the interests of all children. If the students are to be well served, each teacher must continue to grow as a professional by updating skills and knowledge and developing new activity areas. A program that does not include a variety of games, dances, and individual activities in addition to the movement content is not a complete physical education experience.

The physical education content should be integrated with other areas of the elementary school curriculum. If carefully planned, physical education may contribute to reading, math, and other school subjects. A coordinated effort by teachers in various areas of the school curriculum results in favorable outcomes for all areas of the curriculum. For example, movement challenges in the primary grades contribute to math and reading readiness as children explore shape, size, and pathway. Other subject areas also may contribute substantially to the goals of physical education as well.

The content should recognize individual differences in the rate of learning. Within each content area a range of activities should be considered to meet the needs of all the children, those who are able and those whose skills and understandings are below our expectations. The teacher provides a variety of skills and activities for each level of ability within the group. New skills and activities are introduced as children are ready to try them or when something new is needed to maintain interest.

The content should provide for progressions from year to year with each experience leading to the next in complexity. Many activities in the curriculum are offered

on an annual basis. It is important to offer children a progression of experiences that challenge them at each level and meet their changing needs. Progression in the complexity and use of skills, the social interactions required, and the complexity of activities to challenge children cognitively are important if physical education is to remain interesting and enjoyable.

The content should be selected with practical limitations in mind. Although physical education experiences should be offered on a daily basis, often they are not. Every program has its limitations. A program that meets only 2 days per week will not accomplish the breadth and depth of experiences that could result from daily physical education. It is probably better to do fewer things well then to try to give the children a little of everything.

Facilities and equipment may also limit the content of the program. Programs operating with limited financial resources will need to plan carefully to maximize the use of what equipment and facilities are available. Teachers will need to be resourceful in extending the program with the use of community resources.

The geographical location affects the length of seasons and the availability of some activities. Each setting provides unique opportunities for children to learn skills that they can use throughout their lifetime.

The content should be planned with continuity in mind. There should be sufficient time to master the skills and knowledge. In a program that meets 1 or 2 days per week the number of possible units of instruction are limited. Most units require a minimum of eight lessons to provide adequate time for meaningful learning in an activity.

Relationships between activities, motor skills, and the application of movement concepts are important if learning is to be continuous. The integrated curriculum is dependent on continuity from one activity to the next.

The curriculum should meet or surpass the state and professional guidelines. Most states have some regulation regarding the minimal physical education requirement. In addition there may be guidelines developed by the state board of education or the state physical education society that go beyond the state regulations in providing guidance for curriculum development.

Content should consider the development of the whole child. Each activity should be selected with the total development of children in mind. Physical fitness, motor skills, cognitive development, and social skills must all be considered in the selection of the content areas.

Content should be selected to address the needs and interests of children. The selection of content should be based on what we know about children at each developmental level. It should be content for children, not adult activities and games. Activities that children enjoy doing and in which they can find success with regard to motor, cognitive, and social skills required are important if positive attitudes about participation are to result. Input from children periodically can help the teacher see the activities from the children's perspective.

The movement content is the core of the physical education program. At each level the variety of experiences offered should include dance, individual activities, and games. These activities should enable the children to use the skills and concepts in many different movement situations. Figure 4-2 defines the content areas of the elementary school physical education program with relative emphasis by level.

Planning for learning

One of our primary concerns in the integrated curriculum is teaching children to be independent learners, to think, and to analyze ever-changing movement situations. If this goal is to be realized, physical education experiences must be carefully planned and conducted and must incorporate experiences that require higher and higher levels of thought processes.

The physical education experience should have a balance in teacher-centered and child-centered activities. Traditionally physical education has been very much teacher directed. Today there is an increasing emphasis on teaching children in a setting in which they assume more responsibility for their own learning. This does not assume that we throw out the equipment and leave the children to their own devices. Nor does it mean that children decide totally what is to be learned. It does require careful planning if children are to become independent learners. Teachers should be a valuable resource in the process of learning but not the only resource.

Learning experiences are planned in progression to meet the movement process goals discussed in Chapter 3. Experiences in physical education begin with the perception of the task, move to the adaptation and refinement of the task, and progress finally to creative movement: varying, improvising, and composing. One should not assume creative movement occurs only in the upper grades. Each process should occur at each level. At each level there will be perceiving and patterning as children are introduced to new motor skills. Adaptation and refinement follow as they learn to use the skills under varying conditions. Finally, creative responses provide children with the challenge that will keep them moving all their lives.

THE ANNUAL PLAN

Once the goals, content, and processes have been defined, a schedule of units of activity, the ***annual plan,*** is developed. The annual plan enables the physical education teacher to plan the year's experiences in physical education. Through annual planning the teacher:

1. Ensures the relative emphasis for each aspect of the curriculum—games, dance, individual activities, and the movement content
2. Determines the number of lessons to be planned for each activity area
3. Blocks out the daily units of instruction
4. Schedules activities dependent on the availability of equipment and facilities
5. Schedules activities with the seasons in mind
6. Schedules activities so that overall body develpment is assured
7. Schedules activities with prerequisites in mind

At each level in the curriculum the emphasis depends on the needs of children as defined by their age characteristics. In levels I and II considerable time is spent in developing the movement content and fundamental motor skills. In levels III and IV the movement content is totally integrated into dance,

Figure 4-2

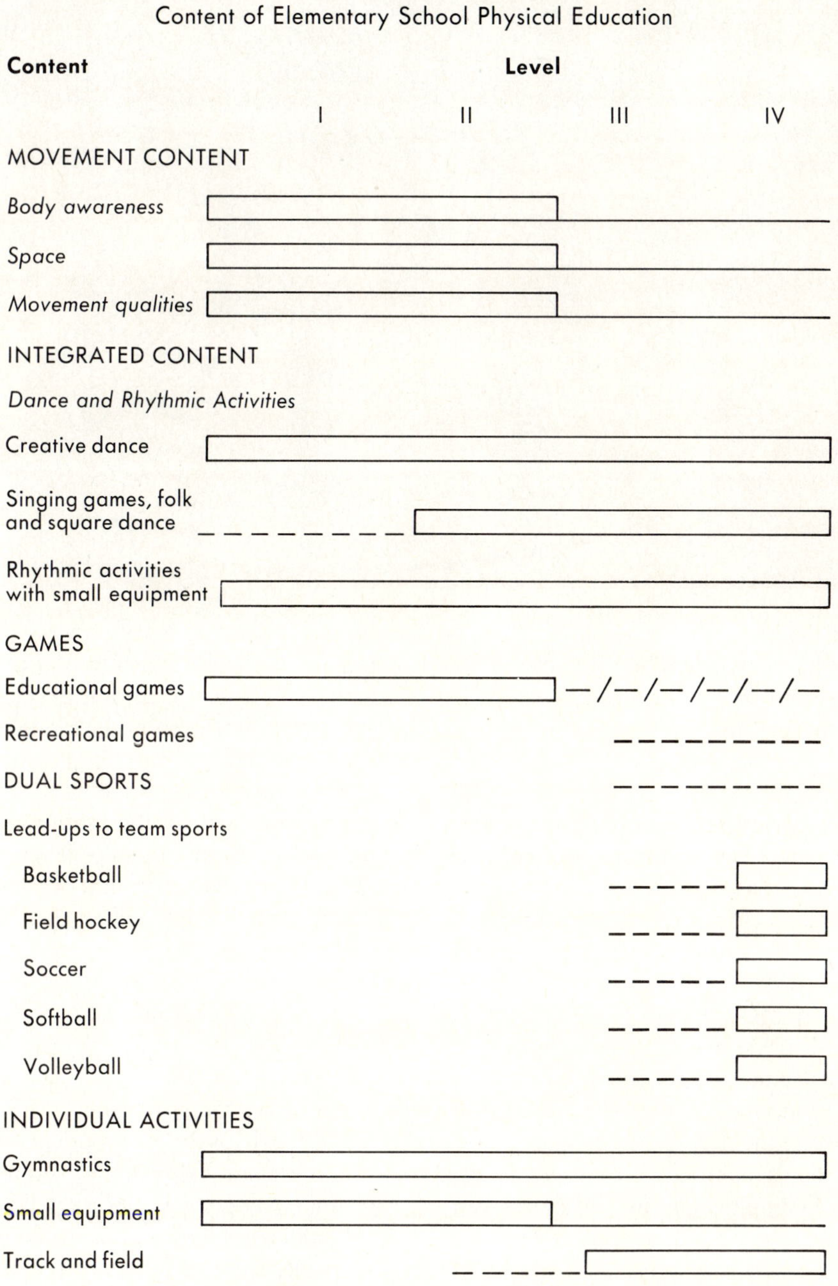

Content of Elementary School Physical Education

Content	Level			
	I	II	III	IV

MOVEMENT CONTENT

Body awareness

Space

Movement qualities

INTEGRATED CONTENT

Dance and Rhythmic Activities

Creative dance

Singing games, folk and square dance

Rhythmic activities with small equipment

GAMES

Educational games

Recreational games

DUAL SPORTS

Lead-ups to team sports

    Basketball

    Field hockey

    Soccer

    Softball

    Volleyball

INDIVIDUAL ACTIVITIES

Gymnastics

Small equipment

Track and field

Introduced _ _ _ _ _ _   Major emphasis ☐

Continued use _____________   Occasional use —/—/—/—/—

games, and individual activities. These are important years for the development of sports and dance skills as well as the continued development of individual activities.

Using the school calendar as a guide, the teacher determines the number of lessons for each unit and writes them into the year's schedule. A sufficient number of lessons is essential if there is to be time for adequate learning. Units generally vary from 8 to 12 or 15 lessons depending on the activity and age level.

In settings where more than one teacher will be responsible for the physical education classes it is helpful if teachers plan the activity schedule together. It may be more economical of time in preparation for classes if classes are involved in the same activities. The preparation of areas for use, such as lining fields, or the arranging of equipment, as in gymnastics, can be accomplished more easily when teachers work together.

Some activities may be considered prerequisites for others. Creative dance activities in which body parts are moved to musical accompaniment are lead-ups to rhythmic activities or folk dance. If stunts and tumbling are taught separately from apparatus activities, the conditioning and body positioning used in tumbling may be considered a prerequisite for later work on apparatus.

Overall body development should be considered in planning. Few units of activity provide the development of all physical fitness components. For example, a unit in soccer that develops cardiorespiratory and muscular endurance might be followed by a unit in stunts and tumbling to develop flexibility.

Two basic methods are used to schedule units of activity to fit within the school calendar: the solid unit approach and the multiple unit approach. In the solid unit approach one unit is introduced at a time. This approach is best when the physical education class is scheduled 3 or fewer days per week. It provides more continuity since it allows sufficient time to be spent on the unit each week. In the multiple unit approach more than one unit is taught per week. This approach is best for a 5-day-per-week program since it allows for more variety within the week. Two units are perhaps the maximum per week if continuity is not to be lost. When multiple units are taught, one unit may complement another. For example, a unit in softball combined with a unit in track provides for the maintenance of fitness better than a softball unit taught alone.

THE UNIT PLAN

The final preparation for teaching involves the development of units of instruction from which the daily lessons will later be devised. A unit of instruction is a series of related learning experiences based on a common theme. The ***unit plan*** enables the teacher to organize a series of related learnings into

COMPARISON OF SOLID AND MULTIPLE UNIT PLANS

SOLID UNIT PLAN

Month	Week	Monday	Tuesday	Wednesday	Thursday	Friday
Sept	3	Soccer		Soccer		Soccer
	4	Soccer		Soccer		Soccer
Oct	1	Soccer		Soccer		Soccer
	2	Soccer		Soccer		Soccer
	3	Tumbling		Tumbling		Tumbling
	4	Tumbling		Tumbling		Tumbling
Nov	1	Tumbling		Tumbling		Tumbling

MULTIPLE UNIT PLAN

Month	Week	Monday	Tuesday	Wednesday	Thursday	Friday
May	1	Softball	Track	Softball	Track	Softball
	2	Track	Softball	Track	Softball	Track
	3	Softball	Track	Softball	Track	Softball
	4	Track	Softball	Track	Softball	Track
June	1	Softball	Track	Softball	Track	Softball

lessons which follow a logical progression. Unit planning involves the following steps:

1. Establishing the unit objectives
2. Determining equipment and facility needs
3. Determining the number of lessons
4. Selecting the content and learning processes
5. Considering the health and safety of the participants
6. Organizing learning materials
7. Organizing the class
8. Creating the block plan which places the content and processes within the number of lessons to be developed
9. Planning the evaluation of the students and the unit

Establishing The Unit Objectives

Objectives are developed on the basis of past experience, future needs, and the present status of the students. The first objectives to be developed are the general outcomes of the unit. Why have we chosen to present this unit? How does this unit contribute to the overall objectives of our elementary school physical education program? What is unique about this experience in the development of children? These objectives are followed by a second set of objectives that deal with the more specific outcomes of the unit. Each of the general goals is broken down into a series of specific learning outcomes. Examples of general goals and their specific objectives follow. These objectives may reflect a progression in development throughout the unit. For example, a beginning skill objective may be concerned with the technique, whereas the *terminal objective* for that skill (the statement of the intended final outcome of the unit) may deal with its use in different situations.

Objectives may be stated qualitatively or quantitatively. *Qualitative objectives* help the teacher to identify the behavior necessary for success by describing how the action will take place. *Quantitative objectives* measure the result of the behavior. For example, a qualitative objective in catching might be stated as follows: To catch a playground ball by getting in line with the ball, reaching out for it, and pulling the ball in toward the body with both hands. A quantitative objective might be stated: To catch the playground ball, thrown at chest height, 8 out of 10 times. Some objectives lend themselves more easily to a quantitative statement, whereas others may be better suited to a qualitative statement. Qualitative objectives may be more important in initial learning, whereas quantitative objectives may be more helpful in advanced stages of learning in which the effec-

UNIT OBJECTIVES

To develop the understanding and use of the concept of general space:
1. To move within the boundaries of general space
2. To move in general space avoiding others
3. To move in a variety of ways while moving in general space
4. To use all the space as the general space increases and decreases.

To develop the basic skills of fielding in softball:
1. To field a grounder by getting in line with the ball, lowering the hips, reaching out with the glove, fingers pointing downward, watching the ball into the glove, and covering the ball with the other hand
2. To field a fly ball by getting in line with the ball, reaching upward with the fingers of the glove pointing upward, watching the ball into the hands, and covering the ball with the other hand
3. To move into position and field ground balls and flies coming to the right, left, in front of, or behind the player

To develop appropriate social skills for participation in basketball:
1. To verbally encourage teammate's efforts during practice and play
2. To make positive statements to others when they make errors
3. To pass the ball to others during play

---

tiveness of the performance may be a more appropriate measure.

Objectives should be written with the age and experience of the youngsters in mind. A catching objective for first graders should vary from that for third graders. In the first grade the teacher may emphasize the use of body parts, as is suggested in the qualitative objective above. In the third grade emphasis may be on the ability to adjust catching to varying conditions, such as balls thrown to the side, in front, or behind the receiver or catching balls of different sizes. In writing meaningful objectives the teacher should:
1. Assess the children's status with the objective to be developed. Is the objective totally new to the children? If not, how much experience have they had with it?
2. Determine the needs or points of emphasis for the present experiences. What do the children need to know to be successful as they begin the unit?
3. Determine where the children should be at the end of the unit. In other words, what is the terminal objective? A series of objectives may be written to describe the development of a particular skill or knowledge in the unit, as described in the box above.

Determining Equipment and Facility Needs

The next step in unit planning is to determine the equipment and facility needs. In doing so the teacher must answer the following questions: What is the minimum amount of equipment necessary for maximum learning? Will additional equipment need to be acquired through purchasing or borrowing from another school? What are the space needs? Are particular field or court markings required?

Setting The Number of Lessons

Based on the objectives of the unit and the relative importance given this activity in the annual plan, the number of lessons required for sufficient experience to accomplish the objectives is determined. Units shorter than eight lessons in all probability will not provide ample time to accomplish the unit objectives. In programs in which physical education time is limited, fewer units of study will be presented. Children need time to develop the skills and understanding and to apply them.

Selecting Content and Learning Processes

Once the unit objectives and the number of lessons have been determined, a list of the activities to be

Table 4-1
Unit planning of content and process for fifth-grade basketball

Skills	Concept	Task analysis	Process behavior	Evaluative criteria (points of emphasis)	Use
Dribbling	Controls force and level; moves in general space avoiding others; changes speed; changes direction and pathway	Dribbles comfortably with either hand	Adapting	Pushes ball with fingertips, head up (not looking at ball), ball low	Sideline basketball
		Dribbles around stationary objects, changing hands	Refining	Keeps body between object and ball	
		Changes speed while dribbling	Refining	Pushes ball a little more ahead as he or she accelerates	
		Dribbles while moving against an opponent	Varying	Keeps body between ball and opponent, opposite hand up	

included is devised. This list includes the skills to be taught, the concepts to be developed, and any special learning experiences in which the children will engage in meeting unit objectives. Examples are given in Tables 4-1 and 4-2.

A task analysis is developed that describes how the children will progress from their present status to the terminal objective. This task analysis gives direction regarding how each skill or concept will be practiced or developed.

Process behavior, as discussed in Chapter 3, is included for each step in the progression. This is dependent on the experience the children have had previously with the skill or concept. If the skill or concept is new to the children, they begin at the perception level. If they have learned the skill or concept previously, they may begin at the adapting, refining, or higher creative levels. Time available and difficulty of the skill or concept determine the processes that may be achieved in the unit.

Evaluative criteria are included for each stage in the learning process to be included in the unit. These criteria become the points of emphasis as the children are learning the skill. In developing concepts, questions to be used as points of emphasis may also be included. These questions challenge the children in developing a variety of responses as well as help to keep the children on task.

The number of different activities included in the unit varies with the type of unit and the difficulty of the tasks. In developing the content and processes one must consider whether it is better to expose the children to a wide variety of activities or to develop a few more fully. For example, in a unit in basketball for the fifth grade, the development of certain game aspects may require that more time be spent on one or two different games so the children may get beyond the learning of the basic rules and have the time necessary to learn the game concepts.

Health and Safety

Some units of instruction require special consideration for the health and safety of the participants. For example, in gymnastics care must be taken to provide the safest possible learning environment for all children. A set of safety rules may need to be written and communicated to the students. In other activities safe use of equipment, such as keeping balls low or keeping equipment in designated areas, may be of concern.

It is assumed children are dressed appropriately for the activity to avoid unnecessary loss of control. To avoid injuries appropriate warm-up activities are

Table 4-2

Unit planning for first-grade space concepts

Concept	Task analysis	Process behavior	Points of emphasis	Evaluative criteria
General space	Explores general space without touching others	Perceiving	"Can you avoid others' self space as you move?"	Moves while avoiding others' self space
	Explores general space using all space available	Perceiving	"Have you been to all parts of the space? Corners? Center? Sides?"	Moves to all parts of the space
	Moves in a variety of ways in general space alone	Varying	"What were some of the ways you moved? (locomotor movements, speed, directions, etc.)"	Uses several different locomotor movements; changes the body parts used to move, speed, direction, etc.
	Increases and decreases available space	Varying	"How did your movements change as space increased? Decreased?"	Adjusts movements to the increase and decrease in size of general space
	Moves with a partner in general space	Varying	"What ways did you move? Were some the same as when you moved alone? Different? Which ways?"	Adjusts movements to those of partner; cooperates in deciding how to move
	Moves in a variety of ways with a ball	Varying	"Which ways were you able to move keeping the ball under control? Which ways were easiest to avoid others? Hardest? Why?"	Keeps ball under control while moving

important. Stretching in gymnastics and warm-ups for the fingers in volleyball are examples of care that must be taken in providing a safe environment. Further discussion of considerations for the safe conduct of physical education activities may be found in Chapter 7 and in the activity chapters.

Organizing Learning Materials

The use of visual aids, demonstrations, or special class projects helps to create and maintain interest in the unit of activity. Additional materials may be needed to enhance the children's learning. Posters, bulletin board displays, rules digests, periodical articles, filmstrips, and other materials may provide additional motivation for students.

Demonstrations and visits by athletes or dancers often help children realize the potential for movement that the unit provides. The children look up to local high school or college athletes, and their visits may have positive effects on the unit outcomes. A culminating learning experience such as participation in a demonstration for other classes, a special event, or a tournament gives additional opportunities to use the new skills and knowledge acquired in the unit.

Class Organization

General procedures for class organization need to be worked out. Some activities lend themselves to individual work, others to work with partners or in small or large groups. Station work may be used, or the entire group may participate in the same activity. Plans for establishing partners and groups will need to be considered. The standard procedures to be followed to begin and end the class must also be determined. Further discussion of organizational strategies may be found in Chapter 7.

Block Planning

The **block plan** is the tentative calendar of events that provides for the all the material to be included in the period of time designated for the unit. Each block in the plan represents one lesson. Activities are arranged in logical progression, with continuity

BLOCK PLAN FOR FIFTH-GRADE FOLK AND SQUARE DANCE

Day 1
Move in time to music
R. 7 Jumps, Christ
Church Bells

Day 2
Move in time to music
Do-si-do

R. Christ Church Bells
Virginia Reel

Day 3
R. Do-si-do
Ladies chain

R. Virginia Reel
Sicilian Circle

Day 4
R. Ladies chain
Right and left through

Sicilian circle

Free choice

Day 5
R. Right and left
through
Move to ¾ time

R. Sicilian circle
Tinikling

Day 6
Move to ¾ time

Tinikling

Day 7
Grand right and left

R. Tinikling
Oh Susanna

Day 8
Grand right and left

R. Oh Susanna

Free choice

Day 9
Corner/partner relationship

Solomon Levi
Oh Johnny

Day 10
Corner/partner relationship
Visiting couple

R. Oh Johnny
Solomon Levi
Birdie in the Cage

Day 11
Visiting couple

Birdie in the Cage
R. Oh Johnny

Day 12
Dance party

Free choice

R indicates review.

planned within each lesson. The block plan includes the introduction of new material and its subsequent review. It includes the skills, concepts, and activities for the day. In determining the amount of time to be devoted to any particular aspect of the unit the teacher must consider the process level to be achieved and the teaching methods to be used.

However, one must remember that the block plan is only tentative. Changes will need to be made in the plan as the unit progresses. Even teachers with a great deal of teaching experience find it necessary to make changes in the block plan. Each group of children differs. Some groups will need more time to develop certain skills and understanding than others. The success of the unit is not determined by the amount of material covered but by the quality of the learning experience. An example of a block plan follows.

Evaluation of the Results

Planning for the evaluation of the unit outcomes is a part of the preplanning. Teachers must determine the most significant outcomes of the unit and devise a method to evaluate their success. It is assumed the teacher has an accurate assessment of student needs before instruction begins. Evaluation is an ongoing process. It goes beyond the need to assess students for the school's reporting system. Evaluation happens daily as the teacher helps each child work toward the accomplishment of the unit objectives.

A second phase of evaluation involves the review of the unit at its close. The teacher determines the extent to which the objectives were accomplished, changes that would make the unit more effective another time, and which activities might be eliminated or which new activities might be added. Evaluation procedures are discussed further in Chapter 9.

SAMPLE LESSON PLAN

Date: <u>September 15</u> Day: <u>2</u> Unit: <u>Educational Games</u> Grade: <u>1</u> Equipment: <u>None</u>

OBJECTIVES

1. To create force in starting by beginning with the feet in a forward stride position and knees bent, leaning forward, with the arms bent at the sides to drive on the start, and pushing off on the balls of the feet.
2. To absorb force in stopping by assuming a forward stride position, bending the knees, and bringing the body weight back over the base.

THE LESSON

Activity and procedure	**Points of emphasis**
Warm-up: running laps (Children enter the area and immediately begin laps; teacher calls out locomotor movements.) "Skip, run, gallop."	Keep space between self and the person ahead Stay to the outside of the gym
"Stop and sit where you are. On the signal and before I count to 3, I want to see how many can find their own space. 1-2-3."	
Practice stopping "On the signal we will move in general space. When I say 'Stop,' I want to see how quickly you can stop on your feet. Then we will begin again. Try different ways of stopping."	Forward stride Knees bent Weight over base
"Did you try to stop with your feet close together? Far apart? Knees bent? Legs straight? Leaning forward? Body over your legs?"	
"Now move to the line and do a good stop." (Children line up in one line at the end of the gym.)	

DAILY PLANNING

With the unit plan completed the final preparations for teaching are made with the development of the daily *lesson plans*. Often the difference between effective and ineffective teaching is a matter of working out the details of the individual lesson. Careful planning is required if teachers are to help students accomplish worthwhile objectives. Continuity is achieved when teachers carefully construct a lesson so that each part leads smoothly into the next. Physical education time is limited. Successful planning can maximize the participation of all through careful organization of the class and smooth transitions from activity to activity. Lesson planning includes the development of:

1. The objectives for the day
2. The activities and learning processes to be utilized
3. The equipment and materials needed
4. The points to be emphasized
5. The procedures to be used in organizing and moving the group

SAMPLE LESSON PLAN

Practice starting
 "Pretend you are in a race and you want to get a fast start. What would be a good position? Take a position you think would be good and be ready to start when I give the signal. Ready, Go. Now stop. Was it a good starting position? Try another. Ready, Go. Stop." (Repeat several times having children try different positions.) "Which position seemed to be the best?"

 (Children practice starts moving in line. As they return to starting line, the class begins Jet Pilot.)

Feet in forward stride
Arms bent to drive
Lean forward
Knees bent

"Are you ready for a fast start?"

Jet Pilot
 "You must have a good stop to be the first one back."

"Let's see who can have the best stop."

Red Light
 (As the children stand in line, the teacher divides them into groups of three with the two outside children holding hands and the third child in the center.)

 "Find a space in the playing area for your group."

"You must stop quickly and be very still."

Squirrels and Trees
 (Two children do not have a tree.)

"Is everyone ready to start? Can you stop quickly in a new tree?"

 "I want to see how many children always get a tree. Think where you want to go before I give the signal."

EVALUATION

Some of the children did not respond quickly to the signals. Emphasize listening next time.
Their use of general space was good. Most moved well without touching others.
The children need to be reminded to use their arms to help them get off to a good start.
In stopping, some are not bringing their weight back over the base and also have their feet
 too close together.

6. The evaluation at the close of the lesson
A sample lesson plan is shown below.

Lesson Objectives

The first task in preparing the lesson is to determine the objectives to be developed. These objectives should include the skills and movement concepts to be introduced or reviewed and, where appropriate, the social behaviors to be stressed. In writing objectives the teacher determines individual and group needs. In developing objectives the teacher considers the process behavior at which the class is functioning regarding each skill or concept to be attained.

Objectives are selected from the unit and describe what is to be worked on for the day. Since they are written in behavioral terms in which they describe the outcome of the performance, these objectives may describe the execution of a skill (how body parts are used) or the use of a skill in a variety of movement situations. The objectives serve as a valuable tool in determining the needs of children in future lessons.

At the close of the lesson the teacher determines how well the objectives were met and makes plans for the next lesson with further emphasis on some objectives and the introduction of new objectives as needed.

Selecting the Activities and Learning Processes

Once the day's objectives have been determined, the teacher then selects the learning experiences that will help each child master each objective. Activity selection is partially based on the process behavior achieved by the children. Activities for children at the perception stage will differ from those at the improvising stage. Sometimes children may progress through several process levels within a lesson. Activities are arranged in order of difficulty, with each activity leading smoothly into the next.

Equipment and Materials

The amount of equipment used should maximize the learning for each child. Where the amount of equipment is limited, a variety of kinds of equipment may need to be used so all children have an equal opportunity for practice. In addition, special materials may be needed. Task cards, posters, pictures, and the like may make the learning more interesting.

Points of Emphasis

The points to be emphasized should be noted for each activity. Learning is not necessarily the result of participation. It is the result of teaching. Sometimes these teaching points will be directed toward the execution of skills, whereas in other activities the understanding and application of movement concepts or the use of motor skills will be stressed.

One must always keep in mind that the activity serves as the means, not the end, to learning about human movement. A summation of the important points should be planned for the close of the lesson. At this time the children should be encouraged to verbally respond to questions recapitulating the day's objectives.

Procedures

Once the activities have been selected, the teacher determines how the class will be organized. The children are to be grouped for maximum learning and participation in each activity. Children may work as individuals or in small or large groups, depending on which grouping will best serve to maximize the movement for all. A smooth transition from one activity to the next must also be carefully planned. Inexperienced teachers often take class organization for granted. Anyone can organize a group of children into a circle or four groups. However, valuable time and attention are often lost when teachers do not think carefully through the moves required for a successful lesson. Suggestions for classroom management are found in Chapter 7.

Evaluation

As soon as possible following the lesson, the teacher should evaluate the learning experience. The teacher must determine the extent to which the objectives were met, which objectives need additional emphasis in the next lesson, and the needs identified for future lessons. Further discussion of evaluation is found in Chapter 9.

SUMMARY

The physical education program comprises the physical education class, the special class, intramurals, and special events. In the physical education class children learn motor skills, develop understanding about human movement, and acquire social skills for successful participation. The special class is provided for children who cannot fully benefit from the physical education class. The nature of the special class varies with the needs of the special learners, serving as a resource room for some and an alternative to the physical education class for others. Placement may be temporary or permanent. The intramural program and special events include all activities outside the class settings. These provide additional opportunities for children to use the skills and knowledge developed in class.

The successful implementation of the physical education program is dependent on careful planning. Each school provides a unique setting for learning because the environment, the school, and the learners themselves influence curriculum development.

Steps in curriculum planning include an analysis of the factors affecting the curriculum, the development of program goals, and the selection of the content and processes to meet these goals. An annual plan is developed to fit the curriculum to the school calendar. The planning process is concluded with the development of units of instruction and then daily lesson plans. Each organizes learning experiences into a logical progression with careful considerations for the needs of individual children and the class.

Planning does not ensure effective teaching, but it is the first step in providing for the needs of children. Teachers must then carry out the plans using their teaching skills to help children become the best they can be.

REFERENCES

1. Jewett, A., and Bain, L.: The curriculum process in physical education, Dubuque, 1985, William C. Brown Co.
2. Jewett, A., and Mullan, M.: Curriculum design: purposes and processes in physical education teaching-learning, Washington, D.C., 1977, AAHPERD.
3. Mager, R.: Preparing instructional objectives, rev. ed. 2, Belmont, Calif., 1984, Pitman Learning Inc.
4. Rink, J.: Teaching physical education for learning, St. Louis, 1985, Times Mirror/Mosby College Publishing.

ADDITIONAL READINGS

Cooper, J., and others.: Classroom teaching skills: a handbook, ed. 2, Lexington, 1982, D.C. Heath & Co.

Instructional planning from writing objectives to teaching skills and concepts, classroom management, observational skills, and evaluation.

Harrison, J.: Instructional strategies for physical education, Dubuque, 1983, William C. Brown Co.

Understanding teaching and learning and the planning process from writing objectives, selecting learning styles, selecting instructional materials, and planning for evaluation to developing units and lessons.

Metzler, M., and Young, J.: The relationship between teachers' preactive planning and student process measures, Research Quarterly for Exercise and Sport 55(4):356, December 1984.

A study of two teachers and the fourth-grade student process behavior differences resulting from different lesson-planning patterns.

Singer, R., and Dick, W.: Teaching physical education, ed. 2, Boston, 1980, Houghton Mifflin Co.

A look at teaching students and teachers and the development of the systems approach, including writing and analyzing performance objectives, evaluation, and planning and carrying out the instructional plan.

Part Three

Conducting the Physical Education Program

Selecting the content and processes is the first step to a successful physical education program. Implementation of the program involves planning the teacher's interactions with the students—selecting methodology, planning the classroom management, establishing an environment conducive to learning, and finally evaluating the outcomes of the program.

5

LEARNING AND MOTOR LEARNING

CHAPTER OBJECTIVES

1 To identify principles of learning and motor learning
2 To apply knowledge of learning principles to the teaching of physical
education

To be an effective teacher one must understand how children learn. *Learning* may be defined as a change in behavior brought about as a result of practice. Children need a rich environment for learning if they are to meet their optimal movement potential. Children are totally involved in the learning process, and although the emphasis is on the cognitive process and the motor response, in physical education children are involved as total beings.

Learning and performance are not synonymous. Performance is a function of learning and other variables. Motor skill performance is related to physical characteristics, motor ability, perceptual ability, cognition, and emotional state. The physical education teacher contributes substantially to the development of children by providing a variety of experiences in which the thinking, moving, and feeling child develops. Motor learning and performance are both handicapped if the physical qualities needed for skilled movement are not present.

Maturation, leadership, learning set, motivation, whole-part learning, practice, knowledge of results, transfer, reinforcement, and retention are factors that require attention in setting the stage for learning. The following pages discuss learning theory and learning principles of concern to teachers.

LEARNING AND MOTOR LEARNING

The critical periods theory of child development suggests that certain times in the developmental process are important for the learning of particular skills. If these skills are not developed at the appropriate time, future success in the performance of these skills is affected. Although this is only a theory, deprivation of opportunities in the elementary school may have a lasting effect on a person's ability to move successfully throughout life. During these early years children need the opportunity to not only master the fundamental motor skills that are the foundation for future dance and sports skills but also to develop the understanding of their own movement important in the transfer of learning.

Learning is often depicted in educational psychology as a performance curve (Figure 5-1). Horizontal lines depict a slow rate of learning, whereas steep vertical rises show active learning. The initial horizontal line represents beginning understanding

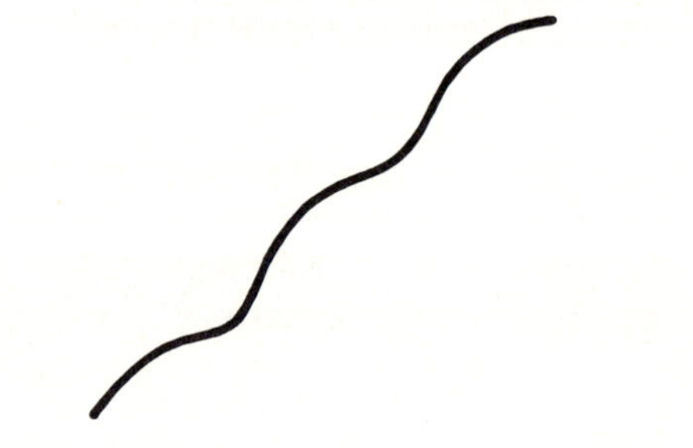

Figure 5-1

Performance curve.

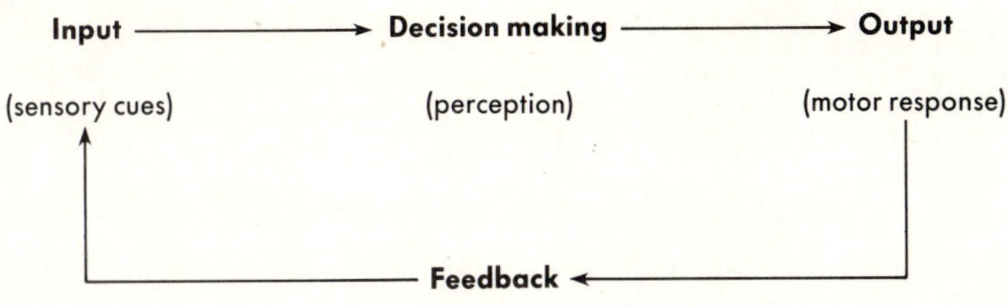

Figure 5-2

Motor learning model.

of the task and body actions. As the child gains insight into the task, improvement in performance results and the curve shows a vertical rise. This rise may represent mastery of parts of the task and enthusiasm for learning. Transfer of learning, motivation, and success all account for this steep rise. Horizontal lines throughout the curve indicate plateaus in learning. These represent declines in the rate of learning. Plateaus may be the result of conditions within the learner or within the learning environment. The student may have lost interest, may need time to integrate the skill, or may have reached a high degree of skill after which improvement will take greater effort. On the other hand, the teacher may be moving too slowly or too rapidly or may need to change method or practice to make it more appealing to students, or environmental factors such as the climate, facilities, or equipment may be a factor. To minimize plateaus the teacher must recognize individual needs, give encouragement and appropriate feedback, avoid excessive anxiety in the learners, and provide interesting experiences to practice the skills.

Figure 5-2 shows a learning model. Through the senses the learner receives certain stimuli, or input. Individual differences in the sensory mechanisms' ability to receive stimuli vary the input from child to child. The second step involves some decision making, which may be labeled perception. This process involves analyzing the sensory data based on present conditions and past experience, which has been stored in the brain. This process is a highly individual matter. Judgments are made and decisions for action considered and selected. A motor response is the result. As the action is taken, the child receives feedback about the affects or result of the response through the sensory modalities, and the process is repeated.

In learning motor skills children generally pass through three stages of learning. In the first stage they begin to grasp an understanding of the sequence of the task, how body parts are used, and control of space and movement qualities for successful performance. This is the time of teacher explanation and demonstration and beginning attempts to explore body movements to accomplish the task and to perform the skill. The second stage is the practice stage, in which children refine the pattern, correcting errors as needed. At this stage feedback is extremely important in helping them have a correct movement. The third stage involves mastery learning and a relatively automatic performance in which the skill is habituated. Now the children can concentrate on the use of the skill in different situations under varying conditions.

Maturation and practice play important roles in the development of motor skills. Maturation provides the capability for learning. Early motor development is dependent on the neuromuscular maturation of the child. Once sufficient neuromuscular maturity has been attained, practice plays an increasingly important role in the development of motor skills. Motor skills improve with age, but the effect of maturation on motor skill acquistion during the elementary school years is not clearly understood.

Considerable variation in motor development exists among individuals at any one age level. The range in individual differences will increase with age. Girls advance in maturity at a faster rate than boys, but this is not necessarily true of the development of motor skills. Cultural effects on motor development are a factor at an early age, since boys have been encouraged to develop motor skills and girls have not. Form in motor skills is an individual matter as children with different physical attributes and body proportions attempt the same skills. In providing for the needs of each child the teacher's focus of attention should be on the analysis of why skills are inefficient, determining whether inexperience, lack of understanding, or the absence of some physical quality such

as flexibility or strength may be the cause. Children progress at their own rate; early success is not necessarily an indicator of future accomplishment.

Motor learning should encourage thinking. Physical education should teach the child to think as well as to move. The teacher must attempt to make the learning purposeful and meaningful, not just a conditioned response in which little or no thinking is involved. The teacher must teach for understanding and skill. Motor skill learning is more than trial and error, with the teacher helping the children to develop the thinking needed for continued success by attending to relevant stimuli. This should include understanding how the body is used and how movements need to be changed under various conditions.

Tension affects learning. The emotional setting must be considered. The emotional state of the learner may facilitate or inhibit performance. Although an optimal level of tension is conducive to learning, the best environment is one in which there is not a high level of anxiety. Too much tension lowers the level of learning because energy is wasted handling the tension. The teacher attempts to arouse students without causing too much anxiety. Stressful settings are more disruptive to learning complex tasks than simple tasks. Through the learning of progressively more difficult skills children are challenged and their confidence level raised. Competition is controlled so that too much anxiety does not result.

Leadership is important in learning. The physical educator plays an important role in the learning of children. The teacher presents a clear picture of the lesson objectives, uses demonstration and verbal explanation to translate the objective to the class, plans interesting practice, is alert in detecting and correcting errors, and is responsive to the individual needs in the group. A sincere interest in children and their efforts is demonstrated in the teacher's behavior.

MOTIVATION

Motivation is the process of getting an individual to act in ways that satisfy a need or desire. The teacher does not give students motivation but rather alters the variables that affect motivation.

The teacher in the process of motivating students alters several variables that affect motivation, namely, interest in learning, level of aspiration, feeling tone, rewards, success, and knowledge of results. Students react differently to the manipulation of these variables. Some students may be more motivated by certain variables than by others. To be successful the teacher must discover which variables individual students respond to best.

Students must be interested in the goal toward which they are working. Interest in learning a particular skill or motor activity may be influenced by several factors. Athletic ability is valued in our American culture. Adequate skill may be important to group membership. An individual may wish to develop skills for leisure time pursuits. There may be interest in improving one's appearance or in improving or maintaining health. All of these plus other factors may influence children's interest in learning.

The student's level of aspiration is an important factor in motivation. Level of aspiration varies with the individual. Some children seek the highest level of accomplishment, focusing most of their energies into the pursuit of one or a few activities. Others are content with a recreational level of skill. A higher level of intended achievement usually yields a higher level of performance. Success results in a rise in the aspiration level, whereas continued failure may lower the desired goal. At times the teacher's view of what a child should accomplish and the child's personal goal for achievement may not be the same.

If there are pleasant feelings associated with the learning, motivation is enhanced. Motivation is related to students' feelings about learning. Feeling tone is important. Pleasant feelings about learning motivate whereas negative feelings reduce motivation. Feelings are affected by the learning environment. If children like and respect the teacher and believe that the teacher views them in the same way, motivation is enhanced. Variety in the way skills are practiced or in the methods of presentation and the selection of activities themselves can result in children viewing physical education as challenging and fun.

Rewards and recognition are powerful motivators. Successful performance yields recognition from both peers and teacher. Although I do not recommend material rewards as a rule, verbal praise and recognition in the group are important. Rewards in physical education should be within the activity itself, as children see the effects of their participation and contribution to the activity.

Success enhances an interest in continuing to learn. Success enhances success. The teacher must be aware of student needs and goals. Activities are selected with the age and maturity of the students in mind. Children enjoy moving, and the teacher assists them in finding ways to move that have meaning for them. The teacher begins where they are, with their developed interests and abilities, and proceeds to help children in setting goals. Student involvement in goal setting increases motivation. A progression of increasingly difficult tasks is provided to meet the needs of the individuals and to guarantee continued success in learning. Feedback regarding the degree of success affects motivation. This is discussed more fully later in this chapter. Confidence is gained and progress is much more rapid as children engage in successful learning.

Students must understand the goal to which they are working if motivation is to be maintained. The students understand what is to be learned and why it is important. The relationship of what is being learned in physical education to other school subjects or use in school, home, or community activities is understood. Students are motivated to learn when they see meaning and relationship in what they are learning. When they are assigned tasks within their ability, they can easily see what they do each day to bring them closer to meeting the goals. Practice of skills is related to their use in the activity. If a particular activity is meaningful and important to them, there is increased motivation for practice.

WHOLE-PART LEARNING

A question that must be addressed in planning learning experiences for children is whether to present the new material as a whole or to divide and present it in parts. A whole may be defined as the largest whole that the learner can grasp. It may be considered the activity itself, for example, soccer, or a particular skill involved in a game, such as the serve in tennis. Skills may also be considered wholes, and some may be practiced in parts. Several factors concerning the task and the learner must be considered in the choice of teaching the whole or part method.

The nature of the task and condition of the learner must be considered in selecting the whole or part method. If the task is simple, if it is made up of integrated parts, if the parts are not meaningful to the learner, or if the parts are performed simultaneously, the whole method is probably best. On the other hand, if the task is complex, if it has independent parts, and if work on segments is necessary, the part method should be the choice. For example, in teaching the backward roll the hand placement on the mat is extremely important to successful completion of the roll. It may be helpful to practice the roll back to the placement of the hands on the mat below the shoulders before attempting the "whole" backward roll.

If the learner is capable of remembering long sequences, is highly skilled, and is able to concentrate over a long period of time, the whole method may be used successfully. When the learner has a limited memory, has a short concentration span, and is having difficulty with one part, making the whole method unsuccessful, the part method may be used to an advantage. A combination of whole and part methods usually works best.

As a general rule children learn motor skills better and faster when they are taught as a whole. It may be more feasible to break games down into specific parts for practice. The teacher begins with the general concept and then breaks it into meaningful parts. Observing a soccer game may give meaning to the learning of particular skills. In developing parts immediate feedback is essential to help the learner fixate on the part being learned.

The parts may only have meaning if the learner sees them as a part of the bigger whole. Seeing a skill used in an activity may give meaning to practicing it alone. The teacher must be careful not to dwell too long on developing parts without putting them back into the whole. Interest in learning may be lost if the children lose sight of the meaning of the practice because too much time is spent on one or more parts.

TRANSFER

Speed in learning is somewhat dependent on one's ability to adapt and apply previous learning. This ability to apply what has been learned in one situation to learning in a new situation is called *transfer*. Although each motor skill is specific, there are general, perceptual, motor, and maturational factors that may be the same and that can enhance learning from one skill to another. Transfer is a critical factor in problem solving, creativity, insight, and reasoning.

Transfer may facilitate or interfere with learning. There is positive transfer when old learnings facilitate new learning, and negative transfer when old learnings interfere with the learning of new material. Positive transfer provides economy in the use of time and energy in learning, whereas negative transfer increases the time and energy spent for new learning.

The teacher must identify the factors that generate positive or negative transfer and structure the setting so those that enhance learning are used to advantage. Four factors have been identified that affect transfer: the similarities between the two learning situations, the association of the old and new learning, the degree of original learning, and the perception of essential and unvarying elements between the old and new learning.[2]

The greater the similarities between the old and new learning situations, the more likely transfer is to occur. To encourage transfer the two learning situations should be as alike as possible. The learning conditions as well as the similarities of the activities must be considered. The feelings, motivation, and set to perform are important factors affecting the students. Conditions that bring about anxiety, such as the threat of a test or a highly competitive activity, may actually interfere with the learning. The "set to perform," the way a student is thinking, results in the student perceiving the situation as similar or different from the previous one. If the previous situation will interfere with learning, the teacher should attempt to structure the situation as differently as possible to avoid the effects of negative transfer. The teacher must decide what conditions are needed to help with positive transfer. The similarity of the methodology, the sensory mode, and the approach to the new learning must be considered. The movement approach encourages perceptions of similarity through discovery teaching and problem solving. In planning for skill practice, the closer the practice simulates the use of the skills in the activity, the more likely transfer is to occur.

When two learning situations are associated, transfer is more likely to occur. Attitudes, feelings, and beliefs affect transfer. If the association is pleasant, such as having fun in the gymnasium, positive transfer is more likely to occur. However, an anxiety-producing situation or failure negatively affects transfer. The teacher can associate past successful experiences with the new material by focusing the children's attention on a previous experience in which they applied the skills successfully. In planning for transfer the teacher determines the students' past experience and how it can be used successfully in the new context.

The more meaningful and purposeful the original learning experience, the greater the likelihood that transfer will take place. The better something is learned, the more appropriately it may be transferred. On the other hand, poorly learned material is transferred inappropriately. With adequate learning of the first task the second task may be learned more efficiently in less time. It is probably better to spend time learning a few things well than to spend the time on learning too many things. Research indicates time spent on successful learning of an easy task yields better transfer to more difficult tasks than spending the same time on difficult tasks.[2] Material partially learned will probably not be applied to new situations.

The identification of similar elements in the old and new learning situations can enhance transfer. The identification of similar elements signals the relevance of previous learning to the new learning. These elements in physical education might be the use of particular body parts, similar functions with different implements, or the use of force, balance, and other movement principles. The elements that receive attention must be important to the new task; focusing on nonessential elements may result in negative transfer. The elements identified must be within the understanding and experience of the learner. Identifying elements helps to focus the learners' attention on critical aspects of the new skill or concept and increases their conscious recognition of these elements in the new situation. Identifying these elements is an essential aspect of teaching for transfer.

If transfer is to occur, the teacher must teach for transfer. Many teachers assume children will transfer learning from a previous situation to present learning opportunities. Transfer of learning is not automatic; it occurs only with careful planning. The teacher is in control of the information to be transferred. In presenting new material the teacher stresses the concept or key points to be learned, facilitates transfer by pointing out the relationships or similar elements with previous learning, and plans practice building on these essential elements. In transfer the effect is positive if the activity calls for an old response to a new stimulus, such as in transferring batting skill in softball to batting in baseball. The effect is negative when a new response is required for an old stimulus, such as in learning tennis skills, which require a firm wrist, after learning badminton skills, which require a flexible wrist. There is contradictory evidence about whether learning basic principles will facilitate learning specific skills. Gestalt theorists support teaching

basic movement principles and generalizations. The movement approach is based on the premise that learning principles will transfer from one situation to another. Teaching for transfer should encourage thinking and problem solving. The age, maturity, and experience of children affect their ability to transfer learning. Young children require more assistance if transfer is to be effective. The teacher must enhance the chance for transfer by pointing out the similarities in the old and new learning and by helping children apply movement principles.

Teaching for transfer is our ultimate goal. Since it is not possible to prepare children for every movement situation that will occur in their lifetimes, one must teach for transfer with the hope the reasoning and thinking skills developed will enhance transfer of learning outside the school.

PRACTICE

We learn by doing. Practice gives us the opportunity to repeat an action numerous times, to develop smooth flowing movement in the best form.

Motor skills are taught, not caught. Moving does not necessarily imply learning. Teachers at times may assume that learning is taking place in an activity because the children are active. An effective practice involves purposeful activity in which the students' attention is focused on what is to be learned. The teacher identifies the key points for successful performance, and the students develop these concepts through conscious effort. Practice makes perfect only if practice *is* perfect.

The quality of the practice is important in developing proficiency of performance. The students must be aware of the goal and the key points to consider in meeting that goal. The practice must be interesting to maintain high motivation. Early analysis and correction of errors are essential to preventing fixation on incorrect form. The students must develop understanding of the task to respond to the teacher's feedback and to analyze their own performances based on the resulting action. Variety in the way the practice is conducted is important in maintaining interest and motivation. Different formations, relationships with partners and opponents, and equipment are used to broaden the understanding and use of the skills being practiced. Problem solving adds to the interest as children attempt to use the skills effectively under varying conditions. Skills should be practiced as they will be used, and each student should have the opportunity to attempt the skill as much as possible in the practice period.

Practice beyond the first correct response yields overlearning, which is important in retention. The object of practice is to increase understanding and perfect performance. Once the skill has been performed correctly, additional practice helps to retain the skill in the correct form. Although errors still may be made following the first correct response, errors should be gradually eliminated in the following attempts to perform the task. Overlearning results in better retention, and long-term retention requires more overlearning. However, there is a point of diminishing returns. Too much practice of any one skill can result in boredom and detract from further learning.

The length of practice is governed by the nature of the skill and the age and level of ability of the participants. Short, frequent practice periods are best during the early stages of learning. Since frustration and fatigue may be the result of early attempts in learning a motor skill, short practice periods may be used to an advantage. However, the practice should be long enough to have meaning. The maturity of the students determines optimal practice times, since young children have a shorter attention span than older children. With young elementary school age children periods of 5 to 7 minutes are appropriate for the practice of one skill. The length of practice for activities requiring strength and endurance is determined by the physical condition of the participants. As children in the upper grades recognize the importance of being well skilled, their interest in practice increases. Once a certain level of skill has been achieved, interest in practice may also increase since there is satisfaction in practicing the skill. Skills requiring a high degree of accuracy or vigorous activity require more frequent rest periods, so short practices may have the best results.

The practice schedule is planned according to the learner's capacity and stage of learning and the difficulty of the skill. **Massed practice** refers to practice periods scheduled close together. **Distributed practice** refers to practices scheduled over a period of time in which time between practices may vary. If exploration is needed or if remembering is important to success, such as in the learning of folk and square dance sequences, massed practice may be best. On the other hand, if the skills are difficult, distributed practice may be best to give the children a longer time to develop the skill and understanding necessary to be successful. For young children during the development of gross motor skills distributed practice appears to be best. Skills learned in massed practice may

be retained by distributed practice once a particular level of skill has been achieved. Distributed practice offers young children more variety in programming, which is important in maintaining their interest.

Practice should proceed at as nearly a normal tempo for the skill as possible. Skills that require both speed and accuracy should be practiced at the required speed when possible. There is some controversy among motor learning specialists about whether one should practice for speed or accuracy first.

KNOWLEDGE OF RESULTS

As an individual performs a motor task, information, or *feedback,* about the success or failure of the performance may be readily available. If, for example, the performer is able to get the ball to the receiver, the effectiveness of the task may be readily seen. On the other hand, if the throw was short or was intercepted by an opponent, the performer receives information about the task's ineffectiveness. Many times the feedback available tells students that they were not successful but not why the performance failed. The teacher provides the information to help improve the performance another time. Perhaps the technique was incorrect or the timing too early or

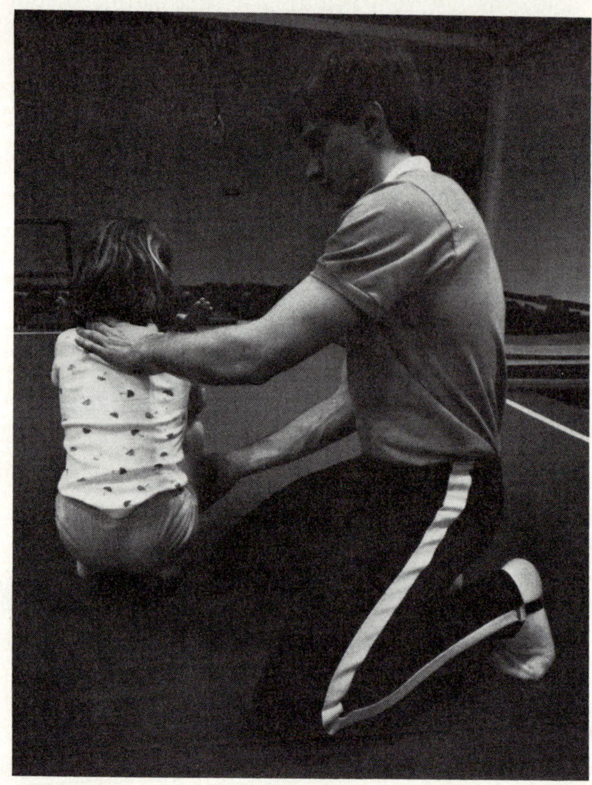

too late. This information supplied by the teacher or other observer of the performance is called *augmented feedback.* Augmented feedback, commonly referred to in the literature as knowledge of results (KR), is important when the available information is inadequate.

Improvement in performance is related to the amount and nature of the feedback received. Augmented feedback is important if errors are to be corrected in the early learning period. This knowledge of results should go beyond a judgment of success or failure. It should be given in an encouraging way, suggesting the changes needed to improve the performance.

The knowledge of results should provide the students with the information needed at their individual level of skill. The teacher must decide what information is necessary to improve the performance depending on the age and maturity of the students and the performance level at which the children are working. Young children can handle limited bits of information at one time. Beginners need information basic to the performance of the task, whereas more advanced performers may need information on some of the finer points of the technique.

Augmented feedback assists the learner in attending to relevant cues. The teacher identifies the most important cues for the student's attention when helping children perfect their technique or improve their use of a skill. If a child is not accurate in throwing to a target, emphasis on the follow-through may be needed to improve the accuracy of the performance. If a child is being left behind by the person he or she is guarding, perhaps watching the opponent's waist may improve the guarding technique. Relevant cues vary with the needs of the individual students and their level of understanding.

REINFORCEMENT

Reinforcement is any event that increases the probability of the occurrence of a behavior or maintains the strength of a behavior. It provides satisfaction or recognition for behaving in a certain way or for doing something.

Reinforcers differ with each individual. Children respond differently to reinforcers. What is a reinforcer for one child may have little effect on another. It is important for the teacher to get to know the students well enough to know what reinforcers work best with each one.

The best reinforcers build feelings of self-worth and enhance the children's self-concept. Positive reinforcers are desired. They may give recognition, opportunities, or special privileges. For example, the teacher may say "That was well done, Mary," "Now that you have completed the assignment, I will help you with a new skill," or "You have done so well that you may have free time now and choose your next activity."

To strengthen behaviors the teacher should respond with sincere praise, recognizing the efforts being made, progress toward goals, and success along the way in learning new skills or activities as well as praise for a task successfully mastered.

Immediate reinforcement is more effective than delayed reinforcement. Reinforcement following the successful completion of a task is most effective. Delaying reinforcement may lead to confusion over which response is being rewarded. After the inital reinforcement is given, a schedule for reinforcing future accomplishments may need to be established. Ratio, interval, variable, or fixed schedules may be used. Reinforcement is given after a set of appropriate responses in the ratio schedule, after a set period of time in the interval schedule, on an irregular schedule in the variable schedule, and on a regular basis in the fixed schedule.

Reinforcers may strengthen appropriate and inappropriate behaviors. Often the inappropriate behavior of children is reinforced by the teacher's response to it. If the negative response of the teacher gives the children the attention they desire or permits them to avoid a situation for which they had anxiety, they may continue to behave in the same manner in the future. The teacher must work hard to reinforce only desirable behaviors. It may be necessary sometimes to plan strategies not only to strengthen appropriate behavior but also to reduce the inappropriate behavior of children.

A behavior may be weakened or extinguished when the behavior is not followed by a reinforcer. Often inappropriate behavior may be extinguished by ignoring the behavior. If a child seeks the teacher's attention by behaving in a particular manner, it will be strengthened by the teacher's responding to that behavior. Ignoring the behavior and carefully rewarding appropriate behavior may encourage the child to seek more acceptable ways of performing.

RETENTION

Retention refers to the degree to which learning is remembered over time.

That which has meaning is retained longer than information and skills that do not. The more meaningful the original learning, the more likely it will be retained. Learning that has personal importance, in which the goal is important to the learner and the learner can see a use, is retained longer than other learning. Providing children with a variety of activities in which to use a motor skill increases its meaning, as does relating its importance to success in an activity the children enjoy.

The degree of success in original learning affects retention. Longer retention is the result of developing a degree of proficiency in a skill. Retention is favored when a skill is not only performed well but is understood as well. Both motor skills and knowledge are retained if the degree of original learning was good. The teacher's use of review and practice aid retention. Summarizing the main points, helping students use the material in new ways, transfering old to new learning, and practicing help students retain skills and knowledge over a longer period of time.

Motor skills are retained longer than other learnings. Each repetition of a skill wears a deeper neuromuscular pathway within the organism. These connections appear to be retained longer than in other forms of learning over a period of time of disuse. Skills in which there is a high degree of sequential and temporal patterning or proficiency will be retained.[8] Timing may be lost with disuse, whereas sequence is more easily retained.

Motivation and feeling tone influence retention. Learning in which there was a felt need and that is related to pleasant experiences will be retained longer than that which created feelings of anxiety or other unpleasantness. The goals for learning in physical education are a quality performance, variety in the use of skills, and the ability to transfer learning from one situation to another. The teacher must help the children think about their actions and to focus attention on the day's objectives. Thinking while doing is important to learning and retention.

SUMMARY

In addition to understanding children and knowing their subject matter, teachers must understand and apply what they know about learning and motor learning if teaching is to be effective. Motor skill performance is related to the physical characteristics, the motor and perceptual abilities, cognition, and the emotional state of the learner. Early motor learning is dependent on the learner achieving the neuromuscular maturation required for the task. Once achieved, learning is affected by factors over which the teacher may have some control. The teacher plays a very important part in the learning process by clearly presenting the material to be learned, providing interesting activities in which learning will take place, giving appropriate feedback to help correct errors, and encouraging children to their best efforts.

Learning is marked by rapid and slow changes in behavior, which are often depicted on a performance curve. Motivation, whole-part learning, transfer, practice, knowledge of results, and reinforcement all affect learning and the retention of what has been learned. Rate of learning varies with the individual and that which is to be learned. Thinking is as important a factor in learning in the gymnasium as it is in the classroom.

Level of aspiration, interest in and understanding of the goals, a pleasant learning atmosphere, rewards, recognition, success, and failure all affect motivation for learning. The teacher cannot motivate students but may alter the variables that affect motivation. Motor learning may involve whole or part learning. Generally a combination of the two is most effective. Relatively simple skills are best taught as a whole, whereas more complicated skills may be best broken down into parts and then put together.

Transfer is the ability to apply what was learned in one situation to other situations. Pointing out the similarities of previous learning to new learning may aid in the learning process. Transfer is not automatic. The teacher must teach for transfer by helping students see the relationships between old and new learning.

Motor skills are learned through meaningful practices that encourage a correct response. The practice of skills should be as similar to their use in the activity as possible. Practice should be planned with the age, maturity, experience, and stage of learning in mind.

Feedback is important in learning. Although the student receives some feedback as a result of the performance, this information may be lacking in helping a student analyze the performance in depth. The teacher provides valuable information, augmented feedback, to assist children in correcting errors and improving the quality of the performance. The information given varies with the age, maturity, and stage of learning, since a beginner may need help with the basic technique while a more advanced performer may need assistance in adapting the skill to a new situation.

Positive reinforcement increases the probability of the recurrence of a behavior. Reinforcement should build confidence and feelings of self-worth. With attention to these factors teachers can effectively assist children in meeting the class goals. Failure in this regard inhibits learning and may even discourage children from active participation in physical education activities.

REFERENCES

1. Caskey, S.: A task analysis approach to teaching, JOPERD **53**(1):59, January 1982.
2. Hunter, M.: Teach for transfer, El Segundo, Calif., 1983, Tip Publications.
3. Hunter, M.: Motivation theory for teachers, El Segundo, Calif., 1983, Tip Publications.
4. Hunter, M.: Retention theory for teachers, El Segundo, Calif., 1983, Tip Publications.
5. Kerr, R.: Psychomotor learning, Philadelphia, 1982, W.B. Saunders Co.
6. Oxendine, J.: Psychology of motor learning, Englewood Cliffs, N.J., 1984, Prentice-Hall, Inc.
7. Robb, M.: The dynamics of motor-skill acquisition, Englewood Cliffs, N.J., 1972, Prentice-Hall, Inc.
8. Singer, R.: Motor learning and human performance, ed. 3, New York, 1980, Macmillan Publishing Co., Inc.
9. Singer, R.: Sport psychology, JOPER **47**(7):24, September 1976.
10. Stallings, L.: Motor learning from theory to practice, St. Louis, 1982, The C.V. Mosby Co.

ADDITIONAL READINGS

Christina R.: The motor learning of children. In National Association for Sport and Physical Education: Echoes of influence, Washington, D.C., 1977, AAHPERD.
Traces the differences in motor readiness of children from 2 to 6 and 6 to 12 years old, including sex differences.

Peterson, A.: Using feedback to develop tennis skills, JOPERD **52**(7):54, September 1981.
Structuring practice to give tennis players immediate feedback on specific errors.

Rarick, G.: Concepts of motor learning: implications for skill development in children. In Albinson, J., and Andrew, G.: Child in sport and physical activity, Baltimore, 1976, University Park Press.
A recap of what is known about motor learning regarding age, maturity, motor ability, practice, retention, transfer, learning specificity, individual differences, and knowledge of results.

Salmela, J.: A human information processing approach of the child and skill. In Albinson, J., and Andrew, G.: Child in sport and physical activity, Baltimore, 1976, University Park Press.
Development of an information processing model, its modification from childhood to adulthood, and its compatibility with the real world.

Scanlan, T.: Motivation and stress in competitive youth sports, JOPERD **53**(3):27, March 1982.
Helping youth to get the most from youth sports by realistic goal setting and putting emphasis on skill development and improvement rather than winning.

Weiss, M.: Developmental modeling: enhancing children's motor skill acquisition, JOPERD **53**(9):49, November/December 1982.
Strategies to enhance learning in children who process visual information more slowly than older children and adults.

6

TEACHING STYLES

CHAPTER OBJECTIVES

1 To differentiate teaching styles available to the teacher of physical education regarding teacher and student decision making

2 To identify the situations in which each style may be used advantageously

3 To describe the steps to be taken in developing movement challenges

Effective teaching results from the combination of carefully planned and organized learning experiences and the teacher's ability to carry the lesson through to successful completion. The teacher must be able to determine the needs of the children in the class and select appropriate learning activities. These activities are then organized in a logical sequence into units of instruction and then into daily lessons. Following this careful planning, the teacher must be able to conduct these activities in a way that is meaningful to children, efficiently uses time, and achieves the stated objectives. The teacher must have the skill or concept objective and the process of learning desired clearly in mind. Once the content and process are known, the teacher then selects the teaching strategy to be used to accomplish the lesson objectives.

If teaching is to be effective, regardless of the style to be selected in a particular learning situation, the teacher must consider each of the following:

The teacher must be concerned with (1) the quality of the performance, (2) variety in the use of skills and knowledge, and (3) the transfer of skills and knowledge to new learning situations. The child's best efforts should be enthusiastically encouraged. The teacher must study why a student's movement is not effective and be able to take action that will result in a more successful performance. Early correction of errors is important.

This does not imply that all children's responses should be the same. In the movement lesson, many different responses may meet the objectives. Furthermore, the teacher should provide a wide variety of experiences to enhance a broader understanding and use of the skills and concepts. Finally, the teacher must help children see the relationship between new learning and previous learning experiences (in other words, must teach for transfer).

Individual differences must be recognized. Variability in skills, understanding, past experience, and rate of learning must be considered in the selection of teaching styles if all children are to benefit from the new experience. The teacher should strive to become skillful in the use of a variety of styles, since no one style is best for all children and in all situations. Several different styles may be used effectively within a single lesson.

The teacher must provide sufficient time for learning, to allow the children to grasp the material before moving on to the next part of the lesson. The teacher must develop a sensitivity about when it is time to move on, allowing adequate time for learning and maintaining the children's interest.

In presenting new material the teacher should avoid giving too much information, which may result in confusion for learners who are attempting to grasp too much too quickly. Material should be presented with attention focused on a few elements at a time. The teacher must be able to analyze the task and to determine what information the children need initially and at what stage they need further information.

The practice of skills should be closely related to the use of skills in the specific unit and should stimulate children's thinking. Children may not see the relationship between the use of skills in the practice situation and the use of skills in the activity. Practice of skills and concepts should prepare children for their use in an activity. Interest in practice is difficult to maintain when practice is dissimilar to activity use of skills and concepts.

The teacher must be responsive to the changing needs of children as the lesson proceeds. The teacher must recognize when a change of pace is needed, when further clarification is necessary, and when a change in the practice procedures would be beneficial.

Regardless of the teaching style, the children should be involved intellectually in the learning process. Although the child-centered styles involve the children more in searching for answers on their own, each style should encourage verbalization by the students and an understanding of why we do things a certain way.

The most effective teachers are those who teach learners how to learn. The results of effective teaching should be a desire in children to continue learning and the development of skills needed to be independent learners. Teachers who help children find success and make learning fun through a variety of interesting and challenging activities enhance future learning.

TEACHING STYLES

In conducting learning experiences for children the teacher may select from a variety of **teaching styles** or teaching methods. These styles are actually strategies for organizing and presenting learning experiences to children. Teaching styles range from direct, teacher-centered approaches to those that are indirect and more student centered. Figure 6-1 places the methods to be included here on a continuum from teacher centered to child centered. At one end of the continuum is a style in which the teacher makes decisions exclusively. At the other end is a style in which the children are the prime decision makers; between the two is a gradual shift in decision making from the teacher to the children.

Generally speaking, child-centered teaching styles take more time to develop. Planning, in which the teacher must anticipate the children's possible re-

Teacher centered				Student centered
Command	Task	Guided discovery	Problem solving	Free exploration
Direct				**Indirect**

Figure 6-1

Continuum of teaching styles.

sponses, must be carefully thought out beforehand. Skill in the use of these approaches takes considerable practice by the teacher. The children also need time to develop skills in solving movement challenges and to gain confidence in their own ideas.

Command

The **command**[4] style has been the most frequently used method in physical education in the past. This style is the most teacher-directed style of teaching. Although the word *command* connotes a dictatorial approach to learning, this is not necessarily the case. The teacher's manner in this approach is dependent on the teacher's personality more than the style itself. In the command style the teacher is the sole decision maker. The teacher decides what to do, how to do it, and the quality of the performance that is acceptable.

The command style is divided into several steps. First there is an explanation and demonstration by the teacher of the task to be accomplished. Any questions regarding the task are answered. The students then practice the task with the teacher moving among the group correcting errors and offering encouragement. At the close of the practice there may be a further evaluation or discussion with the teacher again reinforcing the main points of emphasis before moving on to the next part of the lesson.

An example of the use of the command style follows. The teacher is introducing the chest pass. The group is seated as the teacher explains the chest pass, its use, and the points of emphasis. A demonstration follows, with the teacher executing the pass a few times and again emphasizing the major points in the execution of the skill that the children are to be considering. The children are then divided into partners and begin practice. The teacher moves among the group correcting errors and giving encouragement. At the close of the practice the teacher asks the group

to verbalize the major points once again. The teacher then moves on to the next part of the lesson.

There are several advantages to the command style. It provides the most direct route to the objective. If time is short, it may be the most efficient and effective means to present motor skills. Since the teacher decides on what will be taught and what procedures will be used for practice, there is little time lost in organizing the group. Maximum practice for all can be easily accomplished.

The command style enables the students to see the objectives directly and therefore clarifies the expectations for performance. If the explanation and demonstration are well done, there can be little doubt by the students about which aspects of the performance they should focus their attention on. If a uniform response is desired, this method may be most effective. This style is also effective with large groups, since the class may be organized quickly and all the children are doing the same thing. The command style requires a less thorough knowledge of the material because the teacher alone controls the flow of information. This may be why it is often the choice of inexperienced teachers.

There are also several disadvantages to the command style. This style is insensitive to individual differences and needs. One way is presented and only one response is appropriate. Usually the presentation is geared to the so-called average students, so those who are well skilled or not yet ready for the material are given little consideration.

In addition it does not encourage creative or innovative response by the students, because the teacher tells them how to respond. If understanding and

concept development are the goals of the lesson, the command style is a poor choice because it does not encourage thinking by the students.

Task

In the *task*[4] style the teacher determines the content but the children are allowed some decision making. The teacher designs a series of tasks leading up to the unit outcomes. These tasks are broken down into a series of activities through which the children progress to achieve the final task. These activities should begin at a level below the poorest skilled and progress to a level above the most highly skilled children. The task style may be used at three different levels, with each requiring more decision making by the student. At the lowest level the teacher presents a task, which is broken down into several levels of achievement. All the children work on the same task, but each begins at a comfortable stage in the progression of the activity.

At the second level the teacher may assign individual children tasks on which to work, depending on their level of ability. This may be most effective in gymnastics where individual differences in ability vary greatly. Each child may be given a task card in which several tasks have been developed, designed individually for that student.

At the third level more independence of action is required. The student receives a task booklet that describes all the tasks to be completed in the unit. The children decide individually which tasks they will work on and assume responsibility for working on each task within the unit time. At this level students take more responsibility for determining their needs and work accordingly in meeting unit objectives.

In the task style the teacher must provide resources to aid individual learning. The teacher is a valuable resource, but the children also should have posters, books, loop films, and other aids available to assist them in the learning process. The children must be encouraged to use a variety of resources; otherwise they often depend on the teacher as the most direct path to the information they need.

As tasks are developed for the children, the terminal objective or evaluative criterion must be carefully spelled out. The children must be able to determine when they have accomplished the task. This criterion may be qualitative or quantitative. It may be something that the child or a partner may evaluate, or it may require the teacher's evaluation. It is a good idea to include several means of signing off on tasks.

Having the teacher check each task is inefficient use of the teacher's time. Children need the opportunity to be responsible for their own evaluation as well as to assist in the evaluation of others.

Safety concerns or prerequisite skills should be clearly stated in the description of the task. If spotting is required, a spotter (either student or teacher depending on the activity) should be designated.

An example of a task developed as a part of a gymnastics unit for first grade children follows:

1. Mount the low beam. With a spotter walk forward the length of the beam. Dismount.
2. Mount the low beam. With a spotter walk backward to the end of the beam. Dismount.
3. Mount the low beam. With a spotter walk sideways the length of the beam. Dismount.
4. Mount the low beam. With a spotter walk forward to the center of the beam. Walk through the hoop and continue to the end of the beam. Dismount.
5. Mount the low beam. With a spotter walk to the center of the beam. Stand and turn. Continue walking forward to the end. Dismount.
6. Mount the low beam. With a spotter walk to the center of the beam. Turn and walk backward to the end of the beam. Dismount.
7. Mount the low beam. With a spotter walk to the center of the beam. Turn a ¼ turn and walk sideways to the end of the beam.

Similar tasks would be developed for other pieces of equipment used in the unit.

Tasks may also involve some problem solving. This may be accomplished by asking the children to experiment with different uses of the body or body parts in the execution of skills. In this manner they must find the most efficient way of moving on an individual basis.

The task style allows for individual differences in skill level and recognizes individual needs in working on particular skills. The individual children not only select the task they begin to work on but also select the level at which they begin to work on the task. In this style the teacher's ability to assist is maximized because the teacher is free to circulate among the group helping individuals as they work on various tasks. Since individual children are working on their own, success and failure are known only to the individual. All children, however, should experience success as they work at a level of performance at which they are comfortable.

The task style also permits maximum use of facilities and equipment. This style is extremely helpful

in situations in which the amount of any particular piece of equipment is limited, because it does not require each child to use the same type of equipment at the same time.

The advantage of allowing children to choose the task and to work on their own may also be this style's greatest disadvantage. This style requires increasing independence of action and assumption of personal responsibility for accomplishing the tasks. This may be difficult for some children. The teacher must be alert to the progress the children are making in achieving the tasks and help those who are not self-directed to select and complete tasks along the way.

Guided Discovery

In the *guided discovery*[4] approach teacher-designed movement tasks are utilized but in a manner in which the children are able to make individual decisions about how to move. However, their attention is focused toward a specific movement response, so that the nature of the responses produces similar movements from the entire class. This approach is used effectively in situations in which the teacher is interested in children discovering the most suitable movement response for a given task or in the development of a new skill. In this way children are able to experiment with the use of the body in achieving the objective and developing greater understanding about why particular movements are more efficient and effective. In this style motor activity begins with a general response to a movement challenge and proceeds through a series of steps, each of which narrows the focus of the response until the ultimate movement

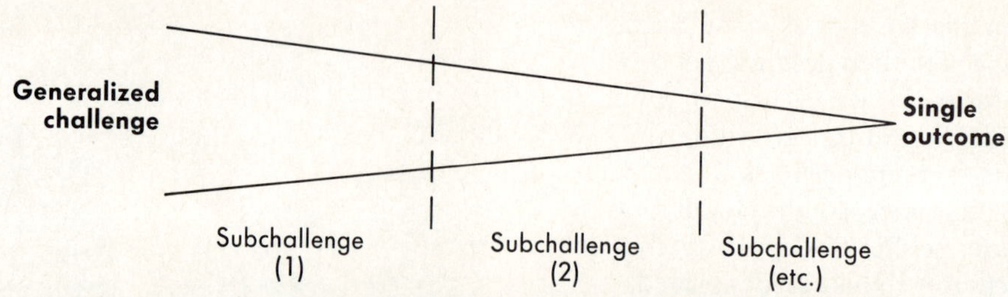

Figure 6-2

Guided discovery.

goal is achieved. Figure 6-2 demonstrates the nature of responses that are a result of this style.

As the children move, limitations are imposed that indicate the content being developed and that limit the range of movement responses. The teacher guides the student in the discovery of how to perform the movement task. The students make decisions on how they will respond.

This is the first style on the continuum that requires higher-level thought processes. Whereas in the previously described styles the teacher determined not only the content but also how it was to be achieved, in guided discovery the teacher only defines the intended outcome of the movement response. This then gives the children the opportunity to experiment with the movement, to make comparisons with other movement responses in their repertoire, and to analyze the possible motor responses.

An example of guided discovery follows. The teacher states the challenge: "Begin in a standing position and jump for distance on the mat." The children experiment with the task. Subchallenge 1 focuses their attention on the landing position: "Try landing in different positions. Land so that all body parts are as far from the starting line as possible. What position seems to be the best?" Subchallenge 2 focuses on the take-off: "How can your feet be positioned to get the best possible take--off?" Subchallenge 3 focuses on the use of the arms in aiding the take-off: "Try using your arms in different ways. Which ways help you jump the farthest?" Subchallenge 4 focuses on the body position: "Try jumping from an upright position. Now try bending your knees and leaning forward. Which position helped your jump the most?" During each subchallenge the children experiment with the use of the body parts

mentioned. Additional questions may need to be asked at each step to help the children focus on the most efficient movement. As the subchallenges are developed, the skill becomes more and more like the standing long jump. Success in this style is dependent on the teacher's ability to respond to the children's experimentation with movement and continue to focus their attention on the task. Suggestions for the development of movement challenges follows this discussion of styles. The result of this style should lead to a positive self-concept by the child since each child will find success in solving the movement challenges. The process of learning that takes place will give the students the tools to apply what has been learned to other movement situations.

A disadvantage to this style is that it takes a great deal of time--time for the children to be guided to the discovery of the movement solution and time for the teacher to think through the steps the children will need to take to get there. This style requires a great deal of patience by the teacher, as do all child-centered methods. Children often take more time than we expect to reach the solution. Teachers must allow children the time they need and not be too eager to give them the answers before they have discovered them themselves.

Problem Solving

Problem solving is similar to guided discovery in approach, but whereas one similar solution to the movement problem was the goal in guided discovery, many different solutions are the outcomes of problem solving. Figure 6-3 focuses on the motor responses obtained using this method.

In problem solving the teacher poses a movement

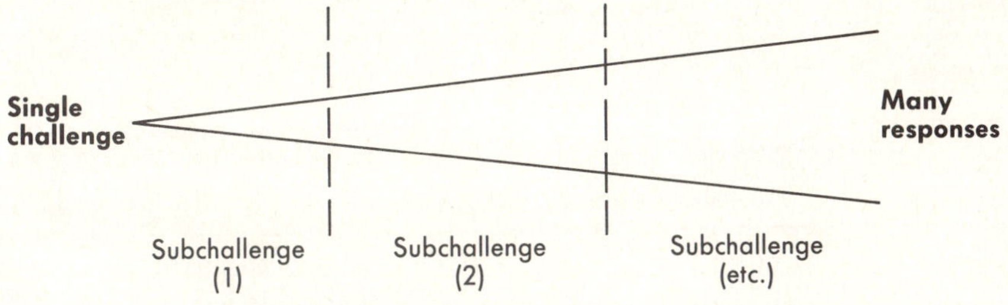

Figure 6-3

Problem solving.

challenge that has some parameters, such as the use of space, pathways, and/or locomotor movements to be used, and the children try to find as many solutions to the problem as they can. Any movement response that meets the criteria of the task is acceptable. Here again the teacher is a resource in bringing the focus of the activity to their attention as needed and in helping individuals work toward possible solutions.

An example of the development of a movement challenge using this style follows. The problem to be solved is to explore moving in a variety of ways in general space with a change of direction. The teacher poses the following questions. Each question follows a period of experimentation with the previous question. As each step is added, a new focus to the movement challenge is added, which broadens the movement responses possible.

1. Staying within the area and avoiding other peoples' self space, move in as many different locomotor movements as you can.
2. What nonlocomotor movements can you add as you move in general space?
3. Can you change direction as you move?

Additional questions may need to be asked to help the children as they experiment with movement in response to the questions stated above. In developing questions to aid the children the teacher must be careful not to let personal expectations for possible solutions interfere with the children's own solutions to the task. This style takes considerable time. Children need time to think, to interpret the challenge, and to explore possible solutions.

This style is exceptionallly well suited for activities in which conceptualization is important. If the challenges are well designed, there is greater cognitive involvement than in guided discovery and greater

individualization of responses as children work to solve the movement challenge on their own.

Movement challenges may vary in complexity with the ability of the group. With younger children the challenge may be relatively simple, with only one or two elements involved. As the children develop skill in these child-centered approaches, challenges become more complex and include subchallenges to solve as well. The outcomes of these movement challenges might be the development of skills, the understanding of concepts and relationships, or variations in skills and strategies.

Exploration

Exploration is the most child-centered style on the continuum. In this style the movement task is de-

Table 6-1
Teaching styles

| Method | Decision making | | Advantages | Disadvantages |
	Teacher	Students		
Command	Exclusively	None	Uniformity of response; most direct method to task, saves time; needs minimal preplanning and knowledge of activity	Does not individualize instruction; little thinking involved
Task			Individualizes instruction; children determine needs; maximizes use of equipment and facilities; performance goals defined and communicated; children move on to new material when ready	Tasks all planned prior to beginning of unit; takes time to develop tasks; requires independent learning skills
Level 1	Develops content	Select entry level		
Level 2	Individualizes tasks for children	Select task on which to work		
Level 3	Develops task content for the unit	Select tasks based on individual needs		
Guided discovery	Determines terminal goal	Decide movement solutions toward goal	Involves thinking; develops understanding of efficient movement	Takes time; requires careful planning; difficult with groups in which there is great variability in skill
Problem solving	Sets parameters of movement challenges and safety; raises questions to stimulate a multitude of responses	Decide how to move within parameter of movement challenge	Very good for conceptual development; enhances cognitive development; develops skills in problem-solving technique; enhances creativity	Does not teach a specific outcome
Exploration	Sets parameters of movement challenges and safety	Free movement responses	Allows children more freedom in moving; enhances creativity in movement	Is inappropriate if specific outcomes are desired

signed to enable the children to move freely as they desire, within the limits of safety. This style is similar to problem solving, but the children explore movement in a more general way with minimal teacher direction. This style may be used to introduce concepts, ideas, new equipment, and the like or to elicit original responses and ideas from the children.

This style is most effective with young children who are involved in their first physical education experience. It enables the children to work on their own and explore their own capabilities. This style is geared for everyone's immediate success and should result in greater confidence in one's ability to move and in moving.

This does not imply that the teacher puts out the equipment and allows the children to have free play. Tasks used in this style are directed by the teacher in some way. For example, the teacher may ask "How many different ways can you move on the balance beam on two feet?" or "Pick a piece of equipment and see how many ways you can use it." It is important for the teacher to be responsive to the children's needs by suggesting new challenges when it is time to move on. It is of value to have the children share some of their movement experiences with others to increase the movement possibilities for everyone.

CHOOSING A STYLE

The style of teaching one may choose is dependent on the particular learning situation. An illustration

Table 6-2

Steps in developing movement challenges

Concept	Outcomes	Activity/instructions	Questions
Creating force	Adjusting force for distance	"With a medium-sized ball, throw to a partner. After 4 successful throws, move a step back and repeat."	"What did you do to get the ball to your partner as the distance increased?"
	Adjusting force to size of ball thrown	"Select 3 different size balls. Practice throwing each to your partner. Move back after 4 throws with each."	"How did your throws change as you used different-sized balls? What changes did you make as the balls got heavier? Lighter? Smaller? Larger?"

of the use of each style in teaching a ball skill is given on pp.78-79. Table 6-1 summarizes the use of each of the previously discussed styles. Factors that influence the style chosen include the age and experience of the children, the stage of learning, the content to be taught, the level of the task, the resources available including the amount of equipment and space, the number of students, the time available, and the personality of the teacher.

BUILDING MOVEMENT CHALLENGES

The success of indirect or child-centered styles of teaching lies in the teacher's ability to develop movement challenges with the children. Many times these challenges are unsuccessful because teachers have not formulated in their own minds what the outcomes of the experience should be. This does not mean the teacher should be looking for a specific or single outcome, but it does mean careful planning must be utilized to enable the children to meet the purpose of the activity.

The first step in planning movement challenges is to identify the movement concepts with which the children will be working and to determine the level of understanding that can be expected by the individual children in the group. Once these concepts and children's needs have been identified, the teacher must determine the outcomes to be achieved. Perhaps the outcome merely is to explore different ways of moving in space. It might be moving in space while changing pathways, speed, or locomotor movements, or it might be creating appropriate force in throwing a ball to a partner under varying conditions.

Once the outcomes have been determined, the teacher designs the activity through which the outcomes will be achieved. These activities might include individual, partner, or even small group work. At this stage the teacher must establish the framework in which the children will work. Often children are unable to meet the outcomes because the teacher is too vague in stating the challenge for them. "Move as the music tells you to move" is the type of statement that can only result in frustration for both the children and the teacher.

Planning must go one step further. It is not enough to put the children into the activity and assume they will achieve the objective. The children may enjoy the activity and really never understand what its purpose was. The teacher must anticipate the outcomes of the children's participation and develop questions that will respond to their movements and keep them on task. This is the most crucial part of planning movement challenges. Questions should encourage creative or innovative solutions to the challenge. They should encourage all to have the courage to try something new. And they should be questions in which a yes or no answer would be inappropriate. Children should be encouraged to verbalize their responses to partners, to small groups, or to the entire group. Beginning teachers may find this a difficult task. However, as the teachers gain experience in working with children, they will be able to draw on past experiences in anticipating the responses children might make. One cannot deny that "If you become a teacher, by your pupils you'll be taught," as suggested in *The King and I*.

When working with and responding to children during the movement activities, the teacher must en-

DEVELOPING THE BALL SKILL OF BOUNCING (DRIBBLING) WITH A VARIETY OF TEACHING STYLES

Objective: To dribble a ball in general space under control by pushing the ball slightly ahead with the fingertips, below waist height, looking up to avoid others and protecting the ball by keeping the body between the ball and an opponent.

COMMAND

1. The teacher gives an explanation and demonstration of the dribble, emphasizing the points above. The children are seated.
2. Each child gets a ball and practices dribbling as the children move in general space. The teacher calls out the change of hands.
3. As the children practice, the teacher offers suggestions for improvement and reinforcement of good dribbling.
4. At the close of the practice session the teacher leads a summation of the important points to remember about dribbling.

TASK

Dribbling: When you complete the unit you should be able to:

1. Execute a dribble with good control with either hand.
2. Protect the ball while dribbling.
3. Dribble into an open space.
4. Dribble around an opponent.
5. Use the dribble to draw an opponent to create space for teammates.

Execution of the skill:

1. Include a reference for them to check.
2. A description of the skill, with common errors cited.
3. Suggest the use of a loop film.

Task 1: Practice dribbling the ball with the preferred hand in the space designated.
   a. Pushes the ball with the fingertips.
   b. Controls the ball just below waist height.
   c. Dribbles the ball without watching it.

Task 2: Practice dribbling the ball with the nonpreferred hand in the space designated.
   a. Pushes the ball with the fingertips.
   b. Controls the ball just below waist height.
   c. Dribble the ball without watching it.

Task 3: Dribble around the cones 5 feet apart, changing hands so the hand farthest from the object is used for dribbling as you pass the object.
   a. Keeps the ball moving.
   b. Keeps the body between the object and the ball.

Task 4: Working with a partner, try to dribble the ball around your partner as your partner attempts to get the ball.
   a. Keeps the body between the ball and the opponent.
   b. Keeps the ball moving.
   c. Dribbles at a level that is easy to control and keep the ball from the opponent.

Task 5: In a group of eight, in the space provided, each dribbles the ball avoiding contact with the others.
   a. Dribbles without watching the ball.
   b. Keeps the ball moving.
   c. Protects the ball.

Task 6: In groups of four to six (three per team), dribble, drawing an opponent to create spaces for teammates.
   a. Keeps the ball moving.
   b. Dribbles without looking at the ball.
   c. Protects the ball against opponents.

GUIDED DISCOVERY

1. Establish a signal for listening.
2. Children are scattered in self space within the assigned boundaries.
3. Each child has a ball.
4. Problems:
   a. Let's see how many different ways you can bounce the ball in your self space. What body parts can you use? Which parts enabled you to have the most control? (Hands) What level was it easiest? (Medium)
   b. Now let's bounce the ball in general space. Try using different body parts, including different parts of the hand. Which enabled you to have the best control? (Fingers) Now let's try to find the level at which to bounce the ball for greatest control. Try it

DEVELOPING THE BALL SKILL OF BOUNCING (DRIBBLING) WITH A VARIETY OF TEACHING STYLES—cont'd

high, low, and in the middle. At which level could you move the easiest? (Low)

c. Move in general space, dribbling the ball. As you move in general space while dribbling, what do you have to do to avoid bumping into others? (Look up)

d. Now we are going to alternately increase and decrease the amount of space we have. How did your dribbling change as the space changed? (Bounced closer to the body, took smaller steps, controlled the height of the dribble, etc.)

5. Summarize the findings of the children regarding an effective dribble.

PROBLEM SOLVING*

1-3. As above.

4. Problems:
   a. How many ways can you move the ball in your self space? Another way? Now move the ball in general space. Can you move it in the same ways? Different ways?
   b. Can you change the body parts used to control the ball in self space? In general space? Did you keep the ball under control?
   c. At what levels can you control the ball in self space? In general space?

EXPLORATION

This method would not be used to develop the dribbling objective.

*This method may not result in meeting the dribbling objective, since the children are not directed toward a specific response.

courage individual children to find their own ways of moving and their own solutions to the movement tasks presented. The teacher must be careful not to pass judgments regarding their movement responses to the children, which results in limiting the possible movement responses of the children. Singling out individual children to show their movements to the group may unconsiously communicate to children that a particular type of response is desired. This is not to say that whatever movement response a child makes is appropriate. As the teacher circulates among the children, additional questions and suggestions may be needed to keep the children on task. The teacher must learn to accomplish this in a way that encourages the individual creative responses of children. Table 6-2 summarizes the steps in developing movement challenges with an example for developing the concept of creating force.

DEVELOPING CREATIVITY

Every human being can be creative. However, self-confidence is required before a child can be creative, and the environment must be one in which creative solutions to challenges are encouraged. Creativity takes time, and ample time must be provided if creative thinking is to take place.

Every physical education experience should encourage creativity. Often creativity is thought to be a part of only the dance experience. Dance does provide the opportunity for the child to express ideas through movement. However, all physical education should require creative thinking, whether it be creating a gymnastic routine, determining a group strategy in a game, or deciding how to outwit an opponent in soccer.

In developing creative ideas a person moves through several steps. The first step involves being interested in something. During this interest phase the children seek as much information as possible. What are the facts? What are the parameters? Once the information is gathered, the children experiment with possible solutions to the challenge until they find one they especially like. This solution may then be developed further. The children have then reached the stage where they wish to share their creation with others. At this point some evaluation by the group may take place, with the teacher encouraging the children to tell what they liked about the ideas expressed.

Creativity can only happen in an environment conducive to creative thinking. The teacher must be the model for such behavior by doing the following:

Encourage the children to develop their own ideas

Demonstrate they value new ideas
Give reassurance to children engaging in the creative process
Have resources available that encourage the children's search for ideas

Encourage risk taking in problem solving
Encourage nontraditional use of the body and objects
Ask questions that require thinking
Not leave creativity to chance

SUMMARY

A number of different teaching styles may be used in the teaching of physical education. These styles involve varying degrees of teacher and child decision making. The command style is the most teacher centered, with the teacher making the decisions of what, how, and when certain skills or concepts learned. In the task style the teacher decides how and what will be learned, but the children also have some decision making in selecting the task or the level at which they work on the learning task. Guided discovery utilizes an approach in which the teacher guides the students through a series of activities leading to their discovery of the correct solution to the movement task. Problem solving and exploration are much more child centered, as the learning allows the children to make more decisions regarding their movement responses. In problem solving the teacher imposes certain parameters such as the locomtor movements, space, and qualities of movement concepts to be used. Movement challenges in the exploration method are general, with a minimum of guidance by the teacher.

Each style has value for learning in physical education. Not all children learn best by the same style. Some material may be better taught by one style than another. The time available for learning and the desired outcomes also affect the selection of teaching style. The teacher must determine the relationship between what is to be learned and the process of learning in selecting the best teaching style for the situation.

Developing movement challenges is an important part of child-centered methods. These must be carefully planned. Steps in planning include identifying what is to be learned and what outcomes are to be sought, selecting the activities, and developing questions to help children stay on task and to clarify the movement tasks.

Creativity, the highest level of learning, should be encouraged in all aspects of physical education. Creative responses will be the result in an environment that encourages thinking and the development of one's own movement ideas.

REFERENCES

1. Cooper, J., and others: Classroom teaching skills: a handbook, ed. 2, Lexington, 1982, D.C. Heath & Co.
2. Dougherty, N., and Bonanno, D.: Contemporary approaches to the teaching of physical education, Minneapolis, 1979, Burgess Publishing Co.
3. Harrison, J.: Instructional strategies for physical education, Dubuque, 1983, William C. Brown Co.
4. Mosston, M.: Teaching physical education, Columbus, 1981, Charles E. Merrill Publishing Co.
5. Rink, J.: Teaching physical education for learning, St. Louis, 1985, Times Mirror Mosby.
6. Singer, R., and Dick, W.: Teaching physical education, ed. 2, Boston, 1980, Houghton Mifflin Co.

ADDITIONAL READINGS

Annarino, A.: The teaching-learning process: a systematic instructional strategy, JOPERD **54**(3): 51, March 1983.
   A plan for achieving instructional goals, including behavioral objectives, content, teaching style, teacher interventions, and evaluation.

Goldberger, M.: Effective learning through a spectrum of teaching styles, JOPERD **55**(8): 17, October 1984.
   A look at teaching styles and the decision-making process.

Metzler, M.: Developing teaching skills: a systematic sequence, JOPERD **55**(1):38, January 1984.
   The use of microteaching to improve teaching skills.

Rink, J.: The teacher wants us to learn, JOPER 52(2):17, February 1981.
   Ways teachers communicate expectations to children during teaching.

Werner, P.: Concept teaching in movement and music, JOPERD **53**(7):49, September 1982.
   An example of how similar concepts may be taught in physical education and music classes.

SAFETY, ORGANIZATIONAL STRATEGIES, AND CLASSROOM MANAGEMENT

CHAPTER OBJECTIVES

1 To identify procedures necessary for a physical education program founded on sound health practices

2 To discuss guidelines for establishing a safe environment for physical education experiences

3 To describe class organization and management techniques that ensure maximum participation for all children in every class

Successful experiences in physical education not only require careful planning of content and activities in the daily lessons but also the establishment of policies that guarantee the safe and healthful participation of all children. These policies must be concerned with the degree to which the children may participate in physical education, the nature of the experiences deemed appropriate for each child on a temporary or permanent basis, and the safe conduct of the physical education program.

POLICIES FOR HEALTHFUL PARTICIPATION
Medical Examinations

Each child should be required to have a physical examination and medical history completed by a physician before participation in physical education. In localities where this request puts an undue financial burden on the families of school children, the school should arrange to have these important examinations completed by a local physician or medical society. These examinations are important not only for participation in physical education but also to guarantee the child's well-being in all aspects of school life.

Results of the school examinations should be kept on file, and periodic examinations should be required throughout the school years. Changes in the health status of children may require even more frequent examinations.

Regarding physical education, physicians should be required to state in writing the extent to which each child may participate. In cases in which a health problem requires some special considerations in physical education, all restrictions must be carefully defined. In dealing with these restrictions it is often best to have the school nurse or the physical educator communicate directly with the physician, since the physician may have little understanding of the activity requirements of various physical education activities. In this way the best possible program can be prescribed for each individual student. An example form for medical clearance for physical education is given in Figure 7-1. A list of the physical education activities to be included in the physical education program may be added to assist the physician in determining the level of participation for a child who will have some restrictions.

```
PHYSICAL EDUCATION PARTICIPATION EXAMINATION

I have examined ___________________________________ on ____________ and

_____________    recommend unrestricted participation in vigorous physical
                 education activities.

_____________    recommend the following restrictions for participation in
                 physical education activities.




                                          _________________________________
                                              Physician's signature


                                          _________________________________


                                          _________________________________
                                              Physician's address

                                          _________________________________
                                              Parent's signature
```

Figure 7-1

Sample form for clearance for participation in physical education.

Identification of Health Problems

Often physical educators or classroom teachers note changes in individual children that may signal potential health problems. Problems in vision or hearing and changes in behavior or reaction to activities may first be observed by school personnel. These changes should be made known to the school nurse or other authority so appropriate action may be taken. Early detection of potential health problems is essential. Often early care results in better health as well as considerable savings in medical costs for remedial services.

Excuses From Participation in Physical Education

It is advisable to select a person, preferrably the school nurse, as the only one who may excuse a child temporarily from participation in physical education.

In responding to requests by family physicians or parents, the school nurse determines the extent to which children may safely participate. In addition this procedure permits adequate health records to be maintained and potential health problems to be brought to the attention of the appropriate personnel. When children's participation in physical education has been restricted, their return to full participation should require the authorization of the school nurse or designated authority.

If a school nurse is not available, excuses or restrictions from activity should be directed to the teacher of physical education, either the physical education specialist or the classroom teacher. Teachers need to communicate the nature of the physical education experiences to help parents make appropriate requests regarding any restrictions in participation of their children. A possible guideline to handle such requests may be that a student may be excused from physical education for 3 days at the parents' request, after which a physician's request is necessary.

Attire

Children should be attired for safe participation in physical education activities. In many elementary schools boys and girls do not change their clothes but are required to wear sneakers. Appropriate footware is essential to safe participation. In some activities and where health policies allow, moving barefooted may be beneficial. If proper footware is not available, going barefooted is much safer than participating in stocking feet. If all children cannot provide their own footware, parents' groups may be enlisted to initiate a fund to provide shoes for those in need. In other situations the teacher may provide a box for shoes that children have outgrown. These shoes may be given to those who need shoes on a temporary or permanent basis.

Children should remove all objects from their pockets before participating in physical education. Failure to do so may cause injury should a child fall or bump into equipment or other children. For safe participation in most activities, long hair should be pulled back and secured to provide unrestricted visual contact with the environment.

Heavy clothing that restricts movement or results in overheating should be removed. Whenever possible, at least in the upper elementary grades, children should change clothes for participation in physical education activities. Changing clothes is important in establishing sound personal hygiene habits. Clothes worn for physical education should be laundered on a regular basis and clean socks should be worn each day. In classes in which the children do change clothes, it is essential to have adequate supervision in the changing areas. A sweater or jacket and long pants or warm-up suits should be available for outdoor play during the fall or spring.

SCHOOL SAFETY

The safety of children at school must be a primary concern. Each teacher must assume responsibility for providing a safe environment for learning and must be consistent in enforcing the safe behavior of children. Teachers should know the activities well enough to recognize the type of injuries that might occur. They must be aware of potential safety hazards and take appropriate measures to minimize the risks to the safety of the children in their care. Few activities are considered naturally dangerous. Most often it is the manner in which an activity is conducted that makes it hazardous.

Regardless of the precautions taken, minor accidents do occur occasionally. In case of an accident emergency procedures should provide care for the injured and supervision for the other children in the class.

Emergency Procedures

All teachers should have training in first aid procedures, including cardiopulmonary resusitation (CPR). Procedures to follow in case of an emergency should be carefully defined for all teachers. Adequate procedures include:

1. Notification of designated school officials (the school nurse or school administrator) of the injury or other emergency
2. The first aid treatment to be administered
3. Who has decision-making authority if local medical emergency services are required
4. How and when to notify parents

For the teacher working with young children, notifying local school personnel may be a problem since the injured child should not be left alone and the other children in the group may be too young to transmit the information to others. Procedures may need to be worked out with a teacher close by so that adequate supervision is provided.

A written report of the accident should include a statement of what happened, the circumstances surrounding the incident, the treatment given, the time of the injury, the witnesses if any, and the activity in which the accident took place. This report should be completed as soon as possible after appropriate care has been given to the injured child. A sample accident report form is given in Figure 7-2. A copy of the teacher's lesson plan for the day should also be filed.

Follow-up measures should be taken immediately to eliminate the cause of the injury and to prevent further accidents. Responsibility for follow-up action should be designated to someone on the school staff. This might include repairs to equipment or facilities if needed.

Most school districts offer low-cost accident insurance for children that covers most school accidents. This insurance is especially important for children who are not covered by any other family medical insurance. Lack of adequate medical coverage is often cited as the reason for suits against school districts as a result of school accidents.

```
                          ACCIDENT REPORT

    Date ________________               School __________________

    Name ________________________________ Age _______  Sex  F ______ M ______

    Parent (guardian)___________________________________ Insurance  Yes ___  No ___

    Address ___________________________________ Company_________________

            ___________________________________ Phone ________________

            _______________________________

    Activity_______________________________ Time of injury______________________

    Nature of injury (include type and body parts involved)

                    Example:  Abrasion—right knee, right elbow

    ________________________________________________________________

    ________________________________________________________________


    Treatment given ________________________________________________

    ________________________________________________________________

    ________________________________________________________________


    Recommendation for further treatment___________________________

    ________________________________________________________________

    Under what conditions did the accident occur?__________________________

    ________________________________________________________________

    ________________________________________________________________

    Where did the accident occur (facility)? ______________________________

    Probable cause of injury____________________________________________

    ________________________________________________________________

    ________________________________________________________________

    Witnessed by____________________________________________________


                                        ___________________________________
                                        Signature of person completing report
```

Figure 7-2

Sample form for accident report.

LEGAL LIABILITY

All teachers share the responsibility for the well-being of all students. Although they are not inherently dangerous in themselves, the nature of physical education activities requires the careful planning and conducting of activities to ensure the safety of all.

Legal liability must be a concern for all who teach. In the case of negligence, one must prove the following:

1. That the individual in charge had the responsibility to assure the safety of the participant
2. That the individual in charge violated this responsibility
3. That an injury did occur
4. That the injury was the result of the violation of the responsibility for the safety of the individual

Since accidents are bound to happen, all teachers should have liability insurance. Insurance provided by the school district most often provides some liability coverage for teachers. Teachers should fully understand their liability, the insurance coverage the school system provides, and the laws concerning liability in their state.

In fulfilling the teacher's duty for the safe participation of all children, three major responsibilities must be addressed: the activity must be appropriately supervised; the activity should be suitable for the participants and carefully conducted; and the environment in which the activity takes place must be one in which safety is controlled. In fulfilling liability responsibilities it is important that policies for healthful participation be followed closely. In addition the following discussion establishes guidelines for each of these important concerns.

Supervision

All persons conducting physical education classes should be appropriately trained. In providing adequate supervision of physical education activities one must first consider the necessary qualifications required of the assigned personnel. The teacher of physical education should have an understanding of human anatomy and physiology as well as the age characteristics of elementary school children. Teachers should be competent in all the activities they will teach. This should include knowledge of the progressions in moving from one level of competency to the next, the prerequisites needed for particular skills, and the awareness of risks that will minimize potential dangers. In addition the teacher should know the potential activity results of specific motor experiences. For example, knowing the specific effects of exercise on body segments, muscles, and other body systems, should enable physical educators to select appropriate experiences for the children in their classes. Appropriate supervision also assumes the teacher has the ability to administer first aid and to react immediately in case of injury.

The supervision provided may be either direct or indirect. **Direct supervision** assumes the supervisor is with the students, whereas **indirect supervision** assumes the supervisor to be in the area where the activity is taking place.

Direct supervision is important in the introduction of a new activity. Teachers stay with the participants until they are familiar with the activity, understand their own capacity to accomplish the task, and understand and adhere to the safety rules. The more inexperienced the participants are in an activity, the greater the responsibility of the teacher. Students must be well aware of the safety factors and understand any risks; it is not enough merely to inform them of risks. Young elementary school children may require more direct supervision since they are not always mature enough to fully appreciate the safety concerns of the teacher. For example, when introducing a new piece of apparatus, such as the horizontal ladder, the teacher should stay with the children until each has had the opportunity to try it, to mount, to move, and to land safely. Both direct and indirect supervision are important in maximizing the participation for all children. As the teaching methods become more child-centered, the teacher may be giving some direct supervision to some children while indirectly supervising the remaining children. Direct and indirect supervision shifts from some individuals or groups to other individuals or groups as the teacher moves throughout the activity area. Station work and use of the task style of teaching involve indirect supervision for at least part of the class.

Any failure by the participants to adhere to safety rules or any change in the condition of participants requires more direct supervision until the condition can be reversed. Indirect supervision assumes the supervisior is located in the immediate area and is accessible to anyone who needs assistance. Teachers must position themselves where they can oversee the entire group. In providing indirect supervision the individual must be alert to any unsafe conditions that may arise. Horseplay should always be discouraged. Equipment should always be used safely, and participants should only work within their ability.

Adequate supervision must be provided for all school experiences. Supervision of the playground activities may be the responsibility of the physical education or classroom teacher. If the children change clothes for physical education activities, supervision must also be provided in locker room areas. Physical education facilities should be locked when supervision is not available. This is especially important when large apparatus or other equipment is being used.

Selection and Conduct of Activities

The activities that are selected should be appropriate to the age, size, physical condition, and ability of those participating. Individual differences must be considered in the selection of activities for any group. Children should be encouraged to work to their level of ability but should not be pressured into attempting activities that they do not feel they are ready to do. Lack of confidence in performing a particular motor activity may result in an injury because of increased anxiety before the attempt.

No child should attempt an activity without careful instruction. Teaching is important. Safety is of utmost importance during the instruction phase, and children should not be asked to take unreasonable risks. Instruction must be geared to the maturity of the students because lack of maturity may jeopardize the children's safety.

Potential risks to safety must be anticipated. Thorough planning is important not only in the selection of activities but also in the manner in which they are conducted. Activities should be organized with special consideration for spacial needs. Children should

be able to move freely. They should not interfere with one another and should be able to move away from obstacles and equipment. In situations in which safety hazards cannot be avoided, activities must be modified. If this modification does not reduce the risks, then the activity should be discontinued. Special concerns for safety are included in each of the activity chapters that follow.

In case of an emergency or when a potentially dangerous situation arises, the teacher must remain calm. The teacher's display of confidence should be reassuring to the children and may even eliminate behavior that can lead to potentially dangerous situations.

The Environment

Rules of safety should be established for all areas of the school, including classroom, gymnasium, and playground. These rules must be consistently enforced by all school personnel. The activities of one child should not endanger others.

The atmosphere in the physical education class should be one in which children not only participate safely but also feel safe. Children who are comfortable in a situation are more willing to participate freely and to behave safely. It must be an environment where children assume responsibility for their own safety and the safety of others.

Protective equipment and other safety devices should be provided and kept in good working condition. Protective equipment should fit the participants using them. In activities in which safety equipment is needed, it should be used always, with the children taught how to use it effectively.

Floors and other surfaces should be inspected for safety on a regular basis. Unsafe conditions should be reported immediately. Repairs should be made promptly and all areas well maintained. Teachers should use good judgment in using facilities and equipment until appropriate repairs are made.

Heat and ventilation should be controlled, with activities moderated where environmental conditions warrant. In some areas monitoring air quality, temperature, or high humidity may necessitate changes in the activities for the day.

Rainy day activities should be related to the units of instruction being taught since children are developing skills and awareness of safety that reduces the risks of injury. However, modifications in activities or equipment may be needed where space is reduced dramatically to ensure the safe participation of all.

Table 7-1

Instructional and management problems in physical education

Problem	Probable cause	Solution
INSTRUCTIONAL PROBLEMS		
Several children in the class are unable to do the skills needed in the unit.	Great variation in ability in group	Plan activities to develop skills in progression for all levels of ability in the group.
In a gymnastics lesson not all children are working.	Loss of interest because skills are too difficult or too easy	Providing a variety of activities to challenge all ability levels.
The class is having some difficulty using a concept.	Not ready for the application	Determine level of understanding. Provide activities at a lower level to prepare students for the movement challenge.
The children do not appear to understand how to perform a skill.	Lack of understanding of what is to be done	Provide another demonstration and explanation of the task and ask questions to determine understanding.
MANAGEMENT PROBLEMS		
Two children are fighting during a game.	Not enough activity	Restructure activity to maximize active participation for all.
A child is not chosen by anyone in the group as a partner.	Child may be unliked by others	Arrange children into partners.
Two children in the rear of the group are not listening.	Not within eye contact or hearing of teacher	Arrange children in close so all can hear explanations and see demonstration.
Several children are unable to follow the instructions given.	Instructions unclear	Repeat instructions; ask questions for clarification.
The class is noisy and not responsive to the signal for listening.	Signal not clear	Clarify signal for listening; practice response to signal.
The class is unable to reorganize for the new activity within the lesson.	Directions unclear; children not listening	Get group's attention. Go over steps in reorganization. Move group.

If the above concerns for adequate supervision, for appropriate selection and conduct of activities and for a safe environment are met, we are well on the way to providing a safe physical education experience for all children.

CLASS MANAGEMENT AND ORGANIZATIONAL STRATEGIES

Successful teaching is the result of careful planning of both instruction and management. *Instruction* is composed of all the activities that the teacher utilizes to meet the lesson objectives. *Management* includes the operations that are required to move the class smoothly from one activity to the next, from the beginning of the lesson to its conclusion.

Many times a lesson is unsuccessful because the teacher fails to manage the class effectively. Regardless of how well the instructional phase is planned, failure to be concerned with management operations only leads to disaster.

It is essential for the teacher to distinguish between instructional and management activities. Instruction involves those activities that include (1) diagnosing class needs, (2) planning and presenting information, (3) asking questions, and (4) evaluating progress. Management activities are those that (1) create and maintain the instructional conditions, (2) reward appropriate behavior, (3) develop teacher-student rapport, and the like.[1]

Problems that arise during the lesson must also be diagnosed. Some may be the result of inadequate planning, whereas others may be problems that are difficult to anticipate. Instructional problems require instructional solutions and management problems require management solutions. Table 7-1 differentiates some typical instructional and management problems that may occur in physical education.

Classroom management skills are essential to good teaching. Good classroom management practices by the teacher result in the development of good self-management skills by the students. Once students learn to be more self-managed, it is easier for the teacher to concentrate on effective teaching. Children must learn to assume responsibility for their own actions and to share responsibility for classroom management. For example, children can learn to be responsible for getting out equipment, taking care of it, and putting it away. They can also learn to work in a group and not distract the work of others. However, these are skills they learn not by chance but through the management activities of the teacher.

In planning the lesson the teacher should identify each part of the lesson in which management skills will be used. These parts of the lesson should be worked out ahead of time to minimize the management time and maximize the learning time. Beginning teachers are often so worried about the content of the lesson that they overlook the necessary management operations. Yet it is in this area the lesson most often breaks down.

As the teacher and students move through the lesson, the teacher uses verbal and nonverbal cues in organizing the class, in moving them from one activity to another and from one formation to the next. These cues are also used in securing, using, and putting away equipment as well as reacting to the behavior of the students on and off task.

The time taken to manage the class or to perform the functions cited above should be minimal. As children learn to become more self-managed, time is reduced further. If the teacher takes too long in the management tasks, there is a greater chance for disruptive behavior by the students. To maximize learning time the teacher must plan carefully the management activities. For example, anyone can organize a group into a circle, but it may take one teacher a few seconds and another a few minutes. The less time available to children while they wait for the next part of the lesson to happen, the greater the chance the move will go smoothly.

Class management techniques should be as unobtrusive as possible so as not to detract from the instructional aspects of the lesson. If well planned, they will move the group quickly into activity and smoothly from one activity to the next. Rather than merely reacting to problems as they occur, management operations should prevent problems from occuring. Several factors affect the selection of appropriate management strategies:

1. The maturity of the students and their relationships to one another must be considered. Are the students self-directed, or do they need more structure within which to learn? Are they well disciplined? Can they follow directions and stay on task with little direct supervision? What has been the nature of their previous learning experiences?

2. The number of students, the amount of space, the equipment, the time constraints, and the goals for the lesson are all considerations in selecting appropriate management procedures.

3. The teacher's personality is also an important factor. What is the teacher's preferred teaching style? What rapport has been established with the group?

The first task in effective management is to develop a cohesive group. The teacher must strive to develop an atmosphere in which teacher-student and student-student relationships are good and everyone is supported by everyone else. In this atmosphere children can feel comfortable in striving to do their best.

Management problems may be of an individual or group nature. Often individual problems may be intertwined with group problems that may cloud the issue in determining strategies to overcome them. In Table 7-2 Cooper and associates[1] define group management problems. Individual behavior problems and strategies to deal with them are discussed in Chapter 8.

The following sections offer suggestions for developing effective class management techniques.

Establishing a Class Routine

One important concern in classroom management is the establishment of a class routine. Children are creatures of habit. The routine should include how the class begins, what signal is to be used to get the group's attention, and what is expected in listening and following directions, in working with others, in the use of space for particular activities, and in special routines for the use of playground, gymnasium, and other spaces.

These routine behaviors are best taught in the early physical education experiences or when several teachers are involved in the physical education instruction at the beginning of the school year. The earlier these behaviors are established, the sooner maximum activity can be achieved. If routines are to

Table 7-2

Group classroom management problems and their behavioral descriptions

1. Lack of unity	The class lacks unity, and conflicts occur between individuals and subgroups, as: (a) When groups split, become argumentative over competitive situations such as games, or boys side against girls; (b) When groups split by cliques or minority groups; (c) When group takes sides on issues or breaks into subgroups; when hostility and conflict constantly arise among members and create an unpleasant atmosphere.
2. Nonadherence to behavioral standards and work procedures	The class responds with noisy, talkative, disorderly behavior to situations which have established standards for behaving, as: (a) When group is entering or leaving room or changing activities, lining up, cleaning up, or going to auditorium; (b) When group is working in ability groups or engaging in committee work; (c) When group is completing study assignments, receiving assignments, correcting papers, or handling work materials; (d) When group is engaged in discussion, sharing, or planning.
3. Negative reactions to individual members	The class becomes vocal or actively hostile toward one or more class members, as: (a) When group does not accept individuals and derides, ignores, or ridicules members who are different; (b) When group reacts negatively to members who deviate from group code or who thwart group's progress; when a member's behavior upsets or puzzles members of the class.
4. Class approval of misbehavior	The class approves and supports individuals, as: (a) When they talk out of turn, act in ways which disrupt the normal work procedures, or engage in clowning or rebellious activities.
5. Being prone to distraction, work stoppage, and imitative behavior	The group reacts with upset, excited, or disorderly behavior to interruptions, distractions, or constant grievances, as: (a) When group is interrupted by monitors, visitors, or a change in weather. (b) When members constantly have grievances relating to others, lessons, rules, policies, or practices they believe are unfair and when settlements are demanded before work proceeds.
6. Low morale and hostile, resistant, or aggressive reactions	The class members engage in subtle, hostile, aggressive behavior, creating slowdowns and work stoppages, as: (a) When materials are misplaced, pencils break, or chairs are upset; (b) When books, money, or lunches are temporarily lost; (c) When there are constant requests for assignments to be repeated and explained; (d) When students constantly complain about behavior of others with no apparent loss of friendship; (e) When children accuse authority figures of unfair practices and delay classwork with their claims.
7. Inability to adjust to environmental change	The class reacts inappropriately to such situations, as: (a) When a substitute takes over; (b) When normal routines are changed; (c) When new members transfer into the class; (d) When stress situations cause inappropriate reactions.

From Cooper and others.

be established painlessly teachers, must be consistent in defining the specific behaviors appropriate in these different situations.

If the children change clothes for physical education, there may be free time at the beginning of the period. This time should be used constructively. Posting a list of activities to work on before the beginning of class is helpful. In this way children may use the time beneficially to further their own development.

Managing the Lesson

Establish a signal for listening. A signal for listening must be established if the class is to begin quickly. A great deal of time can be lost if this routine is not

set. Signals for starting an activity should not be confused with the signal for listening. Often a voice command is all that is needed for beginning, but a louder signal such as a whistle may be more effective for getting the group's attention in some situations. Using the word, "freeze," raising a hand, and dimming the lights are examples of signals used to get the attention of the class. Positive feedback is important in establishing the signal for listening. The teacher should encourage the children to respond quickly and praise their efforts when they do. Such comments as "Good listening, Mary," and "I like the way John is listening" go a long way in establishing good listening skills.

Get off to a good start. To begin the lesson promptly it is important to have all materials ready that will be used in the class before the class begins. Sometimes children may help organize the materials for the lesson. As children gain experience in helping, they will require less time to get out the equipment and other materials, which allows more time to be spent in the instructional phase of the lesson.

In beginning the lesson it is important that the children be arranged in a manner that is conducive to good listening. The class should be seated where all are able to see and hear. When meeting outdoors the class should assemble away from distracting noises. If it is windy, the class should face the oncoming wind so the teacher's voice is projected toward the class. On sunny days the teacher should face the sun so the children do not have to strain or shield their eyes to see the teacher and the demonstrations.

Get the class into activity quickly. In order for the lesson to be most effective, it is important to get the class into activity quickly. Often a lesson never really gets its momentum because too much time is taken for management at the beginning of the lesson. The class should begin on time. When the children enter the gymnasium, the lesson should begin immediately. Once the daily routine is established, children should be able to enter the area and immediately begin the warm-up activities or to receive the instructions for the first activity. Children are eager to get started. Teachers must channel this enthusiasm by getting the children moving quickly in the lesson.

A time-saving method should be used to take the roll if necessary. Often this can be done while the children are engaged in the warm-up activities or the first activity of the lesson.

Instructions should be short and to the point. Minimum time should be used for giving instructions. Momentum is often lost because teachers dwell too long on points of emphasis or other instructions. This is an important time but one in which attention can be lost if instructions take too long.

In moving the group into activity it is important the children listen to all the instructions before moving. Children are eager to get moving and often begin following what they think the instructions are before they are actually completed. When giving instructions it is often a good idea to:

First, tell the children when they will move ("When I give you the signal").

Second, tell them where and how they will move ("I want you to find your own space inside the black boundary lines").

Third, tell them what they will do when they get there ("and sit down").

Often in giving instructions to children, for example to move to a new formation it helps to get a time reference regarding how long it should take. For example, to help children move quickly one might say "When I say go I want to see if everyone can line up on the black line before I count to three. Go. One, two, three."

Children need encouragement to follow the new instructions quickly. Positive feedback is always helpful in establishing good management habits. At times a group may need to be rewarded for responding quickly to instructions, especially when the group is just beginning to develop self-management skills. The reward might be free time during the last part of the period or a choice of a favorite activity.

Establish momentum and keep the lesson moving. An effective lesson is one in which momentum is established and the lesson parts flow smoothly from one to another without breaks where disruptive behavior might occur. Disruptions often occur when there is a break in the activity flow or there is an unnecessary slowdown. These disruptions may be the result of a child's change in behavior for some reason, the occurrence of some unplanned event, stopping an activity before its conclusion, or prolonging an activity beyond its usefulness. It may also be the result of failure to maximize the activity, resulting in the loss of interest of the group. These disruptions may also be the result of the teacher in taking too much time for an explanation or not sensing when it is time to move on.

Occasionally teachers must deal with several events taking place simultaneously. For example, a teacher giving a demonstration of a new skill to the class notices two children are being inattentive. The successful teacher must be able to deal with these two events at the same time if momentum is not to be lost. A question posed to either of the two children, or a remark or an instruction given to the children as the explanation and demonstration continue, will be helpful in keeping the lesson moving.

Teachers should be careful to stay on task and not become distracted by events that occur randomly. There are occasions when circumstances do lend themselves to the "teachable moment," but teachers should most often avoid situations that get them off track.

Teachers must also develop an awareness of when it is time to move on in the lesson. It is important both to permit adequate time for children to develop the skill or concept as well as to move on to the next activity before the children lose interest.

Maximize the opportunities for each child to participate. It is important to maximize the amount of activity for each child during the lesson. Time studies often disclose that individual children have spent far too little time being physically active in the lesson. Teachers must make maximum use of equipment and organize the group so as many children as possible are actively engaged in moving throughout the lesson. Whenever possible teachers should attempt to have all children active at one time. Mass teaching involves organizing the class so all children are working in their own space individually on a particular skill or concept with the teacher circulating among the children giving help where needed. Since skills or concepts are best learned over repeated practice, this approach maximizes individual development. This mass teaching approach is perhaps a little unnerving for beginning teachers since the children may be spread over a large area and the teacher may feel some lack of control over the group. With experience teachers will feel more comfortable in using this technique of organizing the group for individual work.

Often we do not have an adequate supply of any one kind of equipment to allow each child to work alone. Opportunities for practice may be improved by gathering all the balls available rather than insisting on the use of only one type of ball. The children should share the equipment so all have the opportunity to use balls of a variety of sizes and types while practicing the skill.

Another method for maximizing learning opportunities when limited pieces of equipment are available is to use the station approach. The children are divided into several groups with each group practicing different skills; the available equipment is used to its maximum. After a period of practice each group moves on to a new station, to a new skill, and to new equipment. In this manner all the children are actively practicing their skills with little waiting, if any, for a turn. It is important to watch the time carefully so all have an opportunity to work at each station. Children readily display their disappointment at not having an opportunity to try each activity.

Activity modification is another means of maximizing the opportunities for all children. In developing group learning experiences the teacher must determine what is the smallest group necessary to fulfill the activity objectives. A suggested minimal number of participants for each activity is included in the games analyses in Chapters 22 through 28. However, reducing the number of participants per group results in maximum participation only when the teacher substitutes several small group games occurring at the same time for one large group activity.

Increasing the amount of equipment used or the number of active participants in an activity is another way to maximize the opportunities for each child. In this way children will have many opportunities to use their skills in a minimal amount of time. The games analyses in Chapters 22 through 28 suggest the amount of equipment needed to maximize the activity.

Plan the technique for grouping students. Often in a physical education class the teacher wishes to divide the group into partners or small groups. These groupings may be for the entire unit, for a part of the unit, for the day, or for an activity within the lesson. Many times individual work lends itself to a group activity, in which the children work individually on a particular skill but within a small group setting.

Small group work has considerable value in the learning experiences of children. These experiences give children the opportunity to work with less direct teacher supervision. They also provide an opportunity to develop leadership skills. Children may be given responsibility to secure, take care of, and put away the equipment they will be using. It also provides an environment for sharing, planning, and working together. Children may be asked at various times to assume leadership and followership roles.

Several methods may be used to divide children into groups. At no time should any method be used that emphasizes the inadequacy of any child, such as putting the children in a line and having the captains alternately pick their groups. This method is often cited by individuals of all ages as a reason for disliking physical education.

Teachers should not relinquish their responsibility in dividing the class into partners or groups. Saying "Find a partner" does not always have the result the teacher would like. There undoubtedly will be some children who will not readily seek a partner and others who are unwilling to be someone's partner; often the result is that the least secure children end up being together. In many situations this is not the best possible pairing, since the insecure children lack confidence that will limit their success.

Within the class grouping can be attained by numbering off (1, 2, 3, 4, 1, 2, 3, 4 . . .) or grouping children by their birth months, height, weight, or size. Children may also be grouped according to their ability in an activity or by their social behavior. Groups may also be formed by having the children draw colors or numbers out of a box. The teacher may also pick groups randomly by dividing parts of a circle or some other formation into groups.

Often the teacher groups the children before class by matching them heterogeneously or homogeneously depending on the activity. Some activities may call for matching children according to ability to equalize individual as well as team competition. Homogeneous grouping may be effective in gymnastics or when practicing special events like the high jump when raising and lowering the bar for different abilities within the group cuts down on individual practice time. A disadvantge to homogeneous grouping may be that poorly skilled children do not have the opportunity to observe a good performance. In using heterogenous grouping the more able youngsters not only serve as models for performance but

may also be called on to help their less able classmates.

The use of a sociogram as a method for determining groups may also be effective. Children may be instructed, "List three persons you would like on your soccer team." The children respond in writing and the teacher groups them into equal teams ensuring that the children will be with at least one person of their choice. To begin the process of grouping the teacher begins with the children who were not picked by anyone or who were chosen by only a few. The response of the children in selecting those with whom they would like to be grouped varies somewhat with the activity, but this method enables the teacher to have a clear look at what is going on in the class. The teacher can hopefully use the information gathered to affect the social interactions of the group. Another method to use in grouping children in which the children are more actively involved in the process is one in which the teacher or the class elects the captains. The captains then meet privately with the teacher and group selection takes place. In this way the teacher can help the children make individual choices that will benefit the group and yet give them more opportunity in the grouping process. In this manner only the captains and the teacher know who is chosen last.

When grouping children into squads or teams that will be used for more than one day in the unit it may be helpful to assign or, better yet, give the children an opportunity to select a name for their group. This helps them, especially young children, to remember their groups from day to day. A game to play to aid children in remembering their groups is to call quickly the name of a group and ask them to do something. ("Elephants, stand up. Zebras, turn around.") Calling the names quickly and having the children respond to some instruction several times furthers their listening skills as well as helping them to remember their groups.

Organize the skills practice for optimal learning. The skills practice is an important part of the lesson. In games lessons there should be a balance between skill practice and game play. The practice of skills allows the children to repeat the skills, which is important in mastery and may not always be achieved in game play. Often children do not see the relationship between the skill and the game. Therefore the practice of skills should be similar to their use in the activity. This practice should allow time to work in increasingly challenging activities. In determining the practice of skills a task analysis is essential in which the progression in skill development is defined.

A variety of formations may be used to enhance skill development. Once they learn these formations, children may move quickly into place to begin the activity, saving valuable time for the practice of skills. In using any formation for skills practice the teacher should organize the group within the available space, minimizing safety hazards so each group has sufficient space and the activity of one group does not interfere with the activity of another. Teachers should circulate among the groups as they work and position themselves in such a way that all children can see them if there is a need for further clarification. In choosing a formation the teacher should make every attempt to maximize the opportunities for each child. Figure 7-3 shows many of the formations that can be used in a physical education class.

Plan the care and efficient use of available equipment and space. The equipment to be used in the lesson should be collected ahead of time and be ready for distribution at the appropriate time. If several teachers will be using the same equipment, it may be possible to have the first group get it out and the last group put it away. Classroom teachers may also use student or adult aides or paraprofessionals to help prepare the area for the physical education class.

The distribution, care, and collecting of the equipment for the physical education lesson must be carefully planned. If instructions are vague or incomplete, the children may use the equipment in an unsatisfactory way. Often this is where a lesson breaks down. The instructions should always include how the equipment will be obtained and especially what to do with it when it is received.

Children must be taught to assume responsibility for taking care of the equipment. Children not only should learn the routines for obtaining and putting away equipment but also should be taught how to use it in a way in which it will remain in service for a long time. Children need to learn to respect the school's equipment and value its care.

If elementary school children are to use equipment effectively, it should be of appropriate size and weight. Today a variety of elementary schoolsize equipment is available. Apparatus should also be proportional to the size of the children. The use of foam balls increases the safety for children in many activities. Where possible a variety of types of equipment should be available so children have the opportunity to handle them and to learn their properties.

Methods used in securing and putting away equipment include the following:

1. Having the children in a line; one after an-

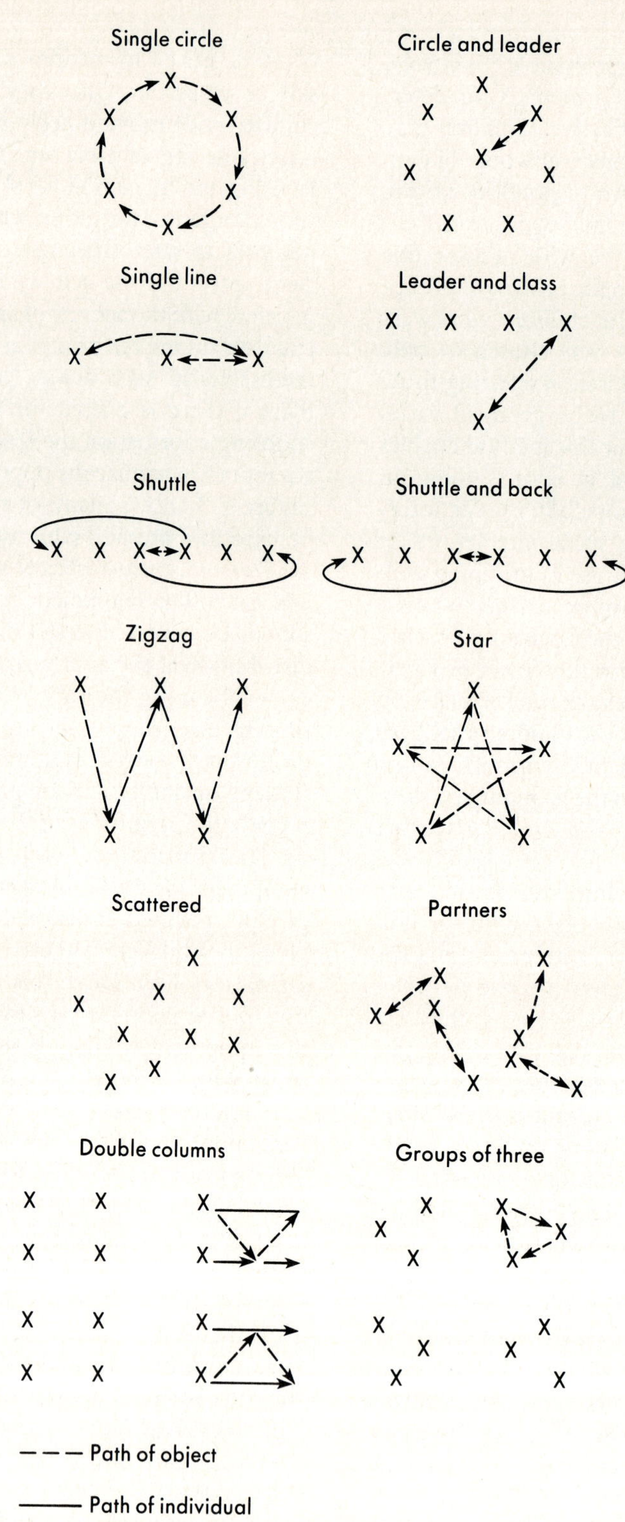

Figure 7-3

Formations to use for skills practice.

other receives or picks up a piece of equipment.

2. Having the equipment arranged in the area to be used; each child goes to a piece of equipment. In this way children are arranged in their own spaces as well.
3. Organizing the class into groups or formations; one member of each group secures and distributes the equipment to the group.
4. Arranging the equipment at various stations; children are assigned to each station, where they go to pick up equipment.

For collecting the equipment at the end of the activity these arrangements may be reversed.

In maximizing the use of space, using the walls often increases the space as well as serves to keep equipment contained in the area. The use of walls also maximizes individual activity and permits variation according to ability since individual children control their own skill work. Using walls often allows for a better practice situation than would be found when working with a partner. Children can also concentrate on the pattern of movement rather than being concerned about where the object goes.

Plan the transitions from one activity to the next. Transitions from one activity to the next must be carefully planned. The teacher should avoid any moves that are not essential to the success of the activity. The children should be moved from one activity and formation to the next as smoothly as possible. The most efficient method of moving the group with as few moves as possible from one formation to another must be determined. The teacher should avoid bringing the children together between each new formation. For example, if the children are arranged in a circle, it is not necessary to bring them in close and then organize them into partners in two lines for the next activity. Dividing the circle in half and putting each half in position facing the other half, or assigning partners in the circle and putting them into position, would be much more efficient. Carefully preplanning the order of activities may avoid needless reorganization of children.

Plan a good ending for the lesson. The lesson should always have a strong finish. As the class period comes to a close, the teacher should plan for good closure. Usually time is taken to summarize the major points of emphasis in the lesson. The teacher also may wish to prepare the class briefly for the next lesson's activities. The group should leave the physical education area in order. If the children do not change clothes, they should move in an orderly way to their classroom. Any issues raised during the physical education class should be addressed and resolved before the children return to the classroom. Physical educators must take the time to be sure the children are ready for the remainder of the school day. Often the physical education class is very stimulating. Children need to be brought down to a level of excitement that enables them calmly to begin the next activity. Often the time taken to summarize the lesson is all they need. In other cases time spent in relaxation training may be important.

Special Concerns When Using Child-Centered Methods

It is important to establish a good working relationship with the class before attempting child-centered methods. Children need to have some expectation of acceptable behavior before developing more independent learning.

Obviously these methods rely heavily on a good signal for listening. The signal to be used with the group must be established. It may be helpful to have the children practice responding to the signal. For example, the teacher instructs the children to move in a variety of ways in general space and to see how quickly they can stop and be ready to listen when the music stops.

The use of imagery when establishing the boundaries or when finding one's own space adds to the fun of the lesson. For example, "Inside the black lines is a big piece of bread. You are all peanut butter. Spread out." One must always present instructions in a way that challenges the children to follow them. They do it because it is the difficult thing to do, not because the teacher tells them they must.

The teacher must develop a sensitivity for the children as they are working. It is important to pose questions or to move on to the next activity at the appropriate time. This should be done when they have had enough time to explore possible solutions but not so much time as to lose interest. The teacher should use a variety of challenges to maintain interest.

One must be certainly aware of previous learning experiences in using this approach. Children who have had only teacher-centered learning experiences have some difficulty at first in using this approach. A teacher must gradually introduce the approach and use it for short periods at first, until the class begins to feel more comfortable in exploring movement and solving problems on their own.

The teacher should encourage performance in

front of the group. The teacher must be sensitive to the children's feeling about their performance and organize it in such a way to prevent the children from feeling overly self-conscious. In the lower grades children may enjoy performing in front of the group. In the middle and upper grades they may be more hesitant. At this level the teacher may organize the class so several children or a group of children perform at the same time, although they are working independently of one another. Once they gain confidence in group presentations, individuals may find performing alone a challenge.

USE OF VOLUNTEERS AND PARAPROFESSIONALS

In recent years the use of volunteers and paraprofessionals in the school setting has increased dramatically. Physical education is one area that can benefit greatly by using aides. Parents, interested adults, high school students, or upper elementary school children may be willing to volunteer in the physical education classes.

These aides may serve in a variety of ways. They may help set up the physical education site by getting out apparatus and other equipment, putting up nets, marking boundaries, and other tasks. They may work with individuals or small groups under the direction of the teacher, which results in greater individual help in skill development. The use of peer teaching in the elementary school has proven to be effective in enhancing learning.

SUMMARY

All teachers share in the responsibility for providing a safe learning environment. Safe behavior must be consistently encouraged. If an accident occurs, the injured child should receive prompt attention and first aid care. Emergency procedures should be carefully developed and communicated to all school personnel. Teachers must be aware of their responsibility in providing adequate supervision of all activities, selecting and conducting activities with safety in mind, and providing a safe environment for learning to take place.

Effective classroom management is essential if learning is to be maximized. Management and instructional problems must be diagnosed and appropriate management or instructional solutions implemented. Effective management includes procedures

for getting the class started, giving meaningful instructions, securing and putting away equipment, organizing and moving the class throughout the lesson, and planning closure for the lesson. There is no substitute for careful planning of management techniques if the class activities are to move smoothly from beginning to end.

REFERENCES

1. Cooper, J., and others: Classroom teaching skills: a handbook, ed. 2, Lexington, 1982, D.C. Heath & Co.
2. Dougherty, N.: Liability, JOPERD **54**(6):52, June 1983.
3. Dougherty, N., and Bonanno. D.: Contemporary approaches to the teaching of physical education, Minneapolis, 1979, Burgess Publishing Co.
4. Dreikers, R., and Cassel, P.: Discipline without tears, New York, 1974, Hawthorn Books.
5. Harrison, J.: Instructional strategies for physical education, Dubuque, 1983, William C. Brown Co.
6. Morris, G., and Stiehl, J.: Physical education from intent to action, Columbus, 1985, Charles E. Merrill Publishing Co.
7. Rink, J.: Teaching physical education for learning, St. Louis, 1985, Times Mirror Mosby.
8. Schurr, E.: Movement experiences for children, ed. 3, Englewood Cliffs, N.J.,1980, Prentice-Hall Inc.
9. Siedentop, D.: Developing teaching skills in physical education, Palo Alto, 1983, Mayfield Publishing Co.
10. Van der smissen, B.: Legal aspects of adult fitness programs, JOPERD **45**(2):54, February 1974.

ADDITIONAL READINGS

Carpenter L., and Acosta, R.: Negligence: What is it? How can it be avoided? JOPERD **53**(2):51, February 1982.
Physical educators' responsibilities for the safe participation of participants in their charge by providing supervision, good judgment, and proper instruction and measures to avoid negligence.

Griffin, P.: Coed physical education problems and promise, JOPERD **55**(6):36, August 1984.
A look at the reasons why some coed programs fail and others succeed.

Kneer, M.: Ability grouping in physical education, JOPERD **53**(9):10, November/December 1982.
Considerations for determining ability groups and how to accommodate them in the curriculum.

Metzler, M.: Developing teaching skills: a systematic sequence, **55**(1):38, January 1984.
Use of microteaching to improve teaching skills by analyzing management and teaching time.

Metzler, M., and Young, J.: The relationship between teachers' preactive planning and student process measures, Research Quarterly for Exercise and Sport **55**(4):356, December 1984.
A comparison of teaching by two teachers using divergent lesson planning patterns, resulting in management procedures that varied the academic learning times for the fourth-grade students in their classes.

Phillips, J., and Carter, J.: Tired of being chosen last? Humanistic alternatives to group division, JOPERD **56**(1):96, January 1985.
Guidelines and methods to divide a class for activity.

8

COMMUNICATION AND THE SPECIAL NEEDS OF CHILDREN

CHAPTER OBJECTIVES

1   To describe teacher-pupil relationships conducive to learning
2   To identify the strategies to use in dealing with behavior problems
3   To apply guidelines to meet the special needs of children
4   To discuss the conduct of activities that assist students to become independent learners

The development of skills for lifelong learning is an important goal of education. Young children are eager to learn about themselves and the environment in which they work and play. Teachers play an important role in structuring the learning environment to maintain interest in learning. They must strive to provide the kinds of experiences in which the love of learning is enhanced. Since the purpose of physical education in the schools is to develop positive attitudes toward physical education and physical activity in general, which will result in a lifetime of active participation, teachers must strive to establish the most favorable environment for these values to be achieved.

To meet the goal for lifelong learning teachers must help students develop learning skills that are not dependent on the teacher interacting directly with the students. In order for independent learning skills to result the learning environment must be one in which there is adequate communication between teacher and learners, it must be free of conflict between the desires of teacher and students, and the needs of individual children must be recognized and met. The following pages suggest techniques teachers may use to help all students get the most from their physical education experience.

COMMUNICATING WITH CHILDREN

Adequate communication is essential in establishing good teacher-pupil relationships. *Interpersonal communication skills* may be defined as a series of specific verbal and nonverbal behaviors that stimulate personal inquiry between two or more persons—inquiry that leads to self-knowledge.[2] Communication may be verbal or nonverbal. Verbally we communicate by the words we use in the verbal message, by the tone of voice, or perhaps by silence, by not answering at all. Nonverbally we communicate in our appearance, our posture, our facial expression, our lack of attention, the distance we put between ourselves and those to whom we are communicating, and in the way we model the behavior we value.

Nonverbal behavior is important. Teachers must be conscious of their own feelings and attitudes as they respond to children. The teacher's posture and facial expressions may communicate to the child an interest or disinterest in what is being communicated

and positive or negative feelings about what is being said.

To enhance communication the teacher must be attentive and a good listener. When listening the teacher must try to distinguish between what was actually said and what was really meant. If a child says, "This isn't any fun," the actual meaning may be "I am frustrated because this is too difficult." If the teacher is not sure of the meaning, the students may be asked questions to help clarify what they are trying to say.

As a result of good communication the teacher gains a better understanding of children and their needs, and children recognize the value of physical activity to healthful living. The box on p. 99 outlines some aspects of communication in physical education for teachers and students.

Physical education teachers communicate the importance of physical activity and the physical education class, the nature of the physical education learning environment, and the value they place on the accomplishments of each child. Teachers, directly or indirectly, communicate feelings about the importance of physical activity in a person's life through their physical appearance, good health, and vitality and in their enthusiasm for the physical activities that make up the physical education classes.

In communicating about the nature of the learning environment in the physical education class the distinction between recess and physical education may need to be clarified. Recess is a time for children to determine which activities, if any, they will pursue. Teachers have the responsibility first for what students learn. Teachers set the standard for performance. They communicate what is to be learned and how it is to be learned. Teachers help children set goals and assess their progress toward these goals. They give encouragement as improvement occurs and help each child reset personal goals for achievement.

The structure of the lessons must be established early. It is important to set the patterns for behavior and the routines early in the physical education experience. Expectations for listening, improving skills, increasing knowledge, establishing relationships with others, and working without direct teacher supervision must be carefully communicated.

The teacher also communicates feelings about the children. Turner and Purkey[17] outline teacher behaviors that invite or disinvite child participation in physical education. Children respond positively to physical education if they feel they are invited to participate by a teacher who they believe views them as able and responsible. Sometimes children perceive the physical educator as one who values only those children who are gifted movers. The teacher must be careful to communicate a sincere interest in all children and their success in physical education.

Students also communicate. The students communicate their interest in learning the particular skills and knowledge, their understanding of what is to be learned and how it is to be learned, their assessment of their progress toward the objectives, and their satisfaction or frustration toward the learning experience. To other students they communicate their likes and dislikes, their feelings toward specific others, and their willingness to work with individual children and to help each other. A good learning environment is one in which the relationship between teacher and students encourages students to express their ideas and feelings in a positive way.

Children need an opportunity to express their thoughts and feelings openly. They may need help in understanding their feelings in a nonthreatening way. When interacting with students the teacher describes rather than judges. The teacher must look at a situation from the students' point of view by being sensitive to their feelings. The teacher should respond in a way that helps the children understand when the teacher's point of view is in conflict with theirs and should do so in a nonthreatening manner. Teachers must be careful to send the desired messages to children by being alert to their own feelings and nonverbal cues.

COMMUNICATION IN PHYSICAL EDUCATION

WHAT IS COMMUNICATED

Teacher
  Value of physical education
  Importance of each child's participation and
    success
  What is to be learned and how
  Expected social behavior
  Willingness to help
  Feelings about the physical education class
Students
  Interest in physical education
  What they can do
  What they know
  Own assessment of achievement
  How they feel about others
  How they feel about their physical education
    experience

HOW IT IS COMMUNICATED

Verbal
  Verbal responses
  Silence
  Tone of voice
Nonverbal
  Facial expression
  Body posture
  Physical space
  Lack of attention
  Modeling
  Appearance

CLASS CONTROL AND DISCIPLINE

An important result of adequate communication is a learning environment in which there is order, in which certain standards of behavior are practiced. Class control is a planned strategy rather than a response to a situation that arises. It is action rather than reaction. The best strategy is to structure the situation so that inappropriate behaviors are avoided. In other words the teacher acts in a manner that prevents discipline problems. Adequate planning is essential for effective class control. If the lesson is conducted with maximum participation and effective transition from one activity to another, and if the lesson objectives and subsequent activities are meaningful to the individual students, behavior problems are minimized. Good management and effective instruction are important ingredients of an effective learning environment.

The school attempts to prepare children to participate in our democratic society. Democracy ensures each individual certain freedoms. Children must learn to accept the obligations and responsibilities associated with freedom and to respect the freedom of others. All societies must have order, with some restrictions placed on their members. Schools develop standards of behavior for the benefits of all chil-dren, to ensure their rights and optimal development. The physical education class has its rules of behavior also, written or unwritten. Rules should be minimal in number and general enough to apply to many different situations. A discussion early in the year to go over the rules and why they are important is essential to getting everyone off to a good start. It may be of value to have the children help to determine the rules they need for successful participation in the physical education class, since they are more apt to follow rules they had a part in determining than those imposed by an adult. Consistency in reinforcing rules is essential. In the beginning of the school year when children are getting acquainted or reacquainted with the rules, the teacher gives more direction in the conduct of the class. As children learn to function appropriately in the class setting, the class becomes more student directed. One must be firm regarding adherence to the rules, especially when introducing new rules at the beginning of the school year. Cracking down later in enforcing rules is much more difficult, since it is frustrating for children who interpret the actions as changing the rules. The importance for certain standards of behavior become apparent as children respond to the teacher's enforcement of the rules.

Occasionally a situation arises in which the teacher needs to reestablish order or alter the behavior of an individual, a group, or the entire class. *Discipline* may be defined as "a process of assisting youngsters to adjust to their environment and develop acceptable inner controls."[9] Teachers must be consistent in their interactions with the students. Teachers also should know what behavior they wish to approve, ignore, or disapprove, so that they consistently respond in a particular manner to a specific behavior. The teacher must strive to respond most often to significant student behavior. All children should be treated fairly. The teacher must respond to a behavior regardless of who the child is; there can be no favorites. If for some reason the teacher responds differently, then the children must understand why.

The first step in dealing with inappropriate behavior is to restore order. Once order is restored, the cause of the behavior must be determined by responding to the following questions:

Is the cause anything the teacher did or did not do?

Are the expectations clear to the students?

Are the activities challenging the students?

Do the planned activities provide maximum activity for all?

Are there distractions in the environment that have resulted in the behavior?

Is the behavior a problem of an individual, a group, or the entire class?

Is the child capable of the behavior desired?

Is the expected behavior important to the child?

What are the child's goals?

Dreikurs and Goldman[5] suggest there are four possible goals of a child's misbehavior: attention getting, power, revenge, and a display of inadequacy. Children may seek the attention of an adult in many ways. If the reward for misbehaving provides the needed attention, even though the adult response is negative, children may continue to seek attention through misbehavior. Children seeking power want to be the boss, to demand their way in a particular situation. Children seeking revenge wish to hurt the teacher, and children displaying inadequacy usually want to be left alone, with no demands put on them. Dreikurs and Goldman go on to suggest that the teacher's natural reaction to the behavior may be the key to determining the cause. If the teacher is inclined to react with annoyance, reminding and coaxing the child to behave in a particular way, it is probably a response to attention-getting behavior. If children provoke the teacher, they seek power over the teacher. If the teacher feels hurt or wants to "get even," the goal is probably revenge, and if the teacher feels despair and helplessness in assisting the child, he or she is probably responding to a display of inadequacy.

Several different strategies may be used to deal with behavior problems once the cause is determined. The solution should be based on the cause. Sometimes a change in organization, a clarification of information, or a modification in activity or teaching method may be all that is needed to correct the situation. In other situations the teacher may need to deal with an individual or group of students to initiate a change in behavior.

Whenever possible the teacher should respond to positive behavior and ignore negative but nondestructive behavior; however, one must respond to the misbehavior when it causes concern for the safety of an individual. Often rewarding appropriate behavior goes a long way to eliminating negative behavior. Responding to desired behavior may help many children learn to be responsible for their behavior.

The teacher should respond promptly to the situation but avoid responding on first impulse. It may intensify the behavior rather than correct it. The teacher should view the behavior from the child's point of view, anticipate what response the child expects, and then not respond in the expected way. The teacher must then take responsibility for the action taken.

It is important to match the reaction to a behavior with the seriousness of the transgression. The teacher should convey recognition that all make mistakes. In dealing with behavior problems the teacher should express concern, warmth, and caring. Knowing the children helps to establish priorities for positive responses. Responses should be directed to specific behavior. It is important to communicate why a behavior is inappropriate at a particular time.

In correcting children the teacher shows disapproval for the behavior, not for the child. Discipline must not lower a child's self-esteem. Negatively singling out a child in front of the group can have serious social implications. Children perceived by their peers as being disliked by the teacher are not liked by their classmates. The teacher should react to the present behavior and not past transgressions and must be careful to determine which child is at fault rather than merely singling out the child who is usually disruptive.

The following teacher behaviors, identified by

Johnson[12] as roadblocks to communication, should be avoided in dealing with the inappropriate behavior of children:

1. Ordering, commanding, and directing: "You quit complaining and just pay attention!"
2. Threatening: "If you guys don't stop messing around, I'm going to have to put you on report!"
3. Preaching or moralizing: "You girls know better than to behave that way!" " Is that any way to behave?"
4. Offering advice or solutions prematurely: "You'll just have to have your mother help you to get your gym clothes ready on time."
5. Judging, criticizing, and blaming: "You are just lazy.". "You two are always causing trouble in this class."
6. Stereotyping or labeling: "Don't act like a fourth grader." "You are acting like a baby!"
7. Interrogating or cross-examining: "What in the world did you do that for?" "How come you didn't ask me first?"
8. Distracting or diverting: "Why don't we talk about it some other time?" "Now just isn't the time to discuss it!"

Hoffman and associates[10] suggest that the way the teacher addresses students about their behavior has certain implications. The "you" messages cited above can only be interpreted in a negative way as an evaluation of the students. An "I" message, such as "I like the way Jane is working," is a statement communicating positive feelings about the student's behavior.

It is important for the teacher to remain under control when correcting children. One must speak calmly and not respond to the children on an emotional level. There should be no ridicule or sarcasm. Teachers should not allow themselves to get involved in arguments with children. The teacher is in control. If a child attempts to confront the teacher in a power struggle, the teacher should withdraw from the situation, which has the effect of dissipating the child's power. The teacher should avoid coercion, forced apologies, detaining children after school, imposing extra work, such as a written report or additional exercise, and corporal punishment.

Modeling is a technique that can have a positive effect on behavior. The teacher targets the desired behavior without mention of the inappropriate behavior. A teacher might say,"I like the way Mary is listening," or " I like the way John is sharing the ball with Mike." In this way positive behavior is reinforced, while the undesired behavior is ignored.

Reality therapy is another technique that may be used successfully. This approach puts the responsibility for behavior on the child. It avoids putting the teacher in the position of judging the appropriateness of the behavior. The teacher assists the child in identifying the inappropriate behavior and the consequences of that behavior. The child then can judge whether the behavior is appropriate and develops a plan to follow to attain the desired goals. For example, a child with poor listening skills meets with the teacher. As a result of poor listening the child does not know what is to be done and is distracting others. A plan is worked out to help the child change the behavior. The child will sit next to the teacher when instructions are being given and away from a classmate to whom the child likes to talk. Reality therapy is concerned with what the behavior is rather than why the child behaved that way.

Reality therapy may also be applied when a change in behavior is needed by a group of children or an entire class. This is called *norm setting*.[9] In this approach the teacher and students share in the goal setting for the class, stating the goals so they are easily understood by all concerned. The next step is to determine what both the teacher and the students will do to meet the goals and the consequences if the goals are not being met. It may be necessary to use reality therapy with individuals as well. Success in working toward the goals should be rewarded along the way. Periodically the group should evaluate progress toward the goals and suggest any changes that may be needed.

Time-out is another strategy for dealing with inappropriate behavior. The misbehaving child is removed from the activity momentarily until he or she is ready to participate within the rules established. Time-out gives children the opportunity to get themselves back under control. Return to the activity is dependent on children assuming responsibility for their behavior. The teacher might put a child out of the activity by saying, "When you are ready to rejoin the group and follow the instructions, you may join the activity."

Loss of privileges is another approach. Children learn to view the consequences of their behavior as the loss of some opportuntity in the class.

Another approach is the *contingency contract*.[9] This approach also helps children assume responsibility for their own behavior. Children are given a reward for appropriate behavior. This approach may work with a group as well as individual children. In essence the teacher directs the children by saying, "If you do this, then you may do that." This approach gives the children a sense of accomplishment in achieving the goal and in receiving the reward.

Punishment has been used to initiate changes in behavior. Although it may stop a behavior, it will not eliminate the cause or reduce the factors that prompted it. Punishment creates a negative relationship between the transgressor and the person administering the punishment and increases anxiety for all. If it is to be used, it should be administered firmly and consistently. There should be no threats of punishment, especially if the teacher does not wish to make good on the threats. Mass punishment should be avoided. Exercise or running laps should never be used as punishment. Punishment is a negative approach to behavior change and should be avoided where possible.

Occasionally children experience behavior problems that do not seem to respond to the various strategies used. The teacher should seek help from other professionals. Often a staff meeting may be called for all teachers working with the child and other school personnel, such as the school nurse, psychologist, and social worker to establish the probable cause of the misbehavior and to plan a strategy to help the child become a more productive member of the class. By working together, the staff may achieve a more consistent effort to help a child overcome the difficulties.

INDIVIDUALIZING INSTRUCTION

Children come to the physical education class at varying stages of development and from many different backgrounds; both factors affect their performance. As the children progress through the elementary school years, these performance differences increase. The teacher of physical education must identify the needs of children in planning and conducting appropriate physical education experiences for each child in the class.

Not all children can meet physical education lesson objectives without some special consideration. Some may have had limited opportunity in a variety of motor experiences outside the school. Other children may not find the objectives challenging to their advanced abilities. Still others may not be able to meet lesson objectives designed for the "normal" child because of a disabling condition. This group of children includes the overweight, the malnourished, those with a low level of fitness, the temporarily or permanently physically disabled, the socially malad-

justed, the developmentally disabled, and children with learning disabilities. Since the goal of education is to help all children reach their full potential, it is the responsibility of the physical educator to plan experiences that will address the special needs of all children in their charge (Figure 8-1).

The first step in individualizing instruction is to gather the information necessary to determine each child's status and needs. This information comes from two sources, the medical examination, discussed in Chapter 7, and the physical education assessment.

Once the medical information has been obtained, the teacher is ready to begin the physical education assessment. This assessment should be based on the objectives of the physical education program and should include an evaluation of the child's fitness, motor skill development, understanding of physical education, and social development. Chapter 9 suggests techniques that may be used in undertaking this evaluation.

After the medical information has been gathered and the physical education assessment made, the teacher determines the needs of each child and how the needs will be met. Many may be met in the physical education class by planning and conducting activities that:

1. Provide a wide range of activities to fit the varied abilities of the children
2. Utilize a progression in learning to guarantee the success of each child
3. Present information in a multisensory approach (visual, auditory, verbal, and tactile) to enhance all possible channels for learning
4. Use a variety of teaching styles

In addition to the regular physical education class two additional programs may be needed: the resource room and the adapted physical education class. In the resource room, children needing help receive additional help from the teacher on a one-to-one basis. A child might come to a resource class on a regular basis, usually in addition to regular physical education, or may come only for help in certain activities. A child who has had limited experiences in gymnastics may come for extra help during that unit. The resource room may also be used to help children improve their health-related physical fitness. The adapted physical education class is for those children who cannot safely or successfully meet the objectives of the regular physical education class. Children may be assigned to the adapted class on a permanent basis or only during the activities in which their participation is not possible. For instance, a blind child may

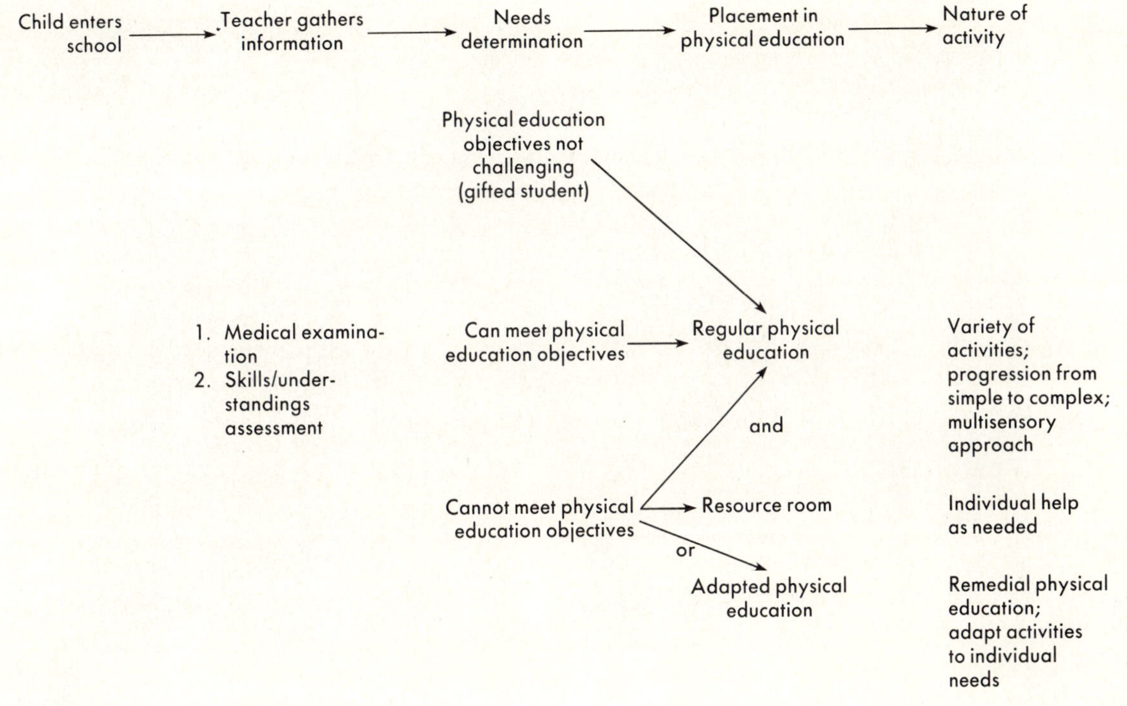

Figure 8-1

Meeting individual needs in physical education.

participate in many of activities in the regular physical education program but be assigned to the adapted class during most of the volleyball unit since safe participation in the game is impossible. A child temporarily disabled by an accident may be assigned to the resource room during rehabilitation or to adapted physical education.

In determining the best possible setting to achieve the educational goals the teacher must consider all aspects of human development: fitness as well as motor, cognitive, and social development. Children and teacher work together to establish short- and long-term goals and strategies to meet these goals. Through a planned progression of motor activities and knowledge and through opportunities to work in increasingly complex social situations, children move successfully to meet these goals.

Mainstreaming

With the introduction of Public Law 94-142, the Education of All Handicapped Children Act of 1975, many physical education programs took on a new responsibility of providing physical education for all students, including the handicapped. In many communities this previously had been the responsibility of special educators rather than physical educators. This law provides the opportunity for children to receive special help in physical education when they need it.

Public Law 94-142 requires an ***individual education plan (IEP)*** for the disabled child and the opportunity for learning in the least restrictive environment. Physical education is the only school subject named in the law. It is important for the physical educator to be involved in setting the IEP. The least restrictive environment in physical education is one in which the child can participate successfully and safely in as near a normal setting as possible. ***Mainstreaming*** provides an opportunity for the disabled to enhance their social, cognitive, motor, and emotional development in a setting with nondisabled children. For the normal child it offers a chance to get to know and understand the disabled as capable and contributing members of society. Although not all children can benefit totally from the mainstream setting, every attempt should be made to provide at least some experiences with their normal peers.

The social integration of disabled children into physical education classes with their normal peers is not automatic. The teacher may need to prepare the other children before a disabled child appears. Helping children understand the disabling condition and the special needs and assistance that will be needed can go along way in helping the children accept the disabled child.

The goals of mainstreaming for the disabled are to:

1. Develop life skills to enable them to be as independent as possible. In physical education children improve fitness and develop motor skills for a productive, active life.
2. Develop a positive self-concept. This is no easy task in a discriminating world. Children develop motor skills for a lifetime of activity with emphasis on what they can do. Physical education helps children accept limitations by development of their skill potential and modification of activities to meet their needs.
3. Learn socially acceptable behavior. Children learn appropriate social behavior relating to play and recreational activities.
4. Develop personal grooming habits. Children learn personal grooming habits relating to active participation and personal hygiene.

Meeting fitness and motor goals

Disabled youngsters often have difficulty in physical education because of past inactivity. Low levels of physical fitness and poor motor development are common. Some children have not been encouraged to be physically active. Sometimes the natural drive of children to be physically active may appear to be subdued. Parental concern may also be a cause of inactivity. Since physical activity may cause discomfort in some conditions, such as asthma, parents may discourage activity in their anxiety for the child's well-being. Some parents may not encourage play with other children in order to avoid awkward social situations. Many of these fears are imagined rather than real. Because of restrictions and parental attitudes, children may not have a self-concept that includes seeing themselves as movers. Their body awareness may be poor. Inactivity has the result of keeping children developmentally behind their normal peers.

Poor motor skill development or low fitness level may necessitate placement in adapted physical education or the resource class. In many activities variations in skill may be accommodated within the activity in the regular physical education class. Some children are intolerant of their less able peers. Modifications within group activities are possible to increase the total success for everyone. The teacher must decide if placement in regular physical education with or without the resource room help will enable the child to be successful in meeting the goals set for the child, or whether temporary or permanent placement in adapted physical education would be better.

Meeting cognitive needs

In placing disabled children in physical education the teacher must also consider the cognitive level of functioning. Children function best in the mainstream setting if they can function on the same intellectual level as their peers. Administrators fail at times to consider this aspect of human development when placing children in physical education. Many disabled children have difficulty with abstract ideas that are a part of the physical education experience. Exploring movement and developing creative solutions to movement challenges are extremely difficult for the deaf because of their limited language development and difficulty in thinking abstractly. Developmentally disabled youngsters may also have difficulty in these activities because of their lack of understanding of terminology and inadequate body awareness.

Many group activities in the upper grades require an ability to understand complex rules and changing relationships of participants. Sometimes a large group activity may be too distracting for satisfactory performance for some children.

Building vocabulary is important in developing the movement curriculum. Teachers should use a variety of ways to present material to help children. Pictures and written words, as well as verbal explanations, provide a variety of approaches to help in developing understanding of concepts and other knowledge.

Developing social goals

Social skills are of concern for both normal and disabled children in the mainstream setting. The teacher must establish an environment in which discriminatory behavior by the children is discouraged and supportive behavior encouraged. Physical appearance is a factor in social integration. The more "normal" an individual appears or the more physically attractive, the greater the chance for social acceptance in the group.

Communication skills are also important for social integration. The deaf and hard of hearing are not easily socially mainstreamed. Communication skills are often limited and the other children may feel awkward in trying to talk or to understand the speech of a child with a hearing loss.

The more contact disabled children have with their peers, the greater the chance for social integration. Some disabled children are only mainstreamed in the physical education setting, whereas others may attend classes with their peers for most of the school day. The more exposure children have to one another, the greater the chance for social acceptance. Adolesence may be a time of greater anxiety for disabled children as they seek the peer relationships so important at this stage of development.

Some disabled children have had little experience with children the same age. These children may not have acquired the social skills needed for successful group activity. The teacher has to carefully structure the situation so appropriate social skills are learned and reinforced.

The teacher should strive to develop independence and avoid being overprotective. The teacher must be well aware of the handicapping condition and activities that might be contraindicated. On the other hand, knowledge about a child's disabilities should not be allowed to limit the opportunity for development of the child's full potential.

Social integration is much more easily accomplished in the class setting than in recess or other periods of free play. Often in the recreational setting children ignore or shy away from their disabled classmates. The physical education teacher will have to be aware of these potential problems in structuring intramural activities to include all children wishing to participate.

Making mainstreaming work

Physical education is required by law for all disabled children. Children should not be indiscriminately placed in regular physical education with little regard for their needs. The teacher must decide which goals can and cannot be met in the mainstream setting.

It is important to get the child off to a good start. A screening device is included in Appendix Five. Some children require special services in addition to those provided in the physical education program. Some children may benefit from physical therapy. Others may require psychological or nutritional counseling to help them overcome some difficulties. If adequate services are provided at an early age, some children may move totally to regular physical education programming during their school years.

An example of an IEP, which is required by law for all disabled children, is found in Appendix D. It should include both long- and short-term goals for the child and the plan for meeting these goals. Periodically a review should be conducted to determine the progress toward meeting these goals. The goals should reflect the overall goals of the physical education program. In placing the disabled child in regular physical education the teacher must plan experiences that will not compromise the educational goals for other children in the class. Teacher aides, adult volunteers, and peer tutors may be used to provide additional individual help in the physical education setting. Older elementary, middle school, or high school students are often used to give assistance. Using school-age assistants is of value in creating better understanding between the disabled and the normal population. These assistants may be used in the assessment of movement potential, in giving individual help in motor skill development, in classroom management, or in controlling behavior.

Since implementation of P.L. 94-142 severely retarded children have been placed in some public schools. Usually these children are not successfully mainstreamed; their special needs require placement in adapted physical education. These individuals need extensive work in the acquisition of motor skills for everyday living, such as going up and down stairs and stepping over objects. Their ability to concentrate is of short duration and the activity period should end before boredom and frustration occur. Retention is limited. Skills need to be repeated frequently with a planned reinforcement schedule for skills previously learned. The children benefit from encouragement, praise, and material rewards. Punishment or withdrawing privileges may be beyond their understanding. Rewards must be given immediately following each successful performance at their maximum capacity if they are to be of value.

The Gifted Child

Gifted child tend to be gifted in all areas. In addition to having exceptional intellectual ability, they tend to be well coordinated, healthier, and better adjusted than their classmates. The physical education program must strive to challenge these children in providing movement activities that maintain interest in physical activity. The program for gifted children is one of enrichment. Within each unit of activity, the teacher plans to introduce more advance skills and knowledge as the children indicate a readiness for more advanced work.

Gifted children may need some assistance in accepting the mistakes and lack of understanding of classmates. They may at times be called on to help other children with skills or strategies, but assisting others does not meet their own needs for physical activity and should not be used to the detriment of their own development.

Gifted children excel not only in the physical education class but in the intramural or special interest club opportunities as well. It is at these levels of participation where their needs may be more fully met as they engage in activities with children of similar abilities outside their own class.

DEVELOPING INDEPENDENT LEARNERS

One goal of education is to produce independent, lifelong learners. The school strives to enhance the children's love for learning by assisting them in developing skills of inquiry and investigation. The physical education program plays an important part in the development of independent learning through individualized goal setting, the children's assumption of responsibility for their own learning, and discovery teaching.

The setting in which independent learning takes place is one in which a good teacher-student relationship has been established. There is mutual trust, a respect for the rights of the individual, and support for one another. The environment provides freedom for learning but also structure. The rules of conduct are defined and the expectations for listening, following directions, and working understood. Safety is carefully considered, with the children understanding safety rules and why they are needed. The children work at their own level of ability in a nonthreatening, friendly, and helping atmosphere.

The child is the focus in the learning experience. There must be flexibility in goal setting and expectations. The students are assisted in setting realistic performance goals. Although they are not given choices in what they are to learn, they may choose how they will work toward the goal, how long they will work, how well they will achieve the goal, and through what activities they will practice. In making these decisions children generally make safe choices. They do not choose to do something for which they do not believe they are ready. In most instances they make a selection that pushes them to greater achievement.

Children come to the school setting varying in self-confidence. Past success and failure affect the children's self-esteem and consequently their confidence to try new things. It is up to the teacher to structure learning in the physical education classroom so all children can be readily successful through careful selection and conduct of activities.

The movement curriculum provides opportunities for children to solve problems within their own skill and understanding. The movement approach to learning utilizing problem solving enables children to process information, to make choices, to act, and to evaluate the results of their action. Sequential learning experiences develop confidence as children are successful at each step in the progression.

The learning environment provides opportunities for children to relate to each other in many ways. Assuming responsibility for staying on task, taking care of equipment, and the like, as an individual or in a small group, are important aspects of the learning experience. When they are ready, children may assume different roles in the group, as follower, shared decision maker, or leader, the responsibilities varying with the maturity of the child. These responsibilities may range from being at the head of the group when moving to a new station to organizing the other children in the group for activity. The learning environment provides a wide variety of experiences geared to the interests and needs of each child, to challenge their abilities, to arouse their imagination, and to develop creative ideas. It is an atmosphere in which questions are raised by both students and teacher and answers are sought rather than given. Emphasis is on personal inquiry and investigation. The teacher does not do for the students what they can do for themselves. Several resources should be available to facilitate learning, including the teacher, other students, books, posters, and the like. These enable the children to seek appropriate help as needed. Children need assistance to evaluate their progress in meeting goals and to reset goals and change the activity for practice as needed.

The teacher helps to direct the inquiry through further questioning. Questions may be raised to help the children establish relationships between old and new learning, to make judgments about structure, appearance, or function, or to suggest experimentation, such as "Is it better to . . . or . . . ?"

Children need time to explore and to discover their answers. The teacher must exercise patience in not helping too soon. At times the teacher may need to assist in alleviating children's frustration at not finding an easy answer or in getting the children back on track if they stray.

Questioning is an important teaching skill. Questions should seek verbal responses that suggest understanding or the lack of understanding rather than yes or no answers. Once the question has been posed, the teacher must give the child sufficient time to respond. Questions should be open ended to provide for a variety of responses within the level of understanding of the child.

The class ideally provides indirectly supervised activity to give children freedom to work on their own. There may be several choices for practice to meet the day's objectives, and the children may work alone or with other children.

Several techniques may be used to help children select appropriate activities. One is the use of a check list. This may be a grand list for the class or preferably an individual list for each child. An individual list designed to meet the needs of each child is most effective. Children are highly motivated when the activities are challenging and yet within their ability to achieve. In using checklists it is necessary to divide the activities into those that the children may check for themselves and those that the determination of mastery will be decided by the teacher. As the children accomplish all the activities on their individual lists, a new list is provided.

Another approach to the checklist is to organize the activities to be included in the unit into separate categories based on difficulty. The first category would include those activities that all the children should be able to accomplish by the end of the unit. These might be called the red activities. The next category, the white activities, would include the activities that the majority of the children would accomplish. The last category, the blue activities, would include those that only the top students in the class might master.

Challenge cards are another approach. A list of

BALL SKILLS CHALLENGES

1. Standing behind the line and using the underhand throw, throw the ball into the basket. How many times can you get the ball in the basket?
2. Move back three steps and try it again.
3. *Throw the ball overhand into the basket.*
4. *Throw the ball between your legs into the basket.*

challenges may be placed at each station for the children to try. Children add new challenges to the list as they develop their own ideas. The box below gives an example of a challenge card.

The teacher gradually relinquishes responsibility for individual learning as the children are able to take more responsibility in the learning process. This is not a laisse faire approach but rather a plan carefully conducted to bring about independence in children. In the beginning children may learn to work in indirectly supervised settings with the teacher assuming responsibility for what is to be learned and practiced. As the children develop their ability to set goals and plan a course of action, more freedom is gradually introduced to accommodate this development. The teacher still remains an active part of the process, providing a variety of experiences and equipment for the students to make choices and to help students when needed.

As children develop independent learning skills, they respond to each new situation by examining the alternatives, risks, and consequences and by choosing a course of action. An evaluation of the result of this action results in new responses. The wide range of skills and activities in which they are interested challenge the children to take risks in learning, to try new skills, and to relate to others. The box below summarizes the changes that take place as the children assume more responsibility for their own learning.

DEVELOPING INDEPENDENCE IN LEARNING

THE LEARNING ENVIRONMENT

Communication between teacher and students
Children and teacher supportive of one another
Safety rules understood and followed
Expectations for listening, following directions, taking care of equipment, and general behavior understood

ACTIVITIES

A variety of activities planned for each lesson
Progression from simple to complex

TEACHER AND STUDENT ROLES

Teacher	Student
Determines goals	Chooses activity
	Determines how long to practice
	Determines level of skill to achieve
Provides resources	Chooses resource: teacher book, poster, video
Evaluates progress to goal	Seeks help in assessing progress
Organizes the group for activity	Assumes responsibility to stay on task
	Assumes role as group member
	Assumes role as group leader
	Assumes role as shared decision maker

SUMMARY

To enhance a love for learning, schools and teachers attempt to establish a learning environment in which there is adequate communication, there is order, and individual needs are of primary concern in planning and conducting the physical education activities.

The teacher must establish a good working relationship with children. In order to do so, there must be adequate communication between the teacher and the students. Teachers and students communicate both verbally in what they say and how they say it and also nonverbally in their facial expression and posture. The teacher must be a good listener, distinguishing between what was said and what was meant.

MOVING AND LEARNING

The Elementary School Physical Education Experience

Times Mirror/Mosby

Essential Elements a to d	Grades K-3		Essential Elements e to g	Grades 4-6	
	Text Page Reference	Lesson Plan Page Reference		Text Page Reference	Lesson Plan Page Reference
1, Physical education development to improve the quality of life	181, 183, 187, 190	Keyed in each lesson	1, Physical education development to improve the quality of life	181, 183, 187, 190	Keyed in each lesson
	Activities throughout text, especially track and field, gymnastics, small equipment activities	Keyed in each lesson		Activities throughout text, especially track and field, gymnastics, small equipment activities	Keyed in each lesson
	182, 183, 188, 192	Keyed in each lesson		182, 183, 188, 192	Keyed in each lesson
2, Motor skills that develop positive body image and confidence	140, 141, 148, 150, 153-154	28-41, 22-26, 106-115, 118-125	2, Motor skills that develop positive body image and confidence	140, 141, 148, 150, 153, 154	22-26, 28-41, 106-115, 118-125
	207, 208, 212, 218, 221, 225-226	42, 44, 46, 126, 128, 130-131		207-208, 212-213, 218, 221, 225-226	42, 44, 46, 126, 128, 130-131
	123, 129, 135			Developed in each activity chapter	2, 10, 14, 86, 94, 100
3, Rhythmic activities that develop coordination, self-expression, creativity, and endurance	313, 330, 335, 371-372, 376, 377	61, 66, 68, 70, 72, 145, 150, 151, 153, 155, 157, 190, 196, 202, 277, 282, 287	3, Rhythmic activities that develop coordination, self-expression, creativity, and endurance	313, 346, 358, 371-372, 375-376, 379	61, 66, 68, 70, 72, 145, 150, 151, 153, 155, 157, 190, 196, 202, 277, 282, 287
4, Skills related to games and sports	420, 424, 428-430, 445, 448, 451, 454, 455, 457, 469, 472-473, 485, 487, 489, 494-497, 508, 511-513, 527, 529	220, 226, 253, 302, 309, 334	4, Skills related to games and sports	420, 424, 428-430, 445, 448, 451, 454, 455, 457, 469, 472-473, 485, 487, 489, 494-497, 508, 511-513, 527, 529	220, 226, 253, 302, 309, 334
	227, 397, 412	80, 166		217, 227, 394, 407, 413	80, 166
	162-173			162-173	
	420, 424, 428-430, 433, 445, 448, 451, 454-455, 457, 459, 469, 472, 473, 476, 478, 485, 487, 489, 494-498, 501, 508, 511-513, 515-516	220, 226, 232, 240, 247, 302, 309, 316, 322, 328		420, 424, 428-430, 433, 445, 448, 451, 454-455, 457, 459, 469, 472, 473, 476, 478, 485, 487, 489, 494-498, 501, 508, 511-513, 515-516	220, 226, 232, 250, 247, 302, 309, 316, 322, 328
	140-141, 148, 150, 153-154	22-26, 28-41, 106-115, 118-125		140-141, 148, 150, 153-154	22-26, 28-41, 106-115, 118-125
5, Sequential gymnastic and tumbling skills	237, 264, 268, 271, 275, 277-278, 280		5, Sequential gymnastic and tumbling skills	237, 264, 268, 271, 275, 277-278, 280	
	237, 264, 268, 271, 275, 277-278, 280			237, 264, 268, 271, 275, 277-278, 280	
	238, 240, 241, 244, 253, 255, 258, 261, 264, 268, 271, 275, 277-278, 280	177, 260, 266		238, 240, 241, 244, 253, 255, 258, 261, 274, 268, 271, 275, 277-278, 280	177, 260, 266

KEY: a, Kindergarten; b, Grade One; c, Grade Two; d, Grade Three; e, Grade Four; f, Grade Five; g, Grade Six.

Fasson®
CRACK'N PEEL Plus™
PATENT PENDING

Teachers communicate the value they place on physical education and each child in the class. The students communicate their likes and dislikes in the physical education class.

Class control is a planned strategy to avoid the need for discipline. The teacher establishes the expected behavior and consistently rewards those children who behave appropriately. Several strategies may be used to deal with inappropriate behavior. All focus on helping children assume responsibility for their own behavior. Reality therapy or norm setting in which children develop a plan to change their behavior, time-out, loss of privilege, and continguency contracts all help children to function in more socially acceptable ways.

Since the needs of children vary in any group, the teacher must individualize instruction, by matching instruction with the needs of each child in the class. Some children find the physical education objectives too difficult, whereas other children of advanced ability find the objectives too easy. Children may be placed in regular physical education classes where a variety of experiences are provided to meet their needs. Other children may be placed part-time in the regular physical education class and in addition may go to the resource room for additional help in areas of special need. Adapted physical education may be scheduled for some children to help them during a period of rehabilitation or to adapt activities to meet their special needs. The goal is to place all children in a physical education experience as close to normal as possible but one in which growth in skill and understanding is assured.

The overall goal of education is learning for a lifetime. If this goal is to be reached, children need to be encouraged to pursue learning on their own, independent of direct teacher intervention. Building confidence, encouraging inquiry, making available alternate resources, and providing for children as they are ready for more complex social interactions must be carefully built into the physical education experience.

REFERENCES

1. Auxter, D., and Pyfer, J.: Principles and methods of adapted physical education and recreation, ed. 4, St. Louis, 1985, Times Mirror/Mosby.
2. Cooper J., and others: Classroom teaching skills: a handbook, ed. 2, Lexington, 1982, D.C. Heath & Co.
3. Dougherty, N., and Bonanno, D.: Contemporary approaches to the teaching of physical education, Minneapolis, 1979, Burgess Publishing Co.
4. Dreikurs, R.: Psychology in the classroom. ed. 2, New York, 1968, Harper & Row, Publishers.
5. Dreikurs, R., and Goldman, M.: The abc's of guiding the child, Chicago, 1967, North Side Unit of Family Education Association.
6. Dreikurs, R., and Soltz, W.: Children: the challenge, New York, 1964, Hawthorn Books, Inc.
7. Estvan, F.: Teaching the very young: procedures for developing inquiry skills. In Anderson, R., and Shane, H.: As the twig is bent, Boston, 1971, Houghton Mifflin Co.
8. Fait, H.: Teaching and evaluating physical education for severely and profoundly retarded. In NASPE: Echoes of influence for elementary school physical education, Washington, D.C., 1977, AAHPERD.
9. Harrison, J.: Instructional strategies for physical education, Dubuque, 1983, William C. Brown Co.
10. Hoffman, H., and others: Meaningful movement for children: a developmental theme approach to physical education, Boston, 1981, Allyn & Bacon, Inc.
11. Jansma, P., and others: Behavioral engineering in physical education, JOPERD **55**(6):80, August 1984.
12. Johnson, D.: Reaching out: interpersonal effectiveness and self-actualization, ed. 2, Englewood Cliffs, N.J., 1981, Prentice-Hall Inc.
13. Liddle, J., and Breihan, S.: What is it like to be handicapped? JOPER **51**(3):36, March 1980.
14. Margo, R., and Davis, K.: Special methods aud disabled students, JOPER **52**(2):82, January 1981.
15. Schurr, E.: Movement experiences for children, ed. 3, Englewood Cliffs, N.J., 1980, Prentice-Hall, Inc. 1980.
16. Siedentop, D.: Developing teaching skills in physical education, ed. 2, Palo Alto, 1983, Mayfield Publishing Co.
17. Turner, R., and Purkey, W.: Teaching physical education: an invitational approach, JOPERD **54**(7):13, September 1983.

ADDITIONAL READINGS

Baker, B.: Can people with impairments overcome society's handicaps? JOPER **48**(6):60, June 1977.
A story of a young handicapped woman's school experience and her attempts to overcome society's labels.

Danaher, P.: Handicap awareness program, JOPERD **54**(3):67, March 1983.
A program to heighten student awareness of handicapped people.

Klesius, S.: How's everything going today? JOPERD **53**(7):45, September 1982.
Use of a behavior change schedule to help children develop better social behavior.

Miller, S.: Do the nonhandicapped have a right to an individualized education program? JOPER **50**(6):19, June 1979.
A plea to meet the special needs of all students, not just the handicapped.

Mizen, D., and Linton, N.: Guess who's coming to p.e.? JOPERD **54**(8):63, October 1983.
Six steps to more effective mainstreaming.

Rink, J.: The key is the learning environment, JOPERD **53**(7):44, September 1982.
A program focusing on skillful movement and independent learning skills.

Stewart, C.: Integrating the physically handicapped into the physical education classroom, JOPER **51**(4):17, April 1980.
Considerations to assure the physically handicapped child success in physical education.

9

ESSENTIALS OF EVALUATION

CHAPTER OBJECTIVES

1 To describe the importance of evaluation in the educational plan in physical education
2 To identify strategies for evaluating pupil status in physical education objectives
3 To describe techniques for evaluating teacher effectiveness
4 To apply guidelines for evaluation to the physical education program

Evaluation is an important part of the educational process. It is the act of making judgments around which educational decisions will be made, decisions about meeting the needs of children, the effectiveness of teaching, and the value of the physical education program itself. It is the means to more effective teaching and learning.

Some think of the evaluation process as the end or final act or judgment. Actually it is an ongoing process that begins the first moment of the first day and is not completed until the end of the lesson, the end of the unit, or the final moments of the school year. Along the way it helps teachers keep abreast of individual and group needs and provides valuable information needed to plan the next steps in learning. It also helps children to see what they have accomplished and to determine the direction for future work. The final evaluation at the end of the school year gives us an indication of the total achievements of individuals and the group.

PLANNING FOR EVALUATION

Evaluation is essential to curricular, unit, and daily planning. A plan to evaluate the outcomes of the program as a whole needs to be developed. Techniques to measure the extent to which unit and daily objectives are being met should be in place before the curriculum is implemented or the unit or daily lessons begun. The planning process includes the development of objectives, the selection of activities and methodologies to be used to meet the objectives, and planning of the process for the evaluation to determine the extent to which the objectives are met. This process of developing objectives, teaching, and evaluating is repeated time and time again as the unit of instruction is underway. Figure 9-1 schematically depicts this process. If the judgment, on the basis of the evaluation process, is that the objectives have been met, the process is repeated with a new set of objectives. These new objectives may be a higher order of objectives based on the same skills, knowledge, or behaviors, or they may be a totally new set of motor skills, knowledge, or social behaviors. If the objectives have not been met, a new course of action may be required. Perhaps the objectives were too difficult or require additional time for mastery. Therefore the objectives may need to be restated or modified so achievement is possible. Additional activities or new teaching strategies may need to be incorporated as well.

The evaluation plan includes the determination of what is to be evaluated, the selection of the measures to be used, the administration of the measures,

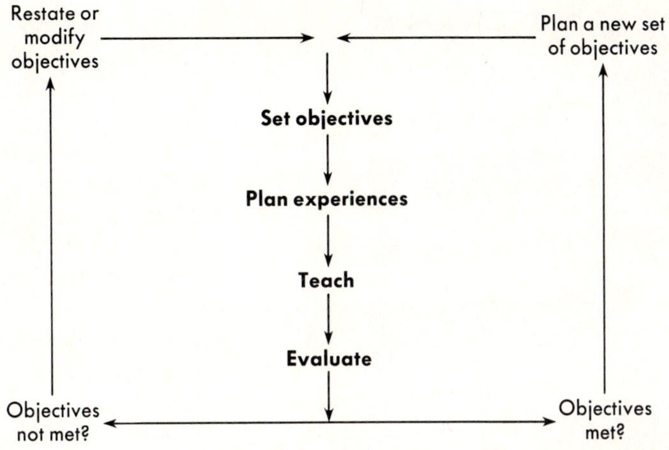

Figure 9-1

Curriculum implementation plan.

the analysis of the results, and the educational decision making based on the judgments made.

Determining What Is To Be Evaluated

All purposes for the evaluation must be determined. Is it to be used to evaluate the effectiveness of the program or the teaching? Is it to measure student achievement? The information gathered may be used to initiate changes in the curriculum, to improve teaching effectiveness, to establish or reestablish individual performance goals, or to communicate to parents, teachers, and administrators the present status of the children's efforts.

Outcomes of the curricular effort or the effects of the use of a particular teaching technique or an assignment given may be studied. It may be a look at the skills, understanding, and/or social behavior of children. The teacher may desire a preassessment before beginning a unit, a determination of status at the end of a unit, an assessment of improvement made during a particular unit of activity, or some prediction of future success.

Selecting Measurement Techniques

Once the purposes of the evaluation have been clearly defined, the measurement techniques to be used are selected. The teacher may choose observational techniques or more formal skill and written tests.

The instruments may be **norm referenced** or **criterion referenced.** In norm referenced measures the

scores may be compared to the scores of other children of similar ages and sex. The AAHPERD health-related fitness tests found in Chapter 13 are an example of norm-referenced tests. Information from such tests is quantitative; it is a numerical score of what the children did, for example, how fast they ran or how far they threw. Criterion-referenced measures tend to be qualitative in that they measure how a person performed rather than the result of the effort. Criterion-referenced information is helpful in determining errors in performance important to improving the effectiveness of skill and in also looking at behaviors that do not lend themselves to a norm, such as certain social behaviors. In the following activity chapters criteria to evaluate the efficiency of skill performance are identified.

Another consideration in selecting measures is to determine the conditions under which the testing will take place. Is a maximum effort required or a typical performance? Will the skills be measured within the activity, in combination with other skills, or in isolation? The number of trials or observations to provide an accurate measure must also be determined.

Administration of Measurements

The teacher should be knowledgeable about the techniques to be used. All materials should be ready and the organization and conduct of the testing session well planned. Sometimes practice with the instrument before use in a class may be beneficial in im-

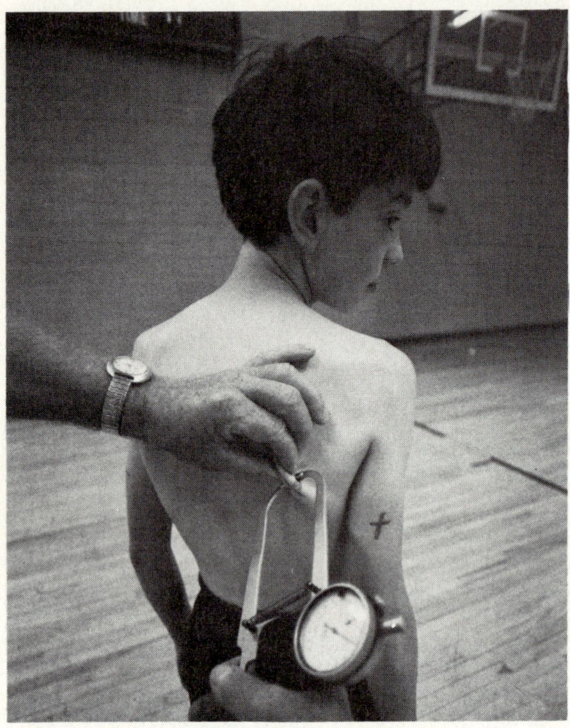

proving the efficiency and effectiveness of the measure being used.

The scoring should be consistent from student to student. It should be fair, treating all students in a similar fashion. The teacher must also be aware of individual conditions that might affect the test results, such as illness, inattentiveness, distractions, cheating, or the teacher's personal feelings about a student.

The test should be appropriately timed. If it is to be used for preassessment to determine the needs at the beginning of a unit, the teacher must know what information students need to yield appropriate results. If it is a test of achievement, the students need to have had sufficient time to have developed their skills before the testing. If it is to be used to help both teacher and student determine needs, it should be placed appropriately in the unit. For instance, giving a written test on the rules of basketball after a few lessons may determine areas of confusion that could be clarified early in the unit to enable the children to use the rules more effectively as they play the game. Testing at the end of the unit tells the teacher and student what has been achieved but does not give direction for future action, since the unit has drawn to a close. It may not be as motivating for students to be tested at the end of a unit since there is no time for further improvement.

Analysis of Information

An analysis of the test results is important after the data have been collected. The information should discriminate between the varying levels of ability of the students. Often test results identify the top and bottom students but do not differentiate the needs of the majority of students who fall between. In all probability the teacher already knows which students are outstanding and which need the most help. If "average" children are to be helped to achieve their movement potential, measures must be used that determine their needs as well.

Another concern in the analysis is whether the results provide important information. Do they tell us what we need to know? Do they serve the purpose for which the test was intended? For example, do they give us an insight into the needs of the children or the degree of improvement during the unit?

Making Decisions

Once the results have been analyzed, the teacher makes decisions about what course of action to take. The teacher must decide what the results of the measurements actually indicate. To what extent are the goals and objectives being met? What changes are suggested to improve teaching? What are the possibilities for curricular change? The teacher looks at the alternatives. Should more time be spent on the items measured? What needs must be addressed? Do the results indicate the children are ready to move on to new material? Is a change in activity or method needed to enhance future learning? The teacher looks at the consequences of each possible alternative. For instance, if more time is spent on a skill, what effect will this have on other unit material? Weighing the consequences of each alternative, the teacher chooses the best solution for the particular situation.

ASSESSING PUPIL ACHIEVEMENT

The primary goal of evaluation is to diagnose student needs so that more effective instruction may be planned. An evaluation of pupil status regarding program goals is essential in determining program direction, in setting individual achievement goals, and in communicating to both students and parents the progress being made. A sample screening device may

BEHAVIORAL OBJECTIVES IN PHYSICAL EDUCATION

QUANTITATIVE

The student will put 8 out of 10 balls into the target area.

The student will jump a minimum of 8 feet.

The student will catch four out of six medium-sized playground balls thrown in the medium level from 10 feet away.

QUALITATIVE

The child will throw underhand holding the ball in the fingers, stepping forward on the opposite foot, swinging the arm in an underhand motion, and ending with the fingers pointing to the intended target.

The child will jump from a standing position, bending the legs at the knees, hips, and ankles, taking off on two feet, swinging the arms forward as the jump is taken, and landing softly with the body forward of the feet.

The student will catch the ball by getting in a direct line with the oncoming ball, reaching out with both hands toward the ball, grasping it in the fingers, and pulling it in toward the body.

---

be found in Appendix Five. Evaluation of student performance is an ongoing process from the beginning to the end of each unit of instruction. It may be used to establish baseline levels of competency at the beginning of a unit, to group children homogeneously or heterogeneously, to diagnose needs throughout a unit, and to determine the total accomplishments at the end of a unit. Since activity time is generally limited, the teacher must minimize the time taken in evaluation. Sufficient time must be set aside to get the job done, but it should not take away from other aspects of the lessons.

The evaluation process begins with the development of meaningful measurable objectives, written in behavioral terms. These objectives may be quantitative or qualitative. Quantitative objectives give students a criterion to aim for in performance and an opportunity to self-test their achievement along the way. Qualitative objectives often require the assistance of someone else to help children describe their performance, at least until they have developed adequate body awareness. Behavioral objectives were discussed in Chapter 4. Several examples follow.

Objectives to be measured should be those most important in the unit of instruction and whose importance has been communicated to the children.

Several techniques may be used to obtain the information necessary to plan appropriate experiences for children. They are summarized in the box below. Teacher observation is one method commonly used in assessing pupil performance. A well-trained ob-server can easily pinpoint the strengths and difficulties through observation of the children in activity. Observations in this context offer a way to compare the performances of children of the same age and experience. Observations are subjective, however, and in that regard susceptible to being influenced by personal feelings toward particular children. To make observations meaningful, it is helpful to use a checklist or scorecard identifying important aspects to be observed. Observations then serve to diagnose specific errors in execution that clearly identify student needs.

The use of *rating scales* is another observational technique. The teacher determines a rating scale for each skill to be evaluated, ranging from an excellent performance to one needing more work. In using a rating scale the teacher must carefully define what each rating means. Rating scales are usually of limited value since they do not identify the specific reasons the children receive a particular rating. A rating scale combined with a space for comments may be of more value in helping to identify and communicate student needs. In using rating scales the observer must plan sufficient time to observe each child and should use the entire scale of ratings to differentiate performance. When using a rating scale with five categories, such as consistently excellent, generally good, average, fair, and needs more work, some children should be classified into each category if the scale is to truly discriminate between the performance of the children. If only the top three categories are used, average

EVALUATING MOTOR SKILLS

CRITERION REFERENCED OR NORM REFERENCED?

Criterion referenced
Qualitative
Easily identifies errors in performance
Self-testing for children (requires maturity to analyze own performance)
Looks at skills that do not lend themselves to norms (such as forward roll)

Requires several performances
May be observed in an activity

Norm referenced
Quantitative
Measures all-out performance
Self-testing for children (score easily interpreted)
Looks at skills in which performance is easily measured in time, number, or distance
May require several trials
Requires a special testing situation
Isolates skill, perhaps in context of activity

CHOOSING THE TECHNIQUE

Teacher observation? (does not require a specific testing situation)
  Checklist
    Identifies specific aspects to be observed
    Helpful in diagnosing specific errors in performance
    Helps children see what specifically they need to work on
    Subjective (some objectivity)
    Requires several observations
  Rating scale
    Establishes a numerical or word description of performance
    Does not identify specific reasons for rating

becomes the lowest observed performance.

Skill tests may also be used. These may be standardized tests found in the literature or teacher-made tests. They should be used only when they can provide information that is not available by any other means. Formal skill testing is motivating, and if the scores are easily understood, they do provide valuable information on performance for the children. Fitness tests fall in this category. In developing or selecting skill tests the following criteria should be considered:

1. The test accurately tests what the teacher wants it to test.
2. It isolates the skill being tested.
3. The test is of suitable difficulty for the group being tested.
4. It tests one student at a time.
5. The test may be administered easily and is efficient in the use of time.
6. The scoring is simple and the scores are easily interpreted.
7. Norms are available for the age and sex being tested.

In administration of skill tests every effort should be made to maximize the activity for all children and to organize the testing so a mimimum amount of time is needed. Often other techniques are more efficient of time and permit the children more activity than formal skill testing.

Another technique is the child self-evaluation. All children are given an individualized checklist of skills. When they feel they have met the criteria, they check them off or seek the teacher to assist them in determining whether the criterion has been met. Positive teacher feedback is important in using this technique. The teacher encourages the children to identify those skills needing more work and encourages them to do

EVALUATING MOTOR SKILLS—cont'd

    Subjective (lacks objectivity)
    Takes time and several observations
Skill tests?
  May be teacher made or standardized
  Performance easily interpreted by students
  Motivating for students
  Require a specific testing situation
  May remove skills from the context of the activity
  Standardized tests not readily available for elementary school children, especially those in
    primary grades
Student self-evaluation?
  Teacher develops list of skills and criteria
  Qualitative or quantitative
  Motivating for students
  Helps students assess own performance
  Helpful in helping students set their own performance goals
  Lends itself to individualizing instruction
  Requires maturity in analyzing own performance
  Requires feedback from teacher
  Takes time to develop lists of skills and criteria

so. A combination of teacher and student checks may be used. The students may check off some skills on their own, whereas a teacher is required to check off other skills. This technique works best after the children have developed sufficient body awareness and the maturity to look at themselves objectively.

Knowledge is also evaluated in physical education. This may be done by observing children's responses to movement problems, questioning, or written tests. The movement content lends itself more easily to qualitative evaluation. In assessing the children's movement responses the teacher must define specifically what he or she is looking for as the children move. The teacher may seek several different responses or a particular type of response. This does not mean the teacher looks for the same response from each child.

Questioning may also be used to seek information about knowledge. Throughout the lesson the teacher raises questions requiring the children to organize their thoughts and respond verbally. Responses should call for more than a yes-or-no response.

Written tests may be given in the upper elementary grades. Tests should be carefully constructed to test important knowledge in a mimimum amount of time. Tests of rules and other important knowledge about games may be given early in the unit to determine those that need clarification to be used effectively. Written tests at the elementary level are short, usually 10 to 15 questions, and require short answers (simple recall), or response to true/false, multiple choice, or alternative response items. They should test important information and be stated clearly and simply.

Evaluating social behavior in physical education does not lend itself to formal testing. Many of the

observational techniques previously mentioned serve the teacher well in obtaining the necessary information. Sociometric forms may be used to determine what is going on in the group and which children need help in developing better social relationships. Anecdotal records are another technique that uses observation of performance. The teacher records incidents or certain events. This method may be of considerable help in evaluating social behavior as the teacher tallies the occurrence of certain social behaviors.

Evaluation data are used throughout the unit to determine the next steps in planning for learning as well as to report pupil progress to the school administration, to teachers who will be working with the students at the next grade level, and to parents.

REPORTING PUPIL PROGRESS

Report forms are the most important instrument of communication between the school and parents. They give tangible evidence of student achievement and areas needing more work. They may be used in conjunction with parent conferences in which the teacher meets with parents to discuss the individual child's progress.

The form of the report card for physical education should conform with what is used in other curricular areas. Marking needs to be interpreted so that the methods of arriving at the marks are known to both pupil and parent. It should reflect the program goals and the progress the child has made in achieving those goals. All areas considered in arriving at a mark and the weighting for each should be made known.

In reporting fitness test results schools often develop a fitness profile in which each year's test scores are recorded, giving parents a picture of how the test scores have changed from one year to the next.

Letter grades are usually not given in the elementary school, but they may be given in the upper elementary grades in some schools. They are not as individualized as other reporting forms. Although many teachers view letter grading as not in the best interests of children, the system still exists, and parents find such grades easy to interpret. Unfortunately grades may discourage the child who needs activity the most. If letter grades are given in all subjects including physical education, physical education is on a par with the other school subjects. On the other hand, if other subjects receive grades and physical education does not, it may appear that physical education is of less value than other school subjects.

Rating scales may be used in place of letter grades. They have some of the same limitations as letter grading in that they are not individualized and may discourage the poor performer. Parents may also interpret a five-category rating scale as letter grades.

A descriptive statement of written comments on performance is probably most meaningful. The teacher can communicate the child's strengths and also the areas in which more work is needed. They require more time to prepare, but they actually tell the parent more than other forms of reporting. Fitness test scores or other performance measures may be included in the written report.

MEASURING TEACHER EFFECTIVENESS

Evaluation to improve teaching effectiveness is essential for all teachers. Systematic evaluation of teaching too often ends with graduation and an undergraduate teaching degree. Throughout teachers' professional careers they may periodically be observed by an administrator, but these sporadic evaluations of teaching usually create momentary anxiety and have little effect on future teaching performances. Although it often seems to have negative connotations, evaluation should be a positive experience.

Beginning teachers must be dedicated to a systematic plan of evaluation if they are to grow as teachers. In planning the evaluation teachers must first determine what they would like to know about their teaching. Student achievement, time spent in the various parts of the lesson, types of interactions with students, and student time on task are some of the information of interest to teachers. Several techniques are possible for collecting data about teaching. Some use self-analysis that is completed by the teacher, whereas others require the help of a trained observer or assistant.

One form of self-analysis is the written daily lesson evaluation. Shortly after the lesson has been completed, the teacher jots down notes regarding what took place. It may include comments about particular students and their needs, management problems, or group problems with the lesson objectives. In a short time the teacher may see trends in teacher behavior by analyzing these daily evaluations. The evaluation of beginning teachers often focuses on their own behavior but not necessarily on its effects on children's learning. If teaching is to improve, teachers must be good observers of their own behavior. Effective use of this form of evaluation is developed over time as the teacher focuses attention on various aspects of teaching.

In another self-evaluation technique the teacher records the lesson on a tape recorder for later playback. A great deal of information can be gathered in the playback. Were the verbal explanations clear? Did the teacher talk too long? Was the class listening? Which students received attention and what was the nature of the attention? How did the teacher respond to class questions? Was the feedback to children related to the lesson objectives or pupil behavior?

With the help of another teacher or older student the teacher can use several additional techniques. A video recording of the lesson may be obtained and analyzed in much the same way as the tape recording.

The teacher may also use an observer who records information in a systematic manner. A duration study may be conducted by recording the amount of time spent on various aspects of the lesson. The teacher may wish to know how much time was spent getting the class started, giving the beginning instructions and demonstrations, moving the class from one activity to the next, or giving feedback during an activity.

Event recording is another observational approach. A list of possible events is made, and the observer tallies the number of times each event occurs. Interactions with students, both positive and negative, correcting or encouraging, may be recorded. Event recording might be done at certain time intervals throughout the lesson. For instance, the observer may record three times for 3 minutes at the beginning, middle, and end of the lesson.

Another recording technique is group sampling. At particular intervals throughout the lesson the observer scans the group and records the number of children engaging in a particular activity.

If periodic observation by administrators is to result in improved teaching effectiveness, teachers and administrators must develop a good working relationship. This relationship must be supportive and nonthreatening. All school personnel have the same ultimate goal—the maximum learning of all children. Personal growth in teaching should be valued highly. The observation of teaching should take place on a regular basis, not just once a year, at the time of annual review. Observers must be careful to praise the aspects of the lesson that were done well in addition to offering suggestions for improving the effectiveness of other parts of the lesson. The result of effective administrator-teacher relationships will be more effective learning for children in an atmosphere in which the continued growth of teachers is assured.

PROGRAM EVALUATION

Program evaluation provides valuable information for determining the quality of the physical education program. It should encompass all aspects of the program including the instructional program, intramurals, special interest groups, and special events. A program review should be undertaken on a regular schedule, usually every 3 to 5 years.

The program evaluation may be conducted within the school by teachers and administrators or with the assistance of consultants from other schools, neighboring colleges of education, or the state department of education. Local, state, or professional criteria may be used. If evaluation is conducted with outside help, approval of the administration and board of education should be sought.

In preparation for the evaluation a program statement is developed that includes all necessary information about the program, including the philosophy of the program, its relationship to school goals and other school curricula, scheduling, equipment and facilities, personnel, activity content, teacher-pupil ratio, and cost. Program goals are listed, and any particular concerns about the program are raised. These concerns may be the reasons the program is being reviewed.

Program goals are broken down into a series of measurable objectives, that identify the questions to be asked and the criteria for evaluation. Social skills and knowledge as well as motor skills and fitness should be included.

Information may be gathered from various sources. Teacher-constructed tests or standardized tests may be used to determine students' comprehension of the objectives. Frequency charts in which the number of times children participate in extracurricular activities may be used. Student interviews and questionaires can be administered. Parents and administrators may be interviewed. Teachers who work with the children at the next educational level (middle, junior high, or high school) may be asked for information regarding their perceptions about strengths and weaknesses. Observations of how children use free time at school may be a reflection on the effectiveness of the physical education program.

Once the information is received, an analysis is undertaken to determine the extent to which the objectives are being met and the implications for program revision. Recommendations should be forwarded to administrators and the board of education.

SUMMARY

Evaluation is an essential part of effective teaching. It is a process that begins the first day of teaching and is not concluded until the school year has come to a close. Evaluation is important to curriculum, unit, and daily planning, helping teachers to plan challenging learning experiences for children.

Curricular implementation involves setting objectives, planning learning experiences, teaching, and evaluating the outcomes. If the evaluation indicates that the objectives have been met, the process is repeated with a new set of objectives and learning experiences. If the evaluation determines that more work is needed on the objectives, the objectives are restated or modified to meet the needs of the children.

The assessment of pupil progress is important if appropriate learning experiences are to be planned. Motor skills, knowledge, and social behaviors should be included as important aspects of the physical education program. Several techniques may be used, including observations, written tests, and motor performance tests. Pupil progress is recorded and reported in written form to administrators, other teachers, and parents.

Another goal of the evaluation program in the schools is the improvement of instruction. Teachers may use a variety of techniques, including self-analysis or peer observations, to help them identify areas in which they could be more effective.

Program evaluation is another aspect of evaluation. Periodic evaluation of the program is conducted by the physical education teachers themselves, with the assistance of administrators, personnel from neighboring schools or colleges of education, or the state department of education. This review provides valuable information to the continued improvement of the program in meeting the needs of children.

Well-planned evaluation in education results in keeping the curriculum up to date, improving teacher effectiveness, and identifying student needs. As a result student learning is enhanced as the physical education program strives to prepare children for a lifetime of physical activity.

REFERENCES

1. Auxter, D., and Pyfer, J.: Principles and methods of adapted physical education and recreation, ed. 4, St. Louis, 1985, Times Mirror/Mosby.
2. Cooper J., and others: Classroom teaching skills: a handbook, ed. 2, Lexington, 1982, D.C. Heath & Co.
3. Dougherty, N., and Bonanno, D.: Contemporary approaches to the teaching of physical education, Minneapolis, 1979, Burgess Publishing Co.
4. Dreikurs, R.: Psychology in the classroom. ed. 2, New York, 1968, Harper & Row, Publishers.
5. Dreikurs, R., and Goldman, M.: The abc's of guiding the child, Chicago, 1967, North Side Unit of Family Education Association.
6. Dreikurs, R., and Soltz, W.: Children: the challenge, New York, 1964, Hawthorn Books, Inc.
7. Estvan, F.: Teaching the very young: procedures for developing inquiry skills. In Anderson, R., and Shane, H.: As the twig is bent, Boston, 1971, Houghton Mifflin Co.
8. Fait, H.: Teaching and evaluating physical education for severely and profoundly retarded. In NASPE: Echoes of influence for elementary school physical education, Washington, D.C., 1977, AAHPERD.
9. Harrison, J.: Instructional strategies for physical education, Dubuque, 1983, William C. Brown Co.
10. Hoffman, H., and others: Meaningful movement for children: a developmental theme approach to physical education, Boston, 1981, Allyn & Bacon, Inc.

ADDITIONAL READINGS

Brown, E.: Visual evaluation techniques for skill analysis, JOPERD **53**:(1):21, January 1982.
Developing techniques for observing motor skills, including vantage point, movement simplification, balance and stability, movement relationships, and range of movement.

Carlisle, C., and Phillips, A.: The physical education teacher assessment instrument, Journal of Teaching in Physical Education **2**:62, Winter 1983.
A technique for evaluating the physical education teacher's performance.

Farley, M.: Program evaluation as a political tool, JOPERD **55**(4):64, April 1984.
In addition to being a valuable tool for program improvement, program evaluation may be used to nurture objectives of accountability, legitimacy, public support, and effective communication of results to the community at large.

Lambdin, D.: Keeping track, JOPERD **55**(6):40, August 1984.
Recording techniques to help students and teachers assess physical education outcomes.

Melville, S.: Teaching and evaluating cognitive skills, JOPERD **56**(2):26, February 1985.
Suggestions for teaching and developing written tests to measure cognitive skills.

Nelson, J., and Dorociak, J.: Reducing administration time while improving reliability and validity of fitness tests, JOPERD **53**(1):63, January 1982.
Suggestions for the efficient administration of fitness tests.

Thomas, J., and Thomas, K.: Strange kids and strange numbers: assessing children's motor development, JOPERD **54**(8):19, October 1983.
Selecting important behaviors and characteristics and appropriate tests and the importance of measures of motor development.

Part Four

Foundations of Physical Education

Several foundational areas of understanding and skills underlie all movement experiences. To move effectively and efficiently an individual must have an understanding of human movement, a repertoire of basic motor skills, appropriate social skills to interact with others, and sufficient health-related fitness to sustain the activity. The objectives of the elementary school physical education program are to develop these fundamentals essential to a lifetime of enjoyable physical activity through a variety of meaningful, fun-filled motor experiences.

10   Understanding Human Movement

11   Fundamental Movement Skills

12   Developing Social Skills

13   Fitness and Movement Efficiency

Understanding Human Movement

The concepts discussed in this chapter are inherent in any movement from the simplest locomotor task to complex sports skills, from the movements of the unskilled laborer to those of a surgeon. These concepts are important in early learning in physical education and are later integrated into the learning of all the physical activities in which one participates throughout life.

The information is meaningful to children, since they are curious about themselves and the movement tasks in which they engage in physical education. These experiences teach children to understand and appreciate their own movement potential. It provides an opportunity for them to develop their own ideas in challenging and enjoyable ways as they attempt to solve movement tasks.

It is important for children to develop a basic understanding of the movement concepts during level I and II experiences in the elementary school physical education program. Integration of the movement concepts into all aspects of the program begins with these early experiences and becomes more and more important as the child progresses through the elementary school grades.

Although the content has been divided into three distinct areas, it must be remembered that all are interrelated and are involved in any movement. The activities included here only represent a few suggestions for the development of the basic understanding of each concept. They are not necessarily listed in order of difficulty. Integration with the other activities is found in the chapters that follow.

PLANNING AND CONDUCTING MOVEMENT EXPERIENCES

1. It is important to establish rapport with the group before attempting a movement approach to learning. Children need a framework within which to work, so it is important for the teacher to have an established relationship with the children before proceeding. When beginning the school year with a new group of children, it is best to plan a few lessons to help establish the rules for expected behavior and the class routine before moving to the less structured movement approach.

2. The teacher should define with the children the space to be used. Often physical education areas may also be used as the cafeteria or multipurpose room, so furniture or other equipment may occupy some of the space. If the teacher wishes the children to avoid some areas, the space needs to be defined

for them by setting the movement boundaries to exclude those places.

3. A signal for listening needs to be established before the children begin moving. It need not be the same signal each day. Practice in responding to the signal may be helpful for young children, such as giving them a chance to move around in the space and stop on the signal a few times. Some teachers refer to the signal as the signal to "freeze" when indicating it is time to listen or to change activities.

4. Generally in the beginning phases of learning, themes of three to five lessons are developed for each concept. In this way, children have a longer time to develop an understanding of a single concept before moving on to the next. This gives the child greater time for learning and understanding the concept through a variety of activities.

5. The success of the children's learning is dependent on the teacher's skill in responding as they are moving. It is not free play. The teacher must be able to ask appropriate questions during the movement activities to keep the children on task and enhance their understanding of the concept involved. These questions are stimulated by the children's response to the challenge that was posed prior to moving.

6. It is important that the children's earliest experiences be centered around the movement content. It is more difficult to get started in the upper grades. As children begin to be more group oriented, they do not respond well to problem solving unless they have had previous experience with this method. If their orientation to physical education has been the traditional activity-centered approach, then the concepts may more easily be grasped through these activities, since it gives the children a framework with which they are already familiar. Problem solving continues to be a viable method in teaching traditional physical education activities.

7. In planning for children the challenges should be kept simple but specific to the outcome we wish to achieve. Challenges that are too general or vague do not develop the understanding for which we are striving. This does not mean that we are looking for a limited number of different responses. On the contrary, we should encourage a variety of responses, but only those that solve the challenge that has been presented.

8. A variety of activities are needed in the development of greater understanding. Exposure to a series of challenges that relate the concept to a variety of movement situations is crucial.

9. Children should be encouraged to think and to develop their own ideas. Success in this regard is closely related to the child's self-concept. Those children with greater self-confidence will be more comfortable in developing their own solutions to movement challenges. Much effort must be made to recognize the efforts of those lacking confidence to help them feel successful.

10. In the early years children are more successful working alone in solving movement challenges. Gradually they learn to work with a partner and later a small group of three or four.

11. Emphasis should be on the quality of movement. Children should be helped to evaluate their own responses to the movement challenges in a nonthreatening way that emphasizes the positive aspects of their performance. The teacher may foster a supportive attitude by asking the children what they liked about the performance.

BODY AWARENESS

The primary purpose of body awareness activities is to acquaint children with themselves as movers—to gain understanding of what the body can do and to increase awareness of the body through movement. Although research in this area is limited, one might expect that the more children understand about the body and its actions, the more effective they might be in solving movement tasks. Moving children may have little conscious awareness of their body parts and their potential for movement. These activities focus the children's attention on themselves and their

BODY AWARENESS CONCEPTS

Names and locates body parts of self and others
   Large parts: arms, legs, back, chest, head
   Small parts: hands, ankles, feet, wrists
   Parts of thigh, knee, calf, shin, forearm, elbow,
      fingers, toes
Body shape
   Straight
   Curled (round)
   Twisted
Movements of body parts
   Bend (flex)
   Straighten (extend)
   Rotate
   Pronate, supinate

Relationship of body parts
   Support/nonsupport
   Action/stillness
   Unison, opposition, sequence
Uses body parts to perform movement tasks
   Locomotor/nonlocomotor
   Stop/start
   Manipulative skills
The body as communicator
   Communicating ideas
   Communicating feelings
   Communicating attitudes
   Conscious/unconscious
Tension/relaxation
   Body segments

moving body parts. The program objectives to be achieved in body awareness activities include the following:

1. Naming and locating body parts of self and others
2. Awareness of possible body shapes
3. Recognizing possible movements of body parts
4. Awareness of the relationship of body parts while moving
5. Using body parts efficiently to accomplish movement tasks
6. Understanding the use of the body in communication (body language)
7. Awareness of body tension and the ability to perform conscious relaxation

It is assumed that appropriate vocabulary and understanding of one's anatomy and physiology is also the result of these experiences. The box above outlines the content for each objective.

Objective One: Names and Locates Body Parts of Self and Others

The naming and locating of body parts is often taken for granted. Yet it is not uncommon for elementary school children as late as second grade to be unsure of where certain body parts are, such as their shins and thighs. Children learn body parts that they use at an early age to manipulate their environment—arms, legs, fingers. They also learn those that may be frequently bumped or banged, such as knees or elbows. They may be unfamiliar with some parts of the arms and legs. This objective should be met during level I.

Activities

1. Move a body part while in self space. Try another. Another. (Often when children get beyond identifying five or six parts, they begin to experience some difficulty in naming others. This demonstrates the degree of awareness they have of their own bodies.)
2. Balance a beanbag on a body part a partner names. Or on how many different parts can you balance a beanbag?
3. Toss a beanbag. Catch a beanbag on the body part a partner names.
4. Working with a partner, move your partner's body part as he or she names it.
5. Working with a partner, one names a body part and the other moves it with the eyes closed.
6. Working with a partner, one is the leader. Move the same body parts the leader moves.
7. Call out the names of body parts—forearm, thigh, shin, wrist, etc. What are they parts of?
8. Name and move body parts that begin with A, B, etc.

Related knowledge

Names and spelling of body parts.

Evaluative criteria

1. Can the child move or point to body parts named by the teacher? (How quickly can you touch your _________?)
2. Can the child name and point to body parts? (This is my _________.)
3. Can the child match body parts to those of a partner?

Objective Two: Awareness of Possible Body Shapes

Familiarity with actions that allow the body to assume shapes important in specific movement tasks is essential to good body awareness. Understanding why certain body shapes aid a movement and others hinder movement is important to efficient use of the body in solving various movement challenges.

The body may assume shapes ranging from straight to rounded or twisted.

Activities

1. Working in self space, can you make a round (curled) shape? A twisted shape? A straight shape?
2. Moving in general space, on the signal make a shape and freeze. Try it again. Again. Were you able to make a shape that you could hold for a long time? What kind of shape was easiest to hold?
3. Make a shape supported on one body part. Try another. Can you make a shape supported on two parts? Another? Three body parts?
4. Use your body to make the shape of a letter of the alphabet. What letter did you make? How would you describe its shape? Try another.
5. Using one or two elastic ropes held by two persons, vary the height of the ropes and try different ways of going over and under the ropes. What body shapes could you assume when you went over the ropes? Under? How did your body shape change as the space got smaller? Larger?
6. Working in self space, make a very large shape with your body. Can you slowly change your shape from large to small? Can you change your small shape to a large one?
7. Working with a partner, make a shape that your partner can go over. Repeat. Now make a shape that your partner can go under. Around.

8. Working with a partner, can the two of you make a curled shape? A straight shape? A twisted shape? Can you make a shape with one of you curled, the other straight? What other combinations of shapes could you try?
9. In a small group of four or five children, we are going to make a machine. One person begins by making an interesting shape; it may have some moving parts and sound effects if you wish. The next person adds on to the machine by touching the first person and making his or her own shape, motions, and sound effects. Continue until all are a part of the machine. Did you use a variety of shapes? Could you make a machine with everyone making the same shape?

Related knowledge

Terminology: round, straight, twisted, curled.

Evaluative criteria

1. Can the child vary the body shape in solving the movement challenges?
2. Can the child adjust the body shape to fit into the available space?

Objective Three: Recognizes Possible Movements of Body Parts

Before children can successfully learn and use motor skills, they must have an understanding of how their body parts function. These activities attempt to help the children realize their movement potential.

Activities

1. Select a body part. Move it in as many ways as you can. Try another. Another. How would you describe some of the ways you were able to move your body parts? Describe how you moved to someone close by.
2. Can you move your legs without touching them to the floor? How many different ways could you move them?
3. Move one (or more) body parts in your self space. Which parts could you bend (flex)? Extend? Rotate?
4. Working with a partner, create a human sculpture. One person is the artist, the other the lump of clay. The artist moves his or her partner's body parts to form the sculpture. What were the ways you were able to move various body parts? Describe them to your partner.
5. While in self space move some body parts that enable you to stay where you are. Now move some parts that move you through general space. Now move in self space. Those are called nonlocomotor or axial movements. Those that move you through general space are called locomotor movements.
6. Bend one body part. Try another. When we bend body parts, we call that flexion. Straighten a body part. When we straighten body parts, we call that extension. When we bend a body part, the muscles we use to bend it are flexed. Some muscles are also relaxed. Can you feel the flexed muscles?
7. Stretch a body part. Try another. Can you feel the muscles that help you stretch?
8. Turn (rotate) a body part. Try another. Which body parts do not turn? Why? Some of the joints of the body allow for rotation and others do not.
9. Working with a partner, one is the leader. The leader tells the partner to bend, stretch, or rotate specific body parts. The partner responds with eyes closed. Take turns being the leader. Were you able to respond to your partner without looking at the body parts you were asked to move?

Related knowledge

Terminology of the types of movement possible: bend, flex, stretch, extend, rotate, pronate (rotate forward and toward midline), supinate (rotate away from midline).

Types of joints: ball and socket, hinge, pivot, condyloid.

When a body part moves, some muscles contract and others relax.

Movements through space are called locomotor movements; those in which one remains stationary are nonlocomotor or axial movements.

Evaluative criteria

1. Can the child move body parts in the correct movement on command? (Flex your wrist.)
2. Can the child verbalize and move body parts in all ways? (My wrist can flex, extend, and rotate.)
3. Can the child describe the type of movements possible in the various types of joints?

Objective Four: Awareness of the Relationship of Body Parts while Moving

The content in this area develops an understanding of the relationship of body parts in three areas: that some body parts may be used for support and non-support functions; that in any action some body parts move while others remain still; and that in any action body parts may move in unison, sequence, or opposition.

Activities

1. With one body part stationary, move in your self space. Try moving again with another body part stationary. Increase the stationary parts to two or three. Try it again.
2. Support your body on one part. Can you use another part for support? Try again. Which two body parts can you use for support? Another two? Now try supporting the body on three different parts.
3. Try a movement using one body part for support. Can you repeat the movement, supporting the body on a different body part? Try it again.
4. Move your body from the waist up. Waist down. Were you able to keep half of your body still as you moved the other half?
5. Working with a partner, move and tell your partner which parts are moving and which are stationary. Repeat with a new activity with your eyes closed. Were you able to tell your partner which parts were moving and which were still without looking at them?
6. Perform a movement skill—locomotor, nonlocomotor, or with an object (manipulative). Which body parts are involved? Which are not?
7. Moving in general space, on the signal become a statue with your (some body part) moving. Move again.
8. Balance a beanbag on some body part and keep

it still. How many different ways can you move other body parts and still keep the beanbag on that part? Try another part for supporting the beanbag and move again.

9. Begin moving one body part. Now add another part and move them in unison. What other two parts can you move together?
10. Can you begin a movement with one body part and continue it with another, so that one part moves and then the other? This is called moving parts sequentially. Which other parts can you move sequentially?
11. Can you move one body part one way and another in an opposite way? Which other body parts can you move in opposition?
12. Can you flex a body part and extend another part nearby?
13. Can you touch two body parts together? Three?
14. Can you make two body parts move away from each other and then meet?

Related knowledge

Terminology: support, nonsupport, unison, sequence, opposition.

Evaluative criteria

1. Can the child accurately respond to challenges that call for keeping some body parts still while others are moving?
2. Is the child comfortable using various body parts for support?
3. Can the child respond to problems that call for body parts to move in unison, sequence, and opposition?

Objective Five: Uses Body Parts Effectively To Accomplish Movement Tasks

When they are learning movement skills, it is important for children to begin to understand how the body is used to accomplish the skills most efficiently and effectively. Greater understanding in this area should better equip children to see the common elements in certain skills and to be able to adapt them more easily as various situations require. More efficient movement and better body mechanics should be the result of these activities.

Activities

1. (Have the children perform some movement skill and name the body parts used.)
2. Working with a partner, select a skill. Move and

tell your partner how you used the body parts to perform the skill.
3. Explore movement skills, using body parts inappropriately (for example, not putting the opposite foot forward on a throw or failing to bend knees in jumping). How was the performance affected? How did it feel?
4. Explore the use of the body in moving from one place to another. Which parts could you use? How many different ways could you get there? Which body parts did you use? Which skills did you use? Which ways took the most energy? The least? In which ways could you move more quickly? More slowly?
5. Explore the use of manipulative skills, using various body parts to project or receive an object. How did you move the body parts to project the object? To control it as you received it?
6. Explore the use of the body in moving with good alignment and moving objects, such as how to push, pull, or carry objects varying in size, either real or imaginary. What body parts did you use if the object was large? Small?

Related knowledge

Understanding of how body parts are used in performing various motor skills.

Evaluative criteria

1. Can the child describe accurately how body parts are used in the execution of various motor skills?
2. Can the child apply what he or she has learned about efficient movement in one task to similar tasks?

Objective Six: Understands the Use of the Body in Communication (Body Language)

This section is designed to help children learn to use their bodies as a means of communicating ideas and to become aware of how we unconsciously communicate to others through posture, facial expression, body movements, and gestures.

Activities

1. Moving in general space, can you move like a person who is happy? Sad? Tired? Energetic? Disgusted? Pleased? How did your movements change as you changed your emotions?
2. Pretend you are a clown. What would you do to make others laugh?
3. Show us how you would feel if you were invited

to a birthday party. If it is Halloween. If you heard a strange noise. If you had an appointment at the dentist.

4. Working with a partner, act out an emotion as your partner acts out the opposite. If one is happy, then the other is sad.
5. Think of something you would like to share with your partner. How could you tell him or her without using words?
6. As a poem is read (that includes a change of moods) act out changing movements to match the moods of the poem. What feelings did it convey? How did you act each of them out?
7. (Use imagery.) You are a snowman melting, an ice cream cone in the sun, a puppet with strings whose strings are cut one by one.

Related knowledge

The body may be used as an instrument for communicating ideas.

Sometimes we communicate feelings to other people that we do not really mean and that hurt their feelings. We must be more aware of how we use our body language.

Evaluative criteria

1. Can the child use the body successfully to communicate ideas?
2. Is there a growing awareness of what we communicate to others through our actions?

Objective Seven: Awareness of Muscle Tension and the Ability To Perform Conscious Relaxation

Perhaps the greatest contribution physical education can make is to develop an awareness of tension and the ability to perform conscious relaxation. This an important aspect of movement not only for the highly skilled but for everyone.

The environment for conscious relaxation must be comfortable, with little in the way of distraction. Generally it is helpful to begin lying on a mat rather than on the floor. Once learned, conscious relaxation may be practiced under many different conditions, but initially it is helpful to be in an environment that is comfortable, sufficiently warm, not brightly lit, and relatively quiet. The leader should have a pleasant, relaxing voice.

Conscious relaxation should not result in sleeping, since the goal is to remain conscious. When working on conscious relaxation the children should be encouraged to tighten only those body parts called

for in the exercise. The leader should move around the room, touching the children to help them become more aware of tension in body parts other than those with which they are working.

Activities

1. Balance on various body parts. Touch those parts where you feel tension.
2. Perform slow relaxed movements. For example, how slowly can you move your arm?
3. (Use imagery.) Pretend you are floating on a cloud. Can you be a snowflake?
4. Working with a partner, match the slow movements your partner makes.
5. Working with a partner, tell your partner which body parts to tense. Check to see that they are tense by touching. Touch other parts. Are they tense too?
6. Conscious relaxation[1]:
   a. Lying on your back on the mat, slowly take a series of deep breaths. Slowly breathe in and out.
   b. Make a fist as you bend your arm at the elbow and hold. Feel the tension in the muscles in the front of your upper arm. Let it go slowly, until your arm feels relaxed. Try it again. (If they have difficulty begin with one arm at a time.)
   c. Point your toes away from the rest of your body. Hold. Feel the tension in the back of your legs. Now slowly let it go. Repeat.
   d. Now flex your ankles so your toes try to point toward your head. Feel the tension in the front of your legs. Hold. Now let it go until your feet fall limply onto the mat. Try it again.
   e. Turn your knees out forcefully. Hold that position. Feel tension in the outer thigh area. Now let it go so your knees turn back into their original position. Repeat.
   f. Rotate your knees inward. Hold. Now relax. Repeat. Do you feel tension in your inner thighs?
   g. Tighten your abdominal muscles, pressing your back into the mat. Hold. Slowly let it go back to your starting position. Try it again.
   h. Press your head back, lifting your upper back off the mat. Hold. Feel the tension in your upper back and neck. Slowly lower your back to the mat and your head to its resting position. Repeat.
   i. Pinch your shoulder blades together, feeling tension in the back of your shoulders. Hold. Slowly relax and sink into the mat. Repeat.

j. Roll your shoulders forward and upward keeping your arms on the mat Hold. Feel the tension in the front of your shoulders. Slowly relax and bring your shoulders back to their resting position. Try it again.

k. Spread your fingers. Hold. Feel the tension in your fingers. Slowly relax and let your fingers fall limply to the mat. Do it once more.

l. Make a fist with both hands. Hold. Feel the tension in your fingers and hands. Let it go and allow your hands to lie limply on the mat. Repeat.

m. Touch your chin to your chest. Hold. Feel the tension in the front of the neck. Slowly return your head to the mat. Repeat.

n. Wrinkle your forehead by raising your eyebrows. Hold. Feel the tension in your forehead. Now slowly relax. Repeat.

o. Close your eyelids as tightly as possible. Hold. Now slowly let it go. Repeat.

p. Open your mouth as wide as you can. Do you feel like yawning? Now slowly close your mouth. Repeat.

q. Pucker your lips as hard as you can. Feel the tension at the edge of your mouth. Now slowly let your lips relax. Repeat.

r. Make a forced smile as you bite down hard. Hold. Feel the tension in your jaw and lips. Now slowly relax. Repeat.

Related knowledge

Terminology: relaxation, tension.

Evaluative criteria

1. Can the child consciously relax body parts called on by the teacher? (The teacher can tell by touching.)
2. Is the child able to tense only those body parts called for by the leader while keeping all others relaxed?

SPACE

The understanding of space is another essential element in the study of human movement. Success in moving is dependent in part on the individual's ability to use space successfully, whether the task is creating a dance or outmaneuvering one's opponent on the soccer field. Program objectives include the study of:

Self space
General space
Level
Direction
Pathways
Range

Each of these objectives is broken down into several learning outcomes in the following material. The box below outlines the content for each objective.

SPACE CONCEPTS

Self space
  Dimensions
  Movements possible
  Relationship between self and general space
General space
  Dimensions
  Movements possible
  Relationship between self and general space
  Relationship between body movements and size of space available
  Use all available space effectively
Level
  High, medium, and low levels
  Movements possible in each level
  Changes level smoothly

  Controls the level of an object
Direction
  Moves in forward, backward, right, left, up, and down directions
  Possible movements in each direction
  Controls change of direction
Pathways
  Moves in straight, curved, or combination pathways
  Possible movements in each pathway
  Recognizes available pathways in space
Range
  Dimensions
  Relationship of range and size of available space
  Controls range of movements

Objective One: Self Space

Self space, or personal space, is the immediate area surrounding a person, including the space within the natural body extensions. Children must have an understanding of their own space if they are to work effectively with others in their spaces.

Activities

The children each have their own space in the physical education area.

1. Show me the size of your self space. How wide is it? How high does it go? How low does it go? Can you touch all parts of your self space? In front of you? Behind you? To the sides?

2. Standing in a hoop, show me the size of your self space. Move out of the hoop and show me your self space. Do it again in the hoop and then out in a new space. Did you notice how your self space goes wherever you go?

3. Can you touch all parts of your self space with a body part other than your hand? Which ones did you use? Did you use your feet? Your elbow? Your knee?

4. How can you move your body parts to take up as much space as possible? As little space as possible?

5. Working with a partner, define your self space while your partner outlines it with a rope. Repeat this, changing roles and using another rope. What was the size of your self space? Was it the same size as your partner's? Others' in the class?

6. Move your self space as close as possible to a child near you. How close can you get without touching (or getting into another person's self space)? How do you feel when you are very close? How did your self space change?

7. How close can you get your self space to everyone in the class without touching? Move your self space away. Now close again. Did you like getting your self space close? Why? Why not? (This could lead to a discussion of individual space needs. Sometimes we don't mind others close; sometimes we need more space.) When do you need more space? Less?

8. Moving in a circle, one behind the other, make your self space as large as possible. Now as small. Be sure you do not touch one another. Keep moving in the circle. How does the circle change as your self space increases and decreases?

9. Move one body part. How many ways can you move it around you in your self space? Try another part. Can it move in the same way? Why? Why not?

10. Can you move more than one body part in your self space? Can you move two body parts in the same way? In different ways? How many can you move at the same time in your self space?

Related knowledge

Terminology: Self space.

Evaluative criteria

1. Can the child demonstrate the dimensions of self space?
2. Can the child move in a variety of ways in self space?
3. Does the child demonstrate that the self space moves as he or she moves in general space?
4. Can the child demonstrate the potential changes in self space as general space decreases or increases?

Objective Two: General Space

General space is the space available for movement, which varies with the physical dimensions of the space, and the number of individuals and/or objects sharing it. An understanding of general space is important in any movement situation, especially when the movement environment contains obstacles, equipment, and other individuals.

Activities

1. (After defining the area to be used, ask the children to move to all parts of the available space without getting into another's self space.) Have you been to the corners? Middle? Sides? How quickly can you stop on the signal? (a good activity for establishing the signal for listening.) Be sure to move to all parts of the space. Did you move to empty spaces?
2. Imagine you are a paint brush. Paint the general space your favorite color. Did you miss any places?
3. We are going to move in general space in as many different ways as we can. Each time I give the signal, change the way you move. What were some of the ways you chose to move? Can you move on one foot? Two feet? Hands and feet? Which ways of moving did you like best? Why?
4. Execute a movement as you remain in your own space. Now do the same movement while moving in general space. Repeat. What were some of the movements you tried? Which movements were you able to do exactly the same while standing and while moving? What kind of movements required you to add other movements so you could move in general space? Which movements did you like best? Why?
5. (Alternately increase and decrease available space as children continuously move in general space.) Were you able to continue moving and keeping your self space away from the self space of others? How did you change your movements as the space got smaller? Larger? Did your self space change? How? Were empty spaces harder or easier to find as the space got smaller? Larger?
6. (Holding the outside edges of a parachute, the children are numbered off by threes. As their number is called, the children move under the chute, covering as much space as possible before it comes down.) Which ways did you move? Which worked best to cover as much space as possible and avoid the self space of others?
7. Pretend you are in a balloon (or in boxes of different sizes). How can you move? How does the size and shape of the space you are in affect your movement?
8. (Half the children or hoops or other objects are scattered throughout the area as obstacles. The remaining children move in the space available.) How did you move in general space? How did your movements change as you moved around the obstacles? Did you look for the empty spaces? Were you able to move without touching the other children and the obstacles? (Increase the number of obstacles or decrease the available space and repeat.)
9. Change the size of your self space as you move through general space. What happens to the general space when we all make our self space as large as possible? Small? Tall? Short? Wide? Narrow?
10. Working with a partner, follow the leader as you move in general space. Use as much space as you can. Did you move to the corners? Middle?

Sides? The leader must always look for the empty spaces. Were you able to follow your leader and keep your self space away from the self space of others?

11. (Mark small, medium, and large circles, [or squares, triangles, or other shapes] on the playing surface, one for each child. Have the children choose a circle and move within its general space.) How many different ways can you move? Now move to a new circle of a different size. Repeat the activity. Change circles again. Repeat the activity. Did you move the same ways in each space? Why? Why not? Which ways did you like best in each size circle?

12. (Make a circle on the floor with a 10- to 12-foot rope for each 8 to 10 children. All the children put one body part inside the circle, then two parts, three parts, their whole bodies, without touching the rope or each other.) How many parts could you all get in the circle? Make the circle smaller and repeat. Which parts did you choose that enabled the group to get as many parts in the circle as possible?

13. Using a general space of different shapes such as a square, rectangle, circle, or triangle, move within the confines of the shape. Which shapes were the most restrictive? Which shape did you like best? Why?

14. (Mark a grid on the floor. Have the children explore the space available in each area marked off in the grid). How did you move? How did the space available affect the way you moved?

15. (Repeat activities 1 through 14 while using a piece of hand apparatus, such as a ball or hoop.) What did you do to keep the hoop or ball under control? (Emphasize control and a variety of ways of using the piece of equipment while moving in general space.)

16. Pass a ball around a circle of four to five persons. Increase and decrease the diameter of the circle. What did you have to do to get the ball to the others in the circle as the general space of the circle became larger? Smaller?

Related knowledge

Terminology: general space, boundaries, empty space.

Evaluative criteria

1. Does the child stay within the designated area? (demonstrates the dimensions of general space)
2. Can the child move with control in a variety of ways in general space alone or with others and/or objects?
3. Can the child demonstrate an understanding of how movements change as general space increases or decreases?
4. Does the child use available space effectively?

Objective Three: Level

Level is height in space: low, medium, and high. The high level may be defined as above the shoulders, the medium level between the shoulders and hips, and the low level below the hips.

Activities

1. Move a body part at the _______ level. Name it as it moves. What other body parts can you move at that level? How many body parts can you move at that level? Try another level and repeat twice.
2. Move a body part at the _______ level. What other ways can you move it at that level? How many different ways can you move it at that level?
3. Can you move a body part at one level? Add another at a different level. Now add a third part at the last level at the same time. Repeat moving two body parts at each level.
4. Move around the gymnasium in general space. On the signal, assume a shape with as many parts in one level as possible.
5. Moving in general space, continue moving on the signal but changing level. What ways can you move at each level? Can you move the same way at two or all three levels?
6. Working with a partner and a ball, what skills can you do at each level? Can you move the ball as you move through general space at the high level? The medium level? The low level?
7. Working with a partner and a ball, what do you do to make the ball change levels? Can you move the ball from the high to the medium to the low level? Medium to high to low? Low to high to medium?
8. With the apparatus, how many ways can you move at the low level? Medium level? High level?

Related knowledge

Terminology: level.

Evaluative criteria

1. Does the child understand that there are three levels in space and knows where each begins and ends?

2. Can the child move in a variety of ways at one, two, or all three levels at a time?
3. Can the child change level smoothly and efficiently?

Objective Four: Direction

There are six directions: forward, backward, right, left, up, and down. Direction is defined by which body surface is leading in the movement.

Activities

1. Scattered in general space, let's see how many different directions you can move. Pretend there is a string attached to some body part and let it pull you through space. What part of your body usually leads when you move forward? Backward? Right? Left? Up? Down? Can you lead with a different part? How do you adjust your body position for the new lead?
2. While moving in general space, on the signal change directions. What directions did you choose? Which did you like best? Why?
3. Standing in a space away from others, move (one, two, three, or four) body part(s) in any direction. Move them in another direction. Can you move one part in one direction while you move another part in another direction? How many parts and directions can you move at once? Start with one part at a time.
4. Select a direction in which you will move. On the signal continue in that direction but change the way you move. What changes did you make? Which did you like best? Now try a new direction. Which ways of moving were easiest? Most difficult? In which direction(s) could you move in the most ways? Why?
5. Moving in general space, change the direction and movement on the signal. Which did you like best? Least? Why?
6. Stand on a line on the floor. Can you move down the line and change direction without losing your balance? Remember, do not look at your feet but at a spot out in front of you. Which directions were easiest and most difficult in staying on the line? Now try it on the balance beam.
7. Moving on lines painted on the floor, change directions and movements each time you move to a new line. Were you able to stay on the lines as you moved from line to line and changed direction?

8. Select three points in the room. Move to each, changing direction as you move from one to the next. Repeat. This time move in a different direction to each point. Which body parts led? Can you change leads and not direction as you move from one point to the next?
9. With a partner, follow the leader, changing direction as you move through space. Was it easy to follow your partner's direction and avoid others? What adjustments did you have to make?
10. Working with a partner, change movement and direction while following your partner. Which movements were most difficult in following your partner and watching out for others?
11. Face your partner. Now move in the same direction he or she moves. Were you able to do it? Which directions were most difficult? Now move in the opposite direction. Were any directions easier?
12. Use any of these challenges and change direction as you move through space while controlling a hoop, ball, or other object. In which directions did you have the best control? Why?

Related knowledge

Terminology: direction, forward, backward, right, left, up, down.

Evaluative criteria

1. Can the student move in all six directions?
2. Does the child move in a variety of ways in all directions alone, with others, and/or with objects?

3. Can the child control movement while changing direction alone or in relation to others or objects?

Objective Five: Pathways

Pathways are the lines of movement in space: straight, curved, or combinations of both.

Activities

1. Find two points in the room. Begin at one and move to the next. How many different pathways could you use? Can you move from one to the other in straight lines only? Combinations of straight lines? Curved lines only? Combinations of curved lines? Combinations of curved and straight lines?
2. (Place many objects as obstacles scattered on the floor. Children move throughout the space, finding available pathways.) Describe the pathways you followed. Were they straight lines? Curved lines? Combinations?
3. Imagine letters of the alphabet in the air and then on the floor. Can you write the first letter of your name on the floor as you walk in general space? Make a letter that is made up of straight lines only. Which did you do? Now try a letter with only curved lines. Try a letter that is made up of curved and straight lines.
4. Working with a partner, decide who is the writer and who is the pencil; the writer stands behind the pencil with hands on the pencil's hips or shoulders. The eyes of the pencil are closed. The writer moves the pencil to make a letter on the floor. The pencil attempts to guess the letter.
5. (Each child has a piece of paper and a pencil or crayon. Each draws an interesting design on the paper with a continuous line. After drawing the design, each draws it on the floor by walking in general space.) How large can you make your design on the floor? How small? Trade designs with someone near you. Draw that design on the floor. How would you describe the design you just made? (for example, a combination of curved lines).
6. Working with a partner, each draw a design on a piece of paper. Take turns telling each other how to move as you trace the design on the floor. Did your partner suggest some ways of moving that were difficult to do? Why?
7. (Each individual has a long rope with which to create a design on the floor and then traces the design by moving along its path.) How many different ways can you move along the pathway you have created? Can you change your movement when you come to a change in the pathway? Move around the room to the pathways your classmates have made. Trace them, moving in a different way along each path. Were any ways of moving more difficult than others? Did you have any favorite paths?
8. (With the children in groups of four or five, one is a plane, one a control tower operator, and the others obstacles. With eyes closed, the plane attempts to follow the control tower operator's instructions in moving through the open paths.) Which instructions were helpful? Which were not?
9. (With the children in groups of three or four, one person is given a piece of paper with a design on it. That person must communicate the design to the group without showing it to them.) Did everyone have the same idea about what was being said? How could the design be explained more simply?

Related knowledge

Terminology: pathways, curves, zigzag.

Evaluative criteria

1. Is the child aware that there are straight, curved, and combination lines in space?
2. Can the child move in a variety of ways in different pathways?
3. Do the children recognize pathways for themselves and others as they move in space?

Objective Six: Range

Range includes the relationship of the body to self space, the relationship of one body part to another, and the relationship of body parts to objects in space: big/little, tall/short, wide/narrow, near/far.

Activities

1. In your own space, make the largest body shape you can. Now the smallest. Repeat. This time see if you can smoothly change your large shape to the smallest possible.
2. Working with a partner and a ball, stand as close to your partner as you can without touching. Throw the ball so your partner can catch it. Now gradually move farther apart, going only as far as you and your partner can still throw and catch the ball successfully. How did your movements

change as you went farther apart?

3. Moving in general space, make a body shape as wide as possible. Keep moving as the space gets smaller. How close together could you be and still keep the wide shape? As the space gets smaller and smaller, adjust your shape so you can continue to move without touching. What happens to your possible range as the space gets smaller?

4. Working with a partner, get as near to each other as possible. Now as far as possible. (Increase the size of the groups, adding one person at a time until you have everyone in the class in one group.) Why was it easier to work with one partner as opposed to the larger group? How did the possible range change as the group got bigger?

5. Working with a partner, execute a movement while your partner copies it but changes the range of movement. Which types of movements were most difficult to change the range? Easiest? Why?

6. Working in groups of three or four, pretend you are cheerleaders. Make up a cheer. After doing it successfully, change its range. Can you do it with as big moves as possible? Small?

Related knowledge

Terminology: range, near, far.

Evaluative criteria

1. Can the child demonstrate the dimensions of range?
2. Can the child understand the relationship of range to the amount of space available?
3. Does the child control the range of movement of body parts?

QUALITIES OF MOVEMENT

Along with developing an understanding of the body and its movement potential and moving in space, children need to experience other factors that affect movement. Many of these qualities of movement require the application of mechanical principles. In the objectives that follow—for balance, force, time, and flow—important mechanical principles are included in the related knowledge. The box below summarizes the content for this section.

Objective One: Balance

All movement through space is the result of moving off balance and then regaining balance again. Since body parts may be used in various ways in shifting

---

> ## QUALITIES OF MOVEMENT CONCEPTS
>
> Balance
>   Balances on different body parts
>   Adjusts body to move off balance
>   Adjusts body to move on balance
> Time
>   Controls speed from very slow to very fast
>   Moves to an imposed rhythm
> Force
>   Creating force
>   Controls force from very little to strong movements
>   Uses body parts to create force
>   Creates force to move the body
>   Creates force to move an object
>   Absorbing force
>   Absorbs the body's force
>   Absorbs an object's force
> Flow
>   Bound
>   Free

from balance to off balance and back again, it is important for children to experience many different kinds of balance challenges that enhance their understanding of principles concerned with this important movement quality. *Dynamic balance* (balance while moving) and *static balance* (stationary balance) should both be studied.

Activities

1. Moving in space, on the signal assume a balanced shape and hold it. Now slowly move your body parts off balance and move again. Try another balanced position this time. Repeat. What position of body parts enabled you to keep your balance easily?

2. Balance on two (three, four) different body parts. Can you lose your balance and then regain balance on the same two (three, four) body parts? On different parts?

3. Move on a line. Try moving in different ways, keeping your balance. Stop and assume a balanced position. Move again. Stop and balance in a new way. How did you keep your balance when you

were moving? When you were still?

4. (Have the children use different locomotor movements and move in general space.) On the signal stop in a balanced position. Vary the speed of movement. What positions helped you maintain your balance best on stopping? Try different ways of stopping.

5. On the signal make a shape. Describe it. Are you on or off balance? What is your base of support? How does your balance change as you make your base bigger? Smaller?

6. Working with a partner, assume a balanced position on one, two, or three body parts and have your partner gently try to push you off balance. What positions enabled you to maintain your balance as your partner gently pushed you?

7. Working with a partner, have the partner tell you which body parts to balance on. Can you balance on your foot and one hand? Which body parts were most difficult to use in balancing?

8. (Make available a variety of equipment such as beanbags, balls of various sizes and composition, hoops, and wands. The children select a piece of equipment and balance it on various body parts.) What did you do to balance the object on big body parts? Small body parts? Take a different piece of equipment and repeat. What objects were easiest to balance? What body parts offered the best balance points?

Related knowledge*

1. Every object has a *center of gravity* about which the body weight in all directions is balanced.

2. A body is balanced when its center of gravity is over its supporting base.

3. The nearer to the center of the base the *line of gravity* falls, the more stable the body.

4. The larger the base, the more stable the body.

5. The lower the center of gravity, the more stable the body.

6. The base should be enlarged in the direction of the moving or opposing force to allow for a decided shift of the center of gravity without the line of gravity falling outside the base.

7. Whenever one body part moves away from the line of gravity in one direction, the center of gravity shifts in that direction. If this shift puts the center of gravity beyond the base, another body part must move in the opposite direction to bring the center of gravity back over the base or balance is lost.

8. External weights added to the body become part of the total body weight and affect the location of the center of gravity, displacing it in the direction of the added weight.

9. In supporting an object, to keep the center of gravity over the base, the person's body shifts away from the object.

10. The closer to the center of gravity the weight is held, the less it changes the location of the center of gravity and the less effort needed to hold it.

Evaluative criteria

Can the child adjust body positions to maintain balance in a variety of balance situations?

Objective Two: Force

Force is the energy required to move an object or individual. As the body or an object is moved, it is acted on by a force initiated through muscle contraction. To stop the movement, the force must be absorbed by the same body parts or others. As children master movement skills, their ability to use them effectively in various situations is partially dependent on their ability to control the force created and to absorb the force appropriately.

Activities
Creating force

1. Use a little force, just enough to get you moving. Now increase the force so you move strongly.

---

*From Broer, M., and Zernicke, R.: Efficiency of human movement, ed. 4, New York, 1973, Holt, Rinehart, & Winston.

Now reduce the amount of force again until you are barely moving. Describe your movements to someone close to you. How did the movements change as you became stronger? Weaker?

2. Move strongly and make a loud noise. Can you move strongly and yet be as quiet as possible?
3. Explore moving strongly. How many ways can you move? Now try moving weakly. What were the differences? How did it feel?
4. Explore creating force for starting. Use your feet in different ways. How did you use your legs to get a good start? Add the use of your arms. What do you do if you want to get a very fast start? Try starting using as few body parts as possible.
5. Explore the use of the body in creating force in executing various locomotor and nonlocomotor movements such as running, jumping, pushing, pulling, or lifting. Which body parts did you use to create force when running? Pushing? Etc.
6. Think of a task that someone in your household performs. Can you pretend to do it? How much force does it take to perform the task?
7. (Creating force with balls.) Working with a partner, practice throwing to one another. Use the fewest number of body parts for the task. Increase the distance. Change the size and/or the weight of the ball used. How did you change the throw as the distance (size or weight) of the object changed? Did you change the skill? Use more or less body parts? Did you consistently throw the ball with just enough force so your partner could receive it easily?
8. Throw the ball to a wall with just enough force for it to come back to you. Can you throw the ball so it rebounds very close to the wall? To a line on the floor?

Absorbing force

1. Run as fast as you can in general space. On the signal stop as quickly as you can. What did you do with your legs as you stopped? What was the position of your body?
2. Practice jumping from or over objects of varying heights. How did your landing change as the distance jumped became greater? Did you land softly?
3. (Falling. See the activities in Chapter 19.)
4. Practice catching a ball, pretending it is a fresh egg or a balloon filled with water. How did you catch it to prevent the egg or balloon from breaking?
5. While practicing catching, vary the distance be-

tween individuals, and/or the size and weight of objects. How did your catching change in these different situations? How did you use your body to soften the force received?
6. Working with a partner, throw a ball so it lands on various body parts of your partner. Can you absorb the force so the ball drops close to your body? What did you have to do as the ball made contact with your body? Which body parts were easiest to absorb the force? Why?
7. Throw a ball against various surfaces (wall, curtain, mat, etc). Which surfaces absorbed the object more easily? What does that tell you about the use of your own body surfaces in absorbing a force?

Related knowledge*

1. The greater the distance and therefore the time over which momentum can be developed, the greater the momentum possible.
2. The longer the force is applied to an object, the greater the force imparted.
3. The more contributing muscles, the more force attainable.
4. The stronger the muscles called into play for a task demanding a good deal of force, the more efficient the action and the less the muscular strain.
5. The more fully a muscle is extended (lengthened), the greater the force it can exert.
6. Force should be applied as nearly as possible in

---

*From Broer, M., and Zernicke, R.: Efficiency of human movement, ed. 4, New York, 1973, Holt, Rinehart, & Winston.

the direction of the desired movement to use minimum energy.

7. If linear motion is desired, the more nearly through the center of gravity the force is applied, the less force required to move a given object.
8. The farther from the center of gravity the force is applied, the less energy necessary to rotate an object.
9. Spin is caused by an off-center application of force.
10. A ball with backspin stays in the air longer, or rises, its roll is shortened, and its bounce is higher and shorter than normal.
11. A ball with forward spin drops more quickly, its roll is lengthened, and its bounce is longer and lower than normal.
12. Ordinarily a ball will rebound at an angle equal to that at which it strikes a surface.
13. Three forces act on a projectile: gravity, air resistance, and the initial force that put it in motion.
14. The distance an object travels depends on its intial speed and the angle of release.
15. When air resistance isn't a factor, the optimum angle of release for maximum distance is forty-five degrees.
16. If the purpose of the projection is speed rather than distance, the angle should be as low as possible to carry the required distance.
17. Injury or rebound can be avoided by reducing the shock of the impact.
18. The force of impact depends on the weight of the moving object and the speed of the object.
19. The more gradual the reduction of this force, the less likely is injury or rebound to occur.
20. Force should be absorbed gradually by increasing the distance and the time over which the force is absorbed.
21. The nearer to the center of gravity the force is received and the more nearly the center of gravity is kept over the center of the base, the more readily balance will be maintained.

Evaluative criteria

1. Can the child select an appropriate amount of force for the task?
2. Can the child adjust the body position to absorb the force of the body or object appropriately?

Objective Three: Time

In exploring time children become aware of time in space as a measure of speed and in moving rhyth-mically to their own rhythm or an imposed rhythm.

Activities

1. We are going to move in general space, changing speed. Select two points in the room. How quickly can you move from one to the other? How slowly? Can you pick a speed between? How did your movements change as you went faster? Slower? What determined how fast you could go as you moved in general space?
2. Moving in general space, respond to the instructions of the teacher. Move very fast. Now slow down. Speed up to a medium speed. Now move very slowly. Speed up just a little. Now move faster. How did you adjust your speed to the instructions?
3. Think of a skill that you know. How slowly can you do it? Move in slow motion. Think of another. Can you move even slower?
4. Responding to clapping, a drumbeat, or recorded music, move in time to the beat. Begin clapping in time and then begin moving and clapping. Were you able to move in time to the clap? Faster? Slower?
5. Moving to a count, can you make a balanced shape on three body parts within the count of four? Take all four counts to get there. Try another. Can you curl in four counts? Stretch? Roll?

Related knowledge

Speed is a measure of time. Speed varies from slow to fast. It is important to select a speed appropriate for the task, one that is not too fast or too slow. One must always control speed while moving.

Rapid acceleration or deceleration may be important in some movement tasks.

Evaluative criteria

1. Can the child move at varying speeds, ranging from very slow to very fast? (Young children often do not have a slow.)
2. Does the child control speed when moving in general space?
3. Can the child move to an imposed rhythm?

Objective Four: Flow

Flow is the ability to combine movements smoothly. Flow may be *free,* in which there is a continuity of movement, or *bound,* characterized by the control or momentary restraint of movement in which the body may be stopped. In the early years children have difficulty in combining movements without a break in the action. As they mature in their motor development, children are able to combine movements in a flowing manner.

Activities

1. Moving in general space. Can you keep moving as you change direction or pathway to avoid others? Can you change locomotor movements on the signal without stopping? How did you plan so you could keep moving? Continue moving, changing speed, level, etc.
2. Can you combine locomotor and nonlocomotor movements as you move in space? Begin from a stationary position, doing nonlocomotor movements. Now begin moving in general space, adding locomotor movements. If you wish, you may continue the nonlocomotor movements as you move or stop them.
3. Combine two different movements into a movement sequence. Can you perform them smoothly? As they are ready, increase the number of movements to be included or add changes in level, direction, force, or time.

Related knowledge

Terminology: flow, movement sequence.

Evaluative criteria

1. Can the child smoothly combine movements?
2. Can the child create a movement sequence?

SUMMARY

The movement content provides the basis for understanding human movement. Three general areas are explored: body awareness, space, and qualities of movement.

Body awareness enhances the children's understanding of themselves as movers. Activities enrich their understanding of body parts, the movement potential of these body parts, and how the body parts move together to perform a variety of movement tasks. Other areas of study include the body as an instrument of communication and tension and conscious relaxation.

Space concepts are important to successful movement. In many individual and group activities in which there is competition between two or more individuals, success is most often achieved through the manipulation of the available space. Topics for study include self and general space, level, direction, pathway, and range of movement.

Qualities of movement include the creation, application, and absorption of force, balance, time, and flow. These elements are controlled by the individual, resulting in effective, efficient movements.

Since these concepts are important to all movement, study begins early in the elementary school experience. Once understood, they may be further developed through a variety of physical education activities.

REFERENCES

1. Auxter, D., and Pyfer, J.: Principles and methods of adapted physical education and recreation, ed. 4, St. Louis, 1985, Times Mirror/Mosby.
2. Broer, M., and Zernicke, R.: Efficiency of human movement, ed. 4, New York, 1973, Holt, Rinehart, & Winston.
3. Gilliom, B.: Cherp Basic movement education for children: rationale and teaching units, Reading, Mass., 1970, Addison-Wesley Publishing Co.
4. Laban, R.: Mastery of movement, ed. 3 (revised by L. Ullman), London, 1971, MacDonald & Evans, Ltd.
5. Logsdon, B., and others: Physical education for children: a focus on the teaching process, ed. 2, Philadelphia, 1984, Lea & Febiger.
6. Rasmus, C., and Fowler, J., editors: Movement activities for places and spaces, Reston, Va., 1983, AAHPERD.
7. Riggs, M., editor: Movement education for preschool children, Reston, Va., 1980, AAHPERD.

ADDITIONAL READINGS

Barrett, K.: Phys ed is movement ed. In NASPE: Echoes of influence for elementary school physical education, Reston, Va., 1977, AAHPERD.
The movement content in elementary school physical education and examples of how the content is implemented.

Cunningham, C.: How we teach it balance challenges. In NASPE: Echoes of influence, Reston, Va., 1977, AAHPERD.
Balance challenges on skates, stilts, and unicylces.

DeSorbe, B.: How do you get the ball from here to there? JOPER **48**(6):35, June 1977.
Using exploration and probelm-solving techniques to teach children about angles and trajectories.

Ratliffe, T.: Using worksheets in physical education, JOPERD **53**(7):47, September 1982.
Developing worksheets that reinforce classroom learning in reading and writing and enhance understanding in physical education.

Sakola, S.: A k-6 progression built on organizing concepts, JOPERD **53**(7):38, September 1982.
Developing skills through progressions that encourage transfer of learning and application of movement conepts.

II

FUNDAMENTAL MOVEMENT SKILLS

CHAPTER OBJECTIVES

1 To discuss concerns for the planning and conduct of activities to develop fundamental movements

2 To analyze the fundamental movements and identify mechanical principles involved in their execution

3 To describe activities for the development of fundamental movements

4 To integrate the movement content in the teaching of fundamental movement

One objective of the physical education program at the elementary school level is the development of motor skills. The mastery of these movement patterns is essential to future success in the development of sports or dance skills that may be used throughout one's lifetime.

The movement content of the previous chapter is an important part of motor skill learning. If it is appropriately taught, body awareness is enhanced in the learning of these motor skills. In addition, children learn to apply space and quality of movement concepts as the particular skills and situations warrant.

As children develop the ability to perform these skills in various situations, they should also begin to understand body mechanics and the laws that govern human movement.

PLANNING AND CONDUCTING FUNDAMENTAL MOVEMENT EXPERIENCES

Learning motor skills requires instruction and the early correction of errors. Children should understand the important aspects of each skill and the consequences of executing skills incorrectly. This will help them begin to analyze their own performance and adjust their body movements to perform various motor tasks. A part of the learning experience should involve the verbalization of the major aspects of the skill, how the body is used to accomplish the task. Without the basic understanding of how the skill should be executed, children who perform a skill well may have more difficulty in adjusting the skill to meet the new demands of various movement tasks and applying what they know about one skill to a similar skill. Children also learn the mechanical principles that apply in the execution of the movement skills. Once they are understood, the teacher should assist the children in applying these mechanical principles to new situations.

Beginning learning experiences should provide the children with an opportunity to explore the use of their bodies and various pieces of equipment. If guided properly, the children acquire a better understanding of the use of the body in performing skills and also the properties of the equipment they are using. As the children are working, the leader should use the movement vocabulary in raising questions. Learning experiences should encourage the children to use what they know about their potential body movement, space, and movement qualities.

"

Equipment used should be of an appropriate size and weight for elementary school children. As a part of the learning experience children should be exposed to a variety of equipment to enable them to adjust their body movements as the equipment demands. A list of equipment for elementary school children is found in the Appendix.

Activities for practicing skills should be arranged to encourage the use of the best possible techniques. For example, targets used for ball skills should be large enough and far enough away so the children must execute the skill correctly to be successful.

To develop fundamental movements children need the opportunity for maximum participation. In many activities all the children may be working simultaneously to perfect their skills. If equipment is being used, it may be necessary to use a station approach to learning, especially if there is not sufficient equipment for all to be active at one time.

Controlling one's movements for the safety of oneself and others is an important part of the learning experience. Taking responsibility for one's movement should be encouraged always. The following sections include the analysis of a variety of movement skills that should be mastered during the elementary school years. Teaching suggestions and activities to aid in the development of these skills are included.

LOCOMOTOR SKILLS
Walk

Although the walk is the *locomotor movement* attempted first by children and generally mastered by the time the children reach the elementary school, the technique continues to undergo refinement through the adolescent years.

The walk in a forward direction is executed by transferring the body weight from one foot to the other as the legs swing alternately in front of the body in an even rhythm. As the leg moves forward, balance is temporarily lost but is regained by the placement of the forward foot on the floor. The body weight is transferred from two feet to one foot, back to two feet, and then to the other foot. The foot placement begins with contact on the heel, moving to the outer edges of the foot and finally toward the toes. One foot remains in contact with the floor at all times. As the forward heel touches the ground, the rear heel is lifted to begin the next leg swing. The toes point straight ahead, and placement of the feet forward is on either side of an imaginary line on the ground that bisects the body. The body is erect with

Figure 11-1

Evaluative criteria for the walk.

- Head is up, body erect.
- Leg swings forward.
- Arms swing in opposition to legs.
- Heel-to-toe placement of foot.
- Toes point straight ahead.

the head up. The arms swing freely at the sides in a forward and backward direction in opposition to the leg movements. The walk may also be executed in a backward direction.

Mechanical analysis
Balance

Walking is a matter of moving the body weight beyond the base of support and the line of gravity and regaining balance by stepping on the forward foot to bring the center of gravity back over the base of support. Since there is a period when both feet are in contact with the ground, stability is easily maintained.

Force

The action is begun with a diagonal push-off backward against the ground with the ball of one foot.

The push of the foot directs the force forward and upward through the center of the body weight.

The force is absorbed gradually over a period of time as the weight is taken first on the heel, then on the outer edges of the foot, and finally on the toes.

Teaching points

1. Keep the body erect with the head up and the eyes facing forward.
2. Point the toes straight ahead.
3. Place the feet a comfortable distance apart.

Movement concepts

Children should experience walking:
1. In general space, avoiding others and recognizing how walking changes with the space available.
2. Forward, backward, and to the side and changing direction without hesitation.
3. In various pathways.
4. Changing the range of step.
5. At various speeds.
6. Varying the force used.
7. Changing the use of body parts to walk in different ways.
8. In relation to others or objects.

Activities

1. Walk in general space controlling your movements to avoid contact with others.
2. Walk changing direction. In which directions is it easiest to walk? Hardest? Why?
3. Walk in a curved pathway. Straight lines. Or combinations of curves, straight lines or both.
4. Walk changing the length of stride. Take big steps. Little steps.
5. Walk changing the speed of your walk. Can you walk faster? Slower?
6. Walk taking heavy steps. Soft steps.
7. Change the amount of space available. How does your walk change as the space gets larger? Smaller?
8. Who can walk like a clown? A happy person? A soldier? A sad person? An old person? A tired person? As if in a parade?
9. Walk leaning forward. Stiff legged. Toeing in. Toeing out. With wide steps. With narrow steps.
10. Walk on your heels. On your toes. Flat footed.
11. Walk as if you were walking on ice. In mud. On glue.
12. Walk with a partner. Now hold hands and walk again. Can you stay together?
13. Walk with a partner moving in step with that person.
14. Walk with a partner standing behind one another. Face to face.

Run

The mechanics of the run are similar to those of the walk. However, in the run the speed of movement is faster, the stride is longer, the arms are used more purposefully to add power to the movement, and there is a time when the individual is airborne.

The run is executed with the head up and the body leaning slightly forward. The support foot contacts the ground close to the body's center of gravity. At slow speeds initial contact is with the heel or the whole foot. At faster speeds the lateral border of the ball of the foot touches first. The foot placement is with the toes pointing straight ahead. On contact the bending of the knee and consequently the increased flexion in the ankle permit a greater thrust of the push-off foot. As the foot is placed on the ground, the push-off sends the body momentarily into the air as the opposite leg swings forward. As the leg reaches forward, the knee swings forward and upward as the lower leg flexes, bringing the heel close to the buttocks. The arms are bent at the elbows and move in opposition to the leg movements, helping to drive the body forward. The arm swing is in a forward/backward direction.

Mechanical analysis
Force

The bending of the knee and ankle on contact allows the leg muscles to extend more forcefully, thus creating greater force, which results in greater speed.

The action of the arms adds to the movement by increasing the contributing muscles involved.

As the body moves forward on contact, the location of the center of gravity forward of the supporting foot permits a greater horizontal component and thus more thrust forward (horizontal) and less force upward (vertical). There is more of a vertical component than in the walk.

Teaching points

1. Keep the head up and the eyes looking forward.
2. Swing the arms in a forward/backward direction.
3. The foot lands softly on the running surface.
4. The length of stride is a comfortable distance.
5. Bring up the heel near the buttocks during the recovery phase.

Figure 11-2

Evaluative criteria for the run.

- Head is up, body leans forward.
- Knee swings forward and upward with lower leg flexed.
- Arms drive in opposition to legs.
- Nonsupport phase with both feet off the ground.
- Foot contact under the center of gravity; toes point forward.

Movement concepts

Children should experience running:

1. In general space avoiding contact with others and recognizing how running changes with the space available.
2. Forward, backward, and to the side and changing direction without hesitation.
3. In various pathways.
4. Changing the range of stride.
5. At various speeds.
6. Varying the force of the run.
7. Changing the use of body parts to run in different ways.
8. In relation to others or objects.
9. For time or distance.
10. Noticing how running changes for sprints and distance running.

Activities

1. Run in place. Then run in general space controlling movements to avoid contact with others.
2. Run changing directions. Can you run forward? Backward? To the right? To the left?
3. Run in a straight line. Now a curved pathway. Can you combine a straight line and a curve as you run?
4. Run changing the length of stride. Take small steps. Take long steps.
5. (Change the amount of space available). How does your running change as the space becomes smaller? Larger?
6. Run changing speed as you go. Can you run slower? Faster?
7. Run changing the speed of the arm movement. How does that affect your run?
8. Run for a specified distance, such as a 30-yard dash.
9. Run for a long distance, such as once around the field.
10. Run a shuttle run.
11. Run for time. How far can you go in 10 seconds?
12. Run for a long time. Can you set a pace and continue to run for 3 minutes?
13. Run around obstacles in an obstacle course.
14. Run leaning forward. Stiff legged. Toeing in. Toeing out. With wide steps. With narrow steps.
15. Run on your heels. On your toes. Flat footed.
16. Run with a partner. Hold hands and run again. Can you stay together?
17. Run with a partner moving in step with that person.
18. Run with a partner standing one behind the other. Now face to face.
19. Run in a group following one another. Can you set a pace where all can stay together?
20. Run in a group of four or five persons, one behind the other. As you run, the last person sprints to the head of the line. Repeat.

Jump

The *jump* has many variations depending on the task to be accomplished. The take-off may be from one or both feet with the landing on two feet. The action may begin from a stationary position, or it may be preceded by a run or walk. The vertical jump and the horizontal jump for distance are described in this section. The standing and running long jump and the high jump are described in Chapter 16.

In preparation for the vertical jump a deep crouch is taken by flexing the hips, knees, and ankles. As the

Figure 11-3

Evaluative criteria for the vertical jump.

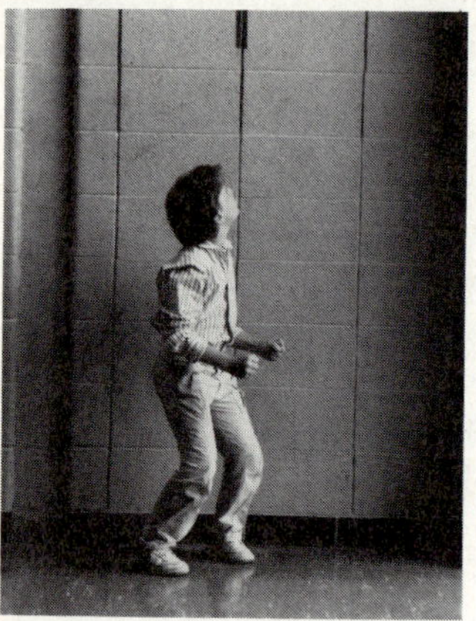

- Flexion in hips, knees, and ankles.

- Forceful extension of legs.
- Arms reach forward and upward.
- Body fully extended.

- Soft landing with flexion in ankles, knees, and hips.

jumping action begins, there is a forceful extension of the legs, and the arms move forward and upward to aid in the lift of the body. The body remains fully extended until the feet are ready to touch the floor on the landing. At that time flexion in the ankles, knees, and hips helps absorb the force for a soft landing.

If the purpose of the jump is to reach or touch an object high above the head, the reaching arm is extended well above the body and the other arm at the height of the jump.

In the horizontal jump for distance the jump is usually preceded by several running steps. The take-off is from one foot, with the landing on two feet.

Before the take-off, flexion in the hip, knee, and ankle allows for greater thrust to propel the body off the ground. The arms move in opposition to the legs during the approach and swing in the direction of the jump during the take-off. The head is up and the body is extended during the take-off and flight. On landing both legs reach forward and the ankles, knees, and hips flex for a soft landing. The arms are bent and may be held out to the sides to aid in balance on landing. The feet are a comfortable width apart.

Mechanical analysis
Force

Flexion in the hip, knee, and ankle permit the force to be applied over a greater distance.

The force is applied downward and backward and results in the body being propelled upward and forward in flight.

Through the flexion of ankles, knees, and hips, the force is absorbed in landing over a greater distance. The arm action aids the jump in that more muscles are contributing to the effort. Each force is applied at the optimal time when the preceding one has made its greatest contribution to the task.

Balance

In jumping for distance, the arms are positioned out to the sides of the body to add stability to the flight and landing.

Teaching points
Vertical jump

1. Drop to a deep crouch before the take-off.
2. Use the arms, timing them with the leg action, to aid the jump.
3. Reach to full body extension at the height of the jump.
4. Land softly by bending the knees.

Horizontal jump for distance

1. Take off from one foot.
2. Perform the approach and the take-off as one continuous action.
3. Swing the arms forward to aid in the jump and

Figure 11-4

Evaluative criteria for the horizontal jump.

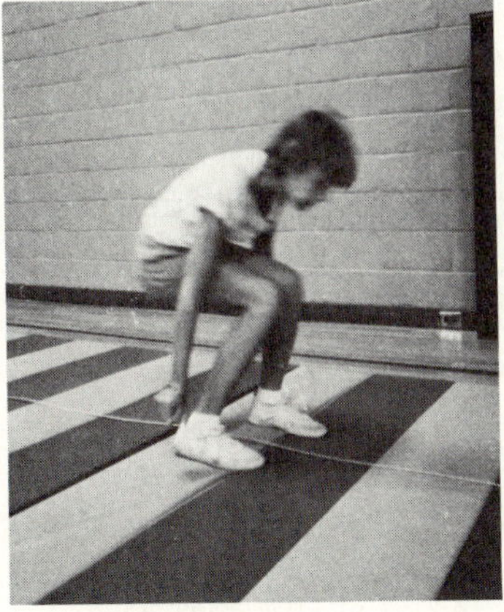

- Body is erect with a forward lean.
- Take-off leg flexed at hip, knee, and ankle.

- Arms swing forward; legs extend forcefully.

- Legs reach forward; arms aid in balance.
- Soft landing with flexion in ankles, knees, and hips.

slightly to the side for balance.
4. Land softly by bending the knees.
5. Reach forward on landing.

Movement concepts

Children should experience jumping:
1. In all directions.
2. Various heights.
3. Various distances.
4. Over objects.
5. Changing the use of body parts to jump in different ways.
6. Varying the approach used.

Activities

1. Jump forward, backward, and to the side.
2. Jump varying the height jumped. (For jumping over objects a bamboo pole or jump rope may be held loosely by supports or children so that it falls if the jumper makes contact with it.)
3. Jump over objects such as beanbags, benches, or boxes.
4. Jump in and out of a hoop placed on the floor.
5. Jump a specified distance such as 3 feet.
6. Jump and vary the distance jumped.
7. Jump with a partner. Now hold hands and jump again.
8. Jump varying the approach used.
9. Jump and turn in place.
10. Jump moving forward and turning while in flight.
11. Vary the landings used: Land on one foot, make a four-point landing, land and roll, land with feet apart, land with feet close together, etc.
12. Jump over a moving object.
13. Execute a series of jumps maintaining momentum.
14. Jump off an object such as a box or bench.
15. Jump onto an object such as a box or bench.
16. Jump and touch an object high overhead, or make a chalk mark on the wall at the height of the jump.

Hop

The *hop* requires good balance and sufficient leg strength to propel the body upward and forward from one leg.

The hop is a push off from one foot and a landing on the same foot. The nonsupporting leg is held up with the knee bent and usually with the foot held back. The body is erect. As the hop is initiated, flexion in the hip, knee, and ankle increases to permit greater force to overcome the body's inertia and project the body into the air. The arms are bent at the elbow and are out slightly from the body to aid in balance. The arms may be moved upward to help increase the height of the hop. The landing should be soft, with flexion in the ankle, knee, and hip to absorb the force. Contact with the ground begins with the forward part of the foot, shifting gradually to the ball of the foot and finally to the heel.

Mechanical analysis
Projectiles

The laws governing projectiles apply to the hop.

To increase vertical distance the angle of take-off should be as close to vertical as possible.

Balance

Since the support is on one leg only, holding the arms out to the sides improves balance.

Force

Flexion in the hip, knee, and ankle allows the leg muscles to extend more forcefully on the push-off.

Flexion at the hip, knee, and ankle on the landing permits the force to be absorbed more gradually over time.

Teaching points

1. Land softly by bending the knees.
2. Use the arms to help propel the body upward.
3. Use the arms to the sides to maintain balance.
4. Establish a rhythm for hopping to hop several times in succession.

Movement concepts

Children should experience hopping:
1. In general space avoiding contact with others.
2. In all directions.
3. In various pathways.
4. Changing the range of step.
5. Varying the height of the hop.
6. At various speeds.
7. Maintaining a steady rhythm to enable them to hop repeatedly on one foot.
8. Changing the use of body parts to hop in different ways.
9. In relation to others or objects.

Activities

1. Hop in general space controlling movements to avoid contact with others.
2. Hop changing direction. In which direction was

Figure 11-5

Evaluative criteria for the hop.

- Body is erect.
- Push-off with one foot.
- Use arms for balance.
- Land bending at the hip, knee, and ankle.

it easiest to hop? Most difficult?
3. Hop in a straight line. Now a curved line. Can you combine straight lines, curves, or both as you hop?
4. Hop changing the length of your hop. Take a short hop. Now a long hop.
5. (Change the amount of space available.) How does your hopping change as the space gets smaller? Larger?
6. Hop changing speed as you hop. Can you hop slowly? Faster?
7. Hop over obstacles such as a rope or low balance beam.
8. Hop around obstacles scattered in the area.
9. Hop in place several times, and then hop in general space the same number of times.
10. Hop and turn in place.
11. Hop on one foot several times; then hop on the other foot the same number. Repeat several times.
12. Hop changing the position of your arms as you

Figure 11-6

Evaluative criteria for the leap.

- Head is up body leans forward.
- Flexion in hip, knee, and ankle to thrust on take-off.

- Arms drive in opposition to legs and upward.
- Legs extended.

On landing there is flexion in the hip, knee, and ankle for a soft landing.

---

hop. Out to the sides. One forward and one backward. Close to your sides. Over your head.
13. Hop in and out of a hoop placed on the floor.
14. Execute a high hop. A low hop.
15. Perform a series of hops with each progressively higher than the hop before.
16. Hop with a partner. Now hold hands and hop again. Can you stay together?
17. Hop in step with a partner.
18. Hop with a partner standing one behind the other. Now face to face.

Leap

The *leap* is similar to the run. However there is a greater vertical component as the body moves through the air in the nonsupported phase of the skill. In the leap the body remains airborne much longer than in the run with the objective being to cover a greater distance while moving through the air. The body is more fully extended than in the run as the performer reaches forward in the air.

The take-off is from one foot with the landing on the other foot. The arms move in opposition to the legs as in the run but move upward as well to increase the height of the leap. During flight the take-off leg is fully extended with the forward leg reaching forward for maximum distance. To absorb force the landing should be soft with flexion in the ankle, knee, and hip of the contacting leg. The arms aid in balance.

The leap is usually preceded by a series of running steps.

Mechanical analysis

The mechanical analysis is similar to the run with increased thrust from the take-off leg to increase the time of the nonsupported phase.

Projectiles

To increase the vertical component the angle of take-off should be closer to the vertical than in the run.

Figure 11-7

Evaluative criteria for the slide.

- Body is erect; head is up.
- Step (leap) to the side (long).
- Draw, transfer weight (short).

- Step (leap) again with the same foot leading (long).

Teaching points

1. The take-off projects the body upward to get maximum height.
2. Use the arm swing to aid getting the body upward.
3. Get full extension of the legs during flight.
4. Land softly by bending the knee.
5. Use the arms to maintain balance on landing.

Movement concepts

Children should experience leaping:
1. In general space avoiding contact with others.
2. In all directions.
3. Changing the range of the step.
4. Varying the height of the step.
5. Changing the use of body parts to leap in different ways.
6. Varying the approach.
7. For varying distances.

Activities

1. Leap over a low obstacle.
2. Leap over two ropes placed on the floor some distance apart.
3. Combine the leap with a series of runs and repeat, for example, run, run, leap; run, run, leap.
4. Leap over a series of obstacles while maintaining momentum throughout.
5. Take small leaps. Wide leaps.
6. Take low leaps. High leaps.
7. Holding hands with a partner, leap together.
8. Leap over a series of obstacles that require varying distances to cover.

COMBINATIONS OF LOCOMOTOR SKILLS

The gallop, slide, and skip are combinations of the locomotor skills previously described that are performed in an uneven rhythm. These skills are often used in children's dance and rhythmic activities found in Chapters 17 through 20.

Slide (gallop)

The *slide* consists of a combination of a short leaping step and a walk. The slide is initiated with a step to the side. This is followed by a drawing or closing

Figure 11-8

Evaluative criteria for the skip.

- Body erect head up.
- Step (long).
- Hop on same foot (short).

- Lead leg lifts.
- Arms swing forward and upward.

The skip is repeated with a step on the opposite foot.

step with the other foot, bringing it to the side of the leading foot. As the weight is transferred to the trailing foot, the lead leg reaches to the side again. The same foot leads each step. The slide is in uneven rhythm with the step being a longer step than the draw phase of the slide.

A slide performed in a forward direction is known as a *gallop.*

Step	Hop	Step	Hop
1	and	2	and
Long	Short	Long	Short

Mechanical analysis

Many of the principles that apply to the walk and the leap also apply to the slide. In addition:

Force

The leaping action generates the force either sideward or forward.

Balance

It is important to keep the center of gravity over the base, especially as the base decreases in size with the drawing foot.

Teaching points

1. Keep the legs relaxed.
2. Keep an uneven rhythm.

• • •

Activities for the slide and gallop follow the discussion of the skip.

Skip

The *skip* combines a walk and a hop in an uneven rhythm. Commonly executed moving forward, it may also be performed while moving backward.

The step is initiated by taking a step forward on one foot. This is followed by a hop on the same foot, during which time the opposite foot is brought forward to begin the next step. The step forward is performed on the first beat in the rhythm, and the hop is actually taken on the upbeat to the next beat. The rhythm is analyzed as follows:

Step	Draw	Step	Draw
1	and	2	and
Long	Short	Long	Short

As the skip is taken, the arms move in opposition to the legs and may be brought upward as well as forward, especially when height is desired in the skipping motion.

For children having difficulty establishing the rhythm of skipping, it may be helpful to have them skip with another child or the teacher.

Mechanical analysis

The mechanical principles of the walk and hop also apply in the skip. In addition:

Balance

The arms held out to the sides add stability to the narrow base of support.

Force

The upward swing of the arms aids in propelling the body up into the air as does the lifting of the non-supporting leg on the hop.

Teaching points

1. Swing the opposite leg forward on the hop.
2. Swing the arms to add height and distance on each skip.
3. Lift the lead leg for height on the hop.
4. Keep the uneven rhythm going.

Movement concepts for the skip, gallop, or slide

When skipping, galloping, or sliding children should experience moving:
1. With control in general space while recognizing how the skip, gallop, or slide changes with space available.
2. Forward, backward, and to the side changing direction without hesitation.
3. In various pathways.
4. Changing the range of the step.
5. At various speeds.
6. Varying the height of the step.
7. Changing the use of the body parts to skip, gallop, or slide in different ways.
8. In relation to others and objects.

Activities for the skip, gallop, or slide

1. Move in general space controlling movements to avoid contact with others.
2. Move in general space changing direction.
3. Move in a curved, a straight, or a combination of pathways.
4. Move changing the length of stride. Take large steps. Small steps.
5. (Change the amount of space available as the children are moving.) How does your movement change as the space becomes smaller? Larger?
6. Move changing speed as you skip, gallop, or slide.
7. Move getting as much height in flight as possible.
8. Move covering as much distance as possible.
9. Move with a partner without holding hands. Now move again holding hands.
10. Move lightly. Heavily.
11. Move around obstacles placed on the floor.
12. Move in step with a partner.
13. Move with a partner standing one behind the other. Face to face.

CONTROLLING ONE'S MOVEMENT
Start

In starting the feet are in a comfortable forward/backward stride position with flexion in the ankles, knees, and hips. The body leans slightly forward; the head is up. The arms are bent at the elbow and ready to drive in opposition to the leg action. At the start there is a forceful extension of the legs and a driving action of the arms in the direction of the start.

Mechanical analysis
Balance

The body lean aids in getting the body off balance and quickly into motion.

Force

The flexion in the ankles, knees, and hips permits a forceful extension of the legs to get the body moving quickly.

The arm action adds momentum to the start.

Movement concepts

Children should experience starting:
1. Using body parts in different ways to affect the start.
2. To move in various directions.

3. To achieve various speeds (varying force).
4. Various locomotor movements.
5. In relation to others or objects.

Activities

1. Practice starting with feet close together. Wide apart. A comfortable distance. Which seems best?
2. Practice starting with the body leaning forward. Standing straight. Leaning slightly backward. Which did you like best?
3. Practice starting with the arms in various positions, such as at your sides, bent and driving at the start, behind your back, over your head. Which helped best to get you off to a good start?
4. Practice starting moving forward. Backward. To the side.
5. Try starting for a walk. A run. A skip. A hop. A gallop.
6. Try to get off to a fast start. A moderate one. A slow start.
7. Holding hands with a partner start together.
8. Start on the signal: Ready, Go.
9. Start from behind a line.

Stop

In stopping, the initial action places one foot out in front of the other in a forward/backward stride position. To absorb force on contact with the floor there is flexion in the ankle, knee, and hip. The arms may be extended slightly to the side to aid in balance. The body weight is brought back and down over the base of support.

Mechanical analysis
Balance

The flexion in the ankles, knees, and hips lowers the center of gravity for greater stability.

The body weight is pulled back so the line of gravity falls within the base of support.

The forward/backward stride position used in stopping, while moving forward, allows the base of support to be enlarged in the direction of the force and thus aids stability.

Force

The flexion in the ankles, knees, and hips permits the force to be absorbed more gradually.

Movement concepts

Children should experience stopping:
1. Using their body parts in different ways to absorb the force.
2. From various speeds.
3. From various locomotor movements.
4. While moving in various directions.
5. In relation to others and objects.

Activities

1. Stop with your feet together. Wide apart. A com-

fortable distance. A forward/backward stride. A side stride.
2. Stop leaning forward. Standing upright. Leaning back slightly.
3. Stop with your arms at your sides. Over your head. Behind your back. Out in front of you.
4. Stop while moving slowly. From a moderate speed. Fast.
5. Stop while skipping. Walking. Running. Hopping. Galloping.
6. Stop while moving forward. Backward. Sideways.
7. Moving with a partner stop together.
8. Stop on the signal.
9. Stop at a line.

Dodge

Dodging involves the quick shifting of the body or body parts away from an object or a person. The direction of movement and/or the pathway of movement may be changed.

When dodging the individual hesitates in moving, bends the knees, and shifts the body weight over the base of support and then in the new direction of movement. This is followed by a push-off with one or both feet to get moving in the new direction of movement.

Mechanical analysis
Balance

The bending of the knees lowers the center of gravity and increases stability before the change of direction.

To increase stability the base is enlarged in the direction of the force.

To move quickly the body leans in the new direction, moving the body weight outside the base of support.

Force

The bending of the knees allows a more forceful extension of the legs in pushing off to move in the new direction.

Movement concepts

Children should experience dodging:
1. Around stationary objects in space.
2. Around moving objects in space.
3. Using body parts in different ways to dodge.
4. While moving at various speeds.
5. In different directions.
6. While moving in various pathways.
7. While moving with various locomotor movements.

Activities

1. Move in general space. Dodge the stationary objects placed throughout the room.
2. Move in general space. Dodge anyone you meet. (Reduce the size of the area and repeat.)
3. Move with different locomotor movements while dodging individuals or objects.
4. Dodge the balls that half of the class roll toward you.
5. Move with a ball in general space. Can you dodge others and the balls they are controlling?

Landing

Landing after a period of flight requires the controlled and gradual absorption of force as body parts contact a surface. In landing on the feet contact is made first with the balls of feet and rolls down the foot to the heels. The force is absorbed by flexion beginning in the ankles, moving to the knees, and finally reaching the hips. The head is up and the upper body is straight. The arms may be extended out to the sides for balance.

Mechanical analysis
Force

Force is gradually absorbed by flexion beginning in the joints closest to the point of contact and spreading to joints farther away.

Balance

Flexion in the ankles, knees, and hips lowers the center of gravity, which aids in stability.

Keeping the head up and upper body straight keeps the center of gravity over the base of support.

Movement concepts

Children should experience:
1. The use of different body parts to land.
2. The controlled relaxation of body parts.
3. The use of body parts in different ways to land.

Activities

1. Land in various positions, such as landing on one foot, two feet, or hands and feet.
2. Working with a partner, jump and land together. Can you land differently?
3. Land in various ways while jumping for distance.
4. Land in various ways while jumping over an object.
5. Land in various ways while jumping from a bench or box.

NONLOCOMOTOR MOVEMENTS

Nonlocomotor, or axial, **movements** are generally performed from a stationary base. However, they may be done in combination with locomotor movements as well as performed in a standing, kneeling, sitting, or lying position.

Bend/Stretch

Bending is a movement around a joint where two body parts meet. It is also called flexion.

Stretching is an extension at the joints. Stretching becomes increasingly important as children mature in maintaining flexibility and in warming up for physical activity to prevent muscle soreness. Static stretching is most effective. After force is exerted in the stretched position, it should be held for a period of time (5 to 30 seconds).

Movement concepts

Children should experience bending and stretching:
1. Various body parts leading to a beginning understanding of the movement potential of each body part.
2. To feel the tension and relaxation in muscles involved in stretching and bending.
3. In varying ranges of movement.

Activities

1. Bend one body part. Now stretch it. Try another. Another.
2. Bend two body parts at the same time. Does one bend more than another? Try two more.
3. Bend several body parts at the same time. Now stretch them. Try it again.
4. Stretch your body as tall as you can. Now bend (curl) to become as small as possible. Try it again, but this time do it while lying on the floor.
5. Jump and stretch. Land and bend.
6. Working with a partner, one is the leader. The leader bends one body part. Can you bend another? Keep going. How many different body parts bend? Now repeat the activity, stretching body parts one at a time.

Push/Pull

The push is a forceful movement that moves an object away from the body or the body away from an object. The pull is a forceful movement of an object closer to the body or the body closer to an object.

Movement concepts

Children should experience:
1. The effects of pushing close to and far from the object's center of gravity.
2. The use of various muscle groups to perform pushing and pulling movements.
3. Pushing and pulling with differing amounts of force.

Activities

1. Push or pull light objects. Moderate objects. Heavy objects. (These may be real or imaginary.)
2. Try pushing an object using different body parts, such as arms only, trunk, or legs.
3. Pull an object using various body parts.
4. Try pushing an object while standing. Sitting. Kneeling. Lying down. Try to pull the object from these positions.
5. Push or pull a partner over the line using various body parts.
6. Push or pull an object quickly. Forcefully. Slowly. Gradually.
7. Push an object through its center of gravity. Above it. Below it. To the side of it.

Swing/Sway

The **swing** is a circular or pendular movement around a fixed center with the axis above the moving part.

The *sway* is a pendular movement with the axis below the moving part.

Movement concepts

Children should experience:
1. Tension and relaxation in body parts.
2. Awareness of which body parts swing and sway.
3. Swinging and swaying at various speeds.
4. Swinging and swaying using body parts in unison, in opposition, or in sequence.
5. Swinging and swaying in various ranges of movement.

Activities

1. Swing or sway different body parts. Swing or sway one body part. Now try another. Another.
2. Swing or sway at different speeds. Can you move slowly? Now increase speed until you move as fast as you can. Now slowly again.
3. Swing and sway in various ranges of movement. Swing one body part with a big swing. Can you swing that same part in a small swing?
4. Swing two body parts in opposition. In unison. In sequence.
5. Swing two or more body parts at the same time.
6. Swing or sway to a beat or musical accompaniment.

Twist/Turn

The *twist* is a rotation of the body or body parts around a stationary base.

The *turn* is partial or full rotation of the body while shifting its base of support.

Movement concepts

Children should experience twisting and turning:
1. Various body parts.
2. In various ranges of motion.
3. At various speeds.
4. Using the body in different ways to maintain balance.

Activities

1. Move one body part in large circles. Small circles.
2. Turn a one-quarter turn. A half turn. A three-quarters turn. A full turn.
3. Twist a body part. Now try another. Another.
4. Twist or turn as you move through space with various locomotor movements.
5. Turn with a partner. Can you twist as well?

6. Twist body parts while standing, sitting, kneeling, and lying down.
7. Try supporting yourself on different body parts. Which parts can you twist or turn on?

MANIPULATIVE SKILLS

Manipulative skills involve the use of body parts to propel an object. A few selected skills are included here. Additional skills may be found in Chapters 14 and 23 through 28.

Vertical Throw

The vertical throw is used by children in their exploration with balls and in a select number of games played at level I.

The ball is held in front of the body in the fingers of two hands, with one hand on either side of the ball. As the throw begins, the ball is lowered and the hips and knees bend to lower the ball further. As the throw begins, the arms are raised and the legs are extended. The arm action is up, with the ball released above shoulder height. The arms continue to follow through straight up following the flight of the ball.

Mechanical analysis
Force

Flexion of the hips and knees permits greater force production for the throw.

The follow-through determines the direction of the flight.

Teaching points

1. Keep the body straight, bending only in the legs.
2. Follow through straight upward.
3. Watch the ball into flight.

Movement concepts

Children should experience:
1. Varying the height of the throw.
2. Using body parts in different ways to perform the skill.
3. Varying the force used to propel the ball.
4. Varying the speed to propel the ball.
5. Throwing balls that vary in size and weight.
6. Controlling the throw so someone else can catch it.

Activities

1. Can you throw the ball so it goes just above your head? Five feet above you? Close to the ceiling

Figure 11-9

Evaluative criteria for the vertical throw.

- Ball held with fingers in two hands.
- Hip and knee flexion as ball is brought down.

- Legs extend.
- Arms are raised.
- Ball released; arms continue to follow flight.

without touching it?

2. How high can you throw the ball and keep it under control?
3. Can your throw the ball forcefully? Softly?
4. Can you throw the ball fast? Slowly?
5. Begin the throw with the ball at different levels.
6. Working with a partner, can you throw the ball up so your partner can run under it and catch it?
7. Can you throw the ball over the rope strung across the gym?
8. Can you throw the ball so the flight is up and in front of you? Back over your head?

Underhand Throw

The underhand throw may be performed using one or two hands to support the ball. In levels I and II many of the children throw a medium-sized ball underhand with two hands since their hands are not yet large enough to control the ball with one hand.

Two-hand underhand throw

The ball is held in the fingers at one side of the body. As the ball is brought back to begin the throw, the body weight shifts to the foot on that side as a step is taken backward. As the ball is brought forward the body weight shifts to the opposite foot, which is forward. The ball is released and the arms follow through in the direction of the throw.

One-hand underhand throw

The one-hand throw is similar to the two-hand throw but the ball is held in the fingers of one hand only.

Mechanical analysis
Force

The backswing and follow-through ensure maximum time to develop force for the throw.

Figure 11-10

Evaluative criteria for the two-hand underhand throw.

- Held in the fingers of two hands.
- Arms swing back; weight shifts back.

- Arms swing forward; step on opposite foot.

- Follow through in direction of the throw.

Figure 11-11

Evaluative criteria for the one-hand underhand throw.

- Ball held in fingers.
- Ball brought back; weight shifts back.

- Arm swings forward; step on opposite foot.

- Follow through in direction of the throw.

The transfer of weight to the rear foot and then to the forward foot permits a greater distance over which to develop force for the throw.

The transfer of weight increases force for the throw because more mass is applied to the throw.

Projectiles

The angle of release of the ball and the velocity of the ball at release determine the distance the ball will travel.

Teaching points

1. Transfer the body weight to the supporting foot on the backswing.
2. Step forward on the opposite foot on the throw.
3. Watch the target throughout the action.

4. The body should face the target on release.
5. Follow through in the direction of the throw.

Movement concepts

Children should experience throwing:
1. At different levels.
2. Various distances.
3. At various speeds.
4. Using body parts in different ways to perform the throw.
5. Varying the force of the throw.
6. Balls of varyious size and weight.
7. With accuracy and control to targets and to partners.

Activities

1. Throw the ball so it hits the wall 5 feet away. Now take a step back and throw again. Continue to move back until you can no longer hit the wall. How did you change your throw to get the ball to the wall?
2. Throw the ball as hard as you can. Now softly.
3. Throw the ball to the high level. The medium level. The low level.
4. Throw the ball as fast as you can. At a moderate speed. Slowly.
5. Throw using the body in different ways. Examples: Throw without the step forward. Hold the ball on top and bottom. Throw without a follow-through.
6. Throw the ball to the target on the wall or into a basket.
7. Throw the ball to a partner. Was your partner able to catch it? Try it again. If you're successful, take a step back and throw again.

Overhand Throw

The overhand throw is a skill that is difficult for some elementary school children. Its success depends on the ability to coordinate the body actions sequentially. In addition the object thrown is relatively small, which requires a great deal of control for accuracy.

Practice should begin at level I, but it is not until levels III and IV that the children begin to use the skill effectively in most games.

The ball is held in the fingers of the throwing hand. As the ball is brought back, initiating the throwing action, the body rotates so the opposite side is presented toward the target and the weight shifts back to the foot on the same side as the throwing hand. The arm is bent at the elbow and the elbow leads slightly as the arm is brought forward for the throw. As the arm comes forward there is a step forward on the opposite foot and the hips rotate forward. The arm extends and the ball is released; the arm follows through in the direction of the throw and finally down across the body. The body is erect and the eyes continue to face in the direction of the throw throughout the throwing action.

It may be helpful to begin young children in a side orientation to the target and straddling a line. In this manner they are already in position for the arm action, the trunk rotation, and the final weight transfer to the opposite foot. Since their side is toward the target, it is natural for them to turn to face the target as they release the ball.

Mechanical analysis
Force

Weight transfer and body rotation increase the distance over which the force is developed.

Projectiles

The angle of release and velocity of the ball at release determine the flight and therefore the distance the ball travels. For maximum distance the ball is released at approximately a 45-degree angle.

Balance

Stability is maintained since the step forward increases the base of support in the direction of the force.

Teaching points

1. Grip the ball with the fingers.
2. Turn the side of the body toward the target.
3. Step forward on the opposite foot.
4. The elbow leads as the arm moves forward.
5. Release the ball as the arm extends.
6. Follow through in the direction of the throw.

Movement concepts

Children should experience throwing:
1. At different levels.
2. Various distances.
3. Varying the force of the throw.
4. The ball at various speeds.
5. Using body parts in different ways to perform the throw.
6. Balls of various size and weight.

Activities

1. (Beginning at a distance for which the children will need a complete arm swing) throw the ball

Figure 11-12

Evaluative criteria for the overhand throw.

- Fingers grip the ball.
- Side to target, weight back.

- Elbow leads.

- Ball release; opposite foot forward.
- Follow through in direction of throw.

to hit the wall. If you are successful, move farther from the wall. Continue to move back until you can no longer hit the wall.

2. Practice throwing so the ball lands on the high part of the wall. The medium level. The low level.
3. Throw the ball as hard as you can to the wall. Now softly. Can you throw the ball so it rebounds to you? So it hits the wall and remains close to the wall?
4. Throw the ball as fast as you can. Slowly.
5. Throw the ball using the body in different ways. Throw with feet parallel. With arms straight.
6. Throw the ball to a target.
7. Throw the ball to a partner. Can you throw it so your partner can catch it? If successful, take a step back and throw again.

Catching

Catching is a difficult skill for elementary school age children, especially catching a small object. Until children can make accurate judgments about the flight of an object, their catching skills are inconsistent. However, they might have more success in catching if the balls they were attempting to catch were thrown with more control and accuracy. Children have more success catching medium-sized balls in the beginning stages of learning. It is not until later development of catching that they catch small balls consistently. Using foam balls may help build confidence in catch-

ing, especially in activities in which children vary the force and level of the throws.

As the object approaches, the child judges where it may be intercepted and moves to a position directly in line with the object at that spot. Eyes are fixed on the object, and the child prepares for the catch by reaching out with both arms toward it. It may be necessary to take one or two steps forward or back to correct for the speed of the object.

As contact is made, the hands are brought in toward the body to absorb the force. The ball should be contacted by the fingers.

Mechanical analysis
Force

Extension of the arms followed by flexion at the elbows as the ball is contacted increases the distance and time over which the force is absorbed.

If the object received is coming forcefully, stepping back with one foot and bringing the arms back to one side of the body allows for a more gradual absorption of force.

Balance

A forward/backward stride position increases stability as the force is received.

Teaching points

1. Move to line up with the ball.
2. Watch the ball into the hands.

Figure 11-13

Evaluative criteria for catching.

- In line with the ball.
- Reaches toward ball with both hands.
- Watches ball into hands.

- Contacts ball and pulls it in toward the body.

3. Gradually absorb the force by pulling the hands in toward the body.

Movement concepts

Children should experience catching objects:
1. Of various sizes and weight.
2. Thrown directly to them, to their left, to their right, in front of, and behind them.
3. Thrown at different levels.
4. Thrown at various speeds.
5. Thrown with varying force.
6. Thrown from close range and from farther away.
7. Using the body in different ways to catch the ball.

Activities

1. (Select several different kinds of objects for the children to catch.) Which objects were easiest to catch? What did you have to do to catch the largest? The smallest? The heaviest? The lightest?
2. Working with a partner, throw a ball back and forth. Throw the ball directly to your partner. Now have him or her move to one side or the other. Back or forward.
3. Practice catching balls at various levels. How did your catching change as you caught a ball coming from the high level? The low level? In which level was it easiest to receive the ball?
4. Working with a partner, begin close together and practice catching. Now move farther apart but only as far as you can be successful in catching.
5. Catch a ball thrown vertically. An underhand throw. An overhand throw. A sidearm throw. Catch a ball that has been struck with the hand. With a paddle.
6. As you catch a ball, take a step forward. Backward. Assume a side stride position before catching the ball.
7. Catch a ball keeping it as far from your body as possible. Now bring it in close.
8. Can you catch the ball with body parts other than your hands?

Striking

Striking is a movement directed toward an object. Various body parts as well as an implement held in the hand may be used. The object to be struck may be stationary or moving. Hand/eye and foot/eye coordination are important to success in striking.

As in throwing, successful striking requires a backswing, contact when optimal speed in the swing has been achieved, and a follow-through in the direction of flight. Usually a forward/backward stride position is assumed with a weight transfer from the rear foot to the forward foot as contact is made with the object. The orientation of the body to the object and the degree of body rotation are dependent on the specific striking action. If an implement is used, it must be gripped firmly to maintain control when contact is made. Practice in striking should begin with the use of the hand and foot. Paddles, bats, sticks, and racquets should be introduced in progression as soon as the children gain control of the action.

Evaluative criteria

Specific striking skills may be found in Chapters 14, 24, and 26 through 28.

Mechanical analysis
Force

The force applied to an object must be great enough to overcome its inertia and the external forces such as wind or friction.

The force produced by the body must be transferred to the object.

The direction of the force applied determines the direction the object will move.

The greater the speed of the implement at contact with the object, the greater the speed of the object struck.

The greater the striking mass at contact, the greater the speed of the object struck. Striking mass is increased by a firm grip on the implement, so the body and the implement become the striking body and the implement become the striking mass.

A force applied to an object above or below its center of gravity results in spin.

The transfer of weight to the rear foot and then to the forward foot increases the length of the arm swing and therefore the amount of force that may be transferred to the object.

The transfer of weight also moves the whole body mass in the direction of the force applied.

Balance

The forward/backward stride adds stability to the action.

Teaching points

1. It is important to have an adequate base of support in striking an object.
2. In preparation for the contact the arm, foot, or object is brought back for a backswing.
3. Contact the object close to its center of gravity.
4. Follow through in the desired direction of flight.
5. Grip the implement firmly.
6. Keep the arm straight prior to contact with the object.

Movement concepts

Children should experience striking objects:
1. With various body parts.
2. With implements varying in size and shape.
3. Varying force.
4. At different points on the object (to learn about spin).
5. At various speeds.
6. That are stationary and moving.
7. Varying in size and weight.
8. From various positions, such as in front of, on top of, to the side of, and behind the object or varying the stance.

Activities

1. Strike a ball using one body part. Strike it again with another body part. Another. What did you have to do to control the object with different body parts?
2. Strike balls or balloons varying in size and weight with your hand, sticks, table tennis paddles, or racquetball or paddle tennis racquets.
3. Strike an object with your hand or an implement so you can strike it again and again. How many times can you hit it with control?
4. Strike an object so it goes to the wall and returns to you.
5. Strike an object as hard as you can. Now softly.
6. Strike an object with just enough force to reach the wall and not rebound.
7. Strike an object so it remains on the ground. Goes into the air. Bounces.
8. Strike an object so it goes directly to your partner. Now to the side of your partner.

SUMMARY

An important goal of the elementary school physical education program is the development of motor skills. Learning begins with the refinement and mastery of motor skills believed to be the basis for many sports and dance skills to be used in later years. These skills include locomotor, nonlocomotor, and manipulative skills as well as those skills used in controlling the body's movement, such as starting, stopping, dodging, and falling.

As children refine these fundamental movements, they learn how the body parts are used to produce efficient and effective movement. In addition they learn to apply and use the movement concepts of body awareness, space, and qualities of movement as they engage in a variety of motor activities designed to enhance their skills and understandings.

REFERENCES

1. Atwater, A.: Cinematographic analyses of human movement. In Wilmore, J., editor: Exercise and sport sciences reviews, vol. 1, New York, 1973, Academic Press, Inc.

2. Broer, M., and Zernicke, R.: Efficiency of human movement, ed. 4, New York, 1973, Holt, Rinehart, & Winston.

3. Corbin, C.: A textbook of motor development, ed. 2, Dubuque, 1980, William C. Brown Co.

4 Gallahue, D.: Understanding motor development in children, New York, 1982, John Wiley & Sons.

5. Roberton, M., and Halverson, L.: Developing children: their changing movement, ed. 2, Philadelphia, 1984, Lea & Febiger.

6. Thomas, J.: Motor development during childhood and adolescence, Minneapolis, 1984, Burgess Publishing Co.

7. Wickstrom, R.: Fundamental motor patterns, ed. 2, Philadelphia, 1977, Lea & Febiger.

ADDITIONAL READINGS

Capon, J.: Perceptual learning stations, JOPER **50**(4):92, April 1979.
The use of stations to enhance motor skill learning.

Heitmann, H.: Integrating concepts into curricular models, JOPER **52**(2):42, February 1981.
A curriculum in which knowledge about human movement is integrated into motor skill learning.

Lewandowski, D.: Shoestrings and shoeboxes, JOPERD **55**(6):34, August 1984.
Homemade equipment to enhance motor skill development.

McClenaghan, B., and Gallahue, D.: Fundamental movement: a developmental and remedial approach, Philadelphia, 1978, W.B. Saunders Co.
A discussion of the development in children of fundamental movement skills, program design, and experiences to enhance their development.

Weiss, M.: Developmental modeling: enhancing children's motor skill acquisition, JOPERD **53**(9):49, November/December 1982.
Strategies for helping children get the most out of demonstrations of motor skills.

Whiting, H.: Acquiring ball skill, Philadelphia, 1971, Lea & Febiger.
A systems analysis of mechanisms involved in ball skill performance.

12

DEVELOPING SOCIAL SKILLS

CHAPTER OBJECTIVES

1 To discuss social development as an important objective of physical education in the elementary school

2 To identify social skills important to success in our society and to successful participation in sports and dance

3 To identify social skills which may be taught in physical education and to select strategies for planned social learning during the elementary school years

4 To describe the importance of play in the development of sex roles

5 To identify stereotyping and discriminatory behavior and strategies to deal with it

The elementary school years are an important period in the emergence of social skills in children. The development of social skills occurs in many different social environments, as identified in Figure 12-1. Each social setting dictates its values and norms for behavior. Through the reinforcement of appropriate behavior and the punishment of inappropriate behavior, the children learn how they must behave. In each setting the role that individuals play, with whom they interact, and how they interact will be clearly determined by significant persons. During childhood these standards of behavior are almost exclusively prescribed by adults.

The children's experiences in school add to their social development. One objective of education in any society is to teach children cultural social values. In the United States these social skills are those required for participation in a democracy. Kindergarten children enter school with little skill in purposefully interacting with others. During the elementary school years children develop many skills important to successful participation in our society.

Since sport and play involve role playing, there is a belief that both are basic contributors to the socialization of children. Piaget believed that games gave children practice with societal rules.[1] Physical educators have included the social development of children as an important goal. Social development has often been considered to be an obvious and automatic result of the physical education group experience. If physical education is to claim the development of social skills as an important outcome of its programs, then the social objectives must be defined clearly. Activities planned and conducted for their achievement and an evaluation process must be in place to determine the extent to which success has been achieved. Social skills to be developed during the elementary school years are listed in Figure 12-2. Physical education experiences that are not carefully planned and conducted not only may result in undesirable behavior but also may be a detriment to continued participation throughout life.

The social objectives of the physical education program focus their emphasis in two directions. First, the physical education experience should foster the development of skills needed to function as a pro-

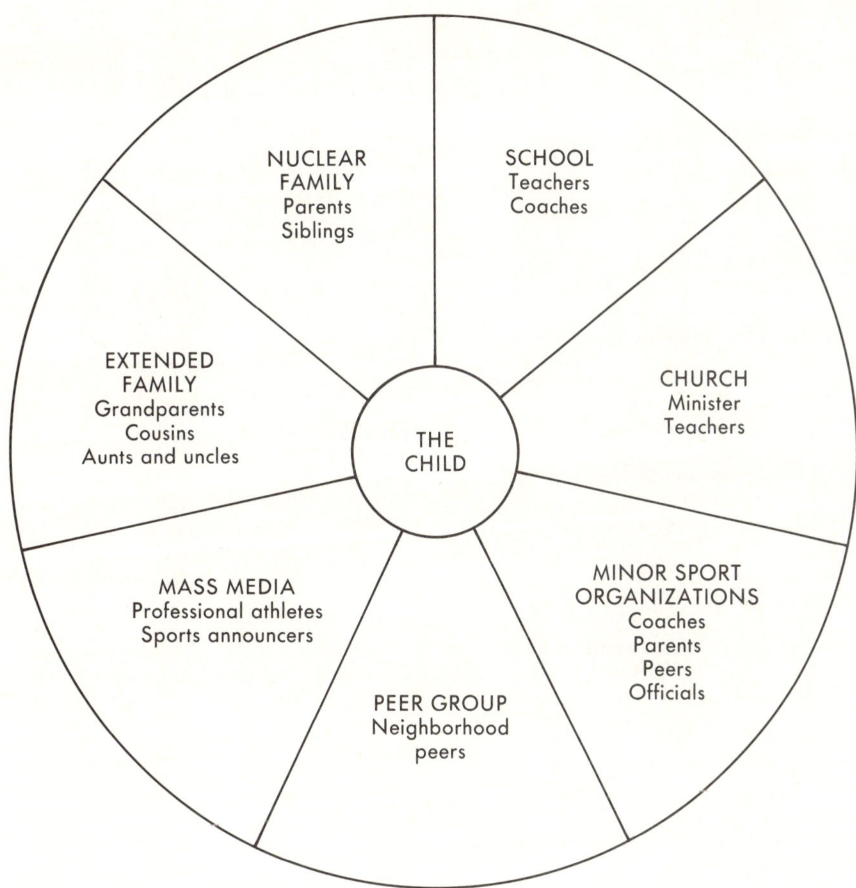

Figure 12-1

Significant others in the social systems in which a child may interact. Modified from McPherson[1].

ductive member of groups in society in general. This objective focuses on the development of skills including assuming responsibility for one's actions and working alone, alongside, and with others. Accepting individual differences and the ideas of others, supporting others, sharing in decision making, and assuming group roles (such as taking on leadership responsibilities) should also be promoted.

Second, the physical education experience should provide for the learning of social skills important for participation in sports and dance. These skills include learning how to compete, how to cooperate, and how to control aggression. Sportsmanship skills such as respect for authority, playing fairly, accepting losing, and being a gracious winner are also important.

Teachers play an important role in the development of social skills. They direct the learning by directly or indirectly interacting with the students, helping them to interact with each other, and reinforcing values and behaviors that occur in the class. Teachers structure the learning environment to foster the positive interaction of children. Teachers serve as models for the behavior they desire in children and recognize and reward the appropriate behavior of the children.

THE SELF-CONCEPT

Before individuals can function effectively as a part of a group or with another person, they must have a good feeling about themselves. These feelings result from experiences with others. Success and failure and the impressions we have about how significant persons in our lives feel toward us help to shape our feelings about ourselves. Relationships with parents, siblings, and others in the home before the school

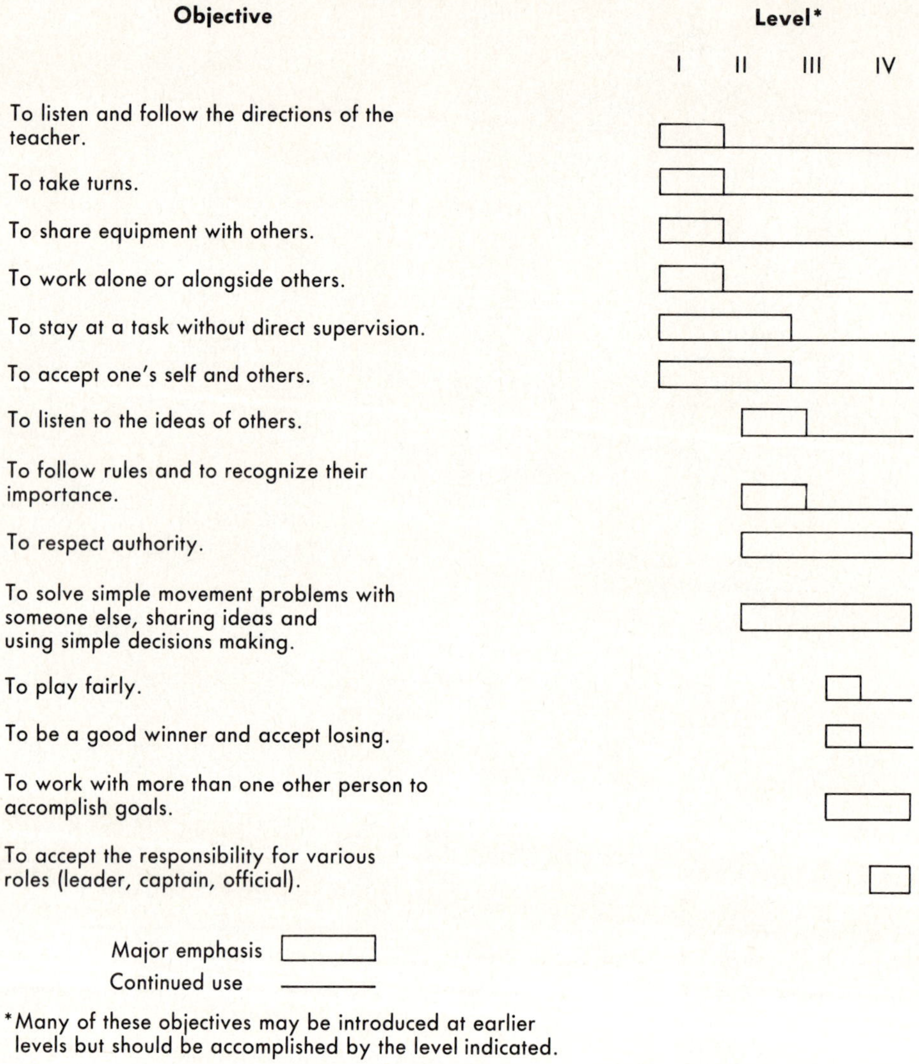

	Objective	**Level***			
		I	II	III	IV

To listen and follow the directions of the teacher.

To take turns.

To share equipment with others.

To work alone or alongside others.

To stay at a task without direct supervision.

To accept one's self and others.

To listen to the ideas of others.

To follow rules and to recognize their importance.

To respect authority.

To solve simple movement problems with someone else, sharing ideas and using simple decisions making.

To play fairly.

To be a good winner and accept losing.

To work with more than one other person to accomplish goals.

To accept the responsibility for various roles (leader, captain, official).

Major emphasis ☐
Continued use ────────

*Many of these objectives may be introduced at earlier levels but should be accomplished by the level indicated.

Figure 12-2

Social objectives.

years begin and the relationships outside the home that develop during the school years are important in establishing the self-concept.

The children's physical being helps to shape their impressions of themselves. Their world is filled with physical activity. Much of the early learning of children is accomplished through physical contact with the environment. Success and failure in these physical or motor pursuits is important in shaping the feelings about the self. Therefore children entering school have some feelings about their own physical potential before beginning formal physical education. Early success is important in viewing oneself as a mover. Successful children want to move and will probably make physical activity an important part of their lives if success continues.

All experiences make their contributions to children's concept of themselves. Learning to deal with disappointment or failure is a part of the maturing process. Individuals must have an accurate concept of self. They must be able to accept both their negative and positive characteristics and they must like themselves as they really are. Self-advocacy is important. Children must see themselves as persons who can do things, persons who have skills. Children who like themselves are willing to make positive statements about themselves, to undertake new tasks with the expectation for success, to be active participants in the group, to take risks, and to become doers.

The self-concept develops in a group setting. Children attempt to validate their feelings of self-worth by seeking experiences with others. It is important that these group encounters be planned and conducted carefully to ensure that they result in helping all children feel good about themselves.

The teacher facilitates the formulation of the feelings of self-worth. Encouragement and positive feedback are important in helping children view themselves as a success. Often physical educators take success for granted. In our eagerness to help children we often look for mistakes or errors in performance to correct rather than to give praise for a job well done. Children need our help to correct errors, but they also need our encouragement when they are successful.

Teacher expectations reinforce both positive and negative behavior. If children perceive that the teacher expects them to act in a particular way, they will. For example, children who perceive the teacher as not expecting them to listen and follow directions probably will not. Children who think the teacher expects them to do well at a particular skill will probably do so. Not only is the teacher's perception of a child's worth communicated to that child by the teacher but also it is eventually communicated to the child by other children, who model the teacher's behavior. Teachers should praise a child's efforts in front of other children, provide equal opportunities for the participation of all children, provide for the organization of teams so that no children are publicly chosen last, and organize the class so all have equal opportunity to assume the various roles and responsibilities during the class activities. The teacher's behavior results in similar child behavior as the children interact with one another.

To enhance the development of a positive self-concept the teacher must:

1. Treat each child as an individual, helping all to reach their movement potential by providing for the needs of each through a series of experiences that result in success for each child.
2. Communicate feelings of worth to each child by being supportive and encouraging supportive behavior by and toward all children.
3. Help children set realistic goals for themselves and communicate these goals to parents.
4. Use a variety of teaching methods, emphasizing those that allow for individual differences in performance.
5. Help all children develop skills that they can use in participation with other children.

As the children mature, progressing through the elementary school grades, they gradually become socialized as a member of the school and society and as a participant in a variety of physical activities.

SOCIAL SKILLS FOR PARTICIPATION IN A DEMOCRATIC SOCIETY

As was stated earlier, the physical education experience provides an environment for learning social skills important to life in our democracy. While democracy offers many individual freedoms, it requires all individuals to assume responsibilities for their actions and to respect the rights and freedoms of others. Life in a democracy depends on the individual assumption of responsibility and adequate social skill in interacting with others. Teachers of physical education must help children develop their potential in an environment where these skills are learned and where discriminatory and sex stereotyping does not exist.

Working Responsibly

In the process of becoming socialized children must adjust to various environments. In physical education certain procedures are established in the best interests of all. The first social interactions involve the children with the teacher, as the authority figure. During these first experiences the children learn the behavior appropriate for the physical education setting. Teachers must be consistent in their expectations if appropriate social behavior is to be learned quickly. Inconsistency in expectations results in confusion and frustration for both the students and the teacher. Some children respond quickly to the expected behavior, whereas others need more help and understanding along the way.

Appropriate social behavior involves developing responsibility in three areas: responsibility for one's own actions, responsibility in caring for school equipment and facilities, and responsibility for acting safely. Assuming responsibility in these areas includes the knowledge of why certain behavior is appropriate and the consequences of actions that are not. The first steps in being responsible for one's own actions include responding to the signal for listening, listening and following directions, staying on task for a reasonable amount of time, and learning to work independently of direct adult supervision. As was noted in Chapter 7, good management skills help children develop responsibility in these areas. One rule in helping children assume responsibility is never to do for them what they can do for themselves.

As children develop social skills during the elementary school years, they may assume more responsibility. They may organize themselves for practice and small group work. They may decide the level of task on which they will work and make other decisions affecting their performance in physical education. Caring for school equipment and facilities is another responsibility children must learn to assume. Children must learn to respect the property of others and take pride in maintaining the environment. They must be taught the consequences of equipment and facility abuse—its impact on themselves, the community, and the economy in general. Children enjoy helping with equipment and should learn to assume responsibility for its distribution, care, and storage.

Behaving safely is also important. Children should learn to assume responsibility for their own safety and for the safety of others. As children begin to assume responsibility for the safe conduct of the physical education class, the learning environment becomes safe and less threatening for everyone.

Activities that enhance the development of these important skills include the following:

1. Allowing children to help get out, to care for, to organize, and to put away the equipment
2. Giving children the opportunity to assume responsibility for their own activity by working as individuals or in a small group with indirect supervision from the teacher
3. Allowing children to define specific goals and to judge their accomplishment
4. Organizing small groups of children to work on a task, taking responsibility to see that all have an equal opportunity for participation
5. Giving children the responsibility to help in formulating rules of behavior for the safe participation of all

As the children learn to work responsibly, they also begin to develop group skills that will help them in working with others. As a result of these early experiences children should develop a sense of belonging to a group and a feeling of cohesiveness.

Interacting with Others

Once children have accepted themselves, they are ready to accept others. Persons who accept their own strengths and weaknesses can realistically accept the strengths and weaknesses of others. An important aspect of the acceptance of others is the recognition that all have certain rights in the social environment. Each child has an equal opportunity for participation, for use of equipment, and for assistance and support of the teacher and others in the group.

The physical education experience should be one in which concern for others is paramount. In their first activities children learn to take turns and to share equipment. Helping and supporting others should be encouraged. These early opportunities prepare children for future group activities in which support for one another in the team effort is necessary.

In the learning environment children are competing for the attention and approval of the teacher. This is not conducive to a supportive environment. The teacher must be an effective model in assisting and supporting each child if a supportive environment is to be the result. Demonstrating the importance of each child in the group is essential.

In the middle school years much attention must be given to developing sensitivity to others' needs and feelings. Children often unknowingly hurt one another by their remarks and body language. Hoffman and others[2] suggest that children need to have the opportunity to work out feelings by answering the following questions:

1. How do I feel when I make a mistake?
2. How do I like people to correct my errors?
3. Would I like someone to help me learn a new skill?
4. What happens when I don't take care of my things?
5. How do I feel when I don't get a turn to do something?
6. Do others feel the same way as I do?

The teacher must reinforce the observed behaviors in which children show sensitivity and support of others. Responding to supportive behavior by saying "I like the way Jim recognizes Joe's effort" will help children to value this type of behavior. Conducting activities in which helping and supporting each other are important to success will go a long way in developing these social skills.

An important part of learning in schools is to develop skill in working with others. In many facets of education today a great deal of emphasis is being placed on meeting individual needs, with little regard for the child as a member of a group. Society has seen the result of this emphasis for the past decade. A strong democratic society requires group effort. Education has a vital role in developing citizens willing and able to assume responsibility for undertaking the process of and accepting group decisions.

The requirements for cooperation begin with sharing an idea with a partner. Working with one other person to solve a simple movement challenge is the next step in learning to work with others. Finally the children become ready to work with others in increasingly larger groups in more complex shared decision making. The development of these skills occurs as the socialized child emerges during the elementary school years. Along the way opportunities for working with others must be planned carefully for each child at each level of social maturity. As children develop group skills, they improve their ability to communicate with others in sharing their ideas. They learn to accept differences of opinion and to disagree without blaming. They learn to value the ideas of others in planning for group action to solve a variety of movement challenges. The solutions for some movement challenges may call for a division of labor or the delegation of different responsibilities in the group.

Elementary school children enjoy and need the opportunity to assume responsibility and leadership within the class. Group or squad leaders can share in the management responsibilities for the class as well as develop leadership skills. In the early grades these leadership experiences may include distributing and collecting equipment, getting the group ready to move on to the next activity, or organizing a small group into activity. In later years children may be involved in checking off skills the group has accomplished, leading a warm-up activity, or assuming responsibility for the rotation of players in a game.

As the social structure of solving movement challenges becomes more complex, specific roles in the group emerge. Some children become group leaders, and others are content to follow. Roles vary as children participate in different groups. Motor skill development appears to be a component of leadership in physical education since often children who emerge as leaders are those who are well skilled. Perhaps the confidence they gain from being well skilled and the value placed on it by other children enable these children to assume leadership roles more easily.

Children model the behavior of significant adults and peers. They become the kind of leaders and followers they have observed. If they observe the democratic process in action, they become democratic leaders. If they view leaders as the ultimate authority, they become more autocratic. As they are ready, children need to assume responsibility in the leadership roles of group leader, team captain, umpire, and/or coach.

Discriminatory Behavior

Prejudice and discrimination occur in every facet of society, including sports and dance. Individuals who look, speak, or act differently from the expected norm are treated differently by individuals and groups. Those receiving differential treatment include minority racial groups, ethnic groups, and those with handicapping conditions ranging from obesity and other physical handicaps to mental retardation. An important part of the educational experience is the recognition and acceptance of individual differences. A positive self-concept is important in accepting others. Often it is the child with poor self-esteem who acts out the most against others who are different.

More role modeling of individuals working together is needed. Teachers must provide the best models if children are to respond in a positive way to all other children. Teachers must avoid giving children labels such as disadvantaged or handicapped. They should respond to stereotyping statements such as "All _______ are good basketball players" or "_______ are all lazy" by correcting such misconceptions. There is no place in the school for ethnic jokes or comments that highlight differences in dress, physical appearance, and the like. Statements that criticize, judge, or devalue people of various cultures must be avoided.

The teacher must help children learn about each other. When children who are different are introduced to a group, children seek information about their differences. Adults are often embarrassed by the questions children ask. Teachers need to learn to deal with these questions. Many times a simple explanation is all that is needed to begin to develop new understanding, and often the child who is different can handle the questions better than an adult.

Schools should assume responsibility to teach children about other races, cultures, or handicapping conditions. As understanding is increased, prejudice, which is based on ignorance, is decreased. Children should be taught the interdependence of cultures, the histories of minorities, and the causes and treatment of handicapping conditions. Children need to become aware of stereotyping and prejudice in our society. They must become aware of social issues from the point of view of the handicapped and the various racial or cultural groups. They need to learn how the dominant culture holds down and penalizes groups and individuals. Games that are popular in other lands or folk dances that are a part of other cultures offer children the opportunity to learn about others.

The physical education class should be structured so that all children have the opportunity to work with all other children in the group. Often the teacher needs to assume responsibility for pairing up children as partners or determining small group composition, if each child is to have the opportunity to work with all others in the group.

Sex Stereotyping

Parents and other significant persons are important influences in the development of sex roles in children. Through the observation of their parents as they interact with each other, children learn the expected behavior for their sex. The roles each sex assumes are determined more by society than biology. Women have been viewed as homemakers, as obedient and subservient wives and mothers, as attractive sex symbols, as dependent and emotional beings. While this image of women still persists today, the roles of women are expanding. The roles acceptable for males as aggressive, domineering, self-confident, tough-mind-

ed, willing to take risks, and unemotional also have not necessarily been in the men's best interest.

In our society sport has long been regarded as a male domain. The girl athlete has experienced role conflicts between the expectations for being a woman and the expectations for being an athlete. Title IX in 1972 was intended to eliminate sex discrimination and segregation in schools, but it did not necessarily result in sex equity.

Society's assumption that being male is best has not had a totally positive influence on sport in general. Girls' programs have been set up to imitate boys' programs, many of which have not always been conducted in the best interests of the participants. Today there are many opportunities for the female athlete. At the elementary school level there may be experiences in equal but separate teams for girls or in activities conducted on a coeducational basis.

The value of play in the socialization of children, especially boys, has long been recognized in the writings of such observers as Margaret Mead and Jean Piaget.[3] During play we observe the development of those sex roles that have been believed crucial to success in society. The play deemed appropriate for girls and for boys has socialized both sexes into their perceived roles in society. In a study of elementary school children's play Lever and associates[3] found the following:

1. Boys played outdoors more than girls. (Eighty-five percent of the boys and 60% of the girls spent more than one quarter of their play time outdoors.) Indoor play is more restrictive and also more private. Boys appeared to gain in independence from the outdoor play experience .

2. Boys played in larger groups. (Seventy-two percent of the boys and 52% of girls played in groups of four or more.) The games boys chose required larger numbers of participants.

3. Boys played in more heterogeneous groups. Eight- to 12-year-olds seemed to prefer sex-segregated age-homogeneous groups, but since boys' activities required larger numbers of participants, they tended to play in more heterogeneous groups than girls. Girls playing in mixed groups tended to play down to the level of the youngest members. Boys, on the other hand, required the younger players to play up to the level of the older children.

4. Girls were more apt to play in predominantly male games than were boys to participate in girls' games. (Many believe that girls are probably not punished early or as severely for inappropriate behavior and therefore feel freer to participate in boys' activities.) Girls played the boys' games seriously, whereas

the boys who participated in girls' games tended to play the part of a tease and not a serious competitor.

5. Boys played competitive games more often than girls. (Sixty-five percent of the boys participated in these activities as opposed to only 35% of the girls.) These games had a set of rules and a specific aim to be achieved, such as scoring a goal. They were games in which a winner was declared.

6. The games boys played lasted longer than the games of the girls. During recess the boys' games often lasted the entire recess period, which was 25 minutes. The girls' games never lasted longer than 15 minutes.

7. The boys' games required higher skill levels that could be developed only over a long period of time. Girls' activities tended to be those such as rope jumping in which skill mastery was acquired in a short time.

8. The boys' activities had more opportunity for surprise and risk taking. The girls' games required taking turns, and in many of the activities no strategy or rules left up to interpretation were involved.

9. The boys appeared better able to handle disputes that came up as they played the games. This may have been the result of modeling of the older boys as they played in heterogeneous-age groups. When disputes arose in the girls' activities, the activities often came to an end.

In summary, Lever and associates concluded that the play of children probably does prepare them to assume different sex roles. The boys' play activities seem to prepare them for a wider range of work settings than does the play of the girls, which is more private and more in the sphere of the home and roles as wives and mothers. The boys' play seems to further independence and encourage the development of organizational skills through the greater complexity of the play and the need to delegate responsibility in various games. The boys learn to play in larger and more diverse groups. They learn to function in a rule-bound environment and to deal with disputes. They learn to take risks in an environment where the payoff is high and the risks are not a life-and-death matter. They receive immediate feedback on the success or failure of their efforts. There may be greater opportunities to develop leadership skills, and they learn how to compete. Both skills may help them in future encounters in the business world.

Girls, on the other hand, seem to develop more delicate socioemotional skills. They work in small, intimate groups in more private play. The age-heterogeneous play develops nurturing skills. Their play is more spontaneous and free from structure and rules. The organization of their play tends to be more co-operative than competitive. The play of girls may be training for future heterosexual courtship; they play more in pairs than in larger groups and tend to have a single best friend. They develop sensitivity and empathy toward each other.

The findings of this study may suggest that perhaps the play of children before entering school gives boys the edge in the skills needed to be a successful participant. As a result boys often dominate in many of the activities included in the physical education program.

The physical education experience should provide opportunities to develop greater understanding between the sexes and to develop their biological potential. To avoid sex stereotyping teachers must:

1. Provide opportunities for boys and girls to work together.
2. Control activities so all children have an equal opportunity to participate and to assume all roles.
3. Positively reinforce the activity of all children.
4. React to stereotypical remarks, such as "Tom throws like a girl."
5. Control activities so that children who are better skilled and more aggressive do not dominate in games.
6. Provide nonsexist role models, such as boys dancing or girls playing basketball.
7. Provide opportunities for all children to learn the skills of cooperation and competition.
8. Provide activities to enhance the ability of both highly skilled girls and boys.

SOCIALIZATION FOR PARTICIPATION

Sports and dance are well established as important aspects of our American culture. Television and radio coverage, newspapers, and magazines report the excellence achieved by individuals and teams. Individuals vary in their activity habits, ranging from spectator to occasional participant to dedicated athlete or dancer. Team sports once thought to be the pastime of high school or college-age persons or professional athletes are a growing part of adult recreational pursuits. Lifetime sports such as tennis and golf continue to be popular leisure time activities. Many forms of dance are also pursued by the adult population through local dance companies, in folk and square dance groups, or as evening entertainment. The variety of recreational sports and dance activities available is expanding rapidly for all ages.

Successful and satisfying participation in many

motor activities is dependent on acquiring some proficiency in the motor skills required and also learning the appropriate social behaviors needed to interact with others. Since the overall goal of physical education is to prepare the individual for a lifetime of physical activity, socialization for participation is extremely important.

In the broader context sports roles are learned through modeling and imitating significant others, such as older children, parents, coaches, and professional athletes. Childhood and adolescence are important years in learning sports roles. Children may assume the role of spectator or participant. Participation is valued if parents, teachers, peers, and others demonstrate that it is important. Children appear to be socialized toward participation by the age of 8 or 9, boys generally earlier than girls. Each sex seems to be influenced most significantly by different groups. Boys seem to be influenced more by peers, followed by family and school. Girls are influenced more by family, then peers and community.[1]

Sportsmanship

Sportsmanship is defined by Webster's New Collegiate Dictionary as "conduct becoming a sportsman." The meaning of the term is vague, and behavior considered to be appropriate at one level of competition might be unacceptable at another. In this text the good sport is one who respects the rules and authority, plays fair, knows how to compete and cooperate, and in winning and losing keeps the game in perspective.

Respecting Rules and Authority

Learning to respect rules and authority is a part of the socializing experience. Throughout life individuals need to adjust to the written (laws) and unwritten rules in dealing with others and persons of authority. All groups need rules to indicate the behavior expectations for members of the group. They permit groups to operate with a minimum of disruption and nonproductive behavior.

Teachers must communicate their rules to the group. Children need to understand the nature and basis for the rules they must follow. Rules that are understood are more apt to be followed than those that are imposed indiscriminately. Within the group there should be a process for formulating and modifying rules. The children should participate in this process. Children need to learn that people make rules and people can change them.

Young school children view rules as being absolute. As they mature during the elementary school years, their experiences with rules help them to understand that rules may be relative as the situation changes. Children learn that rules are made in the best interests of the group and help to balance individual and group needs. When rules are formulated, there should be as few of them as possible and the rules adopted should be broad enough to cover a variety of situations.

Many of the rules in the physical education class relate to safety, equal opportunity for all, and fair competition. Children learn that rules may be modified to serve the players. For instance, we do not need to play by the "official" rules of the game. Children need to be given the opportunity to formulate rules and to suggest modifications for the activities in which they are to engage.

Playing Fair

Playing fair begins with respect for others. Each participant plays within the spirit of the rules. All should always give their best effort without humiliating the opponents. Playing fair includes working with teammates. It also includes playing without distracting or interfering with opponents.

Winning and Losing

Someone said, "There is no such thing as a good loser"; everyone wants to be a winner. Winning is a legitimate goal, but it may prevent children from keeping the game in perspective. To children the game at times may seem to be a life-and-death matter. The value of playing the game must be broadened to mean something more than winning. Putting more emphasis on the process of accomplishing the goal than on the score may make the game experience fun for all. Discussion of the outcomes of games at their conclusion—focusing on how well the team worked together, used skills appropriately, or developed strategy—helps children view the outcome as more than winning or losing.

To maximize the sportsman-like behavior of all, the teacher should equalize competition so that all have an opportunity to win and no one is able to humiliate the others. Goals other than scoring should be stressed, such as working together or supporting teammates. Scoring may be modified by giving points for completion of a specific number of passes or for each team player handling the ball. With these methods the team score represents the team's efforts,

not the mistakes of the other team. In some games players may be rotated from one team to the other so each player is a part of the winning and losing effort.

Participation in motor activities has its rewards. It is fun, and many find pure joy in moving. There are also the feelings of good health and being "in shape"; the pride in accomplishment and the satisfaction of approval of friends and family; and the camaraderie in working with others to achieve a goal. These rewards should be a part of the physical education experience.

Aggression

Aggression, the act of vigorously pursuing a goal,[4] is a learned behavior. It may have positive or negative results. If persons work to achieve the goal in a socially acceptable manner, by doing their best and within the rules of fair play and sportsmanship, aggression is thought of as a positive act. If individuals do not play fairly or attempt to harm their opponents, aggression is believed to be negative.

Society differentially reinforces the aggressive behavior of individuals or groups. In the United States boys and men are reinforced more for aggressive behavior than are girls and women. Lower socioeconomic groups reinforce aggressive behavior more than middle or upper socioeconomic groups. Boys learn that sports are a way to recognition at an early age. The desire to win and the reinforcement of ag-

gressive behavior may push some children into psychologically untenable situations.

Children tend to imitate the behavior they observe. If sports heros such as professional athletes display aggressive behavior, it may influence the behavior of children, especially when they participate in games and other motor activities. While most sports personalities display the type of aggressive behavior we value for young athletes, some do not. At times children may need assistance in determining which behavior they should emulate.

Many times aggressive behavior is the result of frustration. Teachers must watch for the conditions that would result in negatively aggressive behavior and make the appropriate adjustments in the environment to bring about the needed changes in behavior. The rotation of players in positions or on teams and the equalization of competition can go far in promoting desirable behavior.

Cooperation and Competition

Cooperation is the working together of individuals to achieve a goal. The degree of cooperation required varies with the situation. In early cooperative experiences simple delegation and assumption of certain roles in activities may be all that is needed. Later activities may require a higher level of cooperation as children share in the decision making in the development of strategy in a game or in the design and creation of a movement sequence in dance.

Competition refers to a contest between individuals or groups. It may be (1) an individual or group against another individual or group, (2) an individual or group against an object, or (3) an individual or group against a standard. Competition is an acquired aspect of behavior and probably culturally determined. In sport it is the product of an individual's experiences. There is considerable variation in competitiveness among persons, and an individual's competitiveness may vary in different situations. Competitive behavior is reinforced by others. If it is reinforced, it will persist. A higher level of reinforcement for competitive behavior may result in an individual seeking out experiences in which individuals or teams compete with one another such as tennis, soccer, or basketball. Those with a lower level of reinforcement for competitive behavior may tend to select activities in which competitve behavior is minimized, such as hiking or rock climbing.

The schools use competition as a motivational device. Grading, being first, striving for the teacher's attention, and the like may stress competition and

may not be in the best interest of educational goals. Education has put greater emphasis on being an individual than on functioning as a member of a group. A person may have difficulty in our society without group skills. Children need to learn to share, to work cooperatively with one another, to delegate responsibility, and to contribute to and accept group decisions. Children may benefit from competition in some situations, but it may be detrimental in others. In some situations competition in which children try to beat time, distance, or numbers may be preferable to beating people.

Cooperation is also a learned behavior. As children interact with others and become more socialized during the elementary school years, their ability to work with others increases. Play with others places external controls on the behavior of individuals. It reduces freedom of action of the individual while it increases the possibilities for interaction of the group. In group activities individual and group behavior is reinforced. Actions not conducive to the group effort are not reinforced and actually may be punished by the group. Teachers, parents, and others are important in helping children to develop group skills that enable them to work cooperatively.

In physical education competitive situations that involve more than one person on a team require cooperation among individuals or group members to achieve success. Learning to compete and learning to cooperate are important educational goals since our culture is based on both. Learning experiences should foster the development of both, not one at the expense of the other.

The misuse of competition (such as valuing the score more than the people or the way the goal was achieved) does not favor educational results. Too much competition may inhibit learning and personal development. Children may lose interest in a worthwhile activity because of an overly competitive environment. Actually more might be accomplished in a cooperative setting.

Learning how to compete is more than winning and losing. Children need to be taught how to compete in an environment in which the focus is on the process of competition rather than the outcome. Having a single winner and the best performance as criteria may interfere with children's perception of success. We need to foster sharing and involving others in accomplishing group goals, such as passing to teammates. Children may become negative about an activity in which the element of fun is lost in the eagerness to have the best score. Competitive gaming and interest in rule-governed play appears to peek at about the fourth or fifth grade.[5] In order for children to maintain a high level of interest in competition the outcome of the activity must be unpredictable, as when there is an equal probability of winning.

Children may need help in defining goals that go beyond a winning score. Examples of alternate goals include commiting no more than 5 errors, completing 10 passes, or predicting the point spread. With these types of goals the children's attention is focused on a specific outcome rather than the score.

Activities to develop cooperative behavior include working together to achieve some task such as moving a large object from one place to another; keeping an object balanced; helping organize an area for activity by getting out and placing the equipment where needed; including activities where there is a delegation of responsibilities or different positions to be played; developing original games; and using peer teaching. The idea of new games promotes the notion of group cooperation in activities in which there is not a team score.

SUMMARY

The development of social behavior appropriate for life in a democracy is an important goal of education. Physical education has the added responsibility of teaching those social behaviors important for the participant. Appropriate social behavior does not necessarily result from active participation with others. Careful planning and conduct of physical education experiences is essential if appropriate social skills are to be developed. The maturity of the children and the nature of the activities themselves guide the teacher in planning for appropriate social development.

The children's feeling and behavior toward others are influenced by their own feelings of self-worth. The first step in planning for appropriate social behavior is to help each child feel an important part of the class. The teacher must model the appropriate behavior, valuing each child and reinforcing supportive behavior.

The physical education class should enhance those social behaviors taught in other settings in the school. These are social skills important for success in school and in society. They include assuming responsibility for one's own actions; effectively interacting with peers, other children, and adults; and recognizing the worth of each individual in avoiding discriminatory and sex-stereotyping behavior.

In addition the physical educator helps each child develop those skills important to participation as a sportsman, namely playing fair, accepting winning and losing, controlling aggression toward others, and learning to cooperate with and compete against others in socially acceptable and effective ways.

REFERENCES

1. McPherson, B., and others: The social structure of the game and sport milieu. In Albinson, J., and Andrew, G., editors: Child in sport and physical activity, Baltimore, 1976, University Park Press.
2. Hoffman, H., and others: Meaningful movement for children, Boston, 1981, Allyn & Bacon.
3. Lever, J.: Sex differences in the games children play. In Yiannakis, A., and others: Sport sociology: contemporary themes, ed. 2, Dubuque, 1979, Kendall/Hunt Publishing Co.
4. Coakley, J.: Sport in society, ed. 2, St. Louis, 1982, The C.V. Mosby Co.
5. Ellis, M.: Why people play, Englewood Cliffs, N.J., 1973, Prentice-Hall Inc.
6. Calhoun, D.: Sports culture and society, West Point, N.Y., 1981, Leisure Press.
7. Dickinson, J.: A behavioral analysis of sport, Princeton, 1977, Princeton Book Co. Publishers.
8. Leonard, W.: A sociological perspective of sport, ed. 2, Minneapolis, 1984, Burgess Publishing Co.
9. Pooley, J.: Physical education and sport and the quality of life, JOPERD **55**(3):45, March 1984.
10. Seidentop, D.: Developing teaching skills in physical education, ed. 2, Palo Alto, 1983, Mayfield Publishing Co.
11. Synder, E., and Spreitzer, E.: Social aspects of sport, ed. 2, Englewood Cliffs, N.J., 1983, Prentice-Hall Inc.

ADDITIONAL READINGS

Boslooper, T.: Physical assertiveness, JOPER **47**(5):35, May 1976.
The role of society in the development of assertive behavior in men and women and sport participation as a means and an outlet for aggressive behavior.

Duquin, M.: Differential sex role socialization toward amplitude appropriation. In Yiannakis, A., and others: Sport sociology: contemporary themes, ed. 2, Dubuque, 1979, Kendall/Hunt Publishing Co.
A study of the depiction of women in children's books.

Duquin, M.: The importance of sport in building women's potential, JOPERD **53**(3):18, March 1982.
The effects of culture on women in sports and the role sports can play in the development of women for new roles.

Feigley, D.: Is aggression justifiable? JOPERD **54**(9):63, November/December 1983.
A discussion of aggression in sports events and why individuals behave in unsportsmanlike behavior.

Logsdon, B., and others: Physical education for children: a focus on the teaching process, ed. 2, Philadelphia, 1984, Lea & Febiger.
Chapter 3 discusses the age characteristics of children, including the development of aggressive, competitive, and cooperative behaviors.

Schafer, W.: Sport and male sex-role socialization. In Yiannakis, A., and others: Sport sociology: contemporary themes, ed. 2, Dubuque, 1979, Kendall/Hunt Publishing Co.
Discussion of the stereotype of men as successful, strong, objective, and unemotional.

13

FITNESS AND MOVEMENT EFFICIENCY

CHAPTER OBJECTIVES

1 To recognize health-related physical fitness as an integral part of the physical education program

2 To identify the components of health-related physical fitness

3 To select the tools for assessment and the activities for development of fitness based on sound health practices

4 To identify the important movement principles in performing daily tasks efficiently

5 To examine good posture and identify common postural deviations

An important objective of physical education is the development and maintenance of health-related physical fitness. Health-related physical fitness is (1) "the ability to perform strenuous physical activity with vigor without excessive fatigue, and (2) demonstration of physical activity traits and capacities that are consistent with minimal risk or developing hypokinetic disease."[12] (Hypokinetic disease refers to those diseases or disorders, generally of the muscular, skeletal, or cardiorespiratory system, that limit the capability for movement.) An understanding of *body mechanics,* the efficient use of the body in maintaining good alignment and in performing daily tasks, is important in knowing how to use the body in lifting, carrying, pushing, and pulling without undue stress on body segments.

FITNESS

Fitness has been an important aspect of physical education in the United States since its early origins when physicians, the first physical educators, recognized the importance of physical activity for healthful living. In the 1950s in response to an increased impetus for fitness following World War II and the Korean engagement, the American Association for Health, Physical Education and Recreation established a series of tests to assess the motor fitness of youths from 10 to 18 years old. The components tested were believed to be important to a person's overall motor ability. The tests included items to measure agility, power, cardiorespiratory endurance, muscular strength and endurance, and speed. The test items included a 50-yard dash, a shuttle run, a 600-yard run, sit-ups, the standing jump, a softball throw for distance, pull-ups for boys, and a flexed arm hang for girls. National norms were established, and these were revised periodically between 1958 and 1976.

During this time there was often discussion about the test items and their relationship to health. Speed and power were found to be heavily dependent on genetic factors and not particularly responsive to training. Agility, although an important component of some motor activities, has little relationship to health.[12] Some questioned whether the tests actually measured the motor components they were supposed to measure; for example, whether the standing jump measured leg power or the ability to jump from a standing position. Table 13-1 compares the components of motor and health-related physical fitness.

Table 13-1
Physical fitness components

Component	Definition	Motor fitness	Health-related fitness
Agility	Ability to change direction quickly, easily, and with control	X	
Body composition	Percentage of body fat		X
Cardiorespiratory endurance	Maximal functional capacity of the cardiorespiratory system to continue activity over a period of time	X	X
Flexibility	Range of movement in a joint	X	X
Muscular endurance	Ability to continue muscular effort over a period of time	X	X
Muscular strength	Amount of force that can be exerted by a muscle	X	X
Power	Use of strength to apply force in a particular task	X	
Speed	Ability to move the body quickly	X	

Cardiorespiratory endurance has been conclusively linked to coronary heart disease. The relationship of body composition and activity level has been clearly established. With the establishment of the relationship of inactivity to health problems involving the bones, musculature, cardiorespiratory system, and weight control, fitness has become an important concern for individuals of all ages. The activity habits developed as a part of the physical education experiences have lasting effects on an individual's health now and in the future. Those who exercise regularly have a much brighter prospect for a healthy life. Those who choose not to exercise have to assume the consequences.

Health-related Fitness

In 1980 the U.S. Department of Health and Human Services held a conference to address health issues important to our nation. Several of the objectives endorsed are important to physical education and youth fitness. In these objectives the conference set 1990 as a target date for:
1. Improvement in the number of children participating regularly in appropriate physical activities, particularly cardiorespiratory fitness programs
2. Improvement in the number of children and adolescents participating in daily school physical education programs (The National Children and Youth Fitness Study[15] reported in January 1985 that approximately 36% of the children and adolescents in the United States participated in daily physical education.)
3. The establishment of a methodology for systematically assessing the physical fitness of children[18]

Since all the components in motor fitness were not believed to be important to health, a new term, health-related physical fitness, emerged with a redefinition of fitness. Health-related physical fitness includes those components that can prevent disease and/or promote health, namely cardiorespiratory endurance, body composition, muscular strength and endurance, and flexibility. In 1980 the AAHPERD health-related physical fitness test was introduced. The test items were designed to assess these components and are included as the test items suggested in this chapter.

IMPLEMENTING THE HEALTH-RELATED PHYSICAL FITNESS PROGRAM

Pate[12] defines the fitness goals for the child's total physical activity/physical education/health education experience as:
1. Maintenance of good functional capacities in the health-related physical fitness components during childhood
2. Exhibition of a level of habitual physical activity sufficient to stimulate normal growth and development
3. Demonstration of a level of health-related physical fitness that minimizes the risks of later development of hypokinetic diseases
4. Acquisition of the skills, knowledge, and attitudes that optimize the chances of maintaining good health-related physical fitness throughout life

In structuring the physical education experiences

Table 13-2

Potential contribution of physical activities to health-related fitness*

Activity	Cardiorespiratory endurance	Muscular strength and endurance	Flexibility	Body composition†
Movement content	X	X	X	X
Fundamental skills		X		
Educational games	X			
Basketball	X	X		X
Field hockey	X	X		X
Softball		X		
Soccer	X	X		X
Volleyball		X		
Track and field	X	X		X
Gymnastics		X	X	
Creative dance		X	X	
Folk and square dance	X	X		X
Rhythmic activities with balls, sticks, and ropes	X	X		X

*Assumes maximum participation for all.

†Body composition is related to the amount of activity. Activities that require sustained vigorous activity would contribute the most.

to meet the goals for health-related physical fitness the following must be considered:

Fitness is an integral part of the physical education experience. Fitness is not a unit of activity but a part of every activity included in the physical education curriculum.

Fitness is concerned with total body development. Motor activities included in physical education have the potential of developing specific components of health-related physical fitness but not necessarily all. Units of instruction must often be supplemented with additional activities to ensure total body development. Table 13-2 looks at the fitness components that may be developed in various physical activities. It must be remembered the actual contribution an activity makes to fitness depends on the manner in which the activity is conducted. Since activities are designed to work on specific fitness components, a variety of activities are required to ensure total body development.

Fitness should be fun. Often fitness activities have been characterized as a series of boring and tedious exercises and calisthenics or as punishment for minor infractions. Fitness is developed through a variety of physical activities selected to meet the needs and interests of children.

Fitness should be motivated by a desire for self-improvement. All children strive to do their best in an environment in which positive efforts are reinforced and improvement noted.

Fitness should be nonthreatening. The environment should be one in which children and teacher support one another. Each child should be valued. There must be no possibility for ridicule or public judgment of anyone's performance. Testing should emphasize individual improvement rather than rank in class.

Fitness must be vigorous. Each lesson should include vigorous activity in which the children's heart rates are increased and a maximum amount of movement for each child is ensured.

Fitness should be individualized. Children should (1) know their fitness status, (2) be helped to set realistic goals for improvement, and (3) be assisted in establishing a program of activity to achieve their goals. The activity prescription should be based on each individual's initial level of fitness. Those with lower fitness levels should begin with a program of exercise of lower intensity. A fit individual will have to begin at a much higher intensity program if fitness is to be improved further.

Fitness must be progressive. The goal must be to increase the work capacity of each child through a series of progressively more demanding physical activities. An increase in muscle strength requires that the muscle be exercised at higher levels of activity than normal. The heart increases its efficiency as a

result of demands to work harder than usual. Flexibility is improved by increasing the range of movement in the various articulations (joints) of the body.

Fitness requires frequent activity. Three 45-minute periods of vigorous physical activity each week are recommended as a minimum for acquiring and maintaining health-related fitness. Since the 45 minutes are in excess of an optimal period for learning in the early school years, a daily 30-minute period for kindergarten through the third grade is suggested. Since the physical education period is devoted to skill and knowledge development as well as fitness activities, children must be encouraged to be physically active outside school, especially if physical education is not offered on a daily basis.

Fitness should include periods of warm-up and cooling down. Most activities are performed best when the body temperature has been raised slightly, which is the result of warm-up activities. Although young children apparently do not need warm-up activities, in the upper levels children may benefit from warm-ups to prevent muscle and joint injury and soreness as a result of strenuous exercise and to establish the importance and habit of warming up and cooling down. Stretching activities are important in the warm-up and cool-down periods of activity. A series of stretches is found in the flexibility activities in this chapter.

Fitness requires a maintenance program once the desired fitness is reached. If a person stops exercising, the level of fitness achieved is lost in a short time. Therefore an exercise program must be continuous. Since it is easier to maintain fitness than to acquire it, a lower intensity program usually suffices.

Fitness improvement and maintenance require a conscientious effort by the individual. Fitness will not be improved unless individuals value fitness for themselves. All persons must take the responsibility for carrying out their fitness program. Setting realistic goals that include short- and long-term objectives is important. The school can assist by providing programs that encourage fitness activities in and out of school, for instance, a run to the state capitol organized by classroom with individuals running laps that are totaled for a group record. Keeping a log of activities and achievements along the way should help children remain sufficiently motivated and interested to continue working.

As children learn about fitness in physical education, they should be exposed to knowledge that increases their understanding about themselves and the effects of exercise on the body. Much of the knowledge may be included in the elementary school curriculum in other subject areas as well as in physical education. The study of fitness is an example of how the integration of the areas of physical education, health, science, and math may result in greater understanding. Written reports may help internalize and reinforce the value of health-related fitness. The content to be developed in the study of health-related fitness in the elementary school is illustrated on p. 178.

Where possible fitness activities should be built into the development of the unit and related daily activities. Sustaining an activity for longer periods of time, increasing the vigor (speed) of movement, or holding a position for a time is all that is needed to improve fitness. For example, in a basketball lesson the children may be dribbling en masse in general space, responding to the teacher's instructions to change hands, speed up, change direction, or change pathway. The activity is sustained long enough to increase the childrens' heart rates. In a movement lesson the children may be asked to hold a particular shape, which may require stretching or muscle endurance. In this way children work on fitness as they develop skills and knowledge in other areas.

In addition supplementary fitness activities may be organized in several different ways. Fitness activities may be done en masse with the children working in unison. The teacher or a student calls out the activity and the students perform the activity to a count.

HEALTH-RELATED FITNESS CONTENT

VOCABULARY

Fitness
Endurance
Flexibility
Strength

THE HUMAN BODY

Skeleton
Muscles, tendons, ligaments
Cardiorespiratory system
Arteries, veins
Body fat

NUTRITION

Food, the energy source
Carbohydrates, fat, protein
Diet needs

ACTIVITY

Exercise effects:
  Bones
  Muscles
  Heart, lungs
Need for regular exercise

FITNESS

Importance
Fitness testing
Fitness program:
  Acquiring
  Maintaining
Results of being fit
Determining pulse rate

CIRCUIT TRAINING: AN EXAMPLE

Time Interval: 20 seconds per station for primary age children
  (increase to 60 seconds for older children)

Run in place (number of steps)	Sit-ups (number)	Rope jumping (number of jumps)
	or	
	Crab walk in all directions*	
Squat thrusts (number)	Agility run (number of trips) between two points	Pull-ups on low horizontal bar or parallel bars
or		or
Inch worm*		Seal crawl*

*Sustain activity for the entire time.

The activities may be organized so the children perform a series of activities alternated with running or jumping rope. In this way activities to develop various aspects of fitness and using various body parts are alternated with cardiorespiratory exercise. Flexibility, muscle strength, and muscular endurance may be developed as the children move with little break in the activity. An example exercise might consist of running in place, arm circles, running in place, sit-ups, running in place, etc. Activities might also include running in place or rope jumping alternated with some activity performed on the floor, such as alternately curling and extending the body.

Circuit training is another method of organizing for fitness activities. In this technique a series of stations is arranged in the playing area. The children are divided into groups and evenly distributed at the stations. Time intervals of 20 seconds to 1 minute are used, depending on the fitness level and age of the children. On the signal to begin, the children

POSSIBLE MOVEMENTS FOR
AEROBIC EXERCISE

STEPS

Step/run in place
Step, together, step
Hop
Step-hop
Bleking
Schottische
Rocking step, front to back
Jumping jacks
Rope jumping

LEG MOVEMENTS

Knee lifts

Toe touches to side, front, or back
Kick to side, front, or back
Leg kicks (chorus line)

ARM MOVEMENTS

Circles
Swings
Alternate flexion and extension
Raising above head and lowering
Punching

STRETCHING

Overhead, to the sides, forward, back
(standing or sitting)

perform the exercises to be completed at their particular station. They continue to repeat the exercise until time is called. They move on to the next station and begin again on the signal. Activities chosen should be those in which the children may work alone. Individual scorecards may be used on which the children enter their scores before moving on to the next station. Each day the children should make an effort to equal or slightly improve their previous day's performances. More than one activity exercising a particular body segment may be used, but these activities should not be placed too close together. An example of a circuit is given below.

Aerobic exercise performed to music is another way to develop fitness. A simple combination of activities is used, including locomotor movements, stretching, and the like. Children enjoy these routines especially when a catchy tune is used or the music is brought to the class by the students. Exercises should be done to the beat and the phrasing of the music.

Many different movements may be used. Locomotor movements, rope jumping, dance steps, or exercises such as jumping jacks may be performed if the activity keeps going. Adding arm movements or raising the knees generally increases the heart rate. The activity may begin slowly with stretching to music, gradually increasing in aerobic activity and then gradually decreasing once again in effort required. Movements are usually performed in a series of eights to fit the music. Cueing is helpful to assist the children in anticipating the changes in movement and staying with the music. Upper grade children enjoy making up their own combinations of movements. Young children enjoy an aerobic train trip as they follow the leader, performing a different aerobic exercise at each station. Some of the movements that might be selected for aerobic exercise are included above. A simple combination might include a step to which a leg movement is added followed by the addition of an arm movement. An example might be: Step in place (8), add a touch to the side (step, touch) (8), add an arm swing to the side (8), repeat. Another example would be to select a movement and alternate it with a turn to face another direction in four jumps. When building exercises the teacher should remember that arm and leg movements added to the steps increase the demands placed on the body. The boxes below offer suggestions for possible movements and a simple routine.

However they are organized, the activities should be specific to developing total body fitness. Exercises to develop cardiorespiratory endurance, flexibility, and muscular strength of the upper body, abdomen, back, and lower body should be included.

DEVELOPING HEALTH-RELATED PHYSICAL FITNESS

Developing health-related fitness requires a knowledge of body function, an understanding of how each aspect of fitness may be improved, and a means for assessing the degree to which fitness has been at-

SAMPLE AEROBIC EXERCISE

	Count	Number	Activity
Part I			
	16	8	2 count: jumping jacks
	16	8	2 count: step in place (1), kick in front, alternating legs (2)
	16	16	1 count: alternating kicks to the side
	16	16	1 count: alternating kicks to the rear
Part II			
Repeat part I			
Part III			
	8	8	1 count: hop in a circle to the right
	8	8	1 count: hop in a circle to the left
Part IV			

Repeat Part I ending in a side straddle position with arms raised and spread overhead
Music: Anchors Aweigh. From the Greatest College Football Marches, VSD 29/30, Vanguard Record Society Inc. 171 West 23rd St. New York, N.Y. 10010.

tained. The following sections provide this information. The assessment instruments in this text include the following items from the AAHPERD Health-Related Physical Fitness Test: the 1-mile run, the 9-minute run, skinfold measures of body composition, the sit and reach test of flexibility, and a sit-ups test. Additional muscular strength and endurance items included are the pull-ups test for boys and the flexed arm hang for girls from the AAHPERD Youth Fitness Test, and the NCYFS chin-ups test. Although most of the tests have different norms for boys and girls, the teacher may wish to only use the boys' norms for prepubescent children to encourage the girls to a better performance of which they are capable.

Cardiorespiratory Endurance

Cardiorespiratory endurance is the ability to sustain physical exercise and to recover from vigorous physical activity in a reasonable time with no lasting side effects. It is concerned with the ***aerobic efficiency*** of the body, which is the ability of the body to supply fuel and oxygen to the muscles being used. The heart's capacity for pumping blood is a major factor in cardiorespiratory endurance. A conditioned heart is able to exert greater force with each heartbeat, and as a result a greater volume of blood is released into the arteries to be carried through the body.

The efficiency of the lungs to take in sufficient air and to expel carbon dioxide is also an important factor in cardiorespiratory endurance. In order for the body at work to use food supplied by the blood, oxygen is needed. The lungs inhale air, and oxygen from the air is transported to the heart in the blood and then ejected from the heart to be carried to the organs needing oxygen. From the organs the blood carrying carbon dioxide is returned to the heart and finally to the lungs, where the carbon dioxide is released in exhalation.

Improving cardiorespiratory endurance

Frequency: Three to five times per week is required to improve and maintain cardiorespiratory endurance. Exercise on a regular basis may be helpful in establishing an exercise habit.

Intensity: The activity should result in raising the heart rate to 75% of the maximum for a sustained period of time. The ***maximum heart rate*** of elementary school age children is approximately 210 to

220 beats per minute. The heart rate should be raised to approximately 160 beats per minute during exercise if cardiorespiratory endurance is to be affected.

Children in the intermediate and upper elementary school grades can learn to take their own pulse. This may be done at the wrist or at the neck. To find the pulse rate at the wrist, the index and second fingertips are placed on the radial artery, located on the thumb side of the wrist. To take the pulse at the neck, the index and second fingers are placed just under the jaw and slightly above and to the side of the Adam's apple on the carotid artery. The fingers should press easily until the pulse is found. The pulse is counted for 10 seconds and then multiplied by six to find the rate per minute, or a target rate for 10 seconds can be set and compared to the actual rate counted.

Shortly after exercise, in approximately 3 minutes, the pulse rate should drop dramatically back to a nearly normal level. If it does not, a physician should be consulted.

Duration: Activity sessions should last for 20 minutes at the elementary school level. The duration of the activity is related to the intensity of the workout. If the workout is of *low intensity,* such as walking, the activity period needs to be longer. Activity generally begins at a low intensity, with the intensity raised as the children show improvement in cardiorespiratory endurance.

Warm-ups: Stretching exercises of the upper and lower legs.

Activities: Activities in which there is a continuous energy output or those in which high and low intensity activities are alternated are used. Examples include:

Fast walking.

Jogging.

Alternating sprinting and jogging.

A steeplechase course in which the perimeter of the gymnasium or the playing area is set up with imaginary water hazards, obstacles to cross or go around, and areas for sprinting. The children may repeat the course several times, timing each attempt.

Sustained locomotor skills in which the teacher or a student calls out the skills, which may be an extension of the day's unit activities, as the children keep moving: "Skip . . . ; now run . . . ; try hopping."

Running a number of laps around the playing area, attempting to maintain a steady speed: "Run 5 laps."

Running laps for time: "How many laps can you complete in 2 minutes?"

Running in place and then, on the signal, running a lap, repeating several times.

Rope jumping forward or backward: "How many consecutive jumps can you do? How many jumps can you complete in 30 seconds?"

Marching.

Bench step on stairs or a 10- to 14-inch high bench. The individual steps up on the bench with one foot (count 1); brings the other foot next to the first (count 2); steps down with one foot (count 3); brings the second foot next to the first (count 4); and repeats.

Obstacle course including a number of events such as rope jumping and moving over or under obstacles.

Jumping jacks. From a standing position with arms down at the sides, the arms are brought up from the sides with hands touching overhead as the legs jump to a side stride position (count 1). The arms are brought back down to the sides as the legs return to the starting position (count 2).

Aerobic routines to music.

Assessing cardiorespiratory fitness[1]
Distance runs

Purpose: To measure maximal functional capacity and cardiorespiratory endurance.

Either of the two tests may be used. The tests may be administered on a 440-yard or 400-meter track or any other flat measured surface, such as around a measured outdoor play area.

Although norms are given for children in the primary grades for each of the two tests included here, it may be desirable to substitute a shorter run for children in kindergarten through the second grade. Because of their shorter attention span, a 400- or 600-yard run may be more appropriate. Norms may be established by the school or school district from scores collected for 1 or more years and updated as the children's performance improves.

One-mile run The students are organized in partners. On the signal "Ready, start," one of each set of partners runs 1 mile in the fastest time. As the runners cross the finish line, the timer calls out the running time. The individuals not running listen for their partner's running time. Walking is permitted, but the individual should attempt to cover the distance as fast as possible.

The mile is recorded to the nearest second.

Nine-minute run On the signal "Ready, start," runners attempt to run as great a distance as possible before time is called at 9 minutes. Walking is permitted, but the runners should attempt to cover as much distance as possible during the 9 minutes.

The test is scored to the nearest 10 yards or 10 meters.

Body Composition

Body composition refers to the amounts of specific body tissues in the human body. Generally regarding fitness we consider the *lean body weight* and body fat. The lean body weight is made up of the bones, muscles, and internal organs. The body fat is the fat stored in and around the muscles and body.

Body composition, although genetically related to body type, is primarily the result of activity and nutrition. The food we consume is composed of carbohydrates, fats, and proteins. Each of these substances is important to the vital processes that take place in the body.

Carbohydrates provide an energy source for the cells. Carbohydrates in excess of what is needed are converted to fat and stored as adipose tissue beneath the skin.

Fats provide more than twice the amount of energy as an equal proportion of carbohydrates. The fatty layer surrounding the vital organs protects them from trauma, and fat is also a source of insulation protecting the body from cold temperatures. However, in high temperatures excess fat may cause overweight or obese individuals to feel distress sooner than normal weight individuals. Like carbohydrates, excess fats are stored in the body for future use. Although by-products of fats (cholesterol and triglycerides) have been associated with heart disease, fats should not be eliminated entirely from the diet.

Proteins, although they are not an energy source, are important in the growth and repair of cells. They are found in cell walls and the cell nucleus.

The process of breaking down energy sources into glycogen to be used by the cells is called metabolism. The metabolic rate varies with the individual. Some persons appear able to consume large quantities of food without gaining weight. Others tend to gain weight consuming small quantities of food. One might assume that the overweight individual has a more efficient system, requiring little food to provide for its energy needs.

Activity level is also a factor in weight control. Generally overweight children exercise less than children of normal weight. Increasing the activity level is necessary for weight reduction. Sufficient exercise and an appropriate diet bring about the best results in weight control. Childhood obesity is a serious health problem in the United States. Excessive weight has ramifications for the developing child physically, socially, and psychologically. Society values a lean body. As children enter school they quickly become aware of how others react to them. Overweight children are often ridiculed or excluded from group membership. Failure to be accepted influences children's feelings about themselves.

Obese children are handicapped learners in physical education. Vigorous activity is more tiring for them. Obese children heat up more rapidly than their normal weight peers, and chaffing of the legs may make some activities painful. The added weight may interfere with skill development. Ill-fitting clothing may restrict movement.

Screening preschool children may identify early weight problems. Children with weight problems need understanding and counseling. The child and the family may need help in nutrition and diet planning as well as recognition of the importance of daily exercise. A child's overeating may be a reaction to problems at home. Often when children are upset

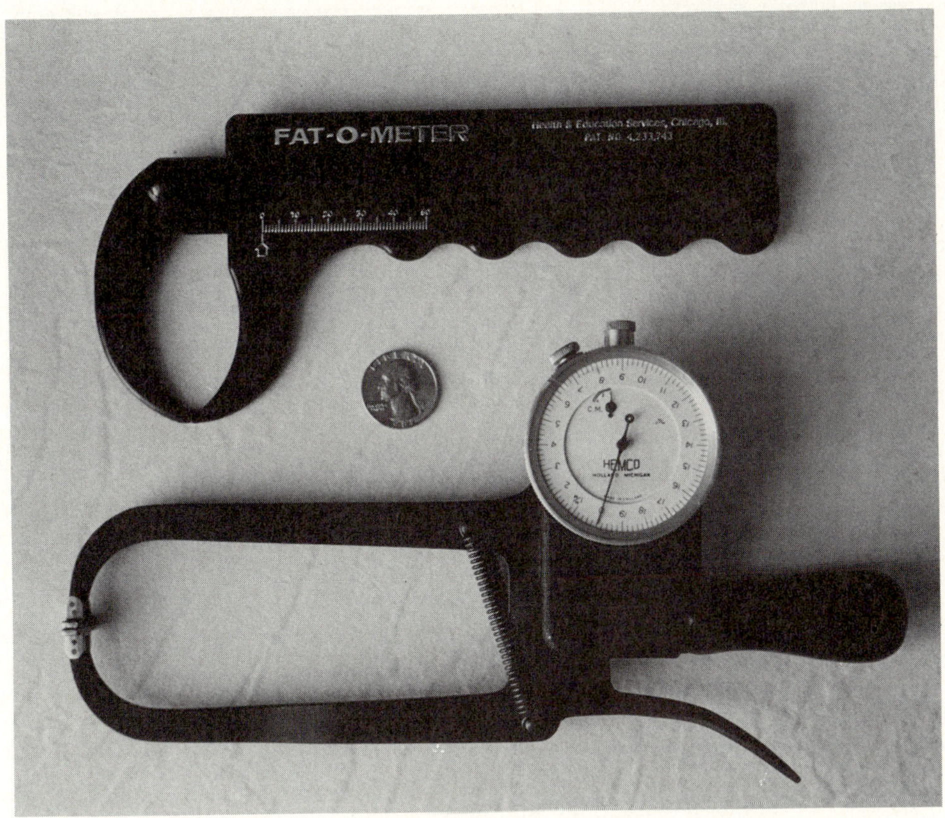

eating becomes a way of coping with their problems. Before a child's weight problem can be dealt with, the cause must be determined. Is it the availability of desserts or other foods with a high sugar content? Is overeating a way of dealing with problems at home? Is poor nutrition the cause of the weight problem? How physically active is the child? What are the child's favorite leisure pursuits?

Overcoming weight problems is difficult for children. It requires maturity, dedication, and often sacrifice. This is only possible if the entire family supports the efforts. Unfortunately it is easier to begin with good habits than to change them.

Improving body composition

Frequency/intensity: Regular daily exercise is required to improve body composition by lowering the percentage of body fat. In working with overweight children it is best to begin with low intensity exercise, which gets them moving but does not result in overheating and other discomforts associated with physical activity. Once an activity habit is established, the intensity of the activity may be increased to moderate intensity. Children with low self-esteem and a body concept in which they see themselves as inept

in physical activity may not be willing participants. Beginning with activities in which fun is stressed and they can feel successful is important. Activities that provide successful social experiences with other children and little pressure to perform at a high level of skill result in greater interest in being physically active. The activity level may then be increased gradually to accommodate weight loss.

Duration: Activity sessions of 30 to 45 minutes suffice. Sessions may increase in duration as the children's condition improves.

Warm-ups: Warm-up activities include stretching for all body segments and light exercise such as walking or jogging.

Activities: Generally all the activities included for cardiorespiratory endurance may be used. Vigorous activity is necessary if children are to metabolize a sufficient number of calories.

Assessing body composition

Skinfold measurements in which the thickness of a section of skin is determined with a *skinfold caliper* are used to measure the percentage of body fat. Several sites on the body are used. The following procedure is used to measure a skinfold[1]:

Table 13-3
Percentile norms for 1-mile run

				Age				
Percentile	5	6	7	8	9	10	11	12
GIRLS								
99	9:03	8:06	7:58	7:45	7:21	7:09	7:07	6:57
75	13:09	11:24	10:55	10:35	9:58	9:30	9:12	8:36
50	15:08	13:48	12:30	12:00	11:12	11:06	10:27	9:47
25	17:59	15:27	14:30	14:16	13:18	12:54	12:10	11:35
5	19:00	18:50	17:44	16:58	16:42	17:00	16:56	14:46
BOYS								
99	7:45	8:15	7:17	6:14	6:43	6:25	6:04	5:40
75	11:32	10:55	9:37	9:14	8:36	8:10	8:00	7:24
50	13:46	12:29	11:25	11:00	9:56	9:19	9:06	8:20
25	16:05	15:10	14:02	13:29	12:00	11:05	11:31	10:00
20	16:37	15:18	14:37	13:56	12:25	11:31	12:02	10:42
15	17:08	15:51	15:06	14:25	13:21	12:11	12:40	11:20
10	17:21	16:56	15:50	15:16	14:19	13:00	13:37	12:07
5	18:25	17:38	17:17	16:19	15:44	14:28	15:25	13:41

From AAHPERD.[1]

Table 13-4
Percentile norms for 9-minute run

				Age				
Percentile	5	6	7	8	9	10	11	12
GIRLS								
99	1584	1980	2340	2260	2300	2240	2170	2370
75	1300	1440	1540	1540	1650	1650	1723	1760
50	1140	1208	1344	1358	1425	1460	1480	1590
25	950	1017	1150	1225	1243	1250	1345	1356
5	700	750	860	970	960	940	904	1000
BOYS								
99	1975	2000	2400	2520	2450	2520	2520	
75	1320	1469	1683	1810	1835	1910	1925	
50	1170	1280	1440	1595	1660	1690	1725	
25	990	1090	1243	1380	1440	1487	1540	
5	600	816	990	1053	1104	1110	1170	

From AAHPERD.[1]

1. Grasp the skinfold between the thumb and fore-finger and lift up.
2. Place the contact surface of the caliper 1 cm (½ inch) above or below the fingers.
3. Slowly release the grip on the calipers, enabling them to exert their full tension on the skinfold.
4. Read the skinfold to the nearest 0.5 mm after the needle stops (1 to 2 seconds after releasing the grip on the caliper).

Girls should wear a loose-fitting tee shirt or halter top. The measurements may also be taken in the locker room when the girls are changing clothes.

There are several calipers on the market. The AAHPERD recommends the Harpenden (Quinton Instrument Co. Seattle, Washington) or the Lange (Cambridge Scientific Industries, Maryland) calipers for measuring skinfolds. Whatever caliper is used, it should be carefully calibrated and should register zero when in the closed position. The Adipometer (Ross Laboratories, Columbus, Ohio) is a less expensive caliper that is affordable for all schools.

Using the calipers accurately takes practice. It may be necessary to test the accuracy of the measurements by repeating the measurements on several individu-als. By repeating the measurements the tester should develop skill using the calipers so there is little dis-crepancy between the repeated readings.

Table 13-5 indicates the percentage of body fat considered to be obese for white elementary school children at various ages.

Sum of skinfold fat[1]

Purpose: To determine the level of fatness.

Two skinfold sites are used for the test: the triceps and subscapular. (Figure 13-1). The triceps skinfold is measured over the triceps muscle of the right arm halfway between the acromion process of the scapula and the elbow. The skinfold is parallel to the lon-gitudinal axis of the upper arm. The subscapular skin-fold is taken on the right side of the body 1 cm (½ inch) below the inferior angle of the scapula in line with the natural cleavage lines of the skin.

Children between the 25th and 50th percentiles should maintain their weight for the current year. Children should hope to score above the 50th per-centile. Children below the 25th percentile need as-sistance in weight reduction to bring their body lean-ness to a more acceptable level.

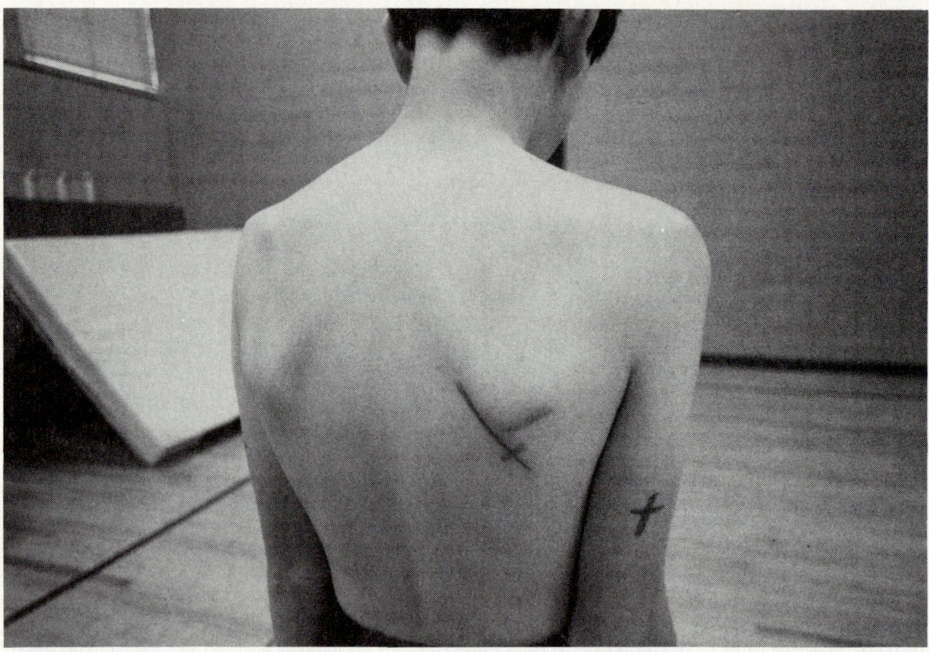

Figure 13-1

Subscapular and triceps skinfold sites.
From AAHPERD.[1]

Table 13-5
Obesity standards for caucasian Americans*

Age	Male	Female
5	12	14
6	12	15
7	13	16
8	14	17
9	15	18
10	16	20
11	17	21
12	18	22
13	18	23
14	17	23

*Minimum triceps skinfold thickness indicating obesity (millimeters).
Adapted from Seltzer and Mayer.[16]

Table 13-6
Percentile norms for triceps skinfold

	Age						
Percentile	6	7	8	9	10	11	12
GIRLS							
75	7	8	8	9	9	9	9
50	9	10	10	11	12	12	12
25	11	12	14	14	15	15	16
5	16	17	20	22	23	23	25
BOYS							
75	6	6	6	7	7	7	7
50	8	8	8	8	9	10	9
25	9	10	11	12	12	14	13
5	13	14	17	20	20	22	23

From AAHPERD.[1]

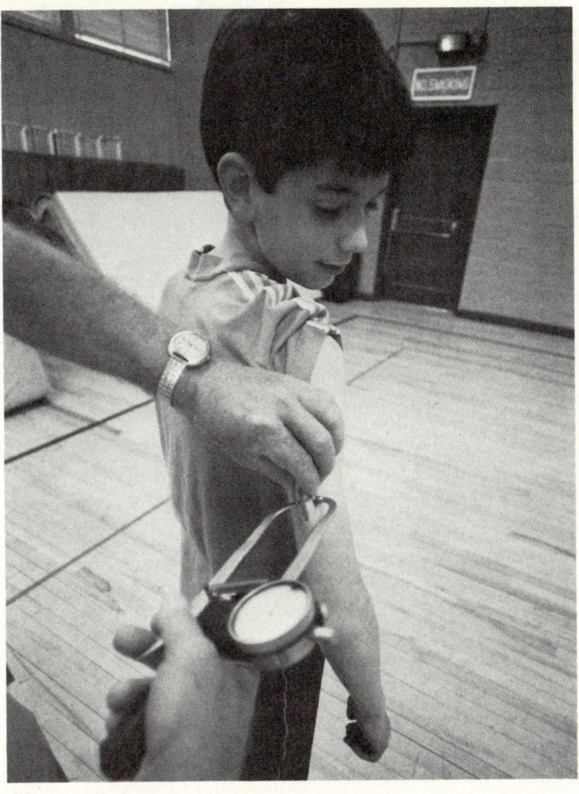

Table 13-7
Percentile norms for sum of triceps plus subscapular skinfolds (millimeters)

				Age			
Percentile	6	7	8	9	10	11	12
GIRLS							
99	8	8	8	9	9	8	9
75	12	12	13	14	14	15	15
50	14	15	16	17	18	19	19
25	17	19	21	24	25	25	27
5	26	28	36	40	41	42	48
BOYS							
99	7	7	7	7	7	8	8
75	11	11	11	11	12	12	11
50	12	12	13	14	14	16	15
25	14	15	17	18	19	22	21
5	20	24	28	34	33	38	44

From AAHPERD.[1]

Flexibility

Flexibility refers to the range of motion in the joints, which varies with age and physical condition. Figure 13-2 shows the difference in flexibility with age and changing body proportions. Since there is great variability, children must be helped to establish realistic goals for themselves and not have the same expectations for performance as other children in the group. Flexibility should not be stressed in the beginning since children vary considerably in this condition and may be discouraged if they are extremely inflexible. Children may also notice a difference in their ability to stretch the two sides of the body.

Flexibility is specific to the particular articulations of the body. A person may have good flexibility in some areas and not in others. Those articulations where the full range of movement is used retain their flexibility; those joints not used in the full range of motion become less flexible.

Adequate flexibility is important to everyday living. It enables one to more successfully complete daily routine tasks. Individuals with good flexibility may be less susceptible to joint injury as well.

Improving flexibility

Frequency: Three to five times per week is recommended.

Intensity: Static stretching is used following the procedures indicated below. The stretch should be repeated several times.

Duration: Stretches should be held for 10 to 30 seconds.

Warm-ups: Easy stretches should be used.

Activities:

Stretching: Stretching is an important activity for warming up and cooling down the body. Slow static stretches are more effective than ballistic or bouncing stretches for increasing mobility in the joints and preventing soft tissue injury. It is vital to stretch the body segments that are important to the specific activity of instruction. The individual begins the stretch to a point of feeling a little tension in the body part being stretched. As the body relaxes, the stretch is extended and held again. Individuals should stretch within their own limits. The stretch should not be strained or painful. Breathing is rhythmical during the stretch, and relaxation is important. On recovery from a bending stretch while standing, the legs

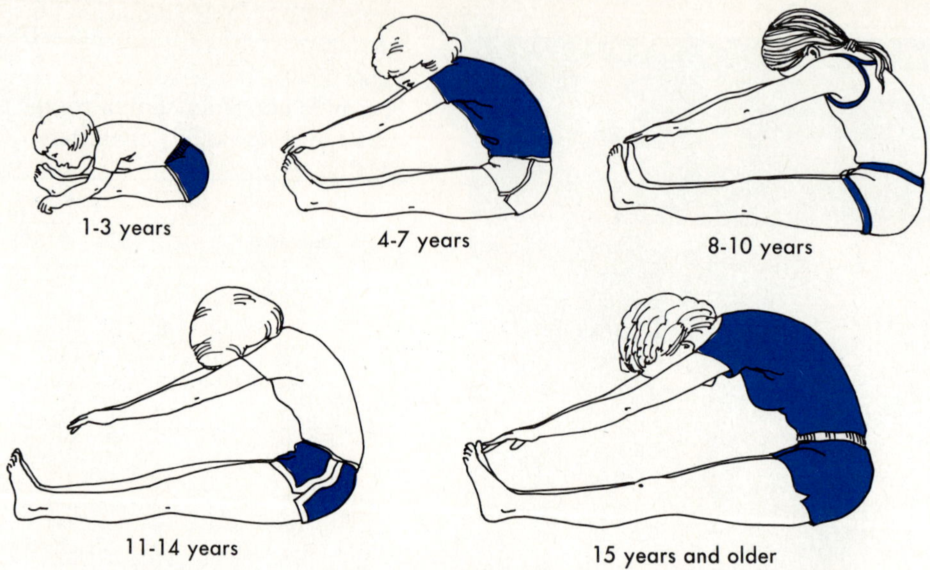

Figure 13-2

Normal flexibility at various ages.
From Kendall, and others.[11]

should be bent slightly to lessen the strain on the lower back.

Stunts: Stunts described in Chapter 15 may be used, including inch worm, bear walk, gorilla walk, ostrich walk, snail, thread the needle, bridge, and back bend.

Movement activities: Many movement activities include potential flexibility activities. Holding freezes in various body positions is fun and at the same time may include stretching.

Miscellaneous activities such as arm circling, bear hug, or squat thrust may also be used.

Assessing flexibility
Sit and reach[1]

Purpose: To evaluate flexibility of the lower back and posterior thighs.

The test apparatus consists of a specially constructed box with a measuring scale on which 23 cm is at the level of the feet. See Figure 13-3 for construction specifications.

The starting position is assumed by sitting at the apparatus in bare or stocking feet with the knees fully extended and the feet shoulder width apart. The feet are placed so they are flat against the board. The arms are extended forward with the hands placed on top of each other. The pupil reaches forward with palms down along the measuring scale four times and holds the position on maximum reach on the fourth trial. The hands must reach evenly.

The score is the most distant point reached on the fourth trial measured to the nearest centimeter.

Muscular Strength and Endurance

Muscular strength refers to the ability of the muscles to do work; muscular endurance is the ability to sustain work over time. Muscular strength and endurance are specific to each set of muscles. Muscles that are used more are stronger and have greater endurance than those that are not used as much. If the muscles continue to be used, the level of strength and endurance is maintained. Reduced use decreases strength and endurance.

The legs, which are used daily to move from place to place, have the strongest muscles. The upper body, especially the muscles of the shoulder girdle, tends to be weaker, and except for a few occupations, it does not have the demands on it to improve and maintain muscular strength and endurance. The abdominal muscles may also be weak. Weak abdominals may be a cause of low back problems. A program should include activities that strengthen and maintain all the muscles of the body.

Improving muscular strength and endurance

Frequency: Three to five times per week is recommended.

Intensity: The workload, or demands on the mus-

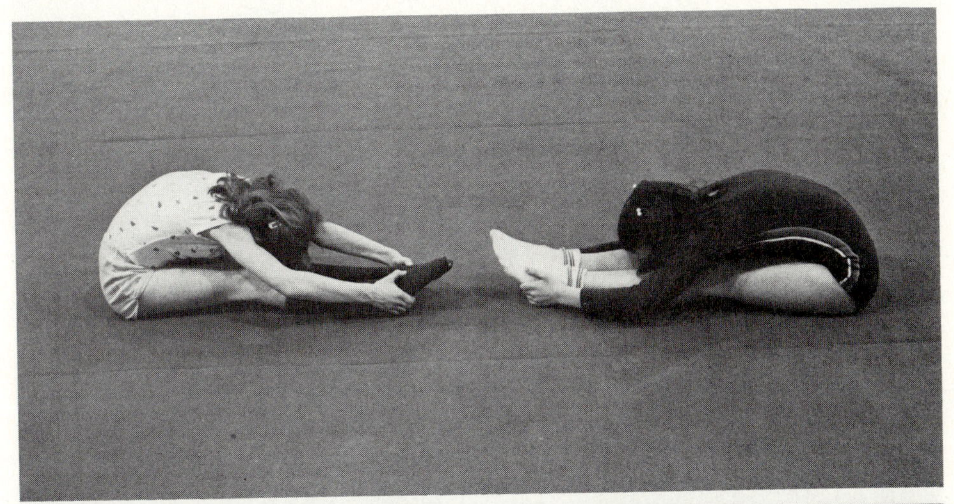

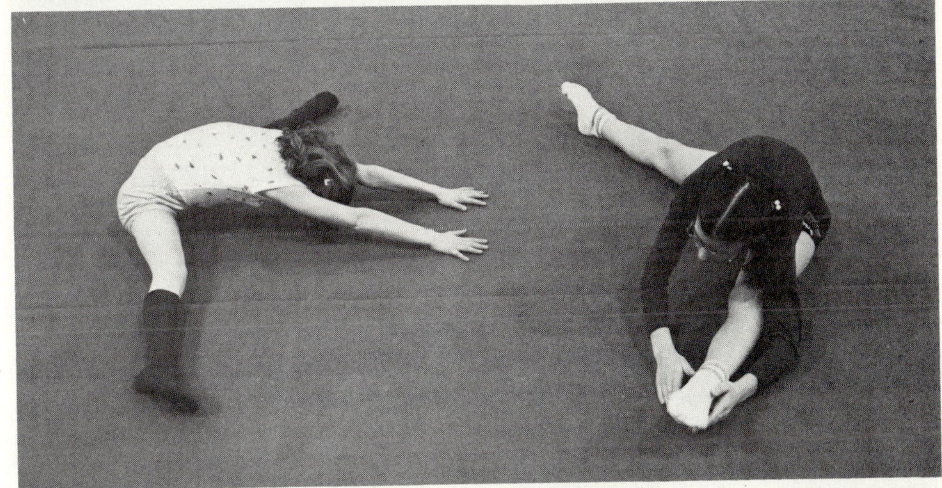

cle groups, should be increased gradually but not too fast.

Duration: The number of repetitions is gradually increased.

Warm-ups: Light activity such as fast walking or jogging.

Activities: For specific body segments the following activities may be used:

For upper body:

Crab walk, seal crawl, coffee grinder, seal slap, bridge, lame puppy walk, bear walk, inch worm, wheelbarrow, mule kick, bridge, or other stunts in which the body weight is taken on the arms (See Chapter 15)

Chinning or bent arm hang on a horizontal ladder, jungle gym, or other climbing apparatus

Traveling on a horizontal ladder or straight arm traveling on parallel bars

Throwing objects and gradually increasing the size and/or weight (a basketball is a heavy object for an elementary school age child), from standing, sitting, and lying positions

Climbing ropes: climbing, pull-ups, or bent arm hang

Push-ups if performed correctly or wall push-aways

Inverted hangs on ropes or horizontal or parallel bars

Table 13-8
Percentile norms for sit and reach

| Percentile | \
 Age | | | | | | | |
|---|---|---|---|---|---|---|---|---|
| | 5 | 6 | 7 | 8 | 9 | 10 | 11 | 12 |
| **GIRLS** | | | | | | | | |
| 99 | 37 | 38 | 37 | 39 | 39 | 41 | 41 | 46 |
| 75 | 30 | 30 | 31 | 31 | 31 | 31 | 32 | 34 |
| 50 | 27 | 27 | 27 | 28 | 28 | 28 | 29 | 30 |
| 25 | 23 | 23 | 24 | 23 | 23 | 24 | 24 | 25 |
| 5 | 18 | 18 | 16 | 17 | 17 | 16 | 16 | 15 |
| **BOYS** | | | | | | | | |
| 99 | 36 | 37 | 38 | 38 | 37 | 37 | 38 | 52 |
| 75 | 29 | 29 | 28 | 29 | 29 | 28 | 29 | 29 |
| 50 | 25 | 26 | 25 | 25 | 25 | 25 | 25 | 26 |
| 25 | 22 | 22 | 22 | 22 | 22 | 20 | 21 | 21 |
| 5 | 17 | 16 | 16 | 16 | 16 | 12 | 12 | 13 |

From AAHPERD.[1]

For abdominals:
  Sit-ups with an increasing workload
  Crab walk, V-sit
  Alternate knee raisers or knee circles
For the back:
  Upper back lift, lower back lift
  Straight back raise
For the legs:
  Jumping for height or distance
  Running in place, jogging, running
  Rope jumping
Combatives provide an opportunity for children to apply mechanical principles and to engage in friendly competition with others as they work on muscle strength and endurance. Children of equal size and weight should be paired. At times they may wish to challenge children with a size advantage, but this should only be allowed within a reasonable range. For safety combatives should be performed on a mat. The following combatives may be performed in the middle and upper elementary school grades when children have acquired the necessary body awareness and control for success:
  Ankle pull: Partners are on hands and knees, next to each other and facing in opposite directions. Each picks up the other's nearest ankle and tries to crawl forward, dragging the partner along.
  Backward goat: Partners are on hands and feet, back to back with hips touching. On the signal

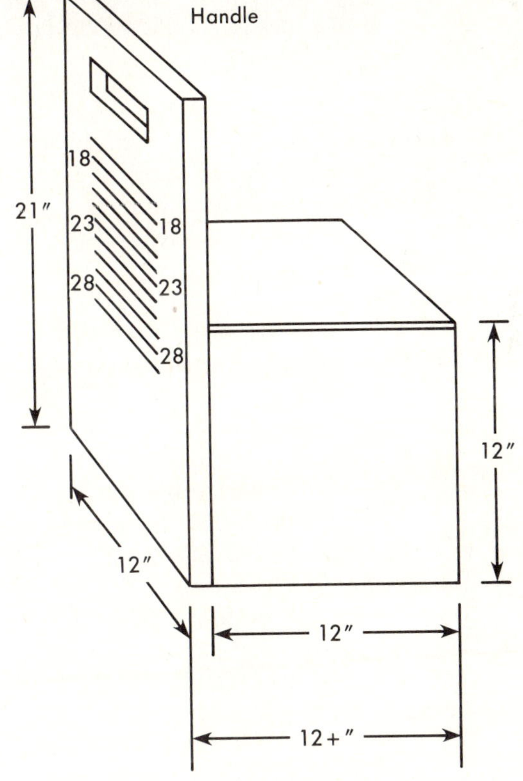

Figure 13-3

Apparatus for flexibility testing.
From AAHPERD.[1]

and using only their hips they each try to push the partner over a line ahead of them. (The hands should be kept well in front of the body to guard against bumping their chins against the mat.)

Bottom's up: Partners begin sitting, facing each other with hands joined, legs spread, and feet touching. Each tries to pull the other so the hips are raised up off the mat.

Chest push: Partners place both hands on each other's chest near the shoulders and attempt to push each other backward over a line.

Foot wrestle: Partners stand facing each other with hands on hips and one foot off the floor; using the free foot, each tries to make the other touch the raised foot on the floor.

Indian hand wrestle: Partners stand facing each other with right hands grasped at the level of the head. With the outer edges of the right feet together and touching and the left foot back for balance, they attempt to push each other, trying to upset the other's stance. If the right foot moves or any part of the body other than the feet touches the mat, the player loses.

Indian leg wrestle: Partners begin lying on the mat on their backs, side by side, and facing in opposite directions. On the signal they raise the inside legs perpendicular to the floor, and each attempts to hook the other's leg at the

knee to cause the partner to roll over.

Lumberjack wrestle: Partners lie down facing each other with legs spread apart, right hands held together with the elbows touching, and left hands behind the backs. Each tries to force the partner's hand to the mat without moving the elbow off the mat.

Stork wrestle: Partners stand facing each other with the left feet raised in back and held with the left hands. With right hands joined, they attempt to pull each other off balance and force the partner to put the left foot down to the mat.

Assessing muscular strength and endurance
Modified sit-ups[1]

Purpose: To measure abdominal strength and endurance.

The starting position is assumed by lying on the back with knees flexed and the soles of the feet on the floor. The heels should be between 12 and 18 inches from the buttocks. The arms are crossed with the right hand at the top of the left shoulder and the left hand at the top of the right shoulder. A partner holds the feet to the floor as the sit-ups are done. (There is some evidence that holding the feet obscures weakness in the abdominals, enabling the student with weak abdominals to perform the sit-up.[10])

On the signal "Ready, go," the individual curls

to the sitting position. The chin remains tucked to the chest and the arms maintain contact with the chest. The sit-up is completed as the elbows touch the thighs. The student then returns to the down position until the midback makes contact with the floor. Students may rest between sit-ups but should be encouraged to do as many as possible in the 60 seconds.

The score is the number of sit-ups that can be completed in 60 seconds.

Pull-ups[8]

Purpose: To measure boys' upper body strength and endurance.

A bar high enough so the individual can hang with arms and legs extended and the feet off the floor is used.

The individual holds the bar with the palms facing away from the performer and raises his body by his arms so his chin can be placed over the bar and then lowered once again to the hanging position. The pull-up is repeated as many times as possible.

One trial is permitted. The body should not swing during the execution of the pull-up. The legs are kept straight and no kicking is allowed.

The score is the total number of pull-ups completed.

Flexed arm hang[8]

Purpose: To measure girls' upper body strength and endurance.

A bar approximately equal to the standing height of the individual is used. Spotters are positioned in front of and behind the girl being tested.

An overhand grip is used. The individual raises her body off the floor to a position where the chin is above the bar, elbows flexed, and chest close to the bar, with the aid of the spotters. This position is held as long as possible.

The score is the total time to the nearest second the position is held. The watch is started as the student assumes the flexed arm hanging position. The watch is stopped when the student's chin drops below the bar, the chin touches the bar, or the head is tilted back to keep the chin above the bar.

Chin-ups[14]

Purpose: To measure upper body strength and endurance.

The same procedure as the pull-ups test for boys is used, except that the bar is gripped with the palms facing the performer.

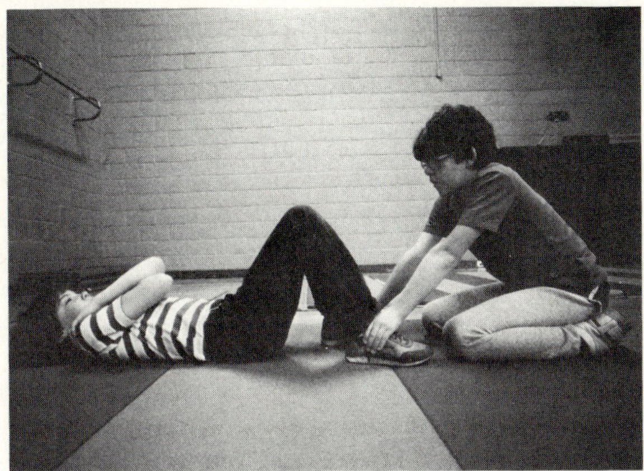

Table 13-9

Percentile norms for modified sit-ups

	Age							
Percentile	5	6	7	8	9	10	11	12
GIRLS								
99	35	42	51	55	51	54	55	61
75	24	28	31	35	35	39	40	41
50	19	22	25	29	29	32	34	36
25	12	14	20	22	23	25	28	30
5	2	6	10	12	14	15	19	19
BOYS								
99	47	47	53	55	52	59	61	68
75	23	26	33	37	38	40	42	46
50	18	20	26	30	32	34	37	39
25	11	15	19	25	25	27	30	31
5	2	6	10	15	15	15	17	19

From AAHPERD.[1]

Table 13-10
Percentile norms for pull-ups (boys)

Percentile	Age		
	9-10	11	12
75	3	4	4
50	1	2	2
25	0	0	0
5	0	0	0
0	0	0	0

From Hunsicker and Reiff.[8]

Table 13-11
Percentile norms for flexed arm hang (girls)

Percentile	Age		
	9-10	11	12
75	18	20	18
50	9	10	9
25	3	3	3
5	0	0	0
0	0	0	0

From Hunsicker and Reiff.[8]

POSTURE

Posture may be defined as the alignment of body parts to maintain an upright position. Posture is dynamic. The skeletal system is comprised of many bones joined and bound together by ligaments, muscles, and their tendons. Movement is possible in a variety of ways, which allows the body parts to be aligned in different ways. In addition, even when it appears to be motionless, the body is constantly adjusting to the pull of gravity. Good posture or body alignment requires each body part to be aligned with the one directly below it so the center of gravity of each part is directly above the one below. In this alignment gravitational stresses are minimized. In good alignment the three major body segments—the hips, trunk, and head—are directly over one another (Figure 13-4).

A plumb line dropped to the side of a standing person should pass through the lobe of the ear, the tip of the shoulder, the center of the trunk, the center of the hips, slightly behind the kneecap, and slightly in front of the ankle bone.

When viewed from the front, the feet are slightly apart (2 to 3 inches), the body weight is carried over the middle of the feet, the knees are straight but not hyperextended, the pelvic girdle is aligned with the feet, the chest is balanced over the pelvis, the shoulder girdle is relaxed with the arms hanging loosely at the sides, and the head is balanced over the upper end of the spine.

Pull-up.

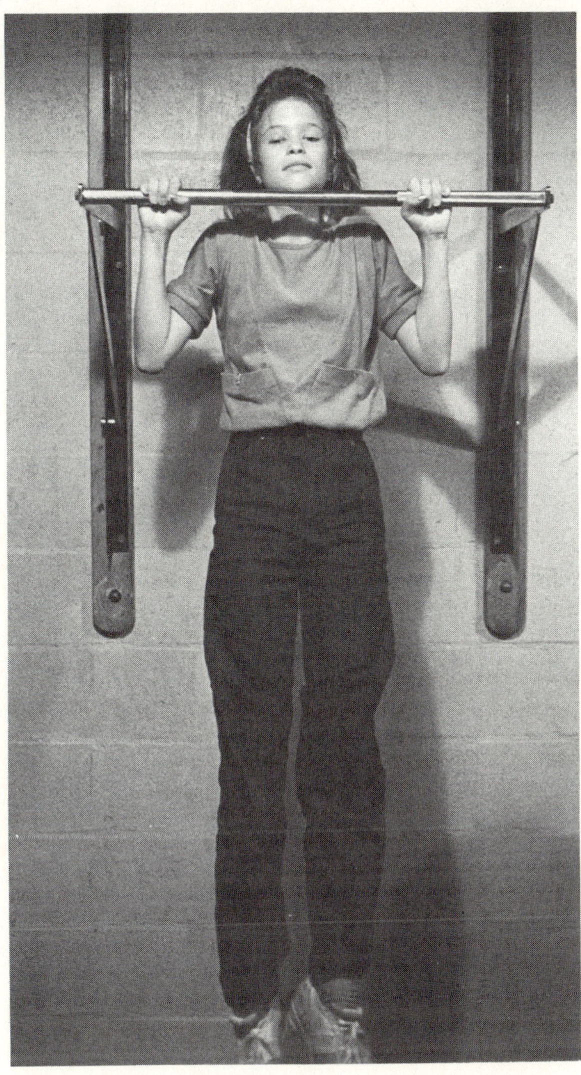

Flexed arm hang.

Table 13-12
Percentile norms for chin-ups

	Age		
Percentile	10	11	12
GIRLS			
99	8	8	8
75	1	1	1
50	0	0	0
25	0	0	0
BOYS			
99	13	12	13
75	4	5	5
50	1	2	3
25	0	0	0

From Ross and others.[14]

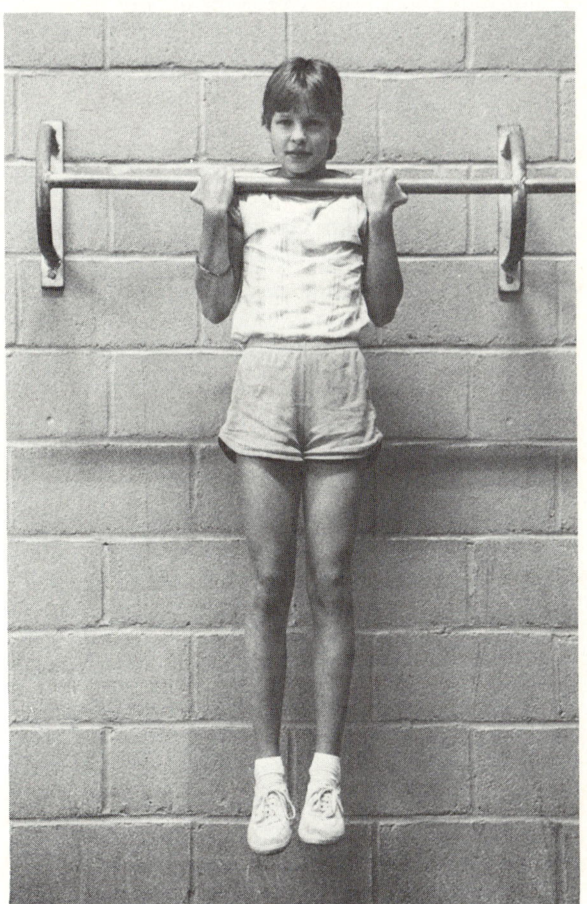

Chin-ups.

When the person is sitting in a chair, the head is aligned directly over the shoulders, the hips are well back into the chair so the thighs are supported, the back is straight and resting comfortably against the back of the chair, the knees are flexed at right angles, and the feet are flat on the floor.

If the chair does not fit, the child's back and thighs may not be supported and/or the feet may not touch the floor. When a child is working at a desk, the top of the desk should be at the level of the elbows. It should be close enough so the child does not have to lean too far forward or sit on the edge of the chair.

Often in physical education students sit on the floor, on mats, or on bleachers, which have insufficient back support. Having children sit next to walls for back support may help. Since children sit for very little time in physical education classes, the chance for poor sitting posture is minimized.

The posture of children differs slightly from the standard recognized as good alignment for adults. Children undergo a series of growth changes from birth to maturity that affect posture. Different segments of the body grow at different rates. As bones grow, the body proportions change. Children have greater mobility and flexibility than adults. The children's range of movement in the joints permits greater momentary deviations in posture than would be considered healthy for adults. This mobility protects children from fixed postural faults to some degree. As children approach adulthood there is a gradual tightening of ligaments and fascia, which begins to limit the range of movement in the joints and consequently increases stability.

In growing children there is an imbalance in the muscle strength of the back and front sides of the body, with the muscles of the back being stronger. As children mature, this imbalance decreases, although generally the muscles of the back of the body remain slightly stronger throughout life. Weak abdominals may contribute to poor postural habits.

Another factor that cannot be overlooked in a discussion of the posture of children is nutrition. Proper nutrition is essential to the healthy development of body tissues. Poor diet has lasting effects on children's posture. Although good diet is important throughout life, it is perhaps of greater significance during the developmental years.

Back problems in adulthood are more often the result of abuse through poor posture and poor body mechanics than the result of an accident. Poor posture may also result in muscle spasms and tension.

Good posture is esthetically pleasing. It conveys the impression of confidence and self-assuredness. It is often a characteristic that gives a favorable first impression. A person's postural habits may be difficult to change. A person may know what good alignment is and yet fail to achieve it for many reasons. Children who are taller than their classmates may slouch so they do not appear to be as big. Adolescents may choose postures common to their group. Small children may walk on tiptoes to appear taller. Good alignment must be valued if good posture is to result.

The physical education teacher is often one of the first to notice deviations in posture. Common faults include the following:

The head held forward of its normal alignment

An increased pelvic tilt, which results in an exaggerated curve in the lower back

Protruding abdomen

Round shoulders

Protruding scapula

One shoulder higher than the other

One hip higher than the other

The feet turned in or out with the weight carried on the inner ankles

Knees turned toward each other

Some postural deviations such as a protruding abdomen or scapula are developmental in nature, appearing at a particular age and developmental period and disappearing without correction. Others may lead to serious problems if not treated.

The largest number of postural deviations occur between the ages of 10 and 15 years. Postural screening is important during this period. The physical education teacher is often responsible for conducting the initial posture screening. Children with postural deviation from the normal standard are referred to the school nurse or their own physician. The physician makes the exercise prescription to be carried out by the physical education teacher. During the adolescent growth spurt spinal deviations may occur. These deviations may be serious and should receive appropriate medical attention promptly to prevent serious and costly medical problems later. Figures 13-5 and 13-6 show normal spinal curves and three common deviations, namely *scoliosis, lordosis,* and *kyphosis.* These conditions should receive immediate medical attention.

Postural Screening

Postural screening should include both the static (stationary) and dynamic (moving) posture. Several observations should be made before an orthopedic referral is recommended. In screening posture the following questions should be answered. If the answer to any of the questions is yes after repeated observations, the child should be referred to the school nurse.

Is the head tilted to one side or forward when walking?

Is one shoulder closer to the ear than the other?

Do the shoulders appear to be tight or positioned forward?

Is one hip higher than the other or appear to be more prominent?

Do the knees turn toward one another? Do they appear to be locked or turned away from each other?

Do one or both feet usually point in or out?

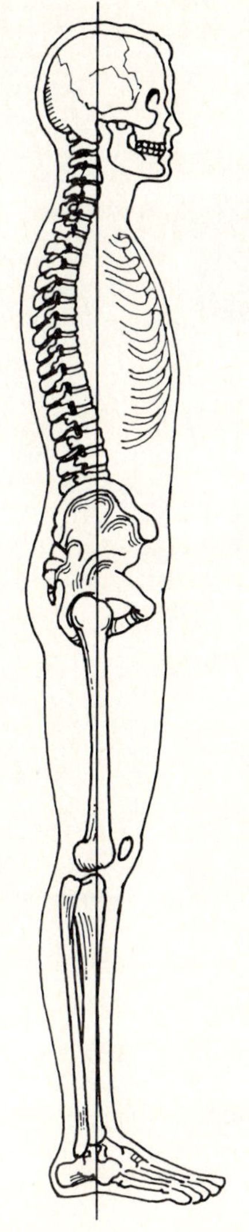

Figure 13-4

Alignment of body parts in standing posture.
Modified From Kendall, and others.[11]

Do the hips protrude in a side view?

The spinal curves in lordosis or kyphosis may be easily seen in the side view of the body. Scoliosis, on the other hand, may be suspected if the shoulders or hips are uneven or if one scapula is prominent and the other does not show. In screening for scoliosis the child bends forward at the waist. The lateral curvature may then be observed in following the spine from the neck to the hips. One side of the body may appear to be higher than the other as well. Girls should wear halter tops for the screening.

BODY MECHANICS

Exercising good body mechanics as we perform daily tasks can aid in preventing strains of muscles and sprains of ligaments. Whenever possible loads should be kept to a reasonable level. For example, putting groceries in two bags rather than overloading one may not only prevent the items from spilling from a torn bag but also avoid undue strain on the body. Careful examination of mechanical principles and their application to daily tasks should result in more efficient use of the body.

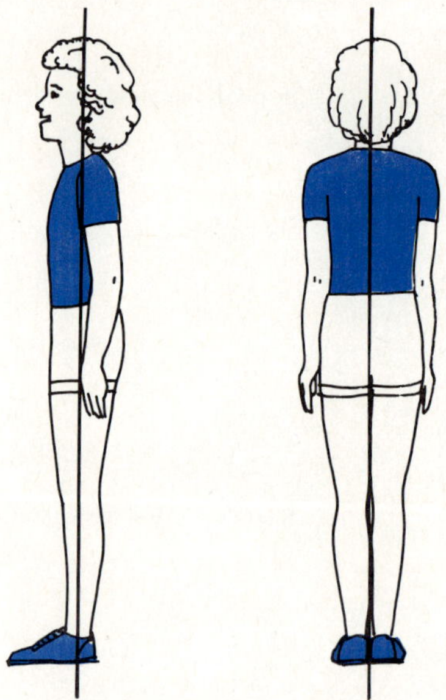

Figure 13-5

Side and back views of normal spinal curves.

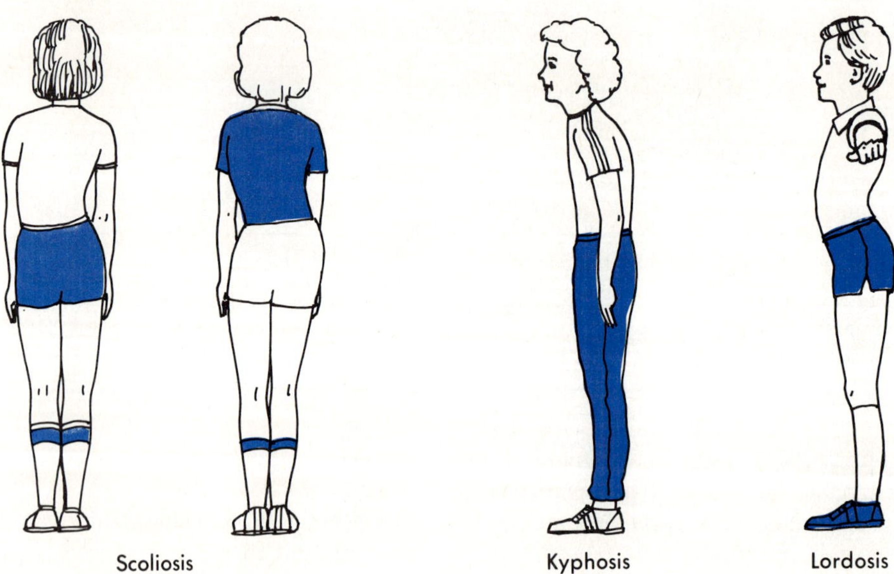

Figure 13-6

Postural deviations. **A,** Scoliosis, total left C curve. **B,** regular S curve. **C,** Kyphosis. **D,** Lordosis.

Lifting

Principle 1: *The heavier the object, the stronger the muscles required to lift the object.*

Principle 2: *An object to be lifted becomes a part of the body weight as it is held.*

Principle 3: *To avoid strain in lifting objects one should attempt to apply all forces vertically through the line of gravity of the body.*

Lifting light objects may require the use of only one body part. Heavier objects require the use of more and stronger body parts. As heavy objects are lifted, the strongest muscles, those of the legs, should be used. This is only possible when the legs are flexed, assuming a stooping position and then straightening as the load is lifted. When the body bends to lift an object, the weaker and smaller muscles of the lower back exert the force for lifting.

Since the object becomes a part of the body weight, it should be held as close as possible to the body.

As the body assumes a stooping posture, the force generated should be applied vertically through the center of the weight. Bending over to lift an object applies the force diagonally upward and backward, which is a mechanical disadvantage for the body.

To lift heavy objects one should stand as close to the object as possible. The feet should be kept in contact with the floor. The legs are flexed and then extended, with the legs doing most of the lifting. The back is kept relatively straight and the object is lifted close to the body.

Carrying Objects

Principle 1: *An object being carried becomes a part of the individual's weight and causes the center of gravity to shift slightly in direction of the added weight.*

The object should be carried as near the individual's line of gravity as possible. The body leans slightly away from the load to counteract the pull of the load and help to maintain balance.

The head and trunk should be kept erect and the abdominal muscles should be tight. When a heavy load is carried on one side of the body, the opposite arm may swing to help relieve the strain of the load.

The object being carried must be controlled to avoid unnecessary swinging or swaying.

Pushing

Principle 1: *In pushing an object the application of force must be continuous, since force must be used to overcome the object's inertia and keep it moving.*

Principle 2: *The force should be applied as near the object's center of gravity and in the desired direction.*

Principle 3: *The heavier the object to be pushed, the stronger the muscles that must be used to move the object.*

Principle 4: *Friction may make it difficult to push objects that are soft or have a large surface area in contact with the ground or floor.*

Some objects are too heavy or too large to carry and must be pushed. Other objects are designed to be pushed, such as grocery carts and lawn mowers.

In pushing an object the back should be kept fairly straight with the body lean beginning at the ankles. The trunk and head are aligned. The feet are in a forward stride position and pointing in the direction of the force. The hips are kept low, the forward knee is bent, and the back knee is straight. The foot pushes against the supporting surface.

Pulling

The principles for pushing apply also to pulling.

Pulling is used for objects too heavy, large, or awkward to lift and where pushing is not desirable or possible. In pulling an object it may be necessary to pull it down from above the shoulders, pull it over ground from above, or pull it horizontally. In pulling the vertical component of force is increased.

In pulling friction is reduced because the vertical component of the force provides a lifting action.

The back should be kept as straight as possible. The knees are bent to add power, the body is inclined slightly forward to allow the body weight to do the work, and the object is grasped firmly.

SUMMARY

The development and maintenance of health-related physical fitness is an important aspect of physical education. Children at the elementary school level not only need to be fit but need to understand why fitness is important and how to test and improve their fitness levels.

Many physical fitness tests are available for use during the elementary school years. The health-related physical fitness test of the AAHPERD measures cardiorespiratory endurance, body composition, flexibility, and muscular strength and endurance of the abdominal muscles. A measure of upper body strength and endurance may also be included. Most of the test items include separate standards for boys and girls. Since there is little evidence that there are significant developmental differences between prepubescent boys and girls, the use of the highest set of norms for both boys and girls should encourage both sexes to their best efforts.

The improvement and maintenance of fitness is an ongoing concern throughout the school year. Many times activities may be built in to the daily lesson by modifying the activity, such as sustaining the activity or holding positions for longer periods.

Since many physical education activities do not provide for optimal fitness development, the teacher must often supplement the daily activities with activities that meet the fitness objectives.

Understanding of good posture and the efficient use of the body in lifting, carrying, pushing, and pulling are also concerns for physical education. The physical education teacher is often responsible for postural screening during the early adolescent years to identify postural deviations, which if untreated may become chronic or permanent conditions of adulthood. Many adult back problems are the result of abuse rather than accident. Children need to be made aware of the importance of good alignment and the appropriate use of the body is performing daily tasks.

REFERENCES

1. AAHPERD: Health-related physical fitness test manual, Reston, Va., 1980, AAHPERD.
2. Anderson, B.: Stretching, Fullerton, Calif., 1977, P.O. Box 2734.
3. Auxter, D., and Pyfer, J.: Principles and methods of adapted physical education, ed. 5, St. Louis, 1985, Times Mirror/Mosby.
4. Bucher, C., and Prentice, W.: Fitness for college and life, St. Louis, 1985, Times Mirror/Mosby.
5. DiGennaro, J.: The new physical fitness: exercise for everyone, Englewood, Colo., 1983, Morton Publishing Co.
6. Getchell, B.: Physical fitness, a way of life, ed. 3, New York, 1983, John Wiley & Sons, Inc.
7. Hockey, R.: Physical fitness: the pathway to healthful living, ed. 5, St. Louis, 1985, Times Mirror/Mosby.
8. Hunsicker, P., and Reiff, G.: AAHPERD youth fitness test manual, rev. ed., Reston, Va., 1976, AAHPERD.
9. Katch, F., and McArdle, W.: Nutrition, weight control and exercise, Philadelphia, 1983, Lea & Febiger.
10. Kendall, F.: A criticism of current tests and exercises for physical fitness, Journal of the American Physical Therapy Association 45(3):193, March 1965.
11. Kendall, H., and others: Posture and pain, Huntington, N.Y., 1975, Robert E. Krieger Publishing Co., Inc.
12. Pate, R.: A new definition of youth fitness, The Physician and Sports Medicine 11(4):80, April 1983.
13. Pollock, M., and Blair, S.: Exercise prescription, JOPER 51(1):30, January 1980.
14. Ross, J., and others: New standards for fitness measurement, JOPERD 56(1):62, January 1985.
15. Ross, J., and others: What are kids doing in school physical education, JOPERD 56(1):73, January 1985.
16. Seltzer, C., and Mayer, J.: A simple criterion of obesity, Postgraduate Medicine 38:101, 1965.
17. Siegel, J., and Manfredi, T.: Effects of a ten-month fitness program on children, The Physician and Sports Medicine 12(5):91, May 1984.
18. Wilmore, J.: Objectives for the nation: physical fitness and exercise, JOPERD 53(3):41, March 1982.

ADDITIONAL READINGS

Blair, S., and others: A new physical fitness test, The Physician and Sports Medicine 11(4):87, April 1983.
An introduction to the health-related physical fitness tests and an interpretation of the test scores regarding acceptable fitness levels.

Dotson, C., and Ross, J.: Relationships between activity patterns and fitness, JOPERD 56(1):67, January 1985.
The effects of physical education curriculum, time in physical education, and community activity involvement on health-related physical fitness test scores.

Gilliam, T., and others: Exercise programs for children: a way to prevent heart attacks, The Physician and Sports Medicine 10(9):96, September 1982.
The effects of a vigorous activity program on the fitness of 6- and 7-year-olds and the resultant changes in daily activity levels.

Jenkins, D., and Staub, J.: Student fitness: the physical educator's role, JOPERD 56(2):31, February 1985.
A program designed to promote fitness and understanding about fitness.

Poehlman, E. Target: Lifestyle, JOPERD 56(2):39, February 1985.
A K-12 program designed to promote good fitness habits and knowledge important to a healthy fitness-oriented life-style.

Ross, J., and others: Maturation and Fitness Test Performance, JOPERD 56(1):67, January 1985.
Developmental trends in cardiorespiratory endurance, abdominal and upper body strength and endurance, lower back and hamstring flexibility, and body composition.

Seefeldt, V.: Physical Fitness in preschool and elementary school-aged children, JOPERD 55(9):33, November/December 1984.
The importance of laying the ground work for physical fitness in the early school years.

Part Five

INDIVIDUAL ACTIVITIES

Individual activities are an important aspect of the elementary school physical education program. Children are challenged through the use of small equipment and large apparatus. These activities promote individual skill development as well as creative use of the body as the children move with or without equipment. The understanding of the body's movement potential is enhanced as children move in space in relation to equipment and apparatus, controlling force, balance, time, and flow.

14

MOVING WITH SMALL EQUIPMENT

CHAPTER OBJECTIVES

1 To provide suggestions for effective teaching and conducting of experiences using small equipment

2 To describe ways of using small equipment to teach and to apply movement concepts

3 To identify a variety of activities using small equipment

4 To describe a variety of sidewalk games for use as playground activities

Children enjoy working with small equipment. They derive much pleasure from manipulating balls, beanbags, discs (Frisbees), hoops, wands, and other small equipment. Scooters, stilts, and balance boards provide challenging play opportunities for children of all ages. Children should be encouraged to develop creative ways to use small equipment as well as skill in using the equipment in more traditional ways.

The application of movement concepts is an important part of the experience with small equipment. Body awareness is enhanced as children develop interesting ways of using body parts in manipulating objects. The use of space provides the additional challenge of moving with a piece of equipment. Controlling force is important in the use of any equipment. New challenges for balance are provided in the use of stilts and balance boards.

Goals that may be developed in the use of small equipment include the following:

1. To develop the use of the body in unique ways to manipulate and control objects
2. To learn the properties of objects and special considerations for their use
3. To apply movement concepts in using small equipment

4. To use equipment as an extension of the body's movement, such as in using paddles, bats, or stilts

SUGGESTIONS FOR TEACHING

The following suggestions for conducting experiences with small equipment should be considered. Additional suggestions may be found in Chapter 7.

When establishing a signal for listening, the teacher should tell the children what to do with the equipment during the period of explanation or clarification. It is difficult for children to hold equipment quietly when instructions are being given. At the beginning of the lesson instructions should be given before the equipment is assigned to the children. During the lesson it may be helpful to have the children put the equipment on the floor in front of them to avoid constant reminders about holding the equipment still. Children might also be challenged to hold the equipment quietly and praised when they do it well. If it is presented as a challenge, most children will do well in holding the equipment when the teacher or others are talking.

It is important to define the area to be used. Some equipment, especially that in which control is easily

"""

MOVEMENT CONCEPTS

The following movement concepts are important in the effective use of small equipment.

BODY AWARENESS

1. To use body parts in a variety of ways to manipulate objects.
2. To use body parts other than those used traditionally in controlling an object.

SPACE

Self/general:
1. To control an object in self space.
2. To control an object while moving in general space.
3. To recognize space needs in controlling objects while performing a variety of tasks.
4. To move in space in relation to an object.
5. To establish the relationship of body parts and an object while performing various skills.
6. To put an object into an empty space.
7. To create a space within which to put an object.
8. To position oneself to cover a space.

Direction:
9. To move in all directions and to change direction while controlling an object.

Pathways:
10. To move in various pathways and to change pathways while controlling an object.
11. To control the path of an object.

Level:
12. To control objects at various levels.
13. To move objects smoothly from one level to another.

Range:
14. To control the range of an object.
15. To vary the range of movement while using a piece of equipment.

QUALITIES OF MOVEMENT

Force:
1. To control the force imparted to an object.
2. To select an appropriate force for the task to be accomplished.
3. To use various body parts to impart force to objects.
4. To vary the force imparted to an object.

Balance:
5. To control balance as one works with an object, both static and dynamic.
6. To use the body in different ways to balance.

Time/speed:
7. To move at various speeds with an object.
8. To vary the speed at which an object is propelled.

lost, such as balls and discs, requires more individual space. In station work each station area should be clearly defined. In individual, partner, or small group work children should be arranged with adequate space within which to work without interfering with the activity of others. The teacher should stress keeping the equipment under control and recognize individual efforts in accepting this responsibility. The teacher should make moving with control a challenge for everyone.

Some equipment or activities require considerable space for the safety of all. The teacher must be sure children are aware of these space needs before equipment is distributed. Children should be taught to use equipment safely. Special safety concerns are identified in the activity descriptions that follow. It may be necessary to discuss uses that are unsafe and why they pose a danger to the group. Children must be taught to assume responsibility for the safety of themselves and all other children in the group.

Many pieces of small equipment may be furnished by the group. Bleach bottles make adequate area boundary markers and objects to hit or maneuver around. Wands may be made from dowel rods. Tin can stilts can be made from large canned food containers. Suggestions for homemade equipment may be found in the Appendix.

MOVEMENT CONCEPTS

The box above outlines the movement content to be developed through the use of small equipment. Beginning movement challenges involve the use of one skill and/or one concept. As the children gain in experience with the equipment, its use, and the movement content, the movement challenges posed become more complex. They may call for the combination of skills and/or the purposeful use of more than one movement concept. In the beginning children may work individually, whereas in later experiences they share in the decision making with partners and small groups of three or four. In this way the possibilities for solutions to movement challenges are expanded beyond the ideas of individual children. Activities may be organized around a theme, for instance, having the children explore a concept such as force using a variety of equipment. Or a number of different concepts might be developed as the children work with various kinds of small equipment.

In the following sections of this chapter activities are suggested for use with a variety of equipment. Some include the movement terminology. As the children explore their own movement in all the activities, the teacher should develop a series of questions to ask to continue to focus the children's attention on the movement concepts.

The activities that follow are but a few of the possibilities for use with small equipment. They are listed in order of difficulty.

BALLS, BEANBAGS, BALLOONS, DISCS, AND RINGS

Balls, beanbags, balloons, discs, and rings are popular equipment for elementary school children. This equipment comes in a variety of sizes, compositions, shapes, and weights. Children should experience working with as great a variety as is available. Often the solutions to movement challenges and the execution of skills vary with the specific piece of equipment being used.

In many schools maximizing the activity for children requires the use of a variety of equipment, such as several types of balls. The teacher should take this opportunity to develop further understanding of the self, the properties of the equipment, and other movement concepts as the children work with many different pieces of equipment. Children may also learn that specific types of equipment may be more suited for use in some activities than in others. For instance, a foam ball is best in dodge ball games or a beanbag might be best in a target toss, where scor-

ing depends on the object remaining in a limited area of the target. The versatility in the use of balls, beanbags, and balloons challenges the youngest as well as the oldest child.

Safety considerations in the use of this equipment include the following:

1. Adequate space is needed for each child or group, so loss of control does not interfere with the work of others. (Balls and discs require the most space.)
2. Control of the object should be a challenge for all children. Children should be encouraged to know their personal limits in controlling an object.
3. Controlling level and force are particularly important if the environment is to be safe for everyone.
4. The group should be organized so the flow of movement in activities involving partners moving the ball from one to the other is parallel to other groups and not through other sets of partners.
5. When these activities are combined with the use of other equipment, they should be placed to one side where walls can help to contain the equipment in an area.

Although each of the following sections includes specific activities for each type of equipment, many of the activities could be used with all three.

BALL SKILLS AND MOVEMENT CONCEPTS

Roll:
  With 2 hands
  With 1 hand
Bounce:
  With 2 hands
  With 1 hand
  Alternating hands
  To another person
Throw:
  Underhand
    With 2 hands
    With 1 hand
  Overhand
    With 1 hand
    With 2 hands (shoulder)
    Overhead
  Vertically
Catch:
  A rolling ball
  A bouncing ball
  A ball in the air
  A falling ball
Kick:
  With the inside of the foot
  With the instep
  Repeatedly (dribbling)
  Punt
  Dropkick
Strike:
  With the hand
    Underhand
    Overhand
  A ball suspended from a rope
Body awareness:
  Use body parts to control a ball.
Space:
  Control a ball in self space.
  Control a ball in general space.
  Control a ball while moving in different directions.
  Vary the path of the ball.
  Control a ball at different levels.
  Move the ball through different levels.
Qualities of movement:
  Control and vary the force used.
  Absorb force with different body parts.
  Vary the speed of the ball.
  Execute skills while moving at various speeds.

Balls

The box above outlines the possible skills and movement content that might be developed in the use of balls. In the beginning the teacher may select one skill, for instance, the bounce with one hand, and have the children explore the use of the body parts involved, movement in self or general space, level, or force. Later challenges might include combining the bounce with one hand with another skill or skills and/or a combination of concepts.

An analysis of the skills used may be found in Chapter 11. The following activities supplement those found in Chapter 11, where emphasis was on developing the technique of throwing and body awareness in the execution of the skill. Using these ball skills and the use of the body in creative ways to manipulate balls, children may:

  Execute skills with balls varying in composition, size, and weight.
  Execute skills while stationary or moving through space.
  Project balls:
    For distance into space.
    To partners.
    To walls.
    To targets varying in level and/or size, varying in distance, varying in the accuracy required (bowling at one or more pins), and rebounding to the target from the floor or wall.
  Execute skills while moving in space, avoiding others and/or obstacles.
  Combine skills to accomplish a task. (Example: Starting from this line, move the ball to the target area and hit the target using three different skills.)

Make up a ball game for three or four people to play using (name) skills.

Combine ball skills with locomotor skills. (Example: Throw the ball in the air, move under it, turn around, and then catch it; or skip as you dribble the ball with your hands.)

Move the ball through space, to a partner, or to a target using body parts other than hands or feet.

Cage ball

Using a cage ball children may:

Work with a partner to push the ball to a line or around obstacles.

Carry it as a group.

Lift or hit it over a rope or net.

Lie on the floor in two lines with feet facing, one line attempting to kick the ball over the heads of the other.

Beanbags

With beanbags children may:

Explore the use of the beanbag while sitting. Standing. Lying down on the back. Lying in a prone position. Kneeling.

Place the beanbag on the floor and move around it. Over it.

Balance the beanbag on different body parts while stationary. Moving in general space.

Balance the beanbag on a body part and move that part, keeping the beanbag balanced.

Balance the beanbag on a body part while performing various skills, such as a crab walk or frog jump, keeping it balanced.

Throw the beanbag from one hand and catch it in the other.

Move the beanbag around the body in the medium level. The high level. The low level.

Throw the beanbag in the air. Do something with the body. Catch the beanbag.

Exchange beanbags with a partner. See how many ways they can do it keeping the beanbag on the floor. In the air. At different levels. While moving.

Move the beanbag with different body parts in general space. To a partner. To a target.

Toss the beanbag from behind the back and catch it.

Toss the beanbag between the legs to a partner. To a target. And catch it in front of the body.

Toss the beanbag as high as possible and catch it.

Catch the beanbag with two hands. One hand. Other body parts.

Pick up a beanbag with various body parts and put it in the hand. Put it in a basket.

Juggle two or three beanbags.

Balloons

With a balloon a child may:

Strike it with various body parts.

Control a balloon in self space while standing or sitting.

Control it at different levels.

Control a balloon while moving in general space.

Hit it to a partner.

Hit it over a net.

Vary the force in hitting it different distances.

In a small group keep the balloon in the air by hitting it. Add another balloon.

Create a game for three players with a balloon.

Discs

Discs, commonly called Frisbees, are a relatively new piece of equipment, having developed popular use in the past three decades. Beginning as a toy used primarily for throwing between individuals, it has evolved as a piece of equipment that may be used in several games, one of which is ultimate Frisbee. It is

also used in competitions in which a variety of skills and routines are tested and creative use of the disc in "free style" activities is judged. The International Frisbee disc Association has identified three levels of proficiency: expert, master, and world class master. The discs come in a number of different styles and sizes, with some meeting the specifications of the IFA.

Discs are difficult for elementary school children to control. They require more space than balls. The safety considerations listed earlier in this section are very important. Because they are difficult to control, disc activities may be more appropriate as level III and IV activities.

Throwing

Cross-body backhand

Grip: Grasp disc as if to fan yourself, with the thumb on the top side and the index finger on the rim.

Execution: Turn the throwing side in the direction of the throw. The weight is transferred to the rear foot. As the backswing is taken by bringing the disc in front of the body and then back, the upper body turns toward the throwing arm. As the forward motion begins, the weight is transferred to the forward foot and the upper body rotates. On the release the index finger points in the direction of the flight. The flight of the disc is parallel to the floor.

Suggestions: Practice the motion without releasing the disc at first.

Sidearm or forehand throw

Grip: Grasp the disc with the thumb on top and the middle and index fingers extended on the bottom, the middle finger against the rim.

Execution: The nonthrowing side of the body is facing the direction of the throw. The disc is brought back to the side. As the disc is moved forward, the weight is transferred to the forward foot. The hips lead the body motion followed by the shoulders and the throwing arm. The wrist snaps as the disc is released, adding force to the throw.

Suggestions: Practice the motion without releasing the disc for a few times.

Underhand throw

Grip: Grasp the disc as in the cross-body backhand.

Execution: The throwing side faces the direction of flight. The disc is brought down and back behind the thrower. The knees are bent. The upper body is slightly rotated in the direction of the throw. As the arm is brought forward, the lead foot steps in the direction of the throw. The swinging and forward motion are primarily from the arm with a snap of the wrist as the disc is released out in front of the body.

Suggestion: This is a difficult throw. It may help to practice the motion slowly to get a feeling for it.

Flights

Several flights are possible with each type of throw. The angle of the disc on release affects the flight. The children should be encouraged to experiment with the angle of the disc as they work on the various skills. The skip flight is the most difficult for elementary school children (Figure 14-1). Note that a skip curve curves to the left for a right-handed backhand, a roll curve to the right.

Catches

Two-hand catch (pancake): Line up with the disc. Reach out and pull it in with two hands, one hand on top, the other on the bottom of the disc.

One-hand catch: Line up with the disc. Reach out and pull it in with one hand.

Between the legs: Used to catch low flights. Face the thrower. Line up with the intended flight of the disc. As the catch is made, the side is facing the throw, there is a jump in the air so at impact both feet are off the ground, the closest leg is up, and the disc is watched into the hand as it is caught under the leg. The thumb is on top of the disc.

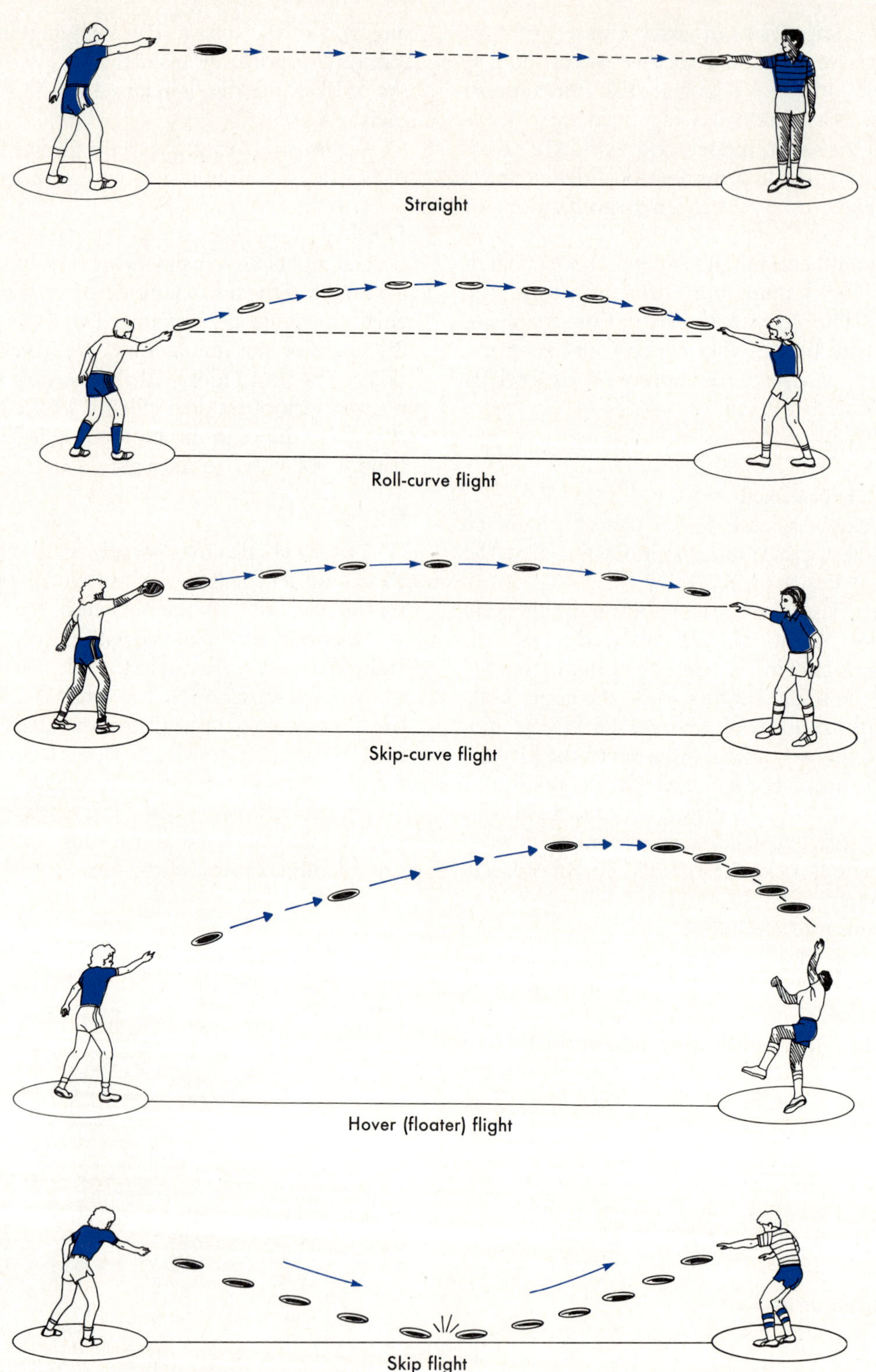

Figure 14-1

Possible disc flights.

Behind the back: Place the feet in line with the flight. Watch the disc as long as possible into the hand. The thumb is on top of the disc.

Fingertip catch: Good for catching high floaters. Match the speed of the disc with the hand or the whole body. Give as the disc is contacted on the index finger. The finger is first placed lightly on the underside of the flight plate of the disc. As the disc slows, the finger spins it to the rim.

Behind the head: Stand either facing the thrower or with your side toward the thrower. Reach behind your neck and make the catch. The thumb is on the bottom, the fingers on top of the disc.

Tipping

Tipping is easiest from hover flights. Tipping can be done as follows:

Finger: Move with the disc or stop its motion. The disc is received on the index finger in the center of the disc. After several contacts it will be necessary to adjust the placement of the finger slightly off center to keep the disc under control.

Knee: Lean back and raise the knee high enough to make a clean contact with the disc.

Head: Tilt the head back to make contact at the hairline. The action of the legs from flexion to extension produces the tipping action.

Toe: This is easiest with a disc dropping from a tip. The action is a kick to the disc with the toe. With this tip one should be able to get the disc high in the air.

Elbow: Lean the upper body to get the elbow straight up.

Heel: Executed to the side of the kicking leg or behind the opposite leg. Timing is important to get a clean tip.

Suggestions: Mark the center of the disc with a felt pen to help in finding the initial striking point.

Activities

With a disc children may:

Using each of the throws execute a straight flight. Roll-curve flight. Skip-curve flight. Hover (floater) flight. Skip flight.

Throw a disc for distance.

Throw a disc through a hoop.

Throw a disc to a target.

Throw a disc into the basket.

Throw and catch a disc with a stationary partner, varying the type of throw and catch used.

Throw and catch a disc with a moving partner, varying the type of throw and catch used.

Throw the disc so that it comes back to the thrower.

Tip the disc on various body parts.

Throw a disc into the wind.

Throw a disc with the wind.

Frisbee golf: Set up a course with the holes marked by discs or natural boundaries agreed on ahead of time by the teams. Players travel the course throwing and moving the disc until they get the disc to the hole. The number of throws taken on each hole constitutes the score.

Ultimate Frisbee: see Chapter 22.

Rings

Rings are available in several different materials. The most common are made of molded rubber, rubber tubing, or a heavy kemp rope.

Rings may be thrown so the ring travels parallel to or perpendicular to the floor or so the ring travels end over end in flight. The grip most commonly used is to shake hands with the ring as it is held perpendicular to the floor.

Many of the activities previously listed in this chapter may be modified for the use of rings. In addition children may:

Twirl one or more rings on various body parts.

Throw the ring on to dowels on a target board.

Pass the ring from different body parts to others in a small group.

Toss rings on to the legs of a chair turned upside down.

Throw rings into several target areas on the floor, using a different type of throw each time.

Toss the ring to a partner who must catch it on a different body part each time.

Make up a game for two or more players with the ring.

HOOPS

Hoops varying in size are available in wood and plastic. Plastic hoops may often be purchased at discount stores. Hoops may be made from 1/2-inch black plastic water pipe. A piece 7 feet 10 inches in length will make a 30-inch hoop. The plastic may be joined together with plastic pipe fitting or with a 3-inch piece of a 1/2-inch dowel glued inside the two ends.

Working with a hoop requires adequate space. Children should explore how the hoop increases their self space and then find a space that does not interfere with the work of other children.

With hoops placed on the floor children may:

In response to a partner, place different body parts in each hoop.

Move through a maze with the hoops placed at different angles.

Hop or jump into hoops placed on the floor in different patterns.

Jump or leap over a hoop placed on the floor.

Hop in and out of a hoop, following its curved path.

See how many children fit inside the hoop without touching.

Hold hands with a partner, one standing in a hoop placed on the floor, the other outside the hoop. The children jump together, one jumping backward out of the hoop while the other jumps in the hoop. Repeat.

Moving a hoop in general space children may:

Roll the hoop in general space.

Roll the hoop while moving in different directions.

Roll the hoop in various pathways.

Roll the hoop at varying speeds.

Roll the hoop and have it come back.

Roll a small hoop through a larger hoop.

Roll the hoop around objects, using one hand to control it. Repeat using other hand.

Children may:

Jump it as a rope.

Twirl a hoop (Hula-Hoop) on various body parts.

Move while twirling the hoop at various body parts.

Balance a hoop on different body parts.

Throw the hoop in the air and catch it.

Bounce a ball through a hoop.

Spin a hoop as it rests vertically on the floor.
Spin a hoop and as it turns do various movements
    in a circle moving around the hoop.
With a partner children may:
    Roll the hoop alternately controlling the hoop.
    Roll the hoop to a partner.
    Throw a hoop to a partner.
    Roll two hoops back and forth.
    Roll three hoops back and forth.
Moving through a hoop children may:
    Move through a stationary or moving hoop with
       various body parts leading.
    Move through a stationary or moving hoop in
       different ways.
    Pass the hoop in a small group while holding
       hands.

PADDLES AND SCOOPS
Paddles

Racquetball and paddle tennis racquets may be used
with some success by elementary school age children
when their hands are big enough to control the rac-
quet without it slipping on contact with the ball. Old
tennis balls, wiffle balls, or small foam balls are easiest
to control. If a variety of balls are available, children
can choose the type of ball that they can control for
the various activities.

It is important to stress safety in use of the paddles. The children should be sure they have a large
enough space to swing the paddles without hitting
other children. As they find a space they should gently
swing the paddle to see the increased space needed.
If they are too close to other children, they must look
for a new space. Control of the swing and the object
projected must always be stressed.

Skills
Forehand drive

The forehand drive is executed on the side of the
body where the paddle is being held. The paddle is
grasped as if shaking hands with the paddle. The V
formed between the thumb and index finger is on
the top as the paddle is held with the paddle face
perpendicular to the floor. As the body moves into
position to begin the stroke, the side is turned toward
the direction of intended flight, with the arm holding
the paddle farthest away. The feet are in a comfortable stride position. The paddle arm is brought back
and the body weight is transferred to the back foot.
As the paddle swings forward, the weight is taken
on the forward foot. Contact with the ball is to the
side and slightly ahead of the forward foot. The paddle is held firmly to prevent the paddle from turning
in the hand on contact. After contact the paddle follows through in the direction of the flight.

    Common errors:
1. Failure to turn the side toward the direction
   of the flight.
2. Stepping forward on the wrong foot.
3. Turning the paddle face up (open) rather than
   perpendicular (closed) on contact.

Figure 14-2

Evaluative criteria and teaching points for the forehand.

- Shake hands with the paddle.
- The body is turned with the opposite side facing the direction of intended flight.

- The paddle is brought back and weight taken on the rear foot.
- Paddle brought forward, weight transferred to forward foot.
- Contact ball to the side and slightly ahead of forward foot.

- Paddle follows through in direction of flight.

Figure 14-3

Evaluative criteria and teaching points for the backhand.

- Hand turned over on the paddle.
- Side turned in direction of hit.
- Paddle back, weight shifted to rear foot.

- Level swing forward as weight shifts to forward foot.
- Contact in front and to the side of forward foot.

- Paddle follows through in direction of flight.

Figure 14-4

Evaluative criteria and teaching points for the serve.

- A forehand grip is used.
- Side facing forward, knees and hips flexed.
- Ball is dropped, paddle brought back at waist height.

- Ball contact at height of bounce, weight transferred to forward foot.
- Paddle swings forward in direction of flight.

4. Failure to hold the paddle firmly on contact.
5. No follow-through.
6. Hitting the ball when it is too close to the body.

Backhand drive

The backhand drive is taken on the opposite side of the body from where the paddle is being held.

The same grip used in the forehand may be used. Most often, however, the hand is turned on the paddle so the thumb is on the back side of the paddle and the back of the hand is on top. As the individual moves to get into position, the side on which the paddle is held is turned in the direction of intended flight. As the paddle is brought back, the body weight shifts to the rear foot. The paddle swings forward and the body weight shifts onto the forward foot. The paddle is held firmly, and contact with the ball is in front and to the side of the forward foot. The paddle continues to move forward in the direction of flight on the follow-through.

Common errors:
1. Being too close to the ball as it is contacted so contact is made in front of the body.
2. Stepping toward the ball rather than in the direction of intended flight.
3. Failure to hold the paddle firmly on contact.
4. No follow-through.

Serve

The serve is the stroke used to put the ball in play. The paddle is held firmly in a forehand grip. Both feet are behind the baseline with the nonserving side facing forward. As the ball is dropped, the paddle is brought back at waist height with the elbow bent and the wrist cocked. The weight is transferred to the rear foot. The paddle swings forward to contact the ball at the height of the bounce with the paddle face perpendicular to the ground. The body weight is transferred to the forward foot, and the paddle swings forward of the body in the desired direction of flight.

Figure 14-5

Evaluative criteria and teaching points for the volley.

Common errors:
1. Failure to hold the paddle firmly on contact.
2. Dropping the ball too close or too far away from the body.
3. Failure to time the paddle swing with the bounce.
4. Opening the paddle face on contact so the ball goes up in the air.

Volley

The volley is used to hit a ball before it bounces on the court. The grip taken depends on whether the ball will be stroked on the forehand or backhand side. The action is similar to the forehand or backhand drive. There is, however, little backswing before contact. The ball is contacted in front of the body with a punching motion, and there is little follow-through of the paddle after contact.

Common errors:
1. Using too much backswing, resulting in too much force.
2. Not holding the paddle firmly on contact.
3. Paddle face is open (angled back) so the ball is lofted too much.
4. Not planting the feet on the volley, but moving through the ball.

Activities

Control is an important goal. As children work, the teacher should relate the activities to the movement content with special emphasis on level, force, range, and placement of the ball to open spaces. In the beginning a small foam ball is easiest to handle. If the children have little experience in striking, it may be best to begin the skills striking with the hand and then using the paddle. With a paddle children may:

Bounce the ball to the floor.

Hit the ball into the air and repeat as many times as possible without losing control. (How did you control the force to keep it going as long as possible?)

Similar to the previous activity but turning the paddle over to alternately hit with a forehand and backhand grip.

Hit a ball at the low, medium, and high level. (How did you change your hit to move the ball to the desired level?)

Using a forehand or backhand drive, hit the ball from a self toss. Hit the ball from a bounce. Receive a toss from a partner and hit the ball to a partner.

Hit the ball to a partner, varying the force of the return as the partner moves closer or farther away.

Follow the leader by repeating the type of hit performed by a partner.

Hit the ball so it bounces before being received by a partner. Continue hitting the ball as many times as possible before losing control. (How did you control the force to keep the ball moving?)

Hit the ball to a space to the right or left of a partner so the receiver must move to the ball. Use both a forehand and a backhand swing.

Vary the force of the hit so that the partner must move up or back to receive the ball. (How did you vary the force to make your partner move forward or backward?)

Hit the ball to targets from various distances. (How did your strokes change as you moved closer or farther away?)

Hit the ball to targets from various positions, such as from the right, left, or directly in front of the target. Vary the strokes used.

Hit a ball suspended from a thin rope using a forehand, a backhand, or alternating the two strokes. (How did you control the force to get as many hits as possible?)

Serve the ball into designated areas of the court. (What changes in your stroke did you make to hit the various areas?)

Games with paddles

The following games may be introduced to use the skills and movement concepts.

PARTNER PADDLEBALL

Equipment: One small foam ball and two paddles.
Area: Two courts 8 by 8 feet, divided by a center line.
Participants: Two players.
Skills: Forehand and backhand drives, volley, serve.
Description: The ball is put into play by one player dropping the ball in the court and serving it with a forehand motion so it lands in the opponent's court. The receiver hits the ball back to the server's court, and play continues until someone fails to return the ball to the opponent's court. A ball landing on the side or end lines is considered inbounds. The ball may be contacted before it hits the floor. A point is scored when the ball is hit so the opponent cannot return the ball within the rules of play. A game is completed when one player scores at least 4 points and wins by a 2-point margin.

Faults:
1. Failure to return the ball so that it lands in bounds in the opponent's court.
2. Contacting the ball more than once in returning the ball to the opponent's court.
3. Hitting the ball so that it lands on the center line.

Penalty: A point is scored for the opponent.

Strategy:
1. Vary the force of the hit.
2. Vary the placement of the ball by hitting it just over the center line or to the back of the court.
3. Hit the ball to an empty space.

Teaching suggestions: Encourage the children to assume a ready position, with feet in a side stride position, one slightly ahead of the other, knees and hips flexed, and paddle held out in front of the body, in the center of the playing area where they can cover the entire court after each hit.

WALL PADDLE TENNIS

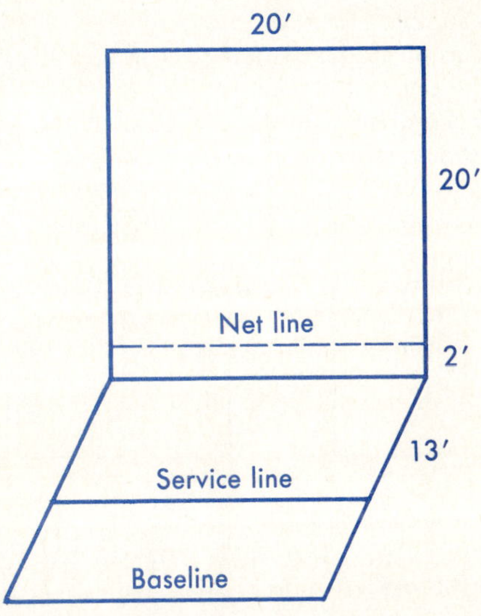

Equipment: Two to four paddles and one small foam ball or an old tennis ball.
Area: A court 26 by 20 feet and 20 feet high, marked as above. A smaller court may be used where space is limited.
Participants: Two opposing players for singles, two teams of two players for doubles.
Skills: Forehand and backhand drive, volley, serve.
Description (singles):   Play is begun by one player serving from behind the baseline. The ball is bounced and then struck so that it hits the wall above the net line. The ball must rebound off the wall beyond the service line and in bounds. After the ball hits the court, the op-

ponent returns the ball by hitting it to the wall above the net line. The ball may rebound anywhere in the playing area. Play continues with each player alternately hitting the ball. A point is scored when an opponent hits the ball out of bounds or commits a fault. Only the server may score. The service continues until the server commits a fault. The game is completed when one player scores 10 points.

Doubles: The rules for singles are followed by team members alternately hitting the ball. A server continues to serve until the team commits a fault.

Faults:

1. Failure to serve or hit the ball so that it hits the wall above the net line.
2. Failure to serve the ball so that it rebounds beyond the service line.
3. Hitting the ball so that it rebounds from the wall out of bounds.
4. Failure of the ball to hit the wall before contacting the floor after the hit.

Penalty: Loss of service or point, depending on which player commits the fault.

Strategy:

1. Vary the force of the hit.
2. Vary the placement of the ball on the wall to change the angle of rebound.

Teaching suggestions: In doubles, those not playing the ball should move back and out of the way.

PADDLE TENNIS

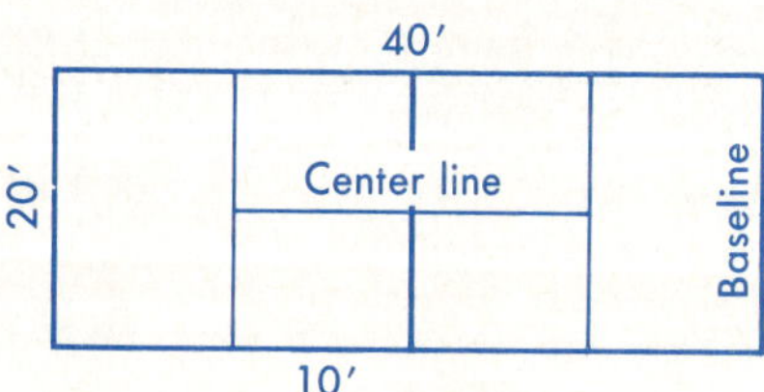

Equipment: Two to four paddles and one small foam ball or tennis ball.

Area: A 20- by 40-foot court with a service line and center line and a net 2 1/2 feet high.

Participants: Two for singles, four for doubles.

Skills: Forehand and backhand drive, volley, serve.

Description: Play begins with a serve from the right-hand court to the right-hand court of the opponent. The server is given two chances to hit the ball into the appropriate court. A ball hitting the top of the net and landing in the appropriate service court is a let serve. Another chance for service is awarded. The ball is returned after it bounces once in the opposite service court. After the serve the ball may be returned into any part of the opponent's court within the boundaries. The ball is served alternately from the right and left courts and to the right and left service courts of the opponent. It may be hit before it hits the court or after it has bounced once. Play continues until a fault is made. A point is scored by the opponent each time a fault is committed. A person serves the entire game. The game is completed when one player has scored at least 4 points and wins by a 2-point margin.

Faults:

1. Stepping over the baseline on the service.
2. Failure to serve the ball into the appropriate service court.
3. Failure to hit the ball over the net.
4. Hitting the ball so that it lands out of bounds.

Penalty: A point is scored for the opponent if a service fault occurs on the first serve for each point, the serve is repeated. If the fault occurs on the repeated serve, a point is scored for the opponent.

Strategy:

1. Look for an empty space to place the ball.
2. Vary the force of the hit.

Teaching Suggestions: Encourage the players to assume a ready position on the court where they can easily cover the court and to assume this position after each hit.

Scoops

Scoops are commercially made of plastic or may be improvised by cutting large plastic jugs. Directions for making scoops may be found in the Appendix.

Many of the activities with balls and paddles may be modified for use with the scoop. In addition children may:

Throw a ball using an underhand, forehand (sidearm), or overhead stroke for distance. To a target varying in size, distance, and level. To a partner.

Throw and catch a ball under the leg.

Catch a ball behind the back.

Throw and catch a ball while moving in general space.

PARACHUTE

The use of parachutes in physical education has become popular in the past decade. Parachute activities are excellent for upper body development, especially for the shoulders, arms, wrists, and fingers. Parachute activities further social development since the cooperation of the children is required to accomplish the tasks.

Parachutes made of silk, nylon, or other lightweight fabrics are available in various sizes and colors through physical education equipment companies. They may also often be obtained from air force installations for a minimal fee. A parachute about 24

Figure 14-6

Holding the parachute.

feet in diameter is easy for a group of young children to handle.

Using a parachute is exciting for children. Care of the parachute should be stressed, with the children taught how to spread it out and to fold it. When the parachute is used outdoors, areas where it can raise dirt should be avoided.

In using the parachute the children form a circle around the parachute, which is spread out on the floor. The children lift the parachute from the floor, holding it with both hands. The parachute may be held with an overhand, underhand, or mixed grip (Figure 14-6). Most of the activities involve lifting the parachute overhead on a signal. Some activities involve the children outside the parachute. Other activities are performed under the raised parachute. The children may:

Move the parachute up and down:

Making waves by holding the parachute and raising it up and down with large arm movements.

Making small ripples by moving the arms up and down in opposition, with one hand going up while the other goes down.

Reaching up as far as possible with the parachute and then bring the edges down to the floor.

Beginning with the parachute close to the floor, lift the parachute up, take two to three walking steps into the center, filling the parachute with air to form a bubble. Walk back out.

Raise the parachute as in the bubble, but release it on a signal so it floats away overhead.

Make an igloo.

Beginning with the parachute close to the floor, lift it up, reaching high in the air with the arms. Quickly pull the parachute down so the edges are on the floor, trapping as much air inside as possible to form an igloo.

Similar to the previous activity, but this time the children lie down as they bring the parachute down with their heads inside the parachute and their bodies on the outside.

Similar to the first activity, but this time a mixed grip with hands crossed is used. As the children bring down the parachute, they turn under their crossed hands to face outside and remain under the parachute as it is brought quickly to the floor.

Rapidly rotate the parachute:

Held at waist height.

Moving with various locomotor movements or dance steps.

Play the following games:

Numbers In: The children are numbered off by fours or fives. The parachute is raised and a number is called. Those with the number

called go into the center and come out at their own places when the center of the parachute starts to come down.

Variation: Performing various locomotor or rope-jumping skills determined by the leader.

Variation: Performing various stunts or tumbling skills while under the parachute.

Variation: Performing various ball skills while under the parachute.

Jaws: One person is the shark and moves under the parachute with one hand up just above the head to form the fin. The shark recruits other sharks by touching those holding the parachute.

Numbers Change: The children are numbered off by fours or fives. The children whose number is called move under the parachute, changing places with someone as they come out as the parachute comes down.

Steal the Bacon: The children are divided into two teams and each team is given numbers. Objects, the bacon, are under the parachute for each team. As a number is called, the children from each team with that number move under the parachute and attempt to retrieve the "bacon" before the parachute comes down.

The children are divided into groups. A number of objects are placed under the parachute. When a team is called, they attempt to go under the parachute and pick up as many objects as possible before the parachute comes down. A variation would include giving point values to different objects and adding up the total points the groups score or designating a specific color of objects to be retrieved.

The group is divided into two teams; one team holds the parachute while the other is positioned under the parachute. As the parachute is rapidly pulled down, the team inside attempts to get out.

The group is divided into two teams, one holding the parachute and the other running around the outside of the parachute. On a signal the group on the outside runs into the middle and then out again, trying not to get caught as the group holding the parachute attempts to catch them inside as they bring the parachute down.

Circle Tug of War: A line is marked under the parachute. Each team tries to pull the other half of the parachute over the designated line. (What body position helps to keep you from being pulled?)

Horse Pull: Similar to the circle tug of war but

with the children standing with their backs to the parachute gripping the parachute with both hands, palms down.

With balls and the parachute the children may:

Holding the parachute at waist height, kick several balls underneath back and forth, trying to keep the balls under the parachute.

With several balls placed on the parachute, bounce the balls on the parachute by raising their arms up and down, trying to keep the balls on the parachute. (How high can you bounce the balls? How long can you keep all balls on the parachute?)

Keep two balls moving on the parachute without touching each other.

Divided into two teams, each holding one half of the parachute, each team attempts to roll a ball so it goes off the parachute on the opposite team's side.

Dodge Ball: Similar to the previous activity, but each team attempts to roll the ball so it touches a player on the opposite team.

Roll one or more balls around the edge of the parachute.

Recite a rhyme as the ball is rolled along the edge of the parachute. When the rhyme is completed, the child closest to the ball suggests a new rhyme. (How quickly can you roll the ball so it does not stop with you?)

Try to roll a small ball through the hole in the center of the parachute.

With an odd number of balls on the parachute and the group divided into two teams, one team on each side of the parachute, bounce the balls on the parachute. On a signal to stop, the team with the fewest number of balls on their side of the parachute wins.

Similar to the previous activity, but this time the children try to bounce the balls off the parachute on the opponent's side. The team with the fewest number of balls bouncing off the parachute on their side wins.

With one or more balls placed on the parachute, count off by twos alternately around the parachute. The ones attempt to keep the ball(s) on the parachute while the twos attempt to bounce it off.

With the group divided into two teams, one team holds the parachute while the other stands outside the parachute. The team holding the parachute attempts to bounce the balls off while the children outside the parachute attempt to keep them on by catching the balls and throwing them back on the parachute.

Kick It Back: The class is divided into two teams with each team numbered consecutively. When a number is called, the opposing players with the number called go under the parachute and attempt to kick a ball back to their teammates before the parachute comes down.

With the group divided into two teams, as the parachute goes up, each team kicks a ball under the parachute to the other team. When the parachute comes down, the team without a ball receives a point.

ROPES

Ropes have many uses in physical education. Many activities with ropes enhance jumping skills and provide excellent activity for developing cardiorespiratory fitness, leg strength, and endurance.

Ropes provide application and practice of movement concepts in individual and group activities. For example, the child's self space is extended in using a jump rope, controlled creation and absorption of force are important in jumping, and timing is essential in coordinating body movements to a moving rope. Creativity should be encouraged by giving the children opportunities to invent new movements for rope jumping.

Safety is a concern is using ropes. Children need to be reminded about the space needed in various activities and should be discouraged from swinging the ropes randomly. In activities in which children are moving a rope for others to jump they should be taught to release the rope at the first feeling of increased tension caused by a rope touching a child's legs. This should avoid tripping on the rope or having the rope wrap around one's legs. In all jumping activities children should be encouraged to land softly.

Ropes may be inexpensively made from No. 8 or 9 sash cord available at hardware stores or from sheeting available at marine supply companies. Ropes are needed in various lengths for individual and group activities. The lengths may be color coded by dipping them in paint or marking them with colored tape. Children and the teacher may then quickly identify the length needed for a particular activity. Ropes may be easily stored in boxes or baskets individually folded and tied in large knots to prevent tangling. Elastic ropes of various lengths are also available for individual and group activity.

Jumping the Long Rope

Long ropes should be from 10 to 14 feet in length. The shorter ropes are easiest for young children to turn.

The children should use wrist action in turning the rope. Children tend to increase speed when turning the rope and need help in maintaining a steady rhythm.

Long rope jumping is easier than jumping the short rope since a child needs only to establish the timing for jumping and does not have to coordinate the turn and the jump. Children having difficulty in establishing the rhythm for jumping may be helped by holding hands with the teacher or another child and jumping together. A double-beat or single-beat jump may be used.

The first step in jumping is establishing the rhythm and relationship to the rope. Repeatedly saying "Jump, jump, jump, jump." may help the children develop a steady even rhythm. If a double-beat jump is used, the first and every other beat from then on are accented.

Activities that may be used to teach long rope jumping include:

Line or stationary rope jumping: The children stand with their sides to the line or rope. On the signal and in the rhythm established by the teacher the children jump back and forth over the rope. On a single-beat jump they pass over the rope on each jump. With a two-beat jump they jump over the rope on the first beat, jump to the side of the rope on the second beat, and jump over the rope on the next beat to begin the two-beat sequence on the other side of the rope.

Cradle: With their side to the rope the children jump the rope, which is gently swung back and forth.

Cradle to a turn: The child begins with the cradle; after the rope is swung several times and the jumping rhythm established, the rope is brought up and overhead to turn as in long rope jumping.

Standing in: A child begins standing with one side to the rope; on the count of three the rope is brought up and around to begin turning.

Run through the front door: The rope is turned so it is moving down and toward the jumper. As the rope passes in front of the jumper, the jumper runs through as the rope moves up and away. The jumper should stand close to the rope to correctly time the move. It may be easier to move through at an angle to the rope rather than straight on.

Run in the front door: This time the jumper moves in but, rather than running through, stops in the

center and jumps the rope one or more times.

Run through the back door: The rope is moving up and toward the jumper. The jumper moves as the rope comes up and passes the jumper's eyes, waits briefly for the rope, jumps the rope then moves out away from the rope.

Run in the back door: Similar to run through the back door, but the jumper stays in to jump the rope several times.

To jump out of the rope the child jumps out of the rope if it is moving down. If the rope is moving upward and away from the jumper, the child jumps the rope and follows the rope out.

Many stunts may be done while jumping the long rope. The children may:

Move in to the rope and jump a specified number of times before moving out of the rope. (Example: first jump once, then twice, then three times, and so on.)

Touch a heel in front while jumping.

Touch a toe behind while jumping.

The child turns while jumping: quarter turn, half turn, three-quarter turn, a whole turn.

Touch a hand to the floor while jumping.

Travel forward and backward while jumping.

Pepper: The rope is turned rapidly.

With a partner, travel backward and forward in opposition or passing each other.

Around the clock: One jumps in place while a partner jumps, moving around the stationary jumper.

Use some of the steps suggested in short rope
jumping.

Jump to rhymes.

Jump a short rope while jumping the long rope.

Make up some new movements for long rope
jumping, alone, with a partner, or for a small
group.

Ball skills may also be used. The rhythm of jumping should be established before the ball skill is begun. The children may:

Play catch with a partner standing outside the
rope.

Bounce or toss a ball to self while jumping.

Play catch with a partner who is jumping with
you.

Activities with two long ropes of equal length

Egg Beater: Two ropes are held perpendicular to
one another with four turners. The ropes are turned
so both touch the floor at the same time. Of the four
corners from which to move into the rope, one is a
front door, one is a back door, and two are mixed.
The front door and back door corners are used to
move into the center to jump, moving in as the rope
passes in front of the eyes.

Double Dutch: Two turners hold the ends of two
ropes. The ropes are turned toward each other so
that as one rope is up the other is touching the floor.
Each time the children jump a rope is passing under
their feet, requiring a single-beat jump. It is easiest
to move into the rope at an angle. Children should
watch the "front door" rope but be prepared to jump
the "back door" rope as they move in.

Double Irish: Similar to double dutch but the
ropes are turned away from each other. The child
moves in at an angle following the "front door" rope
and jumping over the "back door" rope. This style
of jumping also requires a single-beat jump.

Rhymes for jumping

Teddy bear, Teddy bear, turn around.
Teddy bear, Teddy bear, touch the ground.
Teddy bear, Teddy bear, show your shoe.
Teddy bear, Teddy bear, you'd better skidoo.

Brick house, glass house, stone house, tin.
I move out and (name person) moves in.

All in together, Very fine weather.
In (out) goes one, In (out) goes two.
In (out) goes three, and in (out) goes you!

(This may be done with one jumper in on one,
two moving in on two, etc.)

Come, come the kids are calling, calling (name B)
to my door.
(Name B) is the one who's going to have fun, so we
don't need (name A) any more.

The rhyme starts with A jumping. As B is called
he or she comes into the rope. A moves out of the
rope on the last line. It is repeated until all have had
a turn to jump.

Hippity, hippity hop. How many times before I stop?
One, two, three, four, etc.

I like coffee, I like tea.
I'd like (name) to jump with me.

Oh in I run and around I go.
Clap my hand and nod just so.
I lift my knee, and slap my shin.
When I go out, let (name) come in.

(Name, name) set the table.
And don't forget the salt and pepper.

(On the word *pepper* the rope is turned rapidly.)

I have a little duck, his name is Tiny Tim.
I put him in the bath tub to teach him how to swim.
He drank up the water, and ate up all the soap.
He woke up in the morning with a bubble in his throat.
In came the doctor, In came the nurse.
In came the lady with the alligator purse. (Add people
to here.)
"Sorry" said the doctor. "Sorry" said the nurse.
"Sorry" said the lady with the alligator purse.
Out walked the doctor. Out walked the nurse.
Out walked the lady with the alligator purse. (People go
out.)

I'm a little tea pot, short and stout.
Here is my handle, here is my spout.
When I get all steamed up, then I shout.
Just tip me over and pour me out.

Sick in the head, called for the doctor
And this is what he said.
Take two steps forward, turn yourself around.
Do the hokey-pokey and get out of town.

Oh the funniest thing I've ever seen
Was a tomcat sewing on a sewing machine.
Oh, the sewing machine got running so slow. (Slow the
rope)
And it took seven stitches in the tomcat's toe.

Donald duck was a one-legged, one-legged, one-legged
duck.
Donald duck was a two-legged, two-legged, two-legged
duck.
Donald duck was a three-legged, three-legged, three-
legged duck.
Donald duck was a four-legged, four-legged, four-legged
duck.

Jumping the Short Rope

Short ropes for elementary school age children should be cut into 6-, 7- and 8-foot lengths. Some of the taller youngsters in the upper grades may need a 9-foot rope. To select the proper length for jumping the child takes an end of the rope in each hand and steps on the rope. The ends should then reach the armpit for a proper fit. If the rope is too long, it may be wound on the hand.

Once the children have mastered the rhythm of long rope jumping, they are ready to try the short rope. Jumping while turning the rope backward may be easier for some children because it eliminates the tendency to throw the rope with too much force to the floor.

When turning the short rope, the hands should be close to the side with the wrists and hands doing most of the work. It is not necessary to jump high but merely high enough to clear the rope as it hits the floor. The feet should land softly. The body should be erect with the head up.

A single-beat jump, in which the jumper jumps only when the rope passes under the feet, or a double-beat jump, in which the child jumps when the rope passes under the feet and again as the rope is overhead, may be used.

Short rope activities

While turning the rope forward or backward, the children may:

Jump the rope with two feet together.

Jump the rope on one foot.

Jump on first the right and then the left foot alternately.

Move forward or backward while jumping.

Jump while moving both feet from one side to the other (skier).

Jump while moving both feet forward and then backward (bell).

Move the feet to the side and apart and then together while jumping (side straddles).

Move the feet in a forward/backward stride position, alternating the lead leg (forward/backward straddles).

Point a toe to the side while jumping.

Alternately point a toe in front and then behind while jumping.

Touch a heel in front and then to the side while jumping.

Touch a heel in front and then a toe behind while jumping.

Rock back and forth from the left to the right

foot while jumping.

Skip while jumping.

Cross the feet while jumping.

Twist from side to side while jumping.

Do a dance step while jumping, such as the step-hop, bleking, schottische, fling, step-swing, or grapevine.

Turn while jumping: quarter, half, three-quarter, or full turns.

Rope Twirling

In addition to rope jumping skills the rope may be twirled before or during a jumping sequence.

Single-side swing: The rope is held in both hands and twirled vertically on one side of the body.

Double-side swing: Similar to the single-side swing, but the rope is twirled alternately on the right and left sides of the body.

Front swing: The rope is twirled in front of the body.

Figure eights: The rope is twirled in a figure eight in front of the body.

Horizontal swing: The rope is swung horizontally and jumped as it comes around.

Criss-cross: As the rope is jumped, the arms are crossed so the rope is crossed as it passes under the body and then uncrossed as it passes overhead.

Double under: The rope passes twice under the feet on a single jump.

Triple under: The rope passes three times under the feet on a single jump.

Additional Rope Activities

Helicopter: One person stands in the center with a long rope. The rope is swung in a circle by the center person to make the action of the helicopter blade. Children move into the helicoptor by watching the rope and moving when it goes by; then they squat next to the turner. When all are in, they attempt to move back out in a similar fashion.

Jump the Shot: A long rope is used with a beanbag attached at one end. One child turns the rope in a circle parallel to the floor while the other children attempt to jump it as it comes by. The turner may vary the height and/or the speed with which the rope is turned.

Jump the Brook: Two ropes are placed parallel to each other on the floor with the ropes closer together at one end and farther apart at the other. The children begin jumping at the narrow end and continue jumping as the distance between the ropes increases until they can no longer jump the space required.

Jump the Snake: One child wiggles a long rope while other children attempt to jump over it without the rope touching them.

High Water: Two children loosely hold a long rope between them, higher on one end than the other. The other children attempt to go over the rope without touching it as it is gradually raised.

The Bulldog: Four children hold a rope to form the four corners of a square. On a signal each tries to pull the other three corners in his or her direction.

Activities With an Elastic Rope

Elastic ropes of various lengths may be purchased from equipment dealers. With a long elastic rope the children may:

Walk on the rope placed on the floor as a tightrope.

Move under a rope held at various heights in many different ways without touching it.

Move over the rope held at various heights in as many ways as possible without touching it.

Move with another person over or under the rope.

Perform a stunt while moving over or under the rope.

Using two ropes, one held high and the other low and varying the distance between the two ropes, the children attempt different ways to go over one and under the other without touching the ropes.

SCOOTERS

Scooters are popular with children. They provide opportunities for children to control a wheeled object and to explore movements from various positions.

Scooters are available from several manufacturers. They are made of wood with heavy-duty caster wheels. They can be made relatively inexpensively of plywood. Suggestions for the construction of scooters may be found in Appendix Three.

Since they may be a hazard to both the user and the observer, special care must be taken to ensure their safe use. Children should be taught to keep their clothing and fingers away from the wheels and to propel or push the scooter so it remains under control. The children should not stand on the scooters. With a scooter children may:

Assume the following positions to propel the scooter: sitting, kneeling, in a prone position with hips on the scooter.

Move forward, backward, or to the side.

Move with control, varying speed.

Move around objects, through an obstacle course, following lines on the floor, and in various pathways, such as tracing letters on the floor.

Move with a partner in any of the above activities.

Play follow the leader with a partner.

Link several scooters together and move with others.

Explore various ways of stopping and starting.

With a partner make a wheelbarrow.

Play games with scooters, such as Steal the Bacon.

STILTS AND BALANCE BOARDS

Balance activities are challenging for children. Balance boards and stilts involve both static and dynamic balance and balancing at various heights.

In using both stilts and balance boards it may be helpful to have the children work in partners so they can get a balanced position on the equipment with help before attempting to balance alone.

A good surface on which to use the equipment is important. It must not be too slippery. Indoor tile surfaces are generally better than varnished wooden surfaces. A mat may be advisable for use with some balance boards.

Stilts

Stilts provide an opportunity to develop dynamic balance while balancing varying heights from the floor. Stilts may be made of wood or of tin cans to which ropes have been attached. Appendix Three includes specifications for constructing stilts. While balancing on stilts children may:

Move in various directions: forward, backward, or to the right or left.

Move in various pathways.

Follow lines on the floor.

Move over lines or ropes placed on the floor.

Move around objects.

Follow an obstacle course.

Vary the size of the step taken.

Walk, straddling one or two lines.

Walk over objects varying in height (tin can stilts).

Balance Boards

Balance boards provide an opportunity to develop static balance from an unstable base. Several types of balance boards are available. Specifications for constructing balance boards may be found in the Appendix. On a balance board children may:

Hold hands with a partner, who is standing on the floor, and assume a balanced position.

Balance unassisted.

Balance with arms held in various positions.

Balance while assuming various body shapes.

Balance while holding objects of varying weights in each hand.

Balance while balancing beanbags on different body parts.

Balance while performing various ball skills alone or with a partner who is also balancing on a balance board.

WANDS

Wands are 1- to 2-inch dowels 3 feet in length; they may be purchased in hardware stores or building supply centers. They are easily stored in long boxes or baskets which can be brought into the gymnasium for easy distribution.

Safety may be of some concern as the children move with wands. They should be encouraged to keep the wands low when getting them out and putting them away, to be sure they have adequate space with the wand, and to avoid swinging the wands at any level. With a wand children may:

Balance the wand on various body parts.

Toss it vertically from hand to hand.

Step over the wand while holding the wand in both hands and then bring it around the body.

Grasp an upright standing wand with one hand

and duck under the wand without letting go of it.

March with a wand, moving it in various ways.

Imitate a partner's movements with a wand.

Do pull-ups with a partner. One child holding the wand with two hands in front of the body faces and straddles the second child lying on the floor at about shoulder level. The child on the floor grasps the wand with an overhand grip and executes as many pull-ups as possible, bringing his or her chin up to the bar.

Support a wand on two boxes and move under the wand in as many ways as possible without touching it.

Balance a wand on its end on the floor, let it go, and turn around and catch it before it falls.

Pick up objects.

Bring the legs alternately over and under the wand while sitting on the floor, holding the wand in both hands. (Can you do it without touching the wand with your legs?)

Step over a wand held by another at various heights.

While moving in a forward direction attempt to pass under the wand held by two children. The wand is gradually lowered (limbo).

While facing and holding the wand with a partner, stand up and sit down alternately with this person.

Similar to the previous activity, but both sitting and then standing together.

Twirl a wand like a baton.

Jump over it while holding the wand in both hands.

Place the wand vertically on the floor, holding it with one hand. Raise one leg so it passes over the wand, releasing the wand and then regrasping it with the other hand. Repeat with the same leg to return to the starting position. Then try it moving the other leg over the wand.

PLAYGROUND GAMES

Many games using small equipment are ideal for use on the playground during recess and other periods of free play. These games are best suited for small group or partner play. The rules permit some modification and the selection of skills to be used and are well within the ability of the children to organize and conduct.

CHINESE HANDBALL

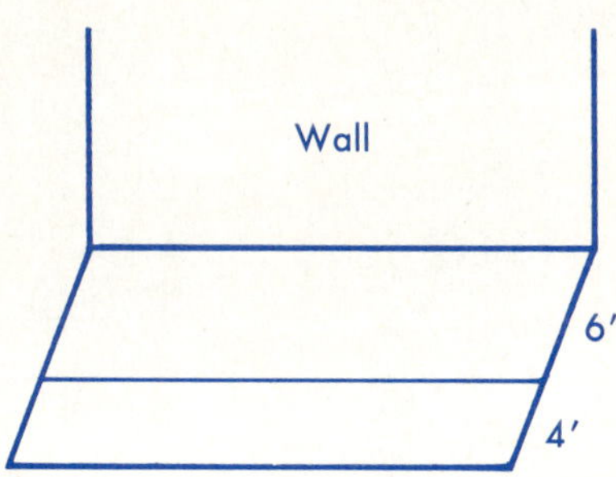

Level: III to IV.

Equipment: One 8-inch utility ball or volleyball.

Area: A wall space 10 feet wide with a floor space 12 feet deep.

Participants: Three players in a file formation.

Skills: Throwing, catching (optional, striking with the hand).

Description: The first player throws the ball to the ground, causing it to rebound to the wall and then rebound into the court beyond the 6-foot center line. The second player catches the ball after one bounce. If the ball is caught, the game continues with the second player throwing the ball to the floor and the first preparing to receive it. If the ball is missed, the third player enters the game and the second goes out.

Fouls:
1. Failure to catch the ball as it rebounds once from the floor.
2. Failure to throw the ball so it bounces from the floor to the wall and back to the floor again.
3. Failure to hit the ball so it rebounds beyond the 6-foot line.

Penalty: Player leaves the game and goes to the waiting line.

Variations: Play begins as above, but after the initial throw the players strike the ball with a downward motion so it hits the floor and then the wall rather than catching and throwing it. The ball may be played from a bounce or from a direct rebound from the wall.

Strategy:
1. Hit the ball with varying force to keep the opponent guessing.
2. Try to position yourself on the court to be able to cover for all possible shots.

Teaching suggestions: Striking the ball with control takes considerable practice. This variation is best suited for children at level IV.

FOUR SQUARE

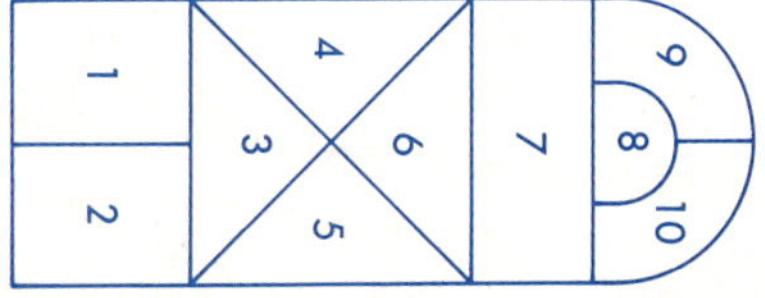

Level: III.

Equipment: One 8-inch playground or four square ball.

Area: Four square courts of four adjoining 8-foot boxes.

Participants: Four per game.

Skills: Striking with the hands, underhand and possibly overhand

Description: One player stands in each of the four playing areas. Player No. 1 begins play by dropping the ball, letting it bounce once and striking it in an underhand motion so that it lands in one of the three other playing areas. The player receiving the ball strikes it in a similar manner so that it bounces in another playing area. Play continues until it cannot be returned, goes out of bounds, or lands on a line. In each case the player at fault moves to area 4 and the other players move up in order so that all areas are covered. The object is to get to and remain No. 1.

Teaching Suggestions: It may be helpful to have the students play two square until they have some control of the ball before using four players. Modifications include using an overhand hit and hitting the ball with little force (teeny-weenys). The player in court No. 1 calls out which shots are legal on each serve. One or two additional players may be incorporated by having them wait outside the playing area and rotating into court No. 4 in turn when someone makes an error. Emphasize control and varying the shots with some deceptions to keep others off guard. Four square may be modified to use paddle striking skills rather than the hand.

HOPSCOTCH

Level: II.

Equipment: A small stone or other flat object to use as the "scotch."

Area: An area of pavement marked out as above.

Participants: Three to four players.

Skills: Underhand throw, hopping.

Description:

Version I: Play begins with the scotch being thrown into square No. 1. The first player then hops into that square, turns without putting down the foot being held up, and kicks the scotch out over the starting line. Play continues tossing the scotch into each successive numbered square, kicking the scotch over the starting line and then hopping in each square passed back to the starting line. When the first player commits a foul, the turn is over and the next player begins the process from square 1. On the second turn for each player play is resumed at the square in which the previous error took place. As play continues farther from the starting line, several kicks may be needed to get the scotch back to the starting line. As the children progress to squares 4 and 5 or 9 and 10, both feet are placed simultaneously in the squares. In these squares the turn is performed by jumping and turning so that both feet land simultaneously in the squares.

Version II: Play begins as in version I with a toss of the scotch into square 1. The player hops through the grid skipping square 1, jumping simultaneously in squares 4 and 5 and then again in 9 and 10 as in version I. On the return the player picks up the scotch while standing on one foot in square 2 and then hops into square 1 and then out of the grid. The player continues throwing the scotch in each square until a foul is commited. On the second round of turns each player begins with a toss to the square in which he or she lost the turn in the previous round.

Fouls:
(versions I and II):
1. Stepping on a line when hopping in and out of the squares.
2. The scotch stopping on a line as it is kicked back to the starting line.
3. Tossing the scotch into the wrong square.
4. Tossing the scotch so it lands on a line.
5. Touching the nonhopping foot to the ground during the turn.
6. Tossing the scotch without assuming the hopping position.

Penalty: Loss of turn.

HORSESHOES

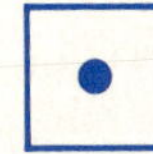

Level: III.
Equipment: A set of junior horseshoes for each player, two stakes secured into the ground.
Area: An area off to the side of the playground 10 feet wide and 25 feet between the stakes.
Participants: Two to four players.
Skills: Tossing the shoes.
Description: To begin play the first participant stands to the side and behind an imaginary line drawn from the stake. Tossing the horseshoe with an underhand mo-

tion toward the opposite stake, the first player attempts to ring the stake with the horseshoe. The next player tosses a horseshoe. Then each player in turn tosses a second horseshoe. Points are awarded after all players have thrown their two horseshoes. A ringer is declared when the horseshoe circles the stake so that a straight edge touching the open ends of the shoe would not touch the stake. Three points are scored for each ringer. If there are four ringers, no score is awarded. The horseshoe closest to the stake wins 1 point if there are no ringers or one ringer for each player. If all horseshoes are an equal distance away, no points are given. A leaning horseshoe does not count more than another horseshoe touching the stake. An official game is 50 points. The number of points if modified should be determined before the game begins.

Scoring is as follows:
Closest horseshoe to the stake: 1 point
Two shoes closer than opponents: 2 points
One ringer: 3 points
Two ringers: 6 points
One ringer and one closest to the stake: 4 points
One player with two ringers against one for the opponents: 3 points
If each player has one ringer, the next closest shoe, if it is within 6 inches: 1 point
Ties: 0 points

Fouls: Tossing the horseshoe from a position in front of the stake.
Penalty: No score for that shoe.
Suggestion: Be sure horseshoe areas are placed near the perimeter of the playing area to avoid children in other activities moving through the area.

SIDEWALK TENNIS

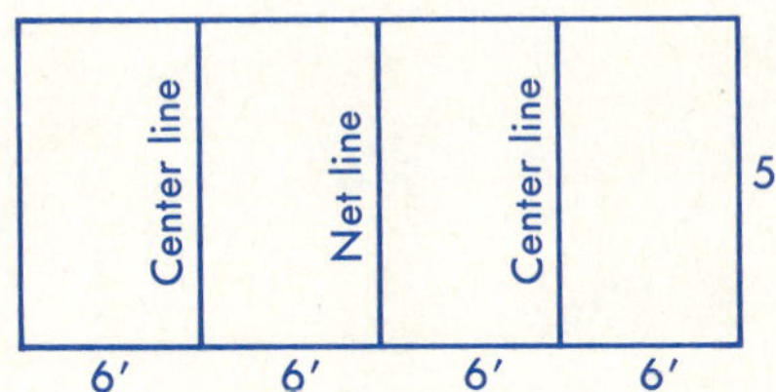

Level: III.
Equipment: One tennis ball.
Area: A paved playing surface 24 feet long and 5 feet wide.
Participants: Two to four players.
Skills: Striking with the hand.
Description: To begin play the serving player drops the ball and then hits it with the hand as it rebounds so it passes over the net line into the opponent's court and lands in the area between the net and the center line. The receiving player returns the ball by hitting it back to the server's court. After the serve the ball may be hit on a fly or after a bounce, and the ball may land

anywhere within the opponent's court. Play continues until one player fouls. Only the server may score. Service is lost when the serving player fouls. Fifteen points constitute a game. A ball landing on the side or base line is considered in bounds. A serve landing on the center line is replayed. When playing doubles teammates alternately hit the ball.

Fouls:

1. Stepping over the center line when serving.
2. Hitting the ball out of bounds.
3. Serving the ball outside the service court.
4. Hitting the ball with a body part other than the open hand.

Penalty: Loss of service or point.

Strategy:

1. Vary the placement of hits to keep the opponent moving.
2. Vary the force of hits to use all of the opponent's court.
3. Place the ball in an empty space in the opponent's court.

Teaching Suggestions: Encourage the players to assume a ready position after each hit to be ready to move to the returning ball.

This game may be played using paddles to strike the ball.

TETHERBALL

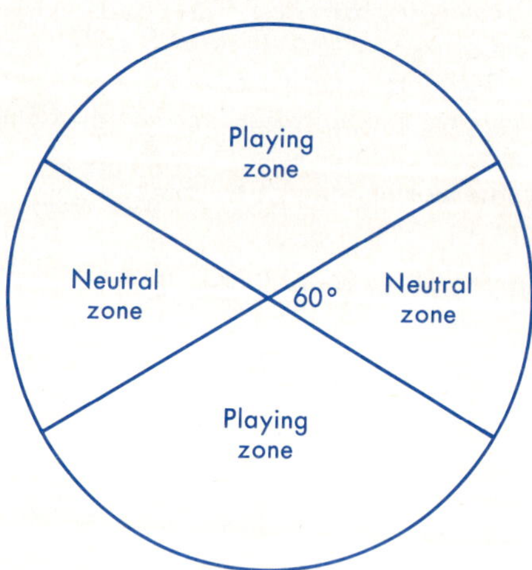

Level: III.
Equipment: A tether ball attached to a pole.
Area: A circle 20 feet in diameter.

Participants: Two to four players.
Skills: Striking with the hand.
Description: The ball is put in play by the first server hitting the ball around the pole. After the ball makes one complete revolution of the pole, the opposing player hits the ball in the opposite direction. Play continues with each player attempting to wind the ball completely around the pole. If teams are composed of more than one player, teammates alternately hit the ball.

Fouls:

1. Hitting the ball with any part of the body other than the hands.
2. Holding, throwing, or catching the ball during play.
3. Touching the pole or rope during play.
4. Playing the ball while outside the court limits or while in the neutral zone.

Penalty: Loss of game.

SUMMARY

Children find work with small equipment challenging. Many activities are self-testing in nature, in that children have the opportunity to test their own ability and to set goals for improvement and challenges for themselves.

These activities provide valuable experiences for elementary school children to apply the movement concepts they have learned, to explore the use of body parts in performing various tasks, to use space concepts, and to experiment with time, force, balance, and flow. In addition to the activities suggested in this chapter, many of the activities in Chapter 11 may be adapted for use with small equipment.

ADDITIONAL READINGS

Bryant, T., and Doss, T.: Tire activities, JOPER **50**(7):75, September 1979.
Ideas for using automobile tires to enhance motor skill and fitness in physical education classes.

Clark, E., and others: Ultimate Frisbee, JOPERD **52**(9):56, November/December 1981.
Rules for ultimate Frisbee.

Corbin, D.: Inexpensive equipment for learning kicking and striking skills, JOPER **51**(5):57, May 1980.
Using materials found around the home to improve kicking and striking skills.

Hardy, R.: Two broomsticks and a ball, JOPER **50**(2):60, February 1979.
A variety of activities for wands and balls.

Plimpton, C.: Hanging hoop maze, JOPER **50**(2):60, February 1979.
Hanging hoops from varying heights and having the children move through and around them in a variety of ways.

REFERENCES

1. Blackwell, D.: So you want to jump rope, Riverton, 1982, The Riverton Ranger Printing Dept.
2. Corbin, D., and Corbin C.: Homemade play equipment for use in physical education classes, JOPERD **54**(6):35, June 1983.
3. Danna, M., and Poynter, D.: Frisbee player's handbook, ed. 3, Santa Barbara, Calif., 1980, Parachuting Publications.
4. IFdA: The discourse: Frisbee flying disc manual for students and teachers, San Gabriel, Calif., 1979, International Frisbee disc Association.
5. Rasmus, C., and Fowler, J., editors: Movement activities for places and spaces, rev. ed., Reston, Va., 1983, AAHPERD.
6. Seker, J., and Jones, G.: Parachute play, Deal, N.J. 1969, Kimbo Educational Records and Educational Activities. K.B.H. Productions.
7. Stafford, R.: Raquetball: the sport for everyone, Memphis, 1984, The Stafford Co.
8. Tips, C.: Frisbee by the masters, Millbrae, Calif., Celestial Arts.
9. Tips, C.: Frisbee disc sports and games, San Gabriel, Calif., International Frisbee disc Association.

15

EDUCATIONAL GYMNASTICS

CHAPTER OBJECTIVES

1 To describe the content of educational gymnastics, including stunts, tumbling, and apparatus activities

2 To provide suggestions for teaching gymnastics to maximize the activity for all and provide a safe environment for learning

3 To identify the movement concepts important to successful participation in gymnastics activities and suggest activities for their further development

Children enjoy climbing, swinging from, and performing stunts on large apparatus as well as rolling, balancing, and performing a variety of stunts. Many playgrounds and gymnasiums are equipped with some types of apparatus to provide for the developmental needs and interests of children. Mats, balance beams varying in width and height, horses and vaulting benches, climbing ropes, and parallel, uneven, and horizontal bars are some of the equipment often provided. Children need to be taught how to enjoy this equipment to its fullest while participating safely.

Gymnastic activities promote a better understanding of body awareness, including how body parts may be used and the relationship of body parts in various spatial orientations and to equipment. Children with little experience in inverted positions often become disoriented when assuming positions other than upright. Balance in different body positions is explored, and the use of body parts to create and absorb force while maintaining body control is enhanced. Using the available space to the fullest and moving in different directions and pathways are required in both mat and apparatus work.

Creativity should be encouraged in each lesson as children make up their own stunts or transitional moves from one stunt to the next. Individual development is enhanced as children develop their own ways to solve the movement challenges with which they are confronted. Since many solutions are possible, all children can find ways of moving that are comfortable for them.

Gymnastic activities also contribute to some aspects of physical fitness. Participation should lead to improved flexibility, agility, coordination, explosive power, and upper body and leg strength.

Gymnastics Goals

The following goals should be realized in the gymnastics program in the elementary school:

1. To develop body awareness in various shapes and spacial orientations.
2. To explore the use of the body to balance; move on and off balance; move from one place to another; move on, along, over and off a piece of equipment; and become airborne and land with control.
3. To discover ways to move on the floor, on mats, and in relation to apparatus.
4. To put a series of stunts together into a simple combination (routine) with flow from beginning to end.
5. To work with others to organize and perform gymnastic activities.

GYMNASTICS CONCEPTS

BODY AWARENESS

1. To use interesting body shapes in creating new moves and in executing transitional moves.
2. To demonstrate use of the following body positions: tuck, pike, straddle, and layout.
3. To analyze the use of body parts in performing gymnastic skills.
4. To use different body parts for support and to determine which are best suited for support in various gymnastics situations.
5. To move smoothly from support on certain body parts to support on other parts of the body.
6. To control muscle tension and relaxation while executing a variety of moves and balances.

SPACE

Self/general:
1. To be aware of body position with different orientations in space.
2. To use all available space.
3. To safely share space with others.
4. To move within the boundaries of mats, beams, et cetera.
5. To move in relationship to partners and/or apparatus.
6. To avoid contact of body parts on apparatus during the performance of some skills.

Direction:
7. To move in a variety of directions on the mat or on the apparatus.
8. To change direction smoothly while performing a combination of skills.

Pathways:
9. To move in interesting and varied pathways while moving on the mat or floor.
10. To change pathways smoothly.

Range:
11. To control the range of movement of body parts while performing skills.

Level:
12. To execute a variety of skills at the low, medium and high levels.
13. To change level smoothly in executing individual or a combination of skills.

MOVEMENT QUALITIES

Balance:
1. To balance on various body parts.
2. To move on and off balance smoothly and with control.
3. To recognize the difference between static and dynamic balance.
4. To recognize how body shape affects balance.

Force:
5. To create force with various body parts.
6. To direct force appropriately when executing skills.
7. To absorb force in landing.

Time/speed:
8. To move in varying speeds while performing skills.
9. To learn how body shape affects speed.
10. To control speed while executing a variety of movements.
11. To learn to use body parts to increase or decrease speed.
12. To accelerate or decelerate as needed.

Flow:
13. To perform smoothly a series of movement skills.

GYMNASTIC CONCEPTS

The movement concepts important to success in educational gymnastics are outlined in the box above. These concepts should be stressed in each lesson as children explore movement challenges, are introduced to new skills, and practice in individual, partner, or group activities.

Movement challenges to aid in the understanding and development of these movement concepts are included in the activities that follow.

TEACHING GYMNASTICS

The gymnastics program poses some special concerns for the teacher. The health and safety of the children must be considered in the conduct of the activities. To meet individual needs the teacher must use a far greater number of different skills than in many other units of instruction. The nature of the activity lends itself to individualized instruction. The following suggestions for teaching address each of these concerns.

Health and Safety
Setting up the equipment

Many activities require the use of mats. Mats should be placed where needed to avoid injury in landing while dismounting from a piece of equipment. Metal supports or other projections on apparatus should be padded in case of accidental falls or uncontrolled landings. Several thicknesses or mats may be needed where children will dismount from a considerable height. Mats should be butted together rather than overlapped or left to gap. Mats should be cleaned on a regular basis. Mats, however, are not the sole protector of the participant. Sound instruction, sequential progression of skills, and spotting complement the use of mats.

Any large apparatus should be checked periodically to be sure it is safe for use. When it is set up all knobs should be tight to avoid movement during use, and it should be properly secured to avoid sliding on the floor. Children should not be allowed under any circumstance to adjust the equipment. Only those versed in the procedure should be permitted to adjust the equipment. Equipment must be placed carefully and should not be too close together, close to walls or other stationary objects, or where there is a poor flow of traffic.

Chalk (carbonate of magnesia) may be used on the palms of the hands to prevent slipping when gripping the apparatus, especially when children are perspiring.

Selecting the content

The selection of stunts should be based on anatomical capabilities. Stunts that put a strain on the ligaments surrounding the knee and hip joint, such as the duck walk, should be avoided. Stunts that involve hyperextension of the spine should not be used excessively. Examples of these activities are bridges and back bends. Partner stunts requiring heavy lifting should also be avoided.

Conduct and supervision

The rules for the safe conduct of the activity should be clearly defined. It may be helpful to have them posted where they can easily be reviewed periodically. No horseplay can be tolerated. Children need to know the consequences of not adhering to the safety rules. Children need to assume responsibility for their own safety and also the safety of their classmates.

In circulating among the children the teacher should always be in a position where the entire group is in view. In this way all activities may be adequately supervised and comments made to children who are far away as well as those who are close by. If maximum participation is provided, supervision is easier because the children are all busy working on something constructive. Many injuries occur when children are waiting for turns and looking for something to do.

The teacher may supervise in a general way by moving among the various groups of children as they are working or combine general supervision with specific supervision by staying with a group of children as they work on a new skill or one requiring the teacher's assistance. When working with a particular child or group of children the teacher must continue to observe and comment on what is happening in other parts of the area. One rule of safety to be stressed in stunts, tumbling, and large apparatus is that no practice periods are permitted without the teacher present.

Many activities require *spotting* during the learning stages. Activities in which there is danger of falling, especially where the body is inverted or is moving through the air unsupported, require spotting. At the elementary school level the teacher must assume responsibility for most of the spotting since the children lack the maturity and understanding to be effective spotters. However, elementary school children may spot headstands or simple balance beam stunts. This assistance may develop an attitude of concern for the safety of others.

For safe participation the number of children assigned to work at a piece of equipment or mat should be limited to an appropriate number to maximize participation.

Children should be taught how to land and to fall when they lose control to avoid injury. Often a roll may be used to absorb force when losing one's balance. Partner stunts are often included in the gymnastic program. In stunts performed with a partner, partners should be of equal size and weight. In activities in which one child supports another the weight should be carried on those body parts capable of supporting the additional weight. For instance, in simple pyramids the weight should be carried on the hips and shoulders.

Organizing the Class

A concern in gymnastics as well as in other activity areas is organizing the activity for maximum participation for all children. Ample equipment should be provided so the children can use the time in practice rather than in waiting for a turn. If equipment or mats are limited, it may be necessary to combine gymnastics activities with activities using small equipment to maximize the activity time for each child. If there are not enough mats for use with the apparatus and tumbling activities, it may be advantageous to separate tumbling and apparatus work into two separate units of instruction.

Some pieces of large apparatus are traditionally used by one sex only; for example, boys compete on the parallel and horizontal bars, whereas girls compete on the beam and uneven bars. However, at the elementary school level all children should have the opportunity to develop skills on all available equipment. Although they may not use some equipment in later years, it is developmentally sound to learn the skills needed, and it teaches children appreciation for the attributes that make participation successful.

In activities using mats it may be possible to have all children working at once. This approach is especially useful when they are learning simple stunts or during movement exploration or problem-solving activities.

Station work is also used in the teaching of gymnastics. Several pieces of equipment are set up in the gymnasium area, and the children rotate from station to station as they accomplish tasks or most often on a signal from the teacher. Children may be assigned to work on specific skills at each station or to solve a particular movement challenge on the various pieces of equipment being used. Children may be heterogeneously or homogeneously grouped for these activities. Sometimes it may be helpful to organize the groups by size to avoid excessive adjustment of the equipment during the lesson to accommodate each child. Station work may also best serve the short attention span of the primary age child.

Children should learn to take some responsibility for helping to set up and put away some equipment. Children should be taught to fold mats correctly and to carry them rather than drag them on the floor. Children need to work together in helping with the mats and apparatus.

Setting up the equipment is a time-consuming task. Classroom teachers, especially those teaching young children, may wish to work together setting up the equipment before school, each class using it throughout the school day, and then helping to put it away as the school day ends. It may also be possible to get aides or upper grade children to assist with equipment.

Children should assume responsibility for their personal preparation for activity, including appropriate dress. Clothing that is loose or too tight may inhibit children's movements. Long hair ought to be pulled back so it does not hinder vision during participation. Sneakers, gymnastic slippers, or bare feet are appropriate for various individual activities. Pockets should be empty and jewelry removed before participation. In classes in which the children do not change clothing for activity the girls may wish to wear shorts under their skirts or dresses.

Effective Teaching

Since the ability of children varies greatly in gymnastics, a variety of activities must be used to provide for the needs of individual children. Some children do not develop their potential because they are forced to work continuously on skills that are beyond them. In their frustration they often quit working and merely watch their more able classmates. Others may not be challenged by the level or variety of skills offered. Gymnastics requires the teacher to look closely at the needs of individuals and to plan accordingly.

Opportunity for creative movement is essential. Children should be encouraged to solve movement challenges in gymnastics and to discover new skills. It is fun to name new creations after the child who developed them, adding them to the gymnastic curriculum. This not only develops a sense of pride in accomplishment but rewards the creative efforts of children.

Warm-up activities that prepare the children for the day's activities are an important part of the lesson. Since there is little vigorous activity in gymnastics, a few activities that increase the heart rate should be included.

The teacher should avoid lifting children onto apparatus. Mats stacked under the equipment have the effect of lowering the apparatus. Children should be helped to find their own ways to mount apparatus. Their attempts may result in some new interesting moves being developed.

The selection of activities should provide for all-around development. Activities requiring flexibility, agility, balance, and strength should be included in each lesson. Excessive time spent in any one type of activity should be avoided. Too much time performing rolls, inverted balances, and some stunts is fatiguing and also may result in dizziness or headaches. Sufficient time should be provided for practice, but the teacher should be ready to move on to a new activity before the children become fatigued or other discomforts result.

In introducing new activities time should be taken to carefully emphasize the technique, critical points, and safety considerations. The skill should be demonstrated if possible. If a demonstration is not possible, talking an able child through the skill will help the group to see how it should be performed. It should be clearly stated if it is an activity to be attempted only with the teacher on hand.

New activities should be related to similar activities that have been taught previously. Before children attempt a new skill, there should be a review of the stunts that are prerequisites for the new activity.

Stunts that are basic or are lead-ups to other stunts should be considered before more difficult activities are taught. Prerequisites should be mastered before children attempt more advanced activities. A stunt should be taught not at a particular grade level but rather when the child is ready to attempt it.

Children need the opportunity to set their own goals rather than the teacher determining what each child will do. In this way all achieve success, and the needs of children with diverse abilities and interests are met. Children should be encouraged to work at their own level of ability. They may need encouragement to do some activities of which they are capable. The selection of new activities should be the joint effort of the children and the teacher. When both the teacher and student feel the time is appropriate, new skills are introduced. New skills should be encouraged but not insisted on.

Good form should be emphasized in the performance of all activities. Each stunt or routine should have a controlled beginning and ending. The teacher should help the children toward pride in their accomplishments with the principle that only through proper practice can one reach a high level of perfection.

Stunts should be put into simple combinations early in learning to give children practice in moving smoothly from one skill to another. This also provides opportunities to develop transitional moves between stunts.

Exploring balance.

STUNTS AND TUMBLING

Stunts and tumbling provide children with the opportunity to use their body parts in a variety of ways. As the children progress through the elementary school grades, an increase in body awareness enables them to perform more difficult skills and to analyze their own movements. Children in the beginning years are not discriminating in their own performances, whereas in later elementary school grades they can better assess their own performance and take action to improve their skill.

Movement challenges contribute substantially to an increased understanding of the body's potential for movement. A few examples of challenges that may be used follow.

Developing the Movement Content

The utilization of movement challenges should constitute much of the time spent in gymnastics, especially at the beginning levels of learning. Children should be given the opportunity to develop their own ideas as they learn to manipulate their body parts and control their body actions. These activities provide challenging opportunities for all since the children individually use the movements they have acquired and no specific gymnastics skills are called for. Examples of challenges for the use of the body without equipment follow:

Balancing on three body parts.

1. Assume a curled shape. In what ways can you move?
2. Make a stretched shape. Can you make a stretched shape with both sides of the body alike? Different?
3. Start with a stretched shape as you move. Gradually move to a curled shape as you continue to move. Did your way of moving change?
4. Can you combine a locomotor movement with a body shape? For example, can you combine a jump and a curl?
5. Vary direction and shape as you move.
6. Can you move in general space and on the signal assume a balanced position? Repeat, moving and balancing. Now move again and balance in a new way. What body parts can you use for support as you balance? What levels?
7. Move and on the signal assume a balanced position. Try it again with a new balanced position. Once more. Repeat several more times. Select one of your favorite ways of balancing. We will try moving in a variety of ways; on the signal balance in your favorite position. Move another way and balance. Now try a new balance position on the signal. Repeat several times, moving and assuming the new position. Repeat once more with a new balanced position and new ways of moving. Now we will combine the three balances. Select a way of moving and balance with the first position on the signal. Move again and balance in the second position. Finally move and then balance in the third position and hold.
8. Can you balance on one body part? Another one? Another? Repeat, balancing on two parts. Three. Can you make up a sequence of balances and moves balancing on one body part, then two, then three?
9. Balance on two body parts. Move the supporting body parts close together and balance once more. Now as close as possible. Now move them far apart. What was the best position to balance easily?
10. Balance on three body parts. Move the supporting body parts in a straight line. Move them as close together as possible. Now apart. How else might you place the three body parts to balance? What positions made balancing more difficult? Easier?
11. Working on a mat, assume a balanced position. Now lose your balance, curling your body to roll to a new balanced position.
12. Can you find different ways to balance with a partner?
13. Can you balance with a partner so that three body parts are in contact with each other? Two? One? Does reducing the number of

contact points increase or decrease the difficulty in balancing?

14. With a partner, balance, lose your balance, and then balance once again.
15. As you move in general space can you change the body parts you use as you travel? Begin moving on your feet. Now change and move on some other body parts. Move once again on your feet. Now other parts.
16. Using different body parts as you move in each direction, can you travel forward? Backward? Sideways?
17. Move on a mat. How many ways can you move from one end to the other with control? Move on different body parts. Vary your body shape, direction, pathway, or speed.
18. Move on the mat, changing levels as you go.
19. Make a curled shape with a partner and move in that shape.
20. Make a stretched shape with a partner and move in that shape.
21. Combine a curl and a stretch with a partner. How did you move to get from the curl to the stretch?
22. Using stunts and tumbling skills you have learned, can you do a forward roll, with head leading? A cartwheel, hands leading in a sideward direction? What body parts lead as you perform various skills? In what directions did you move?

Falling

Falling is a safety skill that should be taught. As children develop skills in gymnastics, they should learn how to control the body when losing balance and landing from apparatus by applying principles of force described in Chapter 10.

1. Early problems might involve rolling as the children purposely lose their balance from a variety of balance positions. For example: Balance on three body parts. Lean until you lose your balance. Curl your body and roll.
2. The children should move in general space. For example: On the signal make a shape and hold. Now fall from the shape to a relaxed position on the floor. Try it again with a new shape and fall. What shapes made falling easier? More difficult?
3. Falling can be combined with locomotor movements. For example: Walk and fall. Run and fall. Skip and fall.
4. Children should explore landing with control from varying heights and then finishing with a roll.
5. Children should learn to fall from a kneeling position.
   Position: Kneeling on a mat, back straight and head up.
   Action: Keeping the back straight, the child falls forward, reaching out with the arms. As the hands touch the mat, the arms bend at the elbows, gradually absorbing the force as the body continues to fall to the mat.
   Suggestions: A soft landing should be encouraged.
6. Children should learn to fall from a standing position.
   Position: On a mat, standing with legs straight.
   Action: The child falls forward as in No. 3, absorbing the force with the arms.
   Suggestions: Arms should be fully extended as contact is made to permit absorption of force over the greatest distance.
7. Children should learn to fall from a height or from apparatus.
   Position: Standing on two or more stacked mats.
   Action: The child falls so the feet land first, absorbing the force by flexing at the knees, ankles, and hips.
   Suggestion: If the landing is off balance, the child should fall forward as in No. 6 or roll.

Animal Walks

Animal walks are simple stunts in which everyone can find success. They are excellent body awareness activities since body parts are used in different relationships. In some animal walks body parts are moved in unison. In others body parts on one side of the body may move at the same time. In still others some parts may be stationary while other parts are moving. They are listed in order of difficulty. Although specific actions are suggested, the children should be encouraged to make up their own interpretations of how various animals move.

Lame dog
Position: On hands and feet.
Action: One foot is lifted off the floor, and the child moves on one foot and two hands or on one hand and two feet.
Suggestion: The child can alternate which hand or

Inchworm.

Crab walk.

foot is held up.

Ostrich walk

Position: Standing, bending at the hips.

Action: Grasping the ankles, the child moves in this position, keeping the legs fully extended.

Snail

Position: Lying on the back with hands at the sides, palms down on the mat.

Action: The body is curled up, bringing the hips and legs up over the head so that the toes touch the mat behind the head.

Bear walk

Position: On hands and feet.

Action: The child moves with the hand and foot on the same side moving forward at the same time, that is, right foot and right hand, then left foot and left hand.

Seal crawl

Position: On the floor in a prone position.

Action: Keeping the body straight and relaxed and using the hands and arms to move forward, the body is dragged along the floor.

Inchworm

Position: On hands and feet with legs straight.

Action: The child walks the hands out as far forward as possible. Keeping the hands stationary, the feet are walked up to hands, keeping the legs straight.

Gorilla walk

Position: Standing with the feet spread shoulder width apart. Bend at the waist, grasping ankles.

Action: With knees straight, walk forward while holding ankles.

Crab walk

Position: On hands and feet with the front of the body facing upward.

Action: Keeping the hips up and back straight, the child walks with the feet leading, head leading, or moving to the right or left.

Seal slap

Position: Body straight and on the floor with the upper body supported on the straight arms and hands.

Action: The child pushes off with the hands and claps the hands together before returning the hands to the floor.

Mule kick

Position: Standing.

Action: With the hands on the mat the child springs from the feet, taking the weight on the hands with arms straight and shoulders shrugged. The head is up. When the hips are above the head, the legs are extended forcibly upward. In the handstand position, the hips are flexed, and the child pushes from the floor with the hands and the shoulders and snaps the legs down. The hands come off the floor for a brief period before the feet touch the mat.

Suggestion: Younger children may perform this stunt without an airborne phase. Control of the up-

Turk stand.

Thread the needle.

ward leg movement is important to avoid throwing the legs over the head, causing the child to fall.

Individual Stunts

The following stunts may be used in addition to the animal walks. They enhance body awareness, balance, and body control. Most may be easily accomplished by everyone. They are listed in order of difficulty.

Heel slap

Position: Standing.

Action: The child jumps into the air, bending the knees and raising the heels behind. The heels are slapped with the hands at the height of the jump. The landing should be soft.

Log roll

Position: Lying on the mat with arms at the sides.

Action: The child rolls over to the side in as straight a line as possible.

Suggestion: This stunt may be performed from a lying position with arms extended overhead.

Egg roll

Position: In a tuck position grasping the legs with the hands.

Action: The child rolls on the mat, moving sideways.

Turk stand

Position: Sitting with legs crossed and hands folded at chest level.

Action: The child leans forward and comes up to

a stand, then lowers the body to sit once again.

Thread the needle

Position: Standing, grasping the hands in front of the body.

Action: The child steps through the arms with one foot and then the other so the hands are behind the back. The action is reversed, coming back to the starting position.

Jump and turn

Position: Standing.

Action: The child jumps into the air, completes a half turn, and lands softly in a balanced position, then jumps, completes a full turn, and lands softly in a balanced position.

Heel click

Position: Standing.

Action: The child jumps, moving the legs to one side and clicking the heels together at the height of the jump. The child may try to click the heels twice or even three times.

Human rocker

Position: In a prone position.

Action: Arching the back, with head up and the hands grasping the ankles, the child rocks forward and back.

Coffee grinder

Position: With the body supported on one hand and extended to the side and the feet touching the floor.

Action: The feet are walked in a circle, pivoting on the supporting hand.

Swagger walk

Position: Standing.

Action: The child walks by alternately stepping forward by bringing each foot behind and to the outside of the supporting foot.

Knee spring

Position: In a kneeling position, with the head up and the back straight.

Action: The arms are forcefully swung forward to jump from the knees to land on the feet in a squat position.

Single leg circles

Position: In a squat position with both hands on the mat. One leg is between the arms, the other extended to the side.

Action: The extended leg swings forward. As it reaches the closest arm, the arm is raised to touch the floor again outside the leg. Shifting the weight to that arm, the leg continues to circle under the other leg and hand and back to the starting position. The back is kept straight and the inside leg bent.

Coffee grinder.

Partner and Group Stunts

Partner and group stunts add the challenge of co-ordinating efforts with others. They are listed in order of difficulty.

Wring the dishrag

Position: Partners facing and holding hands.

Action: Partners lift one arm; both turn toward and under the lifted arm. They continue to turn and end facing each other.

Chinese get-up

Position: Two children of equal size sit back to back with the knees bent and the arms interlocked at the elbows.

Action: The two stand up by pushing equally on each other's back, then sit down again.

Rocker

Position: Partners of equal size facing and sitting on each other's feet with knees bent and the hands holding each other's upper arms.

Action: The children rock forward and back alternately lifting the hips of one and then the other off the floor.

Wheelbarrow

Position: Partners both facing the same direction; one is on the floor on the hands and feet and the other is standing.

Action: The standing child holds the legs of the other. The first child walks forward on the hands, while the standing child walks behind.

Suggestions: The standing child must not push the wheelbarrow but merely supports the legs as the wheelbarrow moves. It may be helpful to hold the legs at the knees to give more support.

Tandem walk

Position: Two children of equal size, facing the

same direction; one is down on hands and feet, while the other squats in front.

Action: Taking the body weight on the hands, the child in front places raised legs on the back of the other child. The upper legs are at the supporting child's shoulders. The children walk forward, the first on hands, the second on hands and feet.

Monkey walk

Position: One child stands with feet apart; the other lies on the back between the legs of the standing child with the feet in front and the head behind.

Action: The standing child bends forward, putting the hands on the mat. The second child wraps legs around the partner's waist, then reaches upward to support the body off the mat by holding on the partner's back. The child in the hands/feet position walks forward supporting the other child beneath.

Suggestion: Moving slowly and keeping the legs wrapped at the waist should be stressed.

Elephant walk

Position: Two children facing one another. One, with hands on the other child's shoulders, jumps up, puts the legs around the partner's waist, and holds the legs in position by wrapping ankles.

Action: The supported child lowers the upper body and with the hands walks the upper body and head between the legs of the supporting child. The standing child bends forward, taking the body weight on the hands and feet. The other child grasps the top of the supporting child's ankles, lifts the head, and extends the arms. The child in the hands/feet position walks forward supporting the other child.

Suggestion: Walking slowly and keeping the legs wrapped at the waist should be stressed.

Camel walk

Position: Two children stand facing the same di-

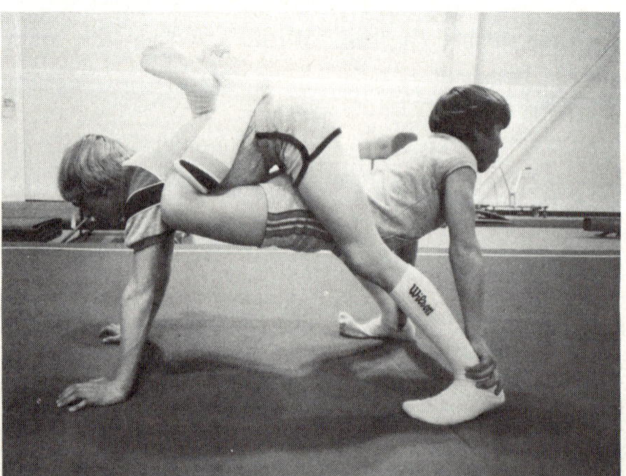

Elephant walk.

rection, one in front of the other. The person in back is holding the other person's waist. With the support of the rear person, the person in front jumps up and wraps the legs around the waist of the rear child.

Action: With ankles crossed to keep the legs in position the child drops down and between the legs of the supporting child. The standing child bends forward and takes weight on the hands and feet. The child on the bottom raises up and grasps the top of the ankles of the other child with arms held straight. The two move forward as the child on top moves on hands and feet supporting the other child.

Partner handstand

Position: Two persons stand facing each other.
Action: One person bends down and places the hands on top of the feet of the other child. The bending child then kicks up into a handstand. The partner supports the handstanding child approximately at the knees and slowly walks forward.

Suggestion: The legs should be straight to avoid kicking the supporting child.

Eskimo roll

Position: One person is lying on the mat with the legs bent at the hips and lifted into the air. The other is standing straddling the down child at the neck and holding the ankles of the down child. The child on the floor grasps the standing child's ankles.

Action: The standing child bends forward and brings the other child's legs and feet to the mat. The child then springs easily and does a forward roll between the legs of the down child. The action results in the reversing of the positions of the two children. The child who was on top is now on the bottom, and the child who began on the mat is standing. The action is repeated several times as the two progress down the mat.

Suggestion: Each child should be able to perform a good forward roll before attempting this partner stunt.

Skin the snake

Position: A group of children stand one in front of the other in a long line with their right hand extended between their legs to hold the left hand of the person directly behind.

Action: On the signal the last person in line lies down on the floor without releasing the hand and the line moves backward, straddling the child lying down. The line continues to move back with each person lying down in turn. When all are down, the last person in the line stands up and begins moving forward, straddling the other persons. Each in turn stands up until all are standing once again.

Monkey roll

Position: Three persons lying parallel on a mat with their heads in a line. They are numbered one, two, and three.

Action: Number one begins the action by raising up slightly and moving over number two to roll on the opposite side of two. One and two continue to roll. Number three moves over one in a similar fashion. Then two over three. They continue to move in this fashion.

Double wheelbarrow

Position: Two children assume the wheelbarrow position, with a third child in position behind the first two and facing in the opposite direction. The third takes the body weight on the hands, lifting the legs and placing them between the hands and ankles of the wheelbarrow couple.

Action: As the wheelbarrow moves forward, the child behind moves backward.

Walking chair

Position: A group of from four to eight children line up one behind the other and facing the same direction.

Action: With their hands on the hips of the person in front of them, all assume a sitting position by bending at the hips and knees and keeping the back straight. They move forward, each stepping first with the right foot and then the left.

Centipede

Position: In groups of three in a line one behind the other.

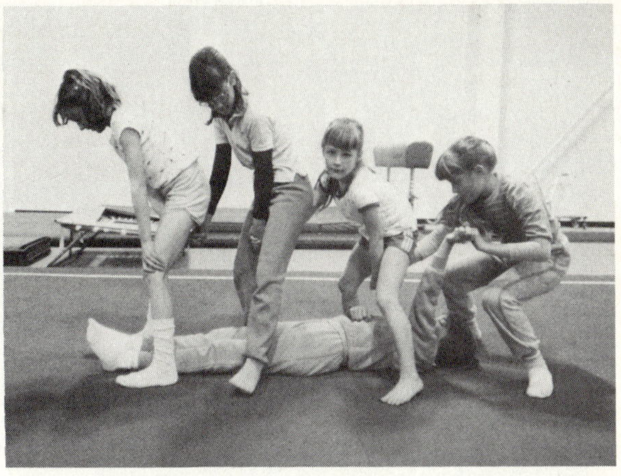

Skin the snake.

Centipede.

Merry-go-round.

Shoulder roll.

Action: The last person in line bends forward and takes weight on the hands and feet. The second person takes weight on the hands and lifts the legs, bending the knees and turning the knees out to each side so they rest on the hips of the person behind. The person in front repeats the action of the one behind, resulting in three persons in line with their weight on all hands and the feet of the last person in line. They walk forward in this position, moving first the limbs on one side and then the other.

Merry-go-round

Position: A group of 8 or 10 children form a circle and hold the wrists of the persons on either side. They number off consecutively. The odd numbers sit on the floor with their legs straight and their feet touching.

Action: On a signal, the even-numbered children take a step backward as the odd numbers raise their hips off the floor, leaning back with their bodies and keeping the legs straight. The even numbers then move around in a circle with the others turning with them by pivoting on their heels. Roles are reversed and the activity repeated.

Thigh mount

Position: Three persons stand side by side facing the same direction. The outside persons with their inside hands hold the center person at the waist; the inside person puts the hands on the shoulders of those on either side.

Action: On the signal the two outside persons bend their inside legs to form a flat surface parallel with the floor. The inside person steps up putting one foot on the inside thigh of the outside persons.

When balanced the inside person extends the arms up and out to the side. Hold the position.

Individual Tumbling Skills

Individual tumbling skills form the basics for beginning combinations in *floor exercise.* Many combinations and variations are possible. Children select skills and make up combinations to fit their abilities. The skills are listed in order of difficulty.

Shoulder roll

Position: Standing with the side to the mat.

Action: The performer drops to the knee closest to the mat, breaking the fall with the hand and arm on the same side. The elbow turns in and the individual lands on back of the shoulder blades. The child continues to roll coming up on the opposite knee and finally to a stand.

Common errors: Rolling on the entire back.

Suggestions: The child should practice slowly at first to get the body position.

Forward roll

Position: In a standing position facing the mat.

Action: To begin the roll the performer assumes a squat position with hands on the mat and the head tucked to the chest and between the legs. With a gentle push with the feet the roll begins with a lift of the hips overhead, the weight shifting from the feet to the hands. As balance is lost, the roll continues with the head well under and the weight taken on the upper back and shoulders. The momentum of the roll should carry the individual back to the standing position. The arms reach upward or are extended

Forward roll.

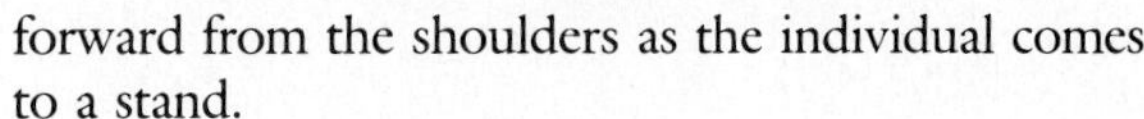
Backward roll.

forward from the shoulders as the individual comes to a stand.

Common errors:
1. Failure to tuck the head to the chest resulting in rolling on the head.
2. Failure to maintain a tuck position throughout the roll.
3. Pushing with the hands a second time at the end of the roll to aid in standing.

Suggestions:
1. To spot the roll, one should kneel next to the tumbler, placing one hand where the neck and back meet and the other on the back of the thighs. In this position the spotter can help in keeping the tumbler in the tucked position and also support the neck if necessary on the roll. Under no circumstances should the spotter push the tumbler into the roll.
2. Most children have little difficulty with the forward roll. Some large children need more assistance in learning to do the roll safely.
3. Beginners should begin the roll from the squat position.

Variations:
Continuous forward rolls: A series of rolls is combined by maintaining the tuck position from one roll to the next.
Straddle: The roll is begun with the legs wide apart and continues in this position, coming up to a stand.
Feet crossed: From the standing position with the feet crossed, this position is continued throughout the roll.
Forward roll step out: One leg is tucked in and the other extended as the roll is taken.

Backward roll

Position: Standing with the back facing the mat.

Action: The body is lowered as if sitting down and the arms are bent with the hands at the shoulders, palms up and fingers pointing in the line of direction of movement. As the hips make contact with the mat, the head is tucked to the chest and the body begins the roll from the hips to the upper back. As the weight is taken on the upper back the hands push to lift the body slightly to get the head under. The roll ends in a standing position.

Common errors:
1. Failure to place the hands in the correct position for the push.
2. Failure to keep tucked as one rolls back.
3. Failure to push or to push evenly with both hands.
4. Turning the head to one side while rolling.

Suggestions:
1. Teaching the backward roll should begin from the squat position.
2. In getting the idea for the roll the children can do the snail but put the hands in the correct position for pushing.
3. The roll is spotted by kneeling next to the individual and holding the tumbler's hips on either side and lifting the hips as the tumbler

Backward roll, *cont'd.*

rolls to the shoulders.

4. Another method of spotting may be used in which the spotter places one hand at the spot where the neck and back meet and the other on the back of the thighs. The spotter lifts the tumbler, supporting the neck in the hand. Under no circumstances should the tumbler be pushed over so the body weight is taken on the neck.

5. The backward roll is much more difficult for children to master. Larger children in the class will need special help.

Variations:

Continuous backward rolls: A series of backward rolls is completed, maintaining the tuck position from one roll to the next.

Straddle: The roll is begun from a standing position with the legs spread apart and the hands between the legs.

Pike: From a standing position, the body is lowered as in a backward roll but bending at the hips and keeping the legs straight. The roll begins from a long sitting position on the mat with the legs swinging overhead as the hands move to the shoulders. The roll continues with straight legs to the standing position.

Back extension: The roll is begun as for a tucked or pike backward roll. As the legs are brought overhead, the hands push and the body extends to a handstand, which is held momentarily. The body then bends at the hips with straight legs to finish in a standing position. This is spotted as a backward roll with hands at the hips helping the lift and handstand position.

Fish flop: Similar to the back extension, but after the body extension the arms bend, lowering the body so it finishes with the back arched and contact on the mat moving from the chest to the lower body.

Cartwheel

Position: Standing with the side facing the direction of movement.

Action: The performer faces forward extending the arms upward and out toward the side. The weight is transferred to the foot away from the line of movement and the other foot lifted. A step is now taken on the lifted foot and the hand on that side of the body is placed on the floor with the fingers pointing to the side of the body. There is a push from the

Cartwheel.

stepping foot as the other leg is swung upward. The legs are in a straddle position throughout the stunt. As the body turns 90 degrees to a side orientation, the second hand is placed on the mat in a line with the first hand. As the movement continues the weight is carried to the second hand and the body begins to drop to the side. The weight is then transferred to one foot and then the other. The cartwheel ends in the standing position with legs and arms spread, the body finishing facing the line of movement.

Common errors:
1. Touching both hands to the mat at the same time.
2. Improper hand placement on the mat, either too near or too far from the front foot.
3. Failure to get the hips over the head.
4. Kicking the leg to the side instead of behind.
5. Landing with feet together or on knees.
6. Inability to keep the arms straight as they take the body weight.
7. Bending the legs as they come up over head.

Suggestions:
1. The sequence is hand, hand, foot, foot.
2. To spot the cartwheel and to help children get the feeling of having the hips overhead one can stand behind the individual with the arms crossed and the hands at the hips. As the child attempts the cartwheel the body is supported at the hips, keeping them up and overhead.

Variation:
One-handed cartwheel: Similar to the two-handed cartwheel, but touching only the first hand to the mat. The body momentum carries the body weight back to the standing position. The sequence is hand, foot, foot.

Round-off

Position: Standing with the side facing the direction of movement.

Action: The round-off is similar to a cartwheel in that the body weight is shifted to the hands and then the feet. However, in the round-off the sequence is hand, hand, and then both feet. A running approach is used in the round-off with a hop step or hurdle step preceding the execution of the skill. As the first hand is brought rapidly to the mat the opposite leg is straight and raised up overhead. As the body weight is taken on the two hands the legs are extended overhead with the feet coming together. There is a slight twist in the body and the hips forcibly flex to bring both feet down to the mat in a snapping action. As the legs snap the hands push from the mat as in the mule kick. In the landing the arms are overhead and the body is facing the starting position.

Common errors:
1. Beginning from a standing position with insufficient momentum to perform the skill correctly.
2. Placing the hands too close or too far from the front foot.
3. Failure to bend the front leg.
4. Failure to get the hips overhead.

5. Not pushing with hands from mat so there is no phase when feet and hands are in the air before landing.
6. Failure to flex hips forcibly.
7. Not bringing legs together overhead.
8. Failure to keep arms straight throughout.

Suggestions:
1. Children can begin learning the skill from a standing position and add a moving approach when ready.
2. The teacher should insist on a moving approach before beginning the skill to develop sufficient momentum.
3. The teacher should emphasize the push with the hands as the hips flex.
4. The cartwheel and mule kick should be practiced before trying this skill.
5. The teacher may draw a line on the mat and have the students practice the round-off by following the line.

Snap-up (kip)

Position: Sitting on the mat with legs straight and toes pointed, hands at the sides.

Action: The body rocks back, bringing the piked legs overhead, and the hands move to a position at the shoulders as if attempting a backward roll. The legs are quickly snapped forward and downward. The back is arched and the hands push forcibly as the leg action is taken. The feet are brought under the body and the upper body is snapped forward. The skill ends in a standing position with the arms extended upward and slightly to the side.

Common errors:
1. Hesitating between the rock back and snap, losing momentum.
2. Failure to push with hands, head, and shoulders as the legs are snapped.
3. Snapping the legs upward and forward rather than forward and downward.

Suggestions:
1. To spot the snap-up the spotter kneels at the tumbler's shoulders, grasping the under side of the upper arm with one hand and the lower back with the other. As tumbler snaps, the spotter lifts until the feet are under the body. A spotter on each side may be used.
2. Another spotting technique involves kneeling at the performer's side and spotting the lower back by the waist with two hands after the tumbler has rocked back. As the tumbler snaps, the spotter lifts until both feet are under the performer.

Forward walkover.

3. The child may begin with a snail to get the proper positioning.
4. A squat position for landing is a simpler variation for beginners.

Bridge

Position: Lying on the back on the mat with hands at shoulders, fingers pointing toward feet.

Action: Pushing with hands and feet, the body is lifted into a back bend and held.

Common errors: Not pushing simultaneously with feet and hands.

Suggestions: This is a prerequisite skill for the front limber, forward walkover, front handspring, and headspring.

Forward limber

Position: Standing, facing the direction of movement.

Action: The skill begins with a kick up into a handstand. Keeping the legs together and straight, the back is overarched and the legs lowered to the mat with the toes turned out. The arms are straight. As the feet touch the mat the hands push off and the body rocks forward to rise to a stand. The arms remain overhead, the head is back, and the back is arched as the performer comes to a standing position.

Common errors:
1. Failure to keep the arms straight.
2. Failure to keep the back arched.
3. Failure to time the push with the rocking forward of the body.

Suggestions:
1. The bridge is a prerequisite skill.
2. One may spot from the side, placing one hand at the upper back and the other ready to support at the waist as the tumbler comes up to a stand.

Forward walkover

Position: Standing facing the direction of movement.

Action: The movement begins with a kick up into a handstand, with the legs split, one forward and the other back. The legs are lowered with the forward leg leading. It is placed on the mat as close to the hands as possible. There is a slight bend at the knee. To come up to a stand, there is a push with the hands and the trailing leg is raised; the hands continue to reach overhead as the performer stands.

Common errors:
1. Failure to keep the arms straight throughout the performance.
2. Throwing the body over rather than lowering the legs with control.
3. Failure to keep the legs split throughout the move.
4. Not placing the foot close to the hands.
5. Failure to push with the hands and to thrust the body forward.
6. Failure to arch the lower back.

Suggestions:
1. The tumbler may think about stepping over an obstacle as the second leg is brought forward and down to maintain an erect position.
2. The spotter places one hand at the base of the neck and top of the shoulders and the other ready to support the lower back as the performer begins to lower the legs.

Back bend

Position: Standing on a mat with arms raised overhead, and head back.

Action: The body is lowered backward, pushing the hips forward and slightly bending the knees. The hands are placed on the mat as close to the feet as possible. The arch is held and the child stands up by thrusting hips forward.

Common errors: Not thrusting the hips forward

to stand.

Suggestion: A spotter should have one hand on each side of the hips to help to control the downward descent.

Back walkover

Position: Standing with the arms raised over head and the back facing the mat. One foot is slightly forward and the weight is on the rear foot.

Action: Reaching back for the mat, the hands are placed on the mat as close as possible to the feet. One leg is raised. Pushing off with the other foot vigorously, the individual assumes a handstand position with one leg forward and the other back. The forward leg is lowered to the mat, the legs remaining in the split position. A push with the hands and a lowering of the trailing leg brings the tumbler back to the standing position.

Common errors:
1. Failure to keep the arms straight throughout the stunt.
2. Placing the hands too far from the feet.
3. Throwing the body over rather than moving with control.
4. Scissoring legs or failure to keep them split throughout the stunt.
5. Failure to swing the leg vigorously as the hands are placed on the mat.

Suggestions:

To spot one stands next to the performer, placing the inside hand on the lower back and the outside hand on the back of the upper thigh of the front leg. In this manner one may support the lower back and also help the leg swing forward by lifting the leg.

Headspring

Position: Standing facing the direction of movement.

Action: The headspring may be performed from a straddle or pike position. The hands are placed on the mat with the head on the mat between the hands. The legs are lifted in the pike or straddle position. The body leans forward and as it does the legs are kicked up and over. As the body continues to move off balance there is a forceful push of the hands to bring the body to its feet. The landing is on the balls of the feet, the knees are slightly bent, and the arms are overhead.

Common errors:
1. Failure to use a two-foot take-off.
2. Failure to get hips beyond head before thrusting legs.
3. Failure to maintain the pike or straddle position.
4. Failure to push with the hands.

Back walkover.

Suggestions:
1. To spot one kneels beside performer, grasping the upper arm with the inside hand and supporting the lower back with the outside hand.
2. This skill is often taught from a rolled mat, which makes it easier for the performer to get the feet under and close to the hands.

Front handspring

Position: Stand, facing the direction of movement.

Action: A moving approach is taken with a final push-off on one foot and a lift of the opposite knee and leg to increase the height of the jump. As the body moves forward and downward the hands are placed on the mat shoulder width apart and the free leg is raised in an extended position. The body is moved quickly through a handstand position, the legs coming together as they move beyond the head and shoulders. As balance is lost the toes reach for the mat and the hands push the body away from the mat. As the feet touch the mat the upper body is raised, ending in a standing position with knees slightly bent and arms overhead.

Common errors:

1. Failure to keep the arms straight throughout the stunt.
2. Failure to push with the shoulders and hands.
3. Failure to keep the back arched.
4. Failure to keep the body in an extended position throughout the stunt.

Suggestions:

1. To spot the front handspring one stands next to the performer, placing the outside arm at the top of the shoulders as the inside arm supports the lower back.
2. This skill may be practiced over a rolled mat for support.

BALANCE STUNTS

Balance activities are an important part of the gymnastic experience. Beginning work on the mats and large apparatus includes balancing in various body positions. Both individual and partner or group balancing activities should be included.

Individual Balances

Skill combinations or gymnastic routines include balance activities. Although they may be held only momentarily, they demonstrate the child's control over the body's movement.

Knee scale

Position: Kneeling on one knee, with the opposite hand on the floor.

Action: The other leg is raised upward and backward, pointing the toes. The opposite arm is extended and the hand forward with the fingers pointing ahead. The head is up.

Arabesque

Position: Standing.

Action: The weight is kept on one foot as the other is lifted back as high as possible. The trunk is bent forward slightly and the back is arched. The hands may assume a variety of positions. The most common is to have the arm on the same side as the lifted leg extending forward and the other back. Both arms form a straight line from the shoulders.

V-sit

Position: Sitting on the floor or a mat.

Action: Both legs are lifted to a V or pike position while pointing the toes. As the legs are lifted the arms swing forward and upward to grasp the ankles. The hands may also be extended to the sides or to the rear.

One-leg balance

Position: Standing with the hands at the sides.

Action: Keeping the weight on one foot, the other leg is raised sideward and upward as high as possible, the heel held with the hand.

Needle

Position: In an arabesque.

Action: The child bends forward, touching the hands to the floor and simultaneously raising one leg backward and upward toward the ceiling. A variation in the hand position commonly used is to grasp the ankle of the supporting foot with one hand while the other touches the floor.

L support

Position: In a long sitting position on the mat with hands touching the mat at the sides of the body and fingers pointing forward.

Action: The body is raised upward and supported on the hands. The legs should be extended forward with the toes pointed and off the mat.

Inverted Individual Balances

Some balancing activities that involve balancing in the inverted position should be included in the gym-

Knee scale.

One-leg balance.

Headstand.

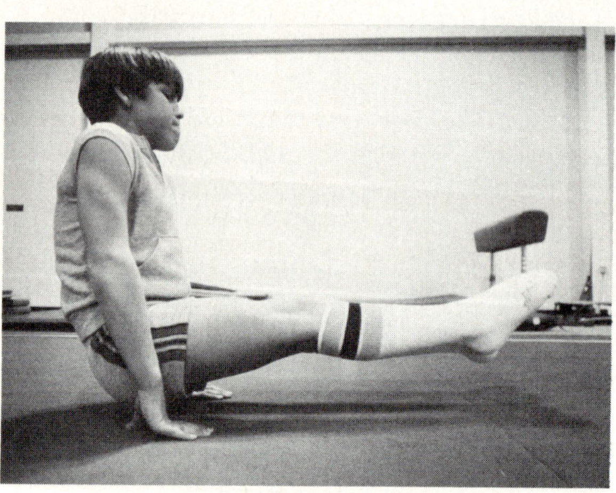

L support.

nastic experience. These challenge the child to control the body while balancing on the head and hands or hands alone.

Shoulder rest

Position: In a long sitting position.

Action: The individual rocks back until the hips are over the shoulders. The legs are extended overhead. The hands support the hips with the elbows on the mat.

Tripod

Position: In a squat position with the hands placed on the mat in front of the feet.

Action: The forehead is placed on the mat out in front of the hands to form a triangle with the hands. The performer rocks forward taking the body weight on the hands and head. The legs are raised and the knees are placed on the bent elbows.

Suggestions:

1. This stunt is a prerequisite to the headstand.
2. The weight should be equally balanced on the hands and forehead. Keep the neck firm.

Headstand

Position: In a squat position.

Action: The headstand begins as the tripod, but instead of placing the knees on the elbows the legs are extended overhead. The back is slightly arched, the legs together, and the weight evenly distributed on the forehead and hands.

Suggestions:

1. Children may assist in spotting the headstand. As the performer raises the legs, the spotter either extends an arm behind the legs or holds the legs until a balanced position is assumed. The spotter should not lift the legs but merely support them until balance is gained.
2. When balance is lost in the headstand, it is easy to curl the body and perform a forward roll.

Variations:

Headstand splits: Once balance is gained in the headstand, the performer moves the legs apart either to the sides or forward and backward.

Headstand turn: Once balance is gained, the performer slowly turns the head and hands to turn 360 degrees in place.

Pike headstand: The headstand begins from a position lying face down on the mat with hands and head in position. Using the abdominal muscles the performer pulls the legs up, bending at the hips to assume a pike position. As the position is attained, the legs continue to move upward, extending overhead to a headstand.

Tip-up

Position: In a squat position.

Action: The hands are placed on the mat in front of the feet. Keeping the elbows bent and the head up, the performer rocks forward, supporting the knees on the outside of the elbows and balancing with the two hands for support.

Tiger stand

Position: In a kneeling position.

Action: The hands and forearms are placed on the mat in front of the knees and parallel to each other. One leg at a time is kicked to an inverted balance position. The back should be arched and head up.

Handstand

Position: Standing.

Action: The performer bends forward, placing the hands on the mat shoulder width apart. One leg swings up and then the other, ending in a position with both legs extended overhead. The arms should be kept straight throughout the stunt.

Suggestions:

1. Children may work in partners, with the spotter standing to the side to take the ankles as they are raised upward. The spotter should not lift the legs but should keep them from continuing to move forward from the overhead position.

2. Once the balance position is attained, the performer may attempt to take a few steps by walking on the hands.

Variations:

Handstand splits: The legs are split in a forward/backward direction.

Handstand straddle: The legs are split in a sideward position.

Stag handstand: The forward leg is bent at the knee and the back leg extended back.

Double stag: Both legs are bent at the knee, one forward, the other back.

Tip-up.

Handstand.

Partner Balances

Partner balances are a challenging activity for children to work together. The partners who are serving as the base should have sufficient strength to support their classmates.

Knee stand

Position: The base kneels on one knee with the thigh of the other leg parallel to the mat.

Handstand straddle.

Stag handstand.

Double stag.

Action: The top person steps up and puts one foot on the knee of the base. The base supports the top person by grasping the upper leg. The top extends the arms out to the side and the free leg is raised back.

Knee-shoulder balance

Position: The base lies on the mat with the knees bent and the feet close to the buttocks. The top stands facing the base and at the base's feet.

Action: The top leans forward, placing the hands on the knees of the base and the shoulders on the outstretched hands of the base. The top then kicks up both feet overhead, arching the back slightly and lifting the head to face the base.

Swan balance

Position: The base lies on the mat with the knees bent; the legs are raised and the hands are reaching upward. The top person stands at the base's feet facing the base.

Action: The top person leans forward, taking the

Swan balance.

Chest stand.

Table stand.

hands of the base and placing the front of the hips on the feet of the base. Straightening the legs, the base lifts the top person into the air. The top assumes a balanced position parallel to the mat and when secure releases the hands and extends the arms out to the side.

Chest stand

Position: The base assumes a hands and knees po-sition on the mat with the top person standing to one side facing the side of the base.

Action: The top bends forward, placing the chest across the back of the base, the chin on the other side of the back, and the hands grasping the partner's lower chest and abdomen. Both feet are kicked upward to assume a balanced position with the legs over head.

Table stand

Position: The base assumes a position on the mat with the legs extended upward at right angles to the mat. The hands are at the shoulders with the palms up. The top person stands at the base's head with the feet in the partner's hands.

Action: The top person places hands on the feet of the base and, pushing downward as the base extends the arms upward, is raised into the air. Both should keep the arms and legs straight as they balance.

Sitting on feet

Position: The base lays on the mat with the hands next to the ears and the palms up. The top person stands on the hands of the base but facing away.

Action: The base lifts the legs, placing the heels on the partner's buttocks and the feet along the back of the thighs. The top person sits on the partner's

Sitting balance.

A four-person pyramid.

feet as the base extends the legs, keeping them at right angles to the mat. The hands of the top person are placed at the hips.

Thigh stand (angel)

Position: The base stands behind and close to the top person. The base squats, places the head between the legs of the partner, and grasps the top person's thighs just above the knees. Coming to a standing position, the partner sits on the base's shoulders.

Action: The base bends the knees and hips and the top person places the feet on the base's thighs. The base holds the other's thighs just above the knees as the top person extends the legs to stand. At the same time the base tucks the head out from between the legs of the top person. The base leans back slightly to straighten the arms. The top person arches the back slightly and extends the arms out to the sides.

Sitting balance

Position: The base lies on the mat with the legs extended upward and the arms at the sides. The knees are bent and the top person stands close to the extended legs facing away from the base.

Action: The base places heels diagonally across the buttocks of the partner and the toes well down on the thighs. The top extends the arms backward to grasp the base's extended arms. With a general push-off from the mat the top assumes a sitting position on the feet of the base. The base straightens the legs and releases the hands. The top person keeps the legs as straight as possible and extends the arms out to the sides at shoulder level.

Pyramids

Pyramid building offers a group activity in problem solving. Pyramids are built by combining individual, partner, and group stunts into an interesting shape. The children work together to choose the overall design and the stunts to be used in putting it together. Pyramids may be made with as few as two persons or as many as are in the group. Although balance stunts are primarily used, various tumbling skills may be included in the making or dismantling of the design.

Pyramids are usually symmetrical in shape, but children may combine stunts into asymmetrical designs as well. They may be of uniform height, high in the middle, high to one side, high on the sides and low in the middle, or whatever is pleasing to the children. They may start by drawing a design on

An eight-person pyramid

paper and then planning the stunts they will use to create it.

An interesting floor pattern may also be used. Although many pyramids are done in a straight line, the stunts may also be formed in squares, circles, triangles, the spokes of a wheel, or other formations.

Pyramids may be formed with moving as well as stationary parts. For example, the merry-go-round, human rocker, coffee grinder, or other moving parts may be added to a pyramid of individual or partner balances.

The parts should be practiced first before the children attempt to put the design together. Once the children are fairly certain of the part they will play, it is time to put the pyramid together.

A good beginning and ending should be encouraged. Once the design and stunts have been decided, the children need to work on the organization for building the pyramid. A planned sequence for adding the stunts is needed. If it entails more than two persons the design is usually built in stages. On a signal, usually counting (1001, 1002), each part is added. After it is complete, the pyramid is usually dismantled to a count as well.

Whenever children construct pyramids in which they support one another, care should be taken to be sure those in the base are strong enough for the task. Weight bearing should only be on body parts that are firmly supported. For instance, in the simple pyramid of three persons, two as base on hands and knees and the third on top in the same position, the top person should place the hands at the shoulders of the bases and the knees at their hips. At no time should the back be used for weight bearing.

The problem-solving approach may be used in building pyramids. For example, the following challenges might be posed.

1. Make a design with one other person. Two. Three.
2. Make a pyramid that is high in the middle. Uniform in height. High to one side.
3. Make a pyramid that is in a straight line. In a square. In a triangle. In a circle. Shaped like the spokes of a wheel.

DEVELOPING A MOVEMENT SEQUENCE

One of the goals of educational gymnastics is to build a combination of movements into a gymnastics rou-

```
                        Floor Exercise
        Name________________________ Music________________

                Skills

        1.___________________________

        2.___________________________

        3.___________________________

        4.___________________________

        5.___________________________

        6.___________________________

        7.___________________________

        8.___________________________

        9.___________________________

       10.___________________________
```

Figure 15-1

Form for recording floor exercise.

tine. In stunts and tumbling this is often referred to as a floor exercise. In a floor exercise the performer moves on a square mat, using as much of the space as possible to perform various skills while moving in different pathways across the mat.

Since these movement sequences are the combination of several skills, children should be encouraged to combine skills throughout the learning process. These combinations may include moving directly from one skill to another or using transitional movements between skills.

Creativity is an important aspect in the development of an exercise. In developing gymnastic routines or floor exercises children should be encouraged to:

1. Choose two or more *stunts and tumbling skills* to be used, including at least one of the most difficult skills the child can perform.
2. Select individual *balances* to provide variation in tempo and level to make the exercise interesting.
3. Use *locomotor skills, nonlocomotor skills, dance steps,* and other movements to creatively form smooth transitions from one skill to the next.
4. Plan for a variation in *level,* performing some skills on the mat, and others in the air (jumps or leaps).
5. Plan for smooth and interesting changes of *direction.*
6. Incorporate a change in *tempo* by performing movements at slow, medium, and fast speeds

(in time to musical accompaniment if used).

7. Use an interesting *floor pattern or pathway* in covering all of the space.
8. Plan a *dynamic beginning,* which sets the stage for the routine and a definite and *interesting ending*.

In developing a floor exercise the problem-solving approach may be used. This permits the children to develop their own creativity as well as work within their own ability. Challenges may be posed to stimulate simple combinations of skills that later may be put together into a longer movement sequence. Creating long movement sequences is difficult for many children. Remembering them also poses a problem for some. Figure 15-1 includes a form that may help children plan a floor exercise. The combinations of young children may vary from two to four or five to seven moves. The sequences will not include all of the components above. Some children at level III and IV have the experience to develop somewhat more complex sequences. Older children may develop an exercise by combining several shorter sequences of skills they have developed over the unit.

Young children are not able to deal with too many components at one time. Keeping the problems simple will gives the children confidence in their ability to combine skills and works to improve the flow of their movements. The children may explore several challenges within the period and at the end of the lesson put a couple of their solutions together. A few movement challenges and some possible solutions follow.

1. Combine a moving stunt with a balance. Examples: Forward roll to a V seat. Backward roll to a knee scale. Headstand to a forward roll.
2. Combine two skills in the low level. Examples: Forward roll with crossed legs to a backward roll. Seal walk to a forward roll. Crab walk, turn over, bear walk.
3. Begin with a skill in the high level and move to a skill in another level. Examples: Cartwheel to a forward roll. Handstand to a chest roll.
4. Move from a low level to a high level. Examples: Backward roll to a back extension roll. Backward roll to a head stand.
5. Move in one direction and then change direction. Examples: Cartwheel to a forward roll. Roundoff to a backward roll.

Another approach to floor exercise is to develop a movement sequence that all the children are able to do. Once they learn the sequence, the children may make substitutions in the routine.

Additional Skills for Building Movement Sequences

Tumbling and balance skills included earlier in this chapter are an important part of the floor exercise routine. The following dance skills and transitional movements add to the flow of the movement sequence. These skills may be developed in levels III and IV.

Attitude

Position: In an erect position with the weight on both feet.

Action: The body weight is shifted to one foot, the other leg raised backward and upward, and the knee turned outward. The arm on the supporting side of the body is extended out from the shoulder with a bend of the elbow bringing the forearm around in front of the body. The other arm is extended upward with a slight bend at the elbow to bring the hand over the head.

Turns. The children should experiment with developing some interesting ways to perform one or a series of turns between the stunts, tumbling skills, and balances they have chosen.

Tour jeté

Position: Standing with the arms down at the sides.

Action: Begin with a step on the right foot, kicking the left leg forward and upward. The body quickly turns 180 degrees with a landing on the left foot as the right leg swings upward and to the rear. The body should be kept erect throughout the movement. The arms move to a position overhead as the left leg swings upward. The head is up with the eyes focusing on a stationary object.

Dance steps. A variety of dance steps may be used to add variety to the movements, such as the schottische, two-step, and polka.

Body wave

Position: Standing with the feet together or one foot in front of the other. The arms are down at the sides.

Action: The arms are lifted forward and upward as the hips and knees bend. The arms swing backward and upward. The arms then continue to move to a position overhead as the body assumes an erect position. The knees are forced forward and the legs straighten by pushing the hips forward. The back is arched, but the shoulders remain back. The shoulders

Split leap

Stag leap.

Double stag leap.

then hunch slightly forward as the legs are completely straightened.

Scissors kick

Position: Standing.

Action: A step forward is taken on one foot and then the other leg is kicked forward as high as possible. As the kicking leg drops, the stepping leg is forced upward so the legs switch positions in the air. The landing is on the kicking leg. The arms are held out to the sides from the shoulders. The body should be kept erect throughout.

Jump with the legs bent to the rear

Position: Standing with the body weight on both feet.

Action: The knees and hips are bent and the child

springs into the air, bringing the heels up to the buttocks. The arms begin at the sides and are raised forward to shoulder height. The landing is soft. The trunk should be kept erect.

Cat jump

Position: Standing.

Action: The performer springs into the air from both feet, raising the knees to the side and touching the soles of the feet under the body. One arm is raised overhead; the other is extended to the side at shoulder height.

Split leap

Position: Standing.

Action: After a couple of running steps, the child leaps into the air with the legs split, one forward and the other back. The arms move in opposition to the legs, one extended upward and backward, the other forward and upward. The head is up and the back is arched.

Stag leap

Position: Standing.

Action: The performer leaps upward and, while in the air, extends the back leg and bends the forward leg back at the knee so the sole of the foot is close to the back knee. The forward arm is straight up overhead; the other is extended diagonally upward and backward. The head is up and the body erect.

Double stag leap

Position: Standing.

Action: Similar to the stag leap, but both legs are bent at the knee. The forward leg is angled downward, the rear leg upward. The head is up and the back straight.

Side leap.

Side leap
Position: Standing.
Action: The movement begins as a split leap, but as the forward leg is raised, the hips are rotated 90 degrees so the body faces to the side of the direction of movement.

LARGE APPARATUS

Playground equipment and large apparatus used indoors are enjoyed by children of all ages. Climbing, hanging from various body parts, swinging, and other movements are challenging for children as they engage in activities that they perceive as risk taking within individual limits of controlled movement.

Many playgrounds are equipped with climbing equipment. Much of the playground equipment constructed today is made of wood. Not only is it constructed to be appealing to the imagination of children and conducive to creative use of the body, it provides a safer environment than the steel used in swings, slides, and teeter-totters, which have been standard playground equipment over the years. Several considerations must be made in planning or constructing playground apparatus. Playground apparatus should be located where it can be easily supervised and does not interfere with other forms of activity taking place on the playground. The surface beneath apparatus should be well-drained and provide for a soft landing as children dismount from the equipment. The base should be anchored to the ground to provide the necessary stability with cement or other material used below the ground surface. The height of apparatus should be appropriate for the size of the children using it. The material used should provide a safe, splinter-free, and nonslippery surface for hand and footholds. A program of preventive

maintenance is important in anticipating and removing potential hazards before they arise.

Many of the activities suggested for use with a horizontal bar or parallel bars may be adapted for use on jungle gyms and other playground apparatus. The physical education program should include movement challenges and traditional activities for the use of this equipment. Emphasis should be placed on the safe use of the equipment so that children will have the knowledge and skill to play on the equipment without direct supervision. It is important to take some time at the beginning of each school year to go over the safety considerations and some of the skills children might need to prepare them to use the apparatus responsibly.

Indoor apparatus may be equally challenging for children. In the sections that follow specific movement challenges and other activities are suggested for use on a variety of apparatus available for use by elementary school children. When possible, equipment should be purchased to fit the size and ability of the children who will be using it. It should also be checked on a regular basis to be certain that it is in safe working condition. Mats should be placed to protect the children from landing on apparatus supports and should extend out from the equipment to provide a safe landing area in all directions.

Creative movement is an important aspect in using large apparatus whether indoors or outdoors. Early experiences should focus on exploration in the use of the body and the movements possible on each piece of equipment. As they learn more traditional activities, children should experiment with new variations and also new ways to move from one skill to the next.

Simple combinations of skills should be attempted in the early phases of learning as in stunts and tumbling. The routine or combination should be built around the essential elements. Each routine should include a mount, moves on the particular piece of equipment, balances or poses, and a dismount. Children should practice the moves in combination. For instance, when they practice a mount, the next move should also be included. In this way children begin to develop movement sequences that have flow from the beginning to the end. As always, a good beginning and ending should be encouraged.

Balance Beam

Balance beams are constructed in both 2- and 4-inch widths and varying in height from a couple of inches to 4 feet from the floor. The height of the beam is usually adjustable, with elementary school age children working no higher than 36 to 40 inches. The narrow beam is adequate for young children but makes many of the skills performed in later grades difficult, since a wider beam offers more support.

When working on the beam the children should focus on the end of the beam rather than looking down at their feet. The hands may be out to the sides for balance, especially if the beam is narrow.

Many of the activities on a low beam do not require spotting by the teacher, but it is desirable to have the children spot for each other to establish the habit of assuming responsibility for each other. Obviously children may spot simple locomotor skills and balances. More complex moves and rolls require spotting by the teacher. When spotting, the child should be positioned next to the beam with the closer arm extended across the beam in front of the performer for the low beam and extended upward for the high beam. In this manner the arm is readily available to grasp should balance be lost. Both spotter and performer move in the same direction with the spotter picking a tempo to stay within an arm's reach of the performer but not so close as to hinder the performer's movements.

Many of the skills on the balance beam can be taught first by using a low beam, 6 to 12 inches in height, with mats stacked to an equal height on both sides of the apparatus and making contact with it. This step should be taken before the skill is attempted on a higher beam. It allows the student to try the skill and alleviates the risk factor and the element of fear.

Moving with equipment may add an additional challenge in the early phases of learning when children are experimenting with balance. Filling bleach bottles or other jugs with varying amounts of sand and then balancing while stationary (static) or while moving (dynamic) should help children learn about balance and what happens when weight is added. Moving and picking up or stepping through or over objects adds to the fun.

Movement challenges

Movement challenges are an important part of learning to use the balance beam. They should be incorporated at all levels of learning to encourage the children's creativity in developing individually designed movements. The examples that follow are but a few of the possibilities.

1. How many different ways can you mount the beam?
2. While on the beam can you make a shape using two body parts for balance? Two others? One foot? Another part?
3. Can you balance on a large body part? A small body part?
4. How many different ways can you travel along the beam?
5. What different ways can you use your arms as you travel along the beam?
6. Can you change direction as you move along the beam?
7. Can you change level as you move along the beam?
8. Carrying one or two jugs varying in weight, what shapes can you make as you balance on the beam?
9. Carrying one or more jugs varying in weight, how many different ways can you move along the beam?
10. Can you pick up a beanbag as you walk along the beam?
11. On what body parts can you balance a beanbag while balancing on the beam? While moving?
12. Can you step over a wand held by a partner as you move?
13. Can you move through a hoop held by a partner?
14. While moving on the beam can you create enough force to become airborne and then land back on the beam, absorbing the force?
15. How many different ways can you dismount from the beam?
16. Can you make a shape in the air as you dismount and still land with control?
17. Can you dismount and land with your back to the beam? Your side? The front of the body?

Skills

Many skills for use on the balance beam follow. They include ways of mounting the beam; movements, turns, and tumbling skills to travel along the beam; poses or balances; and dismounts.

Mounts

Mounting the high beam and mounts in which all body parts are raised require the use of a beat board.

Step-up mount

Position: Standing on the floor or on a low bench at one end of the beam.

Action: The performer steps up on the beam with one foot swinging the free foot forward and upward on to the beam in front of the stepping foot.

Spotting: The spotter should stand next to the beam with an arm extended to offer support if needed.

Front support mount

Position: Standing facing the side of the beam with both hands grasping the top of the beam about shoulder width apart.

Action: With a spring from both legs and a push with the hands the body is brought to a front support with the hips resting on the beam. The hands may remain on the beam or may be momentarily extended to the sides.

One-knee mount

Position: Standing facing the side of the beam. The hands are on top of the beam with fingers pointing away from the body.

Action: With a spring from both feet the performer jumps to a straight arm support with one knee on the beam between the hands and the other leg extended behind. The head is up and the back is arched.

Spotting: The spotter should stand on the opposite side of the beam facing the performer and be ready to give support at the shoulders should the spring carry the performer too far forward.

Squat mount

Position: Stand facing the beam.

Action: A jump is taken from both feet, placing the hands on the beam shoulder width apart and fingers pointing away from the body. Both feet are placed on the beam between the hands as the body assumes a squat position on the beam. The head is up and the back is parallel with the floor.

Spotting: The spotter should stand on the opposite side of the beam and support the shoulders as in the one-knee mount.

Moving on the beam

A good posture, with the body poised and extended and the head up, is important when moving along the balance beam. Using the arms in interesting ways adds to the movements on the beam.

Walk. Forward, backward, sideward.

Hop. Forward, backward, sideward.

Skip. Forward, backward.

Dip walk. As the performer moves on the beam, each leg is dipped to the side as it swings forward by bending the supporting leg and dropping the free leg as it swings forward with the toe pointed.

Chassé. As the performer moves forward, the lead foot slides forward, the rear foot closes to the front foot, and the front foot slides forward once again.

Dip walk.

Toe-touch. As the performer walks forward the toe of the moving foot is extended and touched briefly on the beam in front before taking weight forward on the foot. This may be performed backward by touching the toe backward before stepping on the foot.

Step-hop. A step is taken forward on one foot followed by a hop on the same foot, lifting the opposite knee upward. It is repeated, stepping forward on the other foot.

Grapevine. A step is taken sideward with the right foot. The left is crossed over in front of the right. One more step is taken sideward to the right, finishing by crossing the left behind the right.

The following movements described in the skills for movement sequences may also be performed on the balance beam:

Scissors kick
Jump with legs bent to the rear
Split leap
Stag leap
Body wave

Turns

Squat turn

Position: On the beam facing one end.

Action: The child assumes a squat position on the beam and pivots on the balls of the feet to turn to face the opposite way. The arms are extended to the sides for balance.

Pivot turn

Position: On the beam facing one end.

Forward shoulder roll.

Knee scale.

Action: The performer rises up onto the balls of the feet and pivots to face in the opposite direction. The head is up and the body is extended. The arms may be extended to the sides or one arm may be forward, the other extended to the side.

One-leg turn

Position: On the beam facing one end.

Action: Taking the weight on one foot, the performer turns 180 degrees with the free leg extended forward of the body. The arms are extended out to the sides, the body is erect, and the head is up. As the turn is made, the forward foot is extended behind.

Tour Jeté. Described in skills for floor exercise.

Tumbling movements

The following tumbling skills may be easily adapted for use on the balance beam.

Forward shoulder roll

Position: From a kneeling position, gripping the underside of the beam with one hand on each side of the beam.

Action: One shoulder is placed to one side of the beam. The hips are pulled up in a pike position; then the child slowly rolls forward to finish straddling the beam with the legs straight and toes pointed. The hands regrip the beam in front of the body.

Spotting: Spotters may be used on both sides of the beam, spotting the hips as they come over until the body is balanced over the beam once again. This skill may be adequately spotted by one person as well.

Back shoulder roll

Position: Supine on the beam with the hands gripping the underside of the beam over the head. The arms are bent and the elbows are close together. The head is on one side of the beam.

Action: The legs are pulled up over the head in a pike position. As the legs come over, one knee is placed on the beam. (If the head is on the right side of the beam, the left knee touches first.) As the legs come down, the hands shift to a position grasping the top of the beam. The second leg may be raised behind as in a knee scale.

Spotting: A spotter on each side of the beam supports the hips as they come over until the body is balanced once again. One person can adequately spot this skill.

Balances

The following balances included in balance stunts may be performed on the balance beam:

    Knee scale (with two hands on the beam in front of the body)
    Arabesque
    V-sit
    One-leg balance
    Needle

Dismounts

Some assistance may be needed for dismounts from the balance beam. The spotter should stand ready to

Overhand grip.

Mixed grip.

Reverse grip.

Figure 15-2

Gripping the horizontal bar.

assist on landing but out of the way of moving body parts such as the legs. The teacher should emphasize landing on two feet by slightly flexing the hips and knees to absorb the force.

Jump

Position: Standing anywhere on the beam.

Action: The performer jumps from the beam to the floor (1) with a turn to end with the back, side, or front facing the beam or (2) assuming a pike, tuck, or straddle position in the air.

Knee scale dismount

Position: Knee scale position with two hands on the beam in front of the body.

Action: The body leans slightly forward as the free leg swings down and then backward and upward. The hands push and the body is lifted off the beam. The landing is with the side to the beam, the knees bent, the near hand on the beam, and the other arm extended to the side.

Front vault

Position: A front resting position on the beam with the body supported on the feet and hands. The arms are extended so the upper body is off the beam.

Action: The leg on the side of the landing is kicked upward, followed by the other leg; then the legs swing off one side of the beam to land with the side facing the beam and the near hand on top.

Skill combinations

Beginning combinations include a mount, movement on the beam, and a dismount:

Step-up mount, walk forward, jump dismount.

Squat mount, grapevine step, jump dismount, ending with the side to the beam.

Add a balance:

Step-up mount, dip walk, arabesque, jump dismount.

Front support mount, knee scale, chassé jump dismount.

Add a turn:

Front support knee scale, dip walk, pivot turn, toe-touch walk, V-sit, side seat dismount.

Add an aerial move:

Front support, knee scale, dip walk, squat turn, step-hop, pivot turn, arabesque, knee scale, front vault dismount.

Horizontal Bar

The horizontal bar is often both a piece of playground apparatus and a piece of indoor equipment.

For outdoor use there may be several bars set at varying heights for elementary school children. The indoor bar is most often adjustable for use as a low or high bar.

For most of the skills suggested in this text a bar about shoulder height is desirable. It may be helpful to organize the children according to height when doing station work to avoid the need to constantly adjust the bar to the height of each child.

For safety the children should grip the bar with the thumb on the opposite side of the bar as the fingers. In the *regular grip* the fingers are on top of the bar and the thumb underneath. In the *reverse grip* the thumbs are closest to the performer and the fingers behind the bar. (Figure 15-2). In the *mixed grip* one hand assumes a regular grip, the other a reverse grip. To determine the grip to be used, it is helpful to remember that the individual usually moves around the bar in the direction in which the thumbs point.

Mats should be used under the bar and should extend far enough in front of and behind to provide a safe landing area for a drop from a swing. The bars should be kept clean of chalk and rust. Special care must be taken of outdoor bars because corrosion may make the surface of the bars rough and therefore hazardous.

Prolonged practice of skills in which the performer circles the bar may result in blisters on the hands. Carbonate of magnesium chalk or hand guards should be used to protect the hands.

Spotting the skills is usually at the nearest wrist or over the hand and at the hips. If the bar has been raised, the spotter can stand on one or two folded mats placed to the side of the performer to bring the spotter up to a level suitable to assist the child in performing the skill. Placement of mats should not obstruct the performer in any way.

Movement challenges

Movement challenges encourage the children to discover unique ways of working on the horizontal bar.

How many ways can you find to get on the bar?
Can you hang from two body parts? Two different parts? Three? One?
How many ways can you balance on the bar?
How many ways can you move under the bar?
How many ways can you dismount to land on your feet? To face the bar? To face away from the bar? With your side to the bar?
Can you move from under the bar to the top of the bar?
How many ways can you use a curled shape on the bar?
How many ways can you use a straight shape on the bar?
Can you move from a straight to a curled shape on the bar? A curl to a straight shape?
How many ways can you change direction on or under the bar?

Skills

The following skills may be performed by elementary school children on the horizontal bar.

Mounts

Front support mount. Similar to the front support mount described in balance beam activities. A regular grip is used.

Back hip pull-over
Position: Standing close to the bar with a regular grip, hands shoulder width apart.
Action: One leg is kicked up and over the bar; keeping the arms bent, the body is lifted under and over the bar to end in a front support position.
Spotting: Spotting should be at the shoulders and hips to keep the body close to the bar.
Suggestions: It is important to keep the body close to the bar. There is a tendency to straighten the arms, dropping the body away from the bar, which then requires pulling the body back to the bar before the pull-over can be completed.

Stunts

Single knee hang
Position: Hanging under the bar with a regular grip.
Action: One leg is swung up over the bar. The child hangs from one leg and two hands.
Spotting: The spotter stands at the side, spotting at the near hand and the hips.

Double knee hang
Position: Hanging under the bar with a regular grip.
Action: Both legs are brought up between the arms and then over the bar to hang from two legs and two hands.
Spotting: Spotting is from the side, at the near hand and hips.

Inverted hang: tuck
Position: Hanging under the bar with a regular grip.
Action: Both legs are pulled up between the arms

Pike inverted hang.

in a tuck position and held.

Spotting: Spotting is from the side, at the near hand and hips.

Inverted hang: pike

Position: Hanging under the bar with a regular grip.

Action: Both legs are brought up between the arms in a pike position and held.

Spotting: Spotting is from the side, at the near hand and hips.

Inverted hang: layout

Position: Hanging under the bar with a regular grip.

Action: Both legs are brought up and between the arms in a tuck position. As the legs pass under the bar, they are extended to a layout position perpendicular to the mat.

Spotting: Spotting is from the side, at the near hand and hips. As the body extends upward, the hand at the hips shifts to the front side of the body to assist in keeping the body close to the bar.

Skin the cat

Position: Hanging under the bar with a regular grip.

Action: Both legs are swung up and between the arms. The child stays tucked and touches the feet to the mat over the head, then springs lightly with both feet from the mat, tucks the chin, and returns to the starting position.

Spotting: Spotting is from the side, at the near arm and hip. To assist in coming back to the starting

position one hand is at the hips the other at the back of the neck.

Front support. Similar to the front support described in balance beam activities. This move may be used as a pose on the bar as well as a mount. The arms may be extended to the sides once the balance position has been attained.

Spotting: The spotter stands in front of the performer and spots at the shoulders.

Stride seat

Position: A front support.

Action: One leg swings over the bar to finish extended in front, the other behind. The hand regrasps the bar on the outside of the leg. The body is up off the bar supported on the hands.

Spotting: The spotter stands in front and slightly to the side of the performer, spotting at the wrist and shoulder.

Balance seat

Position: From a stride position on top of the bar with a regular grip.

Action: The rear leg is swung over the bar to end in a sitting position on top of the bar with both legs extended in front, hands gripping the bar. The hands may be extended to the sides once balance is attained.

Spotting: The spotter stands to the side with one hand in front and the other behind the performer.

Bird's nest

Position: Hanging under the bar with a regular grip.

Action: Both legs are kicked up into a tuck position between the arms. As the legs come through, the insteps of both feet stay touching the back side of the bar. The body continues through, ending in a position hanging from the hands and the feet.

Spotting: Spotting is from the side at the near wrist and hips, then shifts from the hips to the front of the body to finish.

Suggestion: As children's body proportions change, this skill may become more difficult on the horizontal bar for children with long legs.

Mill circle (pinwheel)

Position: A stride position on the bar with a reverse grip.

Action: As the circle begins, the arms lift the body up off the bar and the front leg reaches out as if taking a giant step. As the circle continues, the arms pull and the body flexes slightly to bring the body back up to a sitting position.

Spotting: The spotter stands to the side with one hand on the arm and the other at the back of the leg. Spotting is moved to the back during the second half of the stunt.

Dismounts

Rollover dismount

Position: Front support position with a regular grip.

Action: The body leans forward, beginning to circle the bar. As the legs come around, they come off the bar, the hands release their grip, and the performer lands on the mat in a standing position.

Spotting: The spotter stands at the side and spots at the shoulder and near wrist.

Back dismount

Position: Front support.

Action: The legs swing forward under the bar, then backward with the hands pushing away from the bar and releasing their grip. The body remains in a vertical position as the performer moves back from the bar and then to the mat. The knees flex on landing and the arms may be out to the sides for balance.

Spotting: Spotting is from the side at the near wrist.

Swing and drop

Position: Standing slightly away from the bar, which is slightly above the extended arms and hands.

Action: The performer springs up from both feet to take the bar with a regular grip. The hips flex to begin the swinging action of the body. Just before the maximum forward movement the performer drops from the bar to land on the mat in a balanced position, with the knees, ankles, and hips flexing and the arms out to the side for balance.

Suggestion: The performer may choose to drop at the height of the backswing rather than on the end of the forward swing.

Spotting: Spotting is from the side at the waist and midback. Should the performer choose to drop on the backswing, the spotter moves back to assist if necessary with one hand on either side of the body.

Penny drop

Position: Double knee hang with a regular grip.

Action: At the end of the backward swing the hands are released, swinging the arms forward. At the end of the forward swing, with the body parallel to the mat, the knees are brought off the bar and the performer lands on the feet.

Spotting: The spotter stands next to the performer, extending one arm across the chest to assist if more spin is needed. The other hand is across the legs to keep them from straightening.

Skill combinations

A few combinations of skills for the horizontal bar follow.

Front support mount, rollover dismount.

Back hip pull-over mount, front support balance, balance seat, double knee hang, penny drop.

Back hip pull-over mount, straddle seat, balance seat, double knee hang, one-half skin the cat dismount.

Front support mount, stride seat, skin the cat, double knee hang, penny drop.

Front support mount, mill circle, balance seat, double knee hang, tuck inverted hang, single knee circle mount, front support, back dismount.

Parallel Bars

Parallel bars may be part of the playground equipment and set at a fixed height of about 30 inches or may be an adjustable piece of the indoor apparatus. Often in the elementary school the bars are a standard set of bars passed down from the high school. It is important to adjust the height and width of the bars for elementary school children. It may be necessary to use a bench at the end for mounting and several mats piled under the bars to adjust the height for elementary school children. These suggestions should enable the children to mount the bars on their own. Teachers should avoid lifting children up to the bars.

Many of the stunts on the parallel bars require upper body strength, which is often not well developed in elementary school children. For traveling above the bars the spotter needs to help support the upper and lower arm to prevent collapsing of the arm. Skills under the bar are generally spotted by holding one of the child's hands to the bars and helping to lift at the thighs with the other.

Movement challenges

Movement challenges encourage children to find interesting ways of moving. A few of the possibilities follow.

1. Can you mount the bar at one end? From the side of the bars? From underneath?
2. What shapes can you make under the bars as you support yourself with four body parts? Three? Two?
3. What shapes can you make on top of the bars?
4. Can you make a shape as you dismount the bars to end facing the bars? With your side to the bars? With your back to the bars?
5. How many ways can you travel on top of two bars? One? Underneath two bars? One?
6. How many ways can you move from under the bars to on top of the bars?
7. How many ways can you move from the top of the bars to underneath the bars?
8. How many ways can you change direction on the bars? Under the bars?

Skills

The following skills included for horizontal bar may also be performed on the parallel bars. Many of these skills may be performed between the two bars as well as on one bar.

Front support mount
Back hip pull-over mount
Front support
Single knee hang
Double knee hang
Inverted hang: tuck, pike, layout
Skin the cat
Bird's nest
Stride seat
Balance seat
Rollover dismount
Back dismount

Mounts

Jump to a straight arm support
Position: Standing at one end of the bars, with

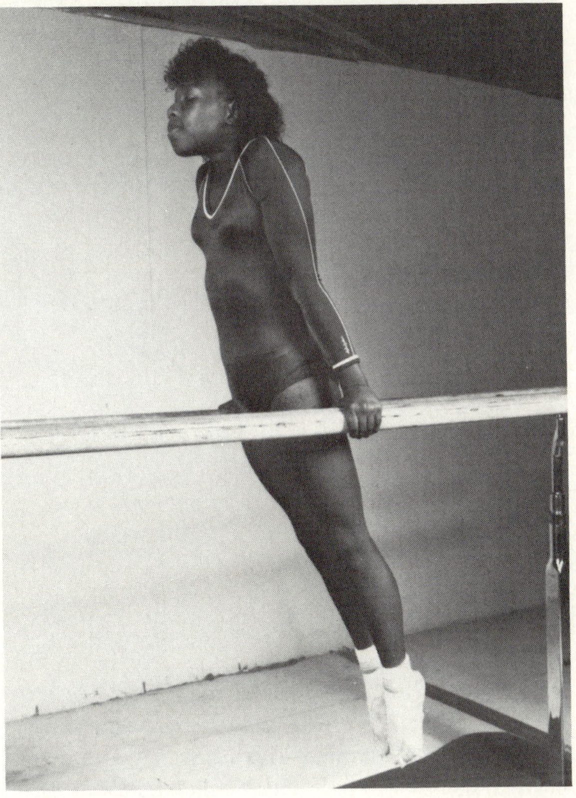

Straight arm support.

hands gripping the top of the bars.

Action: The performer springs from both feet, pushing with the hands to finish with the body extended above and between the bars supported by straight arms.

Spotting: The spotter stands to one side and supports the near upper and lower arm. Another spotting technique is to assist the student from behind by having one hand on each side of the performer's waist.

Swing up from under the bars
Position: At one end of the bars hands gripping the bars from underneath.

Action: The legs are kicked up between the bars, ending with one leg over each bar, gripping the bars behind the knees. The arms are brought up inside the bars and the hands regrasp on top, pulling the body up between the bars to finish in a straddle seat position with one leg over each bar.

Spotting: The spotter stands to one side holding one of the child's hands to the bar and assisting at the thigh with the other hand.

Sloth walk
Position: Under the bars with the hands grasping one bar.

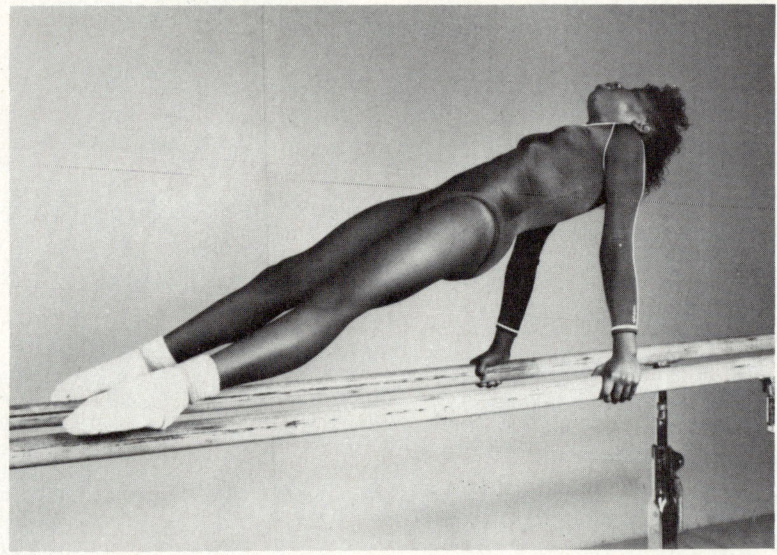

Back foot leaning rest.

Action: The feet swing up to grasp the bar in front of the body. By pulling or pushing with the legs and walking the hands on the bar, the performer moves either head or foot first. This stunt may also be performed using both bars with a hand and foot on each bar.

Spotting: The spotter stands at the side with one hand on the child's hand and the other at the thighs to assist in lifting the legs.

Balances

Angel (knee scale)
Position: A front rest position.

Action: The legs are drawn up onto the bar to a position where the knees are on one bar and the straight arms on the other.

One leg is lifted behind, the back slightly arched, and the head raised. One arm may extend forward.

Spotting: The spotter stands between the bars with one hand at the wrist.

Straddle seat
Position: A straight arm support.

Action: Both legs are swung up over the bars to finish straddling both bars with the legs extended and the toes pointed to the sides. The hands may grip the bars behind the hips or may be extended to the sides.

Spotting: Spotting is from the side with one arm at the upper and lower arm.

Back foot leaning rest
Position: A straight arm support.

Action: Both legs are swung forward and up onto the bar, finishing in a position with the legs extended in front and the upper body supported on straight arms. The head is up and the back is straight.

Spotting: The spotter stands at the side and spots the near upper and lower arm.

Front foot leaning rest
Position: A straight arm support.

Action: The legs are lifted to the bars behind the body, finishing with the legs extended behind and the body supported on the straight arms and feet. The head is up and the back slightly arched.

Spotting: From the side the spotter holds the arm and the front of the thigh to assist in keeping the legs from hitting the bar too hard.

Side rest
Position: A straddle seat position on the bars.

Action: The body is rotated to face one side. The forward leg is flexed at the knee to point back under the bar. The rear leg is extended. The hand on the same side as the forward foot grasps the forward bar; the other arm is extended to the side.

Spotting: The spotter stands to the side and slightly behind the performer and holds the arm on the forward side.

Chest stand
Position: A front support position with the hands grasping the bars underneath.

Action: The upper body drops forward to the far bar with the head on the outside of the bar and the shoulders on the inside. The legs kick up over head to balance with the back slightly arched.

Spotting: The spotter stands in front of the performer with one hand on each side of the hips.

Travel/swing

Straight arm support swing

Position: A straight arm support.

Action: The body swings forward and back to a comfortable and controlled height, the legs coming above the bars on both the forward and backward swings.

Spotting: Spotting is from the side at the near upper and lower arm.

Straight arm walk

Position: A straight arm support.

Action: The hands walk forward or backward on the bars while the body remains straight and the head is up.

Spotting: The spotter stands at the side and holds the near upper and lower arm.

Straddle travel forward

Position: A straight arm support.

Action: The body swings forward, lifting the legs up above the bar. The legs separate to come down in a straddle position over the bars. The hands regrasp the bars in front of the body with the body leaning forward and the legs swinging backward and free of the bars to repeat the action.

Spotting: Spotting is from the side at the near upper and lower arm.

Straddle travel backward. Same as the straddle travel forward, except the legs move from front to back and straddle behind the hands.

Inverted walk

Position: Under the bars with one hand under and on the outside of each bar.

Action: The performer kicks up into a pike inverted hang. Moving the hands one at a time under

Forward roll to a straddle seat.

the bar, the body is propelled forward.

Spotting: From the side the spotter holds the near hand and assists at the hips if needed.

Crab walk

Position: A straight arm support.

Action: The legs are swung forward and up onto the bars in front of the body. From the crab position the hands and feet are walked forward or backward on top of the bars.

Spotting: From the side the spotter supports the near arm and hips.

Hand walk on one bar

Position: A straight arm support.

Action: Rotate the body to one side and regrasp so both hands are on the top of one bar. Walk the hands along the bar, keeping the body straight and the head up.

Spotting: Spotting is from a position behind the performer at the hips.

Forward roll to a straddle seat

Position: In a straddle seat position grasping the bars in front of the body.

Action: Leaning forward, the upper arms are placed on the bars with the elbows on the outside. Keeping the body in a pike position the hips are raised and and brought over the head. The hands are released and regrasped behind the back. The roll is continued to a straddle position.

Spotting: The spotter stands to the side to support the upper back and the thighs.

Suggestions: It is important to have the bar width appropriate for each performer to support the shoulders.

Dismounts

Swing and jump

Position: Between the bars, facing the end, in a straight arm support position.

Action: On a swing forward the body reaches out from the bars and the hands push and release to land with knees slightly bent and the body erect on the mat. The head is up and the hands may be extended to the sides or forward.

Spotting: From the side the spotter supports the near arm.

Side seat dismount

Position: Sitting on the outside of one bar with a hand on each bar, the forward leg bent at the knee, the rear leg extended back, and the toes pointed.

Action: The arms and hips are pushed against the bar to force the body away from the bars. The performer lands with the side to the bars. The near hand may be on the nearest bar.

Spotting: The spotter stands at the side and slightly behind the performer and supports at the hips.

Front vault dismount

Position: From a straight arm support.

Action: The legs are swung well up above the bar behind the body. When the legs are at the height of the swing, the left hand pushes hard and the legs swing over the right bar. After passing over the bars the left hand moves to grasp the right bar as the right moves off the side and is extended to the side. The performer lands with the side to the bars.

Spotting: From the side and in front of the performer the spotter supports the near upper and lower arm.

Rear vault dismount

Position: From a straight arm support.

Action: The legs are swung forward well above the bar. As the legs reach the height of the swing forward, the child pushes with the left hand and swings the legs over the right bar. As the legs cross the bar the left hand moves to grasp the right bar and the right hand is extended to the side. The performer lands with the side to the bars.

Spotting: From the side and behind the performer the spotter supports the near upper and lower arm.

Skill combinations

Combinations include a mount, movements on the bars, and a dismount.

Jump to a straight arm support, swing forward and back, swing to a sitting position on the outside of one bar, side dismount.

Jump to a straight arm support, swing to a straddle seat, straddle travel, jump dismount.

Jump to a straight arm support, straight arm walk, swing to a straddle seat, drop below the bars, pike inverted hang, one-half skin the cat dismount.

Pike inverted hang, layout inverted hang, pull-up to a straddle seat, straddle travel, front vault dismount.

Front support mount, angel, chest balance, straddle seat, straight arm support, straight arm travel, rear vault dismount.

Ropes

Rope activities contribute to upper body strength and coordination of the arms and legs. Children may begin with activities requiring upper body strength before attempting climbing activities. Climbing if done properly uses the muscles of the back and legs to support the body weight so great arm strength is not required.

Ropes are usually of hemp and if not used properly can result in rope burns and splinters. Children should learn to come down the rope with control by using a hand-under-hand method of grasping the rope rather than sliding down. It is helpful to have a rope that extends at least to the floor. The ropes should not be knotted because children tend to use the knots for weight bearing and the ropes become frayed and weakened from this use. Mats should be positioned under the ropes.

Movement challenges

1. How many ways can you support yourself on

Pull-up.

the rope?

2. What shapes can you make as you hang from the rope?
3. What can you do on one rope? Two ropes?
4. Can you do something on one rope and then repeat it using two ropes?

Activities with one rope

Pull-ups

Position: Lying on the mat next to the rope with the hands reaching up and gripping the rope.

Action: Keeping the body straight, the body is lifted to a stand by pulling with the arms and regrasping in a hand-over-hand manner.

Suggestions: Children should be encouraged to keep the body as straight as possible.

Bent-arm hang

Position: Standing next to the rope with the hands reaching and grasping the rope overhead.

Action: With a spring from the feet the body is lifted and held up off the mat, pulling with the arms, which are bent at the elbows. The position is held as long as possible.

Climb

Position: Standing next to the rope, grasping the rope overhead with both hands. The elbows are straight. The rope is positioned to the outside of the ankle, over the foot, and to the inside of the knee of the rear foot. The toe is raised slightly.

Action: The body is pulled up and the body weight is supported by the upper body. The front

Rope climb.

foot crosses over the rear foot and secures the rope between the outer ankles and inner surfaces of the knees. The legs are extended forward from the hips. The body is raised by extending the legs, resulting in the arms bending at the elbows. The body weight is then alternately supported in the legs and then the hands. As the body weight is once again supported in the legs, the arms reach upward in a hand-over-hand manner until the body is again extended. The arms take the body weight, and the legs are pulled up and regrasp the rope. The climb is continued in this manner to the desired height. To descend the rope the arms climb down the rope in a controlled hand-under-hand manner as the legs alternately release and regrasp until the climber is once again on the mat.

Common errors:
1. Attempting to use the arms only to support the body weight.
2. Improper foot position, which is unstable in supporting the body weight.

Spotting: The spotter stands next to the performer as the climb is begun.

Suggestions:
1. The manner of descent should be introduced before the children attempt to climb.

2. Colored tape on the rope at various heights gives the children visual goals as well as sets limits for children during the learning phase when fatigue could be a concern for some.

Rope swing and drop

Position: Standing holding the rope in one hand, bringing the rope several steps back from the vertical position.

Action: As the individual moves forward the hand slides up the rope and the other hand grasps above the first. As the vertical position is reached there is a spring from one foot, jumping upward with the hands reaching up as high on the rope as possible, ending in a bent arm hang. The knees are drawn up and the body leans slightly backward with the back arched and the legs extended forward. As the height of the swing is reached, the body is turned to face downward. The rope is released. On landing the body is carried forward, the knees and ankles bending to land softly.

Common errors:
1. Failure to get a high enough grasp on the rope.

Suggestions:
1. Children love to swing on the ropes. At times it may be necessary to limit this activity to get the children to work on other rope skills.
2. Children may drop at the end of the backswing just before the rope begins to move forward.

Inverted hang

Position: Standing next to the rope grasping the rope in both hands high overhead.

Action: The child springs up with both feet to a bent-arm position and draws the legs up, bending at first and then extending them overhead.

Spotting: From the side the spotter assists at the hips to help lift the legs and to hold them overhead.

Activities with two ropes

Several stunts included in the activities for the horizontal and parallel bars may be performed with two ropes as well. Examples include inverted hangs, skin the cat, and the bird's nest. These are spotted as they would be on the horizontal or parallel bars.

Flying Dutchman

Positions: Holding the ropes back from the vertical position.

Action: This skill is similar to the bird's nest, but preparatory steps are taken, so as the bird's nest position is assumed, the individual is swinging back and forth on the two ropes.

Back hip pull-over mount.

Uneven Parallel Bars

Uneven parallel bars add the challenge of working on a low and high bar and moving from one to the other. Like work on the parallel bars, work on the unevens contributes to upper body strength. In the beginning some children may be hesitant to work on the high bar because of its height from the mat. Many of the skills may be practiced on the horizontal bar, with the bar gradually raised as the children adjust to the new height.

Movement challenges

Exploring movement challenges results in the development of new moves on the bars.

1. How many ways can you get on the low bar? The high bar?
2. What stunts can you do under the low bar? The high bar?
3. How many ways can you balance on one bar?
4. How many ways can you move from the low bar to the high bar? The high bar to the low bar?
5. What stunts can you do between the two bars?

Back pull away.

6. Can you go over one bar and then under the next? Under the first bar to over the second bar?
7. Can you change direction while moving on one bar? On two bars?
8. How many ways can you dismount from the low bar? The high bar?

Skills

Many of the skills performed on the horizontal bar and parallel bars may also be executed on the uneven bars. A few are named in the skills that follow.

Mounts

Front support. Included in the skills for the horizontal bar.

Back hip pull-over mount. Included in the skills for horizontal bar.

Shoot over the low bar
Position: Standing facing the high bar.
Action: The performer jumps to a hanging position on the high bar and swings the legs up and over the low bar to end with the hips resting on the low bar and hands grasping the high bar.
Spotting: The spotter stands behind the performer and lifts at the hips.

Cross seat mount
Position: Standing between the bars facing one end of the bars.
Action: The performer jumps, grasping the high bar with one hand and the low bar with the other. The arm on the low bar is straightened to support the body weight and swing the legs up and over the low bar. The performer ends in a cross seat position, the rear leg extended downward and the forward leg bent back at the knee.
Spotting: Facing the low bar, the spotter supports the arm on the low bar as the legs swing over.

Balances

Balances are no longer used in bar routines, but they are appropriate activities for elementary school children.

Seat balance
Position: Sitting on the low bar with one hand grasping the high bar, facing one end of the bars.
Action: One leg is extended downward to the outside of the low bar and the other foot is drawn close to the hips, bending at the knee. The free hand grasps the low bar behind the hips.
Spotting: The spotter stands to the outside of the low bar and grasps the arm.

V sit. Similar to the V sit described in floor exercise. This is performed on the low bar, facing one end of the bars. One hand is on the high bar, the other on the low bar.

Back pull away

Position: Standing on the low bar facing the high bar, both hands grasping the high bar.

Action: The performer pushes away from the high bar by extending the arms and lifts one leg behind to end in a position with the head up, the back slightly arched, the hands on the high bar, and one foot on the low bar.

Thigh rest

Position: A front support on the high bar, facing the low bar.

Action: The performer bends forward and grasps the low bar in a regular grip. With the arms straight and the head up, the legs slide forward to finish with the thighs resting on the front of the bar. The back is slightly arched.

Spotting: The spotter stands in front of the performer and spots at the elbow.

Arch back

Position: A double knee hang from the high bar facing the low bar.

Action: The low bar is grasped in a regular grip. The arms straighten as the performer arches the body to finish in a position gripping the low bars with the back of the thighs close to the knee resting against the high bar.

Lunge

Position: Standing on the low bar, grasping the high bar in one hand and facing one end of the bars.

Action: One leg is bent at the knee so the upper leg is parallel to the bars. The other leg is extended back so the top of the foot rests on the low bar. The free hand is extended to the side, the head is up, and the back is straight.

Straddle seat

Position: Hanging from the high bar facing the low bar.

Action: The legs are swung up over the low bar in a straddle position, so the thighs are on the low bar. One hand is released from the high bar and placed between the legs onto the low bar. A balanced position is assumed and then the second hand is shifted to the low bar between the legs. The body is lifted off the bars to balance on the hands.

Swan balance

Position: A front support position on either the high or low bar.

Action: The performer assumes a balanced position, lift the hands off the bar, and extends them to the side. The head is up and the back arched.

Swinging/moving

Skin the cat. Described in skills for the horizontal bar.

Skin the cat to a one-leg squat (basket)

Position: Hanging from the high bar with the back to the low bar.

Action: The legs are lifted up and through the hands for a skin the cat. As the legs come over, one foot is placed on the low bar and the other with the top of the foot touching the bar. The performer pivots on the low bar to a one-leg squat with the free leg extended in front.

Spotting: The spotter stands behind the low bar and helps with the foot placement onto the low bar.

Side circle

Position: Straddling the bar facing the end of the bars, with the hands gripping the bars in front of the body in a mixed grip.

Action: The body is lifted slightly off the bar by pushing with the hands. The body is kept stiff while circling sideward around the bar.

Spotting: The spotter stands behind the performer in front of the low bar, ready to assist as the performer comes back up to the bar by spotting at the shoulder.

Suggestions: It is important to move rapidly around the bar to have sufficient momentum to return to the upright position.

Pull-over to high bar

Position: Hanging from the high bar facing the low bar.

Action: One leg is lifted to the low bar and the other straight up between the bars. The foot pushes on the bars and kicks the straight leg up to the high bar. At the same time the arms pull the body up to the high bar. The pull is completed over the high bar, ending in a straight arm support on the high bar facing the low bar.

Spotting: The spotter stands between the bars and pushes the hips up over the bar.

Suggestions: It is important to pull the upper body up close to the high bar as the legs are brought up.

Single-leg flank vault

Position: Straddling the low bar, facing one end of the bars with one hand grasping the high bar, the other on the low bar behind the hips in a reverse grip. The inside leg is extended downward and the outside leg is bent back at the knee with the toes pointed.

Action: The inside leg swings up over the low bar

as the body weight is taken on the hand on the low bar. The landing is with the side to the low bar, one hand on the low bar and the other extended to the side.

Spotting: The spotter stands between the bars and spots the wrist on the low bar.

Pike position shoot-off dismount

Position: Sitting on the low bar facing away from the bars with the legs extended in front of the body in a pike position and the hands gripping the bar next to the hips.

Action: The performer pushes with the hands and momentarily lifts the legs in front before extending the body to land in front of the bars.

Spotting: The spotter stands in front of and to one side of the performer, spotting the performer at the near wrist.

Combinations

Back pull over on low bar, front support, back pull away, forward roll over high bar.

Front support mount, side circle, back pull away, skin the cat to a basket, V sit, single-leg flank vault dismount.

Jump to hang on high bar, pull over to high bar, swan balance, roll forward over high bar to hang, shoot over low bar, pike position shoot off dismount.

Shoot over the low bar mount, straddle seat, swan balance on low bar, straddle seat, single-leg flank vault dismount.

Vaulting

At the elementary level a variety of kinds of equipment are used for *vaulting*, such as benches, Swedish boxes, and horses. These should be of varying heights and adjustable from relatively low for young children to greater heights for older students. A springboard is used to gain lift to get over the equipment. This may be a commercial springboard or a home-made inclined plane.

Spotting is very important in vaulting, and adult spotting is necessary, with the exception of a few movement challenges in which the children are always in contact with the equipment. The spotter should stand on the landing side of the equipment and to the side, being ready to assist at the wrist of the performer. For vaults in which one or both legs are extended to one side, the spotter is positioned on the side away from the legs.

A two-foot take-off is used in vaulting.

Squat mount.

Movement challenges

1. How many ways can you get on the bench?
2. What shapes can you make on top of the bench?
3. How many ways can you find to go over the bench?
4. What body parts touch the bench as you go over?
5. What directions can you move over the horse?
6. How many ways can you move from the bench?
7. What shapes can you make in the air as you dismount?
8. What directions can you face as you land from the horse?
9. Can you change supporting body parts as you move over the horse?

Skills

Knee mount. From the two-foot take-off both hands are placed on the horse with fingers pointing toward the landing area. The performer lands on the knees on the horse.

Courage dismount. From a knee mount, the performer forcefully swings both arms forward and upward, lifting the body up off the horse and landing on the feet in front of the horse.

Children may be hesitant at first to try this skill. The teacher may assist by taking one wrist and helping to swing it forward, lifting the body off the horse.

Squat mount. From a two-foot take-off with both hands on the horse, fingers facing away, the child

Wolf vault.

Handspring vault.

pushes with the hands to help lift the body, ending in a squat position on top of the horse.

The spotter should be ready to assist the children should they fail to get both feet up.

Long-legged children may have more difficulty with this skill.

Jump dismount. The performer stands from a squat mount and jumps to the mat. In jumping to the mat the individual may assume a tuck, pike, or straddle position in the air or may execute a turn varying from a quarter to a full turn before landing.

Squat vault. The child assumes the squat position as in the squat mount but continues over the horse to land in a balanced position on the other side.

Front vault. From a two-foot take-off the hands are placed parallel and positioned on both sides of the horse; the legs are lifted to the rear. The front of the body passes over the horse. The back is arched and the head is up. The landing is with the side to the horse.

Flank vault. From a two-foot take-off the hands are placed on the horse as in the squat vault. The legs are lifted up to the side and over the horse so the side of the body passes over the horse. As the body passes over the horse the upper arm is lifted, taking the weight on the one arm momentarily. The finishing position is facing away from the horse.

Rear vault. From a two-foot take-off both hands are placed on the horse as in the squat vault. The legs are raised up to the side and then over the horse in a pike position. One hand and then the other is lifted as the legs come around and over the horse. The landing is with the side to the horse.

Wolf vault. In the vault the body assumes a squat position with one leg and a straddle with the other.

Handspring. From a two-foot take-off the hands are placed on the horse with the body passing over the horse in a handspring position. See stunts and tumbling for a description of this skill.

SUMMARY

Gymnastic activities are challenging for children of all abilities. A wide variety of activities may be selected including individual, partner, and group stunts and tumbling or work on different kinds of apparatus. Balance beams; vaulting boxes or horses; horizontal, parallel, or uneven bars; and ropes are some of the possibilities. Many schools have outdoor apparatus as well, and many of the skills taught on the indoor apparatus may be adapted for use on jungle gyms or horizontal ladders. Safety is a primary concern and the teacher must take the time that is needed to emphasize the safe use of mats and large apparatus. In a few activities the children may assist as spotters;

in others adult spotters are needed.

Exploring the use of the body in relation to mats and large apparatus is an important aspect of early experiences in gymnastics. Creativity in making up new movements should be encouraged throughout the elementary school years. At the elementary school level a variety of activities should be provided in each lesson to maximize the activity for all children.

REFERENCES

1. Boucher, A.: Educational gymnastics is for everyone, JOPER **49**(7):48, September 1978.
2. Cooper, P.: Feminine gymnastics, ed. 3, Minneapolis, 1980, Burgess Publishing Co.
3. Cooper, P., and Trika, M.: Teaching gymnastics skills to men and women, Minneapolis, 1982, Burgess Publishing Co.
4. Hicks, S.: Basic movement: building a foundation for educational gymnastics, JOPER **50**(6):26, June 1979.
5. Logsdon, B., and others: Physical education for children: a focus on the teaching process, ed. 2, Philadelphia, 1984, Lea & Febiger.
6. O'Quinn, G.: Developmental gymnastics: building physical skills for children, Austin, 1979, University of Texas Press.
7. Reiken, G.: Women's gymnastics teaching and learning progressions, JOPERD, **56**(3):33, March 1985.
8. Szypula, J., and Szypula, G.: Contemporary gymnastics, Chicago, 1979, Contemporary Books, Inc.
9. Wiseman, E.: The process of learning in gymnastics, JOPER **49**(7):44, September 1978.

ADDITIONAL READINGS

Kruger, H.: A focus on body management, JOPER **49**(7):39, September 1978.
Three levels of program objectives for gymnastics to meet the needs of all children.

Mulvihill, L.: Vaulting, JOPER **51**(1):64, January 1980.
Physical prerequisites for success in vaulting, safety in teaching falling, drills, and progressions for teaching vaulting skills.

Parent, S.: To rouse an interest, JOPER **49**(7):32, September 1978.
Developing themes in educational gymnastics.

Sim, L.: Teaching your gymnasts to swing: biomechanics in plain talk for the novice coach, JOPERD **56**(3):39, March 1985.
Application of mechanical principles to swinging in gymnastic activities.

Standeven, J.: More than simply movement experience, JOPER **49**(7):35, September 1978.
The process of learning in educational gymnastics.

Warrell, E.: Safety in using gymnastics equipment, JOPER **49**(7):35, September 1978.
Teaching concerns for establishing and maintaining a safe gymnastics environment.

16

TRACK AND FIELD

CHAPTER OBJECTIVES

1 To explain events included in track and field in the elementary school
2 To identify movement concepts important to track and field events
3 To describe a progression for introducing track and field activities at the elementary school level
4 To provide suggestions for the teaching and organizing of track and field activities

rack and field activities are an extension of the accomplishments of children in the development of the fundamental skills of running, jumping, and throwing and their understanding of human movement. In the elementary physical education program emphasis in developing competency in fundamental motor skills begins in the earliest experiences. These skills are further refined as children learn the running and field events in track and field. In addition the children learn to control body movements and to use balance, the creation and absorption of force, and speed. Space concepts are also important to a successful performance.

Running and field events are highly motivating due to their self-testing nature. Since performance is easily measured children are able to get a clear picture of their level of achievement and can set goals to improve their performance.

MOVEMENT CONCEPTS

The qualities of movement and body awareness concepts are important in track and field. Application of space concepts is a factor in some events. The box below outlines the movement concepts important in track and field at the elementary school level.

Since the use of concepts is important to success in the events, they should be stressed throughout the learning period. Movement challenges to explore the use of body parts in taking off, running, jumping, moving through space, landing, and projecting objects should be used in the early phases of learning, as is suggested in Chapter 11.

SUGGESTIONS FOR TEACHING

The following are suggestions for teaching track and field.

1. Instruction in track and field in the early grades should include an exploration of the use of the body in performing various tasks, such as starting, going over low obstacles, and the like. Short distance runs, the standing jump, and activities such as jump the brook and high water/low water may be used as preliminaries to learning the track and field events of the later years. Table 16-1 lists the suggested activities for elementary school track and field.
2. Warm-ups of easy jogging and stretching must be encouraged to avoid muscle soreness from a strenuous effort.
3. Variation in ability among the children is common. In organizing events homogeneous or

"

MOVEMENT CONCEPTS

BODY AWARENESS

1. To be aware of how the body parts contribute to the movement.
2. To use body segments in unison and/or in sequence in performing the event.

SPACE

1. To increase the range of movement so that the speed and force imparted to an object are increased.
2. To stay within the designated space, such as in a lane while running.
3. To plan movements to fit the space limits, such as the space between hurdles, the space within a baton passing lane, or the area designated for a throwing event.
4. To move in as straight a pathway as possible.
5. To project an object in the desired path for optimal distance.

QUALITIES OF MOVEMENT

1. To use body parts to create force by:
   a. Using all contributing muscles in the event.
   b. Transferring momentum from one body part to another.
   c. Using force to project the body forward and upward as required.
   d. Getting the body moving before the release of an object or before a jump.
   e. Following through to transfer maximum force to an object.
   f. Converting horizontal velocity to horizontal and vertical velocity.
2. To absorb force in landing or stopping.
3. To move the body on and off balance.
4. To use speed effectively in long- and short-distance events.
5. To have a smooth flow of movement from the beginning to the conclusion of the event.
6. To have a smooth flow of movement from one runner to the next when passing the baton.

heterogeneous groups may be used. In running events it is important to have the children run with at least one child of equal ability to maximize their effort. In the high jump homogeneous groups may be of benefit since opportunity for practice becomes limited to those children who can clear the set height. Heterogeneous grouping does have the advantage that all children are exposed to a good performance.

4. Personal improvement in each event is the goal. It is advisable to have numerous opportunities for children to record their performances on individual record cards. An individual record permits the children to chart their own progress in performing their personal best. Some standards for performance are available. In addition, it is challenging for children to set personal, class, and school records that become the school standards.
5. Station work may be used to provide maximum activity for all within the constraints of limited equipment and facilities.
6. Often track and field facilities must be improvised. Specific suggestions for each event are given below.
7. It is important to organize events for maximum safety. Safety concerns are given in the discussions of each event.

RUNNING EVENTS

Running events can be categorized into individual and team events. Individual running events include the short distance races, called **sprints** or dashes, and the middle- and long-distance runs. The team events are the **shuttle** and **pursuit relays**. Running events require an unobstructed path. Adequate space must also be provided beyond the finish line to allow children to run at full speed past the line and to slow down and stop safely. The width of the running area should permit each runner to use full body movements without interfering with others. The running surface should be smooth and free from loose gravel or stones. Grass often provides an adequate surface for running events. Children should be taught to run

Table 16-1

Track and field for elementary school children

Event	Developmental level			
	I	II	III	IV
RUNNING EVENTS				
Sprints	Short distances	20-30 yards	30-40 yards	40-50 yards
Starts	Standing	Standing	bunch, medium	bunch, medium
Distance runs	One time around the area	Mile run	220 yards, mile run	220-440 yards, mile run
Relays		Shuttle 7-10 yards	Shuttle 20-25 yards	Pursuit 100-220 yards
Hurdles		18 inches, 30 yards	24 inches, 30-50 yards	24 inches, 40-50 yards
FIELD EVENTS				
Standing jump		All levels		
Long jump	Jump the brook	Long jump	Long jump	Long jump
High jump	High water	High water	High jump	High jump
Throw for distance	Softball	Softball	Softball, socccer ball	Softball, soccer ball
4-Pound shot			Shot	Shot

in a straight path for sprints to avoid the paths of other runners. In distance events children should watch space carefully to avoid being tripped up or tripping others.

All running events require an efficient running pattern in which the runner moves with a comfortable, even stride and all body actions propel the body in a forward direction. An analysis of the run may be found in Chapter 11.

Sprints

Sprinting requires the runner to cover a short distance in the least amount of time. Since the distance is short, a good start is important and the runner must accelerate quickly and maintain a maximum effort throughout the race. The race may also require a little extra effort at the end to outdistance an opponent. Maximum speed should be maintained well past the finish line. One common error in running events is that runners slow down as they near the finish line.

Elementary school children generally run sprints from 20 to 50 yards, with the younger children running dashes of 20 to 30 yards and the upper elementary school children running 30 to 50 yards. A 100-yard dash is actually a long-distance run for young elementary school children and a middle-distance run for children in the upper elementary grades. Standards for performance for the 50-yard dash may be found in Table 16-2.

Three types of starting positions are usually taught in the elementary school grades. The standing start described in Chapter 11 is used in the lower grades. It may also be taught in the upper grades when the starting surface does not make other types of starts advantageous and for long distance running.

The **bunch** (or crouch) **start** is usually used in sprinting events.

On the signal, "Take your mark," the runner assumes a position behind the starting line as described above. On the next signal, "Get set," the hips are raised and the feet are close together with one foot slightly ahead of the other. On the signal, "Go," there is an explosive push as the legs extend to drive the body forward and gradually upward. The arms move quickly to a position with the elbows bent and drive forward in opposition to the action of the legs. As

Figure 16-1

Evaluative criteria and teaching points for the bunch or crouch start.

• Thumb and fingers parallel to the line, hands below shoulders, knee down next to forward foot.

• Hips up, head and neck in line with trunk, weight forward.

• Legs extend, body rising, arms drive.

Table 16-2

Performance standards for the 50-yard dash (seconds)

Percentile	Age	Girls	Boys	Combined boys and girls
100	9-10	7.0	7.0	7.0
	11	6.9	6.3	6.3
	12	6.0	6.3	6.0
75	9-10	8.0	7.8	7.9
	11	7.9	7.6	7.7
	12	7.6	7.4	7.5
50	9-10	8.6	8.2	8.5
	11	8.3	8.0	8.2
	12	8.1	7.8	8.0

From AAHPER, 1976.

the runner assumes a more upright position the length of stride increases.

The ***medium start,*** which is also used in sprinting, is similar to the bunch start, but the feet are a comfortable step apart. The medium start sacrifices power for a more comfortable stance.

Common errors:
1. The head is facing downward, which may result in loss of balance at the start.
2. The distance between the hands and feet is too great, so power is lost.
3. The legs are straight and the hips too high on the signal, "Get set."
4. The hands are positioned too far forward in front of the body rather than directly under the shoulders.
5. Too much weight is put on the hands, resulting in stumbling out of position.
6. There may be a failure to respond quickly to the signal, "Go."

Distance Runs

Distance races require the runner to accelerate and to find a speed that can be maintained over the longer distance. A common error in distance running is beginning at too fast a speed and tiring before the distance is covered.

The stride is longer in distance running than in sprinting races. Since endurance is a primary factor in long-distance running, a standing start is generally used rather than a crouch or medium start. The runner assumes a forward/backward stride position with the knees bent, the body leaning forward, and the arms ready to drive on the signal, "Go." The crouch or medium start may be used in middle-distance runs. The runner attempts to set a pace that can be maintained throughout the race. As children improve their endurance the pace increases.

While sprinting is performed in a straight line,

Figure 16-2

Comparison of bunch and medium starts.

distance runs involve running in curved paths as well. In running a curved path, the body leans toward the inside of the curve and the outside foot pushes a little harder. The outside arm may also swing slightly across the body as the curve is taken.

If a school does not have a track on which to run, a running area can be measured on the playground with flags or stakes marking the corners. Performance standards for the unique distances may be established over a few years of keeping scores for the various distances used. Performance standards for the mile run may be found in Chapter 13.

Relays

Relays offer a team activity to running events. Four runners comprise a team. In shuttle relays the runners run back and forth between two lines. In the pursuit relay, the racers run an oval course with each runner covering a part of the distance.

The shuttle relay requires less space, with the distance between the lines varying with the age of the runners. Young children may run a shuttle with as little as 20 feet between the lines, while upper grade children may each run 25 yards. In shuttle relays the next runner begins after he or she receives a baton or is tagged on the shoulder.

When passing the baton the runner holds the baton vertically in the right hand, thrusting it out in

Figure 16-3

Evaluative criteria and teaching points for baton passing for the shuttle run.

- Runner in ready position with hand out to the side to grasp baton.
- Runner thrusts baton forward in right hand.
- Right hand exchange.

Figure 16-4

Baton passing in pursuit relays.

• Arm swings upward and into receiver's hand between thumb and index finger, both arms extended.

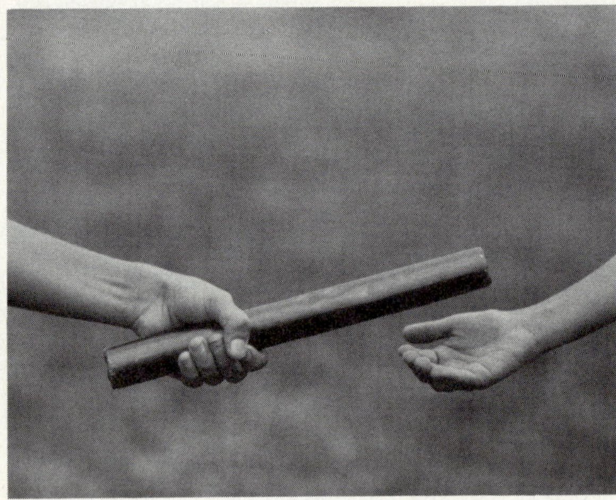

• Or arm swings downward; baton received in open palm, both arms extended.

front of the body. The receiver grasps the baton in the right hand above the runner's hand and then quickly proceeds to the opposite line.

In pursuit relays, passing the baton involves the two runners moving in the same direction in a passing zone, approximately 22 yards long. The receivers may look over their shoulders to see the coming runner or may receive the baton while facing the direction of the run. Although a *visual pass* is slower, it is easier for elementary school children. The *blind pass* is faster, but there is a greater chance for error since the receiver is not looking in the direction of the pass.

Passing the baton in pursuit relays involves a left to right or right to left hand exchange. The runner carries or shifts the baton to one hand and passes it to the receiver's opposite hand.

Note that the baton may be passed in an upward or downward motion. In preparing for the pass the receiver waits in the passing lane close to the oncoming runner. As the runner approaches, the receiver begins to move forward with the receiving hand extended back and in position and the palm turned either up or down. Both runners move in the passing lane, with the receiver accelerating.

The pass is completed with the arms of both runners fully extended. The pass requires perfect timing, and practice is necessary to get a smooth, efficient pass. The passing lane is 22 yards long for the 220-yard relay. The distance to be run is divided into four equal parts, with the passing lane overlapping each of the four distances. The distance will vary with the distance of the race for elementary school children.

Hurdling

Hurdling is a running event with the added challenge of moving over obstacles. Hurdles for elementary school children range in height from 18 to 30 inches. The fear of falling or hitting the hurdles presents a psychological barrier for children. Hurdles must be constructed so that they fall forward if contacted by the jumper. Heavy canvas fastened with Velcro strips to the side supports make excellent cross pieces that "tear away" at impact and reduce the fear of hitting the hurdles. The hurdle height should be adjusted to the height of the hurdler.

Hurdling events vary from 30 to 50 yards in length. The number of hurdles will vary with the distance, with a maximum of four for the 50-yard

Figure 16-5

Evaluative criteria and teaching points for blind pass in pursuit relays.

- Receiver waits at edge of passing zone, hand back ready to move.
- Runner approaches receiver.
- Both run receiver accelerating.
- Arm swings upward and into receiver's hand between thumb and index finger. Both arms extended.

or
- Arm swings downward. Baton received in open palm. Both arms extended.
- Receiver leaves passing zone.

Figure 16-6

Evaluative criteria and teaching points for hurdling.

- Body is propelled forward and upward, forward leg reaching.
- Trailing leg abducted.
- Hurdle cleared landing softly no loss in stride.

Figure 16-7

Evaluative criteria and teaching points for standing jump.

- Toes behind the line. Body bent at hips, knees and ankles. Arms bent at side
- Arms swing back, weight shifts to balls of the feet

- Arms swinging forward and upward, feet pushing off, body reaching forward and upward. The head is up.

- Land with arms reaching forward, heel touch first, legs flexed, body weight forward.

Table 16-3

Standards for the standing jump

Percentile	Age	Girls	Boys	Combined boys and girls
100	9-10	7'11"	6'5"	7'11"
	11	7'0"	8'5"	8'5"
	12	7'0"	7'5"	7'5"
75	9-10	5'2"	5'4"	5'3"
	11	5'4"	5'7"	5'6"
	12	5'6"	5'11"	5'9"
50	9-10	4'8"	4'11"	4'10"
	11	4'11"	5'2"	5'1"
	12	5'0"	5'5"	5'3"

From AAHPER, 1976.

event. The hurdles should be evenly spaced over the distance with a sufficient distance to establish a good stride before encountering the first hurdle, approximately 8 to 10 yards.

In hurdling, the stride should be even between the hurdles so that the same leg leads over the hurdle each time. The action is a leap as the hurdlers project themselves forward and upward. The take-off is on the ball of the foot, and the landing is on the opposite foot. The action should be smooth, with no loss of stride in landing. The trailing leg is up and abducted as it clears the hurdle. The center of gravity is ahead of the driving leg during the lift, which results in the upper body and head well out in front. To determine the lead foot at the start, the hurdler must determine the number of strides to the first hurdle and also the strides between hurdles.

Common errors:
1. Failure to lead with the same leg in going over the hurdles.
2. Breaking stride when approaching the hurdle.
3. Breaking stride when landing from a hurdle.
4. Failure to abduct the trailing leg so that it hits the hurdle.

Teaching suggestions: In developing the hurdling technique, the runner should first practice the start, then run and stop after the first hurdle has been cleared. To get the feeling of the stride before and between hurdles, the runner should move along the side of the course a few times.

FIELD EVENTS

Field events include jumping and throwing skills. At the elementary school level jumping events may in-

Figure 16-8

Evaluative criteria and teaching points for long jump.

- Approaching the board with controlled acceleration.
- Foot plant on board, free leg bent and moving forward, head up.

- Extension of take-off leg, movement forward and upward, chest lifted.

- Both legs reach forward, arms high and reaching forward. Head erect, chest up.

- Balanced landing, heels touch first. Body flexed, weight moving forward.

clude the standing jump, the long jump, and the high jump. The throwing events are the softball and soccer ball throws for distance and the shot put.

Jumping

Jumping events require ample space so that approaches do not interfere with other events. Landing surfaces should be loose and raked to provide an evenly smooth surface. Sand or wood shavings may be used for the standing and long jumps. Net bags filled with pieces of foam, crash pads, or tire tubes tied together and covered with a mat may be used to pad the landing areas for high jumping. High jump standards may be improvised using a bamboo pole or a long rope supported by two adjustable standards. The rope or pole should always be placed so that it falls away from the standards and the jumper if it is accidently touched by the jumper.

The *standing jump* is the first jumping event to be taught. The jumper attempts to cover as much horizontal distance as possible. The jump is measured from the scratch line to the closest point of contact of any body part in the landing area.

The jumper begins with both feet parallel and just behind the starting or scratch line and follows the procedure described in Figure 16-7. As the arms swing forward, an explosive extension of the legs and body and a push with the feet propel the body into the air. The landing should be controlled with the body weight forward, the arms out for balance, and the legs flexing to absorb the force.

Common errors:

1. Failure to coordinate the arm and leg actions.
2. Pushing with the whole foot rather than with the ball of the foot.
3. Not reaching forward with full extension on the jump.
4. Falling backward when landing.
5. Stepping over the scratch line before take-off.

The *long jump* involves a jump for distance after a running start. The measurement of the jump is taken from the scratch line to the nearest point of contact of any body part in the landing area. The take-off surface is a board 4 feet long, 8 inches wide, and 8 inches thick and is flush with the ground.

The approach in the long jump is a run with increasing speed on each step, until a maximum, yet controlled speed is attained. The last stride before take-off is slightly shorter to allow the jumper to prepare for the jump. The take-off is from one foot, and the free leg moves forward and upward to help propel the body into the air. The center of gravity is directly over the board as the take-off foot touches. The forceful extension of the take-off leg completes the upward motion. The angle of take-off is somewhat less than 45 degrees as the body is propelled upward and forward. During the airborne flight both arms and legs reach for maximum distance. The arms and upper body should be kept high with the head up. Maintaining balance and keeping the body weight forward are important in landing.

Common errors:

1. A break in stride in the approach.
2. Failure to achieve a maximum controlled run in the approach.
3. Stepping over the take-off board on the jump.
4. Failure to stretch on the take-off.
5. Head down and failure to lift the chest.
6. Propelling the body forward rather than upward and forward.
7. Loss of balance on landing.

Teaching suggestions:

1. The number of strides for the approach must be determined individually. It should be long enough to attain the desired speed but not too long to be tiring. Each person should determine the number of strides and the point from which to begin the approach.
2. Emphasize running through the board rather than placing too much emphasis on the take-off.

The *high jump* combines a short run with a jump over an obstacle that is raised in height after each successful jump. The jump is measured from the ground upward perpendicular to the top of the cross bar at the point the cross bar is closest to the ground.

Several techniques are used. Those in which the body passes horizontally over the cross bar are the most efficient since the jumper's center of gravity is close to the bar. The Straddle Roll is suggested here because of its movement efficiency. A scissors jump may also be used as a possible lead-up to the fosby flop, a style of jumping often used in competition.

The approach for the straddle roll is a short, deliberate run. The take-off leg is closest to the bar. After the take-off the free leg becomes the lead leg. As the lead arm and leg clear the bar, they rotate upward and away from the bar to facilitate the rotation of the trailing arm and leg upward and away from the bar. The landing should be on two hands and one foot, finishing with a roll to the side and the back.

Common errors:

1. Initiating the turn too soon.
2. Failure to get the free leg or knee high enough to clear the bar.
3. Failure to lead with the upper body after clearing the bar.
4. Failure to lift the take-off leg forcefully and high enough to clear the bar.
5. Running too far or too fast prior to the jump.

Teaching suggestions:

1. Powell[4] suggests the following progression of activities for learning the straddle roll:

   a. With the bar at a low level, the students hop over the bar and the teacher notes the foot on which each hops. The children move to the same side of the bar as the foot they used.

   b. Approaching the bar from a forty-five degree angle, the children hop over the bar once again, checking the hopping foot.

   c. In partners, facing each other, one child holds the non-hopping lower leg and foot of the other. The holding child gently turns the leg toward the supporting foot so that

Figure 16-9

Evaluative criteria and teaching points for straddle jump.

- Approach the bar at a 45-degree angle.
- Take-off on nearest foot, arms back and free leg trailing. Center of gravity behind take-off foot.

- Forceful push-off, arms and free leg move forward and upward as take-off leg extends.

- Body rotates so front of body faces the bar.
- Free leg leading inside arm close to trunk as outside arm and leg reach over bar, arm and shoulder slightly ahead.

- Body continues to rotate, 3-point landing and roll.

the jumper turns away from the holding child.

d. All children practice a short run and hop, turning the opposite direction at the height of the hop.

e. The children hop and turn at the highest point and land on the opposite foot and two hands while forcefully lifting the hopping leg into the air. The head, body, and lifted leg should be in a line. This should help the students get the idea of the body rotation at the height of the jump and the lift of the trailing leg to clear the bar.

f. Finally, the children begin by standing next to a line. They repeat step e, but they land on the opposite side of the line with the lead foot.

2. The teacher should insist on a high kick and knee lift.

3. If the take-off leg consistently does not clear the bar, the child should practice lifting the leg by lying on the floor in a prone position

Figure 16-10

Evaluative criteria and teaching points for scissors jump.

- Bar approached at a slight angle.
- Foot planted away from bar, flexing ankle and knee.

- Leg forcefully extended while free leg swings up to clear bar and arms swing upward.
- Trailing leg is lifted up over bar.

- Legs flex on landing to absorb force, arms out for balance.

Table 16-4

Performance standards for softball throw for distance (feet)

Percentile	Age	Girls	Boys
100	10	167	175
	11	141	205
	12	159	207
75	10	65	114
	11	74	126
	12	80	141
50	10	50	96
	11	59	111
	12	64	120

AAHPER, 1965.

and lifting the leg forcefully to cause the body to roll.

In the scissors jump the body passes in a vertical position over the bar. Success in clearing the bar is dependent on a forceful thrust of the take-off leg and upward swing of the arms. The landing should be on the feet and controlled. This jump is less efficient, and therefore lower heights will be achieved than with the straddle roll.

Common errors:
1. Failure to coordinate the extension of the leg and upward swing of the arms.
2. Taking off too close to the bar, so that the free leg hits the bar as it is brought upward.

Throwing Events

The throwing events in track and field meets include the javelin, discus, and shot put. At the elementary school level throws for distance often include a softball and a soccer ball throw. The javelin and discus are seldom included. A 4- to 6-pound shot is used in the shot put.

Safety is an important consideration in throwing events. The throwing area and the direction in which the throws will be made should be away from the other events. The area should be clearly defined to permit the children to see the restricted area. When more than one person is throwing at a time, a signal for retrieving the objects is used so that the children only retrieve after all objects have been thrown.

Figure 16-11

Evaluative criteria and teaching points for shot put.

• Held at base of four fingers, thumb and little finger supporting.

• Back of hand at clavicle, shot close to neck.

• Semi-squat position, weight over supporting foot, side facing direction of put.

• Forceful extention of knees and arm as shot is pushed outward and upward.

The *throw for distance* may be thought of as an event in itself or as a lead-up to throwing the javelin. An analysis of the overhand throwing pattern that is used in this event may be found in Chapter 11, along with common errors and teaching suggestions. In the early grades a standing throw is used. In the upper grades the throw is combined with a moving approach to maximize the force produced. In all throws a release angle of slightly less than 45 degrees is desired for maximum distance.

Measurement is taken from a point on the starting line to the point of first contact with the ground. Standards for performance in the softball throw are included in Table 16-4.

The softball (fleece ball for younger children) throw is included in all elementary school grades and a soccer ball throw in the upper grades only. While the soccer ball throw is not really a field event, it provides the children with a heavier object to handle which should enhance upper body development. When using a soccer ball the children may need to use two hands to control the larger ball.

The *shot put* may be introduced in the upper elementary school grades. A 4- or 6-pound shot is used. In the elementary school the shot should be put from a standing position. While the shot put is included as a throwing event, it is actually pushed rather than thrown.

The measurement is taken from the starting line or the edge of the circle to the first point of contact with the ground in the landing area.

The shot putter stands in a comfortable position, with the feet about shoulder width apart, behind the scratch line, and the side of the body facing the landing area. The shot is held with the fingers of the hand farthest from the throwing area. To place the shot in the ready position, the arm is straightened overhead and then lowered so that the back of the hand is on the clavicle and the shot is near the neck. Beginning with flexion in the knees, hips, and ankles and the weight over the throwing leg, the shot is released with a forceful extension of the legs and arm in an outward and upward direction and a tranfer of weight to the forward foot. The angle of projection should be about 45 degrees. The putter should be careful not to step over the scratch line or out of the circle as the shot is released.

Common errors:

1. Attempting to throw the shot rather than push it.
2. Letting the shot rest in the palm of the hand.
3. Failure to coordinate leg and arm extension into a smooth, continuous movement.
4. Stepping over the scratch line or out of the circle.

Teaching suggestions:

1. Since the shot is usually put from a circle 7 feet in diameter, this area may be used rather than a straight line.
2. Emphasize the pushing action and the extension of both the leg and the arm to propel the shot.

SUMMARY

Track and field activities involve the adaptation of the fundamental motor skills of running, jumping, and throwing to specialized events. As the children progress through the elementary school years, new techniques are introduced as they are ready. These activities involve the application of the movement concepts to the new skills. Track and field events are self-testing in nature, since performance is easily measured and children can readily see improvements made.

REFERENCES

1. AAHPER: Youth fitness test manual, revised ed., Reston, Va., 1976, AAHPER.
2. AAHPER: Youth fitness test manual, Washington, D.C., 1965, AAHPER.
3. American Academy of Pediatrics: Risks in long-distance running for children, The Physician and Sports Medicine **10**(2):82, August 1982.
4. Powell, J.: Track and field: fundamentals for teacher and coach, ed. 3, Champaign, Ill., 1971, Stipes Publishing Co.
5. Seidel, B., and others: Sports skills: a conceptual approach to meaningful movement, Dubuque, Iowa, 1975, William C. Brown Co.

ADDITIONAL READINGS

Connolly, O.: Shot put and discus, JOPER **51**(1):65, January 1980.
An analysis of the shot and discus events and a training program for beginning athletes.

Cook, T.: Games of a Greek olympiad, JOHPER, **45**(2):59, February, 1974.
Teaching students about the olympics by reinacting an Olympiad from 468 BC.

Tenoschok, M.: Jogging geography, JOPER **49**(6):68, June 1978.
Including learning in geography as a part of a jogging program.

Part Six

Dance and Rhythmic Activities

Dance and rhythmic activities are an essential part of the elementary school physical education program. Several kinds of dance and rhythmic experiences are developed in the following chapters. Creative dance gives children the opportunity to explore the use of the body in communicating ideas. Singing games, American, and international folk dance provide group experiences in moving to the beat and phrasing of the accompaniment. Rhythmic activities present children the opportunity to move with a piece of small equipment to the musical accompaniment. Each experience contributes in a unique way to the goals and objectives of the physical education program.

17

TEACHING DANCE AND RHYTHMIC ACTIVITIES

CHAPTER OBJECTIVES

1 To discuss the importance of dance and rhythmic activities in the elementary school physical education program

2 To define the content of the elementary school dance program based on the development of movement skills and the application of movement concepts with special emphasis on rhythmic elements

3 To provide suggestions which will enable the teacher to plan and conduct appropriate dance and rhythmic activities for elementary school children

Human beings have danced throughout the ages. They have danced to acknowledge the seasons, such as the planting and reaping of the harvest. They have danced in the celebration of their gods, as well as before battle, and dance has often been the medium for demonstrating athletic prowess.

In education, dance has been included in physical education and in music, with physical education assuming the major responsibility for the development of dance and other rhythmic skills. Dance and rhythmic activities have remained unchanged by the introduction of movement education into the elementary school physical education curriculum, since both have always utilized the movement content and the methodology associated with the movement education approach.

THE VALUE OF DANCE AND RHYTHMIC ACTIVITIES IN THE ELEMENTARY SCHOOL PHYSICAL EDUCATION PROGRAM

Dance as an art, and as the expressive entity of creative movement, is vital to the development of the total individual. All of the arts provide ways in which man can bring shape and order to his fragmented and rapidly changing world. But dance provides a primary medium for expression involving the total self, not just a part, like the voice, or totally separated from the physical self like painting or sculpture. Dance and the movement that produces it is "me" and, as such, is the most intimate of expressive media. A child's self-concept, his own identity and self-esteem are improved in relation to such use of his body's movement. If we believe that movement plays a crucial role in the developing life of the child and that all education should foster creativity, body movement as a creative medium in early childhood education attains great significance.[4]

Dance and rhythmic activities make an important contribution to the objectives of the elementary school physical education program. Dance and rhythmic activities are well known not only for their contribution to an individual's skill development but also for their contribution to the further development of the child's creative abilities. Dance is the only area of the physical education curriculum that deals with the arts and aesthetic education. In dance and other

300

rhythmic activities children have the opportunity to use movement to express their ideas and to develop aesthetically.

Children's body awareness is greatly enhanced by the opportunity to create their own movement sequences as they communicate their ideas to others. This body awareness is further developed as children use locomotor and/or nonlocomotor movements in their own dances or in more traditional ones.

Other movement concepts become important as children learn the effective use of space and experiment with the movement qualities of force, balance, time, and flow. The development of rhythmic skills is an important part of the dance and rhythmic activities experience. Children may be using their own natural rhythm or moving to the imposed rhythm of the accompaniment. This imposed time adds another dimension to their understanding of themselves as movers.

Dance and rhythmic activities give children the opportunity to work alone or with others in small groups to solve movement challenges. Sharing in the decision making becomes increasingly important as children move through the elementary school years.

Dance and rhythmic activities are also important contributors to physical fitness. Through these activities agility and flexibility are greatly enhanced, as is cardiorespiratory fitness. Moving to the imposed rhythm of an accompaniment may be one of the more invigorating and physically demanding experiences of the physical education program.

DANCE AND RHYTHMIC ACTIVITIES IN THE ELEMENTARY SCHOOL

The Task Force on Children's Dance in Education formulated the following objectives as desirable outcomes of children's dance. This author believes these objectives also apply to rhythmic activities.

1. To assist the children through movement-centered dance activities and other movement experiences they may be having to:

   Realize their biological urges to experience primal patterns of movement

   Develop an adequate degree of satisfaction in and mastery of their body movements for their own pleasure, confidence, and self-esteem

   Greatly expand their movement resources by offering them many opportunities to explore, discover, invent, and develop different ways of moving and to structure sequences

   Increase their aesthetic sensitivity by emphasizing the expressive and imaginative potential of their movements, as well as the physical and athletic aspects

   Develop their appreciation of dance as art, by relating it to appropriate experiences in music, literature, painting, and sculpture

   Relate their movements effectively to accompanying sounds and to music

   Participate with others in recreational folk and ethnic dances by helping them learn traditional dance steps and understand the different ways they have been used through centuries of people dancing together

Make dances for themselves and others and, when they seem ready for the experience, to perform them for peer audiences

2. To assist the children through audience-centered activities to:

Understand the ancient and honorable tradition of dance as art and ritual

Develop sensitivity to the essence of movement as communication as they observe the performances of their peers

Appreciate the many forms of dance that have evolved in different cultures, all based on common movement resources from which man has drawn for his expressive purposes

Understand, as they grow older, something of the demanding discipline and training of the body necessary for a professional dancer

Enjoy viewing concert and theatre dance and develop a discriminating awareness of movement as an artistic medium[4]

Content of the Elementary School Dance Program

The elementary school dance and rhythmic activity program is composed of several different kinds of experiences. Dance activities include creative dance, singing games, dances of American origin, and international folk dance. Rhythmic activities include movement experiences with balls, ropes, hoops, sticks, and other equipment to musical accompaniment. Besides the activities that are developed in the following chapters, ballet, jazz, tap, break dancing, and other forms of dance may be included in the dance program. Teachers may not always feel qualified to deal with some of these varied forms of dance. Usually help may be found from local dance groups, dance companies, or dance studios.

Dance activities are often integrated with other school subjects. Combining creative dance, art, and music enhances the aesthetic development of children. Folk and square dance are often taught with appropriate units in social studies.

Dance and rhythmic activities are dependent on the use of locomotor and/or nonlocomotor skills and movement concepts. The box below defines the dance content of the elementary school physical education program.

Locomotor skills

Locomotor skills involve the body moving through space from one place to another. The skills are defined as even and uneven movements. The even locomotor movements include the walk, run, hop, jump, and leap. The uneven movements are the skip, gallop, and slide.

The use of locomotor skills is dependent on the type of dance or rhythmic activity in which one is engaged. Locomotor skills may be used singly or in simple combinations as composed by the student. They may also be used in combinations imposed by the teacher or imposed in the execution of dance steps as in the polka, step-hop, two-step, schottische, or waltz. Locomotor skills may be combined with other elements such as nonlocomotor movements, space concepts, rhythmic elements, or other movement qualities. Possibilities for combinations increase with the age and experience of the children. Locomotor movements are analyzed in Chapter 11. An analysis of dance steps may be found in Chapter 19.

Nonlocomotor movements

Nonlocomotor or axial movements used in dance and rhythmic activities include bending, stretching, pushing, pulling, swinging, swaying, twisting, and turning. These movements may be executed individually or in combinations with other nonlocomotor movements and/or locomotor movements. Nonlocomotor skills may be varied in their use with the movement concepts. Younger children use them frequently in singing games as well as in creative dance.

Movement concepts

All movement concepts are utilized in dance activities. Creative dance has traditionally made use of these concepts as the dancer attempts to communicate with the audience. The use of movement concepts in dance has been on a more conscious level than has been their use in other movement activities. The dancer must pay close attention to these concepts in expressing ideas in a meaningful way.

Body awareness is essential in the skillful use of the body in dance and rhythmic activities. The dancer must have full control of the body and its parts in making maximum use of the body in conveying ideas or performing intricate dance steps. Space concepts are important in using space in an interesting manner and in maintaining relationships with other dancers and/or equipment. Movement qualities are important in all dance and rhythmic activities. Force, balance, and time must all be used effectively. The following rhythmic elements are unique to these kinds of experiences:

Underlying beat or pulse beat: The underlying beat is the steady even beat found in any piece of music or rhythmic sequence.

Measure: A measure is a number of underlying beats grouped together into a unit, the number of which is

DANCE AND RHYTHMIC ACTIVITIES IN THE ELEMENTARY SCHOOL

THE CONTENT	MOVEMENT CONCEPTS
Locomotor movements	Body awareness
Walk	Actions of body parts
Run	Relationships of body parts
Hop	Body language
Jump	Space
Leap	General
Gallop	Direction
Slide	Pathway (floor pattern)
Skip	Range
Dance steps	Level
Step-hop	Force
Schottische	Strong-gentle
Polka	Jerky-smooth
Two-step	Tense-relaxed
Waltz	Heavy-light
Nonlocomotor movements	Flow
Bend-stretch	Balance
Swing-sway	Time
Twist-turn	Response to the pulse beat
Push-pull	Response to phrasing
	Tempo
	Even-uneven rhythm

dependent upon the meter.

Meter: Meter indicates the number of beats in a measure such as 2/4, 3/4, 4/4, or 6/8. The upper number represents the number of beats per measure, the lower number the type of note getting the beat. For example in 2/4 time there are two beats to the measure, with a quarter note getting one beat.

Phrase: A phrase is a group of measures which constitute a musical thought.

Rhythmic pattern: The rhythmic pattern is a combination of notes, even and/or uneven which constitute a measure or a phrase.

Tempo: Tempo is the rate of speed—fast, moderate, or slow.

Accent: An accent is emphasis put on a beat. It is usually on the first beat of a measure but it may occur on any beat.

Mood: Mood is the character of an accompaniment which depicts a sadness, gaiety, seriousness, or other feelings.

Intensity: Intensity denotes the loudness, or softness of an accompaniment.

An example of the structure of music is provided in Figure 17-1.

Program Emphasis

The developmental approach to dance and rhythmic activities enables the teacher to plan appropriate activites for children that are based on experience rather than on grade level. Emphasis on each level assumes mastery of the previous level. However, the teacher must select carefully activities that appeal to the maturity of the students.

Level I

During these beginning experiences children master the locomotor skills, by exploring their variations, and begin the exploration and use of nonlocomotor movements. The movement concepts learned in previous units are integrated into the dance and rhythmic activities. The rhythmic elements are introduced

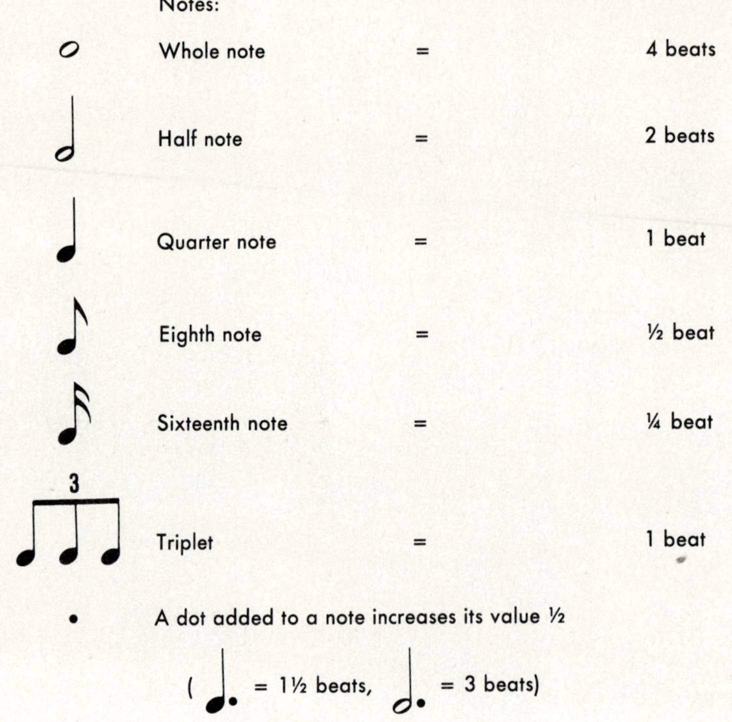

Twinkle Twinkle Little Star

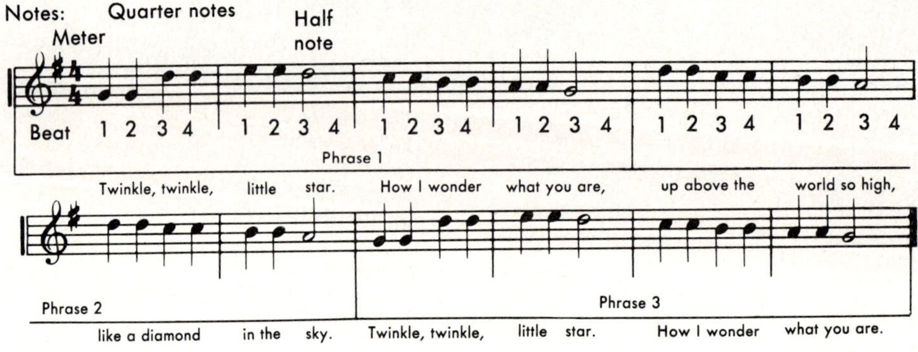

Figure 17-1

Musical structure.

as children move to an accompaniment.

Creative dance is an important part of these beginning dance experiences. Movement challenges deal with concrete ideas within the children's experience. Most of the problem solving is done on an individual basis, but occasionally the children may work with partners.

Singing games and simple folk dances allow children to develop locomotor and nonlocomotor skills in time to music and to develop an awareness of musical phrasing. Simple rhythmic activities with hoops, sticks and balls may be introduced when they gain some control in the use of such equipment.

Level II

During this developmental period children explore

simple combinations of locomotor and/or nonlocomotor movements. Movement concepts are integrated into the creative dance experiences. Individual and partner problem-solving activities continue with occasional work in small groups.

Simple folk and American dances are used at this level, which include mixers in which the children change partners throughout the dance. Some simple dance steps may be introduced toward the end of this level.

Ball control has improved substantially by this time, enabling the children to be more successful in ball rhythms. Work with hoops and sticks continues, and the children may begin to jump rope to accompaniment.

Level III

Creative dance at this level includes challenges in which children are able to use several skills and concepts. The children may now work in small groups as well as individually or with a partner. Children are able to create movement sequences that may be repeated, and the creative dance activities begin to deal with more abstract ideas.

Square dance is introduced and international folk dance and other American dances are continued. A variety of dance formations are used with various partner relationships. Dance figures such as the grand right and left are introduced. The dances included are more demanding in that specific dance steps are used rather than the simple locomotor skills such as the walk, run, or skip, which are used in Levels I and II. The polka, schottische, and step-hop are commonly used dance steps. Line and circle dances without partners may be introduced.

Children at this level enjoy rhythmic activities with sticks, balls, hoops, and ropes. They can make up simple combinations of skills that they may do with a partner or in a small group.

Level IV

Level IV is characterized by further development in all areas. Children are especially interested in group work at this level but there should be time for individual work as well.

Creative dance allows children to use their improved body awareness and knowledge of other concepts and skills in communicating ideas. Folk and square dances include increasingly difficult dance steps and figures, formations, and partner relationships. The two-step and waltz may be introduced at this level. Rhythmic activities include more advanced skills and more complex movement sequences created by the children.

PLANNING AND CONDUCTING DANCE AND RHYTHMIC ACTIVITY EXPERIENCES

Dance instruction requires creative teaching. Success is dependent on the teacher's ability to use problem solving, as well as guided discovery and exploration. Many beginning teachers will feel inadequate in using these approaches. Experience is needed to master these techniques. If confidence in the use of these methods is to be realized, it is necessary for the beginning teacher to plan and to evaluate carefully the outcomes of the lessons.

Elementary school children need vigorous activity. Dance experiences should be planned with a maximum of activity. The lesson should move smoothly from one activity to the next, with some change of pace provided between activities that are vigorous. Generally the activities should be short in duration, although in the upper elementary grades children will remain interested in activities for longer periods of time. Instructions should be simple and to the point to enable the activity to begin quickly.

Individual skills and the understanding and use of the movement concepts should be encouraged. Creativity in finding many different solutions to movement challenges should be promoted. Adequate space must be provided to give children the freedom of movement required to develop their own movement potential. When small equipment is used there must be enough for all children to play, and it must be of appropriate size and weight for the children to control easily. Adequate space is essential if the children are to use the equipment safely.

The dance experiences should include individual, partner, and small group work. Sharing ideas is an important part of the dance and rhythmic activity experience. Children should have the opportunity to work with all their classmates at one time or another. They should be encouraged to participate with different children as the lesson develops.

Movement challenges within the lesson or unit should move from the simple to the more complex. This should be accomplished by working with single elements and gradually combining elements as children are able to deal with more than one element at a time.

In developing movement challenges in dance and other rhythmic activities, the teacher must give the children a framework within which to move. The teacher must think through carefully the objectives

to be developed and the kinds of outcomes that will indicate mastery of the objectives. Children must be given sufficient information to meet successfully the objectives of the dance experience. This does not limit creativity. Without a framework within which to work, there is little creativity. Putting on a record and telling the children to move as the music tells them to move will not result in creative movement responses. It will not only lead to frustration of the children, who are given too many decisions to make, but also to frustration of the teacher, who does not get the appropriate responses. In the younger grades elementary school children work best with concrete ideas. As children progress through the elementary school grades they become increasingly able to deal with more abstract ideas.

Movement challenges should be structured only on the content of the day's lesson or on previously learned material. Within a lesson subchallenges are developed which lead into a culminating activity in which several ideas are used. The lesson usually begins with simple movement challenges in which the children work with a single concept or a movement idea. As the lesson progresses the children add to their solutions by using additional concepts and movements.

Additional concerns for planning and conducting dance and rhythmic activity experiences may be found in the following chapters.

SUMMARY

Dance and rhythmic activities contribute substantially to the objectives of the physical education program in the elementary school. The activities expand the children's understanding of their own movement potential, contribute to their aesthetic development, and provide challenging activities in which human movement is further expanded. Many forms of dance and rhythmic activities may be included. Creative dance, rhythmic activities, and folk and square dance, as well as ballet, tap, jazz, or break dancing, may be a part of the dance experience as children further develop their use of locomotor and nonlocomotor movements and use of the movement concepts.

REFERENCES

1. Dimondstein, G.: Children's dance in the classroom, New York, 1971, Macmillan and Co.
2. Dimondstein, G.: Moving in the real and feeling worlds, JOPERD **54**(7):42, September 1983.
3. Joyce, M.: First steps in teaching creative dance, ed. 2, Palo Alto, Calif., 1980, Mayfield Publishing Co.
4. Murray, R.: A statement of belief. In Fleming, G., editor: Children's dance, Reston, Va., 1981, AAHPERD.
5. Stinson, S.: Aesthetic experience in children's dance, JOPERD **53**(4):72, April 1982.

ADDITIONAL READINGS

Hanson, M.: The right of children to experiences in dance/movement/arts, JOPER **50**(7):42, September 1979.
The value of dance and movement in the education of elementary school children.

Kramer, D.: Dance is physical education too, JOPERD **55**(6):30, August 1984.
Beginning dance experiences as fitness activities to establish interest in dance.

Woodruff, J.: Improvisation for the inhibited, JOPERD **56**(1):36, January 1985.
Using improvisation to expand the dance experience and build confidence using contact with others and props.

Wyckoff, W.: Movement programs and aesthetic education, JOPER, **51**(4):65, April 1980.
The goals of aesthetic education and the nature of movement programs in meeting these goals.

18

CREATIVE DANCE

CHAPTER OBJECTIVES

1   To state the goals of creative dance in the elementary school
2   To discuss suggestions for planning and conducting creative dance experiences
3   To describe the content of creative dance at the elementary school level and suggest movement challenges to develop the content

The dancer is the communicator of ideas, the creator of moods, the entertainer, and the storyteller. To dance requires movements more purposefully executed than in any other movement activity. The dancer is perhaps the most controlled athlete of all. Besides being a skillful mover, the dancer must also understand how to use body parts to accomplish the goals of the dance. In no other movement form are the movements solely the result of the creative genius of the individual, because the dancer uses the body in unique ways controlling space, force, and time to communicate with an audience.

CREATIVE DANCE IN THE ELEMENTARY SCHOOL PHYSICAL EDUCATION PROGRAM

Creative dance is the most neglected area of instruction in physical education. Many teachers feel inadequately prepared to plan creative experiences for children. Yet creative dance is a vital part of the children's physical education experiences. It is the only area in which creativity is a prominent goal. Although the movement-centered curriculum suggested in this book allows the children to develop ideas of their own, the solutions are more often functional than creative. Children learn about movement efficiency rather than the use of movement to express ideas and feelings. The creative dance experience for children should be characterized by a spontaneity in response to the movement ideas posed by the teacher, with the children discovering their own right ways to move.

In creative dance the emphasis is placed on helping children develop their expressive abilities by using the body as the instrument in which the ideas become manifest. Like the artist who paints a picture on a canvas, the dancer expresses ideas through body movement. A child may be skillful in performing various locomotor and nonlocomotor movements and may not be able to use these movements effectively in dance. The emphasis in creative dance is to teach the child to use body movements to communicate dance ideas. In creative dance the child is experimenting with movement rather than learning specific skills. At a later time dance technique may be mastered, but in the beginning stages the focus is on the act of moving itself.

Movement in creative dance is a personal expression. As the children move, their attention is directed inward. The result is not only greater awareness of the body but also of the mind and feelings. This increased awareness of the total being is essential to success in the dance experience.

In creating a dance an individual moves with a series of locomotor and nonlocomotor movements, using the movement concepts to present the ideas. Creative dance extends children's understanding of movement. In analyzing a dance one discovers the dancer moving in space and controlling force and time. The use of these concepts is essential to the development of dances that are pleasing to both the performer and the audience.

The goals to be achieved in the creative dance experience are as follows:

1. To enhance the creative potential of each child
2. To develop skillful and controlled use of the body as a means of expression and communication
3. To develop an understanding and appreciation of dance

The creative dance experience should lead to increased self-esteem and confidence in one's ability to move. As a result, children should be able to move more freely in exploring their movement potential.

SUGGESTIONS FOR TEACHING
Planning the Lesson

The core of each lesson includes activities to enhance the children's awareness of themselves and to develop an understanding of the movement concepts emphasized and provide an opportunity for improvisation. The lesson is usually comprised of a warm-up activity, the presentation of the movements and/or movement concepts to receive attention, an opportunity to experiment with the lesson material, and, finally, the opportunity to use the lesson material in some simple form to create a dance. Continuity in the lesson results in each part of the lesson building onto the next, flowing smoothly to completion. There should be a feeling of closure at the end of the lesson.

Creative dance lessons need structure. Some teachers may feel structure in the lesson deprives the children of a truly creative experience. However, the goals must be clearly defined with appropriate activities and questions to help children develop the lesson material. The children need some place to begin if they are to move creatively. It is a difficult task to be creative in too open an atmosphere. Instructions to move as the music tells them to move will be beyond the comprehension of most children.

Lesson material must be carefully selected with consideration for the age and experience of the children. For example, developing the idea of rag dolls may appeal to first-grade children, but a fifth-grade class may find it too juvenile. Activities within the experience of inner-city children will differ considerably from those for children who live in a rural or suburban setting.

Beginning the Lesson

It is important to get the lesson off to a good start. A signal for getting the attention of everyone is important. While children are working on their own they may need to be reminded about the signal to stop momentarily and why it is important to listen. *After defining the area of the space to be used, warm-up activities related to the lesson objectives should get the children moving.* Vigorous activities involving a movement or concept will not only prepare the children for physical activity but mental activity as well.

Organization of the space may include moving alone, in partners, or in small groups, using all the space or moving in groups from one part of the room to another. The atmosphere of the class will greatly affect the responses of the children. The size of the space, physical obstructions, the distractions of noise and other children, and the like will alter possible reactions to lesson material.

Following the brief warm-up activities the children are ready for the *presentation of the lesson material.* Lessons may be organized around a locomotor or nonlocomotor movement, an action of a limb such as extend or swing, or movement in relation to others. Lessons may also be organized around an idea, such as the wind or trees.

The lesson may be presented verbally or with the use of visual aids or props. Care should be taken to keep vocabulary appropriate to the age of the children, with the teacher determining the most meaningful language to use. The suggested actions should be within the children's ability and understanding.

During this presentation phase of the lesson, the teacher conducts some guided experiences to help children become familiar with the material with which they will work. This should not limit the children's creativity but should serve to stimulate their interest to expand the possibilities for movement. The teacher must develop sensitivity to each child, knowing when to help and what questions to ask. The teacher must also be responsive to the group and be able to judge when the children are ready to move on to the next part of the lesson.

Developing the Lesson

The activity may begin with concentration on one movement or concept and progress to others or combinations of others as the children become ready. For example, the lesson might include exploration of a locomotor or nonlocomotor movement followed by experimentation with the movement in space, varying force or time. There may be exploration of movements in self or general space, moving at different levels, in several directions, varying the degree of force or the time of the movements. Obviously the first combinations must be simple. The teacher may ask, for example: How many different ways can you walk and change direction? This may be a challenge for the inexperienced young dancer. There should be a variety of experiences within each lesson to present a maximum of possibilities for movement.

This development of the lesson material is an important part of the lesson. Children need time to develop an understanding of the lesson material and to interpret it into their own movements under the guidance of the teacher. This is the opportunity for children to explore what body parts to use, how to move them, and where and how to move them in space. As the children work the teacher moves among them, interacting with individual children or with the group as needed. There should be many activities during this phase, with the teacher asking questions and when necessary stopping or restructuring the activity to assist in the development of the lesson material.

It is important for the teacher to *avoid those ex-*

periences that result in imitation or pantomine. "Dance is not about something. It is something in itself."[6] Children should be taught to move as humans and not to imitate the movements of animals and other objects. The objective is human movement that takes on characteristics of the idea presented.

Imagery may inhibit creative responses, so *during the exploratory phase the use of imagery should be limited.* Some images may arise out of the activity. After a period of time working on galloping, the teacher might ask: What moves like that? If the children were exploring locomotor movements it might be more appropriate to have the children move lightly or heavily, or with big or little steps, rather than having them move like a mouse or an elephant. A more satisfactory approach is to explore the movements or concepts to be developed and then relate them to imagery.

Accompaniment may add considerably to the movement experience. However, it too may stifle creativity if presented at an inappropriate time in the lesson. In the beginning of the lesson it may distract the children from the task of exploring movement. After some work on the lesson material it may give a new dimension to their creative efforts.

Children need the opportunity to work as individuals, with partners, and in small groups. In the early years work is almost exclusively of an individual nature. As the children mature, work with partners and in small groups should be included. The teacher must carefully plan to ensure the children have all the social experiences for which they are ready. There may be times when the teacher allows the children some choice about whether they work alone or with others. The teacher must see to it that children are not excluded from working with others if they so desire.

Conducting the Culminating Activity

After a time of exploration and experimentation the children are ready for the culminating activity of the lesson, creating a dance to be presented to the class. All dances should be put into a simple form. Dances should have continuity from beginning to end. They should begin from a definite starting position and should close in a manner that communicates that the dance is completed. Once the starting position is assumed, some signal or accompanying music should mark the beginning of the dance. In the upper grades where a dance may be more complex, the dance should be repeated enough times so the movements

flow continuously. In this way the dance will become a part of the kinesthetic memory rather than requiring conscious effort for each movement.

The dances of young children will be brief and spontaneous. They will be easily forgotten. Dances may be simply the result of the children's exploring the lesson material and then selecting one or two responses they liked best to show to others. In the upper grades children may develop some dances over time, such as the entire class period or a couple of classes. In these dances they will begin working with one or two ideas and gradually add other movements or concepts as the dance is developed. The teacher must know when it is time for each individual or group to move on to new material. These dances are generally movement sequences the children will remember and will repeat. If the dance is to be developed over several lessons, the children may need time at the close of the lesson to make some notes for next time.

The teacher must know the children well to determine how much direction is needed in developing dances. In the beginning the children will be able to concentrate on only one element at a time, such as exploring a locomotor movement or a space concept. The teacher can combine elements only when the children have had sufficient experience with individual elements to feel comfortable in combining them. Combining too many movements or concepts before they are ready will only lead to frustration, because too many decisions must be made.

The teacher should plan carefully to allow sufficient time to explore the lesson material and to make up a dance. Even though the same lesson material may be used in several lessons within the unit, there should be some closure on the lesson material each day.

Young children are relatively uninhibited in performing in front of a group. However, many children in the fourth, fifth, and sixth grades may feel self-conscious when moving in front of others. Individual work may be presented to the group by having several children or one half the class perform at one time. This will help those children who have difficulty in getting up in front of the group, as well as move the presentations along more quickly.

The children should participate in positive analysis and evaluation of the dances presented. The teacher must guide the evaluation of the presentations. Asking children what they especially liked in each dance performance is a good way to begin. Later there may be discussion of how the movements and movement concepts were used in the dances to express the dance ideas.

Evaluation of the creative dance experience is essential and perhaps somewhat more difficult than in other activity areas. Since there is no one correct response, process may be more important than product. Evaluation serves two purposes. The first is to give feedback to the dancer. If the evaluation is to

MOVEMENT CONTENT FOR CREATIVE DANCE

THE BODY MOVES

Body shapes
  Round
  Stretched
  Twisted — Combinations
  Angular
  Symmetrical
  Asymmetrical
Locomotor movements
  Walk
  Run
  Skip
  Gallop
  Leap — Combinations
  Hop
  Jump
  Variations in the use
    of body parts
Body parts and nonlocomotor movements
  Bend
  Stretch
  Push
  Pull
  Swing
  Sway
  Twist
  Turn
  Lift
  Fall
  Variations in the use — Combinations
    of body parts
  Unison
  Opposition
  Sequential
  Away from the body
  Toward the body
  Around the body
  Lead
  Support
  Take body weight

(Combinations)

IN SPACE

Self
General
Direction
  Forward
  Backward
  Right
  Left
  Up
  Down
Pathway
  Curved-circular
  Straight-zigzag
  Combinations of straight
    and curved
Level
  High
  Medium
  Low
Range
  Near-far
  Big-little

WITH FORCE

Strong-gentle
Heavy-light
Tense-relaxed
Smooth-jerky
Accented

IN TIME

Pulse beat
Rhythmic pattern
Phrase
Even, Uneven
Quick, Slow

be effective, the teacher must know the children, their bodies and their movements, and the extent of their understanding of movement concepts. The teacher must be able to give all children the help they need to accomplish the lesson objectives. The teacher must know when the children need help, how to give it, and when the children need more time for work on their own.

The second purpose of evaluation is to determine the extent to which lesson and unit objectives are being met. The teacher needs to ask some questions relating to the lesson: Did the children enjoy the activity? Were the class objectives met? Were the children successful in using the lesson material to create some movements of their own? What did the children each learn about their own ability to move? The teacher must remember that the movements are unique to each child. If the child is to continue to move creatively, the teacher must respect each child's original solutions to the movement ideas posed.

BUILDING THE CREATIVE DANCE LESSONS

Emphasis in the creative dance lesson is on the development of controlled, purposeful movement. Since the development of an understanding of the movement concepts in experiences throughout the school year is suggested, emphasis in this chapter is on the creative development of movement skills with use of the concepts already learned and the introduction of the terminology associated with creative dance. The movement concepts are developed strictly in a way that expands their use as the child begins to use movement to communicate ideas. The box below outlines the movement content of the creative dance experience.

Activity begins with a review of possible body movements and the movement terminology, such as twist or sway. The teacher then might proceed to explore possible variations in the use of body parts in performing these basic movements or possible combinations of these movements. Additional combinations include total body movement in combining body shape and locomotor and nonlocomotor movements. Additional work includes conscious use of space, force, and time. Children in the early grades will work with simple combinations. As the children progress through the elementary school years in their dance experiences, the combinations increase in complexity. The result of these experiences should be increased body awareness and control, the development of a movement vocabulary, and the development of a repertoire of personal movement possibilities.

One approach used in developing dances is the "movement box," in which children select cards with themes such as space, force, or time. Based on their cards, the children develop their dances individually, with a partner, or in a small group.

In developing the lessons the teacher may begin with the selection of movement skills to be developed or the teacher may approach the lesson with an exploration of movements related to a movement theme such as the circus or a child's poem. Movement concepts are used to enhance the movement ideas. Accompaniment and props, such as scarves, may also be used. The following activities are but a few of the possibilities for development in creative dance.

Body Movements
Body shape

The body may assume many different shapes, which may be classified as round, stretched, twisted, or angular. These shapes may be symmetrical or asymmetrical. One body segment may assume a particular shape while another segment assumes a different shape. Body control is important is making and changing body shapes. In evaluating the use of body shape, the teacher should look for shapes which challenge the use of the body as children use body shape in a variety of ways.

The body moves:

Find a body shape. Now try another. Another. (Talk about the kind of shapes the children made.)

Make a shape supported on one leg. An upside-down shape.

Make a rounded shape with the entire body. Make a rounded shape with various body parts.

Make a stretched shape. A bent (angular) shape. A twisted shape. (Try each using various body segments.)

Find a body shape. On the signal assume another shape. (Repeat several more times.) Now begin with a shape you liked, and as I beat the drum slowly change to another shape you enjoyed.

Can you put three shapes together as I beat the drum?

Can you spring into the air and make a shape? Hold it until you land.

What shapes can you make as you walk? As you skip or gallop? Run? Hop? Jump?

As the music plays, slowly make a shape keeping the movement controlled. Hold momentarily. Slowly and with control continue to change shape holding each briefly until the music stops. Hold your final shape.

Make a shape while standing. While lying on the floor. From what other positions can you make an interesting shape?

In space:

Move in general space and on the signal, make a body shape.

Make a body shape and move in that shape in general space.

Make a shape at the low level. Medium level. High level.

Move through general space, making shapes and changing levels as you go.

Make a shape. Move in general space. On the signal stop and make a new shape. Now move in a new direction, keeping your shape.

Make a stretched shape as you move in a straight pathway. A round shape as you move in a curved pathway. Can you combine a stretched and a round shape as you combine a straight and curved pathway?

Make a shape that fills your self space. Now move in general space making a shape that takes up as much space as possible. Try another large shape.

Vary the available space. Make as large a shape as possible. How does your shape change as the space increases? Decreases?

Move in general space. As your name is called stop and make a shape. (Continue until all the children have made a shape.) Were you able to hold your shape?

Half of the group makes shapes, and the other half moves around the shapes. Move as close to the children making shapes as possible without touching them. Could you go over, under, or around the shapes the children made? What was your favorite shape? Why?

With force:

Make a tight shape. Now a relaxed shape.

Make a shape. On the count of 5, tighten your muscles in various body parts, but do not change your shape. What happened to your body shape? How did it feel? Which body parts did you tighten? Could you tighten them all?

Make a shape. Tighten your muscles. Now gradually loosen your muscles, ending in the same shape but as relaxed and loose as possible.

Make a strong shape. A gentle shape.

Change shapes in a jerky fashion. Now change shapes as smoothly as you can, moving from one shape to the next without hesitation.

In time:

Make a body shape. On the count of 4 slowly change to another shape. Hold. Repeat.

Make a shape as slowly as possible. Make the same shape as quickly as possible.

Locomotor movements

Most children begin school with mastery of the locomotor movements of running, walking, hopping, and jumping. They may have had less opportunity for skipping, galloping, sliding, and leaping. Control of movement is emphasized as the children explore the use of body parts to perform the skills, modify the movements in a variety of situations, combine them into simple movement sequences, or use them in combination with other body movements. Emphasis in evaluation should be on the use of locomotor movements in a controlled and purposeful way to communicate dance ideas.

The body moves:

Move in general space with a locomotor movement of your choice. On the signal try another.

Select a locomotor skill to use as you move in general space. On the signal, change the way you do the movement but continue to move using the same locomotor movement. What were some of the ways you could change your movements and continue with the same locomotor movement? Try it again with another locomotor movement. Describe it to someone close by.

Combine two locomotor movements as you cross the floor. What other combinations can you do? Can you combine three locomotor movements as you move? As you move in general space combine a locomotor movement with a non-locomotor movement.

In space:

As you move change the size of your step. Take big steps. Bigger. Now take small steps. Can you combine big and little steps as you cross the floor?

How high can you step? How low? Think of something you might step over. Show us how you would do it.

Move in general space, changing direction on the signal but not changing the locomotor movement you do. Could you move in all directions? Show one movement that was difficult. Now an easy one.

Move with a partner. Hold hands and move side by side. Now one behind the other. Now facing each other.

Vary the size of the space available. Change your movements as the space demands. What happened when the space was small? Large?

Move in self space. Now move in general space.

Change levels as you move. Try another way of moving and change levels.

Move across the room in a curved or straight pathway. Repeat. Could you make the path more interesting for someone to watch? With a partner show each other the path you liked best.

With force:

Vary the force as you move. Move as lightly as you can. How heavy can you move?

Move as relaxed as you can. Now move as tense as you can.

Combine a tense and a relaxed movement.

Move suddenly. Explode as you begin to move.

Pick a locomotor movement and move in general space. Using the same movement move as stiffly as you can. Now as loosely.

On the drum beat you are to move smoothly, keeping the movement going as long as the drum sounds. Listening to a variety of rhythmic instruments, move and continue to move as long as you hear the sound.

Move smoothly and explode on the last beat of the drum.

Make a strong movement. Repeat several times. Make a gentle movement. Repeat. Combine a strong and a gentle movement as you cross the room.

In time:

Pick a locomotor movement and move to the music. As the music changes move in a new way. Which movements worked best with each different piece of music?

Listen to the beat. Move to the even beat of the drum. Take a step on each beat. Try another movement.

Listen to the uneven beat. Move in time to the uneven rhythm. Which movements seem to work best?

The drum will now beat even and uneven rhythms. Listen to the drum and move using an even locomotor movement on the even beats and an uneven locomotor movement on the uneven beats.

Make up a movement sequence combining even locomotor movements.

Make up a movement sequence using uneven locomotor movements.

Make up a movement sequence combining even and uneven locomotor movements.

Make up a movement sequence lasting for 8 beats. Repeat it.

Make up a movement sequence to one phrase of the music. Now to two phrases.

Select a locomotor movement and move as quickly as you can. Now as slowly. Can you combine a slow and a quick movement?

Begin moving at a comfortable speed. Now as you move, gradually move more quickly. Now slow down until the movement ceases.

Body parts and nonlocomotor movements

Besides movements that move the body through space, the body may also perform movements while in a stationary position. Body parts may move to lead a movement, to take the body weight momentarily in a movement, or to support the body. Nonlocomotor movements include bending and stretching, pushing and pulling, swinging and swaying, twisting and turning, and lifting and falling. A description of these movements may be found in Chapter 11. These movements may involve body parts moving in unison, in opposition, or in sequence, with one body part beginning to move followed by one or more body parts. Nonlocomotor movements include movements toward the body, away from the body, and around the body. Many variations and combinations are possible. The teacher should look for unique ways of performing these skills.

The body moves:

Beginning at the head and working downward, explore the movements possible in each part. Discover where the movement is initiated.

Stretch a body part. Now let it collapse. Try another.

Bend a body part. Now add another. Keep adding parts until the body is in an angular shape.

On the drum beat stretch a body part. As the drum continues, slowly bend the same part. Now stretch a body part, and then bend another body part.

Beginning in a standing position, slowly let the body sink to the floor. Now rise again slowly and with control to the starting position.

Swing your arms forward and backward. Now from side to side.

What other body parts can you swing? Try some.

Can you swing the body part in a complete circle? Half?

Stretching your arms overhead, sway back and forth. What other parts can sway?

Twist a body part. Another. Another. Twist the entire body. Can you twist while supported on three body parts? Two?

With a partner, facing each other, one of you move and the other mirror the movements. Move a body part. Keep that part moving as you transfer the movement to another part.

Move body parts from different positions, like standing, lying, and kneeling. How does the body position affect the movements possible?

In space:

Rise and fall from the low level.

Sway as you move in general space.

Sway changing levels.

Swing as large a swing as you can. Now a small swing with the same body parts.

Stretch at a low level. A medium level. A high level.

Begin at the low level and gradually stretch the body to reach the high level. Now bend and with control return to the low level.

With force:

Swing as forcefully as you can. Now gently.

Swing your arms and let the momentum of the swing carry the body either forward or backward. Feel the power in your arms. Repeat while swinging some other body part.

Combine a forceful swing and a gentle swing.

Sway and let the sway turn your body.

Move and stop quickly. How can you use your body parts to stop more quickly?

Move smoothly. Now sharply. Combine a smooth and a sharp movement.

With a partner, one of you move smoothly and the other attempt similar movements but perform them in a jerky manner.

Move a body part with an accent on the beginning of the movement. Can you accent any other part of the movement?

Make a shaking movement with your hand. What other parts can you shake?

In time:

Rise on the count of 5. Now fall on the same count.

Swing in time to the music. Can you move as the tempo changes?

Swing two body parts in unison. Now in opposition. In sequence.

Move two body parts, one quickly, one slowly.

With various rhythm instruments move body parts as long as you hear a sound. How did your movements change with a triangle and a wood block?

Movement Concepts

The movement concepts of space, force, and time are important to the dance experience. While it is suggested in the previous section that they be treated in relation to the movements of the body, they may also be developed as separate aspects of the creative dance experience.

Space

The effective use of space is extremely important in establishing the mood or feeling of the dance. The use of space may produce a feeling of limited or boundless energy. The amount of space used affects the movement by either limiting or expanding the movement potential of body parts. Changing direction and levels adds interest to the dancers' performance. The effective use of pathways, or floor pattern as it is referred to in dance, can contribute to the audience appeal. The careful consideration of the arrangement and interaction of the dancers also adds to the dance.

As dancers move in space, they define the space to the audience, whether the movements are performed in self or general space. Children need to develop an awareness of their own personal space and the surrounding space that may be used.

Moving with others increases an understanding of changing relationships with others or objects. Moving in space helps children increase the awareness of their own movement potential through the exploration of self and general space and the use of direction, level, range, and pathway to express ideas.

Force

Through the study of body movements children develop their awareness of internal force, which their

bodies create, and external force, gravity, to which their body must respond. The control of these forces gives quality to the actions of the body. The child moves in a purposeful and controlled manner as the dance movements are performed. Force may vary from the apparent absence of force in complete relaxation to the production of a force, the maximum the body can produce. In each body movement, force in one or more body parts is produced as the body moves through space and in response to the pull of gravity on the body.

Force may be created and used in a variety of ways. It may be smooth, of a sustained nature, in which there is a constant smooth flow of energy. It may be percussive or jerky, in which the force appears to come suddenly, in an explosive manner, or it may be vibratory or shakey and result in a fluttering, staccato, back and forth action. As the body moves in dance it may give the appearance of lightness, weightlessness, heaviness, or strength. The control of these qualities is essential in conveying the ideas to the audience.

The activities listed in the previous sections may be taken as a study in themselves or as a part of the developing awareness of the body's movement potential.

Time

Time includes the study of tempo, fast to slow, and the study of the rhythmic elements related to music. The rhythmic elements were described in Chapter 17. Since little time is spent on rhythmic elements in other aspects of the program, they should be given attention in the creative dance experience.

The children should develop an awareness of the rhythm of their own body actions and also of the movement that is performed with an external or imposed rhythm, such as moving with another person or moving to an accompaniment.

Moving in response to the underlying beat, rhythmic pattern, and phrasing may be further enhanced through the following activities:

Clap time to the underlying beat, move in place, or move in space.

Perform locomotor or nonlocomotor movements to various meters, including 2/4, 3/4, 4/4, and 6/8 time.

Use rhythm instruments to establish the underlying beat for movement.

Clap the rhythmic pattern of your name. A nursery rhyme. A commercial. Repeat with locomotor or nonlocomotor movements.

Clap the underlying beat of a nursery rhyme. Now clap the rhythmic pattern. Clap one and move to the other.

Combine even and uneven rhythms by clapping. Now move to the pattern.

Make up a rhythmic pattern and plan a movement sequence to go with it, adding other concepts as appropriate.

IDEAS FOR DEVELOPING DANCE LESSONS

Holidays	Nature	Ocean
Halloween	Trees	Waves
Columbus Day	Bugs	Surf
Christmas	Worms	Sand
Valentine's Day	Wildflowers	Seashells
Thanksgiving	Squirrels	Jelly fish
	Porcupines	Crabs
	Skunks	Fish
		Whales
		Seaweed

Seasons	Emotions	Words
Fall	Happy	Ooze
Spring	Sad	Squirm
Winter	Angry	Crash
Summer	Devilish	Screech
	Playful	Tingling
	Jealous	Swishing
	Anxious	Flutter
	Afraid	Creepy
	Lazy	

Texture	Substances	Rhyming words
Soft	Glue	Bright, fight, light
Scratchy	Ice	Blue, glue, moo
Slick	Whip cream	Ball, call, fall
Smooth	Hot fudge	Cool, pool, rule
Sticky	Jello	
Rough	Peanut butter	
Sharp	Lemons	
Fuzzy	Cotton candy	
Hot		
Cold		

Clap the phrases of a piece of music. Now clap the first, move on the second, clap the third, etc.

Move in general space on one phrase, and move in place on the next.

With a partner, one move on the first phrase, the other on the second, continuing to alternate moving on each following phrase.

Contrast movements. On the first phrase take big movements, on the second small movements.

Change level, direction, or pathway on each phrase.

Clap on the accented beat.

Emphasize the step on the accented beat.

Try accenting beat 1, then 2, 3, 4. Accent beats 1 and 3 or 2 and 4.

Move on the accented beat, clap on the others.

Do a nonlocomotor movement on the accent and a locomotor movement on the unaccented beats.

Combine a series of locomotor movements and clap the rhythmic pattern.

Divide into groups assigned whole, half, quarter, and eighth notes, moving to your specified beat as the drum is played. Now try it again as the music plays.

Move in step with a partner with no accompaniment.

In groups, move as if singing a round.

Imagery

The use of imagery may enhance or prevent creative movement. If used too early in the experience, it may limit the movement possibilities for children. But if used after there has been adequate time for exploration of possible movements, it may serve as a stimulus for creative activity. Joyce[6] suggests that images may (1) lead to a movement, (2) arise from a movement, or (3) be the basis for moving. In the first the teacher may use an image to describe the type of movement desired, such as describing a round shape as being round like a ball. Images that arise from movement might be used to develop an idea. For instance, when working on jumping, the teacher might ask the children, "What do you know that jumps?" The teacher might use a story, poem, or theme to stimulate creative movement activity. Possible categories and examples for the use of imagery in developing creative dance lessons are given in the box below.

In selecting appropriate images, the age of the children and their immediate experiences must be considered. Young children enjoy working with nursery rhymes because of their familiarity, their rhyming nature, and also the even meter. Humorous stories or poems are another favorite. Older children may enjoy poetry with an irregular meter, which allows them to establish their own sense of time.

Using Materials To Stimulate Creative Movement

Materials or props may be used to stimulate creative movement. At certain ages some children may be extremely self-conscious when working on their own. The use of some prop may help them to overcome these feelings. Scarves, ribbons, elastic ropes, feathers, and pompoms may be used effectively in dance experiences. An umbrella, a rolling pin, a sponge, or a top are a few of the common objects that might be used to stimulate creative movements.

SUMMARY

Creative dance experiences for children provide further development of movement skills and movement content. Whereas other aspects of the curriculum concentrate on the development of functional movement, creative dance develops movement as a means of personal expression. In creating dances children use body shape and locomotor and nonlocomotor movements as they move in space, with force, and in time.

Creative dance can be a valuable experience in the physical education program. Since it is the only area of the curriculum dealing with aesthetic education, it makes an important contribution to the development of the total child.

REFERENCES

1. Dimondstein, G.: Children dance in the classroom, New York, 1971, The Macmillan Co.

2. Dimondstein, G.: Moving in the real and feeling worlds: a rationale for dance in education, JOPERD 54(7):42, September 1983.

3. Docherty, D.: Organizing and developing movement ideas, JOPERD 53(3):51, March 1982.

4. Fleming, G. editor: Children's dance, Reston, Va., 1981, AAHPERD.

5. Jensen, M.: Composing and guiding creative movement, JOPERD 54(1):85, January 1983.

6. Joyce, M.: First steps in teaching creative dance to children, ed. 2, Palo Alto, Calif., 1980, Mayfield Publishing Co.

7. Logsdon, B., and others: Physical education for children: a focus on the teaching process, ed. 2, Philadelphia, 1984, Lea & Febiger.

8. McColl, S.: Dance as aesthetic education, JOPER 50(7):44, September 1979.

9. Russell, J.: Creative dance in the primary school, London, 1968, MacDonald and Evans, Ltd.

10. Speakman, M.: Teaching modern educational dance, JOPER 49(7):51, September 1978.

11. Trammell, P.: Poetry and dance for children, JOPERD 53(7):75, October 1982.

12. Winter, S.: Creative rhythmic movement for children of elementary school age, Dubuque, Iowa, 1975, William C. Brown Co.

13. Zirulnik, A., and Young, J.: Help them "jump for joy," JOPER 50(7):43, September 1979.

ADDITIONAL READINGS

Hanson, M.: The right of children to experiences in dance/movement/arts, JOPER **50**(7):42, September 1979.
The contributions of dance to the aesthetic education of children.

Minton, S.: Improvisation, JOPERD **52**(7):74, September 1981.
The use of movement exploration or improvisation to discover the body's potential for movement, enhance creativity, and work with others.

Stenson, S.: Evaluate the child: issues for dance educators, JOPER **50**(7):53, September 1979.
The issue of evaluating dance experiences and its use in the learning process to provide feedback for developing self-awareness.

Wiseman, E.: Process not product: guidelines for adding creative dance to the elementary school curriculum, JOPER **50**(7):47, September 1979.
Steps for developing children's dance lessons, including an introductory activity, body actions, skill focus, and group interactions.

Woodruff, J.: Improvisation for the inhibited, JOPERD **56**(1):36, January 1985.
Using improvisation to expand the dance experience and build confidence using contact with others and props.

Wyckoff, W.: Movement programs and aesthetic education, JOPER **51**(4):65, April 1980.
The goals of aesthetic education and the nature of movement programs for meeting these goals.

SINGING GAMES AND AMERICAN AND INTERNATIONAL FOLK DANCE

CHAPTER OBJECTIVES

1 To define the objectives for singing games and American and international folk dance at the elementary school level

2 To discuss suggestions for teaching dances and dance steps and to provide management strategies for dividing the group into partners

3 To analyze dance steps and figures and to define dance terminology, formations, and partner relationships

4 To identify the movement concepts important to success in performing dances

5 To describe a progression of singing games and American and international folk dance to be included at the elementary school level

The dances included in this section represent the potential for a lifetime of activity. Beyond the school years the opportunity to continue to dance may be found in the many folk dance groups, recreation programs, as well as at weddings and other festive occasions.

SINGING GAMES AND AMERICAN AND INTERNATIONAL FOLK DANCE FOR ELEMENTARY SCHOOL CHILDREN

Dance provides the vigorous activity needed for optimum cardiovascular development. Response to musical accompaniment requires the danger to maintain a consistent activity level over the duration of the dance. It is not uncommon for dancers to continue until they are virtually ready to drop. Coordination, balance, and agility are other fitness components important for success in these activities.

In addition, these experiences increase children's understanding of people of other lands, as well as of their own national heritage. The dance unit is often integrated with classroom activities in social studies.

Folk and similar dance activities require partners and small and large groups to work together. Children must be able to adjust their movements to those of other dancers to move effectively with a partner and maintain appropriate relationships with others while moving in different formations.

The progression of activities provides the opportunity for children to learn increasingly difficult dance steps and figures that must be executed to the imposed rhythm of the accompaniment. Increased body awareness and effective use of space and movement qualities are the results of these dance experiences.

The objectives to be emphasized at each level during the elementary school years may be found in the box below.

Several kinds of dances make up the elementary school dance experience:

SINGING GAMES AND AMERICAN AND INTERNATIONAL FOLK DANCE OBJECTIVES IN THE ELEMENTARY SCHOOL*

	LEVEL			
OBJECTIVE	I	II	III	IV
To develop locomotor skills (walk, run, skip, gallop, slide)	———————	------------------------		
To develop nonlocomotor skills	———————	------------------------		
To respond to the underlying beat while executing locomotor and nonlocomotor movements	—————————————————			-----------
To respond to musical phrasing	—————————————————			-----------
To combine locomotor and nonlocomotor movements in time to the music		———————————		-----------
To differentiate even and uneven rhythm	———————	-------------------------		
To learn and use basic dance steps		—————————————————		
To work with a partner and the group in executing dances		———————————		-----------
To move in space maintaining relationships with partners and others in the group	—————————————————			-----------
To vary the range of movement as needed		———————————		-------
To change direction and/or pathway in time to the music	—————————————————			-----------
To control force in moving with another person		———————————		-----------
To change speed smoothly in time to the music		———————————————		-----------

*The solid lines represent emphasis of an objective, the dotted lines, continued use of the mastered objective.

Folk dance: A folk dance is a traditional dance of the people, handed down from generation to generation. Folk dances were often associated with the customs, rituals, and occupations of the people but are now mostly performed for social or recreational purposes. Since American culture is relatively young, these dances are primarily dances of other lands.

Singing games: Singing games are activities for young children that are often the result of putting children's poems to music and imitating the actions described in the song.

American dances: American dances are the dances of colonial America in which popular country tunes of the period were used.

Square dance: Square dances are dances of American origin that are executed from a four couple square set. Since many of the movements used are relatively new, they are not considered to be true folk dances.

SUGGESTIONS FOR TEACHING

Steps in teaching a dance:

1. Teach or review the dance steps and/or figures to be used.
2. Give the name and origin of the dance and any other background information.
3. Teach the words to singing games and other dances that have words before beginning instruction in the dance.
4. Before explaining the dance, arrange the children in the formation to be used. This enables the children to visualize the partner and group

relationships, which will help them in understanding the dance.

5. Break the dance down into logical parts, and have the children move through the dance. If the dance is long, it may be necessary to work with one part at a time, putting it to music, moving on to the next part, putting it with the first, and so on.

6. Listen to the music, and talk the class through the dance. Everyone listens but does not actually do the dance.

7. Try it with the music, slowing the music down if necessary. Move to the appropriate tempo when the children are ready.

Teaching a dance step:

1. Select the best formation in which everyone can see.

2. Demonstrate the dance step, and talk through it as you move. Always move in the same path as the students, even if you are facing them.

3. Have the children first try the step individually and when ready practice with a partner.

4. It may be necessary to slow down the music in the initial phase of learning. As the children begin to master the dance, the music may be gradually brought up to tempo.

5. Put the steps into a movement sequence.

6. Add a change of direction, speed, and so forth.

Methods of selecting and working with partners:

1. Move the children quickly into partners.

2. Change partners often, so children have the opportunity to dance with as many other children as possible.

3. Avoid having the children choose their own partners at random, as it may be embarassing for them; one or two children may be left out and this becomes a threatening situation for them.

4. Several methods may be used for getting partners.
   a. Have the children form a circle or a line. Usually they will be next to someone with whom they would like to dance. You may then designate the partners.
   b. Have the class form two lines facing each other. The children across from each other are partners.
   c. Partners may also be selected by forming a double circle, each circle moving in the opposite direction. On the signal to stop, children closest to each other (one from each circle) are partners.

5. Below the fifth-grade level, do not insist on boy-girl partners. Dance is to be enjoyed, and at some ages students may feel uncomfortable with the opposite sex.

6. Adjust dance positions when necessary. It may be uncomfortable for a short boy to use the varsouvienne position with a tall girl.

7. It is often unnecessary for children to hold hands with partners, especially when moving around the circle. Do not make physical contact mandatory. At some ages this may lead to negative feelings about dance.

8. When boy-girl partners are not used, the use of pinnies, sashes, or vests will help discriminate partners. This is particularly helpful when teaching such figures as the grand right and left.

9. The closed dance position assumes the ability to lead. Since elementary school children find leading to be difficult, dances requiring this position should be modified to use a position more within the children's capability.

10. Some dances do not require partners or may be modified to groups of three. These dances work well at the beginning of the lesson or unit.

Effective teaching:

1. Since children are eager to participate, select dances that may be mastered in a reasonable amount of time.

2. Many of the dances for young children can be learned by merely imitating your actions, so formal instruction may not be necessary.

3. Teach dances in phrases rather than counting steps. Encourage listening to the music. Teach the children to listen for changes in the music that may indicate changes in steps, directions, and so forth.

4. The beginning of the dance and each sequence should be cued just before the time the children will begin or change step, direction, and so forth. Give a starting signal, such as, "One, two, ready, go." Use key words to minimize talking.

5. During the learning phase, it is helpful if the teacher moves with the children, either alone or with a child as a partner.

6. Stress good style. Encourage the children to take short and light steps. Some American dances, such as square dances, use a gliding step, with the feet moving close to the ground. Skipping is not appropriate in this

form of American dance.

7. Vary the pace of the lesson. Dance is an invigorating activity and children will require a chance to rest. Ways to accomplish this might be to allow a group to show their dance to the class while the others observe or for you to review or discuss the background information of the dance.
8. Add the accompaniment as soon as possible.
9. Allow sufficient time to review dances. New dances should be reviewed soon after the initial learning period. Children enjoy doing the dances they have learned in succeeding lessons.
10. Plan for variety to ensure a well-rounded dance experience. Include dances from different countries, as well as those with a variety of steps, figures, and formations.
11. Enhance creativity by giving the children an opportunity to make up their own dances or to modify those they have learned.
12. Another way to introduce dances in the upper elementary grades is to let the children read the dance instructions and see how they would interpret the dance.

DANCE SKILLS

The locomotor skills used in the dances for children are analyzed in Chapter 11.

Dance Steps

Balance: A step forward or backward, followed by a closing step with the opposite foot done in 2/4 or 3/4 rhythm. The weight remains on the stepping foot.

Count: 1, 2(3).

Footwork: Step right forward (count 1). Close left to right (count 2). Hold (count 3).

Count: 1, 2(3).

Footwork: Step back left (count 1). Close right to left (count 2). Hold (count 3).

Bleking: A light springing step in which children hop on one foot while extending the opposite foot forward, heel touching the floor, and toes up. Repeat hopping on the other foot.

Count: 1, 2.

Footwork: Hop right, extend left (count 1). Hop left, extend right (count 2).

Grapevine: A step sideward alternately crossing the feet in front or in back.

Count: 1, 2.

Footwork: Step right to the side (count 1). Cross the left in front of the right (count 2).

Count: 1, 2.

Footwork: Step right to the side (count 1). Cross the left behind the right (count 2).

Polka: A hop, step, close, step, executed in uneven rhythm.

Count: And 1 and 2.

Footwork: Hop right (And). Step left (1). Close

right to left (and). Step left (2).

Count: And 1 and 2.

Footwork: Hop left (And). Step right (1). Close left to right (and). Step right (2).

The polka is a difficult step for children in the closed dance position. To simplify the polka step for elementary school children, a face to face, back to back polka may be used. To teach the polka the following sequence is suggested:

1. Children face a partner with one hand joined (right to left). The movement begins toward the unjoined hands.
2. Children take eight slides facing their partners. Continuing to move in the same path, they turn so that partners are back to back and take eight slides. Repeat the face to face and back to back slides until everyone is comfortable with the changes.
3. Reduce the number of slides to four and repeat as above.
4. Reduce the number of slides to two and repeat. (This is the polka step. The hop is taken on the up beat as the children change direction. The step, close, step follows to the side.)

Schottishe: Three steps followed by a hop taken on the foot taking the last step, executed in even rhythm.

Count: 1, 2, 3, 4.

Footwork: Step right (1). Step left (2). Step right (3). Hop right (4).

Count: 1, 2, 3, 4.

Footwork: Step left (1). Step right (2). Step left (3). Hop left (4).

Step-hop: A step on one foot followed by a hop on the same foot, executed in even rhythm. The next step-hop is taken on the opposite foot.

Count: 1, 2, 1, 2.

Footwork: Step right (1), hop right (2). Step left (1), hop left (2).

The step-hop is difficult for elementary school children. This may be because the skip also uses a step-hop combination but in an uneven rhythm, and it is difficult for children to adjust the step-hop back to an even rhythm.

Two-step: A step, together, step, in uneven rhythm.

Count: 1 and 2.

Footwork: Step right (1). Close left to right (and). Step right (2).

Count: 1 and 2.

Footwork: Step left (1). Close right to left (and). Step left (2).

The two-step is difficult for children, probably because of its uneven rhythm and the failure to transfer the body weight on the close step.

Waltz: A series of three steps taken in an even rhythm to 3/4 time.

Count: 1, 2, 3.

Footwork: Step left forward (1). Step right to the side (2). Close left to right (3).

Count: 1, 2, 3.

Footwork: Step right forward (1). Step left to side (2). Close right to left (3).

Most children have had relatively little experience with 3/4 time. For elementary school children, the waltz step will be easiest to perform in an open dance position. The waltz step may be done as a waltz run, in which the dancer takes three small, even steps forward (without a closing step).

Dance Figures

Allemande left (right):

Position: In a circle or square set with the boy's partner on his right and his corner lady on his left.

Directions: Face your corner. Take your corner's left hand in your left. Walk forward and around your corner. Drop hands and continue to move back to place.

Circle left (right):

Position: Group holds hands in a single circle.

Directions: Move clockwise (counterclockwise) in a circle.

Do-Si-Do:

Position: Children face their partners, with arms bent and held at chest height with their hands on their opposite elbows.

Directions: Walk forward, passing left shoulders with your partner. Continuing to face forward, move around your partner and back to place, passing right shoulders on the return.

Elbow swing (right or left):

Position: Children face partners, extending appropriate arm.

Directions: Hook elbows and turn in a small circle.

Grand right and left:

Position: In a circle or square set.

Directions: Facing your partner, give your right hand to your partner. Walk forward past your partner, giving your left hand to the next person. Continue in this manner, alternately giving the right and left hands to the persons you meet until you meet your partner.

Honor your partner (corner):

Position: Facing partner (corner).

Directions: Acknowledge partner (corner). Boys bow and girls courtsey. (Great variation in this figure exists throughout the United States.)

Ladies chain:

Position: In a square or two couple set with the boy's partner on his right.

Directions: Facing the opposite couple, girls move forward, giving their right hand to the opposite girl. Moving past each other, girls give their left hand to the opposite boy, who puts his right hand on the girl's waist and turns them around to face the opposite couple. Girls repeat the move, giving their right hand to each other and their left to their partner, who then turns them with the boy's right hand on their waist.

Promenade:

Position: Partners stand side by side with the girl on the boy's right. The boy holds the girl's right hand in his right and her left hand in his left.

Directions: Dance is counterclockwise around the set or circle ending in their original position.

Right and left through:

Position: A square or two couple set.

Directions: Two couples walk forward with four steps passing through the opposite couple, passing right shoulders with the dancer directly across from you. Boys take your partner's left hand in yours and put your right hand at her waist. Both turn to face the other couple. Walk forward again passing through the opposite couple, passing left shoulders with the person directly across from you. Turn once more with joined left hands and boys' right hands at the girls' waists.

Sashay:

Position: Facing the center of the circle.

Directions: Move once around partner. Boys move sideways to the right and behind the girl, girls move sideways to the left and in front of the boy.

Star (right or left):

Position: Face the center of the circle or set. Extend right (left) hand into the center joining with the hands of the others. Individuals may hold the wrist of the person in front as they join hands.

Directions: Move clockwise in circle, ending back in place.

MOVEMENT CONCEPTS FOR SINGING GAMES AND AMERICAN AND INTERNATIONAL FOLK DANCE

The movement content to be emphasized in these dance activities is summarized in the box at right. These concepts should be practiced as a part of the learning process for each dance. Special attention should be given to them during the learning phase and before the performance of the dances.

TERMINOLOGY
General

Clockwise: A circular movement in the pathway in which the hands of a clock move.

Counterclockwise: A circular movement in the pathway opposite to clockwise.

Line of direction: Counterclockwise.

Reverse line of direction: Clockwise.

FORMATIONS

Single circle, all facing the center: Dancers form a circle, facing the center, with or without partners. See Figure 19-1, *A*.

Single circle, all facing counterclockwise (or clockwise): Dancers form a circle and all face counterclockwise (or clockwise). See Figure 19-1, *B*.

Single circle, partners facing: Dancers form a circle facing their partners. See Figure 19-1, *C*.

Double circle, partners facing: Dancers form concentric circles facing their partners. The boy is on the inside circle. See Figure 19-1, *D*.

Double circle, partners facing clockwise: Dancers form concentric circles with their partners. All face

CONCEPTS FOR SINGING GAMES AND AMERICAN AND INTERNATIONAL FOLK DANCE

BODY AWARENESS

Body awareness is important in the execution of locomotor and nonlocomotor skills, traditional dance steps, and figures.

SPACE

1. To move in space in relation to partners and others while moving apart and together
2. To move in space in relation to a partner and a group while maintaining the formation and appropriate spacing
3. To change direction smoothly and in time to the music
4. To change or maintain pathways in time to the music
5. To vary the range of movement within the space available and to move with a partner in various formations

MOVEMENT QUALITIES

1. Force:
   a. To move softly to the music
   b. To use appropriate force when moving with a partner
2. Time:
   a. To execute locomotor and nonlocomotor movements to an imposed rhythm
   b. To respond to even and uneven rhythm
   c. To move in musical phrases
   d. To change speed smoothly as the tempo changes
3. Flow:
   a. To combine or change locomotor and/or nonlocomotor movements smoothly

---

clockwise. Inside hands may be joined. The boy is usually on the inside circle. See Figure 19-1, *E*.

Two-couple sets: A double circle of partners alternately facing clockwise and counterclockwise. The boy's partner is on his right. See Figure 19-1, *F*.

Longways set: Two parallel lines of dancers (usually no more than six in each line). Each dancer has a partner in the opposite line. The boys are in one line, the girls in the other. See Figure 19-1, *G*.

Quadrille or square set: A set of four couples forming a square. The boy has his partner on his right. Two opposing couples are the head couples; the other two couples are the side couples. Couples may be numbered one through four. See Figure 19-1, *H*.

PARTNER RELATIONSHIPS

Unless otherwise indicated the boy always has his partner on his right. Unless otherwise indicated, when couples form a double circle, the boy is in the inside circle.

Promenade position: Partners stand side by side with both hands joined (right to right and left to left). See Figure 19-2, *A*.

Open position: Partners stand side by side with inside hands joined. See Figure 19-2, *B*.

Skaters' position: Partners stand side by side facing forward. The boy holds the girl's right hand in his left in front of them, and each puts the remaining hand behind the other's back. See Figure 19-2, *C*.

Groups of three: Groups of three dancers scattered in the area or arranged in a circle all facing the same path. Usually one boy between two girls. See Figure 19-2, *D*.

Shoulder-waist position: Partners face. The boy places both hands at the girl's waist, and the girl places both hands on the boy's shoulders. See Figure 19-2, *E*.

Banjo position: Partners face and stand with right

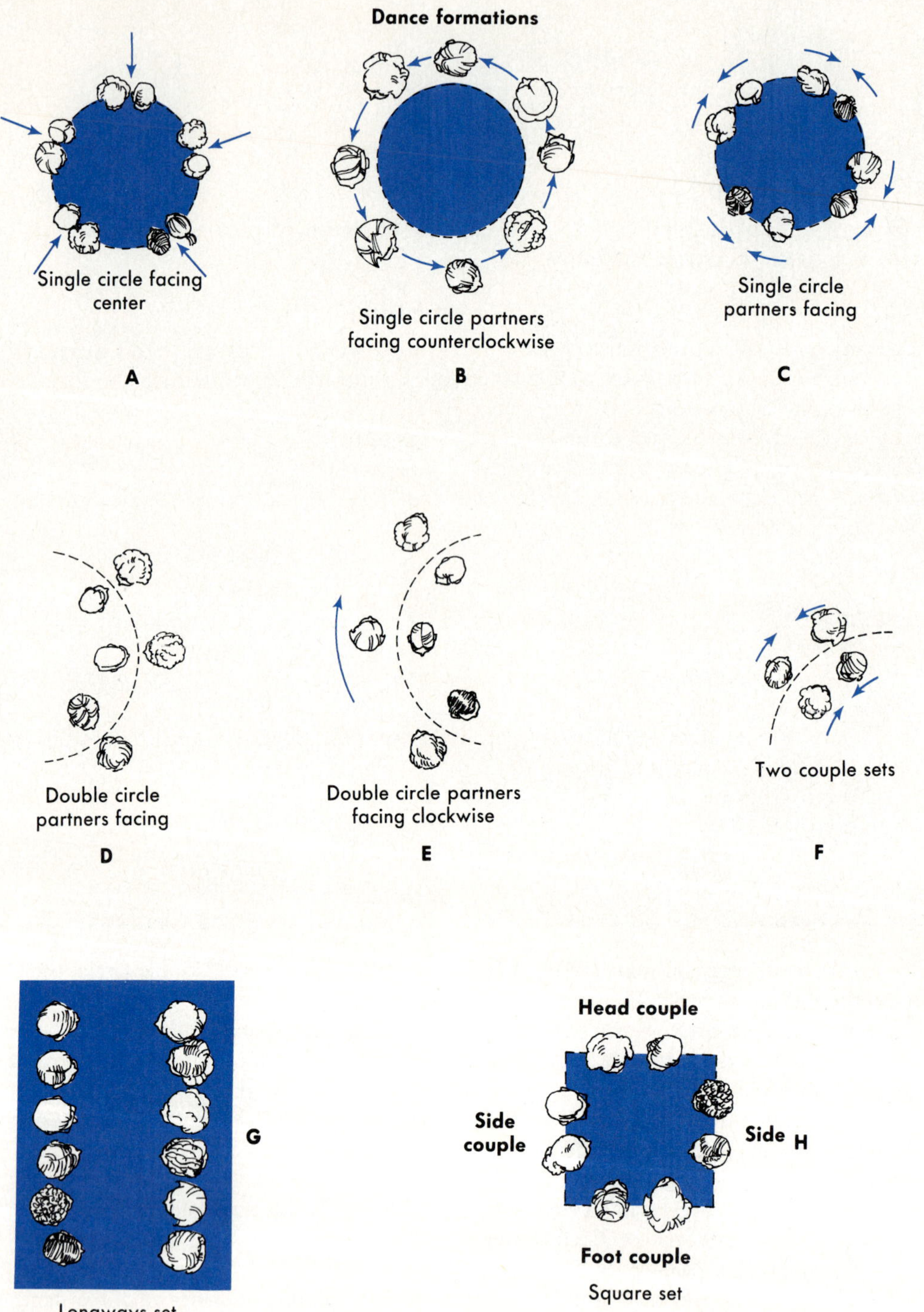

Figure 19-1

Formations for dance activities. **A,** Single circle, facing the center. **B,** Single circle, facing counterclockwise. **C,** Single circle, partners facing. **D,** Double circle, partners facing. **E,** Double circle, partners facing clockwise. **F,** Two-couple sets. **G,** Longways set. **H,** Square set.

Partner relationships

Promenade position
A

Open position
B

Skaters position
C

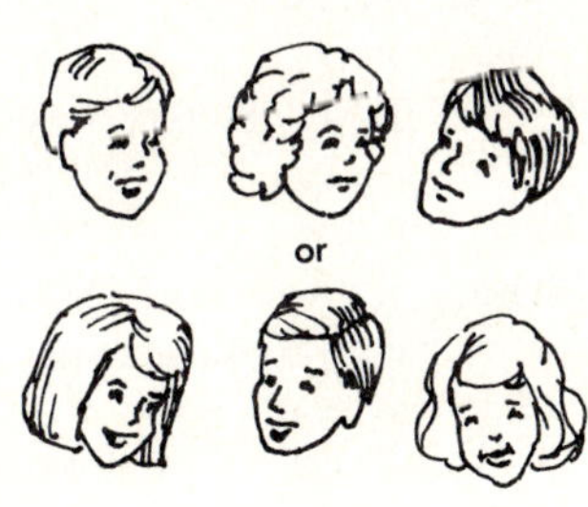

or

Group of 3
D

Shoulder-waist position
E

Figure 19-2

Partner relationships for dance activities. **A,** Promenade position. **B,** Open position.
C, Skaters' position. **D,** Groups of three. **E,** Shoulder-waist position.   *Continued.*

Banjo position
F

Side-car position
G

Varsouvienne position
H

Figure 19-2, cont'd

F, Banjo position. **G,** Sidecar position. **H,** Varsouvienne position.

hips adjacent. The girl's right hand is in the boy's left and her left hand on his shoulder. The boy's right hand is at the girl's waist. See Figure 19-2, *F*.

Side car position: Similar to banjo position, but with left hips adjacent. See Figure 19-2, *G*.

Varsouvienne position: Partners stand side by side facing forward. The boy holds the girl's left in his left, to the side, and her right in his right, slightly above her shoulder. See Figure 19-2, *H*.

SINGING GAMES

BLUEBIRD

Level: I.
Origin: American.
Record: Folkcraft: 1180.
Formation: Single circle, hands joined, and facing the center; one child—the bluebird—stands outside the circle.
Skills: Walk.
Song:
Verse: Bluebird, bluebird through my window.
Bluebird, bluebird, through my window.
Bluebird, bluebird through my window.
Hi diddle, dum dum dee.

Chorus: Take a little boy (girl) and tap him (her) on the shoulder.

Take a little boy (girl) and tap him (her) on the shoulder.
Take a little boy (girl) and tap him (her) on the shoulder.
Hi diddle, dum dum dee.

Action: During the verse the children in the circle raise their joined hands, forming arches through which the bluebird weaves in and out.

At the end of the verse the bluebird stands behind one of the circle players.

During the chorus, the bluebird taps the circle child lightly on the shoulders with both hands. This child becomes the new bluebird when the verse begins again. The old bluebird remains behind the new bluebird, with hands on the new bluebird's shoulders, forming a train. As the chorus continues, the bluebird train moves in various ways in the center of the circle.

Repeat the dance again, adding a new bluebird to the train.

Teaching Suggestions: To avoid a long chain, it may be advisable with young children to begin with a new bluebird once the train has three persons. To maximize activity begin with several bluebirds.

DID YOU EVER SEE A LASSIE

Level: I.
Origin: Scottish
Record: Folkcraft: 1183.

Singing games

Name	Origin	Formation	Basic steps	Suggestions/modifications	Page	Record	Level
Bluebird	American	Single circle, all facing the center	Walk	Begin with a new bluebird when the chain is made up of three persons	330	Folkcraft: 1180	I
Did You Ever See A Lassie	Scottish	Single circle, all facing the center	Walk	Encourage original movements by imitating animals, varying locomotor and/or nonlocomotor movements, and so forth	330	Folkcraft: 1183	I
Gay Musicians	French	Single circle, all facing the center	Walk	Have the children suggest other instruments they might imitate	332	Merit Audio Visual: 1041	I
Looby Lou	English	Single circle, all facing the center, hands joined	Skip	Have the children suggest other body parts they could move in the dance	332	Folkcraft: 1102, 1184 Victor: 20214	I
Oats, Peas, Beans, and Barley Grow	American	Single circle, all facing clockwise; one child, the farmer, is in the center	Walk, skip		332	Folkcraft: 1182 Folkdancer: FD34 World of Fun: 2	I
Pease Porridge Hot	English	Double circle, partners facing	Run		333	Folkcraft: 1190	I
A Hunting We Will Go	English	Longways set	Skip, arch	Sets should be of no more than four to six couples so the dance can be completed within the verse and chorus	333	Folkcraft: 1191 Victor: 45-5064, 22759	II
Go Round and Round the Village	English	Single circle, all facing the center, hands joined	Walk, skip		333	Merit Audio Visual: 1041	II
Grand Old Duke of York	English	Longways set	Slide, cast off, arch		334	Folkcraft: 1191	II
Hokey Pokey	English	Single circle, all facing the center; or a single circle of partners	Walk	As a mixer, one person moving clockwise to a new partner on "And you turn yourself about"	334	Capitol: 6026 MacGregor: 669, 6995	II
Jolly Is the Miller	American	Double circle, all facing counterclockwise	March		335	Folkcraft: 1192 Victor: 45-5067, 20214	II
Shoo Fly	American	Single circle of partners all facing the center, hands joined	Walk, skip	If boy-girl partners are not used, designate one person in each pair with a pinnie or colored sash	335	Folkcraft: 1102, 1185	II
The Snail		An open circle, all facing the center, hands joined, leader on the right	Walk		335	Folkcraft: 1198	II

Formation: Single circle, all facing the center, hands joined; one child in the center.

Skills: Walk and other locomotor and nonlocomotor movements.

Song:

Verse: Did you ever see a lassie, a lassie, a lassie?
Did you ever see a lassie go this way and that?
Go this way and that way. Go this way and that way.
Did you ever see a lassie go this way and that?

Action: Lines 1 and 2: Circle to the left, singing.
Lines 3 and 4: Center child chooses an action to perform, and the children in the circle imitate it.

Teaching Suggestions: Alternate the children in the center, substituting "laddie" when a boy is in the center.

GAY MUSICIANS

Level: I.

Origin: French.

Record: Merit Audio Visual: 1041.

Formation: Single circle, all facing the center.

Skills: Walk and imitate instruments.

Song:

Chorus: I am a gay musician. From (name of town) I come.

Verse: I can play sweet music upon my little drum. Drrum, dum dum. Drrum, dum dum. Drrum, dum dum. Drrum, dum dum. Skipping and playing. Everywhere straying.

Repeat the above chorus and verse.
Repeat the above substituting other instruments, such as:

I can play sweet music upon my violin. Fiddle dee dee. Fiddle dee dee. . . .
I can play sweet music upon my clarinet. Doodle dee doo. Doodle dee doo. . . .
I can play sweet music upon my accordion. Squeeze, squeeze, squeeze. Squeeze, squeeze, squeeze. . . .
I can play sweet music upon my fine trumpet. Tootle, doodle, doo. Tootle, doodle doo. . . .
I can play sweet music upon my big bass viol. Brrum fitz, fitz. Brrum fitz, fitz. . . .

For the last verse each of the children imitate the instrument of their choice.

Action: During the chorus the children walk counterclockwise in a circle. For each of the verses the children stand facing the center of the circle and imitate playing the instrument of the verse.

Teaching Suggestions: Have the children suggest other instruments they could imitate.

LOOBY LOU

Level: I.

Origin: English.

Record: Victor: 20214; Folkcraft: 1102, 1184.

Formation: Single circle, all facing the center with hands joined.

Skills: Skip.

Song:

Chorus: Here we go looby lou. Here we go looby light. Here we go looby lou. All on a Saturday night.

Verse 1: I put my right hand in. I put my right hand out. I give my right hand a shake, shake, shake. And turn myself about.

Verse 2: I put my left hand in. I put my left hand out. . . .

Verse 3: I put my right foot in. I put my right foot out. . . .

Verse 4: I put my left foot in. I put my left foot out. . . .

Verse 5: I put my head in. I put my head out. . . .

Verse 6: I put my whole self in. I put my whole self out. . . .

Action: Chorus: Children skip around the circle to the left.
Verses: The body parts named are moved as suggested by the words of each verse, turning in place on the last line.

Teaching Suggestions: Have the children think of other body parts they could move in the dance.

OATS, PEAS, BEANS, AND BARLEY GROW

Level: I.

Origin: American.

Record: Folkcraft: 1191; World of Fun: 2; Folkdancer: FD 34.

Formation: Single circle, all facing clockwise; one child, the farmer, is in the center of the circle.

Skills: Walk and skip.

Song:

Verse 1: Oats, peas, beans, and barley grow.
Oats, peas, beans, and barley grow.
Do you or I or anyone know?
How oats, peas, beans, and barley grow?

Verse 2: First the farmer sows his seed.
Then he stands and takes his ease.
Stamps his foot, and claps his hands.
And turns around to view the land.

Verse 3: Waiting for a partner. Waiting for a partner.
So open the ring and take one in. While we all gaily dance and sing.

Verse 4: So now you're married you must obey.
You must be true to all you say.

You must be wise, you must be good.
And help your wife to chop the wood.

Action: Verse 1: All sing, clapping hands, while moving to the left. End facing the center.
Verse 2: Pretend to sow the seed. Then stand with arms folded. Stamp your foot, then clap you hands and turn around in place, shading eyes as if viewing the land.
Verse 3: All stand and sing while the farmer walks around in the ring, choosing a partner on the last line.
Verse 4: With hands joined, all skip to the left. The two persons inside the circle join hands in the skaters' position and move around inside the circle in the opposite direction. The person chosen becomes the new farmer, and the original farmer joins the circle as the dance is repeated.

PEASE PORRIDGE HOT

Level: I.
Origin: English.
Record: Folkcraft: 1190.
Formation: Double circle, partners facing.
Skills: Run.
Song:
Verse: Pease porridge hot. Pease porridge cold.
Pease porridge in the pot. Nine days old.
Some like it hot. Some like it cold.
Some like it in the pot. Nine days old.

Action: The song is sung twice.
First time—Line 1: Clap own hands to thighs; clap own hands together; clap partners hands. Repeat.

Line 2: Clap hands to thighs; clap own hands together; clap right hand to partners right; clap own hands together. Clap partners left hand; clap own hands together; clap both hands to partners hands.
Lines 3 and 4: Repeat the actions of the first two lines.
Second time—Partners join hands and run around in a small circle to the right for the first two lines. Reverse direction on the last two lines.

A HUNTING WE WILL GO

Level: II.
Origin: English.
Record: Folkcraft: 1191, Victor: 45-5064, 22759.
Formation: Longways set.
Skills: Skip, arch.
Song:
Verse: Oh, a hunting we will go. A hunting we will go.
We'll catch a fox and put him in the box.
And then we'll let him go.

Chorus: Tra, la, la, la, la, la, la. Tra, la, la, la, la, la.
Tra, la, la, la, la, la, la, la. Tra, la, la, la, la, la.

Action: Verse: Head couple joins inside hands and skips between the lines to the end of the set. They change hands and return to the head of the set. All other children clap while the head couple is active.
Chorus: The head couple skips around the left side of the set, with all couples following. When the head couple reaches the end of the set, they form an arch by facing each other, joining two hands and holding them high in the air. All other couples proceed through the arch reforming the set with a new head couple.
Teaching Suggestions: The sets should be formed with four to six couples to enable the dancers to stay with the music.

GO ROUND AND ROUND THE VILLAGE

Level: II.
Origin: English.
Record: Merit Audio Visual: 1041.
Formation: Single circle, all facing the center with hands joined; one or more dancers scattered outside the circle.
Skills: Walk, skip.
Song:
Verse 1: Go round and round the village.
Go round and round the village.
Go round and round the village.
As we have done before.

Verse 2: Go in and out the window.
Go in and out the window. . . .

Verse 3: Now stand and face your partner.
Now stand and face your partner. . . .

Verse 4: Now kneel to show you love (like) her (him).
Now kneel to show you love (like) her (him). . . .

Verse 5: Now follow me to London.

Now follow me to London. . . .

Verse 6: Shake hands before you leave me.
Shake hands before you leave me. . . .

Action: Verse 1: Circle players walk clockwise, while those on the outside walk counterclockwise.

Verse 2: Circle dancers stand raising joined hands to form arches or windows. Outside players move in and out of the circle passing through the arches, finishing on the inside of the circle.

Verse 3: Dancers in the inside of the circle choose a partner and stand in front of the partner, clapping hands or joining hands with the partner and swaying from side to side.

Verse 4: Inner dancers kneel on one knee and make motions with hands clasped to heart and arms extended to express love.

Verse 5: The chosen dancers follow their partners moving in and outside of the circle, through the·arches formed by the remaining circle players, or skip hand in hand on the inside or outside of the circle.

Verse 6: The partners shake hands, with the original dancer joining the circle of dancers, the chosen partner becoming the new dancer moving to the outside of the circle.

GRAND OLD DUKE OF YORK

Level: II.
Origin: English.
Record: Folkcraft: 1191 (A Hunting We Will Go).
Formation: Longways sets of no more than six couples.
Skills: Slide, cast off, arch.
Song:
Oh, the Grand Old Duke of York, he had ten thousand men.
He marched them up to the top of the hill, and he marched them down again.
And when they're up they're up.
And when they're down they're down.
And when they're only half way up they're neither up nor down.
Hail, Britannia, Brittania rules the waves.
Britons never, never, never, never shall be slaves.

Action: First couple joins hands in the center and slide eight steps down the set and eight steps back.

First couple turns away from each other and lead his or her line around the outside and down toward the bottom of the set; all follow.

First couple forms an arch by joining hands and holding them high in the air at the bottom of the set. All others meet their partners and move through the arch to form a new set with a new head couple.

HOKEY POKEY

Level: II.
Origin: English.
Record: Capitol: 6026; MacGregor: 699, 6995.

Formation: Single circle, all facing the center, or a single circle of partners.
Skills: Walk.
Song:
Verse 1: You put your right foot in.
You put your right foot out.
You put your right foot in.
And you shake it all about.
You do the hokey pokey.
And you turn yourself around.
And that's what it's all about.

Chorus: You do the hokey pokey.
You do the hokey pokey.
You do the hokey pokey.
That's what it's all about.

Verse 2: You put your left foot in.
You put your left foot out. . . .

Verse 3: You put your right hand in.
You put your right hand out. . . .

Verse 4: You put your left hand in.
You put your left hand out. . . .

Verse 5: You put your right elbow in.
You put your right elbow out. . . .

Verse 6: You put your left elbow in.
You put your left elbow out. . . .

Verse 7: You put your head in.
You put your head out. . . .

Verse 8: You put your right hip in.
You put your right hip out. . . .

Verse 9: You put your left hip in.

You put your left hip out. . . .

Verse 10: You put your whole self in.
You put your whole self out. . . .

Verse 11: You put your back side in.
You put your back side out. . . .

Action: Verse: You put the body part named into the circle. You take it out. You put it back in and shake it toward the center of the circle.

Place palms together above your head and rumba hips. You turn around in place as you shake your hands above your head.

Clap four times.

Chorus: Raise your arms over head and lower arms and head in a bowing motion while shaking your hands from front to back.

Kneel on both knees and raise arms above head and lower arms and head in a bowing motion. Then slap the floor six times.

Teaching Suggestions: This dance may be used as a mixer. With partners in a single circle, one person moves clockwise to a new partner, following the turn on "And you turn yourself around".

JOLLY IS THE MILLER

Level: II.
Origin: American.
Record: Victor: 45-5067, 20214; Folkcraft: 1192.
Formation: Double circle, all facing counterclockwise, inside hands joined; one person, the miller, is in the center.
Skills: March.
Song:
Verse: Jolly is the miller who lives by the mill.
The wheel goes around with a right good will.
One hand on the hopper, the other on the sack.
The right steps forward and the left steps back.

Action: Line 1: All march counterclockwise with inside hands joined.
Lines 2 and 3: The children in the inside circle extend their left arms sideward to form a mill wheel as they continue moving in the circle.
Line 4: The children drop hands and change partners, with the children on the inner circle stepping forward, and the children on the outside circle stepping back. At this time the miller chooses a partner and moves into the circle of couples. The person without a partner becomes the new miller.

SHOO FLY

Level: II.
Origin: American.
Record: Folkcraft: 1102, 1185.
Formation: Single circle of partners, all facing the center, hands joined.
Skills: Walk and skip.

Song:
Shoo fly, don't bother me. Shoo fly, don't bother me.
Shoo fly, don't bother me. I belong to company G.
I feel, I feel, I feel, I feel like a morning star.
I feel, I feel, I feel, I feel like a morning star.

Action: Line 1: Walk four steps toward the center, swinging arms back and forth. Walk four steps back to place, swinging arms.
Line 2: Repeat the action of line 1.
Line 3: Partners face, taking hold of both hands, and turn in a small circle ending in the opposite position (the partner on the left now has a new partner on their right).
Teaching Suggestions: If boy-girl partners are not used, it may be necessary to designate one partner with a pinnie or sash.

THE SNAIL

Level: II.
Record: Folkcraft: 1198.
Formation: An open circle, all facing the center, hands joined, leader on the right.
Skills: Walk.
Song:
Verse 1: Let's join hands and make a shell. A place for our small snail to dwell.
Round and round we'll creep and sing. Closer, closer, wind each ring.
Here's our house we built it well. Little snail crawl in your shell.

Verse 2: Little snail now turn about. Find a hole and lead us out.
Round and round we'll creep and sing. Winging out of every ring.
Little snail we're out in time. Here we are back in our line.

Action: Verse 1: The leader winds the group into a close spiral, finishing in the center.
Verse 2: The leader reverses direction and unwinds the spiral finishing in a large circle.
Repeat with the child on the left leading the group.

AMERICAN AND INTERNATIONAL FOLK DANCE

DANISH DANCE OF GREETING

Level: I.
Origin: Danish.
Record: Merit Audio Visual: 1041.
Formation: Single circle of partners all facing the center.
Skills: Run.

Action: Part I: Clap (your own hands). Clap (again). Bow (to your partner). Clap (your own hands). Clap (again). Bow (to your neighbor). Stamp right foot. Stamp left foot. Individuals turn around in place with four little steps.

Table 19-2
American and international folk dances

Name	Origin	Formation	Basic steps	Suggestions/ modifications	Page	Record	Level
Danish Dance of Greeting	Danish	Single circle of partners all facing the center	Run		335	Merit Audio Visual: 1041	I
Nigarepolska (Nixie Polka)	Swedish	Single circle, all facing the center, several scattered inside the circle	Bleking		340	Merit Audio Visual: 1041	I
Shoemakers Dance	Danish	Double circle of partners facing one another	Skip		340	Merit Audio Visual: 1042	I
The Thread Follows the Needle	English	Single lines of about seven to eight children, hands joined	Walk		341	Victor: 22760	I
The Wheat	Czechoslavakian	Sets of three in a circle, facing counterclockwise	Walk, elbow swing		341	Merit Audio Visual: 1041	I
Tra La La Ja Saa	Norwegian/ Swedish	Single circle, one person in the center	Walk, elbow swing	More than one child may begin in the center	341	Merit Audio Visual: 1044	I
Ach Ja	German	Double circle, partners facing counter-clockwise, inside hands joined	Walk, slide		342	Folk Dancer: 34	II
Bow Belinda	American	Longways set of up to six couples	Right- and left-hand turns, do-si-do, slide		342	Folkcraft: 1189 World of Fun: 2	II
Carrousel	Swedish	Double circle, all facing the center	Slide		342	Merit Audio Visual: 1041	II
Chimes of Dunkirk	French	Double circle, partners facing	Stamp, balance, walk	This dance may be used as a mixer	342	Folkcraft: 1189 World of Fun: 4 Merit Audio Visual: 1042	II
Cshebogar	Hungarian	Single circle of partners all facing the center, hands joined	Slide, walk, skip	This dance may be used as a mixer	343	Merit Audio Visual: 1042 World of Fun: 6	II
Galopede	English	Column of four to six couples, facing forward; couples are numbered from 1 to 6 from the head of the set	Walk, skip, two-hand swing		343	Folkcraft: 1331	II
Greensleeves	English	Double circle of partners all facing counterclockwise; in two-couple sets	Walk, right-hand/left-hand star; arch		343	World of Fun: 1 Merit Audio Visual: 1042	II

Table 19-2

American and international folk dances—cont'd

Name	Origin	Formation	Basic steps	Suggestions/ modifications	Page	Record	Level
I See You	Swedish	Two lines of partners standing one behind the other, facing the opposite line	Skip		344	Merit Audio Visual: 1041	II
Jump Jim Jo	American	Double circle, partners facing	Jump, slide	This dance may be used as a mixer	344	Merit Audio Visual: 1041	II
Kinderpolka	German	Single circle, partners facing with hands joined	Step-draw, walk	This dance may be used as a mixer	344	Merit Audio Visual: 1041	II
Noriu Miego	Lithuanian	Two couple sets, facing the center (in a square, one person on each side)	Bleking, right-hand/left-hand star		344	Merit Audio Visual: 1042	II
Polly Wolly Doodle	American	Double circle of partners facing one another, hands joined	Slide		344	Merit Audio Visual: 1041	II
Pop Goes the Weasel	American	In sets of three in a circle of sets, all facing counterclockwise	Skip, walk	This dance may be done as couple and square dances as well	345	Merit Audio Visual: 1043 World of Fun: 2	II
Savila Se Bela Loza	Serbian	Single lines of six to eight dancers	Schottische, run	The schottische may be considered a grapevine, crossing in front of the second step	345	Folkcraft: 1496	II
Skip to My Lou	American	Single circle of partners, all facing the center	Walk, skip, swing, promenade		345	Folk Dancer: FD 34 Folkcraft: 1192	II
Turn the Glasses Over	American	Double circle of partners, all facing counterclockwise, skater's position	Walk		345	Folkcraft: 1181 World of Fun: 2	II
Ace of Diamonds	Danish	Double circle, partners facing	Step-hop, polka		346	World of Fun: 4 Merit Audio Visual: 1044	III
Bingo	American	Double circle of partners, all facing counterclockwise	Walk, slide, grand right and left		346	Folkcraft: 1189 Merit Audio Visual: 1043	III
Buggy Schottische	International	Two-couple sets, one in front of the other, all hands joined	Schottische, step-hop	Variation: rear couple moves forward under the arch formed by the lead couple, "wringing the dish rag"	347	Merit Audio Visual: 1046	III

Table 19-2
American and international folk dances—cont'd

Name	Origin	Formation	Basic steps	Suggestions/ modifications	Page	Record	Level
Cherkassiya	Israeli	Closed or broken circle, hands joined	Grapevine, cherkassiya step, step-hop	Lines of six children may be more appropriate for elementary school children	347	Merit Audio Visual: 1043	III
Christ Church Bells	English	Double circle, partners facing, arranged in two-couple sets	Walk, or run, slide, cast off		347	World of Fun: 5	III
Gustaf's Skoal	Swedish	Square set of four couples	Walk, skip		347	World of Fun: 7 Merit Audio Visual: 1044	III
Hopp Mor Anika	Swedish	Double circle, all facing counter-clockwise	Walk, skip, polka		347	Merit Audio Visual: 1042	III
Horah	Israeli	Single circle, hands on shoulders of persons on either side	Grapevine, hop	Small groups may work best for elementary school children	347	Merit Audio Visual: 1043	III
La Raspa	Mexican	Partners scattered around the room, facing each other, hands joined	Bleking, skip; optional: polka, grand right and left		348	World of Fun: 6 Merit Audio Visual: 1043	III
Moskrosser	Danish	Two-couple sets, facing each other, arranged in sets around the circle; couple 1 facing clockwise, couple 2 facing counter-clockwise	Schottische ladies chain, right and left star		348	Merit Audio Visual: 1044	III
Norwegian Mountain March	Norwegian	Sets of three, with the center person in front, and the other two (partners) stand behind; each holds a handkerchief, which is held by another of the set	Waltz or step-hop	The waltz step is preferable, but it may be too difficult for elementary school children	348	Merit Audio Visual: 1044	III
Oh Susanna	American	Single circle of partners, all facing the center	Walk, grand right and left	A partner swing may be substituted for the grand right and left	349	Merit Audio Visual: 1043	III
Seven Jumps		Single circle, all facing counterclockwise	Step-hop	This dance may be used with younger children if the skip is substituted for the step-hop	349	Merit Audio Visual: 1043 World of Fun: 4	III

Table 19-2
American and international folk dances—cont'd

Name	Origin	Formation	Basic steps	Suggestions/modifications	Page	Record	Level
Sicilian Circle	American	Two-couple sets, in a circle, alternately facing clockwise and counterclockwise (duple minor set)	Walk, ladies chain, right and left through	A right- and left-hand star may be substituted for the ladies chain and a do-si-do with opposite and partner for the right and left through	349	World of Fun: 1	III
Teton Mountain Stomp	American	Single circle of partners, hands joined	Step-close, walk, two-step or buzz step	The buzz step may be substituted for the two-step to be appropriate for level IV	349		
Tinikling	Phillipines	Groups of three to six with one set of poles	Walk, leap	It may be helpful to have the children practice the steps using parallel lines on the floor before using the sticks	350	Merit Audio Visual: 1047	III
Heel and Toe Polka	American	Couples in the varsouvienne position	Polka, two-step	This may be used as a mixer	354	MacGregor: 5003-B	IV
Highland Fling	Scotch	Individuals scattered in the room	Fling		354	Merit Audio Visual: 1045	IV
Jessie Polka	American	In lines of two or more with hands on waist of person in front	Two-step or polka	This may be used as a mixer	354	Folkcraft: 1093	IV
Maitelitza	Russian	Sets of three, inside hands joined, facing counterclockwise	Hop, slide		354	Educational Dance Recordings: FD-2	IV
Mayim	Israeli	Single circles, hands joined and held down	Grapevine, hop, run		355	World of Fun: 6	IV
Miserlou (Kritikos)	Greek	A large broken circle, hands joined; leader at the right end of the line	Grapevine, two-step	Smaller groups may be more successful than one large group	355	Merit Audio Visual: 1046	IV
Virginia Reel	American	Longways set of six couples	Walk, do-si-do, reel, slide	Children must be reminded that reeling is always done with the line opposite the one they are in	351	Merit Audio Visual: 1043	III
Black Nag	English	Longways set of three couples, all facing the head of the set	Run, slide, right and left elbow swing, hey		351	World of Fun: 6	IV

Table 19-2
American and international folk dances—cont'd

Name	Origin	Formation	Basic steps	Suggestions/ modifications	Page	Record	Level
Crested Hen	Danish	Sets of three, hands joined to form a circle	Step-hop		352	World of Fun: 4 Merit Audio Visual: 1042	IV
Cumberland Square Eight	English	Square set of four couples	Gallop, star, basket	A skipping step may be substituted for the basket	352	World of Fun: 5	IV
Fireman's Dance	American	Two couples in a line facing two couples; sets in a circle as the spokes of a wheel	Slide, galop, ladies chain, right and left through		353	World of Fun: 1	IV
Five Foot Two	American	Double circle, all facing counter-clockwise	Two-step, walk, bal-ance		353	Folkcraft: 1420	IV
Gathering Peascods	English	Single circle of part-ners, all facing the center, hands joined	Slide, walk		353	Merit Audio Visual: 1045	IV
Road to the Isles	Scotch	Double circle of partners in the varsouvienne po-sition, all facing counterclockwise	Schottische, step-hop, grapevine		355	World of Fun: 3 Merit Audio Visual: 1043	IV
Sicilian Tar-antella	Italian	Two-couple sets, men standing side by side, fac-ing their partners	Step-hop, do-si-do, skip, star		355	Merit Audio Visual: 1045 World of Fun: 6	IV

*Additional dances, instructions not included.

Repeat the action of Part I:
Part II: Chorus: Join hands with partner and move to the left for the first phrase (16 steps). Change directions and circle to the right for the second phrase (16 steps).

NIGAREPOLSKA (NIXIE POLKA)

Level: I.
Origin: Swedish.
Record: Merit Audio Visual: 1041.
Formation: Single circle, all facing the center; several chil-dren scattered inside the circle.
Skills: Bleking.
Action: Measures 1 to 4: With hands joined, all spring lightly onto the left foot while extending the right foot forward with the heel on the ground and the toe up (bleking step). Bleking right. Bleking left. Bleking right. (These steps are executed slowly.)
Measures 5 to 8: All clap hands once and shout, "Hey." Center dancers then run around the inside of the circle looking for a partner. They join hands with the partner and run lightly in place to finish the phrase.

The dance is now repeated with the center dancers and their partners holding two hands on measures 1 to 4. On measures 5 to 8, the circle dancers move behind their partners and put their hands on the shoulders of their partners. The two move into line to choose a new partner and the dance continues.
Each time the dance is repeated, the line adds one additional person and reverses so that there is a new leader each time.

SHOEMAKER'S DANCE

Level: I.
Origin: Danish.
Record: Merit Audio Visual: 1042.
Formation: Double circle of partners facing each other.
Skills: Skip.
Action: Measures 1 to 4: Wind, wind, wind, the bobbin. (Partners execute a winding motion with the hands and arms.) Wind, wind, wind the bobbin. (Reverse winding motion.) Pull. Pull. Tap. Tap. Tap. (Pull hands away from each other to the sides twice and tap

one hand on the other three times.)
Measures 5 to 8: Repeat the action of measures 1 to 4.
Chorus: Join inside hands with free hand on hips and skip counterclockwise (16 steps).

THE THREAD FOLLOWS THE NEEDLE

Level: I.
Origin: English.
Record: Victor: 22760.
Formation: Single lines of seven or eight children, hands joined; each child is numbered consecutively.
Skills: Walk.
Song:
Verse: The thread follows the needle. The thread follows the needle.
In and out the needle goes. As mother mends the children's clothes.

Action: The first child (1) is the needle and leads the other children. The needle leads the line under the raised arms of the last two children (7 and 8). When the line has totally passed under the arms the children turn and face the opposite direction, letting their arms cross in front of them. This forms a stitch.
The leader repeats the action passing under the arms of 6 and 7. This is repeated until the entire line is sewn, completing the last stitch.
The stitch is then ripped by having all children raise their arms and turn to their original positions.
Repeat the dance with a new leader.

THE WHEAT

Level: I.
Origin: Czechoslovakian.
Record: Merit Audio Visual: 1041.
Formation: Sets of three in a circle, all facing counterclockwise.
Skills: Walk and elbow swing.
Action: Part I: All walk forward (16 steps).
Part II: Center dancers hook right elbows with their right-hand partners and turn twice around (eight skips). Repeat with partner on the left.

TRA LA LA JA SAA

Level: I.
Origin: Norwegian/Swedish.
Record: Merit Audio Visual: 1044.
Formation: Single circle, one person in the center.
Skills: Walk and elbow swing.
Song:
I am waiting, I am hoping. That someone will join me in the ring.
Oh won't you come and be my partner. While the others clap and sing.

Tra la, la, la, Ja Saa; Tra la, la, la, Ja Saa.
Won't you come and dance the way I do. Or must I reverse and go with you.

Action: Line 1: The center person walks counterclockwise inside the circle and sings.
Line 2: The center person chooses a partner who comes into the circle.

Line 3: All turn around in place, stamping on "Ja" and clapping own hands on "Saa." Repeat.

Line 4: The couple in the center hook right elbows and walk around. Reverse with a left elbow swing.

The dance is repeated with each of the center dancers looking for a new partner.

Teaching Suggestions: If the group is large, it may be best to begin with several children in the center of the circle.

ACH JA

Level: II.

Origin: German.

Record: Folk Dancer: 34.

Formation: Double circle partners facing counterclockwise, hands joined.

Skills: Walk and slide.

Action: Part I—Measures 1 and 2: Partners walk counterclockwise (eight steps).

Measures 3 and 4: Partners drop hands, face each other, and bow. Then turn back to back and bow.

Measures 5 to 8: Repeat measures 1 to 4.

Part II—Measures 1 and 2: Partners join hands and take four slides counterclockwise.

Measures 3 and 4: Partners take four slides clockwise.

Measure 5: Partners drop hands, face each other, and bow.

Measure 6: Child on the inside of the circle walks counterclockwise to a new partner.

Repeat the dance with new partners.

BOW BELINDA

Level: II.

Origin: American.

Record: Folkcraft: 1189; World of Fun: 2.

Formation: Longways set of up to six couples.

Skills: Slide, right- and left-hand turns, and do-si-do.

Song:

Verse 1: Bow, bow, O Belinda. Bow, bow, O Belinda. Bow, bow O Belinda. Won't you be my partner?

Verse 2: Right hand around, O Belinda. . . .

Verse 3: Left hand around, O Belinda. . . .

Verse 4: Both hands around, O Belinda. . . .

Verse 5: Back to back, O Belinda. . . .

Verse 6: Promenade around, O Belinda. . . .

Verse 7: Through the tunnel, O Belinda. . . .

Action: Verses 1 to 5: The head boy and foot girl do the action, followed by the head girl and the foot boy.

Verse 1: Move to the center of the set with four running steps, bow, and return to place.

Verse 2: Forward to the center, take right hands, turning once around and then back to place.

Verse 3: Forward to the center, take left hands, turning once and then back to place.

Verse 4: Forward to the center, turn with both hands, and return to place.

Verse 5: Forward to the center, do-si-do, and back to place.

Verse 6: Partners join hands in the skaters' position facing the head of the set. All follow the first couple out to the left, skipping straight down the set, turning sharply at the foot, and promenading up the center of the set back to place.

Verse 7: Couples remain in place, joining hands to form an arch. The head couple goes under the arch to the foot of the set.

The dance is repeated with a new head couple.

CARROUSEL

Level: II.

Origin: Swedish.

Record: Merit Audio Visual: 1041.

Formation: Double circle, all facing the center; inner circle joins hands, outer circle places their hands on the shoulders of the child in front of them.

Skills: Slide.

Song:

Part I: Little children young and gay. Carrousel is running.

It will run til evening. Little ones a nickel.

Big ones a dime.

Hurry up, get a mate or you'll surely be too late.

Part II: Ha, ha, ha. Happy are we. Anderson and Henderson and Peterson and me.

Ha, ha, ha. Happy are we. Anderson and Henderson and Peterson and me.

Action: Part I: All sing and slide slowly in a clockwise direction.

Part II: Continue in a clockwise direction sliding in time to the music which increases in tempo.

Change direction and continue sliding.

Repeat the dance with the inner circle changing places with the outer circle.

CHIMES OF DUNKIRK

Level: II.

Origin: French.

Record: Folkcraft: 1188; World of Fun; 4; Merit Audio Visual: 1042.

Formation: Double circle, with partners facing.

Skills: Walk, stamp, and balance.

Action: Measures 1 and 2: Stamp three times.

Measures 3 and 4: Clap three times.

Measures 5 to 8: Join hands with partner and turn clockwise in place (with eight steps).

Measures 9 and 10: Join right hands and balance (step forward with the right foot, step back on the left).

Measures 11 and 12: Repeat measures 9 and 10.

Measures 13 to 16: With both hands joined, turn clockwise in place (with eight steps).

Repeat the dance.

Teaching Suggestions: This dance could become a mixer by having the child on the inside of the circle, circle with partner in measures 13 to 16 and continue walking forward to a new partner.

CSHEBOGAR

Level: II.

Origin: Hungarian.

Record: Merit Audio Visual: 1042; World of Fun: 6.

Formation: Single circle of partners, all facing the center, hands joined.

Skills: Walk, slide, and skip.

Action: Part I: All slide eight steps to the left, then eight slides to the right.

Part II: Three steps forward into the circle. Stamp. Three steps back to place. Stamp. Repeat.

Part III: Partners join hands, arms extended at shoulder height. Take four slow step-draws (step-close) sideways toward the center of the circle, while lowering and raising arms. Repeat returning back to places.

Now take two step-draws into the center, and two out.

Part IV: Partners face, placing right hands around each other's waist (or hooking right elbows). With left hand held high in the air, turn in place with eight running or skipping steps.

Teaching Suggestions: This dance may become a mixer by having one of the dancers (the one facing counterclockwise) turn once with his or her partner in Part IV and continue on to the next person, who becomes the new partner.

GALOPEDE

Level: II.

Origin: English.

Record: Folkcraft: 1331.

Formation: Column of four to six couples, facing forward; couples are numbered from one to six from the head of the set; partners facing, hands joined in each line.

Skills: Walk, skip, and two-hand swing.

Action: A—Measures 1 to 4: All walk three steps forward, bow, and walk back to place with four steps.

Measures 5 to 8: Release hands. Partners change places with eight steps, passing right shoulders and turning to the right to face partners.

Measures 1 to 8: Repeat measures 5 to 8 returning to places.

B—Measures 1 to 8: Partners join hands and do a two-hand swing with skipping steps.

C—Head couple swings down between the two lines to the foot of the set, skipping. All other couples move up one position while clapping.

Repeat the dance with a new head couple.

GREENSLEEVES

Level: II.

Origin: English

Record: World of Fun: 1; Merit Audio Visual: 1042.

Formation: Double circle of partners, all facing counterclockwise; in two-couple sets.

Skills: Walk, right- and left-hand star, and arch.

Action: Part I—Measures 1 to 8: Walk forward (16 steps).

Part II—Measures 1 to 8: The couple in front turns to face the couple behind, each turning individually. All four join right hands for a right-hand star and walk (eight steps) clockwise.

Now drop hands and join left hands for a left-hand star, proceeding (eight steps) counterclockwise. On the last count the lead couple faces forward again.

Part III—Measure 1 to 8: Rear couple joins inside hands, forming an arch. The rear couple walks four steps forward, while the lead couple walks back four steps under the arch.

Reverse roles with the new front couple backing under the arch, while the new rear couple walks forward forming the arch.

Repeat turning the sleeves two more times.

I SEE YOU

Level: II.
Origin: Swedish.
Record: Merit Audio Visual: 1041.
Formation: Two lines of partners standing one behind the other, facing the opposite line.
Skills: Skip.
Song:
I see you. I see you. Tra la, la, la, la, la, la, la.
I see you. I see you. Tra la, la, la, la, la.

You see me and I see you.
Then you take me and I'll take you.

You see me and I see you.
Then you take me and I'll take you.

Action: Lines 1 and 2: The twos play peek-a-boo with the opposite twos by first looking over their partners' left shoulders and then their right shoulders.
Now twos nod their heads from left to right in time to the music.
Repeat lines 1 and 2.
Lines 3 and 4: Twos clap hands sharply, move past their partners to the left, skipping to the center of the space. Join hands with the opposite two and skip in a circle once to the left.
Lines 5 and 6: Twos clap once more, turning toward their own partners. Join hands with them and turn ending in reverse positions, with the twos in front of the ones. The dance is repeated from the beginning with the ones active.

JUMP JIM JO

Level: II.
Origin: American.
Record: Merit Audio Visual: 1041.
Formation: Double circle of partners, facing each other; hands joined.
Skills: Jump and slide.
Song:
Jump, jump, oh jump Jim Jo.
Take a little whirl and around you go.
Slide, slide and point your toe.
You're a sprightly little fellow when you jump Jim Jo.

Action: Line 1: Progressing counterclockwise, take two slow jumps, followed by three quicker jumps.
Line 2: Release hands and turn once in place with four little steps. Finish facing your partner and join hands.
Line 3: Progressing counterclockwise, take two sliding steps. These are followed by tapping the toes of the outside foot three times.

Line 4: Release hands. Take four running steps forward in the line of direction. Face partner, join hands, and end with three jumps sideways, progressing counterclockwise.
Teaching Suggestions: This dance may be made into a mixer by having the inside dancer move sideways on the last three jumps, while the outside dancer jumps in place.

KINDERPOLKA (CHILDREN'S POLKA)

Level: II.
Origin: German.
Record: Merit Audio Visual: 1041.
Formation: Single circle, partners facing with hands joined and arms extended sideways, at shoulder level.
Skills: Step-draw and walk.
Action: Measures 1 and 2: Couples take two step-draws toward the center of the circle (step close, step close) and three steps in place.
Measures 3 and 4: Take two step-draws out and back to place, ending with three steps in place.
Measures 5 to 8: Repeat measures 1 to 4.
Measures 9 and 10: Slap thighs with both hands. Clap own hands. Clap partner's hands three times.
Measures 11 and 12: Repeat measures 9 and 10.
Measures 13 and 14: Place right heel forward and shake right forefinger at partner three times as if scolding. Repeat with the left foot and finger.
Measures 15 and 16: Turn in place with four little steps, ending facing your partner, and stamp three times.
Teaching Suggestions: This dance may be used as a mixer by having the child facing counterclockwise move forward to the next dancer, while the inactive dancer stamps during the last measure.

NORIU MIEGO

Level: II.
Origin: Lithuanian.
Record: Merit Audio Visual: 1042.
Formation: Two-couple sets facing the center, in a square, with one person on each side.
Skills: Bleking and right- and left-hand star.
Action: Part I: All spring onto the left foot, placing the right foot forward, with the heel down and the toes pointing upward (bleking right).
Bleking left.
Four quick bleking steps—right, left, right, left.
Part II: Clap own hands twice and form a right-hand star in the center. Move forward eight steps clockwise. Clap twice again. Form a left-hand star and move counterclockwise for eight steps.
Repeat the dance from the beginning.

POLLY WOLLY DOODLE

Level: II.
Origin: American.

Record: Merit Audio Visual: 1041.
Formation: Double circle of partners, facing one another, hands joined.
Skills: Slide.
Song:
Oh, I went down south for to see my Sal.
Sing Polly Wolly Doodle all the day.
My Sal she is a spunky gal.
Sing Polly Wolly Doodle all the day.

Fare thee well. Fare thee well.
Fare thee well, my fairy fay.
For I'm off to Louisiana for to see my Susyanna.
Singing Polly Wolly Doodle all the day.

Action: Line 1: All slide four steps counterclockwise.
Line 2: Drop hands and turn individually in place with five stamps (slow, slow, quick, quick, quick).
Lines 3 and 4: Repeat the action of lines 1 and 2, but moving clockwise.
Line 5: Both partners bow. Boys have hands on hips; girls hold skirts.
Line 6: Partners move away from each other, moving backward with four walking or skipping steps.
Line 7: Both dancers move diagonally forward to their own left to meet a new partner.
Line 8: Join hands and skip around in place.
Repeat the dance with a new partner.

POP GOES THE WEASEL

Level: II.
Origin: American.
Record: Merit Audio Visual: 1043; World of Fun: 2.
Formation: Several formations may be used, including sets of three children, partners, or as a square dance.
Skills: Skip and walk.
Song:
Round and round the cobbler's bench, the monkey chased the weasel.
In and out and 'round about. Pop goes the weasel.

Action: In sets of three, spaced in a large circle, inside hands joined; all facing counterclockwise.
Line 1: All walk forward while singing.
Line 2: Join outside hands to make a circle, and circle clockwise. On the words "Pop goes the weasel," the center dancer is "popped" under the joined hands of the outside dancers and moves on to join the twosome in front to form a new group. In a double circle in two-couple sets, partners join inside hands. Couples numbered: Couples facing clockwise are 1, couples facing counterclockwise are 2.
Line 1: All step forward four steps and back four steps.
Line 2: Couples join hands and circle to the left. On the word "Pop" couple 1 pops under the arch formed by couple 2 and moves forward to join the couple ahead to make a new set.

SAVILA SE BELA LOZA

Level: II.
Origin: Serbian.
Record: Folkcraft: 1496.
Formation: Single line of six to eight dancers.
Skills: Schottische and run.
Action: Part I—Measures 1 to 10: Face slightly to the right and move right with small running steps (20).
Measures 11 to 20. Immediately turn toward the left and move back to the left with small running steps.
Part II—Measures 1 and 2: Face the center and take one schottische step to the right, beginning with the right foot.
Measures 3 and 4: Repeat the action of measures 1 and 2 but moving to the left, with the first step on the left foot.
Measures 5 to 12: Repeat the pattern of measures 1 to 4, twice more.
Teaching Suggestions: Savila Se Bela Loza means "a vine entwined itself." The schottishe is almost a grapevine step, with the foot crossing in front (second step).

SKIP TO MY LOU

Level: II.
Origin: American.
Record: Folkdancer: FD34; Folkcraft: 1192.
Formation: A single circle of partners, all facing the center.
Skills: Walk, skip, swing, and promenade.
Song:
Verse 1: Boys to the center. Skip to my Lou.
Boys to the outside. Skip to my Lou.
Boys to the center. Skip to My Lou.
Skip to my Lou, my darling.

Verse 2: Girls to the center. Skip to my Lou.
Girls to the center. Skip to my Lou.
Girls to the center. Skip to my Lou.
Skip to my Lou, my darling.

Verse 3: Swing your partner, skip to my Lou. . . .

Verse 4: I've lost my partner, now what'll I do. . . .

Verse 5: I've got another one, prettier too. . . .

Action: Verse 1: Boys walk four steps toward the center of the circle. Then take four steps backward to their places. Repeat to the center and back.
Verse 2: Girls repeat the action of the boys in verse 1.
Verse 3: Partners join hands and skip or swing in place.
Verse 4: Partners release hands. Girls walk forward, boys turn and walk in the opposite direction.
Verse 5: Children promenade with their new partners.
Repeat the dance with a new partner.

TURN THE GLASSES OVER

Level: II.
Origin: American.
Record: Folkcraft: 1181; World of Fun: 2.

Formation: Double circle of partners, all facing counter-clockwise, in the skaters' position.

Skills: Walk.

Song:

Verse: I've been to Harlem. I've been to Dover.
I've traveled the wide world all over.
Over, over, three times over.
Drink all the lemonade, and turn the glasses over.

Chorus: Sailing east, sailing west.
Sailing over the ocean.
You better watch out when the boat begins to rock.
Or you'll lose your girl in the ocean.

Action: Verse 1: Couples promenade counterclockwise with a walking step. On "Turn the glasses over," they perform a dishrag turn by raising their arms, keeping their hands joined, and turning under their arms, making one complete outward turn.

Chorus: Girls continue walking counterclockwise; boys turn and walk clockwise. Any extra dancers join the children moving in the circle. On the last line children quickly get a partner. Those without a partner move inside the circle for the repeat of the dance.

ACE OF DIAMONDS

Level: III.

Origin: Danish.

Record: Merit Audio Visual: 1044; World of Fun: 4.

Formation: Double circle, partners facing.

Skills: Step-hop and polka.

Action: Measures 1 to 4: Clap hands once, hook right elbows with partners, and walk around with partner clockwise (six steps).

Measures 6 to 8: clap hands once, hook left elbows with partners, and walk around with partner counterclockwise (six steps).

Measures 9 to 12: With arms folded high, all take four slow step-hops toward the center, the boy moving backward and the girl moving forward.

Measures 13 to 16: Take four step-hops back to place.

Measures 17 to 24: Join inside hands and polka counterclockwise around the circle, moving face to face, then back to back. . . .

Variation for measures 9 to 16: A bleking step may be substituted for the step-hop. The rhythm is slow, slow, fast, fast, fast, fast.

BINGO

Level: III.

Origin: American.

Record: Folkcraft: 1189; Merit Audio Visual: 1043.

Formation: Double circle of partners, all facing counterclockwise.

Skills: Walk, slide, and grand right and left.

Song:

A big black dog sat on the back porch and Bingo was his name.
A big black dog sat on the back porch and Bingo was his name.
B I N G O, B I N G O, B I N G O, and Bingo was his name.
B I N G O.

Action: Lines 1 and 2: In the promenade position, partners walk counterclockwise around the circle (16 steps).

Line 3: As they spell Bingo, they form a single circle

by having the dancers in the inside back out. Joining hands, they then slide counterclockwise (12 slides).
Line 4: Partners face each other. Spelling Bingo very slowly they give their right hand to their partners, move past them, and give their left to the next. They continue the grand right and left until they reach a person on "O," who becomes their new partner.
The dance is repeated with a new partner.

BUGGY SCHOTTISCHE

Level: III.
Origin: International.
Record: Merit Audio Visual: 1046.
Formation: Two-couple sets, one couple in front of the other, all hands joined.
Skills: Schottische and step-hop.
Action: Part I: Take two schottische steps forward, boys beginning on their left, girls on their right.
Take four step-hops forward, swinging free foot forward.
Part II: Take two schottische steps forward.
Take four step-hops, during which the lead couple drops their hands but remains holding the hands of the couple behind them. The lead couple casts off, the boy moving left, the girl right, to move in behind the other couple.
The couple in the rear now joins hands and the dance is repeated.
Variation: Instead of casting off the lead couple backs under the arch formed by the rear couple. Without dropping hands they turn as if "wringing the dishrag."
Variation: Instead of casting off, the rear couple moves forward under the arch formed by the lead couple. Without dropping hands they turn as if "wringing the dishrag."

CHERKASSIYA

Level: III.
Origin: Israeli.
Record: Merit Audio Visual: 1043.
Formation: Closed or broken circle, hands joined.
Skills: Grapevine (cherkassiya step) and step-hop.
Action: Chorus: the cherkassiya step, a form of the grapevine is used. The dancer crosses the right over the left with a stamp, takes the weight on the right; takes a very short step with the left to the left. Next, the right foot crosses behind the left, taking the weight on the right and finishes with another very short step on the left to the left. This step is repeated for a total of four times.
The chorus follows each part of the dance.
Part I: Traveling to the right, each dancer steps to the right with the right foot, with the left foot extended to the side.
They then cross the left foot behind the right, taking the weight on the left foot and bending the knees

slightly. This step is done very quickly, almost as a running step (eight times).
Part II: The "horse trot." All face to the right and step-hop, leading with the right foot (eight step-hops).
Part III: The "Susie Q." Keeping both feet together, all dancers move their toes to the right and then, without lifting the feet, move their heels to the right (eight times).
Part IV: "Scissors forward." Beginning with the right foot, dancers kick their feet alternately forward while remaining in place (right, left, right, left) (16 times).
Part V: "Scissors backward." Repeat the action of Part IV, but kicking the feet backward in place.
Part VI: "The train." All face the right and bending the knees but keeping the trunk erect, walk counterclockwise (14 steps), ending with a high jump on both feet, facing the center.

CHRIST CHURCH BELLS

Level: III.
Origin: English.
Record: World of Fun: 5.
Formation: Double circle, partners facing; arranged in two-couple sets; boys on the inside; couple 1 facing counterclockwise, couple 2 facing clockwise.
Skills: Walk or run, slide, and cast off.
Action: Part I: Boy 1 turns girl 2 with a right hand round (eight counts), then turns own partner with a left hand turn (eight counts).
Boy 2 turns girl 1 with a right hand round (eight counts), then turns own partner with a left hand turn (eight counts).
Part II: All join hands and slide to the left (eight slides) to finish in original places. Clap own hands, clap right hand of partner, clap own hands, clap partner's left (four counts).
Part III: "Cast off." Couple 1 turns outside away from each other and passes to the outside of couple 2 as couple 2 walks forward. Each couple now faces a new couple.
The dance is repeated from the beginning.

GUSTAF'S SKOAL

Level: III.
Origin: Swedish.
Record: World of Fun: 7; Merit Audio Visual: 1044.
Formation: A square set of four couples, with two head couples (facing and with their backs to the music) and two side couples.
Skills: Walk and skip.
Action: Measures 1 to 4: Head couples take three steps forward and bow solemnly to each other. Then take three steps back to place and bow to their partners.
Measures 5 to 8: Side couples repeat the action of the head couples.
Measures 1 to 8: Repeat the action of the head and side couples.

Measures 9 to 16: Side couples face and form an arch by joining hands and raising them high in the air. Head couples skip forward.

Boy 1 takes girl 2, and boy 2 takes girl 1 by the hand and turn to face the side couples. The two new couples now skip under the arches they are facing.

After passing under the arch the couples separate by turning away from each other and skip back to their original places. Everyone swings their partner for the remaining measures.

Repeat the action with the head couples forming the arches and the side couples active.

HOPP MOR ANIKA

Level: III.
Origin: Swedish.
Record: Merit Audio Visual: 1042.
Formation: Double circle, all facing counterclockwise, inside hands joined.
Skills: Walk, skip, and polka.
Action: Part I: Swinging hands forward and backward, and free hand on hips, walk forward (16 steps).
Part II: All skip forward (16 steps) and finish facing partner.
Part III: Stamp right foot and clap right hands simultaneously. Clap own hands.
Stamp left and left hands.
Clap right, clap own, clap left, clap own. Repeat.
Clap right, clap own, and stamp three times.
Part IV: Join inside hands, do a face to face, back to back polka counterclockwise (eight polka steps).
At the end, the inside person moves forward to take a new partner and the dance is repeated.

HORAH

Level: III.
Origin: Israeli.
Record: Merit Audio Visual: 1043.
Formation: Single circle, hands on shoulders of persons on either side.
Skills: Grapevine and hop.
Action: Moving counterclockwise, step right to the side, place left behind right, and step right.
Kick left in front of right while hopping on the right.
Step left to the side, kick right across left while hopping on the left.
Repeat. The music gradually increases in tempo.
Teaching Suggestions: Small groups may work best for elementary school children.

LA RASPA

Level: III.
Origin: Mexican.
Record: World of Fun: 6; Merit Audio Visual: 1043.
Formation: Partners scattered around the room, facing each other, hands joined.

Skills: Bleking and skip. Optional: polka and grand right and left.
Action: Part I: Partners execute one bleking with the right foot forward, one bleking with the left foot forward. Repeat right, left, right. The rhythm is slow, slow, quick, quick, quick. Pause.
Part II—Variation 1: Clap hands once, hook right elbows, and skip around with partner (eight skips). Clap again, hook left elbows, and turn again with eight skips.
Variation 2: Join inside hands and do the face to face, back to back polka (16 steps).
Variation 3: In a circle formation, face partner. Give your right hand to your partner, walk forward past your partner, and give your left hand to the next person, doing a grand right and left around the circle.

MOSKROSSER

Level: III.
Origin: Danish.
Record: Merit Audio Visual: 1044.
Formation: Two-couple sets facing each other, arranged around the circle; couple 1 facing clockwise, 2 facing counterclockwise.
Skills: Schottische, ladies chain, right- and left-hand star.
Action: Couple 1 with inside hands joined take two schottische steps forward, passing between couple 2, who drops hands and walks forward two schottische steps to the outside of couple 1.
All move back to place, with couple 1 dropping hands and passing couple 2 on the outside, couple 2 joining hands and passing between couple 1 (two schottische steps).
Ladies chain with eight schottische steps.
Dancers form a right-hand star by placing right hands in the center and moving around in a circle for four schottische steps. Reverse with a left-hand star for four schottische steps.
Couples face. Holding inside hands and moving counterclockwise, take one schottische step moving away from each other, followed by one schottische step moving toward their partner.
Couples take the shoulder-waist position. They step-hop in the direction they were originally facing, turning as they move around the circle. All couples pass by the couple originally in their set and face a new couple, with whom they will repeat the dance.

NORWEGIAN MOUNTAIN MARCH

Level: III.
Origin: Norwegian.
Record: Merit Audio Visual: 1044.
Formation: Sets of three, with the center person in front, the remaining two behind; each holds a handkerchief between their joined hands.
Skills: Waltz or step-hop.
Action: Part I—Measures 1 to 8: Take eight step-hops

(or waltz) forward beginning with the right foot. The first beat of each step is slightly accented. The lead dancer turns to the right and left, looking at the dancers behind.

Part II—Measures 9 and 10: Dancers in the rear form an arch with their inside hands. The lead dancer, continuing the stop-hop (or waltz), moves backward under the arch.

Measures 11 and 12: Dancer on the left, moving clockwise, dances across and under the lead dancer's right arm.

Measures 13 and 14: Dancer on the right turns left under the lead dancer's right arm.

Measures 15 and 16: Lead dancer turns right and under own right arm. The group should now be in its original position.

Measures 17 to 24. Repeat measures 9 to 16.

Teaching Suggestions: This dance represents a guide leading climbers up and down the mountainside and should be performed with this in mind. Most important is keeping the chain untangled and unbroken.

A waltz step is preferrable in this dance, but this may be too difficult for many elementary school children.

OH SUSANNA

Level: III.
Origin: American.
Record: Merit Audio Visual: 1043.
Formation: Single circle of partners, all facing the center.
Skills: Walk and grand right and left.
Song:
Measures 1 to 4: Oh, I come from Alabama with a banjo on my knee.
Measures 5 to 8: And I'm goin' to Louisiana for my true love for to see.
Measures 9 to 16: It rained all night the day I left. The weather it was dry.
I cried so hard I broke my heart. Susanna don't you cry.

Chorus: Oh Susanna, Oh don't you cry for me.
For I come from Alabama with a banjo on my knee. Repeat.

Action: Part I—Measures 1 to 4: Girls walk forward four steps and back four steps as boys clap.
Measures 5 to 8: Boys walk forward four steps and back as girls clap.
Part II—Measures 9 to 16: Partners face each other. All do the grand right and left, giving their right hand to their partner and walking forward to give their left hand to the next. Continue until the chorus "Oh Susanna" is reached (approximately the seventh person).
Measures 17 to 32: At the chorus, join hands with new partner and walk counterclockwise around the circle. (The chorus is repeated.)
Repeat the dance from the beginning with a new partner.
Teaching Suggestions: If the children are not ready for the

grand right and left, a swing with their partners may be substituted.

SEVEN JUMPS

Level: III.
Origin: Danish.
Record: Merit Audio Visual: 1043; World of Fun: 4.
Formation: Single circle, all facing counterclockwise.
Skills: Step-hop.
Action: Beginning with the chorus, the children step-hop counterclockwise (eight step-hops). Reverse direction and take eight step-hops clockwise. The chorus is repeated after each figure.
Figure 1: With hands on hips, raise right knee and hold.
Figure 2: With hands on hips, raise right knee and hold. Raise left knee and hold.
Figure 3: Repeat figure 2 and add kneeling on the right knee and hold.
Figure 4: Repeat figure 3 and add a kneel on the left knee and hold.
Figure 5: Repeat figure 4 and add touching the right elbow to the floor. Hold.
Figure 6: Repeat figure 5 adding touching the left elbow to the floor. Hold.
Figure 7: Repeat figure 6 and touch your head to the floor. Hold.
Teaching Suggestions: Since each hold is for differing amounts of time, encourage the children to listen carefully. If the skip is substituted for the step-hop, the dance becomes suitable for younger children.

SICILIAN CIRCLE

Level: III.
Origin: American.
Record: World of Fun: 1.
Formation: A double circle of two-couple sets, couples alternately facing clockwise and counterclockwise.
Skills: Walk, ladies chain, and right and left through.
Action: Partners join inside hands and walk forward three steps, bow, and move back to place.
All join hands in the set and circle once around to the left.
Ladies chain across and back to place.
Right and left through across and back to place. Partners walk forward and pass through the opposite couple, passing right shoulders with the opposite person. Each couple now faces a new couple.
Repeat the dance in the new sets.
Teaching Suggestions: A right- and left-hand star may be substituted for the ladies chain; a do-si-do with the opposite and then with the partner for the right and left through.

TETON MOUNTAIN STOMP

Level: III.
Origin: American.

Record: Folkcraft 1482.

Formation: Single circle of partners, facing each other; hands joined.

Skills: Step-close, walk, and two-step or buzz step.

Action: Measures 1 to 4: Step toward the center of the circle; close the opposite foot to the first. Step once more toward the circle and stamp with the following foot. (Side, close, side, stamp.) Repeat moving away from the circle.

Measures 5 to 8: Step toward the center once again. Stamp the opposite foot close to the stepping foot. Repeat moving away from the center. Partners shift to a banjo position (right hips adjacent) and walk four steps counterclockwise, the boy moving forward, the girl moving backward.

Measures 9 to 12: Partners shift to a sidecar position (left hips adjacent) by making a half turn to the right. Boy remains on the inside and is now facing clockwise. Boy walks four steps backward while girls walks four steps forward.

Partners shift back to the banjo position by making a half turn to the left. Immediately they release from each other, with the boy moving counterclockwise four steps to meet a new partner.

Measures 13 to 16: New partners join hands and do two two-steps, turning while progressing counterclockwise. Four pivot steps are then taken to the right, so the boy ends up facing the line of direction.

Teaching Suggestions: A buzz step may be substituted for the two-steps and pivots. The dancers then take about eight steps while swinging.

TINIKLING

Level: III.

Origin: Philippine.

Record: Merit Audio Visual: 1047.

Formation: Groups of three to six, each group having a set of poles.

Skills: Walk and leap.

Action: Two long bamboo poles about 9 feet long are needed for each group. These poles may rest on blocks of wood about 2 inches thick and 30 inches long. An individual sits at each end of each pole holding one in each hand. The sticks should be held with the thumb and fingers on the sides of the stick (not underneath). The poles are operated in the following rhythm:

Count 1: Strike sticks together.

Count 2: Strike sticks on the floor or supporting blocks about 18 inches apart.

Count 3: Strike sticks apart one more time.

Variation 1: Dancers straddle sticks. On count 1 they jump with both feet apart on either side of the sticks. On counts 2 and 3, they jump with feet close together between the sticks.

Variation 2: Dancers stand with their sides next to and outside the poles.

Count 1: Pause as the poles are struck together.

Count 2: Leap sideways into the poles, touching the floor first with the foot closest to the poles in the starting position.

Count 3: Touch the other foot to the floor between the poles as the first foot is raised slightly from the floor.

Count 1: Continuing in the same direction, step out from between the sticks to the opposite side with the foot closest to the side, while raising the foot taking the step on count 3.

Count 2: Move in between the sticks as in count 2 above but from the opposite side.

Count 3: Repeat count 3 above continuing to move in the new direction.

Continue stepping out from between the sticks on count 1 and stepping with alternating feet on counts 2 and 3.

Variation 3: Dancers move continuously clockwise around and in between the poles.

Counts 1 to 3: Walk parallel to the sticks on the outside as stick handlers beat together-apart-apart. With the right side toward the sticks, step left, right, left.

Counts 1 to 3: Step right and pivot to face down between the sticks (count 1). Step in between the sticks with the left foot, which is now nearest the sticks (count 2); and with the right (count 3).

Step out with the left on count 1 and repeat the beginning sequence of stepping along and on the outside of the sticks. Four persons may do this at a time by

having each one begin at one of the corners, with two moving immediately through the sticks while the other two begin by stepping parallel to the sticks.

Variation 4: Line a series of pairs of sticks parallel to each other. The children proceed down the series of sticks as in variation 2, except that they must cross one over the other to stick into every other set of sticks.

Variation 5: Similar to the variation above, but children turn between each set of sticks, so that the right foot enters first for one set, the left the next.

Variation 6: Arrange two sets of sticks so they cross in the center. Children proceed as in variation 3, but will step in between a set of sticks for each measure.

Teaching Suggestions: It is helpful to have the children practice the steps using parallel lines on the floor before trying them with the moving sticks. There is a tendency for the children operating the sticks to go faster and faster. The children will need help in maintaining a steady tempo.

VIRGINIA REEL

Level: III.
Origin: American.
Record: Merit Audio Visual: 1043.
Formation: Longways set of no more than six couples.
Skills: Walk, do-si-do, and slide reeling.
Action: Part I: Boys join hands in their line, and girls in theirs. All walk forward four steps and then back to place.
Repeat the action above.
All walk forward, join right hands with partners, turning once around clockwise, and then walking back to place.

Repeat the action, joining left hands.
Repeat the action, joining two hands.
Walk forward to meet partner, do-si-do, and walk back to place.
Part II: The first couple joins hands and slides eight slides down the center of the set and eight slides back to place.

First couple begins the reel by hooking right elbows, circling once and a half around, clockwise, so they end facing the opposite line. They then drop elbows and hook left elbows with the next person in the opposite line. They come back to their partners with a right elbow turn and then on to the next in line, preceding down the set until couple 1 reaches the foot of the set. Couple 1 then joins hands and slides down toward the head of the set.

Part III: Facing toward the head of the set, the first couple casts off, turning away from each other and toward their own line. They then lead their own line to the foot of the set. The first couple then joins hands and forms an arch through which each of the following couples pass. Couple 1 remains at the foot of the set, with couple 2 now becoming active.

The dance is now repeated from the beginning. Couple 2 assumes the original position of couple 1 and will become active in Part II.

Teaching Suggestions: It is important that the children realize that when reeling they always reel with their partner and the line opposite from the one in which they are standing.

BLACK NAG

Level: IV.
Origin: English.

Record: World of Fun: 6.
Formation: Longways set of three couples, all facing the head of the set.
Skills: Run, slide, right-left elbow swing, and hey.
Action: Part I (A)—Measures 1 to 4: "Forward and back a double." Each couple, holding right hands, takes four running steps forward (beginning with the right) and four steps back.
Measures 5 to 8: Repeat the action of measures 1 to 4.
Part I (B)—Measures 1 and 2: Partners face each other, joining both hands at shoulder height. The first couple slips sideways with four sliding steps, toward the head of the set.
Measures 3 and 4: The second couple moves up four slides sideways.
Measures 5 and 6: The third couple takes four slides.
Measures 7 and 8: All "turn single." Releasing hands, dancers turn individually to their right with four steps.
Measures 1 to 8: Repeat the action of measures 1 to 8 beginning with the third couple sliding back to their original position. Then the second and finally the first couple. All "turn single."
Part II (A)—Measures 1 to 8: "Siding." Partners pass each other with four steps, passing left shoulders and return, passing right shoulders. Repeat. (On the fourth step partners turn to face each other so they face each other on the way back.)
Part II (B)—Measures 1 and 2: The first boy and the last girl (diagonals) change places with four sliding steps, with right shoulders leading and passing back to back.
Measures 3 and 4: The first girl and the last boy (diagonals) do the same, with four sliding steps.
Measures 5 and 6: The second man and lady do the same.
Measures 7 and 8: All "turn single."
Measures 1 to 8: Repeat the action of measures 1 to 8 with all dancers in turn returning to their places. All "turn single."
Part III (A)—Measures 1 to 8: "Arm right" and "arm left." Partners turn each other first with a right elbow swing followed by a left elbow swing, with eight steps for each turn.
Part III (B)—Measures 1 to 8: "Men's hey." Couple 1 faces down the set, couples 2 and 3 facing up the set. The first and second boy start by veering to their left, so they pass right shoulders with each other, continuing around a large loop into the center. The third boy waits for about two counts, giving the first two boys a chance to pass each other. Boy 3 then begins his "hey" by moving to the right and into the center. Continuing in the figure eight, they end in their original places.
Measures 1 to 8: "Ladies hey." Girls repeat the action of the boys. On the last two measures the boys turn single with four steps.

Teaching Suggestions: The name of this dance probably originated in the English tradition of naming taverns with animal names.

CRESTED HEN

Level: IV.
Origin: Danish.
Record: World of Fun: 4; Merit Audio Visual: 1042.
Formation: Sets of three dancers, hands joined to form a circle.
Skills: Step-hop.
Action: Part A: Moving clockwise, step-hop in a circle, take a vigorous stamp on the first beat. Dancers lean away from the circle (eight steps).
Jump bringing feet down sharply on the first beat, step-hop in a circle moving counterclockwise (eight steps).
Part B: Continuing to step-hop, outside dancers drop hands. Placing their free hand on their hips the right-hand dancer step-hops through the arch formed by the center dancer and the dancer on the left.
The center dancer turns under own left arm following the right-hand dancer through the arch, followed almost immediately by the left-hand dancer turning under own right hand so that the dancers do not have to release hands.
Repeat the action by having the left-hand dancer begin the move moving through the arch formed by the center and right-hand dancers.
Repeat the sequence once more beginning with the right-hand dancer, and ending with the left-hand dancer.

CUMBERLAND SQUARE EIGHT

Level: IV.
Origin: English.
Record: World of Fun: 5.
Formation: Square set of four couples, designated as head, foot, and side couples.
Skills: Galop, star, and basket.
Action: Head and foot couples, with partners facing, join hands and galop across the set in eight slides, boys passing back to back.
Return to position with eight galops, girls passing back to back.
Repeat the action with the side couples.
Head and foot couples come together in the center of the set forming a right-hand star (eight counts) and then a left-hand star back to place (eight counts).
Side couples repeat the right- and left-hand stars.
Head and foot couples form a basket (the boys join hands with each other behind the girls' backs; the girls extend their hands behind and under the boys' arms and join hands with each other in front of the boys).
Circle to the left and then back to place with two steps (16 steps).
Side couples repeat the action by forming a basket. All

join hands and circle to the left (16 counts).

Promenade back to their original position (16 counts).

Teaching Suggestions: In place of the basket, the two couples may join hands and skip vigorously to the left in a circle.

FIREMAN'S DANCE

Level: IV.

Origin: American.

Record: World of Fun: 1; Folkcraft: 1131.

Formation: Two couples in a line facing two couples in a line, arranged in a circle as the spokes of a wheel.

Skills: Slide, galop, ladies chain, and right and left through.

Action: Part I (A)—Measures 1 to 4: Both boy 1 and the opposite girl 1 (nearest the center of the circle) step forward and join both hands. At the same time boy 2 and the opposite girl 2 (at the other end of the line) take one step back. The active ones slide eight steps down the center, between the lines, while the active twos take eight slides individually behind the lines.

Measures 5 to 8: They return to their places with eight slides, ones on the inside, twos on the outside.

Measures 1 to 8: Repeat the action of measures 1 to 8 but with the twos on the inside and the ones on the outside.

Part II (B)—Measures 1 to 8: Simultaneously the 1 couples do a right and left through, while the 2 couples do a ladies chain, all couples ending in their original places.

Measures 1 to 8: Repeat the action but with the 1 couples doing a ladies chain and the 2 couples doing the right and left through.

Part III (C)—With hands joined in lines of four, all advance four steps forward, shouting, "Fire, fire, fire," and walk back four steps shouting, "Water, water, water." They then release hands, walk forward, and pass through the opposite line, passing right shoulders with the opposite dancer, progressing to begin the dance with a new line.

FIVE FOOT TWO

Level: IV.

Origin: American.

Record: Folkcraft: 1420.

Formation: Double circle, all facing counterclockwise in the promenade position.

Skills: Two-step, walk, and balance.

Action: Part I: Promenade. Measures 1 and 2: Take two two-steps in the line of direction.

Measures 3 and 4: Walk forward four steps in the line of direction.

Measures 5 and 6: Repeat measures 1 and 2.

Measures 7 and 8: Drop left hands. Boy walks four steps forward, turning to face out of the circle on the last two steps. Girl walks four steps backward, turning

to face inside of the circle. All join hands in one large single circle.

Part II: Balance and walk around. Measures 9 and 10: Balance forward, balance back.

Measures 11 and 12: Drop left hands. Walk four steps around partner, moving clockwise to change places. Girls now face out, boys in. All join hands in a single circle.

Measures 13 and 14: Repeat the action of measures 9 and 10.

Measures 15 and 16: Drop partner's hand. Each boy takes the girl on his left for a new partner and both walk four steps to face in the line of direction in the promenade position.

GATHERING PEASCODS

Level: IV.

Origin: English.

Record: Merit Audio Visual: 1045.

Formation: Single circle of partners, all facing the center, hands joined.

Skills: Slide and walk.

Action: Part I: All take eight "slips" (slides) to the left. Drop hands and "turn single" (individually turn in place with four small steps).

Repeat, taking eight "slips" to the right and "turn single."

Part II: Boys step forward to form an inner circle, join hands, and take 12 "slips" to the left, returning to their original positions.

Girls form an inner circle and take 12 "slips" to the left, returning to their places.

Part III: Boys "double" (walk) forward three steps and clap.

Girls "double" forward and clap as boys return to their places.

Girls "double" back as boys "double" forward.

All "turn single," the boys returning to their places as they turn.

Repeat Part III.

Part IV: Partners face and "side" (take eight steps forward, passing left shoulders, turn, and pass right shoulders on the return). "Turn single."

Repeat the "siding" and "turn single."

Part V: Repeat Part II, with the girls forming the circle first and then the boys.

Part VI: Repeat Part III, with the girls leading the first "double" and boys leading the repeat.

Part VII: Partners "arm" (elbow swing) with right elbow (eight steps). "Turn single."

Partners "arm" with left elbow (eight steps). "Turn single."

Part VIII: Repeat Part II.

Part IX: Repeat Part III, ending with a final "turn single."

Teaching Suggestions: This is one of the many old English dances that were danced in the court of King James I.

Later these dances became popular with the country people, who danced them on the village green for pleasure, not spectacle.

HEEL AND TOE POLKA

Level: IV.
Origin: American.
Record: MacGregor: 5003-B.
Formation: Couples in the varsouvienne position.
Skills: Fling.
Action: Beginning with the outside foot, touch the heel forward, toe behind, and take a two-step forward (heel, toe, step, close, step).

With the inside foot, touch heel forward, toe behind, and a two-step forward (heel, toe, step, close, step). Partners take four polka steps.
Teaching Suggestions: The polka step may be taken forward or in the face to face, back to back manner. If the polka step is taken in the open position, the children will need some practice in doing the step as they move forward. This dance may be used as a mixer by arranging the dancers in a circle, moving counterclockwise on the polka step. On the last step the girl takes the step in place, while the boy moves forward to a new partner.

HIGHLAND FLING

Level: IV.
Origin: Scottish
Record: Merit Audio Visual: 1045.
Formation: Individuals scattered in the room.
Skills: Fling.
Action: First step—Measures 1 and 2: Spring on the toes; then with the left arm raised overhead and the right hand on the hip, hop on the left foot, bringing the right foot behind the left leg. Hop again on the left foot, bringing right foot in front of left leg. Hop again on the left, bringing the right foot behind again.

Measures 3 and 4: Repeat from the beginning, hopping on the right foot and reversing hands.

Measures 5 and 6: Repeat measures 1 and 2.

Measures 7 and 8: Place both hands on hips and repeat measures 3 and 4, turning once around in place to the right.

Measures 9 to 16: Repeat measures 1 to 8, beginning with the left foot hop, but raising the right arm first. Second step—Measure 1: Spring on the toes again, landing on both feet.

Measure 2: With left arm raised, hop on the left, touching the right toe forward and to the side. Hop again on the left, bringing the right foot in front of the left leg.

Measures 3 and 4: With both hands on hips and with right-foot hops, turn once around in place to the right (measures 7 and 8 above).

Measures 5 to 8: Repeat measures 1 to 4, beginning with the right-foot hops and raising the right arm. This time turn to the left.

Measures 9 to 16: Repeat measures 1 to 8.

JESSIE POLKA

Level: IV.
Origin: American.
Record: Folkcraft: 1093.
Formation: In lines of two or more with hands on the waist of the person in front.
Skills: Two-step or polka.
Action: Part I: Heel step. Measure 1: Beginning left, touch the heel in front, then step left in place.

Measure 2: Touch the right toe behind, then in place, or swing it forward, keeping the weight on the left.

Measure 3: Touch the right heel in front, then step right in place.

Measure 4: Touch the left heel to the left side; sweep the left across in front of the right. Keep the weight on the right.

Part II: Two-step or polka. Measures 5 to 8: Take four two-steps or polka steps forward in the line of direction.
Teaching Suggestions: This dance may become a mixer by having couples, alternating girl, boy in the line. On the last two steps the girl turns out to her right and falls into line behind her partner. The last girl rushes to the head of the line.

MAITELITZA

Level: IV.
Origin: Russian-American.
Record: Educational Dance Recordings: FD-2.
Formation: Sets of three, inside hands joined, facing counterclockwise; in a circle as the spokes of a wheel.
Skills: Hop-swing and slide.
Action: Part I (A)—Measures 1 to 8: Stamp on the right foot. Hop on the right, swinging the left foot lightly across in front. Stamp left, swinging the right foot across. Repeat the action three times more. Each group then moves forward for three steps.

Part II (A)—Measures 1 to 8: All turn to face the center (making a quarter turn to the left). Each joins hands with the person on the right and left sides, making three concentric circles. All slide eight steps to the right and then eight steps back to the left.

Part III: (B)—Measures 1 to 8: All turn to face counterclockwise and join hands in the original threes. The middle and left persons form an arch by raising their joined hands, and the person on the right walks slowly forward, under the arch, and back to place with eight steps. On the last four steps the middle dancer turns under his or her own arm following the right-hand dancer. The middle dancer then forms an arch with the right-hand dancer and the pattern is repeated with the left-hand dancer going under the arch.

Teaching Suggestions: In Part II the circles may slide in opposite directions (inner circle to the left, middle circle to the right, outer circle to the left).

MAYIM

Level: IV.
Origin: Israeli.
Record: World of Fun: 1046.
Formation: Single circle, hands joined and held down.
Skills: Grapevine, hop, and run.
Action: Part I: Grapevine (tscherkessia). Measures 1 to 4: Moving clockwise, cross the right in front of the left (count 1); step left to the side (count 2); cross right behind left (count 3); step left to the side with a light springing step, accenting the step (count 4). Repeat three more times.

Part II: Center and back. Measure 5: Beginning right, take four running steps to the center, leaping slightly and bending the knee on the first step. Lift joined hands gradually above heads as dancers move to the center. Measure 6: Beginning right, move away from the center with 4 running steps, lowering arms as they move. Measures 7 and 8: Repeat measures 5 and 6.

Part III: Run, toe, touch, Clap. Measure 1: Beginning right, move clockwise with three running steps (counts 1 to 3); turn to face the center, weight remaining on the right (count 4).

Measure 2: Hop on the right and touch the left across in front to the right side (count 1). Hop on right and touch left to the side (count 2). Hop right, touching left in front to the right side (count 3). Hop right touching left to the side (count 4).

Measure 3: Repeat measure 2.

Measure 4: Hop on left, touching right in front to the left side and clap hands directly in front at arms length (count 1). Hop on left, touch right to side and swing arms out to the sides at shoulder height (count 2). Hop left, touch right in front to the left side, and clap hands directly in front at arms length (count 3). Hop left, touching the right to the side and swinging arms out to the sides at shoulder height (count 4).

Measure 5: Repeat measure 4.

MISERLOU (KRITIKOS)

Level: IV.
Origin: Greek.
Record: Merit Audio Visual: 1046.
Formation: A large broken circle, hands joined, the leader is at the right end of the line.
Skills: Grapevine and two-step.
Action: Measure 1: Beginning right, step in place (count 1); hold (count 2); pointing left toe in front of right make a circular out and motion to the left toward the right heel (counts 3 and 4). (Group movement is counterclockwise.)

Measure 2: Step left behind right (count 1); step right to the side (count 2); step left across in front of right (count 3); pivot counterclockwise a half turn on the left to face clockwise (count 4).

Measure 3: Beginning right and moving clockwise take one two-step.

Measure 4: Step back on left (count 1); step right to the side, body facing the center (count 2); step left across in front of right (count 3); hold (count 4).

Teaching Suggestions: Smaller groups may be more successful at the elementary school level. A variation for measure 4 commonly used is to substitute a two-step moving backward, for the movement described above.

ROAD TO THE ISLES

Level: IV.
Origin: Scottish.
Record: World of Fun: 3; Merit Audio Visual: 1043.
Formation: Double circle of partners in the varsouvienne position, all facing counterclockwise.
Skills: Schottische, step-hop, and grapevine.
Action: Part I: Point, grapevine. Measure 1: Point left toe forward to the left.

Measures 2 and 3: Step left behind right (count 1); step right to the right side (count 2); step left in front of right (count 1); hold (count 2).

Measure 4: Point right toe forward to the right.

Measures 5 and 6: Step right behind left (count 1); step left to the left side (count 2); step right in front of left (count 1); hold (count 2).

Measures 7 and 8: Point left toe forward (body leans backward); point left toe back (body leans forward).

Part II: Schottische. Measures 9 to 12: Beginning left, take two schottische steps in the line of direction. Without releasing hands, turn clockwise on hop (count 2, measure 12) to face the reverse line of direction. The girl is now on the boy's left.

Measures 13 and 14: Beginning left, take one schottische step in the reverse line of direction. Without releasing hands, turn counterclockwise on the hop to face the line of direction. The girl is now back in the original position on the boy's right.

Measures 15 and 16: Stamp in place, right, left, right.

Teaching Suggestions: The Scottish style of precise and small foot work should be encouraged. Kicking the heel up on the hop of the schottische step as if to flick the kilt is also characteristic of this dance.

SICILIAN TARANTELLA

Level: IV.
Origin: Italian.
Record: Merit Audio Visual: 1045; World of Fun: 6.
Formation: Two-couple sets, boys standing side by side, facing their partners.
Skills: Step-hop, do-si-do, skip, and star.
Action: Part I: In place, each person steps on the right foot, hops on it, swinging the left foot forward and at

the same time claps own hands (or strikes a tamborine).
Repeat the step-hop on the left foot, swinging the right
foot forward and clapping.

In place, take four quick running steps, snapping fingers or shaking a tamborine overhead.

Repeat the above three more times.

Part II: Snapping fingers or shaking tamborines, dancers bend forward and take four running steps toward
their partners, straighten up and raise their arms. Take
four steps backward, lowering arms and bending forward.

Repeat three more times.

Part III: The head boy and the foot girl (diagonally
across from one another), clap their own hands, run
forward, hook right elbows, turn once, and return to
their places.

The foot boy and the head girl repeat the action.

The action is again repeated for both sets but with a
left elbow swing.

Part IV: The head boy and the foot girl do a right
shoulder do-si-do (pass right shoulders only) and return to places.

The other couple repeats the action.

The do-si-do is repeated for both couples but this time
passing left shoulders.

Part V: Dancers face their own right, and with hands
on waist all skip forward counterclockwise for eight
steps in the circle. Turning about, they skip clockwise
for eight steps.

All four dancers join left hands for a left-hand star and
skip counterclockwise for eight steps. They turn, joining hands for a right hand star for eight steps.

They return to their starting positions to begin the
dance again.

SQUARE DANCE

Square dance calls are of two types: ***patter*** and ***singing*** calls. Patter calls are those in which the caller
gives the instructions of the dance in a rhythmic manner, with folksy sayings added for color. Patter calls
give callers more opportunity to individualize the
dance by adding their own sayings. These calls generally rhyme and fit the rhythmic pattern of the music,
but the music used varies with the caller. Singing
calls are those in which the caller gives instructions
to the dancers by singing the call to a familiar tune.
There tends to be less variation from caller to caller,
since these dances are written to particular tunes.

A square dance is divided into several parts:
namely, the introduction, the main figure, the break,
and the closing. The introductory calls are those that
get the dancers moving. The break consists of the
actions that are generally called half way through the
main figure. The closing includes the actions that will
terminate the dance. In pattern calls, the beginning,
break, and closing are called at the discretion of the
caller. They are not standardized in any way, as they
are in singing calls. The main figure includes the
primary actions from which the dance received its
name.

Square dance figures may be structured in several
ways. Some dances use what is known as a ***visiting
figure.*** In these dances, individuals, a couple, or several couples execute the figure with each couple in
succession. For example, the visiting person(s) from

Table 19-3
Square dances

Name	Call	Figure	Skills	Page	Record	Level
Birdie in the Cage	Patter	Visiting couple	Circle, swing	358	Educational Record: Sq.3	III
Duck for the Oyster	Patter	Visiting couple	Circle, arch	358	Educational Record: Sq.2	III
Irish Washerwoman	Singing	Symmetrical	Do-si-do, allemande left, grand right and left, swing, promenade	358	Educational Record: Sq.2A	III
Just Because	Singing	Symmetrical	Do-si-do, allemande left, grand right and left, swing, promenade, ladies chain	359	Educational Record: Sq.3	III
Pop Goes the Weasel	Singing	Single visiting	Circle, swing, promenade	359	Educational Record: Sq.3 World of Fun: 2	III
Red River Valley	Singing	Visiting couple	Allemande left, grand right and left, promenade, circle, swing	359	Educational Record: Sq.2 World of Fun: 1 MacGregor: 1204	III
Solomon Levi	Singing	Accumulative	Swing, allemande left, grand right and left, promenade	359	MacGregor: 1204	III
Take a Peek	Patter	Visiting couple	Circle, swing	360	Educational Record: Sq.4	III
Alabama Jubilee	Singing	Symmetrical	Allemande left, grand right and left, promenade, sashay, swing	360	MacGregor: 638, 640, 1204 Old Timer: 8041, 8043 Windsor: 4414, 4444	IV
Coming Round the Mountain	Singing	Symmetrical	Ladies chain, swing, allemande left and right promenade	360	Educational Record: Sq.4	IV
Dip and Dive	Patter	Visiting couple	Circle, arch, swing, promenade	361	Educational Record: Sq.4	IV
Divide the Ring and Tunnel Through	Patter	Split-the-ring	Bow, swing, forward and back, arch, do-si-do	361	Educational Record: Sq.3	IV
Hot Time in the Old Town	Singing	Accumulative	Circle, allemande left/right, grand right and left, sashay, swing, promenade	362	Folkcraft: 1037 MacGregor: 652, 004-4, 445-4	IV
Hurry, Hurry, Hurry	Patter	Line	Circle, ladies chain	362	Educational Record: Sq.4	IV
Jessie Polka Square	Singing	Arching	Arch, allemande left, star, promenade swing	363	Folkcraft: 1263 MacGregor: 657	IV
Oh Johnny	Singing	Symmetrical	Circle, swing, allemande left, do-si-do, promenade	363	MacGregor: 6525, 1204 Old Timer: 8041 Folkcraft: 1037	IV
Smoke on the Water	Singing	Symmetrical	Allemande left, grand right and left, swing, circle, sashay, star, bow	363	MacGregor: 1204	IV
Texas Star	Patter	Star	Forward and back, right and left star, swing, promenade	364	Educational Record: Sq.4	IV

couple 1 begin by going to couple 2 and executing the figure. They then move on to couple 3 and finally to couple 4 to repeat the main figure two more times. Then the next visiting person(s) begin the action moving from couple to couple. The main figure is concluded when all four couples or individuals have traveled to each of the other couples to repeat the dance.

In some dances all four couples simultaneously perform the actions of the dance. These dances are referred to as *symmetrical figures.* Other dances use the *star, split-the-ring,* or *arching figures.* In the star figure, individuals or couples grasp hands in the center of the set to form a star. In split-the-ring, a couple moves across the set to pass through between the two dancers of the opposing couple. In arching figures, one or more couples form an arch by raising joined hands and one or more couples pass under the arch. In many of these dances the couples alternate forming and passing through the arches.

The following section includes a variety of square dances that may be used at the upper elementary school level. Only the main figure is included for dances that use a patter call, since the beginning, break, and closing vary in the records available.

BIRDIE IN THE CAGE

Level: III.
Call: Patter.
Figure: Visiting couple.
Record: Educational Recording: Sq.3.
Skills: Circle and swing.
Action: Main figure:
FIRST COUPLE OUT TO THE COUPLE ON THE RIGHT. CIRCLE FOUR FOR HALF THE NIGHT.

Couples 1 and 2 join hands and circle half a circle so couple 1 is facing in toward the center of the set; couple 2 is facing toward the outside of the set.

NOW BIRDIE IN THE CAGE, THREE HANDS ROUND.

The girl of couple 1 drops hands and steps into the circle made by the three other dancers. The three dancers circle around the "birdie."

BIRDIE FLY OUT, THE CROW HOP IN.

The girl backs out of the circle to join hands with the other dancers, while her partner steps into the circle. The three dancers circle the "crow."

NOW THE CROW HOP OUT, SWING YOUR OWN, BOTH COUPLES SWING.

The dance is repeated with couple 1 moving to couple 3 and finally to couple 4.
The entire sequence is then repeated for couples 2, 3, and 4.

DUCK FOR THE OYSTER

Level: III.
Call: Patter.
Figure: Visiting couple.
Record: Educational Recordings: Sq.2.
Skills: Circle and arch.
Action: Main figure:

FIRST COUPLE OUT TO THE COUPLE ON THE RIGHT. CIRCLE FOUR FOR HALF THE NIGHT.

Couple 1 goes to couple 2, the four join hands, and circle to the left half way around so couple 1 faces in toward the set and couple 2 faces the outside of the set.

DUCK FOR THE OYSTER, DUCK.

Couple 1 with hands joined moves under the arch formed by couple 2 and backs back to face the set again.

NOW DIVE FOR THE CLAM, DIVE.

Couple 1 forms an arch and couple 2 with hands joined moves under the arch and backs out again.

AND DUCK ON THROUGH AND ON TO THE NEXT.

Couple 2 forms an arch again, couple 1 moves under the arch and on to couple 3 to repeat the action again. The dance is repeated with couple 1 moving on to do the dance with couples 3 and 4. Following this sequence the dance is repeated with couples 2, 3, and 4 becoming the visiting couples in turn.

IRISH WASHERWOMAN

Level: III.
Call: Singing.
Figure: Symmetrical.
Record: Educational Recordings: Sq.2A.
Skills: Do-si-do, allemande left, grand right and left, swing, and promenade.
Action: Introduction:

NOW DO-SI-DO WITH THE CORNERS ALL, BACK TO BACK AROUND THE HALL. DO-SI-DO WITH THE PARTNERS TOO, SQUARE YOUR SET, HERE'S WHAT YOU DO. ALLEMANDE LEFT WITH YOUR LEFT HAND, RIGHT TO YOUR PARTNER, GO RIGHT AND LEFT GRAND. PROMENADE. THE RIGHT FOOT UP, THE LEFT FOOT DOWN, PROMENADE AROUND THE TOWN. SQUARE UP HERE WE GO.

Main figure:

ALL FOUR BOYS YOU LEAD TO THE RIGHT, HONOR THE LADIES SO POLITE.

All boys move to the girl on the right (past partner).

DO-SI-DO, ON HEEL AND TOE. READY NOW AWAY WE GO.

Do-si-do with the right-hand lady.

STEP RIGHT UP AND SWING HER AWHILE, STEP RIGHT BACK AND WATCH HER SMILE.

Boys swing the girl and then take the girl's right hand in their right and step back away from her.

STEP RIGHT UP AND SWING HER AGAIN. STEP RIGHT BACK
AND WATCH HER GRIN.

Swing the girl again and promenade her to the boy's
home position as his new partner.

The dance is repeated three more times, until the boys
are back to their original partners.

JUST BECAUSE

Level: III.
Call: Singing.
Figure: Symmetrical.
Record: Educational Recordings: Sq.3.
Skills: Do-si-do, allemande left, grand right and left,
swing, promenade, and ladies chain.
Action: Introduction:

DO-SI-DO YOUR CORNER, SHE'S A DARLING. AND THEN
YOU DO-SI-DO YOUR PARTNER, DO THE SAME. ALLE-
MANDE LEFT TO THE CORNER. GRAND RIGHT AND LEFT,
GRAND CHAIN 8 HALF WAY ROUND YOU GO. DO-SI-DO
YOUR PARTNER, SHE'S A DARLING. SO SWING THAT PRET-
TY BABY ROUND AND ROUND. PROMENADE AROUND
THAT HALL, JUST WALK AROUND YOU GO. BECAUSE, JUST
BECAUSE.

Main figure:

HEAD 2 LADIES CHAIN DOWN THE CENTER OF THE SET.
NOW TURN THE LADIES, CHAIN 'EM BACK IN TIME.

Couples 1 and 3 do the ladies chain over and back.

AND NOW THE SIDE 2 LADIES CHAIN DOWN THE MIDDLE
OF THAT RING. NOW TURN THE LADIES, CHAIN 'EM BACK
IN TIME.

Couples 2 and 4 do the ladies chain over and back.

DO-SI-DO YOUR CORNER, SHE'S A DARLING. DO-SI-DO
YOUR PARTNER, DO THE SAME. LET'S TAKE THE CORNER
MAID AND WITH HER PROMENADE. BECAUSE, JUST BE-
CAUSE.

The dance is repeated three more times. For the second
time through the head couples begin the chaining first
on the third and fourth times, the side couples begin
the ladies chain first.

POP GOES THE WEASEL

Level: III.
Call: Singing.
Figure: Single Visiting.
Record: Educational Recordings: Sq.3; World of Fun: 2.
Skills: Circle, swing, promenade.
Action: Introduction, break, closing:

ALL JOINS HANDS AND CIRCLE LEFT, CIRCLE LEFT, CIR-
CLE LEFT WITH THE WEASEL. ONCE AROUND TIL YOU
COME HOME, SWING WITH THE WEASEL. SWING YOUR
PARTNER ONCE AROUND, PROMENADE THE TOWN.
PROMENADE EIGHT AND PROMENADE ALL, SQUARE YOUR
SETS WITH THE WEASEL.

Main figure:

FIRST GIRL GO OUT TO THE RIGHT, CIRCLE THERE LIKE
THUNDER. THREE HANDS AROUND WE GO. POP THE
LADY UNDER.

The first lady and couple 2 circle to the left for one
half turn. Then couple 2 raises their joined hands and
lady 1 moves under the arch and on to couple 3.

GO TO THE NEXT, THE BOY WILL FOLLOW, CIRCLE LEFT
LIKE THUNDER. THREE HANDS AROUND WE GO. POP THE
COUPLE UNDER.

Repeat the action above but this time boy 1 waits
outside the circle, so when couple 3 makes an arch he
and his partner pop under.

ON TO THE NEXT, THE BOY WILL FOLLOW, CIRCLE THERE
LIKE THUNDER. THREE HANDS AROUND WE GO, POP THE
COUPLE UNDER. GIRL COME BACK, THE BOY COME ON
CIRCLE 4 LIKE THUNDER. FOUR HANDS AROUND WE GO,
POP THE COUPLE UNDER.

Come back to couple 4 and repeat the action. This time
all four dancers circle.

The dance is repeated with the second, third, and
fourth couples becoming active in turn.

RED RIVER VALLEY

Level: III.
Call: Singing.
Figure: Visiting Couple.
Record: Educational Recordings: Sq.2; World of Fun: 1;
MacGregor: 1204.

Skills: Allemande left, grand right and left, promenade,
circle, swing.
Action: Introduction and closing:

NOW YOU ALLEMANDE LEFT ON THE CORNER. AND THE
GRAND RIGHT AND LEFT HALFWAY ROUND. WHEN YOU
MEET WITH YOUR PARTNER PROMENADE HER. AND
PLACES ALL, LISTEN TO MY CALL.

Main figure:

THE FIRST COUPLE TO THE RIGHT AND CIRCLE. CIRCLE
TO THE LEFT, THEN TO THE RIGHT. NOW YOU SWING
WITH THE OTHER FELLOW'S PARTNER. NOW YOU SWING
WITH YOUR RED RIVER GAL.

Partners swing.

The dance is repeated two more times with couple 1
moving to couples 3 and 4 in turn. Then the entire
sequence is repeated with couples 2, 3, and 4 becoming
active.

SOLOMON LEVI

Level: III.
Call: Singing.
Figure: Accumulative.
Record: MacGregor: 1204.

Skills: Swing, allemande left, grand right and left, promenade.

Action: Introduction and closing:

NOW EVERYBODY SWING YOUR HONEY, YOU SWING HER HIGH AND LOW. THE ALLEMANDE LEFT WITH THE OLD LEFT HAND, AROUND THE RING YOU GO. A GRAND OLD RIGHT AND LEFT, WALK ON YOUR HEEL AND TOE. YOU MEET YOUR HONEY AND GIVE HER A TWIRL AND AROUND THE RING YOU GO. SINGING, OH SOLOMON LEVI, TRA LA LA LA LA LA. OH SOLOMON LEVI, TRA LA LA LA LA LA.

Main figure:

NOW THE FIRST OLE COUPLE SEPARATE, GO ROUND THE OUTSIDE TRACK.

Girl and boy 1 go around the set, the girl moving counterclockwise, the boy clockwise.

A KEEP A GOING AROUND THE SET. YOU PASS A COMIN' BACK.

Pass partner at the opposite side of the set and continue moving to your home position.

YOU PASS RIGHT BY YOUR PARTNER, SALUTE YOUR CORNERS ALL. YOU TURN AROUND AND SWING YOUR OWN, AND PROMENADE THE HALL. SINGING OH SOLOMON LEVI, TRA LA LA LA LA LA. OH SOLOMON LEVI, TRA LA LA LA LA LA.

The dance is repeated with couples 2, 3, and 4 becoming active in turn. Then couples 1 and 3 become active, 2 and 4, and finally all four couples.

TAKE A PEEK

Level: III.
Call: Patter.
Figure: Visiting couple.
Record: Educational Recordings: Sq.4.
Skills: Circle, swing.
Action: Main figure:

COUPLE NUMBER 1 GO OUT TO THE RIGHT. FACE THE SECOND COUPLE. GO 'ROUND THAT COUPLE AND TAKE A LITTLE PEEK.

Couple 1 separate, lady peeks around the right side of couple 2 and the boy peeks around the left.

BACK TO THE CENTER AND SWING YOUR SWEET. GO 'ROUND THAT COUPLE PEEK ONCE MORE. BACK TO THE CENTER AND SWING ALL FOUR. BOTH COUPLES SWING.

The call is repeated for couples 2, 3, and 4.

ALABAMA JUBILEE

Level: IV.
Call: Singing.
Figure: Symmetrical.
Record: MacGregor: 638, 640, 1204; Old Timer: 8041, 8043; Windsor: 4414, 4444.

Skills: Allemande left, grand right and left, promenade, sashay, and swing.

Action: Opening and closing:

ITS THE ALLEMANDE LEFT, GO ALL THE WAY ROUND. RIGHT HAND AROUND THE NEXT GAL AND DON'T YOU FALL DOWN.

Right hand to the partner and grand right and left.

A LEFT HAND AROUND THE NEXT LITTLE GAL, A RIGHT HAND AROUND THE NEXT, SHE'S THE SWEETEST LITTLE PAL. IT'S A LEFT HAND, A RIGHT HAND, NOW DON'T YOU BE SLOW. ALL AROUND THAT LADY IN THE CALICO. MEET YOUR HONEY AND YOUR PROMENADE, TAKE A LITTLE WALK WITH THAT SWEET LITTLE MAID, TO THE ALABAMA JUBILEE.

Main figure:

FOUR LITTLE LADIES PROMENADE THE INSIDE OF THE RING. BACK TO YOUR HONEY AND GIVE HIM A SWING. SASHAY AROUND YOUR CORNER GIRL. BOW TO YOUR HONEY BOYS, GIVE HER A WHIRL. NOW FOUR GENTS PROMENADE THE INSIDE OF THE HALL BACK TO YOUR HONEY AND SASHAY ALL. SWING THAT CORNER GAL AROUND, TAKE A LITTLE WALK AROUND THE TOWN, TO THE ALABAMA JUBILEE.

The main figure is repeated three more times until the dancers return to their original partners. On the second and fourth times the boys begin the action by promenading in the inside of the ring.

COMING ROUND THE MOUNTAIN

Level: IV.
Call: Singing.
Figure: Symmetrical.
Record: Educational Recordings: Sq.4.
Skills: Ladies chain, swing, allemande left and right, and promenade.
Action:

THE HEAD TWO COUPLES LADIES CHAIN, SIDE COUPLES SWING. CHAIN THEM ROUND THE MOUNTAIN, CHAIN THEM HOME. THE SIDE TWO COUPLES LADIES CHAIN, HEAD TWO COUPLES SWING AGAIN. CHAIN THEM ROUND THE MOUNTAIN, CHAIN THEM HOME. ALLEMANDE LEFT YOUR CORNERS. ALLEMANDE RIGHT YOUR PARTNERS. COME ALL THE WAY AROUND YOUR PARTNER TO THE NEXT GIRL ON THE RIGHT.

All give their right to their partner, walk around their partner, and continue moving forward to the next person.

SWING THIS LADY UP AND DOWN, SWING HER ROUND AND ROUND AND ROUND. AND PROMENADE THAT PRETTY MOUNTAIN GAL.

Promenade with the new partner to the boy's home position.

The dance is repeated until the dancers are with their

original partners. The second time the action begins with the head couples chain; the third and fourth times the dance begins with the side couples chain.

DIP AND DIVE

Level: IV.
Call: Patter.
Figure: Visiting couple.
Record: Educational Recordings: Sq.4.
Skills: Circle, arch, swing, and promenade.
Action: Main figure:

FIRST COUPLE TO THE RIGHT AND CIRCLE FOUR.

Couple 1 goes out to couple 2, they join hands, and all four dancers circle left half way round, so couple 1 faces in toward the set and couple two faces the outside of the set.

THE INSIDE COUPLE ARCH. ITS DIP AND DIVE, AND AWAY YOU GO. WITH THE INSIDE HIGH AND THE OUTSIDE LOW. HURRY, HURRY, HURRY, LET'S GO. DUCK OVER AND BE-LOW.

Couple 2 makes an arch and couple 1 ducks unders it. Couple 1 continues forward, makes an arch. Couple 4 ducks under the arch. Meanwhile, couple 2 turns to face the set, the boy's partner on his right. Couple 4 makes an arch, couple 2 ducks under. This over and under action is repeated until the first couple is back in the center.

NOW DUCK ON THROUGH TO THE OPPOSITE TWO AND CIRCLE FOUR WITH THEM.

On the last move couple 1 ducks under the arch formed by couple 2 and moves on to couple 3. They circle half

way round with them.

YOU DUCK TO THE NEXT AND CIRCLE FOUR.

Couple 3 forms an arch and couple 1 ducks under to move on to couple 4. Couple 1 circles half way round with couple 4.

INSIDE COUPLE ARCH. IT'S DIP AND DIVE AND AWAY YOU GO. WITH THE INSIDE HIGH AND THE OUTSIDE LOW. HURRY, HURRY, HURRY, LET'S GO. DUCK OVER AND BE-LOW. NOW DUCK ON THROUGH AND HOME YOU GO.

The action is repeated with couples 1, 4, and 2 doing the "dip and dive."

AND EVERYBODY SWING. YOU SWING YOUR PRETTY LIT-TLE RED WING, AND PROMENADE HER AND SERENADE HER.

The dance is repeated for couples 2, 3, and 4.

DIVIDE THE RING AND TUNNEL THROUGH

Level: IV.
Call: Patter.
Figure: Split-the-ring.
Record: Educational Recordings: Sq.3.
Skills: Bow, swing, forward and back, arch, and do-si-do.
Action: Main figure:

NOW FIRST COUPLE, NUMBER 1 BOW AND SWING, WE'LL HAVE A LITTLE FUN.
GO DOWN THE CENTER, SPLIT-THE-RING, AND GO ROUND THE SIDES.

Couple 1 walks forward and passes between couple 3, where they separate, the girl turning to her right, the boy to his left. They continue to move around the outside of the set.

JOIN UP WITH THE SIDES, WITH LINES OF THREE.
FORWARD 6 AND BACK.

> They end by passing the side couples and standing next to them, the girl next to couple 2, the boy next to couple 4. The two lines of dancers take four steps forward toward each other and then four steps back with hands joined.

NOW FORWARD 6 AND MAKE AN ARCH.

> The two lines take four steps forward again. The dancers then join hands with the opposite dancer to form a tunnel.

THIRD COUPLE TUNNEL UNDER AND DON'T YOU BLUNDER, SWING ON THE OTHER SIDE.

> Couple 3 passes under the tunnel and swings on the other side (couple 1's home position).

NOW THIRD COUPLE TUNNEL BACK, AND EVERYBODY SWING WITH PARTNER ALL, AND EVERYBODY WHIRL.

> Couple 3 moves back to place under the tunnel and everybody swings.

DO-SI-DO YOUR CORNERS ALL AND DO-SI-DO YOUR PARTNERS TOO.

> All dancers back in their home positions do the do-si-do first with their corner, and then with their partner. The dance is repeated for couples 2, 3, and 4.

HOT TIME IN THE OLD TOWN

Level: IV.
Call: Singing.
Figure: Accumulative.
Record: Folkcraft: 1037; MacGregor: 652, 004-4, 445-4.
Skills: Circle, allemande left and right, grand right and left, sashay, swing, and promenade.
Action: Beginning:

ALL JOIN HANDS AND CIRCLE EIGHT AROUND.
BREAK AND TRAIL ALONG THAT LINE.

> Drop hands and continue moving left, one after the other in a circle.

WHEN YOU GET HOME, EVERYBODY SWING.
THERE'LL BE A HOT TIME IN THE OLD TOWN TONIGHT.

> Main figure:

FIRST COUPLE OUT, AND CIRCLE FOUR AROUND.
PICK UP TWO AND CIRCLE SIX AROUND.

> Boy 1 breaks the circle by unclasping left hand and takes the right hand of the couple 3 girl. Couple 3 now joins the group and circles with them to the left.

PICK UP TWO AND CIRCLE EIGHT AROUND
THERE'LL BE A HOT TIME IN THE OLD TOWN TONIGHT.

> Boy 1 breaks the circle again picking up couple 4 to join the group. All eight circle to the left.

ALLEMANDE LEFT WITH THE LADY ON THE LEFT.
ALLEMANDE RIGHT WITH THE LADY ON THE RIGHT.
ALLEMANDE LEFT WITH THE LADY ON THE LEFT.
AND GRAND RIGHT AND LEFT ALL AROUND.
WHEN YOU MEET YOUR PARTNER, SASHAY ONCE AROUND.
TAKE HER IN YOUR ARMS AND SWING HER ROUND AND ROUND.
PROMENADE AROUND WITH THE PRETTIEST GIRL IN TOWN.
THERE'LL BE A HOT TIME IN THE OLD TOWN TONIGHT.

> The dance is repeated, with couples 2, 3, and 4 becoming the visiting couples.
> Ending:

ALLEMANDE LEFT WITH THE LADY ON THE LEFT.
ALLEMANDE RIGHT WITH THE LADY ON THE RIGHT.
ALLEMANDE LEFT WITH THE LADY ON THE LEFT.
GRAND RIGHT AND LEFT ALL AROUND.
WHEN YOU MEET YOUR PARTNER, SASHAY ONCE AROUND.
BREAK UP YOUR SETS AND DANCE HER 'ROUND AND 'ROUND.
THERE'LL BE A HOT TIME IN THE OLD TOWN TONIGHT.

HURRY, HURRY, HURRY

Level: IV.
Call: Patter.
Figure: Line.
Record: Educational Recordings: Sq.4.
Skills: Circle and ladies chain.
Action: Main figure:

THE FIRST COUPLE GO OUT TO THE RIGHT AND CIRCLE FOUR HANDS ROUND.
NOW LEAVE THE GIRL, GO ON TO THE NEXT, LET'S MAKE IT THREE HANDS ROUND.

> Couple 1 circle with couple 2. Boy 1 goes on to couple 3 and circles to the left with them. Girl 1 stands in a line of three with couple 2.

NOW TAKE THIS COUPLE WITH YOU LET'S MAKE IT FIVE HANDS ROUND.

> Boy 1 and couple 3 move on to couple 4 and all five circle to the left.

YOU LEAVE THEM THERE AND JOIN THE LINE OF THREE. STAND BY YOUR PARTNER.

> Boy 1 leaves couples 3 and 4 standing in a line facing couple 2 and girl 1. He joins partner, to form two lines facing each other.

CHAIN THE LADIES ACROSS THE SET, BUT DON'T YA BE SLOW.

> Girls give their right hands to the opposite girl, walk by them, giving their left hands to the opposite boys, who turn them around (a three-quarter turn) to face down the line.

NOW CHAIN THE LADIES DOWN THE LINE, WALK ON
YOUR HEEL AND TOE.

Ladies now chain with the couple they are facing (the
couple they were standing next to in the line of four).
The boys again turn them with a three-quarter turn.

CHAIN THE LADIES ACROSS THE SET, AND KEEP ON MOV-
ING ROUND.

Ladies chain with the couple across the set, once again
with a three-quarter turn.

AND TURN AND CHAIN YOUR PARTNER BACK TO PLACE.
SQUARE YOUR SET.

Chain once more ending with the original partners.
The dance is repeated with couples 2, 3, and 4 taking
their turns to lead the figure.

JESSIE POLKA SQUARE

Level: IV.
Call: Singing.
Figure: Arching.
Record: Folkcraft: 1263; MacGregor: 657.
Skills: Arch, allemande left, star promenade, two-step,
and swing.
Action:

NOW THE SIDE COUPLES ARCH, HEAD COUPLES DUCK
RIGHT UNDER.
AND YOU DIP AND YOU DIVE, HOME YOU GO AND DON'T
YOU BLUNDER.

Couples 2 and 4 make arches and move clockwise
around the square as couples 1 and 3, moving counterclockwise, duck under the arches. Couples 1 and 3
make arches as 2 and 4 duck under. Repeat until they
reach their home positions.

NOW YOU ALLEMANDE LEFT, PUT YOUR ARM AROUND
YOUR PARTNER IN A STAR PROMENADE DO THE JESSIE
POLKA DANCE.

All give their left hands to their corners and do the
allemande left. When the boys return to their partners
put a hand around her waist (girl does a half turn to
face the same direction as partner). Boys form a left-
hand star and walk forward, counterclockwise. (Star
promenade.)

IT'S HEEL AND A TOE, YOU START THE MUSIC JUMPIN'.

Couples do the Jessie Polka: Touch left heel forward
(count 1). Step left in place (count 2). Touch right toe
back (count 1). Touch right beside left (count 2).
Touch right heel forward (count 1). Step right in place
(count 2). Touch left heel forward (count 1). Swing
left foot across instep of right (count 2).

AS THE LADIES ROLL AWAY, CAN'T YOU SEE THE BUSTLES
BUMPIN'.

Couples take four two-steps forward, the girls turn to
the right and back to the boys behind them on the last

two two-steps.

OH YOU DANCE THROUGH THE NIGHT AS THOUGH IT
WERE A MINUTE.

Repeat the Jessie Polka.

YOUR HEARTS ARE REALLY IN IT. THE JESSIE POLKA
DANCE.

Couples repeat the two-steps with the girls turning
back on the last two two-steps.

NOW WATCH THAT CORNER MAID AND AS SHE COMES
AROUND
TAKE HER IN YOUR ARMS AND SWING HER 'ROUND AND
'ROUND.

As the girls roll back the third time, they swing with
that boy (original corner).

THEN YOU PROMENADE HER HOME, KEEP HER FOR YOUR
PARTNER.
YOU BALANCE AND YOU SWING 'TIL THE MUSIC STARTS
AGAIN.

Keeping their new partners they promenade to the
boy's home position and balance and then swing.
The dance is repeated three times until the dancers are
back to their original partners.

OH JOHNNY

Level: IV.
Call: Singing.
Figure: Symmetrical.
Record: MacGregor: 6525, 1204; Old Timer: 8041;
Folkcraft: 1037.
Skills: Circle, swing, allemande left, do-si-do, and prom-
enade.
Action:

OH YOU ALL JOIN HANDS AND YOU CIRCLE THE RING.
STOP WHERE YOU ARE AND YOU GIVE HER A SWING.
NOW SWING THAT GIRL BEHIND YOU.
GO BACK HOME, AND SWING YOUR OWN IF YOU HAVE
TIME.
ALLEMANDE LEFT WITH THE CORNER GIRL, DO-SI-DO
YOUR OWN.
NOW YOU ALL PROMENADE, WITH THAT SWEET CORNER
MAID.
SINGING OH JOHNNY, OH JOHNNY, OH.

The call is repeated until the dancers are back to their
original partners.

Teaching Suggestions: This dance may also be done using
a single circle of partners.

SMOKE ON THE WATER

Level: IV.
Call: Singing.
Figure: Symmetrical.
Record: MacGregor: 1204.
Skills: Allemande left, grand right and left, swing, circle,

sashay, star, and bow.

Action: Introduction and closing:

NOW YOU ALLEMANDE LEFT YOUR CORNER AND YOU
PASS RIGHT BY YOUR OWN.
RIGHT HAND SWING OLE SALLY GOODIN, A LEFT HAND
SWING YOUR OWN.

Sally Goodin is the girl of the couple to the right.

LADIES STAR RIGHT IN THE CENTER, 'TIL YOU MEET YOUR
CORNER MAN.
AND YOU ALLEMANDE LEFT YOUR CORNER, PARTNER
RIGHT, AND A RIGHT AND LEFT GRAND.
THERE'LL BE SMOKE ON THE WATER, ON THE LAND AND
ON THE SEA.
A RIGHT HAND TO YOUR PARTNER, TURN AROUND AND
YOU GO BACK THREE.
YOU'LL DO A LEFT, RIGHT, AND A LEFT HAND SWING, GO
ALL THE WAY AROUND.
SWING ON THE CORNER, TAKE HER HOME AND SETTLE
DOWN.

Main figure:

FOUR GENTS CENTER, MAKE A CIRCLE AND YOU TURN IT
ONCE AROUND.
HOME YOU GO, SASHAY YOUR PARTNER, STAR WITH THE
RIGHT WHEN YOU COME DOWN.
TURN THAT STAR OUT IN THE CENTER, 'TIL YOU MEET
YOUR CORNER GAL.
ALLEMANDE LEFT THE CORNER, RIGHT AND LEFT GO
ROUND THE WORLD.
YOU'LL WALK AROUND THAT CIRCLE JUST AS PRETTY AS
CAN BE.
A RIGHT HAND TO YOUR PARTNER, TURN AROUND AND
YOU GO BACK THREE.
YOU'LL DO A LEFT, RIGHT, A LEFT HAND SWING, GO ALL
THE WAY AROUND.
SWING ON THE CORNER, TAKE HER HOME AND SETTLE
DOWN.

HEAD GENTS BOW TO YOUR PARTNER AND YOU SWING
HER ROUND AND ROUND.
PASS RIGHT THROUGH, RIGHT DOWN THE CENTER, SEPA-
RATE GO ROUND THE TOWN.
WHEN YOU MEET YOUR LITTLE LADY, SASHAY PARTNERS
ONE AND ALL.
YOU ALLEMANDE LEFT THE CORNER. RIGHT AND LEFT GO
ROUND THE HALL.
THERE'LL BE SMOKE ON THE WATER, ON THE LAND AND
ON THE SEA.

A RIGHT HAND TO YOUR PARTNER, TURN AROUND AND
YOU GO BACK THREE.
YOU'LL GO LEFT, RIGHT, A LEFT HAND SWING, GO ALL
THE WAY AROUND.
SWING ON THE CORNER, TAKE HER HOME AND SETTLE
DOWN.

Repeat from:

HEAD GENTS BOW TO YOUR PARTNERS.

But this time the side gents are active.

TEXAS STAR

Level: IV.
Call: Patter.
Figure: Star.
Record: Educational Recordings: Sq.4.
Skills: Forward and back, right and left star, swing, and
promenade.
Action:

NOW LADIES TO THE CENTER AND BACK TO THE BAR.
AND GENTS TO THE CENTER WITH A RIGHT-HAND STAR.
TAKE THE RIGHT HAND OUT, PUT THE LEFT HAND IN,
COME BACK AGAIN.

Boys reverse directions, changing to a left-hand star.

NOW MEET YOUR PARTNER, GONNA PASS HER BY.
PICK UP THE NEXT ONE ON THE SLY WITH THE ARM
AROUND HER WAIST.
NOW KEEP YOUR ARM AROUND HER WAIST.

Continue moving the star counterclockwise with the
girl by the boy's side.

THE MEN BACK OUT AND THE LADIES COME IN WITH A
TURN AND A HALF.
AND LADIES STAR WITH A RIGHT-HAND CROSS.
AND EVERYBODY SWING AND EVERYBODY WHIRL.

Boys break the star, couples turn moving counterclockwise once and a half. The girls form a right-hand star
in the center.

SWING WITH THE LADY ROUND YOU GO, AND THE ACE IS
HIGH AND THE DEUCE IS LOW.

Girls break the star and swing with their new partners.

PUT HER ON THE RIGHT LET'S PROMENADE, WALK
AROUND THAT HALL.

The dance is repeated until the girls are returned to
their original partners.

SUMMARY

Singing games and American and international folk
and square dance are an essential part of the elementary school dance and physical education experience.
Not only do they provide an excellent cardiorespiratory fitness activity but also contribute to the development of motor and social skills. In addition,
they provide an important activity for the application
of the movement content as the children work in
various partner relationships and formations and per-

form a variety of locomotor and nonlocomotor skills to many different tempos and rhythms. Teaching these forms of dance requires very careful preparation. Dances should be selected that challenge the children but that can be mastered in a relatively short period of time. Organization for getting into partners must be carefully planned to avoid embarassing situations for upper-grade girls and boys. Children should be given many opportunities to repeat the dances they have learned for the enjoyment of moving to the music.

DANCE GLOSSARY

allemande left (right) A dance figure in which the boy gives his left hand to the corner girl, and walks around her and back to his partner.

arching figure A square dance figure in which one or more couples pass through an arch formed by one or more couples by raising held hands.

balance A step forward, close, hold; step back, close; hold executed in 2/4 or 3/4 time.

banjo position Partners face with right hips adjacent, girl's right hand in the boy's left, and her left hand on his shoulder; the boy's right hand is at the girl's waist.

bleking A light hop on one foot extending the opposite heel forward, which is repeated several times alternating feet.

circle left (right) Group forms a single circle facing the center, takes the hands of dancers on either side, and moves in a circle clockwise (counterclockwise).

clockwise Moving to the left in a circle.

counterclockwise Moving to the right in a circle.

do-si-do A dance figure in which couples walk toward each other, with hands crossed at chest level, passing right shoulders; continuing facing forward, they move back to place passing left shoulders.

elbow swing Face partner, join right or left elbows, and turn with small steps.

grand right and left A dance figure in which the dancers move around the circle, boys moving counterclockwise, girls clockwise, giving first the right hand to their partner and left and right hands to those they meet until once again with their partner.

grapevine A step to the side alternating putting the trailing foot across in front of and then behind the other foot.

groups of three Three dancers, usually one boy with a girl on either side.

honor your partner (corner) Face partner, boys bow and girls curtsy.

ladies chain A dance figure in which girls give right hands to each other, their left to the opposite boy as the girls pass, and then turn with boy to face their partner and the opposite girl.

line of direction Counterclockwise.

longways set An arrangement of dancers into two lines with partners facing one another.

open position Partners stand side by side with inside hands joined.

patter call A square dance call in which the caller gives the instructions to the dance in a rhythmical fashion, with folksey sayings added for color.

polka A hop, step, close, step, executed in uneven rhythm.

promenade Partners stand side by side, the girl on the boy's right. Holding each other's right hand and left hand the two proceed around the set and back to their original place.

quadrille A square set; four couples arranged as the sides of a square.

reverse line of direction Clockwise.

right and left through Two couples facing, walk forward, passing right shoulders with the opposite dancer, turn with partner and pass left shoulders on the way back to place where they turn to face the opposite couple.

sashay Moving around partner, boy moving to the right and then behind the girl, girl moving to the left and then in front of boy.

schottische A step, step, step, hop, in even rhythm.

shoulder-waist position Partners face; boy places both hands at the girl's waist, and the girl places both hands on the boy's shoulders.

sidecar position Partners face, left hips adjacent; girl's right hand in the boy's left, with her left hand on his shoulder; his right hand is at her waist.

singing call A square dance call in which the dance instructions are sung to a familiar tune.

skaters' position Partners stand side by side; the boy holds the girl's right hand in his left in front of them, and each puts the remaining hand behind the other's back.

split-the-ring A square dance figure in which a couple moves across the set and passes between the opposite couple.

star A dance figure in which the dancers move to the center of the group, extending right (or left) hands to touch each other, or, with a wrist grasp on the dancer in front of them, they move in a circle.

step-hop A step and a hop on the same foot executed in even rhythm.

symmetrical figure A square dance figure in which all four couples execute the figure at the same time.

two-step A step, together, step, in uneven rhythm.

varsouvienne position Partners stand side by side; the boy holds the girl's left hand in his left to the side, her right in his right slightly above her shoulder.

visiting figure A square dance figure in which the figure is executed by one couple moving to each couple in the set in turn to perform the figure.

waltz A step forward on one foot, a step to the side on the other, and a close executed in 3/4 time.

REFERENCES

1. Harris, J., and others: Dance a while, ed. 5, Minneapolis, 1978, Burgess Publishing Co.
2. Hipps, R., and others: World of fun manual of instructions for world of fun records, Nashville, 1970, Division of Education, Board of Discipleship, The United Methodist Church.
3. Kraus, R.: Folk dancing: a guide for schools, colleges and recreational groups, New York, 1962, Macmillan Co.
4. Napier, P.: Square dancing—Kentucky mountain style, JOPERD **55**(7):39, September 1984.

ADDITIONAL READINGS

Forbes, J.: Early American dance instruction, JOPERD **55**(7):34, September 1984.
A discussion of dance forms in early American life.

Ramsay, J.: Folk dancing is for everyone, JOPERD **55**(7):37, September 1984.
The value of folk dancing in fulfilling the need for cooperative, recreational activity.

Withers, A.: Teaching clogging, in the elementary physical education program, JOPERD **55**(7):43, September 1984.
The history of clogging and eight basic steps.

20

RHYTHMIC ACTIVITIES WITH SMALL EQUIPMENT

CHAPTER OBJECTIVES

1 To specify a progression of rhythmic activities using balls, jump ropes, rhythm sticks, and hoops
2 To describe rhythmic activities using a parachute
3 To discuss suggestions for teaching and organizing rhythmic experiences for elementary school children

Rhythmic activities provide an opportunity for children to use small equipment such as balls, ropes, sticks, hoops, and the like and to move themselves and the equipment to an accompaniment. Each individual brings a somewhat different movement background to the physical education experience. As children work to create combinations of skills and creative movement sequences, they have the opportunity to grow in the understanding of movement and of themselves as movers.

RHYTHMIC ACTIVITIES FOR ELEMENTARY SCHOOL CHILDREN

Children enjoy using small equipment. Rhythmic activities provide the dual challenge of creating interesting ways of using the equipment and using it to the rhythm of the accompaniment.

Body awareness is enhanced as children learn to work within their own abilities and to control objects as the objects are moved. The rhythmic activity experiences should result in learning new ways to use body parts when attempting to control objects.

Space concepts are developed as children learn to control objects. These activities should include opportunities for children to work in their own space as well as in general space and also in relation to other children and the objects they hope to control.

Movement qualities are important aspects of the rhythmic activity experience. Time becomes important as children learn to move themselves and objects within the structure of an imposed rhythm. Children learn not only to respond to the underlying beat but also to respond to tempo changes, rhythmic patterns, and phrasing. In addition, force, flow, and balance are important movement qualities that must be used effectively if children are to be successful in these activities.

The objectives to be developed in rhythmic activities may be found in the box on p. 368. To meet these objectives children should be given the opportunity for maximum participation. Creativity must be encouraged, and children should work as individuals, with partners, and in small groups.

CONDUCTING RHYTHMIC EXPERIENCES

Suggestions for organizing and conducting rhythmic activity experiences for elementary school children may be found in Chapter 7 and 11.

RHYTHMIC ACTIVITY OBJECTIVES IN THE ELEMENTARY SCHOOL*

OBJECTIVE	LEVEL			
	I	II	III	IV
To control a piece of equipment in space	———	———	- - -	- - -
To incorporate space concepts and movement qualities while using small equipment	———	———	———	
To respond to a pulse beat by listening and by manipulating a piece of equipment	———	———	- - -	- - -
To maintain a steady rhythm by carefully listening and responding	———	———	———	- - -
To respond to changes in tempo		———	———	- - -
To respond to accents		———	———	- - -
To respond to musical phrasing		———	———	- - -
To imitate a movement sequence of another person		———	———	- - -
To combine rhythmically body movements and movements of small equipment		———	———	- - -
To work in unison with a partner or in small groups			———	———
To respond to the rhythmic pattern of the accompaniment			———	———
To develop simple combinations of skills creatively			———	———
To put a movement sequence together and to repeat it several times without hesitation			———	———

*The solid lines represent emphasis of an objective, the dotted lines continued use of the mastered objective.

Developing Movement Sequences

1. Early activities with a piece of equipment should help children become acquainted with the properties of the object, such as its weight, shape, and how it can be used in space.
2. Encourage the children to find interesting ways to use the equipment and to develop their own movement sequences.
3. Teach in phrases. Meters of 2/4 or 4/4 are easier for children in their early experiences than are 3/4 rhythms.
4. Cue the beginning so all children get started on the beat, for example, "One, two, ready, go."
5. Begin with using single skills to accompaniment. Move on to simple combinations and finally to more complex combinations when the children are ready. The steps in developing a movement sequence are:

Step 1: To begin, practice single skills without accompaniment. When children have developed some control in their use of skills add accompaniment.

Step 2: Combine two skills in a simple sequence.

DEVELOPING A MOVEMENT SEQUENCE

Step 1:	Step 2:	Step 3:	Step 4:		
Practice individual skills	Develop movement combinations	Add time reference	Add additonal elements		
Practice individual skills without and with accompaniment	Develop several possible combinations; have children give some ideas after a few examples are given	Examples: 4 beats; 4 measures of 4 beats; 4 measures of 3 beats	Locomotor/nonloco-motor	Space	Qualities
			Walk Swing/sway	Self	Force
			Run Bend/stretch	General	Balance
			Skip Turn/twist	Direction	
			Gallop Push/pull	Direction	
			Hop	Pathway	
			Jump	Range	
			Slide	Level	

EXAMPLE: BALL SKILLS

Step 1:	Step 2:	Step 3:	Step 4 (Add one at a time):		
Bounce (catch)	Bounce, bounce, bounce, catch	4 measures of 4 counts each:	Locomotor/nonloco-motor	Space	Qualities
				Move forward the first time through.	Accent the first beat of the measure
Vertical throw (catch)	Throw, catch, bounce, catch	Bounce, catch, bounce, catch; Bounce, bounce, bounce, catch. (Repeat once) Throw catch, bounce, catch; Bounce, catch, throw catch. (Repeat once)	Do the sequence from a stationary position first, then walk the second time through	Move to the side the second time	

Try several possible combinations. After one or two examples are given, ask the children for additional possibilities.

Step 3: Give the sequence a time reference. For example, combine two skills into a 4-beat sequence or combine skills to one phrase of the music. This provides a beginning framework for their movement sequences.

Step 4: Gradually add other elements: space concepts, body movements, change in force, or other movement qualities. The box on p. 369 includes the steps and an example of the development of a movement sequence using balls.

6. In developing movement sequences it may be helpful to begin by giving the children a combination with which to work, such as the following 4-beat sequence for sticks:

Standing, beginning the movement from right to left, hit sticks overhead to the right side (1); moving sticks slightly to the left, hit sticks overhead (2); continuing to move to the left, hit sticks overhead slightly to the left (3); and hit sticks overhead to the left (4).

The children all begin with this combination and add one or more 4-beat sequences to it. For example, they might repeat the movement moving from the left to the right, varying the sequence by moving forward or backward, or using some other combination of their choice.

Refining Tasks

1. Allow sufficient time to have children develop answers to movement challenges. Partner or group work may take longer, since it takes more time to agree with others on movement possibilities.
2. A good beginning and a definite ending are important aspects of a movement sequence.
3. Emphasis should be placed on the smooth transition from one movement to the next and smooth combinations of locomotor and non-locomotor skills while using the equipment (flow).
4. A variety of accompaniments should be used. Children may be asked to bring in records or tapes of music they like. The children should be exposed to a variety of meters as well as types and tempos of musical accompaniment.

BALLS
Equipment

Children should have an appropriate size ball so they can easily control it. A variety of balls may be used. The properties of some types of balls may make them difficult for some children to bounce or control. To be successful in rhythmic activities, children must use equipment they can easily control.

Teaching Suggestions

1. The ball should not be grasped but should rest on the front part of the palm and fingers.
2. When catching the ball, contact should be made with the fingertips, letting the ball roll into the hand as the arms and body give to absorb force.
3. The entire body is used when bouncing the ball.
4. The body should follow the path of the ball. As the ball is moved away from the body it should appear as a natural extension of the body's movement.
5. The children should be encouraged to work with both right and left hands.
6. The action should begin before the beat so the throw or contact on the bounce will be on the beat.
7. Incorporation of movement concepts is a natural part of the activity. Challenges should encourage variety in level, force, self and general space, floor pattern (pathway), direction, and body awareness.
8. Ball rhythms should be introduced early in the teaching of ball skills. Many activities require considerable skill in handling objects and coordinating body parts, and when music is added the difficulty of the activity increases. Therefore, the children must have some opportunity to explore the various ways of controlling the ball using a variety of ball skills before attempting to use the balls in a rhythmic activity. Some prerequisite activities are suggested in Chapter 11.
9. Beginning combinations should be simple (combinations of two to three skills maximum) and should include the repetition of the sequence several times.
10. Beginning combinations may also involve changing hands while executing skills (that is, bouncing the ball twice with the right hand and twice with the left).
11. Accompaniment should have a distinct beat and an appropriate tempo.

Activities
Individual activities

1. Bounce the ball in front of the body and catch.
   a. Bounce to the side of the body and catch.
   b. Bounce the ball under one leg and catch (O'Leary).
   c. Bounce the ball between the legs from the rear to the front.
2. Toss the ball in the air with a two-hand underhand motion and catch.
3. Bounce, bounce, bounce, catch.
4. Bounce the ball forcefully, run under the ball, then catch it.
5. Bounce the ball, turn around in place, then catch it.
6. Throw the ball vertically in the air, arms stretching upward, and catch it.
7. Throw the ball vertically in the air but slightly forward. Move under it and catch it.
8. Throw the ball vertically in the air, turn around in place, then catch it.
9. Throw the ball vertically in the air, turn around in place, let it bounce, then catch it.
10. Throw the ball vertically, touch the floor, then catch it.
11. Bounce the ball in a circle around the body.
12. Roll the ball from one hand to the other, side to side.
13. Make a design with the ball as you move it through space.
14. Do a nonlocomotor skill as you work with the ball (bend and stretch).
15. Execute a ball skill in place, stop, do a locomotor movement, stop, repeat.
16. Execute a ball skill as you skip, gallop, hop.
17. Execute a ball skill as you perform a dance step, such as step-hop, schottische, polka.
18. Bounce the ball in front of the body, moving the ball from the left hand to the right hand.
19. Similar to the last activity, but sliding to the side as you bounce the ball.
20. Execute ball skills while changing level in space.
21. Execute ball skills while moving in various pathways.
22. Vary the time (fast, slow) of the ball skills but keep in time to the music.
23. Roll the ball down one arm, across the shoulders and down the other arm, and catch it.
24. Move the ball in a figure eight in front of the body, changing supporting hands as you cross the midline of the body.
25. Throw, clap, clap, catch, hold. (Slow, fast, fast, slow, hold.)
26. Throw, catch, throw, catch, throw, clap, catch (two small throws, one high throw).
27. Throw the ball from side to side over head, from one hand to the other.
28. Respond to various rhythmic patterns.
   a. Slow, slow, quick, quick, slow.
   b. One, two, three. One, two, three.
29. Move the ball while changing direction.
30. Move the ball on the beat.
31. Move the ball on the off-beat.
32. Drop the ball in front of the body, with the arms continuing downward and circling the ball on its downward path, and catch it.
33. Move the ball around the body at different levels.

Individual ball combinations

1. Bounce, catch, bounce, catch (1, 2, 3, 4). Bounce, bounce, bounce, catch (1, 2, 3, 4).
2. Vertical throw and catch (1, 2). Bounce and

catch (3, 4). Bounce and catch (1, 2). Vertical throw and catch (3, 4).

3. Vertical throw, catch while lowering the ball (1, 2). Vertical throw, catch while lowering the ball (3, 4). Diagonal bounce (left to right), catch (1, 2). Diagonal bounce (right to left), catch (3, 4).

4. Bounce, turn, bounce, catch (1, 2, 3, 4). Bounce, bounce, bounce, catch (to the right side) (1, 2, 3, 4). Bounce, bounce, bounce, catch (to the left side). (1, 2, 3, 4).

5. Diagonal throw over head left to right, catch (1, 2). Diagonal throw over right to left, catch (3, 4). Diagonal throw over head left to right, catch (1, 2). Diagonal throw over head right to left, catch (3, 4). Bounce, bounce, bounce, catch (1, 2, 3, 4). Bounce, bounce, bounce, catch (1, 2, 3, 4).

Combinations of locomotor and ball skills

1. Walk forward four steps, bounce the ball in place four times. Walk backward four steps, bounce the ball in place for four steps.

2. Walk forward two steps, bounce the ball two times, walk forward two steps, toss to self and catch. Repeat.

3. Take two slides to the right, bounce the ball on the right side two times. Take two slides to the left, bounce the ball on the left two times.

4. Take two step-hops forward, toss the ball and catch, toss again and catch. Take two step-hops forward, bounce, bounce, bounce, catch.

5. Take two bounce-catch combinations while standing in place. Take four steps forward bouncing the ball alternating hands (right, left, right) and hold on the fourth step.

Partner ball activities

1. Sitting: Roll the ball to a partner, catch, and hold.

2. Sitting: Roll the ball to a partner, stretching the arms and ball high overhead on the catch.

3. Bounce the ball to a partner, catch, and hold.

4. Throw the ball underhand to a partner, catch, and hold.

5. Bounce the ball three times, then throw to a partner.

6. Throw the ball to self three times, bounce to partner.

7. Turn around and roll the ball between the legs to partner.

8. Turn around and throw the ball overhead to partner.

9. Holding the ball over head, bend from side to side (left, right, left) and then throw to partner.

10. Bounce pass to partner, catch, bounce to self (two times), throw to partner, catch, bounce to self (two times). Repeat reversing the throw and bounce pass.

11. Throw the ball from behind your back to a partner.

12. With each child having a ball and working in pairs, repeat the above skills with both children throwing in unison.

Group routines

The above skills and combinations may be combined into interesting group routines. By using double lines, square formations, circles, or concentric circles, these skills then become an interesting movement sequence.

HOOPS
Equipment

Hoops are available in sizes varying from 2 ½ feet to over 3 feet in diameter. They may be constructed of laminated wood or of plastic. The plastic hoops are inexpensive but must be handled with care if they are not to lose their shape.

Teaching Suggestions

Hoops require more individual space than most equipment. Children may need help in identifying their personal space when using hoops so all have sufficient space within which to work. Hoops may be unfamiliar to most children. Adequate time must be given for exploration in the use of hoops to enable the children to use them effectively.

Activities
Individual activities

1. Holding the hoop in two hands, make circles in front of the body by moving the hoop to the side, up, to the other side, and down.

2. Roll the hoop from one side to the other taking a step to the side as the hoop is rolled.

3. Similar to the last activity but sliding to the side so you can move the hoop farther in a side direction.

4. Twirl the hoop on one forearm or wrist to

one side. Turn it clockwise and counterclock-wise.

5. Twirl the hoop on the wrist or forearm in front of the body changing arms.
6. Step to the side (lunging step) and stretch the hoop overhead to that side. Lunge to the other side and repeat.
7. Holding the hoop in two hands, jump through the hoop as if jumping rope (forward and backward).
8. Step to the side and turn around as the hoop is held high over head and parallel to the floor.
9. Execute dance steps while moving with a hoop.
10. Execute dance steps in a hoop placed on the floor.
11. Move the hoop overhead from left to right.
12. Move the hoop from side to side, making an arc downward and ending on each side with full extension upward.
13. Move around a stationary hoop with various locomotor movements or dance steps.
14. Move in and out of a stationary hoop with various locomotor or dance steps.

Individual combinations

1. Circle the hoop in front of the body two times (1, 2, 3, 4, 1, 2, 3, 4). Jump through and turn the hoop as if jumping rope four times (1, 2, 3, 4, 1, 2, 3, 4).
2. Roll the hoop in front of the body to the left as you slide four slides to the left (1, 2, 3, 4). Roll the hoop to the right as you slide four slides to the right (1, 2, 3, 4). Skip forward while rolling the hoop (1, 2, 3, 4). Skip backward while rolling the hoop (1, 2, 3, 4).
3. With the hoop on the floor move around outside the hoop with four skips (1, 2, 3, 4). Move forward through the hoop with two skips (1, 2). Move backward through the hoop with two skips (3, 4).
4. Stretch the hoop high overhead (1, 2). Stretch to the left (3, 4); Stretch to the right (1, 2). Bring the hoop down in front (3, 4). Walk forward rolling the hoop (1, 2, 3, 4, 1, 2, 3, 4).

Partner activities

1. Roll the hoop to a partner. Catch.
2. Roll the hoop to a partner. On the catch,

ROPE JUMPING SKILLS

Turning the rope	Basic jumps	Special steps
Forward	Single beat	Side to side (skier)
Backward	Double beat	Forward and back (bell)
Single side swing	Rocking step	Side straddle
Double side swing	Running	Forward/backward straddle
Horizontal swing	Shuffle step	Cross feet
Front swing	Skipping	Point your toe to the side
Criss cross		Toe to toe
Double under		Heel to heel
Triple under		Heel and toe
		Toe touch to rear

Turns	Dance steps
Twister	Step-hop
Quarter turn	Bleking
Half turn	Fling
Full turn	Schottische
	Step-swing
	Grapevine

stretch the hoop while overhead.

3. One holds the hoop as the partner moves through the hoop.
4. Move in and out of a stationary hoop doing various locomotor movements, with one going in while the other goes out.
5. Walk side by side rolling a hoop between two partners. Alternate rolling the hoop.
6. Walk side by side, each rolling a hoop.
7. Two partners roll a hoop to each other at the same time.

Partner or group combinations

Interesting combinations or skills may be developed. The use of various formations and the incorporation of space and other movement concepts add to the challenge of developing a movement sequence that is fun to do as well as fun to watch.

ROPES
Equipment

The ropes used in rhythmic activities may be long or short. A discussion of the use of ropes and appropriate lengths for elementary school children may be found in Chapter 14.

Teaching Suggestions

1. Ropes require a large activity area for safe participation. Children may need to be reminded about the amount of space required individually to work safely with their ropes.
2. Rhythmic rope jumping requires considerable skill. Children should have the basic jumping skills well under control before they can expect to be successful when jumping to music. Children at levels III and IV should have the skills necessary to enjoy rhythmic rope jumping.
3. The skills in this chapter are described in more detail in Chapter 14. The box summarizes some possible rope jumping activities.
4. Double-beat or single-beat jumps may be used, although single-beat jumps seem to be preferred.
5. Rope jumping is a strenuous activity especially for those children who may be having difficulty. Provide a change of pace so the children can think through possible combinations and have the opportunity to watch each other jump.
6. Provision should be made for a warm-up period at the beginning of the lesson in which children may jump on their own.
7. Some of the skills may be practiced sequentially,

beginning without a rope, introducing a long rope (where appropriate), and finally using a short rope.

8. As in ball skills, music in 2/4 or 4/4 meter is somewhat easier for beginning jumpers.

Activities

Individual combinations

1. Combine a single or double side swing with a front swing.
2. Combine a single or double side swing with a criss cross.
3. Combine a side straddle with a forward/backward straddle.
4. Combine a point your toe to the side with a toe touch to the rear.
5. Combine single- and double-beat jumping.
6. Combine a side to side with a forward and back.
7. Combine the side swing with forward jumping, side swing, backward jumping.
8. Combine single-beat jumping with a double under: jump 1, 2, 3, 4; double under, jump 2, 3, 4.
9. Combine a basic jump or dance step with a turn.
10. Combine a basic jump with a special foot placement. For example, combine four single-beat jumps with four side to side jumps.
11. Combine two schottische steps with four step-swings.
12. Combine the schottische and rocking step.

Group jumping

By using a longer rope several additional jumpers may stand in front of, to the sides of, or behind the turning child. Many of the individual combinations mentioned previously may be executed by the group with one rope.

Partner jumping

The following relationships may be used in partner jumping:

1. Stand face to face: the partner may run in and out of the rope while performing the jumping sequence.
2. Stand one behind the other: the turner may be in front or behind.
3. Partners stand side by side, with one rope; each holds the rope end with the outside hand.
4. Partners stand side by side with two ropes;

one rope is held by each child with the left hands, the other rope with the right hands.

Long rope jumping

Children may find it is easier to perform rope jumping sequences with long ropes than with short ropes. Children may also jump the short rope while standing in the long rope for an added variation.

STICKS
Equipment

Rhythm sticks may be made by cutting 1- to 1½-inch dowels, broom handles, or plastic tubing into 1-foot lengths. Rolled magazines or newspapers secured with masking tape can be used when a quieter atmosphere is required. Children also enjoy making and decorating their own sticks. Most of the activities included below require two sticks per child.

Teaching Suggestions

1. The children may be arranged in a circle, scattered in the area, or facing partners. In the upper grades groups of three or four may be used.
2. The children should be arranged so that all can see the teacher easily.
3. The sticks should be held with the fingers, which are usually placed on the lower half of the sticks.
4. Action begins before the beat so that the tapping or hitting of sticks is on the beat.
5. Begin with individual activities and progress to partner or group activities as the children are ready.
6. The tips are the upper edges of the sticks, and the ends are the lower edges of the sticks.

Activities
Individual activities

The following skills assume each child is using a pair of sticks:

1. Thrust sticks forward.
2. From a standing position, bend and touch sticks to the floor.
3. Stretch high over head and tap sticks together.
4. Bend from side to side, tapping sticks over head.
5. Bend forward and backward, tapping sticks.
6. Thrust elbows back twice, bring sticks in front, and tape them together.
7. Hit sticks under and over one knee.
8. Hit sticks in front and behind legs.
9. Hit sticks behind back and then in front of body.
10. Twist body from side to side and hit sticks.
11. Swing arms from the front to back and hit sticks.
12. Swing arms forward and backward alternately (one goes forward as the other goes backward).
13. Swing arms from side to side and hit sticks.
14. Combine hitting sticks with locomotor movements such as walking, running, skipping, or galloping, hitting as you move.
15. Combine hitting sticks with locomotor movements, moving and then hitting while standing still (walk, walk, walk, tap, tap, tap . . .skip, skip, tap, tap . . .).
16. Swing and cross sticks in front of body.
17. Circle arms in front of body.
18. Swing with backward extension.
19. Swing sticks in a figure eight, forward to backward or high to low.
20. Circle sticks above head, each stick making its own circle.
21. Perform the arm action of jumping jacks, hitting sticks overhead.
22. While sitting, tap sticks in front on the floor with either the tips or ends.
23. While sitting, tap sticks right on left, left on right.
24. While sitting, clap sticks together.
25. While sitting, tap the ends to the sides.
26. While sitting, tap sticks together with arms bent in front, arms straight, or arms stretched overhead.
27. Tap sticks on various body parts.
28. While sitting, tap sticks to the floor in front or behind your back.
29. Flip sticks by touching the tips to the floor, turning sticks toward you and regrasp, touching ends to floor.
30. Similar to the last activity, but flip sticks out to the sides.

Movement sequences

1. Have the children perform various tapping movements to the underlying beat of the music, such as tapping on front or to the sides.
2. Have the children tap the rhythmic pattern of the accompaniment.
3. Have the children tap in various rhythms:
   a. Tap, tap, tap, rest. Tap, tap, tap, rest.
   b. Rest, tap, rest, tap. Rest, tap, rest, tap.

    c. Tap . . ., tap. Tap . . ., tap. (Long, short, long, short.)

4. The teacher or a child taps a rhythm. The children then tap the same rhythm.
5. Have the children develop a four-beat pattern that they will repeat several times.

Beginning stick combinations

Four-beat combinations:

1. Standing, hit sticks in front of the body two times (1, 2); hit the sticks behind the body (3, 4).
2. Extend arms and sticks to side (1); hit sticks together in front of body (2); hit sticks high over head (3); hit sticks low in front of body (4).
3. Sitting, hit tips of sticks to the floor at the sides (1); hit tips of sticks to the floor in front (2); hit sticks together (3); hit sticks over head (4).
4. Sitting, hit ends to the floor in front (1, 2); hit tips to floor in front (3, 4).

    Three-beat combinations:

1. Hit both sticks to the right side (1, 2, 3); hit both sticks in front (1, 2, 3); hit both sticks to the left (1, 2, 3); hit both sticks in front (1, 2, 3).
2. Sitting, hit end of sticks to the ground (1); hit sticks together (2, 3).
3. Hit sticks to the sides (1); hit sticks together (2); hit sticks over head (3).
4. Sitting, hit ends of sticks to the ground (1); hit sticks together (2); exchange sticks (toss right stick to left hand, left stick to right hand (3).

Stick routines

The following are 16-count routines:

1. Hit tips to ground in front, hit sticks together; repeat. Hit tips to ground to the side, hit together; repeat. Vertical exchange (right to left, left to right) hold; repeat. Hit tips to ground in front, flip sticks in hands; repeat.
2. Holding sticks in the middle, hit the length of the stick to the floor in front, hit sticks together, hit flat sticks to right side, hit together. Hit flat sticks to the left side, hit together, hit flat sticks in front, flip sticks. Hit flat sticks to the right side, flip, hit flat sticks to the left, flip. Hit flat sticks in front, hit together, cross sticks and hit to side together.
3. Hit tips to ground in front, hit together, hit tips to ground in front, flip. Hit tips to ground in front, hit together, hit tips to side, flip. Hit tips to ground in front, hit together, hit tips to ground in front. Holding sticks parallel to the ground, switch sticks in hands.

4. Hit tips to ground in front, flip, repeat. Hit tips to ground in front, hit together, hit tips in front, hit tips to the side. Cross sticks and hit to side, uncross and hit to side, hit behind, hit to side. Hit tips to ground in front, hit together, hit tips in front, flip.
5. Hit tips in front, flip, hit tips to the right, flip. Hit tips to left side, flip, hit tips in front, hit together. Hit to side, hit together, hit to side extended, hit together overhead. Hit right tip in front and flip right, hit left tip in front and flip left.

LUMMI STICKS

This stick game probably originated with a small tribe of Indians in northwestern Washington. Sticks used were approximately 12 to 14 inches long and carved, painted, and burned similar to totem poles. Lummi sticks is similar to a stick game played by the Maori Indians of New Zealand. The sticks are held perpendicular to the floor between the tips of the thumbs and index fingers, with the remaining fingers adding support.

Lummi sticks may be performed in partners seated Indian style facing one another or in groups of four forming a square. Each person has two sticks. When working in groups of four, one pair begins the routine, the second pair then begins on the third beat of the first measure (A) to avoid all four hitting sticks in the middle at one time.

When tossing sticks, the sticks should be placed in the air toward the receiver so they remain perpendicular to the floor. When both sticks are tossed at the same time, one person should toss the sticks close together in the center, while the other separates the sticks and tosses them on the outside.

Several variations are listed below for possible combinations of skills. All are performed to the tune suggested below, which is in 3/4 time.

1. Hit ends to floor, hit own sticks, hit partner's right stick. Hit ends to floor, hit own sticks, hit partner's left stick. Repeat sequence three more times.

2. Hit ends to floor, hit own sticks, hit partner's right stick. Hit partner's left stick. Repeat sequence five more times.
3. Similar to the first sequence, but toss stick to partner rather than hitting partner's stick.
4. Similar to the second sequence, but toss sticks rather than hitting partner's sticks.
5. Hit ends to floor, hit own sticks, toss both sticks to partner. Repeat seven times more.
6. Hit ends of sticks to the ground in front; hit own sticks together; hit partner's right stick; hit partner's left stick; hit partner's right stick; hit partner's left stick. Repeat three more times.
7. Similar to the sixth sequence, but toss sticks, right, left, right, left, instead of hitting partner's sticks.
8. Hit tips to the floor in front; flip sticks toward you; hit end of sticks to the floor; hit own sticks; hit partner's right stick; hit partner's left stick. Repeat three more times.
9. Similar to the eighth sequence, but toss right and left sticks rather than hitting sticks with partner.
10. Hit tips of sticks to the side; flip sticks toward you; hit ends to floor at the side; hit tips to floor in front; flip; hit ends to floor in front; hit partner's right stick; hit partner's left stick; hit ends to floor in front; hit own sticks together; hit partner's right stick; hit partner's left stick. Repeat once more.
11. Hit ends of sticks on the floor; hit own sticks together; pass sticks clockwise by passing the left stick across to partner, transferring the right stick into the left hand. Repeat seven more times.
12. Similar to the eleventh sequence, but complete two passes each time.
13. Similar to the eleventh sequence, but pass until all have their two original sticks.

PARACHUTE
Equipment

Parachutes are available in various sizes. The parachute should be a size that can be handled easily by the children. Smaller parachutes enable the children to work in smaller groups and provide more opportunity for individuals to offer suggestions for possible activities or combinations of skills.

Teaching Suggestions

1. The children will need to be reminded to keep the parachute taut as they move.
2. Teach in phrases as if you were teaching a folk dance or singing game.
3. Cue the sequences so the children may change the

activity or direction in time to the accompaniment.

4. Rhythmic activities using a parachute provide a challenging opportunity for children to work together. Emphasize the need to coordinate efforts to accomplish the tasks.

Activities

1. Execute locomotor movements while moving clockwise or counterclockwise holding the parachute.

2. Move in time to the music while moving with the parachute and varying direction (in and out), tempo, and so forth.

3. Do Ring Around the Rosie with a parachute.

4. Perform simple singing games and folk dances while moving with the parachute.

Additional activities to use in the development of parachute movement sequences may be found in Chapter 14.

SUMMARY

Rhythmic activities provide a creative experience with small equipment. Children apply their rhythmic skills as they develop movement sequences individually, with partners, or in small groups. Some children who feel inadequate in moving alone creatively find confidence in using the equipment as they explore various movement challenges. Since children enjoy working with balls, hoops, ropes, sticks, and the parachute, the added dimension of working to an accompaniment adds a new challenge. Suggestions for musical accompaniment may be found in the Appendix.

REFERENCES

1. Geiger, J., and Popper, E.: Musical ball skills, Freeport, N.Y., 1969, Educational Activities, Inc.

2. Keeleric, K.: Danish ball rhythms (primary), Freeport, N.Y., 1968, Educational Activities, Inc.

3. Glass, H., and Hallum, R.: Rhythm stick activities, Freeport, N.Y., 1974, Educational Activities, Inc.

4. Smith, P.: Rope skipping, rhythms, routings, rhymes, Freeport, N.Y., 1969, Educational Activities, Inc.

ADDITIONAL READINGS

Schmid, A.: Rhythmic gymnastics: new olympic sport, JOPERD 55(5):70, May/June 1984.
The history of rhythmic gymnastics as an olympic event and a description of the event and scoring.

TICS
UNFREEZE FREEZE

Part Seven

EDUCATIONAL GAMES AND TEAM SPORTS LEAD-UPS

If appropriately selected and conducted, games can be a valuable educational experience for elementary school children. Games provide an opportunity for children to use and adapt motor skills, to apply movement concepts in ever-changing game situations, and to develop cooperative and competitive skills in a group setting. Children enjoy games and are challenged by the motor, cognitive, and social opportunities they offer.

21

TEACHING EDUCATIONAL GAMES AND TEAM SPORTS LEAD-UPS

CHAPTER OBJECTIVES

1 To discuss the values of games and team sport lead-ups in meeting the goals of the elementary school physical education program

2 To identify the important aspects of games in the selection of appropriate activities for each group of children

3 To provide suggestions for the planning and conducting of games and team sport lead-ups in the elementary school physical education program

Games are a popular form of play for children, especially children between 6 and 12 years of age. Games provide an opportunity for children to demonstrate their skills to other children and to test their ability as they confront others in game play. Children invent games of many descriptions, some for one person, others for groups varying in number, age, and ability. The games range in complexity according to the ability of the creator, but generally rules are minimal and limited to those needed at that particular moment. Rules are often modified as the game progresses to offer the most favorable opportunity for success by everyone. Occasionally there may be special rules that are applied only on an individual basis as differences in ability are considered by the group.

Children are able to play their games without adult supervision, to choose teams with a great deal of fairness (although their methods may be unorthodox), to abide by the rules set by the group, and to work out most differences of opinion in a reasonable manner. Occasionally disagreements do end the game or worse.

Scoring may be given little importance, and when the game ends, no real winners are declared. Children's personal satisfaction comes from being physically active and having given their best efforts in the play just completed.

THE VALUE OF GAMES AND TEAM SPORT LEAD-UPS IN THE ELEMENTARY SCHOOL PHYSICAL EDUCATION PROGRAM

When used effectively, games can make a substantial contribution to the objectives of physical education and consequently to the development of elementary school children. The values of games are not inherent in the games themselves. Games become educational when they expand the children's understanding of their own movement and the application of space and quality of movement concepts.

Games provide an opportunity for children to put their motor skills to use in many ways in achieving goals. Not only are a variety of skills used, but also children learn to adapt them and assess their effectiveness in different situations.

Games offer a challenge to accomplish a goal. Game play enhances children's ability to analyze a situation and to plan and to act based on that analysis.

It provides for creative thinking as strategy is developed and/or changes are made to make the game better for players of varying abilities or for larger or smaller groups.

Games provide an opportunity to share ideas and to work together to solve challenges in achieving the game objectives. They provide chances for children to assume both leader and follower roles.

The game's environment is one where children can learn about themselves, their strengths and weaknesses, as they attempt to meet the game's goals. Success in games requires children to find appropriate solutions to game challenges based on their individual skill repertoire. Outside the school environment recognition of individual differences enables children to modify rules so players of varying abilities may all find success. Everyone does not necessarily have to play by all the same rules.

Children may take risks in games in a fun way. Games allow the children to move into areas of uncertainty and insecurity without the real threat of failure, since the outcome of the game is not an important or life and death matter. "Games are effective as expressive models for gaining experience in the mastery of dangerous emotions very largely because of their miniature scale and their playful context. They are rendered safe by remaining on a plane of unreality in which 'reality consequences' do not have to be faced."[1]

Games offer an opportunity for play within the parameters of rules and boundaries. Recognition of the importance of rules for everyone and a willingness to play within the rules established requires self-discipline of all participants. Assuming responsibility for the enforcement of rules by acting as the leader or official should encourage children's respect for authority in later games.

GAMES ANALYSIS

Since each group of children is unique, it is necessary when selecting games or lead-ups to match game elements to the characteristics of the particular group of children with whom one is working. Morris[3] has suggested a method of analyzing games that has been modified in this text to include the following categories in activity selection: (1) the physical requirements of the game—equipment, space, and organizational pattern; (2) game structure—game classification, number of participants, modifications, and strategy; and (3) personal requirements—motor skills, movement concepts, and social structure. An additional category—level—is added further to aid the teacher in matching the game to each group of children. See Table 21-1 for examples of games analysis.

Physical Requirements

Equipment: Recommendations that consider size and texture of balls and height of baskets or nets, for the

Table 21-1
Games analysis

Name	Game classification	No. of participants	Equipment	Space and organizational pattern	Motor skills
Sharks and Barracudas	Tag game	Up to 25	None		Stopping Starting Running Tagging Dodging
Club Guard	Ball game	Six to eight per game	Eight-inch playground ball; 1 Indian club for each group	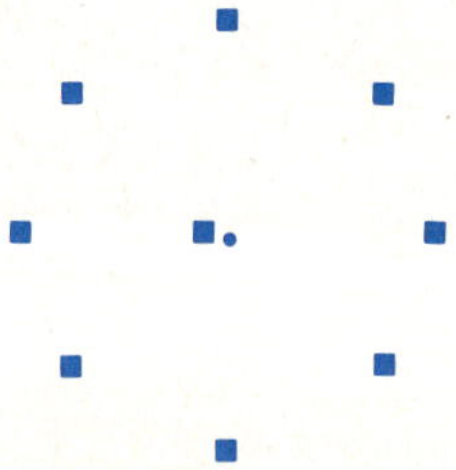	Passing Catching Guarding a pin

Modifications	Movement concepts	Social structure	Strategy	Level

Vary locomotor movements used	Self/general:
	  Moves oneself within the boundaries of the playing area
	  Uses all areas of the available space
	  Moves to an open space while moving in general space
	  Moves with control to avoid others' self space
	Direction:
	  Quickly changes direction to avoid contact with others
	  Quickly changes direction to intercept others
	Pathways:
	  Changes pathways while moving in space
	  Recognizes available pathways within which to move
	  Anticipate the pathways of others to intercept or avoid that path
	Force:
	  Controls force in tagging
	  Creates force efficiently when starting
	  Absorbs force safely in stopping
	Time/speed:
	  Changes speed smoothly and efficiently
	  Matches the speed of a person moving in space to intercept him or her
		Parallel play II	Wait until opponents get close before giving the signal	I

Could designate a particular type of throw to be used	Self/general:
	  Makes one's self space as large as possible
	  Keeps one's self space between the ball and an object to be guarded
	  Places the ball in an empty space
	Direction
	  Quickly changes directions to guard an object
	Pathways:
	  Recognizes available paths within which to move the ball
	Level:
	  Throws the ball at an appropriate level where it can be easily received
	Force:
	  Control force in passing
	  Absorbs force in catching
		Social interaction II	Teamwork is necessary to get the pin; pass quickly to get the ball behind the guard	III

success and safety of all participants.

Space and organizational pattern: The space and the organization of players in the playing area for the smallest number of participants needed for successful play.

Game Structure

Game classification: Games may be categorized in many different ways, from the type of formation used (circle games, line games), the skills used (running games, ball games) to the nature of the game itself (educational, skill, and lead-up).

Educational game: A game involving large or small groups that uses basic motor skills, has few rules, and involves varying degrees of group cooperation to achieve the game goal.

Skill games: An activity the primary purpose of which is the practice of one or a limited number of skills.

Lead-up game: A game that includes some of the skills, rules, and strategies associated with a team sport.

Number of participants: To maximize the opportunity for all children, the smallest number of participants per team is suggested, assuming several games are being played at the same time.

Modifications: Changes that may be needed to maximize or individualize the game or to emphasize certain skills.

Strategy: Points to be emphasized in the game, which may be brought out indirectly or directly by the leader.

Personal Requirements

Motor skills: Important locomotor and/or ball skills for the practice of which the game might be selected.

Movement concepts: Body awareness, space, and/or qualities of movement components essential to game success.

Social structure: The degree to which interaction and cooperation with others is required in the game.

Parallel play I: Children may play in a small or large group, but activity requires little cooperation for an individual's success.

Parallel play II: Similar to I, but each child goes one-on-one with another, usually It or a matched opponent.

Social interaction I: Some simple cooperation, such as working together to cover space for tagging; requires little group planning; and marks a beginning group effort (team score).

Social interaction II: Requires group decision on limited offensive and/or defensive strategy (for example, who will carry the ball).

Social interaction III: Requires group planning in developing group offensive and defensive strategy and delegation of responsibilities when activity requires that several jobs be done.

Level: A composite classification according to difficulty indicated by the previous categories.

Level I: Represents activities in which simple motor skills are needed, rules and concepts are few, there is little strategy, and social dependence is absent. These activities are generally associated with children in the primary grades.

Level II: Represents activities of simple combinations of skills, greater understanding of rules and concepts needed, group strategy, and some group decision making and cooperation. These activities are usually appropriate for intermediate grades.

Levels III: Characterized by increasingly difficult skills and combinations of skills, an increasing number of concepts and rules, and greater dependence on the group for the development of strategy and game success. These activities are usually appropriate for upper elementary school children.

Level IV: The most advanced level to be achieved during the elementary school years. Children are required to use more complex motor skills and combinations to adjust skills to an ever changing environment and changing player relationships. The use of movement concepts is more complex, and the development of strategy is more important for success in games. These activities are appropriate for children in the upper grades. Achievement to this level is dependent on the type and extent of the physical education program.

The game analysis approach in the selection of games may aid the teacher in more carefully matching games with the characteristics of a particular group of children than with a grade level classification of games. Since there are great variations in exposure to motor skills and movement concepts, in social development, and in actual game experience within a group, as well as from group to group, a closer look at games must be made if the needs of children are to be adequately met.

PLANNING AND CONDUCTING GAMES AND LEAD-UP EXPERIENCES

Adults are often eager to get children involved in adult games, with little consideration of where children are in their games development. Success in games is dependent on the leader's attention to game analysis. Failure to consider any one of the categories may result in an unfavorable response by the children as they attempt to play the game successfully. The following suggestions should be of help in adapting games for elementary school children and creating a positive learning experience for all.

An appropriately sized space must be provided. In team sports, children are often asked to play on adult-sized fields with adult-sized goals, although physically they may have only half the size and strength of more mature individuals. If the space is too large, children may not be able to use their skills effectively or to cover the space well on defense. If the space is too small, children may have more success with their skills and space coverage on defense but may have great difficulty using the space effectively in working with teammates because they tend to be too close together. A goal size that enables the defender to cover the space and that provides a space large enough for the offense to have a fair opportunity to score is essential.

Boundary lines must be established far enough from obstacles (4 to 6 feet) to ensure a safe distance for stopping. Children should be encouraged to play within the boundaries and to stop on boundary lines. Some space beyond the boundaries is essential for those children who forget or who misjudge their ability to stop on the line.

Safe play should be stressed at all times. Appropriate footwear is essential to safe participation. Learning to be responsible for one's safety and the safety of others is important. In ball games, especially dodgeball types, rules may need to be established that encourage keeping the ball low. Being under control at all times is an essential trait to be encouraged.

The size, weight, and softness of balls must be considered when selecting appropriate equipment to be used in games. How many times have elementary school children lost interest in playing a game because the ball was too hard when it hit them or when they

tried to catch it or it hurt them when they attempted to strike it? Selecting equipment that allows all children an opportunity for success without developing fear of it is essential.

A prime reason for selecting games is the practice of specific skills. Because certain skills are used in a game does not ensure their practice during the playing of the game. Therefore, special attention must be given to these skills before the beginning of play as well as throughout the game.

In each game the understanding of movement concepts contributes substantially to successful play. Although often many concepts could be identified, the teacher must emphasize the few that are of greatest importance before and during game play.

The games lesson should include practice of the skills and movement concepts, in addition to the games selected to enhance the skills and concepts. Objectives must be continuously emphasized throughout as the games become the means to greater understanding of the objectives. Each activity is chosen for its contribution to the day's objectives, and a variety of experiences should be planned for the development of each objective.

Once play is under way the most important teaching takes place. During play time the teacher guides the children in the game experience by reinforcing the lesson objectives and raising questions (but not providing answers) to help the children develop strategies and solve game challenges.

Developing strategy and establishing the part to be played by each team member are important learning experiences that are a part of games. Children should be encouraged in these efforts through questions posed by the teacher or through brief discussion sessions. Game experience is important in this decision-making process, and the teacher must be patient and give children sufficient experience in the game so they begin to see possible strategies they might use.

Emphasis must be on the development of each individual's potential through maximum opportunities for participation. Often games calling for many players do not afford equal opportunity for active involvement by all the children, because play can become limited to one area of the playing field or to the most aggressive players on the court. Small group activities encourage children to take more responsibility for the game's success and to become more self-directed. If all children are to have the opportunity to practice and use their skills, efforts must be made to maximize participation by reducing the numbers in the game to the fewest possible needed to achieve successfully the game goals and to equalize competition among the players in each game. By having several small groups playing the game simultaneously in the available space, maximum opportunity will be provided to all. Increasing the number of balls used is another way to increase participation in ball games.

Modification of rules may benefit all children. During informal play, children often modify rules of a game for individuals of varying ages and abilities to ensure fair and equal opportunity for success. Adults seldom consider this a possibility. In many games, modification of rules for individuals is acceptable to the group and easily administered. All children are encouraged to play by the most challenging rules for their ability and yet no children are destined to failure by rules that they are unable to meet.

Social aspects of games must not be be overlooked. Many games require group cooperation, sharing in decision making, and the ability to relate to many players in the playing area. One has only to observe a pick-up game of basketball of elementary school children to recognize the lack of group cooperation in the game. Often the one or two most aggressive and/or well-skilled children dominate play while the others move aimlessly around the court, not knowing where to go and seldom, if ever, receiving a pass or becoming actively involved. Teamwork is not automatic. It must be planned for. Many times rules must be added to ensure team play. For example, there must be three passes before shooting for a goal. Games that are highly competitive and those that encourage speed rather than good skill performance should be avoided or used with caution. Games should provide competition to improve, not to prove.

It is important to get the children into the game as quickly as possible if maximum activity for the lesson is to be attained. After the skills and movement concept objectives have been presented, or reviewed, and practiced, the children are ready for the game experience. Whenever possible, the children should be organized into their teams and sitting in formation before the game is introduced. Suggestions for organizing the group may be found in Chapter 7. Children's questions should be answered only after the explanation and demonstration of the game are complete, since most questions will be answered by this time.

Children should be taught to conduct their games without direct supervision of adults. Children can be given the responsibility of conducting their games if properly prepared. Early games have few rules and once learned children can play the games with decreasing assistance from teachers. Children may begin by being given the opportunity to review the rules of the game for the class. Small group play with indirect supervision by the teacher encourages the children to act more independently. Upper elementary school children are also capable of serving as referees or umpires for their games, which not only provides an opportunity to make decisions about rules but also teaches respect for officials.

In a game unit, repetition of games is important. For children to see possible strategies that could be developed, there must be adequate exposure to a game, not necessarily for long periods but at least for frequent periods of time. In organizing units involving lead-ups to team sports, an even more limited number of games should be included. Perhaps one or two lead-up games should receive the most emphasis to afford children the opportunity to understand the rules, the use of skills and concepts, and the development of offensive and defensive play.

When reviewing games it is important to have the children as actively involved in the review as possible. The teacher might ask the group to recall the rules verbally or have one child review the game with the group. These are good techniques to help children develop skill in teaching games and increase their ability to organize and verbalize information.

Evaluation of objectives should include not only the children's ability to execute a particular skill or understand a movement concept, but also their ability to use them in a variety of game situations. Objectives should be stated in such a way as to identify the behavior that indicates the children can use the objectives effectively. The following questions might serves as a guide to the teacher in evaluating the outcomes of games:

1. How well were the specific skills executed?
2. Was each skill used appropriately?
3. Was there evidence that the children understood and applied the important movement concepts in the game?
4. Was there evidence of the children's ability to think in action? Were they able to analyze the situation and plan a course of action?
5. Was there evidence of appropriate social skills? Did they share with others, play by the rules, share in the decision making, and so forth?

Games become educational only when the above suggestions are implemented. Games can be a valu-

able learning experience for children. The teacher must carefully select games and conduct the game experiences so that each child receives the full benefit of the activity, not just some children at the expense of others.

LEAD-UPS TO TEAM SPORTS

To participate successfully in team sports, children must have acquired the following:

Physical skills: The ability to effectively select and execute locomotor and ball handling skills, which may be used singly or in combination to move the ball individually or to teammates.

Social skills: The ability to recognize the need to work together, to share in the game effort, and to relate to many players in the playing area.

Intellectual skills: The ability to analyze the ever-changing game situation and to make decisions about a course of action, to see position play, to understand and put movement concepts into practice, to comprehend a variety of offensive and defensive strategies, and to understand and play by a complex set of rules.

Since elementary school children do not possess all of the prerequisites for successful play, teachers must plan a progression of experiences from which will emerge the ability to participate successfully in the team sports of their choice. Lead-up games are an essential part of the team sports progression in that they allow the children to work on single or simple elements of the game at a simple level of understanding. The progression of activities allows for the gradual introduction of the skills, concepts, rules, and strategy that are essential to successful participation in the game.

In developing sports skills, both technique and use of the skills must be considered. In evaluating performance, the teacher must decide whether errors are the result of failure to execute the skills correctly or the inability to select and use skills appropriately in the game situation. Practices are then organized for the correction of errors, emphasizing either the teaching points important to the skill performance or the use of the skills in gamelike situations. Once the techniques are mastered, emphasis on effective use of the skills through practice and game coaching becomes increasingly important.

Many movement concepts may be identified as essential to a particular team sport. Obviously it is not feasible to develop all concepts in any one unit. Therefore the teacher must carefully select the most crucial concepts for development at each stage in the sport progression.

Rules of games should be adapted and modified to meet the needs of individuals. In many of the games rules may be established for individuals to equalize play for all. Modifications for individuals may be found in each sport progression in the chapters that follow.

Lead-ups also provide for the gradual increase in

complexity of the social environment. Beginning lead-up games will require little social interaction and team work, whereas games used later in the progression require greater dependence on each member of the team for successful play.

Children are generally more interested in playing games than practicing their skills, If lead-up activities are organized for maximum participation and at an appropriate level of difficulty, they may serve an important role in the development of skills and knowledge important to the team sport. Lead-up games will also help children become aware of the goals toward which they are working.

Maximum participation and equalization of competition are important in team sport development. Large group activities that minimize individual development should be used with caution. Children should be matched by ability for competition to ensure each child an equal opportunity for success. In games in which there is a differentiation of individual responsibilities, a standardized plan of rotation should be used to enable all participants to play all positions.

SUMMARY

Educational games and team sport lead-up activities are an important element in the elementary school physical education program. They provide an opportunity for children to use motor skills and to apply knowledge learned in physical education to a group activity. They challenge children to use these skills and knowledge in new ways as the games increase in complexity over the elementary school years. Games and lead-ups also provide an environment in which to learn and to use social skills that are essential to successful participation throughout life.

Games may be selected to reinforce the motor skills the children are learning or to teach concepts. The selection of appropriate games is dependent on the teacher's ability to analyze games with regard to the motor and social skills and concepts needed for success. The game analysis approach is important if games are to be of value in meeting the lesson objectives.

The value of games is not inherent in the games themselves. It is the result of careful planning and conducting of the games experiences. Teachers must maximize the opportunity for individual development by organizing games for maximum individual participation, equating competition, modifying game rules to match the players' abilities, encouraging children to work together, providing a safe, nonthreatening environment in which to play, and helping children to see the relationships between the skills and knowledge they have acquired and the games they are playing.

The progression of lead-up activities for team sports gives children the opportunity to grow in their performance of motor skills and understanding of movement concepts, rules, and strategies over the elementary school years with guaranteed successful participation for all. As skills are refined and more complex understandings are developed, the children gradually move to increasingly complex activities requiring the ability to relate to more participants in the playing area and the development of offensive and defensive play.

REFERENCES

1. Devereux, E.: Backyard versus little league baseball: some observations on the impoverishment of children's games in contemporary America. In Yiannakis, A., and others, editors: Sport sociology: contemporary themes, ed. 2, Dubuque, Iowa, 1976, Kendall/Hunt.

2. Kulewicz, S.: The children, not the games, JOPER **52**(4):67, April 1981.

3. Morris, G.: How to change the games children play, ed. 2, Minneapolis, 1980, Burgess Publishing Co.

ADDITIONAL READINGS

Bean, D.: Outdoor games teaching: a key to effectiveness, JOPERD **54**(9):54, November/December 1983.
Relating skills development to their use in games.

Marlow, M.: Motor experiences through games analysis, JOPER **52**(1):78, January 1981.
Using games analysis for teachers and students to modify games for participants.

22

EDUCATIONAL GAMES

CHAPTER OBJECTIVES

1   To identify principles for conducting educational game experiences
2   To list the movement concepts important in educational games
3   To suggest activities to develop movement concepts in the context of educational games
4   To describe running, tag, and ball games, with suggestions for teaching

Educational games provide the first group experiences in the physical education of elementary school children. Games offer a challenging opportunity for children to put their motor skills to use and to test their skills against others first on a one on one basis, as in avoiding being tagged, and later in more complex group interactions. As children move through the elementary school grades the rules, skills, and social structure of their games increase in complexity with their growth in maturity.

EDUCATIONAL GAMES FOR ELEMENTARY SCHOOL CHILDREN

In addition to the suggestions for planning and conducting games given in Chapter 21, the following principles should be kept in mind:

Equal and maximum participation for all should be considered in selecting games. Many circle games provide activity for only one or two children at any one time and therefore allow very little partiipation for all children.

The elimination of players during the game should be avoided. Games provide equal opportunity for all children to develop and use their skills only when all have equal playing time. Penalties for being tagged, hit with the ball, and the like should not be the elimination of any child from play. Sometimes a change in role, for example, from dodger to thrower, or developing a point system for the number tagged may be all that is necessary to ensure equal playing time for all.

The use of different formations is important in maintaining students' interest by varying the situations in which skills and concepts are used.

In games where some differentiation of responsibility of players is made, a rotation plan should be in operation that gives each child the opportunity to assume each of the different roles. In some games good strategy might necessitate the division of responsibility into offensive and defensive assignments or, in simpler games into the "its" and those being chased. Within the lesson all children should have the opportunity to play as many different roles as possible to enable them to develop their skills to the fullest.

It is important to get the game off to a good start. In beginning play, the first group leader or "It" should be someone who will be successful in a short period of time. Increasing the number of children who are "it" in tag games will help to keep the game moving. This is important if the interest level is to remain high as the children play the game.

As a rule it is best to change the activity when the interest level is high. The timing of each game is important to the success of the game experience. If

the game is played too long, children will not only lose interest at that time but also may play the game less enthusiastically in following lessons. In the upper grades the game must be played long enough for the children to learn the rules and to develop appropriate strategy. For the development of strategy it may be best to play the game often for short periods rather than occasionally for long periods of time.

Children should be encouraged to invent their own games and to modify known games to make them more challenging. Creating new games is an important part of the educational games experience. The class might begin with a known game played in small groups. Following a short period of play, the children are encouraged to modify the game they are playing or to make up a new game. In creating a new game the teacher may wish to suggest certain parameters. The use of a particular skill or movement concept or a particular player arrangement may be suggested. As children gain experience and confidence in creating new games, they will need fewer suggestions from the teacher.

During the elementary school years, several problems may arise in the conduct of games. If uncontrolled they may effect the outcome of the game or the social interaction of the children.

In the beginning stages of game play, some children may have difficulty staying within the boundaries of the playing area. This may be observed in their running outside of the lines to avoid being tagged, failure to run close to the circle in circle games, or not stopping on the end line. This may be the result of the child's need for more space, a lack of control in stopping, or most probably the child's lack of understanding in the use of general space. Movement activities in the exploration of space in which the size of space and the type of movement used are varied will help children to develop this concept. Exploring activities in how to keep the body in control, as in stopping or changing direction, may also be helpful. Sometimes a penalty such as considering children tagged if they go out of the playing area or do not stop on the end line may need to be imposed.

Children need to learn the importance of playing by the game rules. In tag games some children may not attempt to avoid being tagged. Others may not admit to being tagged or hit by the ball in dodge ball type games. If children appear to want to be tagged, this may be an indication that the game is moving too slowly or is not challenging enough for the children. Children need to be encouraged to play by the rules and to avoid being tagged. Emphasis on being a good dodger, asking, "How may did not get tagged today?" or choosing a new leader from those not tagged are ways children may be encouraged to play by the rules. For the child who will not admit to being tagged or hit with the ball, the teacher will usually see who has been tagged or hit and in a casual, friendly way can indicate that the tag or hit was ob-

MOVEMENT CONCEPTS FOR EDUCATIONAL GAMES

BODY AWARENESS

Body awareness concepts are inherent to the understanding of how each skill is executed and used in different ways in games.

SPACE

Self and general space
1. To move one's self and/or a ball within the boundaries of the playing area
2. To use all areas of the available space
3. To move to an open space while moving in general space
4. To move with control to avoid others' self space
5. To move in general space in relation to an object to be avoided
6. To make one's self space as large as possible while covering general space
7. To recognize one's own area of the general space to be defended
8. To keep one's self space between the ball and the goal or between the ball and an object to be guarded
9. To place a ball in an empty space in the opponent's playing area or goal
10. To close spaces open to opponents or a ball
11. To create open spaces while moving in general space

Direction
12. To change direction quickly to avoid contact with others or a ball
13. To change direction quickly to intercept others or a ball
14. To assume a position that enables one to move in any direction
15. To change direction quickly to guard a space or an object
16. To anticipate direction changes of others

Level
17. To throw the ball at an appropriate level into the open space
18. To throw the ball at an appropriate level where it can be easily received
19. To throw the ball at an appropriate level below the waist when throwing at others

Pathways
20. To change pathways while moving in space with or without a ball
21. To recognize available pathways within which to move one's self
22. To recognize available pathways within which to move the ball to score a goal or to intercept a teammate or opponent
23. To anticipate the pathways of others or a ball to intercept or avoid that path
24. To recognize a straight line as the shortest pathway between two points
25. To recognize the shortest path in running around a circle
26. To close paths available to opponents
27. To change the expected path of the ball

QUALITIES OF MOVEMENT

Force
1. To control force in tagging while moving through space
2. To create force efficiently when starting
3. To absorb force safely in stopping
4. To use an appropriate amount of force when throwing
5. To absorb force in catching
6. To control force when striking an object

Time and speed
7. To change speed smoothly and efficiently while moving in space
8. To anticpate the speed of a person moving in space or a ball to avoid them
9. To match the speed of a person moving in space or a ball to intercept them

served. Game rules need to be enforced in a way that is not intimidating to children and with emphasis on how well the game is being played rather than on declaring a winner.

Sharing in running and ball games should be encouraged. Choosing someone who hasn't had a turn to be "it" and handing the ball to a child who has not had the opportunity to throw it should be standard procedures in any game if a cooperative spirit with concern for others is to develop.

Being a good winner or loser may become a problem with some youngsters in the intermediate grades. Keeping winning in perspective is important to a healthy society. Emphasis should be on perfecting the use of skills and concepts and working together in the best effort rather than on winning. Grouping children so that competition is equal for all participants will help. Often poor social behavior is the result of unequal competition in which one team humiliates the other. Matching opponents for competition gives everyone an equal opportunity for success and the challenge of giving their best effort.

SKILLS

Educational games provide an opportunity to use the motor skills children are learning. Analyses of skills used in low organized games and activities to aid in development may be found in Chapter 11.

MOVEMENT CONTENT

The application of movement concepts is an important aspect of game experience. The box below identifies the movement content for educational games. Several concepts may be applied in each game. The teacher determines the concept needs of the boys and girls in the class. After some work on the concept, the children play the game during which it is emphasized further. The movement concepts in the games analysis tables found before each games sections in this chapter identify the concepts as numbered below.

ACTIVITIES TO DEVELOP CONCEPTS FOR EDUCATIONAL GAMES
Space
Running and tag games

Define boundaries. Children are scattered within the boundaries. On the signal, the children move around in general space, avoiding the self space of

others and covering as much of the area as possible. On the signal, the teacher may ask the children to change locomotor movement, direction, or pathway. (The teacher may ask, "Did you cover all the space? The corners? Sides? Middle? Which locomotor movements enabled you to cover the area fastest? In which directions or pathways could you move the easiest?")

Children are scattered in the general space in which many hoops or ropes tied in circles have been placed. The children move freely in the area, covering as much space as possible. On the signal, they attempt to move into an empty hoop (the open space). Repeat. After a few times, remove hoops and repeat the activity with the children looking for their own empty space. ("Did you all find an empty space? How did you make sure you found one? Did you have to keep looking for an open space as you were moving around? What did you do if someone got there first?")

Children are scattered within the space. On the signal, they move in general space. When they come to another person they quickly move to a new open space. ("How did you move to find a new empty space? How did you anticipate the movements of others to avoid getting into their self space?")

Children are scattered in the space. On the signal, they move in general space. On the signal to stop, they attempt to cover as much space as possible by making a large self space. ("Where are the open spaces?")

Children are scattered within the boundaries. Half are stationary (one foot must remain in contact with the floor at one spot). The other half move in general space, covering as much space as possible and avoiding the tags of the stationary children. ("What did you do to get from one place to another and avoid being tagged? Can you think of another way? Did you look for the empty space? Change positions and repeat.")

Moving in general space, children move in one direction. Each time they meet a person or a boundary line they jump out of the way and continue in a new direction. ("In which direction was it most difficult to avoid others?")

Designate some children as movers, the others as followers. All move freely in the general space changing direction. On the signal, the followers go to the closest person and follow that person, moving in the same direction. On the next signal, all children move freely again. Repeat. ("What did you do to anticipate the direction changes of the person you were following?")

Using grids or hoops scattered on the floor as safety areas, half of the children move from spot to spot while the others try to tag them, each moving in the direction indicated by the leader. Those tagged change places with "it." ("In which direction was it easiest to move? How did you avoid being tagged?")

Children are scattered in the general space and there are two taggers. The teacher calls the direction in which all will move. Those tagged change positions with "it." ("In which direction was it easiest or most difficult to avoid the tag?")

With a partner, one is "It." "It" chases the other partner, following the child's movements and directions. ("In which direction was it easiest to follow? To avoid "It?" When was a good time to change direction?")

With a partner scattered in general space, child A, moving in a curved line, tries to tag child B, who is moving in a zigzag. Then they reverse roles and pathways ("What happened to your pathway as you moved in general space with others? In which pathway was it easiest to anticipate the tag?")

In partners, one is stationary in a position about half way between two lines. On the signal, the moving child moves from one line toward the other. Nearing the stationary partner, the moving partner quickly changes pathways to move around the stationary partner and then straight for the other line. Repeat several times. Have the stationary children extend one arm to the side as the partners draw near. ("How did you quickly respond to the change in available space?")

Half the children are "it." Papers with various pathways on them are drawn from a bag by the other children, who must get across the general space along the pathway indicated and without being tagged. They then exchange pathways and try again. Then reverse the roles and repeat. ("What did you do to avoid being tagged? In which path was it easiest to tag? To avoid being tagged?")

Children are arranged in partners on two lines facing each other. On the signal, the partners move toward each other. As they get close together the teacher gives a signal for one line to be chasers, the other fleers. Change the signal again and the partners switch roles. Repeat several times. ("What did you do to reverse your pathway quickly?")

Three circles at least 10 feet in diameter are placed within the playing area, in each of which one "it" stands. Children move in general space and in and out of the circles. The "its" try to tag any children moving through their circle. If tagged, "it" changes place with the child tagged. ("What did you do to avoid being tagged? To tag? For example, change locomotor movement, directions, speed or pathway? Could you do anything else? Were you able to anticipate the pathways of the children moving through the space? What were the clues you used?")

Children are scattered in the general space. Half are taggers, the other half are those being tagged. Designate a locomotor movement, direction, or pathway for each child to move. "Its" may only tag those moving in the same manner as they. Then they change movements and repeat. ("Was it easy to spot those moving as you were moving? Which movements made tagging easier? More difficult? Were some movements easier to use as you moved around others in general space?")

Ball games

In partners, standing 10 to 20 feet apart, children face each other. One child rolls the ball toward or slightly to the side of the other, who attempts to stop it. ("What did you do to stop the ball? Intercept its path? What body position was best as you moved to the side?")

In partners, one child guards an area of wall space. The other has a ball and attempts to hit the wall within the reach of the guard. Increase the space and try again. Repeat several times. Change positions. ("How large an area could you cover? What position enabled you to cover the space best?")

Cones are placed in a box formation in several parts

of the space with one child assigned to protect each box. The children outside the boxes attempt to throw bean bags into the boxes, while the child in the box tries to keep them out. ("What did you do to protect your box? How did you get the bean bags in?"

Assign one third of the group an area of general space to cover in the center of the playing area. The remaining two thirds are located on either side of the guarded space, and they attempt to roll balls through the guarded area. Change groups. ("What did you do to best protect the area? Throwers, where did you place the ball? What problems arose covering the space? Throwing the balls?")

With a partner, one moves in a limited area, but in all directions. The other attempts to get the ball behind the moving player. ("What did you do to get the ball past your partner?")

In partners, one child has a ball. The child with the ball tries to roll the ball between the legs of the other, who is at first stationary and then sliding from side to side. ("What did you have to do to get the ball between your partner's legs? At what level did you throw? Where did you try to roll the ball? At what speed? Pathway?")

In partners, one child guards a duck pin. The other attempts to throw the ball past the other and knock over the pin. (Use more than one pin if the children have difficulty knocking them down.) Change partners several times so each child has an opportunity to throw against several different children. Change guards and throwers. ("How did you successfully guard your pin? What did you do to get the ball past the guard?")

Several groups of three children are designated who move in general space. The remaining children attempt to throw balls to hit the middle person in each group below the waist. ("How were you able to protect the middle person in your group? Throwers, what did you do to successfully hit the moving and guarded target?")

With a partner, determine a level at which each will throw to the other (a different level for each). They throw back and forth. Change levels. ("Which level was easiest to receive the ball? To throw to your partner? Where would you best like to receive the ball?")

One child A throws the ball to a partner B at a designated level. Child A then runs to a pylon and back to the starting position before child B can catch the ball and try to hit child A with the ball (below the waist). Vary levels of throwing. ("Which levels gave you the most time to get back to your position safely? Why?")

In a circle of four or five, the children pass the ball quickly around the circle for a certain period of time, counting passes in the level indicated. Change levels and repeat. ("In which level could you get rid of the ball quickest and have the most passes? In which level was it easiest to receive the ball?")

Qualities of Movement
Running and tag games

Children are scattered in general space with many duck pins scattered in the area. The children move around the general space at speeds indicated by the leader tagging as many pins without knocking them down as possible before the signal to stop is given. ("At what speeds was it easy to control the tag without knocking down the pin? Which the most difficult? What did you have to do to keep from knocking down the pins?")

Similar to 1 above, but several children are "it." "Its" try to tag other children who are safe only when touching (not grasping) an Indian club.

Children are scattered in the general space. One third of the group are "it." On signal they attempt to tag others softly, using body parts other than hands, such as forearm, or elbow. ("Which body parts were easiest to tag with softly? Hardest? Why?")

Children practice stopping on signal as they move through general space. They should try different positions for stopping, use different locomotor movements, and move at different speeds. ("Which position was best for stopping while skipping? Running? Moving slowly? Moving fast? How did your position change as you moved faster?")

Ball games

Children stand various distances from a wall. They throw the ball so that it rebounds directly to themselves. ("As you move closer and farther away from the wall how did you change your throw so it came back to you?") A modification is to roll the ball varying the distance to the wall so there is no rebound. Roll the ball so it rebounds one foot. Two feet.

Children throw to partners several times using a particular pass. They count successful catches. Then they move closer or farther away and repeat. Repeat several times changing distances. Then they try it again with a different kind of pass. ("What

did you do to get the ball to your partner with a particular throw as the distance changed? Did you reach a point where the distance made the pass difficult? What passes worked best for short distances? Medium? Long?")

Children throw a foam ball to partners, who must stop the ball with a different body part each time. ("How can you keep the ball close as you use different body parts? How did you absorb the force? Which parts were easiest to control the ball? Hardest?")

GAMES ANALYSIS

Table 22-1 includes a games analysis for running and tag games. The games analysis for the ball games (Table 22-2) may be found before the section on ball games. The movement concepts refer to the movement concepts numbered in the box on p. 393.

RUNNING AND TAG GAMES

BARNYARD UPSET

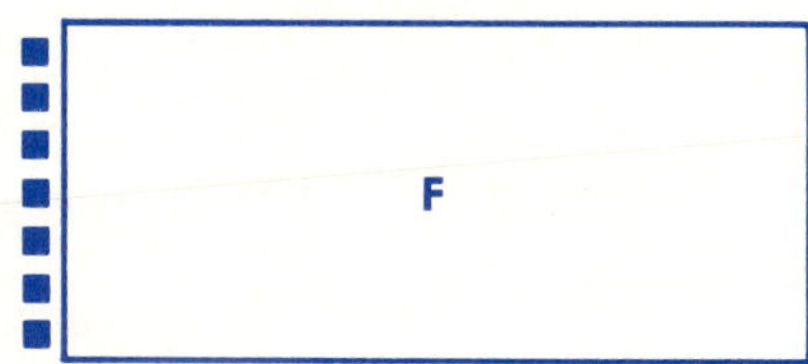

Level: I.
Equipment: None.
Participants: Up to 25.
Skills: Running, starting, stopping, dodging, tagging.
Description: The children are lined up behind the starting line, with "it," the farmer, facing the group. All children secretly select a farm animal that they will be. The farmer calls the name of a farm animal. Those children

who have chosen that animal run to the opposite line, avoiding the farmer, who tries to tag them. If tagged, they must go to the corral. After all children's animals have been called, the game begins again with a new farmer selected from those not tagged. As the game begins again, all children who were tagged rejoin the game. During the game the farmer may call, "barnyard upset," when all children whose animal has not been called must run to the opposite line.

Teaching Suggestions: Emphasize good starts, controlled stops, and tagging softly. Encourage children to try to avoid being tagged. Asking, "How many did not get tagged today?" may be helpful.

BUSY BEE

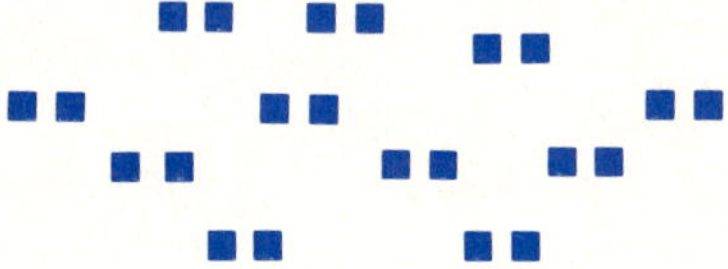

Level: I.
Equipment: None.
Participants: Up to 25.
Skills: Stopping.
Description: The children are scattered with partners in the playing area, with one extra person who is the leader. The leader calls the name of body parts, such as "back to back," "knee to knee," and so forth, and the partners match those parts named. When the leader calls "busy bee," each person finds a new partner. The one without a partner becomes the new leader.

Teaching Suggestions: Emphasize listening carefully to the leader. Encourage the children to think of as many different body parts as possible.

JET PILOT

Level: I.
Equipment: None.
Participants: Up to 25.
Skills: Running, stopping, starting.
Description: The children are lined up behind the starting line with the leader (the control tower operator) off to one side. The control tower operator calls, "Control tower to pilots, control tower to pilots, all planes wearing (color) take off." On the signal, "off," the children wearing the color called run to the far boundary line and back. The first person with a good stop on the starting line becomes the new control tower operator

Table 22-1
Running and tag games analysis

Name	Game classification	No. of participants	Equipment	Space and organizational pattern	Motor skills
Barnyard Upset	Tag	Up to 25	None	Corral	Running Stopping Starting Dodging Tagging
Busy Bee	Running	Up to 25	None	Scattered in partners	Running Stopping
Jet Pilot	Running	Up to 25	None		Starting Stopping Running
Red Light	Running	Up to 25	None		Stopping Starting Running
Sharks and Barracudas	Tag	Up to 25	None		Running Stopping Starting Tagging Dodging
Squirrels In Trees	Running	Up to 25	None		Stopping Starting Running
Bird Catcher	Tag	Up to 25	None		Starting Stopping Running Tagging Dodging
Chinese Wall	Tag	Up to 25	None		Starting Stopping Running Tagging Dodging

*Numbers refer to the concepts given in the box on p. 393.

Modifications	Movement concepts*	Social structure	Strategy	Level
Vary locomotor movements used; have more than one farmer be "it"	Self/general: 1, 2, 3, 4, 6, 10 Direction: 12, 13, 14, 16 Pathways: 20, 21, 23, 24 Force: 1, 2, 3 Time/speed: 7, 8, 9	Parallel play II		I
Vary locomotor movements used	Self/general: 1, 4 Direction: 12 Pathways: 20, 21 Force: 3	Parallel play II		I
If the first back has had a turn, let him or her choose someone else (who has not had a turn) to be "it," or take the second back, and so forth; vary locomotor movements used	Self/general: 1, 4 Pathways: 20, 21, 24 Force: 2, 3	Parallel play I	Control tower operator may vary timing on command to "take-off"	I
Eliminate or reduce the numbers counted; have helpers or teacher's assistance in seeing who is moving	Self/general: 1, 4 Force: 2, 3	Parallel play II	Can you move when the leader is not watching?	I
Vary locomotor movements used	Self/general: 2, 3 Direction: 12, 13 Pathways: 20, 21, 23 Force: 1, 2, 3 Time/speed: 7, 9	Parallel play II	Wait until group gets very close before giving the signal	I
Use a variety of locomotor movements; change signal calling for colors they are wearing, birthday months, and so forth	Self/general: 1, 2, 3, 4 Direction: 12 Pathways: 20, 21 Force: 2, 3	Parallel play I		I
Vary locomotor movements used	Self/general: 1, 2, 3, 4, 7, 10 Direction: 12, 13, 15, 16 Pathways: 20, 21, 23, 24, 26 Force: 1, 3 Time/speed: 7, 8, 9	Social interaction I	With helpers how can you cover the space to get more tagged? What must you do now to avoid the tag?	II
Vary locomotor movements used	Self/general: 1, 2, 3, 4, 7, 10 Direction: 12, 13, 15, 16 Pathways: 20, 21, 23, 24, 26 Force: 1, 3 Time/speed: 7, 8, 9	Social interaction I	With helpers how can you cover space to get more people tagged?	II

Continued.

Table 22-1
Running and tag games analysis—cont'd

Name	Game classification	No. of participants	Equipment	Space and organizational pattern	Motor skills
Circle Race	Tag	Up to 25	None		Running Starting Stopping Tagging
Color Tag	Tag	Up to 25	Colored squares in at least three or four colors	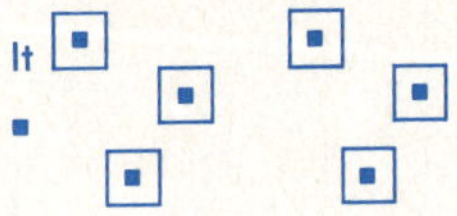	Running Stopping Starting Dodging Tagging
Fox and Hound	Tag	Up to 25	None		Running Starting Stopping Tagging Dodging
Gardener and Scamp	Tag	Up to eight per game	None	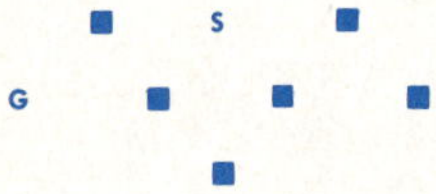	Running Tagging Dodging
Midnight	Tag	Up to 25	None		Running Tagging Dodging Stopping
Sharks and Minnows	Tag	Up to 25	None	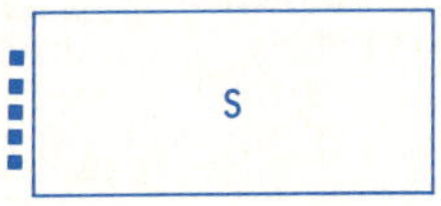	Running Tagging Dodging Stopping
Steal the Bacon	Tag	Six to eight per game	One Indian club/game	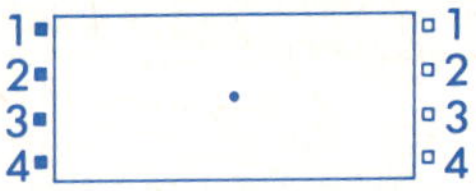	Starting Stopping Tagging Dodging
Two Deep	Tag	Eight to ten per game	None		Starting Stopping Running Tagging

Modifications	Movement concepts	Social structure	Strategy	Level
Vary locomotor movements used	Self/general: 1 Pathways: 25 Force: 2, 3 Time/speed: 9	Parallel play II	Run as close to circle as you can	II
Vary locomotor movements, directions, or pathways used	Self/general: 1, 2, 3, 4 Direction: 12, 13, 16 Pathways: 20, 21, 23 Force: 1, 3 Time/speed: 7, 8, 9	Parallel play II		II
Vary locomotor movements used	Self/general: 1, 2, 3, 4 Direction: 12, 13, 16 Pathway: 20, 21, 23 Force: 1, 3 Time/speed: 7, 8, 9	Parallel play II	Be ready to get into a tree if it gets close	II
Vary locomotor movements used	Self/general: 1, 2, 3, 4 Direction: 12, 13, 16 Pathways: 20, 21, 23 Force: 1 Time/speed: 7, 8, 9	Parallel play II	Move in a path difficult for the gardener to follow	II
Vary locomotor movements used	Self/general: 1, 2, 3, 4 Direction: 12, 13, 16 Pathways: 20, 21, 23, 24 Force: 1, 3 Time/speed: 7, 8, 9	Social interaction I	Wait until the group is close and far from end line before calling "Midnight"	II
Vary locomotor movements used	Self/general: 1, 2, 3, 4, 6, 7, 10 Direction: 12, 13, 16 Pathways: 20, 21, 23, 26 Force: 1, 3 Time/speed: 7, 8, 9	Social interaction I	Look for the open spaces to avoid being tagged	II
Could be played on gym scooters; vary scoring: (1) a point for getting pin only or (2) a point for getting pin or tagging	Self/general: 1, 3 Direction: 12, 13, 16 Pathways: 20, 21, 23 Force: 1, 3 Time/speed: 7, 8, 9	Social interaction I; social interaction II if second scoring method used	Develop deceptive moves in getting the pin to avoid being tagged	II
Vary locomotor movements used	Self/general: 1 Pathways: 25 Force: 1, 3 Time/speed: 7, 8, 9	Parallel play II	Run close to circle	II

Continued.

Table 22-1
Running and tag games analysis—cont'd

Name	Game classification	No. of participants	Equipment	Space and organizational pattern	Motor skills
Uncle Sam	Tag	Up to 25	None		Starting Stopping Running Tagging Dodging
Crows and Cranes	Tag	Up to 25	None		Starting Stopping Reversing pathways Tagging Dodging Running
Touchdown	Tag	Up to 25	One small object that can be concealed in the hand		Running Stopping Tagging Dodging
Stealing Sticks	Tag	Up to 25	Six to eight sticks or Indian clubs		Running Tagging Dodging

(CTO). If desired, the CTO may call, "All planes with all colors," so everyone runs.

Teaching Suggestions: Encourage good starting and stopping. Promote good listening for the signal by having the CTO change the speed at which he or she says, "take off," or hesitating between the two words. If a child is first back and has already had a turn, have the second one back, or first child who has not had a turn become the new CTO.

RED LIGHT

Level: I.
Equipment: None.
Participants: Up to 25.

Skills: Stopping, starting, running.
Description: The children are lined up behind the starting line, with the leader in front of the group. The leader facing away from the group calls, "green light," and counts to ten. The children move forward on the signal, "green light." The leader then calls, "red light," turning to face the other children as they stop quickly. Anyone caught moving after the signal red light, when the leader turns around, must go back to the starting line to begin moving again. The first child to reach the opposite line without being seen moving is the new leader.
Teaching Suggestions: Encourage a balanced stopping position. For young children the game may be more successful by eliminating the counting or reducing the count. Young children may not see those who are moving out at the sides of the group, so they may need helpers to spot or the teacher's assistance. This game may be more successful if played in small groups.

Modifications	Movement concepts	Social structure	Strategy	Level
Vary locomotor movements used; change the signal to color of hair, birthday, and so forth	Self/general: 1, 2, 3, 4, 7, 10 Direction: 12, 13, 15, 16 Pathways: 20, 21, 23, 24, 26 Force: 1, 3 Time/speed: 7, 8, 9	Social interaction I	When Uncle Sam has helpers, how can you cover the space to get more people tagged?	II
Vary locomotor movements used; use long/short vowel sounds as signal; use odd and even numbers or math problems as signal	Self/general: 1, 3, 4 Direction: 12, 13, 16 Pathways: 20, 21, 23, 24 Force: 1, 3 Time/speed: 7, 9	Parallel play II	Be ready to move in either direction	III
Vary locomotor movements used	Self/general: 1, 2, 3, 4, 7, 10, 11 Directions: 12, 13, 14, 15, 16 Pathways: 20, 21, 23, 26 Force: 1, 3 Time/speed: 7, 8, 9	Social interaction II	What can you do to create space for ball carrier, close space on defense, or cover each opponent?	III
	Self/general: 1, 2, 3, 4, 7, 10, 11 Direction: 12, 13, 14, 15, 16 Pathways: 20, 21, 23, 26 Force: 1, 3 Time/speed: 7, 8, 9	Social interaction II	Work together when planning offense; designate responsibilities for defense	IV

SHARKS AND BARRACUDAS

Level: I.
Equipment: None.
Participants: Up to 25.
Skills: Stopping, starting, running, tagging, dodging.
Description: The children are divided into two groups, the sharks and the barracudas. Each group has a leader, who remains facing the opponents. The sharks turn their backs to the barracudas, who sneak up close to the sharks. When they are close, the head shark gives the signal, "Here come the barracudas," and the sharks turn and chase the barracudas back to their line, trying to tag as many barracudas as possible. Those tagged become sharks. Repeat, reversing roles for sharks and barracudas. When the sharks are close, the head barracuda gives the signal, "Here come the sharks," and the barracudas give chase.

Teaching Suggestions: Encourage children to assume a position in which they can reverse their pathway quickly to give chase or to avoid being tagged. Emphasize controlled stops and tagging. Help children to develop the strategy of waiting until opponents are close before giving the signal to run.

SQUIRRELS IN TREES

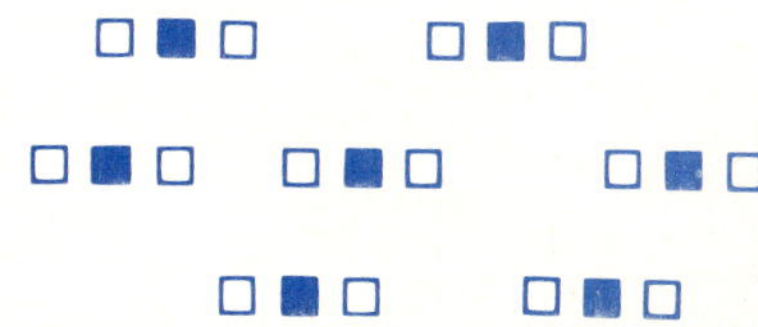

Level: I.
Equipment: None.
Participants: Up to 25.

Skills: Running, stopping, starting.

Description: Children are scattered in the playing area in groups of three with one or two extra players. One person is designated as the squirrel in each group and stands between the other two. On the signal, "change trees," the squirrels leave their trees and go to a new one, and the one or two unassigned squirrels do as well. The object of the game is to always have a tree. After repeating the procedure a few times, children change positions in the group and begin again. Change once more so all have a chance to be squirrels.

Teaching Suggestions: Encourage good listening and controlled movements. Use other locomotor movements in addition to running. The signal could be changed to calling for squirrels by naming the colors the children are wearing, their birthdays, and so forth to encourage good listening.

CHINESE WALL

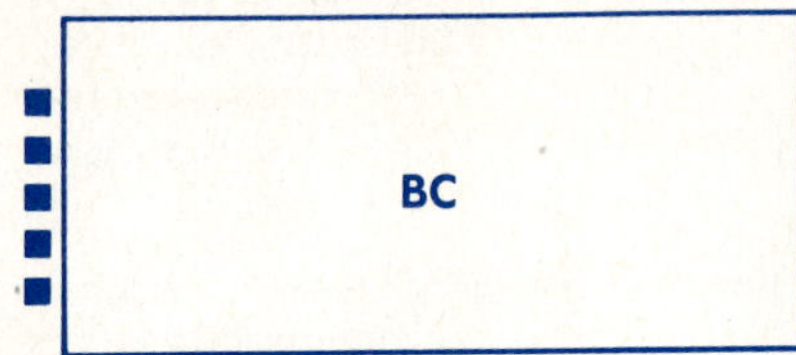

Level: II.

Equipment: None.

Participants: Up to 25.

Skills: Running, stopping, starting, tagging, dodging.

Description: The children are lined up behind one end line with the "bird catcher" out in front. Each child secretly selects a type of bird. The bird catcher calls out the names of birds (robin, sparrow, and so forth), and those children who have selected that bird attempt to cross safely to the opposite line without being tagged. Those tagged help the bird catcher. After everyone has crossed to the opposite line, the game is repeated with a new bird catcher selected from those not tagged.

Teaching Suggestions: Encourage controlled stops and tags. Raise questions to help children develop strategy to cover the space to tag as many as possible and to avoid being tagged.

BIRD CATCHER

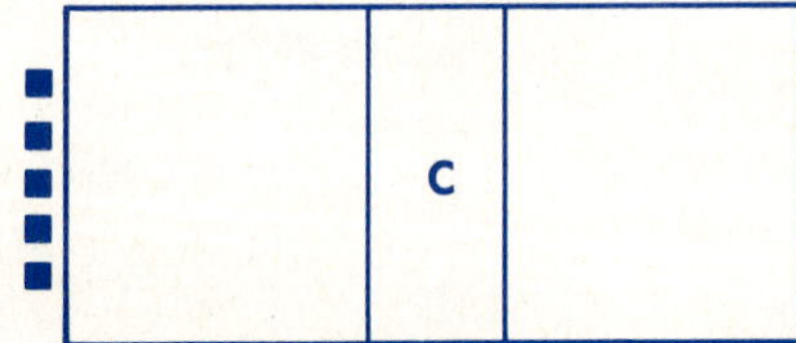

Level: II.

Equipment: None.

Participants: Up to 25.

Skills: Running, starting, stopping, dodging, tagging.

Description: The children are lined up on the end line facing "it." On the signal, they attempt to cross the wall without being tagged. Those tagged help "it." After four or five have been tagged, a new "it" is chosen to guard the wall from those not tagged.

Teaching Suggestions: Emphasize controlled stops and tags. Encourage strategy for guarding the wall and avoiding being tagged.

CIRCLE RACE

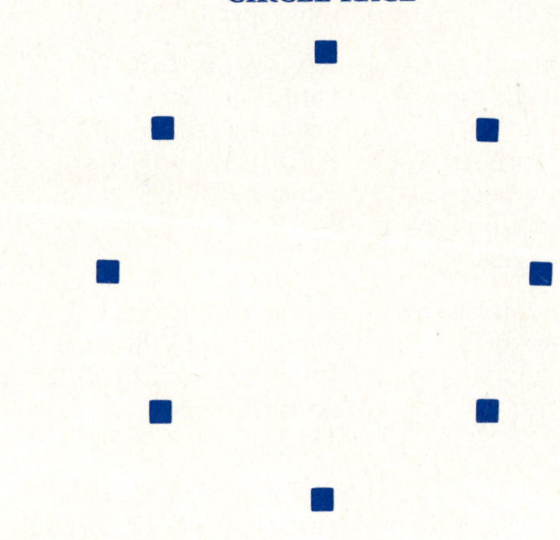

Level: II.

Equipment: None.

Participants: Up to 25.

Skills: Running in a circle, starting, stopping, tagging.

Description: Children are arranged in a circle and numbered off by threes. When the leader calls a number, the children with that number leave their places, run around the circle once and back to place, trying to tag as many children in front of them as possible.

Teaching Suggestions: Encourage running as close to the circle as possible and having controlled tags and stops.

COLOR TAG

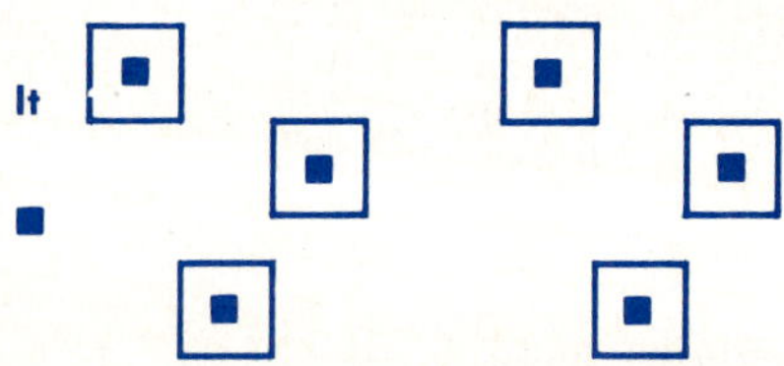

Level: II.

Equipment: Colored squares or hoops in at least three or four colors.

Participants: Up to 25.

Skills: Stopping, starting, dodging, tagging, running.

Description: The children are divided into color groups of equal size. Colored squares or hoops for each color group are scattered throughout the playing area, numbering one less than the number of children in each group. One person from each group is designated as "it." The children of each color group attempt to move from one square to another while "it" tries to tag them. The children are safe when they are touching the square or are in the hoop of their color only. "It" may tag only those in the same color group. After a few tries, a new "it" is selected for each group or "it" changes positions with the child tagged.

Teaching Suggestions: Emphasize looking out for others as they move throughout the playing area and tagging softly. Color groups may be ability grouped to provide a challenge for everyone.

FOX AND HOUND

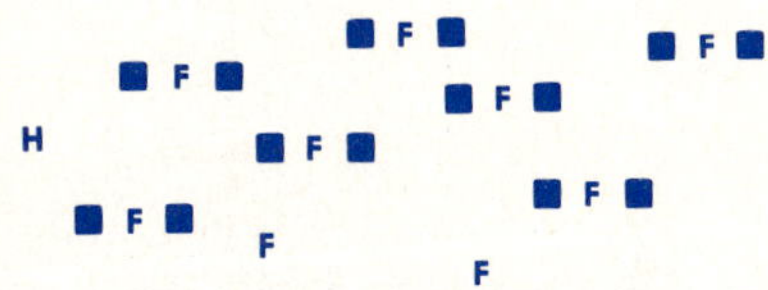

Level: II.
Equipment: None.
Participants: Up to 25.
Skills: Running, starting, stopping, tagging, dodging.
Description: The children are organized in groups of three, with one person designated the fox in each group and the other two the tree. In addition, one or two foxes without trees and an "it," the hound, are needed. The hound attempts to tag the free fox, who may go into a tree to escape. Only one fox may be in a tree at a time, so when the fleeing fox enters the tree, the fox already there must leave. If the hound tags the fox, the two exchange places, with the former fox becoming the hound. After a few tries have the fox change places with one member of the tree and again later to ensure that each child has an opportunity to be a fox.
Teaching Suggestions: Stress controlled stops and tags. Encourage the use of all space in avoiding the hound and changing direction and pathways. A variety of locomotor movements may be used.

GARDENER AND SCAMP

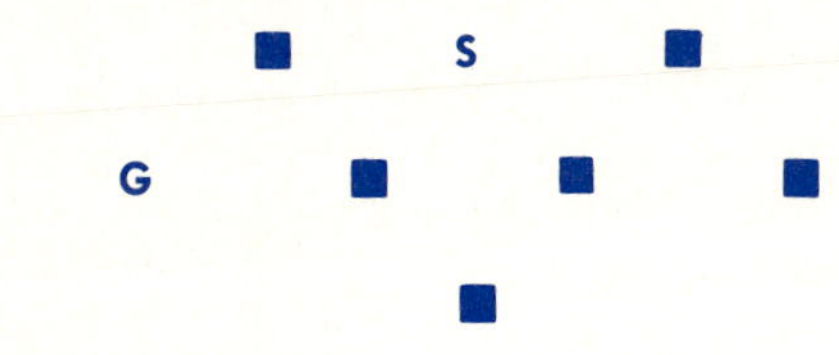

Level: II.
Equipment: None.
Participants: Up to eight per game.
Skills: Running, tagging, dodging.

Description: Children in each group are scattered in their playing area. On the signal, the gardener ("it") attempts to tag the scamp, who runs through the area in and out of the stationary players, by chasing scamp in the same path the scamp took. If tagged, the two change places. After a few minutes a new gardener and scamp are selected in each group.
Teaching Suggestions: The leader may call for scamp and gardener to switch positions without a tag being made, which requires listening and a quick response to the signal to change. The active children will tire quickly, so frequent changes in the group are important. Emphasize making a path difficult to follow and for the gardener to watch the path carefully. Encourage maximum use of available space. This is a good transition game following vigorous activity since all are not active at once.

MIDNIGHT

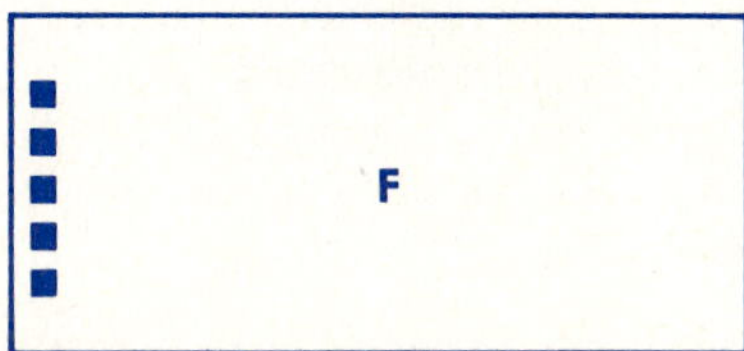

Level: II.
Equipment: None.
Participants: Up to 25.
Skills: Running, tagging, dodging, stopping, reversing pathways.
Description: The children, the chickens, are lined up at one end of the playing area with "it," Mr. Fox, out in front of the group facing away from them. The children move up behind Mr. Fox as the fox walks toward the opposite side of the playing area. The children ask, "What time is it, Mr. Fox?" to which the fox replies, "Two o'clock," or some other time. The children continue walking and asking the time. When Mr. Fox replies, "Midnight," the fox turns and chases the chickens back to the starting line. The game begins again with those tagged helping Mr. Fox. After six or so are tagged, a new Mr. Fox should be selected from those not tagged.
Teaching Suggestions: Encourage controlled stops at the starting line and soft tags. If children appear to be wanting to be tagged, modify the game so that only those not tagged get to be Mr. Fox and there are no helpers. Emphasize thinking about what they can do to avoid being tagged and looking for the open spaces (change path, directions, and so forth). "Its" should think about how they can work together to get more tagged.

SHARKS AND MINNOWS

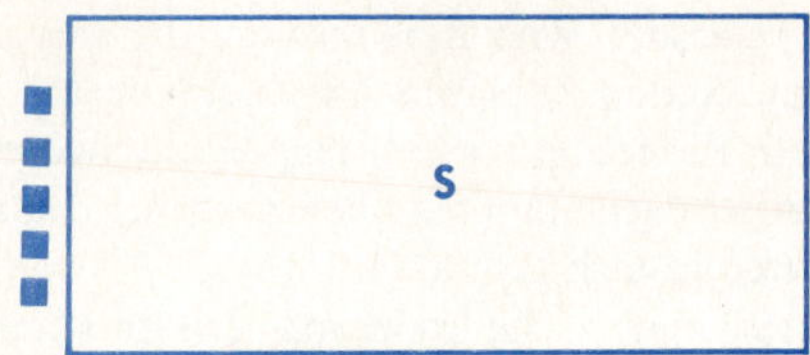

Level: II.
Equipment: None.
Participants: Up to 25.
Skills: Running, dodging, tagging, stopping.
Description: Children are lined up at one end of the playing area. "It," the shark, calls the minnows to "cross my sea." Minnows attempt to cross without getting tagged. Those tagged are changed into "seaweed" and stand at the spot where they were tagged. They now help the shark, but must keep one foot stationary at all times. The game continues until all are tagged. The last one tagged is the new shark.
Teaching Suggestions: Encourage controlled tags and stops. Emphasize looking for the open spaces and available pathways to avoid being tagged.

STEAL THE BACON

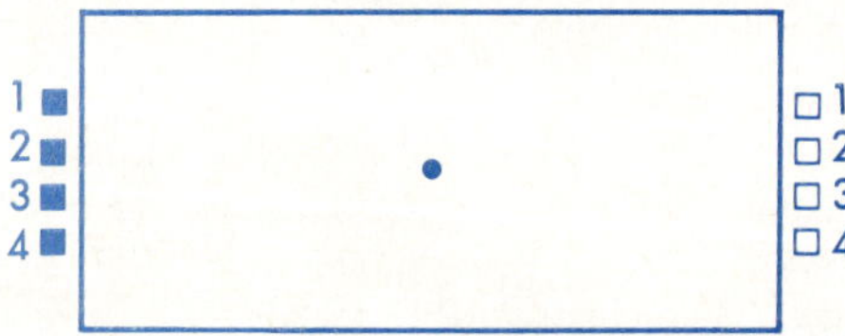

Level: II.
Equipment: Two duck pins per game.
Participants: Six to eight per game.
Skills: Tagging, dodging, stopping, starting.
Description: The children on each team are numbered consecutively beginning with one, are lined up behind their own boundary line. The leader calls a number, and the players from each team with that number come out and attempt to pick up the pin and bring it back across the line before the player not getting the pin can tag them. The game may be scored by either (1) receiving a point only when the club is safely over the end line or (2) receiving a point by bringing the club safely over the end line or by tagging the person with the club.
Teaching Suggestions: Emphasize controlled tags and stops. Have the children try different ways of getting the pin without getting tagged. What movements worked best? Opponents should be matched for ability to provide a challenge for all. Several small groups may play at the same time with the leader calling the numbers. For example, all the twos would go after the pins for their games at the same time.

TWO DEEP

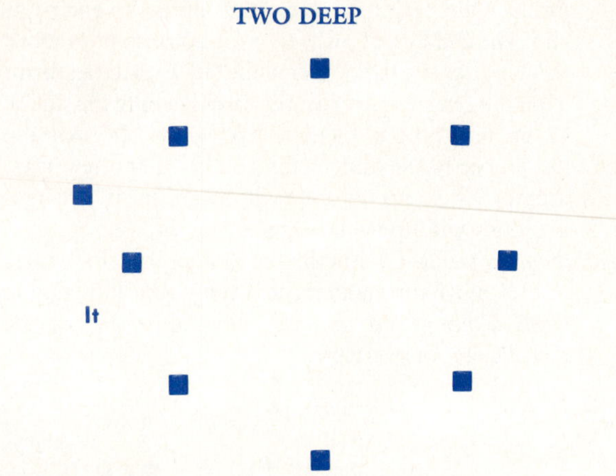

Level: II.
Equipment: None.
Participants: Eight to ten per game.
Skills: Starting, stopping, running, tagging.
Description: The children are organized in a circle, with one player designated as "it" and one other who is being chased. "It" begins the chase. The player being chased may step in front of any player in the circle (two deep) to avoid being tagged. The circle player whose place is taken must then run to avoid being tagged. When the leader calls, "change," "it" becomes the one being chased and the one formerly chased is now "it."
Teaching Suggestions: Encourage running close to the circle and controlling the tag. This is a good transition game following vigorous activity, since all are not active at one time.

UNCLE SAM

Level: II.
Equipment: None.
Participants: Up to 25.
Skills: Running, starting, stopping, tagging, dodging.
Description: The children begin lined up behind the line, with one person designated as "Uncle Sam" facing them. The children call to Uncle Sam, "Uncle Sam, may we cross your river?" to which he replies, "Yes, if you have (color) on." The children wearing the color called attempt to run to the opposite line without being tagged. Those tagged help Uncle Sam as the game progresses. A new Uncle Sam, chosen from those not tagged, should be selected after five to eight people have been tagged.

Teaching Suggestions: Encourage controlled stops and tags and avoiding being tagged. Raise questions to help children cover the area on defense to get as many tagged as possible and also to avoid being tagged when this coverage is made.

CROWS AND CRANES

Level: III.
Equipment: None.
Participants: Up to 25.
Skills: Stopping, starting, tagging, dodging, running.
Description: The group is divided in half, with one group being the crows and the other the cranes. Both teams line up facing each other at the center of the playing area. The leader calls, "crows," and the crows chase the cranes to their end line, trying to tag as many as possible. If the leader calls, "cranes," the cranes chase the crows to their end line. Those tagged join the team that tagged them.
Teaching Suggestions:
1. At first it may be difficult for the children to keep track of which team they are on and which way to run on the signal. If the leader points in the correct direction, it may be helpful.
2. This game may be modified to work on language arts or math concepts by (1) having one group be long vowel and the other short vowel sounds, with the leader calling words with either sound; (2) having one team be odd numbers and the other even; or (3) with odd and even numbers, the teacher gives math problems (add, subtract, multiply or divide numbers), the answer determining which group runs and which group chases.
3. Encourage a ready position, which enables the children to quickly move in either pathway. Emphasize controlled tags and stops.

TOUCHDOWN

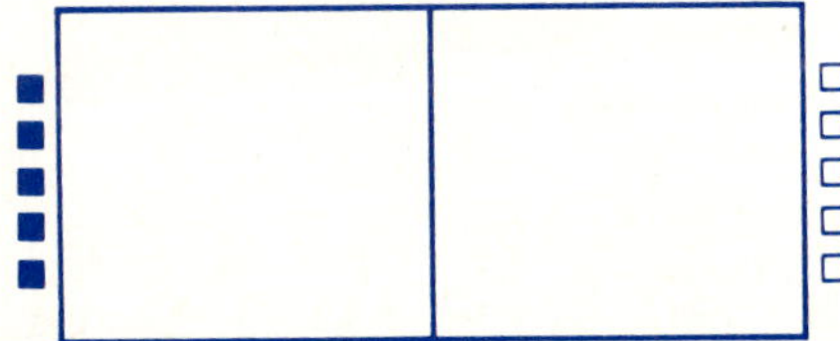

Level: III.
Equipment: One small object that can be concealed in the hand.
Participants: Up to 25.

Skills: Running, tagging, dodging, stopping.
Description: Two teams are gathered on each side of the playing area. One team is given the "football." They huddle and determine the strategy they will use to get the football over the opponents' goal line. The other team plays defense. If the player who has the football is able to get it across the opponents' goal line without being tagged, the team scores 6 points. The football may be concealed from the other team, and tagged players do not have to admit having or not having the football until all are tagged or the football is safely past the line.
Teaching Suggestions: In the beginning the children may be more concerned about who will carry the football than with the group effort to get it safely across the goal line. After one or two times they should begin to see how important it is to work together. On defense it may also take a few times before they will plan strategy. Creating spaces and closing spaces are important aspects of offensive and defensive strategy. This game may be played in smaller groups of six per team. Encourage controlled stops and tags and watching out for others during play.

STEALING STICKS

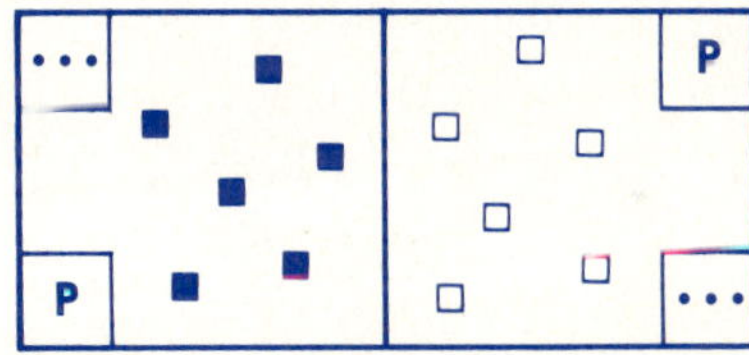

Level: IV.
Equipment: Six to eight sticks approximately 12 inches long.
Participants: Up to 25.
Skills: Running, tagging, dodging.
Description: The group is divided into two equal teams, each team scattered in its half of the playing area. Each team attempts to get to its opponents' sticks without being tagged. If a player touches an opponent's stick without being tagged, the stick may be brought back safely to the player's own half of the playing area. Only one stick may be taken at a time. If tagged, players go to their opponents' prison. Prisoners may be rescued by teammates getting to the prison area without being tagged. The first prisoner caught is the first released. Only one prisoner may be released at a time. Once a player has gotten safely to the prison area, both have safe passage back to their half of the playing area. The first team getting all their opponents' sticks wins.
Teaching Suggestions: This game may be slow getting started at times, because children may hesitate in crossing over into their opponents' territory. Children should be encouraged to work together in trying various offensive and defensive strategies.

Table 22-2
Games analysis for ball games

Name	Game classification	No. of participants	Equipment	Space and organizational pattern	Motor skills
Snowball	Ball	Up to 25	A large number of softball-sized fleece or foam balls	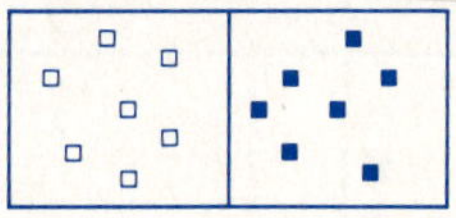	Overhand throw
Stride Ball	Ball	Six to eight per game	One 8-inch ball per group		Underhand throw Catching
Boundary Ball	Ball	Up to 25	Six to eight 8-inch balls, preferably foam	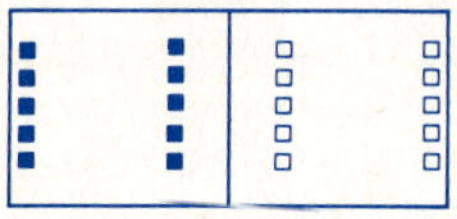	Shoulder or underhand throws Catching
Dodge Ball	Ball	Ten to 12 per game	One foam ball per four players	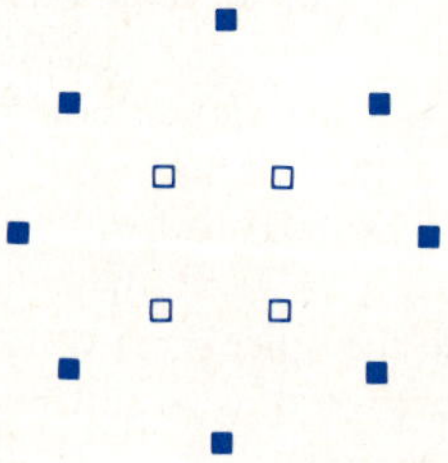	Throwing at a moving target Catching Dodging
Numbers Change Ball	Ball	Two teams of seven to eight players	One foam ball for each player		Throwing at a moving target Dodging
Bombardment	Ball	Up to 25	One 8-inch ball for each player, four players, up to 12 Indian clubs	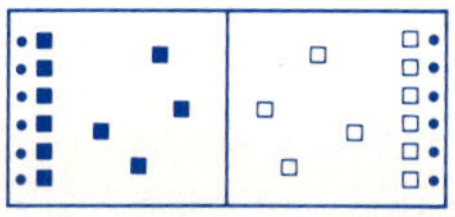	Underhand throw Catching Guarding a pin
Bull in A Ring	Ball	Eight to nine players	One or two foam balls per game	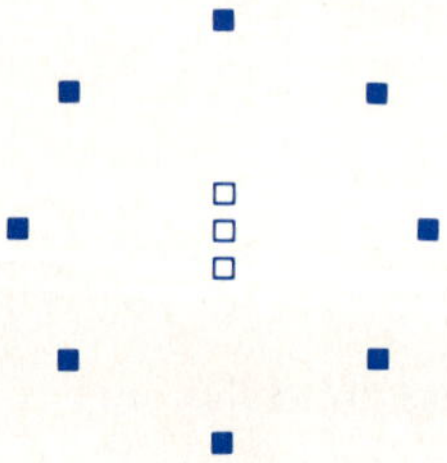	Throwing at a moving target Dodging

*Numbers refer to the concepts given in the box on p. 393.

Modifications	Movement concepts*	Social structure	Strategy	Level
	Self/general: 1, 2, 4, 9 Pathways: 22, 23 Force: 4	Parallel play I	Look for the empty space in which to put the ball; How can you best cover all space on your side of the playing area?	I
Add another ball to each game	Self/general: 9, 10 Level: 17, 19 Pathways: 22, 26, 27 Force: 4, 5	Parallel play II	Look for unguarded space; look one way and pass another	I
	Self/general: 1, 2, 6, 7, 8, 9, 10 Direction: 13, 14, 15 Level: 17 Pathways: 22, 23, 27 Force: 4, 5	Social interaction I	Designate responsibility for some to guard the line, others to be throwers; How can you best cover the space? Get the ball?	II
	Self/general: 2, 5 Direction: 12, 16 Level: 19 Pathways: 20, 22, 23, 27 Force: 4, 5 Time/speed: 7, 8, 9	Parallel play II	Move the ball quickly; anticipate the path and speed of the center players and place ball ahead	II
	Self/general: 1, 2, 3, 5 Direction: 12, 16 Level: 19 Pathway: 20, 22, 23 Force: 4 Time/speed: 7, 8, 9	Social interaction I	Aim ball slightly ahead of the runner	II
Could allow rebounds from walls	Self/general: 1, 2, 6, 7, 8, 9, 10 Direction: 13, 14, 15 Level: 17 Pathways: 22, 23, 27 Force: 4, 5	Social interaction I	Designate responsibility for some to guard the pins, others to throw	III
	Self/general: 1, 2, 5, 8 Direction: 12, 14, 15, 16 Level: 17 Pathways: 20, 22, 23, 27 Force: 4, 5 Time/speed: 7, 8, 9	Social interaction II	Leader must move to keep self between balls and tail; pass ball around to keep bull moving	III

Continued.

Table 22-2

Games analysis for ball games—cont'd

Name	Game classification	No. of participants	Equipment	Space and organizational pattern	Motor skills
Club Guard	Ball	Six to eight per game	One 8-inch ball and one Indian club per game		Chest pass Underhand throw Catching Guarding a pin
Guard the King	Ball	Seven to eight per game	One 8-inch ball per game	 G K	Throwing at a moving target Catching Guarding a moving target Dodging
Kickball	Ball	Two teams of six players	Four bases, one 8-inch playground or soccer ball	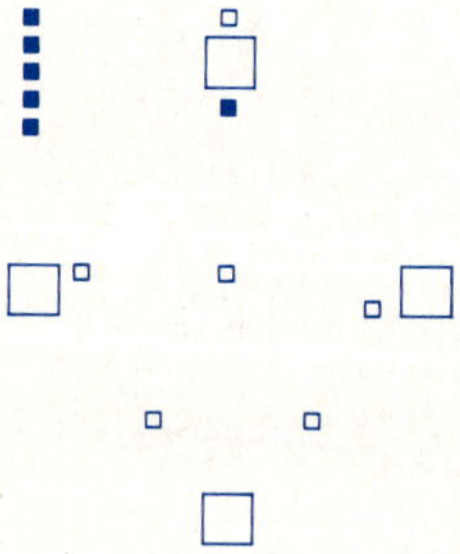	Kicking Catching Throwing Base running
Poison Ball	Ball	Two teams of five to six players	Four to six 8-inch playground balls, two different color balls		Throwing at a moving target Passing Catching
Keep Away	Ball	Three to five per team	One ball per game		Passing Catching
Medic	Ball	Two teams of 10 to 12 players	Six to eight foam balls	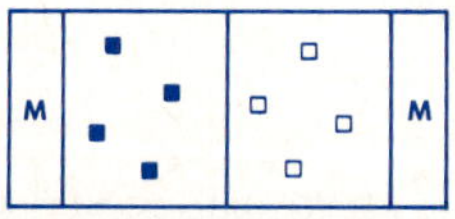 M M	Throwing at a moving target Dodging Catching

Modifications	Movement concepts	Social structure	Strategy	Level
	Self/general: 6, 8, 9 Direction: 15 Level: 18 Pathways: 22, 23 Force: 4, 5	Social interaction II	Team work is necessary to get to the pin and pass the ball quickly; try to get it behind guard	III
Increase number of balls	Self/general: 2, 3, 5, 6, 8, 9 Direction: 12, 14, 15, 16 Level: 19 Pathways: 20, 22, 23, 26, 27 Force: 4 Time/speed: 7, 8	Social interaction II	Work together to get king by passing to those in a better position	III
	Self/general: 1, 2, 7, 9, 10 Direction: 13, 14, 15 Level: 18 Pathways: 22, 23, 24, 26, 27 Force: 3, 4, 5, 6 Time/speed: 9	Social interaction I	Look for empty spaces in which to place the ball; infielders position yourselves to cover the infield area	III
Increase number of poison balls	Self/general: 1, 10 Pathways: 22, 23 Force: 4 Time/speed: 9	Social interaction II	Pass the ball to teammates in a better position to hit the poison ball	III
Dribbling may be allowed	Self/general: 1, 2, 3, 4, 8, 9, 10, 11 Direction: 12, 13, 14, 16 Level: 18 Pathways: 20, 21, 22, 23, 26, 27 Force: 4, 5 Time/speed: 7, 8, 9	Social interaction III	Pass quickly and move to an open space; close spaces on defense	IV
If the ball is caught on the fly, the thrower is considered hit	Self/general: 2, 5 Direction: 12, 14, 16 Level: 19 Pathways: 20, 22, 23, 27 Force: 4, 5 Time/speed: 7, 8, 9	Social interaction III	Protect medic; develop group strategy for getting the medic	IV

BALL GAMES

SNOWBALL

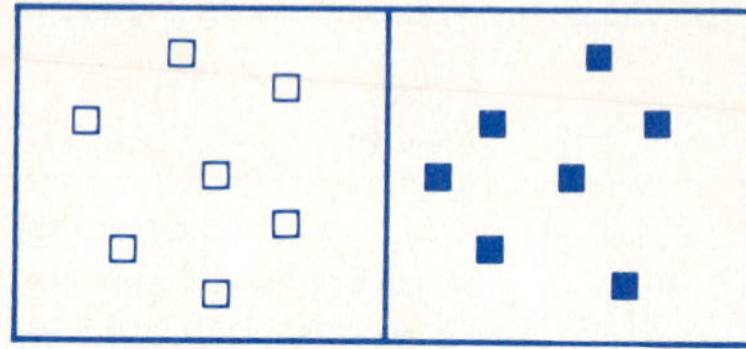

Level: I.
Equipment: An uneven number of fleece balls, at least one for every two children.
Participants: Up to 25.
Skills: Overhand throw.
Description: Half the children are scattered over each half of the playing area. On the signal to begin, the children throw the fleece balls into the opposite side of the playing area. They continue to field and throw the balls until the signal to stop is given. On the signal to stop, each child with a ball holds it high in the air. Any balls thrown after the signal to stop are returned to the side from which they were thrown. The team with the fewest balls on their side wins.
Teaching Suggestions: Emphasize using an overhand throw. A discussion of which are the best areas to throw to may be helpful between games. Emphasis might also be placed on how to cover the space so all balls may be fielded and thrown quickly. Encourage holding the balls up on the signal where they can be easily counted.

STRIDE BALL

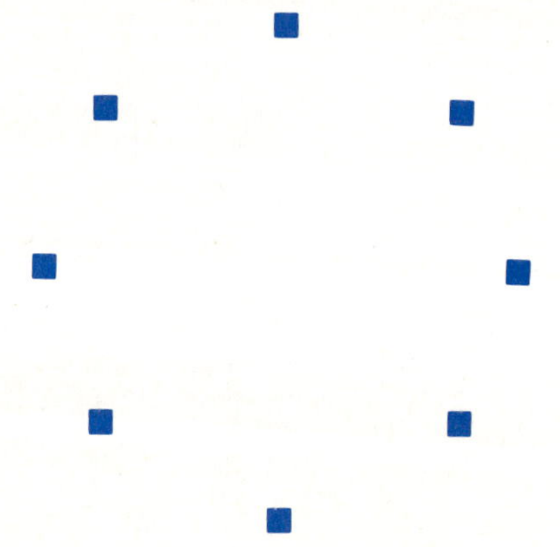

Level: I.
Equipment: One 8-inch ball per game.
Participants: Six to eight per game.
Skills: Underhand throw, catch.
Description: The children are arranged in a circle with feet spread to the side, just touching their neighbors' feet and hands on knees. One child has the ball and begins the game by attempting to roll the ball underhand

between the feet of a member of the group (but not the children directly next to them on either side). The children may stop the ball only with their hands. If the ball goes through or a player moves to use the feet to stop the ball, a point is scored for the thrower.
Teaching Suggestions: Encourage the children to throw quickly and to catch the ball when it comes to them, rather than batting it away. As skill improves, some children may also learn to be more deceptive in their throws by looking one way and throwing another.

BOUNDARY BALL

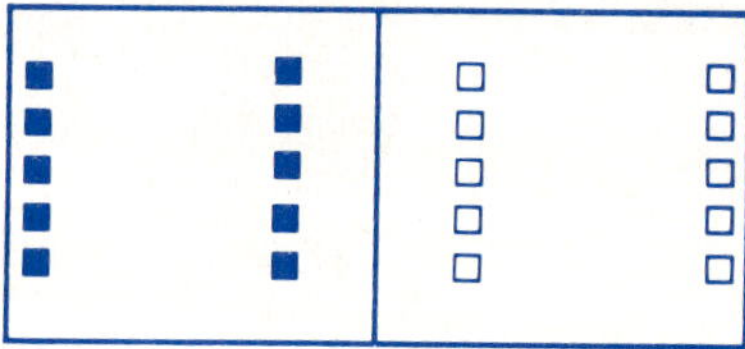

Level: II.
Equipment: Six to eight 8-inch playground or preferably foam balls.
Participants: Up to 25.
Skills: Underhand throws, catching.
Description: Children are divided into two equal groups, each group scattered within its half of the playing area. Each team begins with three to four balls. One player on each team is designated as scorekeeper to count the balls scored by its side. Each team attempts to throw the balls below the head level of the opposite team and across the opponents' end (boundary) line. One point is scored for each ball crossing the line.

Teaching Suggestions: In beginning play children will try to guard the line and also throw to their opponents' side without much success. After a few minutes of play, a discussion might be conducted to help the children analyze the situation and solve the problems raised. The teacher should lead the children in recognizing that a delegation of responsibility as throwers and guards might be helpful (but not tell them directly). As responsibilities are delegated, the children should be able to play both as throwers and guards by rotating positions periodically during the game. Encourage the children to control their throws and to throw at an appropriate level (below head height).

DODGE BALL

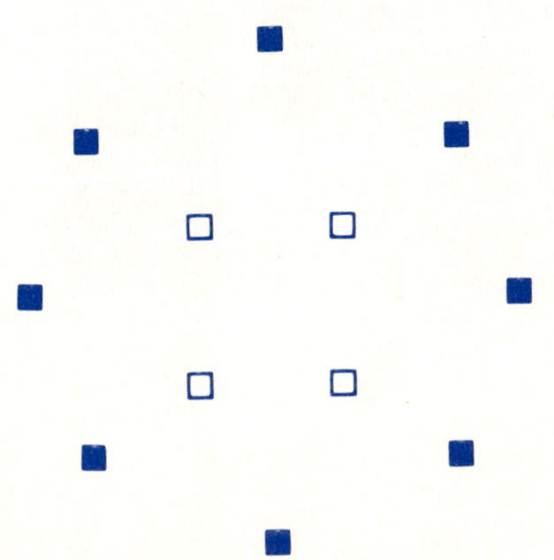

Level: II.
Equipment: One foam ball for each four players.
Participants: Ten to twelve per game.
Skills: Throwing at a moving target, catching, dodging.
Description: The children are arranged in a circle with one-third of them in the center. Children on the circle attempt to hit inside players below the waist or on the lower arms as they move in the circle. When hit with the ball, the player changes places with the thrower.
Teaching Suggestions: Emphasize throwing the ball quickly and keeping the ball low. Encourage sharing the ball on the circle so all have a chance to throw. Throwers should place the ball slightly ahead of the players so they move into the ball.

NUMBERS CHANGE BALL

Level: II.
Equipment: One foam ball for each thrower.

Participants: Two teams of seven to eight players each.
Skills: Throwing at a moving target, dodging.
Description: The players are divided into two teams, each team numbered consecutively. Two persons on each team are designated as throwers. The leader calls one or two numbers, and those players move through the playing area exchanging sides. The throwers attempt to throw the balls and hit the moving players on the opposite team as they move through the area. Only hits below the waist or on the lower arms count. Each team keeps track of its hits.
Teaching Suggestions: Emphasize keeping the balls low and aiming the ball slightly ahead of the runner.

BOMBARDMENT

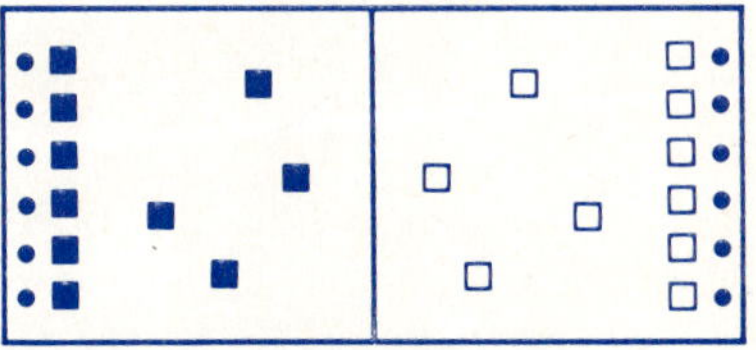

Level: III.
Equipment: One 8-inch ball per four players, up to 12 duck pins.
Participants: Up to 25.
Skills: Underhand throw, catching, guarding a pin.
Description: The children are divided into two teams. Each team is scattered on its half of the playing area. The six duck pins for each team are placed on the back boundary line an equal distance apart. Each team begins with one half of the balls in its possession. Each team attempts to throw the balls to knock down the duck pins of the opponents. Once down, a pin remains down until the end of the game. The team with the most pins standing at the end of the playing period wins. If players accidently knock down pins on their own side, they remain down.
Teaching Suggestions: As in Boundary Ball, the children may at first not designate responsibilities for being throwers or pin guards. A discussion for group decision making may be necessary after a few minutes of play. ("How can we make the game more effective?") A rotation of positions is important. Encourage controlled throws at an appropriate level. The game may be modified to allow balls rebounding from walls and hitting pins to count.

BULL IN A RING

CLUB GUARD

Level: III.

Equipment: One to two 8-inch foam balls per game.

Participants: Eight to nine players per game.

Skills: Throwing at a moving target, dodging.

Description: Players are arranged in a circle with three persons (the head, body, and tail) representing the bull and holding on to each other at the waist. On the signal, circle players attempt to hit the bull's tail by throwing the ball at waist height or below. The head and body attempt to fend off, protecting the tail. All body parts must remain in contact. If the tail is hit, the successful thrower becomes the head; the head, the body; and the body, the new tail.

Teaching Suggestions: Encourage the head player to stay between the balls and the tail and circle players to pass the ball quickly to others in a better position.

Level: III.

Equipment: One 8-inch playground ball and one duck pin per game.

Participants: Six to eight per game.

Skills: Chest pass, underhand throw, catching, guarding a pin.

Description: The children are arranged in a circle with one person in the center designated as club guard. The circle players attempt to throw the ball and knock down the duck pin. If the pin is knocked down, the two players change positions. If the guard accidently knocks down the pin, the guard changes positions with the person who has the ball.

Teaching Suggestions: This game requires teamwork. Encourage passing to get the ball behind the club guard.

GUARD THE KING

Level: III.

Equipment: One 8-inch foam ball per game.

Participants: Seven to eight per game.

Skills: Throwing at a moving target, catching, guarding a moving target, dodging.

Description: The children are arranged in a circle, with one person designated as king and one as guard in the center. The children try to throw the ball so that it hits the king below the waist as the guard attempts to protect the king from such hits. The player who hits the king becomes the king and chooses a new guard.

Teaching Suggestions: Encourage teamwork in attempting to hit the king by passing the ball to others in a better position.

KICKBALL

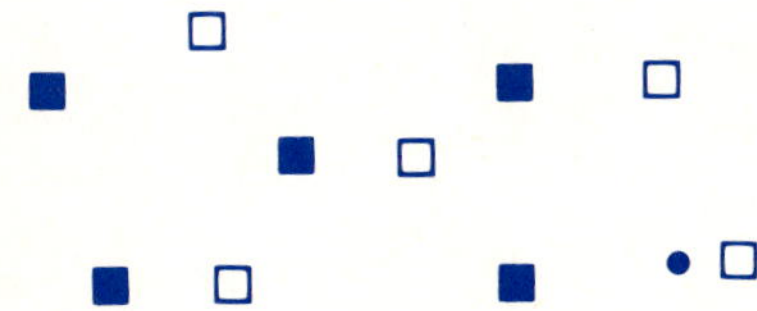

Level: III.

Equipment: One 8-inch playground or soccer ball, four bases.

Participants: Two teams of six players.

Skills: Kicking, throwing, catching, base running.

Description: The pitcher rolls the ball to the batter, who kicks the ball into the playing area (inside the first and third bases). A fly ball caught is an out. The batter then runs as many bases as possible without having the ball beat the runner to the base. If the ball gets to the base before the runner, the runner is out. All outs are force-outs (the player with the ball touching the base before the runner gets there). The player on base waits to finish the run home until the next batter bats. A run is scored each time a player completes the run around the bases. When each of the six players has had a turn at bat, the fielders and batters change places.

Teaching Suggestions: Encourage looking for empty spaces in which to kick the ball. Players waiting to bat should stand outside the playing area near the first base line. Fielders should spread out to cover as much of the infield as possible.

POISON BALL

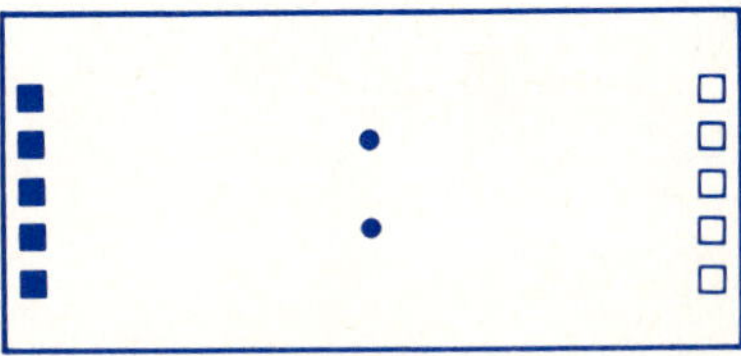

Level: III.

Equipment: Four to six 8-inch playground balls, two poison balls of a different color.

Participants: Two teams of five to six players.

Skills: Throwing at a moving target, passing, catching.

Description: Two teams are lined up behind their respective goal lines. The poison balls are placed in the center of the space between the two teams. On the signal, the teams attempt to throw the playground balls at the poison balls, forcing them over the opponents' goal line. Only the balls may be used to stop the poison balls. A player may hold the ball for no more than 5 seconds before throwing it or passing it to a teammate. A point is scored each time a poison ball crosses the opponents' goal line. Once past the goal line the ball is put back into play by the leader, and play continues.

Teaching Suggestions: Encourage team work in protecting the goal line by passing the ball to those in a better position.

KEEP AWAY

Level: IV.

Equipment: One 8-inch playground ball per game.

Participants: Two teams of three to five players each.
Skills: Passing, catching (possibly dribbling).
Description: One team begins in possession of the ball. They attempt to pass the ball to their teammates, counting the number of passes completed. The other team attempts to intercept a pass and begin its own passing game. If the ball goes out of the playing area, possession is forfeited to the other team. When possession is regained, counting begins again with one. There should be no personal contact or walking with the ball.
Teaching Suggestions: Emphasize quick passes and moving to an open space to receive the ball. Encourage the team on defense to experiment with different ways to close available spaces.

MEDIC

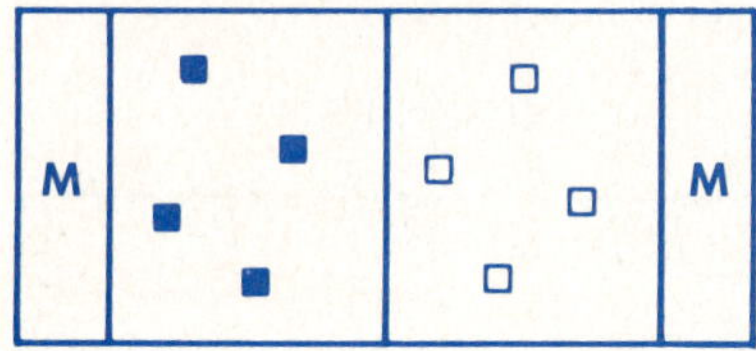

Level: IV.
Equipment: Six to eight 8-inch foam balls.
Participants: Up to 25.
Skills: Throwing at a moving target, dodging, catching.

Description: The group is divided into two teams, with each team designating one person as their medic. The area behind the end line is the hospital area, in which the medic is safe. All balls are placed on the center line dividing each team's playing area. On the signal, the players run up to the line, pick up a ball, take it back to their hospital area, and then move out on their half of the playing area. Each player throws the balls, attempting to hit as many opponents as possible below the waist or on the lower arms. Those hit squat down on the spot where they were hit, raise one hand, and call for the medic. The medic then comes out from the hospital area and takes the player by the hand back to the hospital. The hit player may then return to the game. The game proceeds until time is called or until all the players on one team are hit, including the medic.

Teaching Suggestions:
1. This is a game that usually takes several times before the children become daring and also begin to develop strategy to protect or hit the Medic.
2. It is probably appropriate not to call the attention of the group to what happens if the medic is hit at first and let that information evolve out of game play. From that point, strategy for protecting their medics, as well as strategy to hit the medic, will begin to emerge.
3. The game may be modified by having the throwers considered hit if the opponents catch the balls thrown at them.

SUMMARY

Educational games are one of the first group experiences in physical education. They provide children the opportunity to work in large and small groups with the dependence of the players on each other increasing as they move through the elementary school grades. Educational games are a favorite activity of elementary school children. If carefully selected and conducted, game playing becomes a valuable learning experience for children. Motor skill and concept development are important outcomes of games if these elements are stressed throughout the games lesson. The class begins with a review of the motor skills to be used and a practice period if needed. Movement challenges emphasizing concept use in the context of the games are introduced to focus the children's attention on the movement content to be stressed in the lesson. The games are then played with reinforcement of skill and movement concepts throughout the game play.

The game lesson must be carefully planned and conducted to ensure the safe and equal participation of all children. The teacher must be ever alert to the social environment of games so all children benefit positively from the game experience. Staying within the boundaries, playing by the rules, sharing equipment with others, and learning to win and lose gracefully are important outcomes of games if they are carefully taught.

REFERENCES

1. Council of the National Association for Sport and Physical Education: Games teaching, Reston, Va., 1978, AAAPERD.
2. Fluegelman, A., editor: The new games book, Garden City, N.Y., 1976, Dolphin Books, Doubleday & Co., Inc.
3. Werner, P.: A movement approach to games for children, St. Louis, 1979, The C.V. Mosby Co.

ADDITIONAL READINGS

Benson, J.: Creating games for learning, JOPER, **52**(2):22, February 1981.
Teacher-created interdisciplinary games using available materials for equipment.

Werner, P.: Interdisciplinary experiences through child designed games, JOPERD **53**(7):50, September 1982.
Math, art, language arts, and physical education teachers working together to provide interdisciplinary experiences through games created by the students.

23

BASKETBALL

CHAPTER OBJECTIVES

1   To discuss modifications in basketball necessary for elementary school children

2   To analyze the skills of basketball and suggest activities for their development

3   To discuss the relationship of the movement content to the game of basketball and provide activities to further the understanding of human movement through basketball-type activities

4   To provide a series of progressively more difficult lead-up activities for use during the upper elementary school years

Basketball, a game which originated in the United States, is a popular game of youth and young adults. Its high recreational appeal stems from the challenge of competing against another person or persons; it can be played in a relatively small area and is easily adapted for as few as two players.

Basketball is a complex game. To be successful, basketball players must have the ability to execute a variety of ball-handling skills including passing, catching, shooting, and dribbling. They must also be able to run, jump, change direction (pivot), stop, and start in combination with ball-handling skills as defense and offense require and must have the endurance to sustain activity over an extended period of time. The ability to work together and to relate to nine other moving individuals is a must if the player is to be effective.

Cognitively the players must be able to understand and play within the parameters of the game rules, to comprehend and use a variety of offensive and defensive strategies, and to recognize and put into effective use the movement concepts essential to the game.

BASKETBALL FOR ELEMENTARY SCHOOL CHILDREN

Basketball is a popular game with elementary school children. However, their success is often limited unless the game is adapted for them. Basketball lead-up activities may be successfully introduced in the intermediate grades after the children have acquired the fundamental motor skills prerequisite to basketball.

Equipment: Utility balls that are not too bouncy, soccer balls, or volleyballs should be used in the early years of development, because their size and weight enable them to be successfully handled by intermediate school children. Junior-sized basketballs should be introduced as children are able to handle them, usually by fifth or sixth grades. Baskets should be about 7 or 8 feet high to offer more opportunity for success in shooting. Adjustable baskets are available and should be standard equipment in the elementary school. The free throw line should be moved closer to the basket for young players.

Skills: Basketball requires the use of a variety of ball-handling and locomotor skills. These skills are

used in combination, and good body control is important if a player is to avoid traveling and personal contact. Since there is great variability in ball-handling and locomotor skills of elementary school children, it is important to adapt the rules to the needs of individuals. Being under control to avoid personal contact should be stressed with everyone. However, *traveling* might be called on an individual basis, with stricter adherence to the rule as children's skills improve. The ***double dribble*** is another rule in which some children experience difficulty. In games, opponents should be matched according to ability to provide the best opportunity for all.

The game: Basketball is a game requiring a great deal of team cooperation. Team work takes time to develop, and the basketball progression should be built with a gradually greater dependence on others for success in mind. Often in beginning games there is little evidence of team play. A few more-aggressive players dominate the game and little passing is observed. Rules must be introduced to ensure that play is evenly distributed among all the players. Requiring several passes or several individuals handling the ball before a shot is taken or requiring that no players may take two shots in succession are two modifications that might be needed. Offensive and defensive tactics should be taught. During these developmental years the following should be stressed in appropriate lead-up activities. The role of the offense is to:

1. Maintain possession of the ball.
2. Score points by successfully making baskets.

Offensive tactics that should be stressed include:

1. Moving the ball toward the basket.
2. Passing to a space in front of teammates and in a manner in which the ball can be easily received.
3. Moving to an open space to be free to receive the ball.
4. Remaining spread out to make the work of the defense more difficult.
5. Always being on the move, so players cannot be guarded easily.

The role of the defense is to:

1. Regain possession of the ball.
2. Prevent the opposing team from scoring.

Children should be encouraged to:

1. Stay between opponents and the basket.
2. Take up as much space as possible when guarding.
3. Continuously shift position in relation to the basket as opponents and the ball move on the court.
4. Guard a player who has dribbled more closely than one who has not.

5. Shift quickly to offense when gaining possession of the ball.

BASKETBALL SKILLS

Movement concepts are an important aspect of skill development. Body awareness and qualities of movement must not be overlooked in the learning process. In learning the skills of basketball, children should be encouraged to develop an awareness and understanding of how body parts are used most effectively in executing various skills. Body awareness should be encouraged by emphasizing the evaluative criteria and teaching points in the presentation, practice, and review of each skill. When time permits, problem solving in the use of body parts should be encouraged. Body control should be stressed, including the use of an appropriate amount of force for the task at hand. Children should be helped to apply principles of balance, laws of motion, and projection in the learning process.

Dribbling

Dribbling is used to move the ball on the court while legally maintaining possession of the ball. The ball is pushed to the floor slightly ahead of the moving player with the fingers of one hand so that it rebounds to about hip height where it may be pushed again and on each successive rebound.

Common errors:
1. Slapping the ball with the palms rather than pushing with the fingers.
2. Failing to look where they are going.
3. Bouncing the ball too high.
4. Stopping the dribble and then beginning again.
5. Bouncing the ball too close to the feet.

Activities to practice dribbling

Good ball control while moving requires a great deal of practice. Whenever possible, maximum activity should be provided by having as many children dribbling at a time as possible. It may be necessary to use many different kinds of balls when supplies are limited.
1. Each child has a ball. On the signal, they begin dribbling within the defined space. Activities include changing hands, moving from slow to fast speeds, changing direction, and varying the height of the bounce. Stationary obstacles

Figure 23-1

Evaluative criteria and teaching points for dribbling.

- Pushed with fingertips. Body erect, eyes looking forward.
- Ball projected forward.

such as cones and hoops may be added to the space around which the children must move. Emphasis should be on maintaining control of the ball and looking up to see where they are going. (The teacher should ask questions regarding speed, change of direction, and bounce height to ensure greater understanding.)
2. Parallel lines are drawn about every 10 to 15 feet. The children begin at line 1 and dribble up to line. They do a *reverse turn* and continue to dribble back to line 1. Then they go to line 3, back to 2, up to line 4, back to 3, and so forth. With each change of pathway a

Figure 23-2

Evaluative criteria and teaching points for chest pass.

- Fingers spread, thumbs behind ball.
- Arms at sides, elbows at waist height.

- Step forward
  Ball pushed forward equally from both arms.

- Arms fully extended, hands rotated inward, thumbs pointing down.
- Ball received at chest level.

Figure 23-3

Evaluative criteria and teaching points for two-hand bounce pass in addition to the criteria for the chest pass.

- Ball lands three-quarters of distance toward the receiver.

- Arms fully extended, hands rotated inward, thumbs down.

reverse turn is made. Dribbling should be practiced with one hand and then the other. (What did you do to keep the ball under control as you dribbled and then reversed your pathway?)

3. Whirl dribble: Cones are scattered in the general space. Each child with a ball dribbles to a cone, pauses with the foot opposite the dribbling hand forward, and pivots on the forward foot to turn away from the cone. The dribbler than fakes one dribble back away from the cone, changes hands, and completes the turn around the cone. (Were you able to keep the dribbling going? Did you complete the dribble around the cone?)

4. Hot-shot dribbling: Challenge the children by providing opportunities to practice dribbling behind their back or between their legs while stationary or moving.

Catching

Catching skills are analyzed in Chapter 11.

Passing

The *chest pass,* the most frequently used pass in basketball, is a short, quick pass and is particularly advantageous because it allows the receiver to catch the ball and throw it in one continuous movement. To begin, the ball is held just in front of the chest. As the ball is released there is a snap of the wrists and fingers, which gives power to the throw. The follow-through is in the direction of the throw with arms fully extended toward the receiver's chest.

Common errors:
1. Grasping the ball in the hands with thumbs on the side of the ball.
2. Extending elbows out from the sides.
3. Pushing with one hand more than with the other.
4. Not fully extending the arms on follow through toward the receiver's chest.
5. Not controlling the force of the throw by throwing it too hard or not using enough force to reach its destination.
6. Releasing the ball too soon or too late.

The chest pass requires considerable shoulder gir-

Figure 23-4

Evaluative criteria and teaching points for shoulder pass.

Ball held with fingers spread on either side of the ball.
- Elbows in, arms at sides.

- Step forward on opposite foot.
- Arms extended in direction of flight.
- Ball is received at chest height.

dle strength, often lacking in elementary school children. Children often compensate for this lack of strength by pushing the ball more from one side of the body than the other, which enables them to use trunk rotation to produce additional force. It may be helpful to have them begin the throw from a forward stride position with a shift of their weight to the rear foot before beginning the throw and a transfer of weight to the forward foot on the throw to add power. Making a downward circle with the ball before the forward extension of the arms should give them added power as well.

The *two-hand bounce pass* is similar to the chest pass in its execution and in its use as a short, quick pass. It is easier for children to catch, since the bounce allows more time and expends some of the ball's force. Executed like the chest pass, on releasing the ball the arms and hands follow through forward and downward toward the spot on the floor where the ball will land.

Common errors:
1. Projecting the ball downward rather than forward and downward.
2. Having the ball bounce too close or too far from the receiver.
3. Pushing the ball more with one hand than with the other.

The *shoulder pass* is generally used for long passes down court but may be used by children for short passes as well. It is usually a successful pass for elementary school age children, because more body parts may be used to project the ball than in the chest pass and using two hands affords greater control of the larger ball. The ball is held on one side of the body at shoulder level. The arms are extended forward with a wrist snap as the ball is released and follow through in the direction of the flight.

Common errors:
1. Grasping the ball in the hands.
2. Failing to step forward on the opposite foot.
3. Not following through in the direction of flight.
4. Releasing the ball too soon or too late.

The *two-hand overhead pass* is used for short, high

Figure 23-5

Evaluative criteria and teaching points for two-hand overhead pass.

- Hold ball in fingers over head.
- Step forward as throw is initiated.

- Extend arms with wrist snap.
- Follow through in direction of flight.

passes. The ball is held directly over head with one hand positioned on either side of the ball and with elbows bent. As the throw is initiated there is a step forward as both arms extend forward with a wrist snap on release.

Common errors:
1. Pushing with one side of the body more than with the other.
2. Using trunk flexion rather than a step forward to impart force.
3. Not following through in the direction of the intended throw.
4. Releasing the ball too soon or too late.

Because of a lack of shoulder girdle strength this may be a difficult throw for many elementary school children. Special emphasis may be needed on points 1 and 2 above.

Activities to practice passing

Body control in passing should be stressed, with the responsibility for a successful pass placed primarily on the thrower. In evaluating their success as passers, children should respond to the following questions: Did the ball get to the spot where it was supposed to go? Was the amount of force appropriate so it could easily be received by the catcher?

Activities that permit the children to experiment with the use of different types of passes at varying distances and forces enhance their ability to select a pass for a particular situation. The following examples illustrate these goals.

1. With a partner a short distance away, select a pass to be used and practice it, increasing the distance between the two children when they have completed five successful passes. Contin-

Figure 23-6

Evaluative criteria and teaching points for two-hand set shot.

- Fingers spread, thumbs behind the ball.
- Arms bent, elbows down.

- Ball pushed equally from both hands.
- Arms fully extended upward.
- Arch drops ball into basket.

ue increasing the distance until they can no longer complete five throws. (How did you use your body parts to increase the force needed as the distance became greater? Did this affect your accuracy? Now try another type of pass and repeat the activity.) This may be repeated several times. (Which passes were most effective for short, medium, or long distances? Why were some more difficult? Which were easier for your partner to receive?) Although generalizations can be made about which passes are best in particular situations, there may be individual preferences for certain types of passes. No one pass is best for all, and teachers should encourage children to discover which works best for them.

2. Each child has a ball and is facing a wall that is about 10 feet away. They practice throwing the ball to the wall so that it rebounds just to themselves or to some designated spot on the floor. Try different passes, move closer or farther away from the wall. The children could also experiment with different kinds of balls used in the basketball progression. (What did you do to control the force to get the ball to rebound as you wanted it to? Which throws were easiest to control? At which distances were you most accurate?)

3. Odd and Even: Six to eight children are organized in a circle and numbered off beginning with 1. The even numbers constitute one team, the odd numbers, the other. Each team has a ball. On the signal, each team attempts to pass the ball around the circle to each of its members in turn, counting each successful pass. If the ball is dropped, counting must begin again with 1. At the signal to stop, the team with the highest number of consecutive passes wins. Reverse passing order. Select specific passes to be used each time. (What did you have to do to keep the ball moving so that it could be caught each time? Where did you like to receive the ball?)

4. Galloping Lizzie: Children are arranged in groups of four or five in a circle with an additional person in the center. Circle players attempt to pass the ball quickly to anyone in the circle. The center player attempts to tag the person holding the ball. If "Lizzie" tags a player, the two exchange places. Specific passes may be designated for use. (Where did you want to receive the ball so that you could get rid of it quickly? Which types of throws were easiest to catch and throw again?)

Once children have an idea of the techniques and controlling force, the practice of passing to moving

Figure 23-7

Evaluative criteria and teaching points for lay-up shot.

- Take last step on opposite foot.
- Jump straight up with the shooting knee raised.

- Extend shooting side arm for soft touch on backboard.
- Controlled landing.

players should begin. The activities found later in this chapter for working on space concepts will help children work on passing in a game-like situation.

Shooting

Success in shooting during the elementary school years is limited. The weight of the ball, the height of the basket, and the lack of strength in the arms and shoulders all influence children's shooting abilities. Even with appropriately sized equipment and height of baskets, shooting is difficult.

The *chest shot* (or *two-hand set shot*) is used as a short or long set shot. Because the child can use both hands, more force can be imparted to the ball to get it up to the basket. Although this shot is no longer used at higher levels of basketball, it is one of the most successful shots during the elementary school years. The chest shot is executed as the chest pass but with arm extension upward to give a higher arch to the ball so that it drops down into the basket. It may or may not touch the backboard. If the ball does hit

the backboard, it must be a soft contact to avoid rebounding away from the basket.

Common errors:
1. Pushing more with one hand than with the other.
2. Failing to fully extend the arms upward.
3. Not giving enough arch on the ball.
4. Contacting the backboard too hard so that the ball rebounds away.

The *lay-up shot* is a fundamental shot. Since it is taken while moving it is a more difficult shot for elementary school children. Since this is a shot taken on the move, the last step should be taken by the foot opposite the shooting hand. Raising the knee on the shooting side aids in gaining height on the take-off. The ball is initially held in two hands, and then one hand continues to reach with the ball, being fully extended as the ball is "laid" up softly against the backboard. The ball should be released with the right hand when shooting is from the right, and the left when the shot is taken from the left. This normally keeps the ball farthest away from the person

Figure 23-8

Evaluative criteria and teaching points for one-hand set shot.

- Ball is held at chin height with the fingers of the shooting hand behind the slightly under the ball.
- Knees bent, lead foot forward.

- Knees straighten. Full extension of shooting arm upward and forward.
- Ball arch drops ball into basket.

guarding the player.

Common errors:
1. Traveling before releasing the ball.
2. Watching the ball rather than the basket on the approach.
3. Throwing the ball too hard against the backboard.
4. Stopping before shooting.
5. Releasing the ball without full extension of the shooting arm.

The *one-hand set shot* is more difficult to perform than the two-hand set shot, because only one hand is used to impart force to the ball. The ball is held with the fingers of both hands opposite the chin and in front of the lead foot. The wrist of the shooting hand is cocked back, and the ball rests on the outspread fingers. The nonshooting hand supports the ball at the side and bottom. The knees are bent and the back is relatively straight. As the movement begins, the legs straighten as the ball is taken in the shooting hand, the arm extending forward and upward and pushing the ball toward the basket. The ball is released with a soft backspin. The lead foot should be on the same side as the shooting hand. The follow through is forward and upward.

Common errors:
1. Resting the ball in the hands.
2. Stepping forward on foot opposite shooting hand.
3. Not fully extending the shooting arm.
4. Using too much body action to get the ball up.
5. Hitting the backboard forcefully, causing the ball to rebound rather than score.

Figure 23-9

Evaluative criteria and teaching points for reverse turn and pivot.

Reverse turn:
• One foot forward.

Pivot:
• Turn away from forward foot.
• Pivot foot remains stationary.

• Turn around pivot foot.

Activities to practice shooting

In beginning development of basketball skills, children should be encouraged to develop some of the basic principles of shooting. Not all children will be successful at any particular type of shot. They will need to experiment with the various types of shots to determine which is best for them at this time.

How can they get the ball up to the basket? At this level, emphasis on where they want to put the ball and putting it there softly so that it goes into the basket should be stressed, because they will not all be successful at getting the ball up to the basket in the same way. To maximize the activity, no more than six or seven children should work at one basket.

1. Mass Shooting: Each child has a ball and all attempt to make as many baskets as they can within the time period. (From which places on the court were you most successful? What type of shot worked best? Did you control the force to get the ball into the basket?)

2. Around the World: Numbers from 1 to 10 are marked randomly on the floor in the basket area. Each child begins at 1 and attempts a shot at the basket. If made, the child moves to 2 and so on. To provide maximum activity children may begin at any number and proceed to the next until they have shot from all 10 numbers. (Which ways did you try that were successful at scoring a basket? Did you use the same type of shot near and far from the baskets, from the side, and in front of the basket?)

3. Take A Chance: Seven numbers are marked randomly on the floor around the basket area. Children are divided into partners or groups of three, with one ball for each group. The first person in each group begins at 1 and shoots for a basket. If made, the player may "take a chance" and attempt to shoot a basket from the next number. If made, they continue to move up the numbers; if missed, the next person begins, and the players who missed must go back to 1 when it is their turn again. If they choose not to "take a chance," then they begin their next turn at the number to which they advanced. (How did you change your shots as you moved to different locations on the floor? Did you change the type of shot taken? Where did you try to put the ball?)

4. One-On-One: Each child has a partner. One has the ball and attempts to move the ball to the basket while the other is the guard and attempts to keep the other from shooting. Personal contact should be avoided. (How did you move to get free of the guards to get your shots away? How did you watch the forwards to anticipate their movements?)

Figure 23-10

Evaluative criteria and teaching points for guarding.

- Body crouched, knees bent.
- Comfortable side stride, one foot slightly ahead.
- Hands up to protect space.
- Can move in all directions.

Reverse Turn and Pivot

The **reverse turn** and **pivot** are used to change direction legally while holding the ball. The reverse turn is used to reverse pathways. The feet are in a forward stride position. Weight is on the balls of the feet as the turn is made toward the rear foot.

Common errors:
1. Moving around in a circle rather than turning on the balls of the feet.
2. Lifting a foot on the turn.

Before beginning the pivot the weight is evenly distributed on both feet, with the ball held firmly in two hands. One foot is designated as the pivot foot. The player may turn in either direction as long as the pivot foot remains on the floor and is not dragged from its original position.

Common errors:
1. Not having the body under control before beginning the pivot.
2. Dragging the pivot foot.
3. Changing the pivot foot.

4. Using the entire foot rather than the ball of the foot.

Activities to practice reverse turn and pivoting

1. Dribbling in general space. On the signal do a reverse turn and proceed in the new pathway. Repeat several times. Change lead foot and repeat.
2. In groups of two, one person is the pivot person and has a ball. The other takes a position to one side of the player, but not too close. Slowly at first, the pivot player pivots to keep the other from tying up the ball. As skill improves, pick up speed. (How did you move to keep the ball away from your opponent?)

Guarding

Since half of the time in any game one team is trying to gain possession of the ball, effective *guarding* techniques are a must for each player. The player assumes a slightly crouched position, with feet in a comfortable side stride position slightly larger than the width of the shoulders. One foot may be slightly ahead of the other, and body weight is supported on the balls of the feet. Hands and arms are extended generally with one hand up forward and the other at shoulder level. Players must be alert to movements of the forwards they are guarding so that feet and arms may be moved to guard the player effectively. The guard plays farther away from a player who has not moved than one who has stopped dribbling. Eyes should focus on player's hips to determine where the move will be made.

Common errors:
1. Body erect with no knee bend.
2. Weight supported on the entire foot so it cannot be moved easily.
3. Guarding players who have not dribbled too closely so they are able to move around the guard.
4. Flailing the arms rather than purposeful movement.
5. Running rather than sliding to stay with the opponent.

In the early games in the progression, the concern in guarding is to keep the ball out of a particular space by covering the space to block or to intercept throws. Later when children begin to work against an opponent in a one on one situation, guarding an individual becomes important.

Activities to practice guarding

1. The group faces the leader and assumes a good guarding stance. On the movement by the leader, who moves forward, backward, or to the side, the group responds by moving as if they were trying to contain the leader. (How did you move to stay with the leader? What cues did you use to anticipate which way they would move?)
2. Partners face each other. First without and then with a ball, one attempts to move to some designated area on the floor, while the partners or guards attempt to keep them out. Guards may be asked to use feet only at first with hands behind the back. Later add the use of the arms in guarding. (What did you have to do to keep partners out without using personal contact? Where did you watch so you could anticipate which way they were going to move?)

Movement Skills

The movement skills important to basketball (stopping, jumping and dodging, sliding) are analyzed in Chapter 11.

BASKETBALL CONCEPTS

Application of the movement content is essential to success in basketball. The box below outlines the concepts identified to begin development at the elementary school level. The importance of the application of body awareness and quality of movement concepts has already been stressed in the execution and use of basketball skills. These are enhanced further as children adapt skills for use in various game situations. Space concepts are also important as children move on the court in ever-changing relationships with others.

Each lesson should include activities that enhance the application and use of movement concepts in basketball activities. In addition to emphasis on the movement content as it relates to skill development, activities should help children to see the relationships between these concepts and play in basketball lead-up games. Specific activities that maximize the activity for all children should be used. These activities may actually be mini-aspects of the games themselves. The closer these activities are to the use of the concepts in the games the greater the chance for transfer to these games as the basketball unit is developed. As the children move on in the lesson to the lead-up activities, the teacher must continue to emphasize the concepts developed in earlier parts of the lesson.

Basketball Concept Activities

Space:
Each person dribbles a ball in general space. Emphasis should be placed on either using all space available or moving to an open space on signal.
Similar to above, but now space is alternately increased or decreased. Children continue moving and dribbling, but they modify movement as space changes. (How close can you get together and continue moving without touching? What did you do differently as space increased or decreased to keep the ball under control? What problems did you encounter as the space got smaller?)
One half with balls are dribbling in space, and the other half is stationary. Players keeping one foot stationary attempt to knock the ball away from the dribblers. No personal contact is allowed. (What must you do to keep the ball from the opponents? How did you protect the ball?)
One third of the group assumes a stationary position and are scattered in the general area. The other children are divided into partners, with one ball for each set of two. The partners move in the available pathways, dribbling and passing to each

BASKETBALL CONCEPTS

BODY AWARENESS

Body awareness concepts are applied in the analysis of all skills in which the part played by different body segments is understood.

SPACE

Self and general space:
1. To move oneself and the ball within the boundaries of the court
2. To move in general space in relation to teammates, opponents, and the ball
3. To move around teammates and opponents to an open space
4. To move with control to avoid personal contact
5. To protect the ball as one moves among opponents by keeping body between the opponents and the ball
6. To keep self space beweeen one's opponent and the goal or the ball and the goal, while on defense
7. To pass the ball to an empty space in front of the receiver
8. To use as much space as possible on offense to keep the defense spread out
9. To make one's self space large to cover as much of the court as possible on defense
10. To close spaces open to opponents and the ball especially near the basket, while on defense
11. To create open spaces for oneself, teammates, and the ball by drawing an opponent
12. To reconize one's area of space in which to play or defend

Direction:
13. To assume a position that enables one to move in any direction
14. To change direction quickly to avoid contact with others
15. To change directions to get around an opponent or to stay with an opponent
16. To change direction to open up spaces
17. To change direction to move the ball to the basket
18. To change direction to intercept the ball
19. To anticipate direction changes of teammates and opponents

Level:
20. To move the ball at an appropriate level (where the open space is and where it can be easily received)
21. To protect all levels when on defense

Pathways:
22. To change pathways while moving in space with and without the ball
23. To recognize available pathways within which to move the ball or to score a goal
24. To anticipate the pathways of the ball, teammates, and opponents so that the path may be intercepted offensively or defensively
25. To close pathways available to opponents
26. To change the expected path of the ball
27. To open pathways to the goal on offense

Continued.

BASKETBALL CONCEPTS—cont'd

QUALITIES OF MOVEMENT

Force:
  1. To use an appropriate amount of force in dribbling, passing, and shooting
  2. To absorb force in catching, jumping, and rebounding

Time and speed:
  3. To change speed smoothly and efficiently while moving in space
  4. To alter the tempo of the game by speeding up or slowing down
  5. To judge the speed of the ball, teammates, or opponents to intercept, close an open space, or meet a pass

Flow:
  6. To created and absorb force alternately in dribbling
  7. To combine skills into a continuous movement

other as the stationary (defensive) players attempt to intercept. (How did you anticipate the movements of your partner and successfully pass in the available pathways? What cues did you use?)

Four players are spaced along the foul shooting lane. One person has the ball and passes to a person and cuts for the empty space on the lane. (Were you able to keep track of the empty space? Were you always attentive to where the new empty space was?)

Variation: Number the players so 1 passes to 2, 2 to 3, and so on.

Four players are spaced along the foul shooting lane. One person has the ball and passes and moves away from the ball toward another player, who moves to the empty space. Try this slowly at first, then speed it up once they can do it. (Were you ready to move so you could quickly change places with the arriving player? Was it easy to find the empty space?)

Four persons dribble, one behind the other. On the signal, they must break for an open space. On the next signal, they return to file and repeat. (How did you control the ball and look out for others as you moved to the open space?)

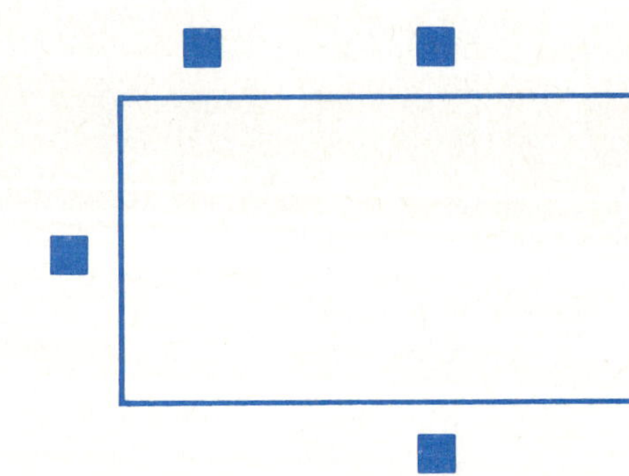

In groups of three, one person is stationary as if throwing the ball in from out of bounds. One is the receiver and attempts to move to an open space to receive a pass, while the third child attempts to intercept the pass. Change positions after a few attempts. (How did you move to get free of the defender? Were you able to pass to a space in front of the receiver? How did you anticipate where to throw the ball?)

Variation: Throwing players move on the court while a third attempts to intercept.

Four persons with balls are in an area the size of the foul shooting lane. Each dribbles, trying to knock away the balls of others while protecing their own. (What did you do to protect the ball?) No personal contact is allowed. Players should attempt to time knocking the ball away when it is out of the hands.

There are four persons, two on each team, and one ball. Each team attempts to see how many consecutive passes they can complete, while the other team attempts to intercept. No personal contact is allowed. Change size of area. (Which was easier, the smaller or larger space? Why?)

Children have partners, one person guarding a grid about 6 feet square. The player outside the grid tries to dribble the ball through the grid as the partner tries to keep him or her out. (What did you do to protect your space? What did you do to move the person out of the space?)

Two or three stationary guards are in the goal area. Two or three forwards attempt to pass and shoot, avoiding interception by the guards. (What did you need to look for as you tried to move the ball to the basket?)

Two on One: Two attempt to move the ball toward the goal, while one attempts to intercept a pass. (What did you do to move the guard out of the way to have an unguarded shot for the basket?)

Qualities of movement:

Similar to the first above, but emphasis is on changing speed. On the signal, they "break" quickly to an open space, then resume normal dribbling.

Additional activities may be found in the suggested practices for basketball skills.

BASKETBALL LEAD-UP GAMES

Table 23-1 includes a game analysis for all the games included here.

ENDBALL

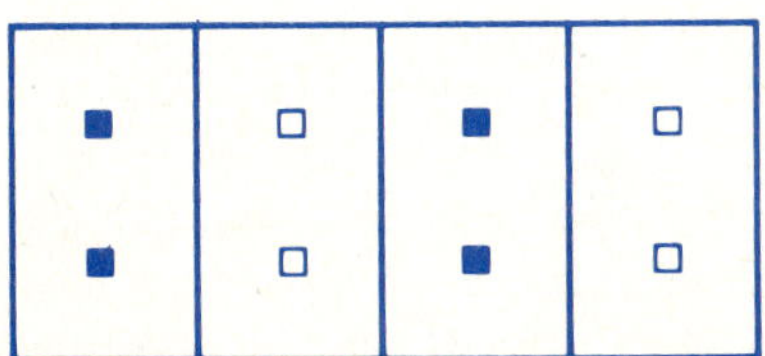

Level: III.

Equipment: One 8-inch utility ball, soccer ball, or volleyball.

Area: A rectangular area divided into four courts, the court on each end being the goal area. The size of the playing area is dependent on the ability of the players.

Participants: Four to six per team.

Skills: Passing, catching, dribbling, guarding.

Description: Play is begun by giving the ball to a player in one of the inside areas, who attempts to pass the ball to a teammate in the goal area. One point is scored when the ball is thrown to a teammate in the goal area so that it may be caught on a fly or after one bounce. After any score or a missed attempt at scoring, the ball is given to the opposing team in the adjacent court. If the ball is intercepted by the opponents in the scoring effort, they attempt to throw the ball to their players for a score.

Violations: Stepping out of the assigned area, walking with the ball, holding the ball more than 3 seconds, illegal dribble.

Penalty: The ball is given to the opponents.

Strategy:
1. Move the ball quickly toward the goal.
2. Move as close as you can to throw the ball to players in the end zone.
3. Cover the entire area on defense.
4. Move to an unguarded area to receive the ball.

Teaching Suggestions:
1. Rotate players periodically so that each has an opportunity to play both positions.
2. Emphasize moving the ball to a better throwing position by dribbling or passing to a teammate in the same zone.

BASKET ENDBALL

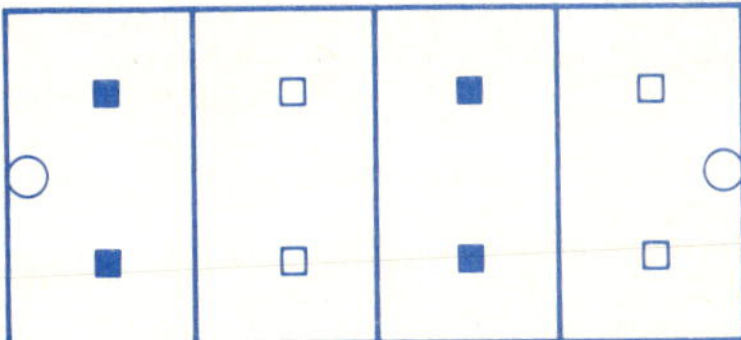

Level: III.

Equipment: Two 7- to 8-foot baskets and one soccer ball or volleyball per game.

Description: The rules of Endball are used with the addition of one chance to shoot a basket after a successful catch. If the basket is made, two additional points are scored. Encourage the children to move close to the basket after receiving the pass to attempt their shots.

Table 23-1
Basketball games analysis

Name	Game classification	No. of participants	Equipment	Space/organizational pattern	Motor skills
Endball	Lead-up	Four to six per team	One 8-inch utility, soccer, or volleyball		Passing Catching Dribbling Guarding
Basket Endball	Lead-up	Four to six per team	Soccer or volleyball; two 7- to 8-foot baskets		Passing Catching Dribbling Guarding Shooting
Zone Basketball	Lead-up	Four to five per team	One soccer, volleyball or, junior basketball; two 7- to 8-foot baskets		Passing Catching Dribbling Guarding Shooting
Basketball Relay	Skill	Four to six per team	One volleyball, soccer ball, or junior basketball per team; one 7- to 8-foot basket for two teams		Passing Catching Dribbling Shooting
Toss-Up Basketball	Lead-up	Four to six per team	One junior size basketball, soccer or volleyball; one 7- or 8-foot basket		Passing Catching Dribbling Shooting Guarding

*Numbers refer to the basketball concepts in the box on pp. 431-432.

Modifications	Movement concepts*	Social structure	Strategy	Level
1. Rotate players so all have a chance to play all positions 2. Limit types of throws used	Self/general: 6, 7, 8, 9, 10, 12 Direction: 13, 16, 18 Level: 20, 21 Pathways: 22, 23, 24, 25, 26 Force: 1, 2	Social interaction I	1. Move the ball quickly 2. Cover the entire area on defense 3. Move to an unguarded area to receive the ball 4. Move the ball to a better throwing position before attempting to throw to teammates in the goal area	III
1. Rotate players so all have a chance to play all positions 2. Limit types of throws used	Self/general: 1, 7, 8, 9, 10, 12 Direction: 13, 16, 18 Level: 20, 21 Pathways: 22, 23, 24, 25, 26 Force: 1, 2	Social interaction I	1. Move the ball quickly 2. Cover the entire area on defense 3. Move to an unguarded area to receive the ball 4. Move the ball to a better throwing position before attempting to throw to teammates in the goal area 5. Move close to the basket before taking your shot	III
1. Rotate players so all have a chance to play all positions 2. Limit types of throws used 3. Match opposing players of equal ability in the court areas	Self/general: 1, 2, 3, 4, 5, 6, 7, 8, 9, 10, 12 Direction: 13, 14, 15, 16, 18, 19 Level: 20, 21 Pathways: 22, 23, 24, 25, 26 Force: 1, 2 Time/speed: 3, 5	Social interaction I	1. Move the ball quickly 2. Cover the entire area on defense 3. Move to an unguarded area to receive the ball 4. Move the ball to a better throwing position before attempting to throw to teammates in the goal area 5. Move close to the basket before taking your shot 6. Keep between opponents and goal when on defense	III
1. Match opposing players by ability 2. Designate a particular pass to be used	Self/general: 4, 7 Direction: 14, 17 Level: 20 Pathways: 22, 24 Force: 1, 2	Social interaction I	1. Pass quickly 2. Begin with pass to player furthest from basket and move ball toward the basket on each throw	III
1. To avoid collisions ball must bounce first before catching it on initial ball toss 2. Distance for free throw adjusted for ability of players 3. It is helpful to call out the number of passes	Self/general: 1, 2, 3, 4, 5, 6, 7, 9, 11, 12 Direction: 13, 14, 15, 16, 17, 18, 19 Level: 20, 21 Pathways: 22, 23, 24, 25, 26, 27 Force: 1, 2 Time/speed: 3, 4, 5 Flow: 1	Social interaction I-II (depending on the number of players called)	1. Move ball toward the basket 2. When on defense, stay between opponent and basket (after the two passes are completed) 3. Move to an unguarded area to receive the ball	III

Continued.

Table 23-1
Basketball games analysis—cont'd

Name	Game classification	No. of participants	Equipment	Space/organizational pattern	Motor skills
Sideline Basketball	Lead-up	Four to five per team	One junior size basketball; two 8-foot baskets		Passing Catching Dribbling Shooting Guarding Pivot, reverse turn Rebounding
Alley Basketball	Lead-up	Five per team	One junior size basketball; two 8-foot baskets		Passing Catching Dribbling Shooting Guarding

ZONE BASKETBALL

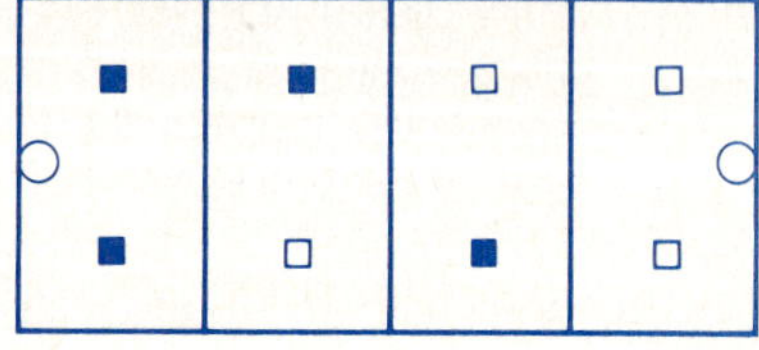

Level: III.

Equipment: One soccer ball, volleyball, or junior basketball and two 7- to 8-foot baskets per game.

Area: A rectangular area divided into four courts as shown, the size depending on the ability of the players. The end courts are the scoring areas.

Participants: Four to five per team. (The number of courts may be increased to accommodate 5 players.)

Skills: Passing, catching, dribbling, guarding, shooting.

Description: Play is begun by giving the ball to a player of one team in the inside court farthest from the team's goal area. Players attempt to complete a pass to a teammate in the next zone or in the goal area. A point is scored when a player in the goal area catches the ball on a fly or after one bounce. If caught successfully, one shot for goal may be taken. If made, an additional two points are scored. After a score or attempted score, the ball is given to the opponents in the adjacent court.

Violations: Stepping out of the assigned area, walking with the ball, holding the ball more than 5 seconds, illegal dribble, personal contact.

Penalty: The ball is given to the opposing team at the nearest sideline.

Fouls: Personal contact.

Penalty: One unguarded throw given to the player fouled against.

Strategy:

1. Move the ball quickly toward the goal.
2. Move as close as you can to throw the ball to players in the end zone.
3. Cover the entire area on defense.
4. Move to an unguarded area to receive the ball.
5. Move close to the basket before attempting to shoot.
6. Keep between opponents and the goal area while on defense.

Teaching Suggestions:

1. Rotate positions so that all have an opportunity to play each position.
2. Match players of equal ability in the inside court areas.

Modifications	Movement concepts*	Social structure	Strategy	Level
1. Match opponents by ability 2. As individuals become ready, call more than one number at a time 3. When calling more than one number, begin play with a jump ball	Self/general: 1, 2, 3, 4, 5, 6, 7, 8, 9, 10, 11 Direction: 13, 14, 15, 16, 17, 18, 19 Level: 20, 21 Pathways: 22, 23, 24, 25, 26, 27 Force: 1, 2 Time: 3, 5 Flow: 1	Social interaction II	1. Move ball toward the basket 2. When on defense, stay between opponent and basket (after the two passes are completed) 3. Move to an unguarded area to receive the ball 4. Use sideline and teammates on court	IV
1. Match opponents by ability	Self/general: 1, 2, 3, 4, 5, 6, 7, 8, 9, 10, 11, 12 Direction: 13, 14, 15, 16, 17, 18, 19 Level: 20, 21 Pathways: 22, 23, 24, 25, 26, 27 Force: 1, 2 Time: 3, 4, 5 Flow: 1	Social interaction II	1. Move ball toward the basket 2. When on defense, stay between opponent and basket (after the two passes are completed) 3. Move to an unguarded area to receive the ball	IV

BASKETBALL RELAY

Level: III.

Equipment: One volleyball, soccer or junior basketball per team; one 7- to 8-foot basket for two teams.

Area: A rectangular playing area with a basket at one end for each game.

Participants: Four to six per team.

Skills: Passing, catching, dribbling, shooting.

Description: Each team is lined up along opposite sides of the court area. Individuals on each team are given a number. When a number is called, the two players, one from each team, run out to the basketballs placed in front of each team, pick them up, and pass them to each member of their team. When the passing is completed, each shoots for a goal and continues to shoot until one is successful. The team scoring first is awarded two points.

Strategy:
1. Begin passing with person farthest from the goal and move the ball to the basket.
2. Make short, quick passes.

Teaching Suggestions: This is a good activity to use before the introduction of Toss-Up or Sideline Basketball. Match players of similar ability to provide equal competition for each member. Any number of teams may participate at the same time, with no more than two teams per basket.

TOSS-UP BASKETBALL

Level: III.

Equipment: One junior basketball, soccer ball, or volleyball for each game and one 7- to 8-foot basket.

Area: A rectangular area half the size of an available basketball court.

Participants: Four to six per team.

Skills: Passing, catching, dribbling, shooting, guarding.

Description: Each team is numbered off and lined up along opposite sidelines. The teacher calls a number and tosses the ball in the air. The players from each team with that number attempt to catch the ball after it has bounced once, complete passes to at least two teammates on the sideline, and attempt one shot at goal. If made, two points are scored; if missed, play is stopped and a new number is called. The person not getting the ball attempts to gain control by intercepting a pass. If successful, a shot on goal may be attempted after passes to two sideline players. Whenever possession of the ball changes, two passes must be made before attempting a shot on goal.

Violations: Stepping outside the playing area, ball going out of bounds, traveling, illegal dribble, shooting before two passes are completed.

Penalty: Ball is put in play by a sideline player of the opposite team.

Fouls: Personal contact.

Penalty: One free throw awarded. One point is scored if the shot is made. If missed, play resumes with a new number being called.

Strategy:
1. Move toward the basket.
2. When on defense, stay between opponent and basket.
3. Move to an unguarded area to receive the ball.

Teaching Suggestions:
1. Distance for free throw should be appropriate for the ability of the players.
2. Children should be matched with others of equal ability.
3. It may be helpful to count orally the number of passes for them as they play the game.

SIDELINE BASKETBALL

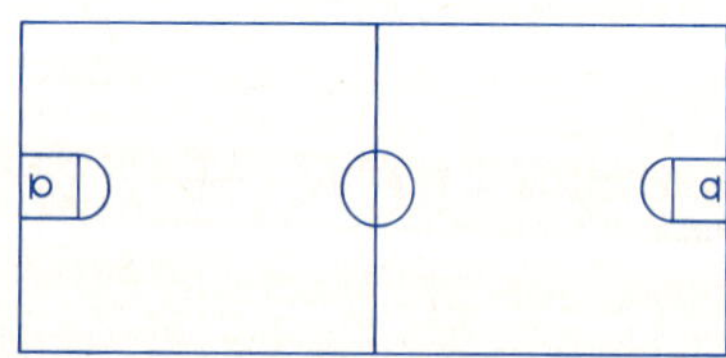

Level: IV.

Equipment: One junior basketball for each game and two 8-foot baskets.

Area: An appropriate sized basketball court for the ability of the players.

Participants: Four to six players per team.

Skills: Passing, catching, dribbling, shooting, guarding, rebounding, jump ball.

Description: Each team is numbered and lined up along opposite sidelines. The leader calls two numbers. Play begins with a jump ball between two opposing players. Passes must be made to two different team members, including the other player on the court and/or sideline players before an attempt for a basket may be made. If the basket is made, play continues with two new numbers being called. If the basket is missed, the ball is in play. If a member of the shooting team receives it, that player may shoot again immediately if he or she wishes. If a member of the opposing team receives the ball, that player must complete at least two passes in moving the ball to his or her own basket before shooting.

Violations: Traveling, illegal dribble, moving self or ball out of bounds, shooting before two passes are completed.

Penalty: Ball is put in play from the sidelines by the opposite team.

Fouls: Personal contact.

Penalty: One free throw awarded the opposite team. If made, one point is scored; if missed, play resumes with new numbers being called.

Strategy:
1. Move the ball quickly toward the goal.
2. Move to an unguarded area to receive a pass.
3. Stay between the opponent and the goal when on defense.
4. Cover as much area on defense as possible.
5. Keep the offense spread out.

Teaching Suggestions:
1. This game may be played one-on-one, two-on-two, three-on-three, and so forth as individual player's ability warrants.
2. If available space is limited, it may be played as a half-court game, with the ball moving to the opposite end (center line) if rebounded by the defensive team.
3. Children should be matched with others of equal ability.
4. It may be helpful to count out orally the number of passes made for them as they play the game.

ALLEY BASKETBALL

G	f	F	g
C	c		
G	f	F	g

Level: IV.

Equipment: One junior basketball for each game and two 8-foot baskets.

Area: An appropriate sized basketball court for the ability and size of the players divided into three alleys.

Participants: Five per team: one center, two forwards, and two guards. The center plays the entire length of the center alley, and the two forwards and two guards play only to the mid-court line.

Skills: Passing, catching, dribbling, guarding, shooting.

Description: Play begins with a jump ball between the two opposing centers at mid court. They attempt to tap the ball to one of their teammates. Play continues with each team attempting to pass and, when in position, to shoot for a basket. If a basket is made, two points are awarded. After a score, play continues with the opposing team passing the ball in from behind the nearest endline.

Violations: Stepping out of the alley, walking with the ball, holding the ball more than 5 seconds, illegal dribble, center taking possession of the ball on the jump.

Penalty: The ball is given to the opposing team at the nearest sideline.

Fouls: Personal contact.

Penalty: One free throw awarded the opposing team to be taken by the player fouled (if it is a forward or center). If a guard is fouled, the shot is taken by a forward or center on the team. If made, one point is awarded. If made, play resumes with the opposing team putting the ball in play from behind the endline.

Strategy:
1. Move the ball quickly toward the goal.
2. Move to an unguarded space to receive a pass.
3. Stay between the opposing forward and the basket while on defense.

Teaching Suggestions:
1. It may be necessary to require two or more passes before shooting to encourage teamwork.
2. After a goal is scored, children should rotate positions in a clockwise manner or in some other way to ensure matching opponents.
3. Emphasize continually moving in the alley to be free to receive a pass.
4. This game may be modified to allow all five players to move in their alleys the entire length of the court.

SUMMARY

Basketball is a popular activity with children. For elementary school children to be successful, modifications of the playing area, equipment, and game are necessary. A smaller playing area, 7- or 8-foot baskets, and junior basketballs or utility balls are used. Since 10 players on the court at a time require an understanding of a complex relationship of teammates and opponents, the numbers are reduced beginning with a simple one on one and gradually increasing the number of players actively involved. The court may be divided into specific areas of play for individual teams as in Endball or for opposing players as in Zone and Alley Basketball.

The movement content is extremely important to success in basketball activities and should be stressed during skill development and game activities. Activities that emphasize the application of the movement content should be introduced to enhance the children's understanding and use of the movement concepts in basketball games as they practice skills and participate. A progression of lead-up activities are used to assist children to develop the skills and knowledge associated with basketball.

REFERENCES

1. Athletic Institute, editors: Youth league basketball: coaching and playing, New York, 1984, Athletic Institute.
2. Barnes, M.: Women's basketball, ed. 2, Newton, Mass., 1980, Allyn & Bacon, Inc.
3. Seidel, B., and others: Sports skills: a conceptual approach to meaningful movement, ed. 2, Dubuque, Iowa, 1980, William C. Brown.
4. Sullivan, G.: Better basketball for boys, New York, 1984, Dodd, Mead & Co.

ADDITIONAL READINGS

Barnes, M.: Conditioning, JOPERD **54**(1):30, January 1983.
Basketball drills to develop strength and endurance, some of which could be used or modified for elementary school children.

Farrell, J., and Weikart, P.: The forgotten skills: add them to your conditioning program, JOPERD **54**(1):32, January 1983.
Activities to develop the body control skills of moving in all directions, changing direction, moving on the diagonal, and changing the support foot.

Gudger, J.: The daily dozen, JOPERD **54**(1):36, January 1983.
Basketball drills, some of which can be adapted for elementary school children.

24

FIELD AND FLOOR HOCKEY

CHAPTER OBJECTIVES

1 To analyze field hockey skills, provide activities and suggestions for their development, and discuss modifications for floor hockey

2 To apply movement concepts to hockey and identify activities in which these concepts may be developed through the games of field and floor hockey

3 To identify a progression of lead-up activities to be used in the elementary school to introduce the games of field or floor hockey

Field hockey was introduced in the United States in the early 1900s and has become a popular activity for girls and women, particularly on the east coast. Internationally it is played by both men and women. Originally its popularity was predominately in countries where Great Britain was involved in early colonization, such as India and South Africa. It is now popular on the European continent with both men and women, especially in Holland. In 1984 a men's as well as a women's team from the United States participated for the first time in the Olympic Games in Los Angeles.

Success in field hockey depends on the participant's ability to control the ball with one side of the stick while moving it in all directions and pathways. This must be accomplished without *obstructing* the opponent (getting one's body between the opponent's body and the ball). The player must be able to vary the force, as in a soft pass to a teammate or a hard shot on goal. Using space effectively is also essential to success in field hockey. The participant is continually adjusting to the changing relationships of teammates, opponents, and the ball.

Since it is a large-group activity with 11 players on each team complex interactions of players are required. Recently the game has been adapted to in-door play with six players on a team. The game requires a team effort; each player has a particular role to play as well as supporting teammates in other positions. In the past two decades, many new styles of play have been introduced that have added to the complexity of the game.

HOCKEY FOR ELEMENTARY SCHOOL CHILDREN

Field hockey is well established in some schools, and floor hockey is becoming increasingly popular as an indoor activity throughout the United States. Hockey offers children one of the few opportunity for a group experience in which the ball is moved with an implement—the hockey stick.

Equipment: Teaching field hockey in the elementary school requires the use of light-weight junior sized sticks. Plastic sticks with a rounded blade may be substituted if the children are taught to use only one side of the stick when contacting the ball. Wooden sticks are preferred. With wooden sticks, regulation balls should be used. Wiffle balls may be used with the plastic sticks. For indoor play, soft or foam balls will allow greater control on a smooth surface. Shin guards should be required of all players, and goalkeepers must wear protective equipment. When plastic sticks are used, shin guards may not be needed. The size of the field should be reduced according to the age and ability of the players, with each lead-up game requiring a different size space. The surface should be as smooth as possible with the grass cut short. An 8- to 10-foot goal is large enough for elementary school children to defend.

In floor hockey plastic sticks with a curved or flat blade may be used. The sticks are often longer in length than those used in field hockey. Wiffle or foam balls or plastic pucks may be used.

Skills: At the elementary school level emphasis in skill development should be placed on stick handling and ball control. Recent changes in skills, such as the introduction of Indian dribbling (described later in this chapter) call for greater versatility in the use of the stick, and this new use should be introduced at an early age. Floor hockey may permit controlling the ball with either side of the stick. Emphasis should also be placed on controlled use of skills. The player should not merely hit the ball as hard as possible, but only hard enough for the task at hand. Therefore, the push pass should be introduced before the hit. In developing skills, it is best to begin work on the techniques with a stationary opponent. Later, as skill is acquired, practice should include working against another person who is actively involved in trying to prevent the skill from being successfully executed. Safety in the use of the stick must also be stressed. Keeping the stick down, holding it correctly, and purposive, controlled movements with the stick will need to be encouraged throughout the unit to avoid unnecessary injuries.

The game: Field hockey is an activity in which the large number of partipants and the large playing area pose problems for elementary school children. The complexity of position play as players interact with one another is difficult for elementary school children to understand. *Marking* (being responsible for an opponent while on defense) must be carefully taught and reinforced throughout the activity. Learning to position and reposition one's self in space in relation to opponents, teammates, the ball, and the goal is not an easy task and takes time to develop. This is best accomplished by breaking down the game into smaller segments in which fewer participants are involved and gradually increasing the number of players and the complexity of the situation as skill and understanding develop. This is also true for the development of the game of floor hockey.

In both games the responsibilities of the offense are to maintain possession of the ball and to score goals. To accomplish this the team must:

1. Move the ball toward the opponent's goal.
2. Control passes to teammates.
3. Move to open spaces to receive passes.
4. Rush each shot on goal.
5. Change the expected path of the ball to keep the defense off guard.
6. Be on the move to adjust one's position in relation to teammates, opponents, and the ball.
7. Keep the ball until a defense player has become committed to make spaces for the ball and teammates.

The responsibilities of the defense are to prevent the opponents from scoring, regain possession of the ball, and quickly move the ball away from the goal they are defending. To be successful the defense must:

1. Stay between the opponents, ball, and goal.
2. Continually move to reposition oneself to close spaces to opponents.
3. Advance to tackle or harass the opponents.
4. Move the ball quickly away from the goal area.
5. Mark opponents closely in the goal area.
6. Watch closely the opponent being marked and not the ball.
7. Anticipate the movements of opponents, teammates, and the ball.
8. On receiving the ball, pass it quickly to the offense.

HOCKEY SKILLS

Hockey skills demand good body awareness as individuals attempt to control a small ball with a stick while they move on the field. Space concepts and qualities of movement also come into play as individuals maintain an appropriate relationship of body, stick, and ball; combine skills smoothly; and vary the force as the situation demands. When teaching hockey skills, control of the stick must be stressed always. In the following pages field hockey skills are presented with suggestions for their use in floor hockey.

Dribbling

Dribbling: is used to move the ball without the help of teammates when a good pass is not possible. It is also used to draw an opponent out of position or to maneuver around an opponent.

The left hand controls the movement of the stick,

Figure 24-1

Evaluative criteria and teaching points for the dribble.

- Lay stick on ground with flat side down. Grasp stick with left hand.

- The right hand is 4″ to 8″ below the left. The left wrist and forearm form a straight line, wrist firm, arm out away from the body.
- The stick is held at a 45 degree angle to the ground, the ball 18″ to 24″ diagonally in front of the right foot.

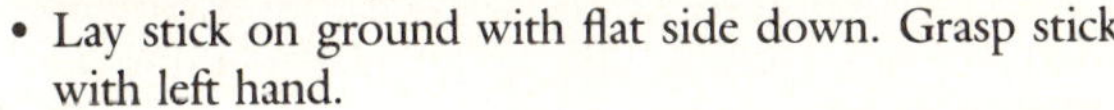

The ball is moved by a series of light taps as the player moves down the field; the head is up and body fairly erect.

while the right hand acts as support. The dribbler's body leans slightly forward, and the head should be up to watch the ball and the field of play. The ball is controlled 18 to 24 inches diagonally in front of the right foot.

Common errors:
1. Facing the back of the left hand in the line of the dribble.
2. Bending left wrist so it is not in a straight line with the forearm.
3. Holding the stick vertically to the ground or laid back.
4. Pushing the ball against the stick rather than tapping it.
5. Bending the body over the ball, with eyes on the ball only.
6. Dribbling the ball too close or too far away from the body.
7. Placing the right hand too far down the stick.

In floor hockey the dribble is executed by alternately contacting the ball with each side of the stick.

Indian dribbling allows the ball to be controlled in front of the body rather than to the side. It is used to move the ball around an opponent's stick or to move it to a more favorable position. The ball is tapped alternately with a forehand and then a reverse stick. Indian dribbling is a difficult skill and will require considerable practice to develop proficiency.

Figure 24-2

Evaluative criteria and teaching points for Indian dribble.

- Left hand grips stick from above, the right hand is 4″ to 8″ below the left.
- The ball is positioned in front of the player, the stick at a 45-degree angle to the ground.
- The ball is tapped to the left.

- The ball is tapped to the right with the reverse side of the stick.
- Ball stays within the width of the body.

The result is better stick control, and this skill should be introduced as soon as the children are ready.

The stick is gripped so that the back of the left hand points upward toward the right and the back of the right hand points backward. Contact is made with the ball by first tapping it in the conventional manner toward the left. The next tap is taken with a reverse stick by turning the stick over the ball in a counterclockwise direction with the left hand and with the ball moving forward to the right. The Indian dribble is called the "over-over" dribble, which helps the student remember the stick movement. The right hand grips the stick loosely to allow the stick to turn under it. The stick is then turned back again for a tap on the forehand side and play continues alternately hitting from the forehand and reverse stick positions. As the ball is tapped diagonally to the right and to the left it stays within the body's width.

Common errors:
1. Facing the back of the hand in the line of the dribble.
2. Placing the right hand too far down the stick.
3. Tapping the ball so it moves well beyond the width of the body.
4. Watching the ball instead of looking ahead.
5. Rolling the right hand rather than letting the stick move under it for the reverse stick tap.
6. Having the stick angle to the ground too vertical.
7. Turning the stick clockwise rather than counterclockwise when changing to reverse stick. This is critical because if the stick is turned clockwise it is impossible to execute a reverse stick hit or push correctly.

In teaching this technique it may help to begin practice by moving the stick to and from the reverse stick position without actually hitting the ball. Have children place a ball directly in front of the body with the stick at a 45-degree angle to the ground and feet shoulder width apart. Begin turning the stick over the ball without touching it, using only the left hand, and then return it to its original position. Repeat a

Figure 24-3

Evaluative criteria and teaching points for push pass.

- V formed between thumb and fingers on hooked side of stick, with the right hand 6'' below the left the left wrist and the forearm straight.
- Feet in a forward-backward stride, shoulder width apart, left foot in front; knees are bent; trunk leaning slightly forward; weight on the rear foot.
- The stick is behind the ball at a 35- to 45-degree angle to the ground; ball is midway between the legs, slightly closer to the front foot.
- Left shoulder points in the line of the push; weight shifts to forward foot as arms sweep stick forward.

- Follow through is long and low in the direction of the hit.

The pass should be directed to a space in front of the intended receiver.

few times. Now add the right hand as a stabilizer, and let the stick turn under the grip. When ready, they should try dribbling the ball from both positions controlling it within the width of the body.

Indian dribbling is an excellent activity to help develop stick control. Indian dribbling is not used in floor hockey, since both sides of the stick may be used to contact the ball.

Activities to practice dribbling:

1. Each child has a stick and a ball. Dribble in general space. (What must you do to avoid others? How did you use your stick to keep the ball under control as you moved?)

Variations:

a. Increase and decrease the available space. (What changes did you make in your dribbling as the space got smaller? Larger?)
b. Change speed on a specified signal. (Did your relationship with the ball change as you went faster or slower? What did you have to do to keep the ball under control at all speeds?)
c. Tapping the ball to the left and to the right (Indian dribbling), on the signal combine with regular dribbling. (How did you move your body to stay with the ball? Which side was easier? Why?)

Figure 24-4

Evaluative criteria and teaching points for the hit.

- Hands together at the top of the stick.
- Feet shoulder width apart, ball is off left foot for a hit to the left; twist trunk so right shoulder is pulled back, ball diagonally off right for a hit to the right.
- Left shoulder faces the direction of the hit. Stick drawn back, left arm straight, right arm relaxed and bent at the elbow, wrists cocked, weight on right foot.

- Stick is pulled to ball, weight shifts to left. Wrists straighten and are firm at contact. Arm and stick in a straight line; eyes on the ball.

- Follow through is long and low in the direction of the hit.

Striking Techniques

The *push pass* is used for passing short distances. It should be the second skill introduced and taught immediately after dribbling. When dribbling, the push pass may be executed quickly in any direction.

The passer has both hands on the stick, with the back of the left hand facing forward. The push may be taken from many positions, but the greatest accuracy and power are produced from a forward-backward stride position. The left wrist and forearm are straight. The sweeping action is initiated by both arms and then continues with the right to give added power. Power comes from the strength of the forearms and a whipping action of the wrists. The ball should be pushed along the ground.

Common errors:
1. Facing the front of the body, rather than the left shoulder, to the push.
2. Assuming too high a position behind the ball.
3. Placing the stick vertically behind the ball.
4. Using a backswing so it is a hit rather than a push.
5. Pushing with the ball to far behind or too far in front of the body.

The *hit* is used for long-distance passing and shooting for a goal. In preparation for the hit, the right hand slides up to touch the left. The back of the left hand faces the line of the hit. The ball is a comfortable distance away so the stick can swing freely. The stick is drawn back in a straight line, the arms not touching the body on the backswing. The wrists are firm and cocked, bringing the stick slightly above the left hand and the toe of the stick pointing upward. The stick speed accelerates as it approaches the ball.

Common errors:
1. Positioning the ball to close or too far away for the hit.
2. Not hitting through the ball. (Topping the ball is usually caused by not watching the ball.)

Figure 24-5

Evaluative criteria and teaching points for the scoop.

- Hands apart on stick held in shoveling fashion.
- Right foot in front, ball in front of left foot, knees bent.
- Stick laid back with blade well under the ball.

- Left arm bent at the elbow.
- Legs straighten as ball is lifted.
- Follow through is low and in the line of the scoop.

3. Having elbows tucked in.
4. Raising the stick too high on the backswing or follow through.
5. Placing hands apart on the stick.

At times the hit is misused in hockey. Players often use the hit when a push pass to nearby teammates would be more accurate and much easier to control. The hit should not be introduced until players have learned to control the ball by dribbling and can push pass with ease.

Bending the elbow on the backswing and reaching forward on the follow through will help the children keep the stick low on the hit.

The *scoop* may be used to lift the ball over an opponent's stick or shoot for goal when in close range.

The hands are apart and moved around the stick to the left, which permits using the stick as a shovel. The feet are shoulder width apart. The ball is raised by lifting the stick as the legs straighten.

Common errors:
1. Holding stick too vertically.
2. Lifting ball too high.
3. Stick coming up high in the front after lifting the ball.

Control should always be stressed. The scoop should be kept low, because high scoops may be dangerous. This skill should be used sparingly.

The scoop is not used in floor hockey.

The *flick* is an effective shot for goal, since the flight of the ball makes it difficult for the receiver to control. It may also be used in passing.

Figure 24-6

Evaluative criteria and teaching points for the flick which utilizes the same grip and stance as the push pass.

- Stick laid back under the ball at 45-degree angle to the ground; stick behind the ball.

- Weight shifts forward, stick imparts force to the ball by left arm pull to body as right moves forward and sideways.

- Strong wrist movement turns stick over on long, low follow-through.

The starting position for the flick is similar to the push pass. The right leg is low to the ground. The left shoulder points in the direction of the flick, and the right shoulder is dipped. The ball is in front and farther from the left foot than in the push pass. The weight shifts to the right leg before the action begins. The stick imparts force to the ball by an explosive lever action of the left arm pulling toward the body as the right arm moves forward and sideways. A strong wrist action at the end causes the stick to turn over as final impetus is given to the ball.

Common errors:
1. The body facing the flick rather than the left shoulder.
2. Assuming a position too close or too far away from the ball.
3. Placing the stick vertically behind the ball.
4. Not getting low and under the ball.
5. Not using wrist action.

The flick is a difficult field hockey skill. Considerable time must be spent in practice if it is to be used effectively. Only a few elementary school children will be ready to try it.

The flick is not used in floor hockey.

Receiving

In *receiving* a ball in field hockey the player must be able to get the ball quickly under control by absorb-ing its force and putting it into position for the next movement.

The stick is held as in dribbling, with the hands apart. The stick should be inclined slightly forward, lined up with the oncoming ball, and on the ground. The stick reaches for the ball and on contact gives sufficiently to keep the ball on the stick. The ball should be received in front of the right foot. This necessitates the use of a reverse stick by turning the wrists so the blade faces a ball coming from the right. A ball coming from behind is received as it moves in front of the body.

Common errors:
1. Placing hands too close together on the stick.
2. Failing to line the stick up with the ball's path.
3. Having the stick vertical or laid back rather than inclined forward.
4. Not giving sufficiently with the stick on impact, resulting in the ball rebounding from the receiver.

Activities to practice striking and receiving techniques:
1. In partners scattered in the general space, push pass to each other increasing and decreasing the space between the partners. (Were you able to get the ball to your partner so it could be received easily each time? How did you change the push pass as the distance changed?)
2. In partners, push pass while moving in general

Figure 24-7

Evaluative criteria and teaching points for receiving.

- The stick is held with hands apart.
- Player lines the stick up with the oncoming ball, reaching for it, stick on the ground and inclined slightly forward.
- On contact with the ball the stick "gives," thus controlling the ball on the stick.

space. (Were you able to get the ball to your partner each time? Could you find the empty spaces? Where do you want to receive the ball to keep moving?)

3. Children each have a ball and a wall space. Push pass the ball to the wall so it rebounds to themselves. (How many passes can you make in 30 seconds? What did you have to do to be able to receive the ball and push it back to the wall quickly?)
4. Similar to 3 above, but have two or three lines of varying distances from the wall. Each child begins in one line, pushes the ball to the wall, moves back to the next line, receives the ball, pushes it once again to the wall, and so on. (How did you change your push pass as you moved from line to line so it could be received easily?)
5. In groups of three with one ball, one player

Figure 24-8

Evaluative criteria and teaching points for passing.

- Look up to see where the pass might be made.
- Pass ahead of intended receiver.
- Receiver moves to meet the ball.

is the defense, who stands in a position in front of the other two who are forwards. One forward begins by dribbling the ball, passes a flat pass to the other forward who controls the ball and passes a through pass behind the defense to which the first forward cuts to receive the ball. The forwards must watch the defense player to be sure there is adequate space for the flat pass. Begin at first with an inactive defense player. After the forwards have successfully executed the drill several times the defense players should attempt to position themselves for an interception. The forwards should vary the passes used depending on the position of the defensive player.

6. Similar to 5 above, but this time a flat pass is followed by a diagonal pass.

Offensive Skills

Passing is a very important skill and must receive emphasis with beginning players. Elementary school children tend to play as individuals rather than as team players. Often they will keep the ball to themselves rather than pass to teammates.

Successful passing requires the cooperative efforts of both the passer and the receiver. An individual should maintain possession of the ball until an opponent begins to move into position to attempt to take the ball away. The passer should look up to see which players are free or who can get free to receive a pass. Theoretically there should be no intercepted passes, since only the passer knows where the ball will be directed. Generally it is the errors of the passer that result in the opponents taking the ball. Passers must look for the empty space in which to place the ball. They must judge the speed of the receiver and use the appropriate amount of force to direct the ball to a spot ahead of the receivers where it can be received easily. The passer may have to hold back slightly while teammates get free to receive the pass. It is important that the pass be disguised if possible so opposing players do not have the opportunity to move into the space through which the ball will travel.

Types of passes:

Upfield pass: A pass at any angle to a teammate who is closer to the goal.

Through pass: A pass parallel to the side lines in which the passer places the ball straight ahead and the receiver moves forward past the opposing player and cuts for the ball.

Square or flat pass: A pass parallel to the end line used when upfield or through passes are not possible.

Give and go: The passer draws the opponent, passes a square pass to a teammate, moves past the opponent, and receives a return pass.

Figure 24-9 diagrams the passes listed above. In all passes, the receivers should initiate the movement by positioning themselves so they are free or by starting to cut.

Common errors:

1. Failing to look up and plan the pass.
2. Passing the ball to the player rather than to a space in front of the receiver.
3. Passing the ball so hard it cannot be received and controlled.
4. Passing the ball too far ahead of the player.
5. Moving in the direction of the pass before passing so the opponents can cover the pass.

Activities to practice passing are included in Activities To Practice Striking Techniques.

The offensive team must take every opportunity to *shoot* for goal. Any of the techniques included in the section on striking techniques may be used in shooting for goals, although the hit and flick are most frequently used.

The first shot at goal should be taken as the ball enters the circle. All forwards have their sticks down

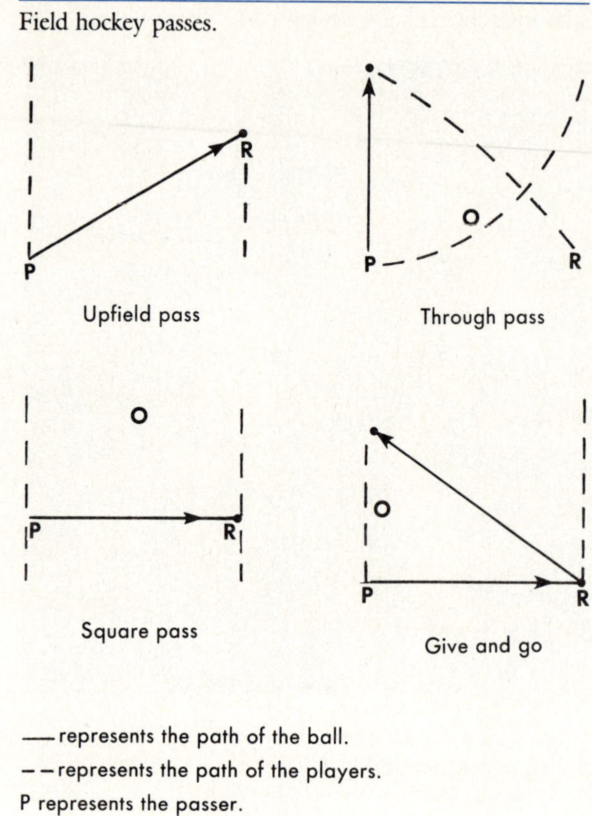

Figure 24-9

in a position where the ball can be played quickly. The ball should be played with as little ball handling as possible before the shot. Forwards should rush the shot to give the goalkeeper little time to control the ball and to increase the possibility of a second attempt should the first one fail. When shooting, forwards should place the ball away from the goalkeeper and preferably into the corners of the goal.

Common errors:

1. Directing the ball at the goalkeeper.
2. Too much ball handling in the circle, so the opportunity for a shot on goal is lost.
3. Carrying the stick up in the air in the circle.
4. Passing to another player when a shot should be taken.

Success in scoring in hockey requires considerable determination by the attack players. They must play aggressively in the circle, and scoring must be their highest priority.

Figure 24-10

Evaluative criteria and teaching points for shooting.

- First attempt taken as the player enters circle.
- Player takes the shot and forwards rush the goal.
- Sticks down in position to quickly play the ball.
- Shot aimed away from the goalkeeper and into the corners of the goal.

Activities to practice shooting:

1. In partners, 10 to 15 feet apart, moving down the field, hit the ball to each other. One partner quickly returns the ball to the other partner as he or she receives it. The one who has the ball at the edge of the circle shoots for a goal. Change sides and repeat. (Where did you try to place the ball to your partner? Where did you want to receive it? Was it easier to hit to the left or right? Where did you want the ball for a pass to the right? To the left?)

2. In three's lined up across the field, children move the ball down the field, alternating the use of push passes and hits. When they get to the edge of the circle, they shoot for a goal with all three players rushing the shot. Change positions and repeat at least two more times. (Did you control the force for the push pass and the hit? Did you accurately judge the speed of your teammates so your passes were put accurately into the space ahead of them? Where did you want to receive the ball? What did you do on receiving the ball prior to the shot on goal?)

3. Children are in partners, with several balls. One push passes to the other who receives it and scoops it into a target area (a hoop on the ground). Vary the distance to the target and the relationship (move to one side of the target or the other). (What must you do to get the ball consistently into the target? Were you able to keep the ball low?)

4. Individuals push pass to the wall, control the rebound, and scoop it to the wall. A goal with a goalkeeper or tires on the goal line may be used instead of the wall. (How quickly were you able to control the ball and scoop for goal? Did you scoop the ball into the empty space past the tires or goalkeeper?)

5. Individuals flick into a target on a wall, varying the distance from the wall or the orientation to the target (to the left or right of it). (What did you do to flick the ball to the target?)

6. Individuals flick into a goal where tires have

Figure 24-11

Evaluative criteria and teaching points for stick side dodge.

• Ball pulled to the left as step is taken to the left.

• Ball tapped forward as step is taken forward on the right foot.

been placed in the center. (What did you do as you positioned yourself to flick into the corners?)

7. Several cones are scattered in the circle at one end of the field hockey field. Each individual dribbles to the edge of the circle, dodges the nearest cone, and shoots for a goal through the spaces between the remaining cones. (Were you able to see the open spaces? How did you move to get open for a shot on goal?)

8. Balls are rolled across the goal area. An individual rushes into the circle with the stick down. The roller calls the placement of the shot into the goal, such as left front corner or high right corner. The rushing player attempts to put the ball into the designated area. (Did you plan your placement as you rushed the goal? How did you adjust your position to hit to different areas?)

9. A player pushes or rolls the ball across the field just outside the circle. A forward moves in, receives the ball with one contact to bring it into the circle, and then immediately shoots for goal. Where did you want to receive the ball so you could get the shot off with one contact?)

Dodging is another important offensive skill. Dodging is the skillful control of the ball around an opponent while dribbling. There are times in hockey when a player wishes to maintain possession of the ball and in doing so must get around an opponent who is blocking the path. It is important for offensive players to be able to dodge using several different techniques if they are to be successful on numerous occasions during the game. In dodging, the player may wish to move the ball to the opponent's stick side or non-stick side. Several options for dodging follow.

In the *stick side dodge* the dribblers draw the ball well to their left and around the opponent's stick. The dribblers pull the balls to their left as they step to the left with the left foot. A second tap is taken, sending the ball straight forward as the right foot steps forward. The ball should be drawn well around the opponent's stick.

Common errors:
1. Pulling the ball too forcefully to the left and out of control.
2. Failing to step to the left as the ball is pulled to the left.

In the *non-stick dodge* the ball is pushed to the right just hard enough for the dribbler to move

Figure 24-12

Evaluative criteria and teaching points for non-stick dodge.

- Ball is pushed to space to the left of opponent.

- Forward follows ball past opponent.

Figure 24-13

Evaluative criteria and teaching points for direct dodge.

- Reverse stick tapping ball to the right.
- Step to the right, keeping shoulders square.

- Tap the ball straight ahead stepping forward on left foot.

around the opponent. The dribblers push the balls ahead and to the left of the opposing players. The dribblers accelerate and pass the defenders on their right to regain control of the ball.

Common errors:
1. Pushing the ball too hard so control is lost.
2. Obstructing by placing one's body between the opponent and the ball (the dodger moving to the same side as the ball).

A *direct dodge* may be executed by dribbling forward, using a quick reverse stick to move the ball to the dribbler's right, and then continuing straight ahead to move around the opponent on the dodger's left side.

In the direct dodge the dribbler uses a quick reverse stick to pull the ball to the right, stepping to the right on the right foot and keeping the shoulders square and facing the opponent. The ball is then tapped straight forward as the move around the opponent is completed, and the dribbler continues by stepping forward with the left foot.

Common errors:
1. Pulling the ball too hard so it travels out of the dribbler's control.
2. Obstructing by turning the left shoulder between the ball and the opponent.

Besides the above dodges, a dribbler may choose to dribble the ball toward the opposing player, then sharply change paths to move the ball either to the left or to the right. As the opposing player commits to the new path, the dribbler quickly moves the ball in the opposite direction and around the would-be tackler.

Another type of dodge involves a movement of the stick over the ball as if pulling the ball to the dribbler's left. When the opposing player moves in the direction of the fake, the dribbler moves quickly forward and around the player. In floor hockey the ball is pulled to the left or right of the opponent, since either side of the stick may be used.

Activities to practice dodging:
1. Each individual has a stick and a ball and is scattered in the playing area. Individuals dribble, pulling the ball to the left or right as designated by the teacher. (Were you able to control the ball? How did you tap the ball to keep it in control? How did your legs and stick work together as you moved the ball to the left or right?)
2. Cones or tires are scattered in the playing area. Each participant has a stick and a ball. The leader calls out the particular dodge to be

Figure 24-14

Evaluative criteria and teaching points for marking.

- Maintain relationship with forward between the player and the goal.
- Move with opposing forward with stick down.
- Move to the ball side of a player without the ball.

used. Individuals dribble in the area and perform the designated dodge as they approach each cone. (Were you able to dodge without hitting the cone with the ball? How far away from the cone did you begin your dodge to avoid contact?)

3. In partners, each has a stick and one has a ball. The individuals with the balls dribble toward their partners, dodging them when they get close. At first the partner should offer little defense against the dodge. As the dodger becomes more skillful in the movements, the partner should become more active in attempting to anticipate the dodge. (How far from your partner did you need to be to begin a successful dodge? Did you use a change of speed to help you get around your opponent? How did you disguise your dodge so your partner was unsure which way you would go?)

4. Several players are in a line one behind the other and scattered over the length of the playing area. The dribblers begin at one end of the playing area and attempt to dodge each player in turn as they proceed to the other

end. Change positions until all have had the opportunity to dodge several times. A different dodge may be executed with each player the dribbler meets if desired. (How far away were you when you began each dodge? Did your opponent anticipate which dodge you would use? How did you disguise the dodge?)

Defensive Techniques

In playing defense, the team must develop several skills to contain the offensive efforts of their opponents. *Marking* is the skill of positioning oneself (1) to prevent an opponent from getting possession of the ball or (2) if that is not possible, to be close enough to get to the ball before the opponent can control it. If the ball is under control, marking involves shadowing the player, forcing the opponent to move the ball away from the intended path on the field.

When marking, defensive players maintain a position with their back to the goal and with their body between the goal and the opposing player. The marking player may move slightly to the ball side of a player without the ball to cut off any passes that may be directed to the opponent. Marking players are constantly in motion, adjusting their position to the movements of the opposition and the ball. The stick is down in position for a tackle or interception. The marking player watches the opponent and the ball carefully, attempts to anticipate the movements of each, and is ready to move as needed. In the circle the defense should mark their opposing forward as closely as possible to intercept or tackle should the marked player receive the ball.

Common errors:
1. Watching only the ball and not the movements of the opposing player.
2. Failing to stay in a position with the back to the goal and between the ball, the opponent, and the goal.
3. Carrying the stick up, not ready for the interception.

The team who does not have the ball must develop the skill of taking the ball away from the opponents. Although several different tackles have been developed over the years, today the most commonly used tackle is the straight tackle.

The *straight tackle* is used to take the ball from an opponent who is coming directly toward the tackler. The tackler assumes a balanced position, with the feet apart and one foot slightly ahead of the other.

Evaluative criteria and teaching points for straight tackle.

- Tackler lines up with dribbler.
- Feet are shoulder width apart, knees bent, stick down.
- Ball is contacted when it is off opponent's stick.

The hands grasp the stick as in dribbling, 4 to 6 inches apart. It may be necessary to move backward with the forward maintaining a position between the ball and the goal until an opportunity to tackle is available. As the ball is contacted it is tapped easily to the side and then controlled by the tackler, who dribbles or passes to a teammate.

Common errors:
1. Failing to line up with the opposing player and the ball.
2. Not watching the ball.
3. Hitting the opponent's stick rather than the ball.
4. Contacting the ball to hard so it cannot be controlled easily by the tackler.

Activities to practice tackling
1. Working in partners, facing each other, each has a stick and one has a ball. One dribbles the ball toward the partner. The tackler moves up and tackles the dribbler. The dribler should offer no resistance to the tackle until the tackler has performed the tackle successfully several times. (Where was the ball when you successfully go it away from your partner?)
2. Children are scattered in the playing area.

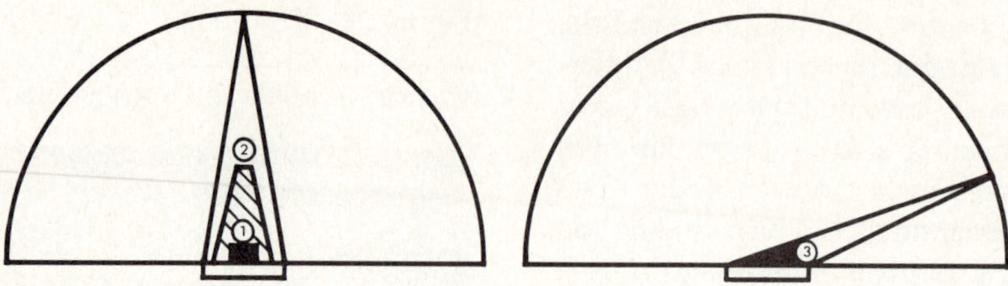

Figure 24-16

Shooting angles.

Each has a stick and half the group have balls. Those with the balls dribble within the area. Those without balls attempt to tackle the dribblers and gain control of the ball. If successful, the two individuals change roles. If a ball or dribbler goes out ot the playing area, it is considered a successful tackle and the two players change roles.

Goalkeeping

Goalkeeping in field hockey is a skill that is limited at the elementary school level. Before goalkeepers may be added to the game, protective equipment must be available. This includes kickers, pads for the legs, a mask, and a helmet. Since goalkeeping equipment is not available in small sizes, children will have to be at least at the fifth or sixth grade level before equipment will fit them. If tennis balls are used and striking is limited to push passes, goalkeepers may be added to the game using shin guards for protection.

In games where goalkeepers will not be used, putting cones or preferably old tires in the goal will help make scoring more challenging. The rules would then prohibit hitting these obstacles on a shot on goal. However, a rebound off the tire may be converted into a score by hitting the ball into the open space.

The goalkeeper assumes a ready position with the stick in the right hand and the flat side forward. The left hand is positioned with the palm forward. The feet are in a comfortable stride position with the hips, knees, and ankles flexed. The eyes are on the ball, and the goalkeeper shifts position to be always between the ball and the goal as the ball moves on the field.

Figure 24-17

Evaluative criteria and teaching points for single leg clear.

- With support foot turned out, inside of foot is lined up with ball.
- Opposite leg sweeps along the ground.
- Contact with big toe joint.
- Follow through, taking weight on kicking foot.

Goalkeepers should position themselves to cut down the angle for shots at goal. Figure 24-16 demonstrates the goalkeeper's position in relation to the ball and the angle for shooting.

In the *single leg clear* the goalkeeper controls the

ball, sending it out to either side of the goal. The kicking leg swings along the ground toward the ball across and in front of the supporting leg. The kicking leg swings through so the momentum carries the body forward, taking the body weight on to the kicking foot. A ball coming from the left is cleared with the right foot, and a ball coming from the right is cleared with the left foot. This is not an easy skill and will take practice for the children to acquire the timing necessary to be successful, as well as the ability to remain in a balanced position ready for the next shot. The single leg clear may be practiced using shin guards only if tennis balls are used and all shots on goal are push passes.

FIELD HOCKEY CONCEPTS

The movement concepts outlined in the box below are important for success in field hockey activities. Activities to help children see the relationship of the movement content of field hockey follow.

Field Hockey Concept Activities

Space

2 points for each pass intercepted. (How did you control the passes to keep the defense moving? Where did the defense person try to stay to cover the space?)

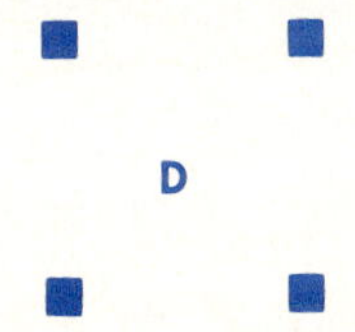

Three players are arranged as the three sides of a square with one empty corner. Each person is numbered. Number 1 passes to 2, 2 to 3, and 3 to 1. The ball is always placed in the empty corner and the receiver moves to that space to pick up the ball. (Was the receiver able to get the ball each time? Why? Why not?)

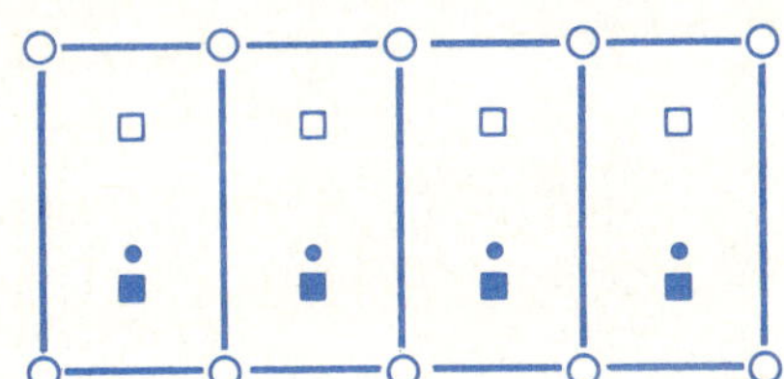

The field is divided into small playing areas marked off by four cones. Each two participants have their own area of play. On the signal, the one with the ball tries to dribble the ball over one end line, while the other attempts to intercept the ball and take it to the opposite end line. The ball should only be taken when it is off the opposing player's stick. If the player in possession of the ball or the ball goes out of the playing area the ball is given to the other participant. (What did you do to get away from your opponent? How did you move to prevent your opponent from scoring?)

Four players are arranged in a square, with a fifth defending player in the center. The four outside players use flat passes to attempt to move the defense out of position so a pass may be made across the center of the square (diagonal pass). A point is scored for each successful pass. The defense earns

Two forwards attempt to move the ball down field against one defense player. The forwards dribble and pass, attempting to create spaces in which to put the ball or themselves as they move down field. The defender tries to cover the space so the for-

FIELD HOCKEY CONCEPTS

BODY AWARENESS

Body awareness concepts are important in the analysis and execution of each skill. In field hockey children must learn to use body parts effectively to move the stick in the desired manner for each skill.

SPACE

Self and general space:

1. To move oneself or the ball within the boundaries of the playing area
2. To move in general space in relation to teammates, opponents and the ball
3. To use all available space
4. To move to an open space while moving in general space
5. To move with control to avoid personal contact
6. To keep one's self space between the opponent and the goal or the ball and the goal while playing defense
7. To recognize one's own area of the general space in which to play
8. To pass the ball to an empty space in front of a teammate
9. To place the ball in an empty space in the opponent's goal
10. To use as much space as possible on offense to deep the defense spread out
11. To close spaces open to the opponents and the ball, especially near the goal area when on defense
12. To create open spaces for oneself, teammates, and the ball while moving in general space by drawing an opponent out of position

Direction:

13. To change direction quickly to avoid contact with others or to move around an opponent
14. To change direction quickly to move into position to play the ball and to move the ball toward or away from the goal
15. To change direction quickly to cover one's area of the field
16. To change direction quickly to open up spaces
17. To change direction quickly to stay with an opponent
18. To anticipate the direction changes of teammates and opponents

Pathways:

19. To change pathways while moving in space with and without the ball
20. To recognize available pathways within which to move one's self or the ball
21. To anticipate the pathways of teammates or opponents to intercept or avoid that path
22. To close pathways available to opponents
23. To change the expected pathway of the ball
24. To establish a pathway away from the goal while on defense
25. To open pathways to the goal on offense
26. To anticipate the pathway of the ball to intercept that path.

QUALITIES OF MOVEMENT

Force:

1. To use an appropriate amount of force in dribbling, passing, shooting, tackling, and dodging
2. To absorb force effectively in receiving the ball
3. To vary the force imparted to the ball or goal tending.

Time and speed:

4. To anticipate the speed of a teammate,
5. To change speed smoothly and efficiently while moving in space
6. To match the speed of a ball or an opponent to meet a pass, intercept, or tackle
7. To alter the tempo of the game by speeding up and slowing down

Flow:

8. To combine skills effectively into a continuous movement, such as dribbling and passing or receiving a ball and shooting.

wards cannot pass successfully. (Where was the best place to position yourself to cover the space? What position prevented a flat pass? A through pass? How did you create spaces for the ball?)

Three on two. Similar to 4 above. Add shooting for a goal as the forwards get down to the circle.

Three on three. The players of each team are numbered, and players with matching numbers are responsible for marking each other. The team who has the ball attempts to complete several consecutive passes, with 1 passing to 2, 2 to 3, and 3 to 1. The opposing team attempts to intercept the passes and gain possession of the ball. (How were you able to move to keep free of your opponent? How did you disguise your passes so the opponents were not sure where the ball would go?)

A number of cones or other obstacles are scattered in the field. Groups of two or three players move the ball down field, passing to each other through the spaces between the obstacles. Receivers should cut to open spaces to receive the ball. (How did you identify the spaces into which you would place the ball?)

Children are arranged in teams of three players, two teams to an area. Teammates attempt to pass to each other and to intercept the passes of the other team. Each team counts the number of consecutive passes. If the ball goes out of the playing area or is touched by the other team, passing must begin again with number 1. (Were you able to find the empty space in which to put the ball?)

In groups of three, the person with the ball passes it across the field so it passes at the head of the circle. As the pass is made the passer gives a signal, "go." One player stands behind the end line to play defense, the other is at the 25-yard line. On the signal, both players rush the ball. The forward attempts a shot at goal and the defense player attempts to prevent the goal. (On defense, where did you position yourself not to allow the forward a good shot at goal? On offense, how did you move to an open space for the shot?)

Each player has a ball. Each one attempts to push pass so the ball hits the balls of the other participants as they dribble and push pass in the area. (Were you able to find the empty spaces in which to move yourself and the ball to avoid others and avoid having your ball hit?)

Two on two in a limited area. The offensive team attempts to move down the field passing. The defensive team attempts to intercept passes and force the offense toward the sidelines. One point is scored for each interception, 2 points for each time the offense is moved toward the sidelines. (How did you position yourself to limit the space of the offensive team?)

Qualities of movement

Groups of three pass as they move down the field, alternating using push passes and hits. One point is scored each time an appropriate force is used in executing a successful pass. The players on the outside should alternate their passes to the player next to them and to the player farthest away. Repeat, rotating positions. (What did you need to think about as you passed the ball various distances? What kind of pass was easiest to receive?)

In partners, children have one ball and move down the field. Players attempt to dribble, pass, and receive as they move. (How smoothly were you able to dribble and pass in one continuous movement? Receive the ball and get started dribbling? What passes were easiest to control so you could get moving quickly? Where did you want to receive the ball so you could continue moving?)

Additional activities that may be adapted to field hockey may be found in Chapter 26.

FIELD HOCKEY LEAD-UP GAMES

An analysis of the games to be included in this section is given in Table 24-1.

SIDE LINE HOCKEY

Level: III.

Equipment: One stick for each participant, one hockey ball, two hockey goals or four cones to mark the goal areas, pinnies or vests to designate teams.

Area: A rectangular area 30 by 60 feet with an 8-foot goal area centered at each end.

Participants: Four to six for each team.

Skills: Dribble, push pass, receive, shoot.

Description: The participants on each team are numbered. The leader calls a number and the participants with that number come out. One player is designated to begin with possession of the ball. The team with the

Table 24-1
Field hockey games analysis

Name	Game classification	No. of participants	Equipment	Space/organizational pattern	Motor skills
Side Line Hockey	Lead-up	Four to six per team	One stick per participant; one hockey ball; two goals or four cones to mark the goal areas; pinnies or vests		Dribble Push pass Receiving Shooting
Advanced Side Line Hockey	Lead-up	Four to six per team	One stick per participant; one hockey ball; two goals or four cones; four to six tires; pinnies or vests		Dribble Marking Push pass Receiving Shooting Tackling
Alley Field Hockey	Lead-up	Five per team	One stick per participant; one hockey ball; two goals or four cones; four to six tires; pinnies or vests		Dribble Dodge Hit Marking Push pass Receiving Shooting Tackling
Advanced Alley Field Hockey	Lead-up	Six per team	One stick per participant; two goals or four cones; vests or pinnies; four to six tires (optional); goal keepers equipment (optional)		Dribble Dodge Hit Marking Push pass Receiving Shooting Tackle Goalkeeping (optional)
Modified Field Hockey	Lead-up	Seven per team	One stick per participant; one hockey ball; two goals; vests or pinnies; goal keepers equipment		Dribble Hit Dodge Push pass Receiving Shooting Tackle Goalkeeping

*Numbers refer to the movement concepts given in the box on p. 458.

Modifications	Movement concepts*	Social structure	Strategy	Level
	Self/general: 2 to 6, 8, 11 Direction: 13, 14, 16 to 18 Pathways: 19 to 23, 26 Force: 1 to 3 Time/speed: 4, 6 Flow: 8	Social interaction I	1. Move to an open space to receive a pass 2. Stay between your opponent and the goal and the ball and the goal on defense 3. Create a space for the ball by keeping a space between the person with the ball and the receiver	III
	Self/general: 2 to 6, 8 to 12 Direction: 13, 14, 16 to 18 Pathways: 19 to 26 Force: 1 to 3 Time/speed: 4 to 6 Flow: 8	Social interaction II	1. Move to an open space to receive a pass 2. Stay between your opponent and the goal and the ball and the goal on defense 3. Create a space for the ball by keeping a space between the person with the ball and the receiver 4. Rush your shot on goal	III
1. Require a number of passes before a shot for a goal may be taken 2. Increase the number of alleys to five	Self/general: 1 to 12 Direction: 1 to 6, 18 Pathways: 19 to 26 Force: 1 to 3 Time/speed: 4 to 6 Flow: 8	Social interaction II	1. Pass to a space ahead of the receiver 2. Move to an open space to receive a pass 3. Defense should hit the ball away from the goal area 4. Use side alleys to bring the ball down field, centering it near the goal 5. Mark closely in the area near the goal 6. Offense should maintain possession until defense is drawn to create spaces.	III
1. Add a goal keeper to each team if equipment is available 2. Require a number of passes before a goal may be attempted	Self/general: 1 to 12 Direction: 13 to 18 Pathways: 19 to 26 Force: 1 to 3 Time/speed: 4 to 7 Flow: 8	Social interaction III	1. Keep a space between you and teammates to create space for the ball 2. Defense should back up forwards on the attack to give support 3. Forwards should drop back to support defensive efforts	IV
	Self/general: 1 to 12 Direction: 13 to 18 Pathways: 19 to 26 Force: 1 to 3 Time/speed: 4 to 7 Flow: 8	Social interaction III	1. Keep a space between you and teammates to create space for the ball 2. Defense should back up forwards on the attack to give support 3. Forwards should drop back to support defensive efforts 4. Use as much space as possible on offense to keep defense spread out	IV

Continued.

Table 24-1

Field hockey games analysis—cont'd

Name	Game classification	No. of participants	Equipment	Space/organizational pattern	Motor skills
Floor Hockey	Lead-up	Six per team	One stick per participant; one ball or puck; two goals; vests or pinnies	Icing line	Dribble Dodge Pass Receiving Shooting Tackle Goalkeeping

ball attempts to complete passes to at least two side line players before attempting the shot on goal. The opposing player tries to gain possession by intercepting one of the passes or picking up a loose dribble. Tackling or hitting sticks is not allowed. If possession is gained by the opposing player, that team must complete passes to at least two teammates before shooting. When a goal is scored, or time is called, a new number is called. The team not scoring, or if time is called the one not receiving the ball in the previous play, is given possession of the ball when play resumes.

Violations: Hitting the ball over the end line and not into the goal.

Fouls: Hitting the ball so it rises dangerously into the air or at another player, personal contact, tackling, hitting the opponent's stick, obstruction (putting the body between the opponent with the ball and the ball), raising the stick dangerously (usually above shoulder height).

Penalty: A member of the opposite team's side line players is given the ball for a free hit (unmarked).

Strategy:
1. Remember to move to an open space to receive a pass.
2. Try to stay between the ball and the goal and the ball and the potential receiver while on defense (goal-side, ball-side).
3. Create spaces for the ball by keeping a space between the person with the ball and the receiver.

Teaching Suggestions:
1. Stress passing with appropriate force so the ball can be controlled easily and passing to a space ahead of the receiver.
2. The stick should be kept down to be ready to receive or intercept a pass.
3. Emphasize the use of space, either creating space on offense or covering space on defense.
4. Emphasize timing when taking the ball from an

opponent so contact is made when the ball is off the opponent's stick to avoid hitting sticks.
5. Encourage control of the ball and the sticks throughout play.
6. Opposing players should be evenly matched in ability.
7. During indoor play the ball should rise no more than 6 inches from the floor except on a shot for goal.

ADVANCED SIDE LINE HOCKEY

Level: III.

Description: Advanced Side Line Hockey is similar to Side Line Hockey, but two or more numbers are called depending on the ability of the players. Passing to two players may now include teammates whose numbers have been called. Two or three tires should be placed on the goal line in the center of each goal. To score, players must now aim for the sides of the goal. The tires provide a surface from which there will be rebounds. Attack players should be encouraged to rush shots on goal so rebounds may be turned into goals.

ALLEY FIELD HOCKEY

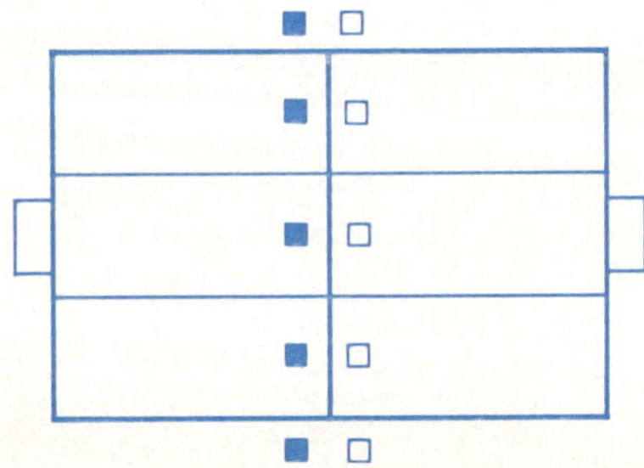

Level: III.

Equipment: One stick for one participant, one hockey

Modifications	Movement concepts*	Social structure	Strategy	Level
	Self/general: 1 to 12 Direction: 13 to 18 Pathways: 19 to 26 Force: 1 to 3 Time/speed: 4 to 7 Flow: 8	Social interaction III	1. Keep a space between you and teammates to create space for the ball 2. Defense should back up forwards on the attack to give support 3. Forwards should drop back to support defensive efforts 4. Use as much space as possible on offense to keep defense spread out	IV

ball, two goals, two or three tires placed at the center on each goal line, pinnies or vests to designate teams.

Area: A rectangular playing area 45 by 80 feet, with three alleys 15 feet in width and an 8- to 10-foot goal centered at each end.

Participants: Five players for each team, three within the playing area and one side line guard on each side line.

Skills: Dribble, dodge, hit, mark, push pass, receive, shoot, tackle.

Description: Play begins with a center alley player passing the ball to a teammate. The ball may not cross the center line until it has been touched by someone other than the person taking the hit. The team with the ball attempts to score by moving the ball down field passing and shooting into the opponent's goal. A shot on goal must be touched by the offensive team in the circle in front of the goal before entering the goal to score. The team on defense attempts to prevent a score by intercepting passes or tackling and then moving offensively to the opposite goal. After a score the ball is awarded to the nonscoring team and play begins again at the midfield line. After a goal is scored each player rotates one position clockwise.

Out of bounds: If the ball goes out of bounds it is put into play by the nearest side line guard of the opposing team. A push pass or hit may be used with the nearest player 5 yards away from the spot where the hit is to be taken. The ball may not rise in the air. The penalty for fouls on the hit is a hit awarded to the opposing team.

Fouls: Raising the stick above shoulder height, obstruction, hitting the ball so it rises dangerously in the air or at another player, personal contact, hitting opponent's stick, moving outside the alley.

Penalty: A free hit is awarded the team fouled against. All other players must be 5 yards away.

Strategy:
1. Remember to pass to a space ahead of the receiver.
2. Remember to move to an open space to receive the ball.
3. The defense should stay between the opponents and the goal and mark closely in the area close to the goal.
4. A forward should maintain possession of the ball by dribbling until an opponent makes a commitment before attempting a tackle.
5. Defense players should hit the ball away from their goal area as quickly as possible.
6. Use all alleys. Use the side alleys to bring the ball down field and center the ball as you near the goal.

Teaching Suggestions:
1. Encourage players to keep spacing and not play too close to their alley lines.
2. To ensure teamwork it may be necessary to require several passes before attempting a shot on goal.
3. Increase the number of alleys to five.
4. Match opponents by ability to provide an equal opportunity for all.
5. Control of the ball and the stick should be stressed throughout the game.

ADVANCED ALLEY FIELD HOCKEY

Level: IV.

Description: Advanced Alley Field Hockey is similar to Alley Field Hockey, with the addition of a defense player in each alley. Players now are named: left half-back, center halfback, right halfback, right wing, center, and left wing.

Teaching Suggestions:

1. Only two players should play the ball at any one time. Halfbacks mark forwards. At no time should two forwards be laying the ball.
2. When a defense player has the ball, the forwards of the same team should move to a position where they might receive a pass and make a space for the ball.
3. Defense players should play in a position behind their forward line to give support to the attack.
4. Add a goalkeeper to each team if goalkeeping equipment is available or when using a tennis ball and push passes only.
5. Increase the number of alleys to five and add two forwards (inners) and two fullbacks.

MODIFIED FIELD HOCKEY

Level: IV.

Description: Modified Field Hockey is similar to Advanced Alley Field Hockey, but the alley lines are removed. Each team consists of seven players: three forwards, three defense, and one goalkeeper. Encourage players to keep their positions and use as much space as possible.

FLOOR HOCKEY

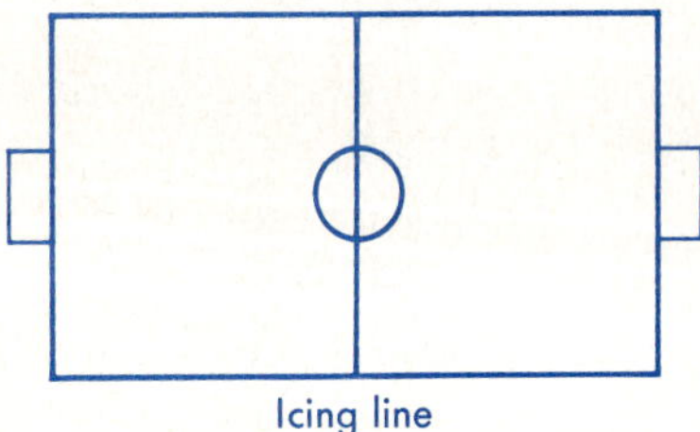

Level: IV.

Equipment: One hockey stick for each participant; two 6-foot goals or four cones to mark goal areas; one puck, floor hockey ball, or small foam ball.

Area: A rectangular area 30 by 60 feet with a 6-foot goal centered at each end; a center face off circle and a midcourt dividing line (the icing line).

Participants: Six players per team: one center, two wings, two defensemen, one goalkeeper.

Skills: Dribble, dodge, hit, pass, receive, shoot, tackle.

Description: Play begins with a face off in which the official drops the puck between the two centers in the face off circle. Each center attempts to pass the puck or ball to teammates, moving the ball toward the opponent's goal for a shot on goal. If the walls mark the boundary lines, the puck may be played off the wall as in ice hockey. A goal is 1 point and play resumes with a face off in the center after each score. Shots for goal must be made on the opponent's half of the court (past the icing line).

Fouls: Personal contact, hitting sticks, raising the stick dangerously, tripping, raising the puck in the air.

Penalty: Players go to a penalty area at one side of the playing area for a designated period of time or to do a penalty, such as jumping rope a certain number of times, and so forth. The team that is penalized plays short until the penalty has been completed. On completion of the penalty the penalized player rejoins the team.

Strategy:

1. Encourage moving to a space to receive a pass.
2. Stay between the goal and the ball and opponents while on defense.
3. The defense should move the ball quickly to the attack.

SUMMARY

Field and floor hockey offer elementary school children the opportunity for a group experience in which a ball is controlled with an implement. Both games require modification and a progression of activities leading up to modified field hockey or floor hockey in the upper elementary school grades. Control of the stick and ball-handling skills are stressed as the children develop a variety of skills and learn increasingly more complex games. The movement concepts important to success are introduced and stressed in both skill development and game play.

REFERENCES

1. Arrighi, M.: Spatial concepts of game play: field hockey, JOPER 47(7):26, September 1976.

2. Cadman, J., and van Heumen, W.: Indoor hockey, tactics, technique, training, London, 1978, Pelham Books.

3. Gros, V.: Inside women's field hockey, Chicago, 1979, Contemporary Books, Inc.

4. USFHA: USFHA manual for coaches, Colorado Springs, 1979, United States Field Hockey Association.

5. Wein, H.: The science of hockey, ed. 3, Topsfield, England, 1984, Merrimack Publishing Co.

6. Wein, H.: The science of hockey, ed. 3, Topsfield, England, 1984, Merrimack Publishing Co.

ADDITIONAL READINGS

Enos, M.: Goalkeeping: an art and a science, JOPER 51(5):30, May 1980.
Teaching positioning to goalkeepers to cut down the angle to the goal.

Fong, D.: The coach's collection of field hockey drills, West Point, 1982, Leisure Press.
An excellent book of drills for developing specific skills and team play.

Hughes, C.: Soccer tactics and teamwork, South Yorkshire, 1979, EP Publishing, Limited.
A book of soccer strategy that has implications for the teaching of field hockey. Includes systems play and suggestions for building the attack and defense.

Tyler, S.: Building systems play through drills, Women Coach 1(3):8, May 1975.
Practice drills to develop space and qualities of movement concepts in field hockey.

25

FLAG FOOTBALL

CHAPTER OBJECTIVES

1   To analyze the skills of flag football and introduce activities to be used in their development in the elementary school

2   To identify the movement concepts important to success in flag football and describe activities to enhance their development

3   To identify a progression of lead-up activities to introduce the skills and concepts of flag football in the elementary school

Football is a popular activity in the United States. Children and youth find it exciting in its use of a ball that is not round, the physical contact it entails, and the use of strategy to move the ball to the goal.

In football, an individual uses specialized skills. The quarterback must be able to pass accurately, to hand the ball to others undetected, and to run with the ball. Some players are ball carriers, who move with the ball given to them in the hand-off or after receiving a pass. Others are line players, who must protect the ball carrier and create a space through which the ball carrier will run. Still others will make up the defense to prevent the opponents from scoring. They must not give the offensive team any space in which to run or to receive the ball on a pass. Constant analysis of the situation is important in the game. Football is one of the few games in which the players have the opportunity to plan and organize what they will do on each play or down.

FOOTBALL FOR ELEMENTARY SCHOOL CHILDREN

Football activities on the elementary school level require modification to guarantee the safety of each child and to take into consideration the difficulty of the skills and game fundamentals. At this level personal contact, as in blocking and tackling, should be discouraged.

Equipment: The shape and size of an official football makes it difficult for elementary school children to control. Junior sized or small foam footballs should be used. Since blocking and tackling are not used, helmets and protective padding are unnecessary. The size of the field should be reduced to fit the players and the games played. Flags or pieces of cloth tucked in at the waist are needed for the most advanced game—flag football.

Skills: Football allows play with the ball with both hands and feet. Passing and kicking skills should be developed as well as the ability to carry the ball in either hand while running.

The game: A progression of games should be used to develop the skills and knowledge associated with football. The rules are modified for the safety and ability of the players. The most advanced game suggested here is Flag Football. This game is similar to Touch Football. However, the use of the flags leaves no doubt about when a ball carrier has been contacted, and the game permits more twisting and turning as the ball carrier attempts to avoid the tag. All games require the learning of both offensive and defensive skills, which are important in the game of

Figure 25-1

Evaluative criteria and teaching points for forward pass.

- Ball is held slightly behind the middle with 2 or 3 fingers on the laces. The side is turned in the direction of the throw. The ball is brought back with the weight transferring to the rear foot.

- Ball is brought forward in an overhand motion, elbow leading, index finger pointing toward line of flight, weight transferred to forward foot.

- Ball is released with a wrist snap, with thumb turning under and toward the outside. Follow through in direction of flight.

football. The responsibilities of the offensive team are to maintain possession of the ball and to score touchdowns. Children should be encouraged to:

1. Vary the offensive strategy used to include both passing and running.
2. Move to an open space to receive the ball.
3. Make spaces for the ball carrier.

The defense tries to prevent the opponents from scoring and to regain possession of the ball by interception, possession on a fumble, and by keeping the offensive team from making the necessary yardage to keep the ball. On defense players should be encouraged to:

1. Close spaces open to opponents.
2. Cover possible ball receivers.
3. Respond quickly to the snap, giving the offense as little time as possible to make their play.

FOOTBALL SKILLS

The following football skills may be developed at the elementary school level.

Ball Handling Skills

The *forward pass* is an effective skill for moving the ball down field and scoring. In football, the pass must be initiated while the passer is behind the ***line of scrimmage*** (an imaginary line extending across the width of the field marking the position of the ball). The flight of the ball should be a spiral to lower the air resistance and to make the pass easier to catch.

Common errors:

1. Holding the ball in the palm of the hand.
2. Placing the hand too far forward on the ball.
3. Failing to turn the nonthrowing side in the direction of the throw.
4. Overthrowing or underthrowing the receiver.
5. Failing to use a wrist snap as the ball is released.
6. Failing to release the ball for a spiral flight.

Teaching Suggestions: Children may be challenged by attempting to increase the distance and accuracy of their passing. The smaller the hand the farther back on the ball the fingers should be to begin the throw. Several different pass patterns may be used in football lead-up games. Figure 25-2 describes the most common pass patterns.

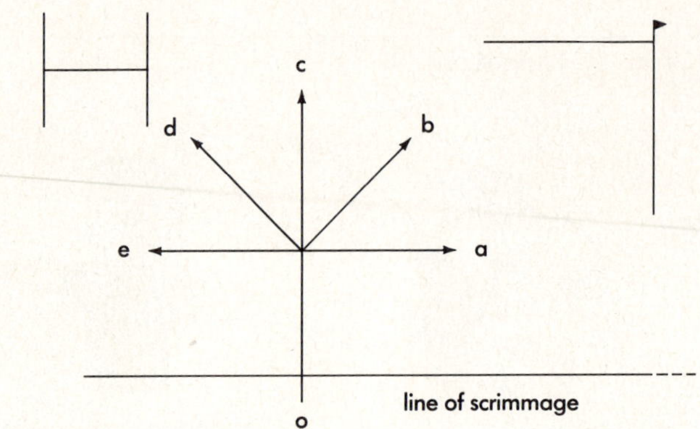

Figure 25-2

Pass patterns. **A,** Out cut (down and out). **B,** Flag. **C,** Streak. **D,** Post. **E,** In cut or in curve (down and across).

Figure 25-3

Evaluative criteria and teaching points for catching.

- Looking over the shoulder toward the passer and the ball, arms and hands extended forward and upward in front of the face.

- Watching the ball into the hands, fingers spread, elbows bend.

- Pulling the ball in toward the body.

When *catching* a forward pass in football activities, the receiver may be facing the passer and the oncoming ball or may be moving away from the passer to the ball, which has been thrown to a space in front of the receiver.

Catching a football while facing the passer uses the same body action as described in Chapter 11.

Catching a football while moving away from the passer requires timing and watching the ball carefully as it comes into the hands. The arms and hands are reaching diagonally forward and upward in front of the face. As contact is made with the ball the elbows bend and the hands cradle the ball in toward the body. The ball is quickly moved to the carrying po-

Figure 25-4

Evaluative criteria and teaching points for lateral toss.

- Ball is held in both hands and is brought back to the opposite side from the throw.

- An underhand motion brings the ball across the body.
- Follow through in the direction of the throw.

sition. When facing the passer, the thumbs are together for a high pass, little fingers together for a low pass. The little fingers are together for a high pass when the receiver is moving away from the passer.

Common errors:
1. Failing to time the run with the ball so the ball is over or under run.
2. Not pulling the ball into the body, but carrying it too high and out in front of the body.
3. Failing to keep the eyes on the ball until it is secured.
4. Catching the ball too close to the body so it rebounds away.

Teaching Suggestions: The hands should be in front of the eyes so the ball may be seen as it is caught. The *lateral toss* is used to pass the ball in a slightly backward or sideward motion. The lateral may be used from any place on the field. The ball is held in both hands and is brought to the opposite side of the body from the throw in preparation for the throw. An underhand action bringing the ball across the body is used with a release about waist height, the index finger pointing in the line of light. The weight is transferred in the direction of the throw and the arms follow through in the direction of flight. A spiral flight is desirable.

Common errors:
1. Failing to bring the ball to the opposite side before the throw.
2. Releasing the ball too high or too low.
3. Lateraling the ball forward.

Activities to practice passing and catching:
1. The children are divided into partners scattered in the general space. One is the passer, the other the receiver. The teacher calls the type of pass to be performed and the children practice the passes from a stationary position. Once the children have an idea of the skills and the relationship between passer and receiver the skills are practiced with the receiver moving in the space to receive the ball. Passers and receivers must look out for others as they complete their passes.
2. In partners, one is the passer, the other the receiver. The passer throws a forward pass to the receiver, who moves closer or farther away on each pass. The two change roles on each pass.
3. The children are in groups of three: the center, the receiver, and the quarterback. On the signal from the quarterback, the ball is snapped by the center, with the receiver moving forward to receive the pass. Vary the distance and path of the throws.

Figure 25-5

Evaluative criteria and teaching points for pitch out.

- Extend arm in direction of pitch.
- Ball moves end over end.

Figure 25-6

Evaluative criteria and teaching points for hand-off.

- Ball is shifted to one hand, arm extended toward receiver.
- Hands in cradling position, upper thumb against chest, wrist rotated so palm is out.
- Ball handed to receiver.

Figure 25-7

Evaluative criteria and teaching points for carrying the ball.

- Hand is in cradling position.
- Ball handed to receiver.

4. The children are in threes, similar to 3 above. The three determine the pathway the receiver will run, and the quarterback attempts to put the ball into the space to which the receiver is running.

The *pitch out* is a pass either to the side or to a player behind. It is taken behind the line of scrimmage. As the ball is received on the snap, it is brought up to the chest with two to three fingers of the passing hand on the laces and the other hand acting as support. As the pitch out begins, the arm is extended in the direction of the pitch. On release, the thumb rolls under the ball with the wrist rotating downward and outward. The flight of the ball is end over end.

Common errors:
1. Holding the ball in the palm of the hand.
2. Failing to extend the arm fully in the direction of the pitch.
3. Failing to roll the thumb under the ball resulting in the flight of the ball not being end over end.

The *hand-off* gives the option of giving the ball to a teammate rather than having the quarterback passing or running with the ball. This should be accomplished in a way to make it difficult for the opposing team to detect who has the ball. The hand-off may be faked also to keep the opponents guessing.

The hand-off is initiated by holding the ball in

Figure 25-8

Evaluative criteria and teaching points for punting.

- Ball held in front of and away from the body, the end facing downward. Step on kicking foot.

- Ball dropped parallel to the ground. Step on left foot.

- Ball contacted on the instep and slightly to the outside of the right foot, with the toe pointed and body leaning away

- Kicking leg follows through upward and in the direction of the kick.

both hands. As the receiver approaches, the ball is shifted to the hand closest to the receiver. The arm is bent at the elbow, and the lower arm is turned out toward the receiver. The ball is handed to the receiver as the two pass. It is not tossed.

Common errors:
1. Holding the ball too far away from the body before the hand-off.
2. Tossing rather than handing the ball to the receiver.

The receiver has the hand away from the quarterback in the cradling position ready to receive the ball, with the upper-hand thumb against the chest, the wrist rotated so the palm faces out. As the ball is received the receiver secures the ball into the carrying position, accelerates, and moves away.

Common errors:
1. Reaching to receive the ball.
2. The receiver failing to secure the ball before moving on.

Figure 25-9

Evaluative criteria and teaching points for place kick.

- Ball is on the ground and held with the index finger so the upper edge angles toward the kicker.
- Ball approached, last step on foot opposite the kicking the foot.

- Kicking leg swings forward, contacting the ball on the instep.

- Leg follows through in the direction of the kick.

Teaching Suggestions: The children must be encouraged to assume the cradling position before receiving the ball and not reaching for it. Young players may have more success completing the hand-off with the use of two hands throughout the handing motion.

When *carrying the ball* the ball must be held securely to maintain possession of it. The ball is cradled on the inside of the carrying arm and in at the inside of the elbow. The ball is held on the right side of the body when running to the right and on the left side when running to the left. In this way the body may be kept between the ball and the defenders.

Common errors:
1. Failing to hold the football in close to the body.
2. Placing fingers too close together so the ball is not held securely.

Teaching Suggestions: The children should practice carrying the ball on both the right and left sides of the body.

Activities to practice ball carrying:
1. Set up an obstacle course of cones or other objects. The ball carriers move through the obstacle course carrying the ball first on one side and then the other.

Kicking Skills

Punting in football is similar to the skill used in soccer. At the elementary school level it is used in a number of lead-up activities. As the ball is received from the snap, it is moved to a position out in front of the body, with the end turned slightly downward and to the inside. A step is taken forward on the right (kicking) foot. The ball is held with the right hand on the side and slightly to the rear. The left hand supports the ball on the opposite side. The kicking leg is then brought forward to contact the ball. The ball is projected forward and upward as the kicking leg follows through in an upward motion.

Common errors:
1. Throwing the ball rather than dropping it.
2. Dropping the ball too close to the body so contact is made on the leg or ankle.
3. Kicking with the toe.
4. Failing to point the toe.
5. Kicking the ball straight up rather than forward and upward.

Teaching Suggestions: Practice the drop without kicking the ball first. Emphasize beginning with the weight on the left foot, stepping right, left, and then kicking with the right. Children should practice punting for distance and also for accuracy.

Figure 25-10

Evaluative criteria and teaching points for centering.

- Assume a stride position with knees bent and body weight forward and over the ball.
- Ball is held in two hands.
- Toes point straight ahead.

- Arms extend back between legs.
- Release ball from finger tips.

The *place kick* is similar to the instep kick in soccer, with the ball held in position by a teammate. This is also called the soccer-style kick or side winder. In the placekick the ball is held by placing one end on the ground with the laces facing away from the kicker. The kicker approaches the ball, placing the opposite foot to the side and slightly behind the ball. The kicking leg swings forward, contacting the ball, and projecting the ball forward and upward.

Common errors:
1. Failing to be on the appropriate step when reaching the ball.
2. Kicking with the toe.
3. Failing to follow through in the intended direction of flight.

Teaching Suggestions: Children may practice place kicking for both accuracy and distance.
Activities to practice kicking:
1. In partners, practice kicking, varying the distance between the two individuals.
2. In partners, practice kicking the ball away from the receiver, to the right or left.

Offensive and Defensive Skills

Centering is the means of putting the ball in play after a down. The center, on the signal from the quarterback, lifts the ball from the ground and tosses or hands it between his or her legs to the quarterback. At the elementary school level the **shotgun** is usually used in which the quarterback is positioned several yards behind the center. However, **a direct snap,** in which the quarterback is over the center with his or her hands under the center, may be used.

The center assumes a position behind the line of scrimmage with the ball on the ground directly in front of the center. The throwing hand is on the ball as it would be for passing, with the other hand on the opposite side of the ball to help guide the ball on the snap. On the signal from the quarterback, the center extends the arms backward between the legs and tosses the ball to the quarterback, who is standing directly behind and (in elementary school games) some distance from the center.

Common errors:
1. Lifting the ball off the ground before the signal from the quarterback.
2. Releasing the ball too soon so it goes too low.

Figure 25-11

Three- and four-point stance.

Figure 25-12

Evaluative criteria and teaching points for blocking.

- Begin in three-point stance.
- Cross arms with hands grabbing shoulders.
- Stride forward.
- Keep head up when contacting opponent.

3. Releasing the ball too late so it goes too high.

The *three-point* and *four-point stances* are used for offensive and defensive positioning, respectively. In the three-point stance the feet are shoulder width apart, with the feet parallel or one foot slightly ahead. (The foot that is back is on the same side as the hand that is down.) The knees, ankles, and hips are flexed. The body weight is forward and is resting on the fingers of the down hand but not too heavily. The head is up, the eyes looking forward. The nonsupporting arm is up and the lower arm is resting on the upper leg. The elbow is bent, and the hand is in toward the supporting arm. The four-point stance is similar to the three-point stance except that the body rests on two hands and both feet. In this position the body and head are aligned and parallel to the ground.

Common errors:

1. Failing to assume a balanced position by having too much weight forward.

Blocking at the elementary school level is limited to moving the body into the path of an opposing player, or to intercept the ball. When blocking, the player moves from the three-point stance to a forward stride position, the feet a comfortable distance apart

FOOTBALL CONCEPTS

BODY AWARENESS

Body awareness concepts are applied in the analysis of each of the skills as the children learn to understand how their body parts are used in successfully performing these skills.

SPACE

Self and general space:

1. To move oneself and the ball within the boundaries of the field
2. To move in general space in relation to teammates, opponents, and the ball
3. To move to an open space to receive the ball or while running with the ball
4. To kick the ball to an open space
5. To pass the ball to an empty space in front of the receiver
6. To use as much space as possible on offense to keep the defense spread out
7. To close spaces open to opponents and the ball while on defense

Direction:

8. To change direction quickly to avoid contact with others, get around an opponent, and move the ball to the goal line
9. To change direction quickly to move into position to receive the ball
10. To change direction quickly to stay with an opponent
11. To change direction quickly to intercept the ball
12. To anticipate direction changes of teammates and opponents

Pathways:

13. To change pathways while moving in space with or without the ball
14. To recognize available pathways within which to move the ball either passing or running
15. To anticipate the pathways of the ball, teammates, and opponents so that the path may be intercepted offensively or defensively
16. To close pathways available to opponents
17. To change the expected path of the ball
18. To open pathways to the goal line while on offense

QUALITIES OF MOVEMENT

Force:

1. To use an appropriate amount of force when passing or kicking
2. To assume a position to get off to a good start on the signal
3. To absorb force effectively when catching the ball

Time and speed:

4. To anticipate the speed of the ball and teammates when receiving a pass or when passing
5. To change speed smoothly and effectively while moving in space
6. To match the speed of the ball and an opponent to intercept or to tag

Flow:

7. To combine skills effectively, such as the handoff and running or catching and running, into a smooth, continuous movement

---

and knees bent. The arms are crossed, and the hands grasp the shirt at the shoulders; the elbows are down and in close to the body. The eyes are on the opponent. The head is up as contact is made with the opponent's upper body.

Common errors:

1. Placing feet too close together so the body is not balanced.
2. Keeping legs straight, body too erect.
3. Keeping elbows up or away from the body.
4. Keeping head down.

Teaching Suggestions: Have the children practice going from the three-point stance to the blocking position several times before attempting to block another player.

FOOTBALL CONCEPTS

The movement content important for success in football is outlined in the box above. Activities to develop these concepts should be used in each lesson to help children apply the movement concepts to football activities. A few suggested activities follow.

Football Concept Activities

Space

The area is marked off into 5-yard squares with cones marking the corners. An offensive and a defensive player are located in each square. On the signal from the leader, the offensive player attempts to move around the defensive player. The defense player tries to move into the intended path of the moving player. Repeat, changing roles. (How did you move to create a space with in which to move around your opponent? What did you look for on defense to anticipate the path the runner would take?)

Repeat above activity, but this time use a ball carrier, and the defense must now take the flags. (How did you move to get free of the defense?)

Children are in groups of three: a quarterback, a receiver, and a defense player. The quarterback passes to the moving receiver, while the defense player attempts to intercept the ball. (What did you do to move to an open space to receive the ball? What did you do to anticipate the pass so it could be intercepted?)

Similar to above activity, but there are two receivers. The pass is now made to the receiver that is free. (How did you anticipate where to throw the ball?)

An area is marked off into 10-yard sections, one defense player in each. The ball carrier attempts to run from one end of the area to the other through the 10-yard areas without losing flags in his or her belt. (What moves did you make to make a space in which to run?)

FOOTBALL LEAD-UP GAMES

An analysis of the football lead-up games which follow may be found in Table 25-1.

FOOTBALL END BALL

This game is played like End Ball in basketball except that a football is used and running with the ball is not penalized. See Chapter 23.

PUNT BALL

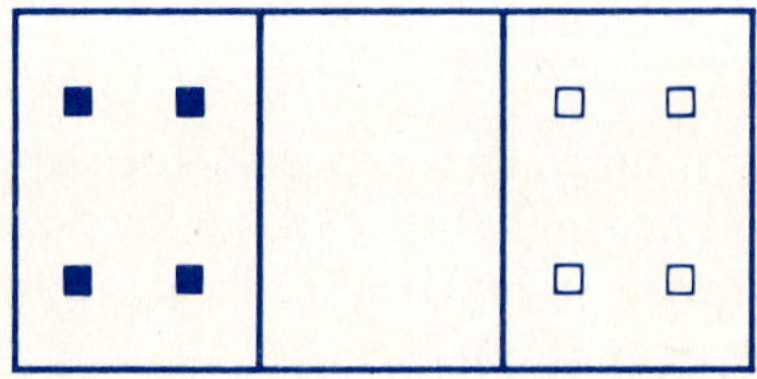

Level: III.
Equipment: One junior sized or small foam football.
Area: A playing field 35 feet wide by 75 feet long with a neutral area 25 feet wide in the center of the field.
Participants: Four to five players per team.
Skills: Punting, catching.
Description: One team begins play by kicking the ball to the opponents' end of the field. If the ball goes over the goal line in the air 3 points are scored for the kicking team. The opposing players attempt to catch the ball coming into their third of the field between the neutral zone and the goal line. If the ball is caught, they punt the ball back to the other team from the spot where it was caught. If the ball is dropped, the kicking team scores 1 point. If dropped, the receiving team kicks the ball from the spot where it first touched the ground.
Fouls:
1. Kicking the ball so it lands in the neutral zone or out of bounds.
2. Walking with the ball after the catch.
Penalty:
1. Opposing team takes possession of the ball and kicks from anywhere in its area or, if out of bounds, from a spot closest to where the ball went out side the boundaries.
2. Move back to the appropriate spot and kick the ball.
Teaching Suggestions:
1. Encourage the receiving team to cover its entire area for possible catches.
2. Encourage the receivers to call for the ball when they will attempt to catch it.
3. Number players and have them kick in turn to ensure that all have an equal opportunity.
4. Reduce the length of the field to allow for more field goals to be scored.
5. Modify scoring so the receiving team scores points for successfully catching the ball.
6. Use place kicking instead of punting.

ZONE FOOTBALL

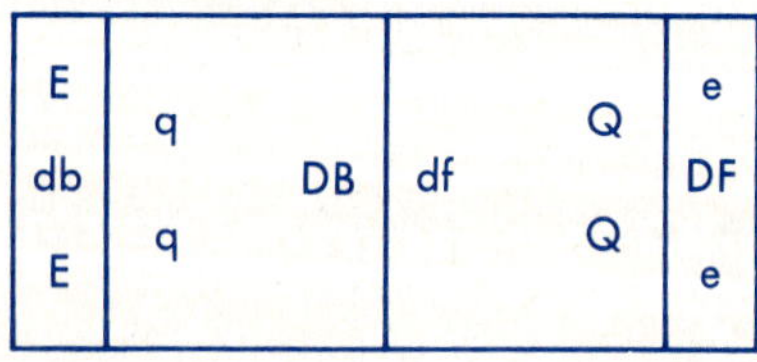

Level: III.
Equipment: One junior sized or small foam football.
Area: An area 30 feet wide and 60 feet long divided in the center and 10-foot areas marked off at each end of the playing field.
Participants: Six players per team: two ends, two quarterbacks, and two defensive backs.

Skills: Passing, catching.

Description: One team with the ball begins play. A quarterback attempts to score by throwing the ball to one of the ends. A pass may be completed to the other quarterback on the team if the ends are not free. A point is scored if the ball is successfully caught by an end. After a score the ball is given to a quarterback on the other team to begin play. If the ball is intercepted, the defensive back quickly throws the ball to a quarterback on the same team and play continues. If the ball is dropped it is given to the opposing team.

Fouls: Personal contact with a member of the opposing team.

Penalty: Ball is awarded to the opposing team's quarterback.

Teaching Suggestions:

1. Add an additional defense player to each of the middle zones.
2. Reduce the size of the playing field.
3. Encourage the children to pass the ball quickly.

PASS PUNT AND KICK

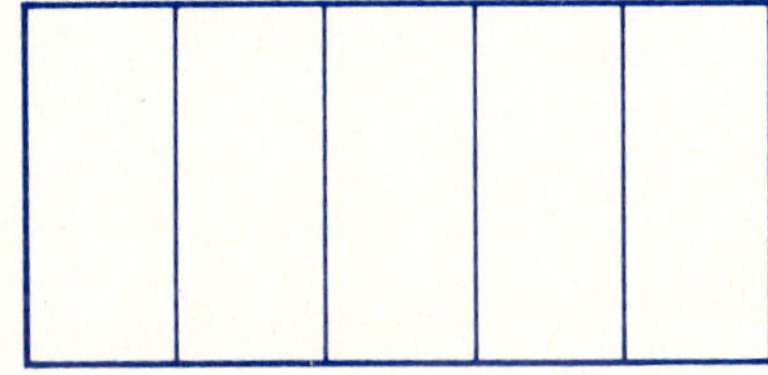

Level: IV.

Equipment: One junior sized or small foam football.

Area: A field space 20 yards by 50 yards with 10-yard lines indicated and a goal line at each end.

Participants: Five per team, numbered from 1 to 5.

Skills: Punt, forward pass, place kick, catching.

Description: One team has the ball in its half of the field and attempts to move the ball over the opponents' goal line in the air. Player 1 begins play by punting, passing, or place kicking the ball toward the opponents' goal line from the 10-yard line. If the ball is caught by the opposing team on a fly or after it touches the ground without going over the goal line play continues with the player 1 on the receiving team using one of the three skills to move the ball toward the other goal line. Players assume responsibility for moving the ball in turn, with the number 2 players coming into action next and so on. If the ball is caught in the air the team may move three steps forward before passing, punting, or place kicking the ball. A punt over the goal line scores 1 point, a pass 2 points, and a place kick 3 points.

Fouls:

1. Moving forward away from the spot where the ball touched the ground or more than three steps after it was caught.

2. Kicking or passing the ball out of bounds.

Penalty:

1. Move to the appropriate spot and execute one of the skills.

2. The receiving team begins at the spot where the ball went out of bounds.

Teaching Suggestions: Encourage the receiving team to move quickly to the ball to get possession as close as possible to the opponents' goal line.

ONE DOWN FOOTBALL

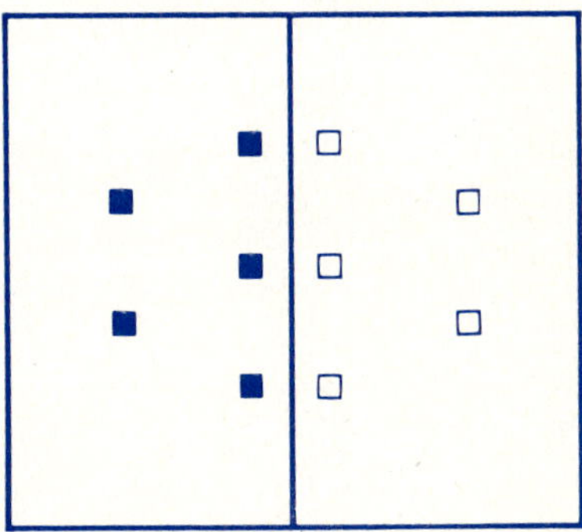

Level: IV.

Equipment: One junior sized or small foam football; two flags for each player.

Area: A playing field 20 yards wide and 25 yards long divided into two equal halves

Participants: Five per team: three line players, two backs.

Skills: Passing, catching, tagging (taking the flags), carrying the ball.

Description: To begin the game, one team is given the ball at the line of scrimmage. On the signal, "hike," from one of the backs they attempt to run or pass any number of times to move the ball to the goal line, without being tagged. The defending team attempts to get both flags from the player with the ball or to intercept a pass. If it is successful in getting the flags or a pass is incomplete the defensive team takes possession of the ball and play begins at the spot where the last flag was secured or the ball was thrown. If the pass is intercepted play continues with the intercepting team attempting to score at the opponents' goal line. If it does not score it is given one more play (down) to do so. If a touchdown is scored play begins once again at the line of scrimmage, with the nonscoring team beginning the play. A touchdown scores 6 points.

Fouls: Pushing; using the hands, hips, or shoulders to block another player.

Penalty: On the defense, replay the down if scoring did not result. On the offense, loss of down, opponents take possession where the infraction occurred or where the ball was downed, whichever is closer to the opponents' goal line.

Table 25-1

Games analysis

Name	Game classification	No. of participants	Equipment	Space/organizational pattern	Motor skills
Football Endball	Lead-up	Three to four per team	One junior or small foam ball	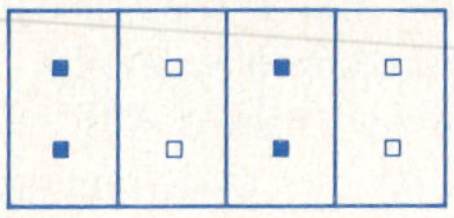	Passing Catching
Punt Ball	Lead-up	Four to five per team	One junior or small football	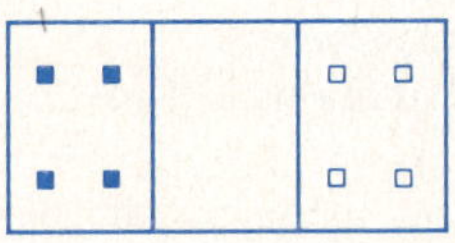	Punting Catching
Zone Football	Lead-up	Six per team	One junior or small foam football	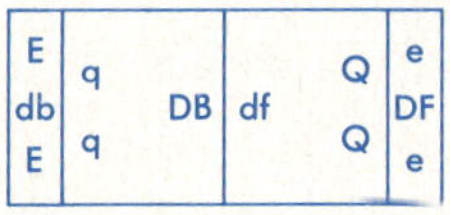	Passing Catching
Pass, Punt, and Kick	Lead-up	Five per team	One junior or small foam football	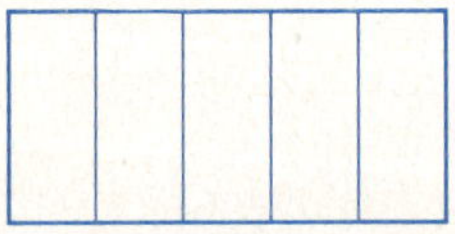	Punt Forward pass Place kick Catch
One Down Football	Lead-up	Five per team	One junior or small foam football	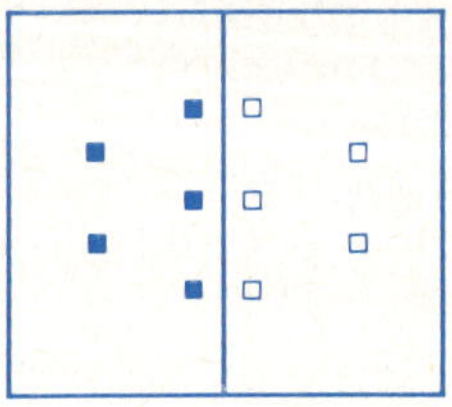	Passing Catching Carrying the ball Tagging
Flag Football	Lead-up	Six per team	One junior or small foam football		Centering Place kick Punt Forward pass Lateral Hand off Blocking Carrying the ball Pitchout

*Numbers refer to concepts given in the box on p. 475.

Modifications	Movement concepts*	Social structure	Strategy	Level
1. Rotate players so all have a chance to play all positions	Self/general: 1, 3, 5 to 7 Direction: 9, 11, 12 Pathways: 14 to 17 Force: 1, 3 Time/speed: 4	Social interaction I	1. Move the ball quickly 2. Cover the entire area on defense 3. Move to an unguarded area to receive a pass 4. Move the ball to a better throwing position before attempting to pass to a teammate in the goal area	III
1. Number players (each kicks in turn) 2. Reduce length of field to allow more scoring 3. Modify scoring so receiving team receives points for catching the ball 4. Use place kicking instead of punting	Self/general space: 1, 4, 7 Direction: 9 Pathways: 15 to 17 Force: 1, 3	Social interaction I	1. Receivers stay spread out to cover the entire area 2. When kicking, look for open spaces within which to punt the ball	III
1. Add one defense player to each of middle zones 2. Reduce the size of the playing area	Self/general: 1 to 3, 5 to 7 Direction: 8 to 12 Pathways: 13 to 17 Force: 1, 3 Time/speed: 4	Social interaction I	1. Offense should stay spread out and moving to get away from defenders	III
	Self/general: 1, 4, 7 Direction: 9 Pathways: 14, 17 Force: 1, 3 Time/speed: 4, 6	Social interaction I	1. Move quickly to the ball to receive it as close as possible to the opponent's goal line.	III
	Self/general: 1 to 7 Direction: 8 to 12 Pathways: 13 to 18 Force: 1 to 3 Time/speed: 4 to 6 Flow: 7	Social interaction II	1. Move to an open space to receive a pass 2. Offense keep spread out to increase space defense must cover	IV
	Self/general: 1 to 7 Direction: 8 to 12 Pathways: 13 to 18 Force: 1 to 3 Time/speed: 4 to 6 Flow: 7	Social interaction II	1. Move to an open space to receive a pass 2. Use a variety of skills on offense to keep the defense guessing	IV

Teaching Suggestions:

1. Encourage the offense to stay spread out to create spaces for runners and the ball.

2. The defense should attempt to cover the space but avoid blocking the opponents.

3. Add additional downs to give more opportunities to score.

FLAG FOOTBALL

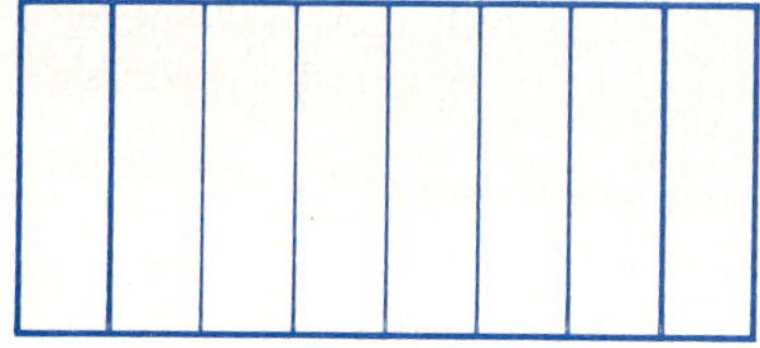

Level: IV.

Equipment: One junior sized or small foam football; two flags for each player.

Area: A playing field 30 yards by 60 yards with 10-yard lines indicated the length of the field and two end zones 10-yards wide at either end.

Participants: Six players per team: four line players and two backs; two of the line players are ends and are eligible to receive passes.

Skills: Passing, catching, ball carrying, centering, hand offs, pitch-out, place kick, punt, blocking.

Description: The game begins with one team kicking off from behind their own goal line with a place kick to the other team. All players on the kicking team must be behind the goal line as the ball is kicked. The receiving team attempts to catch the ball or gain possession of it after it touches the ground and move the ball to the opposite end zone before the ball carrier can have both flags taken. The kicking team attempts to down the ball by taking the flags of the ball carrier. If the ball should be fumbled at any time, the team who first touches the loose ball gains possession and play begins at that spot. Once the ball is downed after the kick-off, the offensive team has four downs to move the ball to the next zone. Each down begins with the ball being centered to one of the backs who gives the signal, "hike." The ball may be passed, handed off, or run on each of the downs. If a forward pass is used to move the ball it must be thrown from behind the line of scrimmage. Each team may "huddle" before each play to decide the strategy it will use. If a team fails to move the ball to the next zone in four tries, the other team takes over and play continues. On the fourth down a team may punt but must indicate their intention to do so before centering the ball. Neither team may cross the line of scrimmage until after the ball has been kicked. Six points are scored for a touchdown. After a touchdown the scoring team may have one attempt to gain an extra point by taking an additional down from 3 yards out from the goal line. An extra point is earned if it successfully runs or completes a pass on this play to move the ball past the goal line. If the ball is downed behind the team's own goal line the opposing team is awarded 2 points. If the kick-off goes into the end zone a player from the receiving team may touch the ball to the ground behind the goal line for a touchback. Play then begins at the receiving team's 20-yard line.

Fouls:

1. The ball going out of bounds on the kick-off.
2. Forward passing on the kick-off return.
3. Failing to indicate the intention to punt.
4. Passing beyond the line of scrimmage.
5. *Off-side:* a player of either team beyond the line of

scrimmage before the ball is centered.

6. Pushing of blocking with the hands, hips, or shoulders.

Penalty:

1. Kick the ball again. If it goes out of bounds on the second kick the receiving team begins play on its 20-yard line.

2. Ball downed. Begin at the point where the ball was caught on the kick-off.

3. Five-yard penalty.

4. Five-yard penalty.

5. Five-yard penalty.

6. Fifteen-yard penalty.

Teaching Suggestions:

1. Encourage the children to use a variety of skills (passing, running, and hand offs) to keep the defense guessing.

2. The defense may use a man to man or zone coverage.

SUMMARY

Flag football offers elementary school children the opportunity to work with a ball that is not round. It is a team game in which children have the opportunity to plan a course of action before each play. The skills and knowledge of football are difficult and take time to develop. Football is a very physical game, and care must be taken to provide the safest environment for all by carefully and consistently enforcing the safety rules, particularly concerning physical contact.

Football activities provide another activity in which application to the movement content should be made. Key concepts of space and qualities of movement should be an important part of each lesson. While it is considered to be a sport primarily played by men and boys, girls enjoy the lead-ups as well.

REFERENCES

1. Arnheim, D., and Pestolesi, R.: Elementary physical education: a developmental approach, ed. 2, St. Louis, 1978, The C.V. Mosby Co.

2. Fuoss, D.: Complete handbook of winning football drills, Newton, Mass., 1984, Allyn & Bacon

3. Kirchner, G.: Physical education for elementary school children, ed. 6, Dubuque, Iowa, 1985, William C. Brown, Publisher.

4. Schurr, E.: Moement experiences for children, ed. 3, Englewood Cliffs, N.J., 1980, Prentice-Hall.

ADDITIONAL READINGS

Bahneman, C.: Pass Football, JOPER **49**(2):53, February 1978.
   A game derived from flag football in which several different scoring options are included.

Gustafson, J.: Razzle dazzle football, JOPER **50**(6):69, June 1979.
   A version of flag football, with the option of passing at any time.

26

SOCCER

CHAPTER OBJECTIVES

1   To identify the modifications necessary to make soccer a successful activity for elementary school children

2   To analyze the skills of soccer to be taught at the elementary school level and to describe activities to be used in their development

3   To identify the movement content important for success in soccer and to suggest activities to help children apply the movement concepts in soccer activities

4   To describe a series of progressively difficult lead-up games to be developed in soccer units at the elementary school level

Soccer, an important international game, is a popular physical education activity in the elementary schools in the United States. This popularity is probably due to several factors. It is a game that provides for large-group participation, requires little equipment, and is an outdoor game commonly played in the fall. In some areas of the country it is an important interscholastic and collegiate sport as well. Soccer is a complex game. It provides the rare opportunity for children to use body parts other than the hands to control the ball. It encourages perhaps more creative use of body parts, many of which children have not considered as usable in ball games. The skilled player must be able to control the ball received at all levels and vary the force as the situation demands.

Participants must be able to relate to many players, opponents, and teammates, moving over a large area, and recognizing the role each must play if teamwork is to be successful. Players must know how to use space, maintaining appropriate relationships with teammates and opponents and moving effectively to open and close spaces as they move offensively and defensively.

Soccer also requires excellent cardiorespiratory conditioning, as it is a game where everyone remains active in moving the ball from one end of the field to the other.

SOCCER IN THE ELEMENTARY SCHOOL

Soccer is an enjoyable game for children and provides an activity for progressively larger groups and specialization of responsibility over its development.

Equipment: Soccer is an economical game in that little equipment is needed. Soccer balls are now produced in varying sizes to fit the size of the players. At the elementary school level, the smaller balls will permit better control and use of skills. For indoor play, foam balls can be more easily controlled on the smooth floor surface. When introducing the skill of heading, foam balls enable the children to master the technique without fear of injury.

Playing areas and goals must also be adjusted to the size of the players. An 8- to 10-foot goal area is large enough for an elementary school child to cover. The size of the field should allow for successful use of skills, permit the development of team play, and provide the opportunity for growth in the use of important movement concepts. Each lead-up game has its own space requirements.

Skills: Soccer requires almost total use of the body in controlling the ball. Although the feet are most often used, the child must learn to receive and control the ball with many other body parts, including the head. With an appropriate sized ball most children will achieve success in mastering the skills.

In the beginning children should learn to understand the behavior of the ball under different conditions. Proper execution and timing should be stressed. Passes to teammates should allow for easy reception. Speed should not be stressed. The maximum opportunity for children to develop personal skills should be provided within the limitations of time and space.

Ball control or **collecting** are terms that refer to a player's ability to receive a ball and to bring it under complete control. It includes the term *trapping* which generally denotes receiving and stopping a ball between the leg or foot and the ground. In early experiences when children are beginning to learn ball control, trapping should be encouraged. Keeping the ball low is important in the games played at the beginning levels. Later, ball control skills in which the ball is not stopped but merely controlled will become more important in the games.

The game: Soccer offers the complex interaction of a large number of players. Relating to 21 other participants, each with slightly different responsibilities in the game, is confusing to elementary school children. Soccer may also be an inactive game for many at the elementary level, since children are only beginning to develop team play and to learn to use the large space available. Therefore, it must be broken down into smaller group activities if each child is to have an equal opportunity to develop to the fullest. As children progress in the game, a larger space, more players per team, and more advanced rules may be introduced.

The responsibilities of the team on offense are:
1. To score goals.
2. To maintain possession of the ball to prevent the opponents from scoring.

Offensive tactics that should be stressed in the elementary school program include:
1. Keeping one's feet going in the direction of the goal.
2. Passing ahead to an open space.
3. Controlling passes so they may be easily re-

Figure 26-1

Evaluative criteria and teaching points for dribbling.

- Head up, upper body inclined forward.
- Run on the balls of the feet.
- Ball is contacted with inside of the foot, outside of foot or instep.
- The ball is kept within playing distance always.

ceived and controlled by a teammate.
4. Moving to meet the ball.
5. Rushing a shot on goal.
6. Changing the path of the ball to keep defense off guard.
7. Always moving, repositioning in relation to the ball, teammates, and the defense.
8. Maintaining a constant surveillance of teammates, ball position on the field, and its relationship to the goal.
9. Keeping the ball until a defense player has committed to the player with the ball but before one is about to be tackled.

The responsibilities of the defense are to:
1. Prevent the opposing team from scoring by tackling, intercepting passes, and closing space close to the goal.
2. Get the ball to their offensive teammates as quickly as possible.

Defensive tactics to be stressed include:
1. Staying between opponent and goal.

Figure 26-2

Evaluative criteria and teaching points for inside of the foot pass.

- Supporting foot next to ball with toes turned slightly inward; both knees bent.
- Body and head over ball; eyes on the ball.

- Kicking leg brought back, ankle firm, toes up and leg turned to the side.
- Contact the center of the ball with inside of foot.
- Leg follows through in direction of pass.

2. Continually repositioning to close spaces.
3. Advancing to tackle or harass the attack.
4. Clearing the ball away from the goal as quickly as possible.
5. Moving more closely to mark opponents as they near the goal.
6. Anticipating the movement of the ball and opponents.
7. Passing quickly to the attack.
8. Watching the player one is marking, not the ball.

SOCCER SKILLS

Body awareness concepts are extremely important in the mastery of soccer skills, since more body surfaces may be used to play the ball. Creating and absorbing force with body parts that children have little experience in using is challenging for elementary school children.

Dribbling

Dribbling is a skill in which an individual player maintains control of the ball while moving the ball downfield. It may be used to move in for a shot on goal, to create a space by drawing a defender or to allow a teammate time to get free for a pass. The ball is moved down the field with a series of taps with the inside, outside, or instep of the foot. The ball is kept a comfortable distance from the feet but always within the immediate playing area.

Figure 26-3

Evaluative criteria and teaching points for outside of foot pass.

- Supporting foot is placed beside and away from the ball, with toes pointing in the direction the runner is moving.
- Eyes are on the ball as contact is made through the center of the ball with the outer edge of the foot, toes pointing inward, ankle flexed and firm.

- Leg follows through in the direction of the pass.

Common errors:
1. Looking down at the ball only.
2. Contacting the ball with too much force, so the player must run after it.
3. Dribbling too long so it is taken away by an opponent.
4. Dribbling toward the person to whom a pass will be made.
5. Disrupting the rhythm of running while dribbling.

Teaching suggestions: Dribbling is a skill often overused in soccer. It should be used only when good opportunities for passing do not exist, since it slows down the offense. Children need coaching during play. They should be encouraged to dribble or pass at the appropriate times. When dribbling around an opponent, players must learn to use body movements to disguise their intent. Maximum ball control is required for these maneuvers.

Activities to practice dribbling:
1. Each child has a ball and dribbles in general space using as much space as possible, controlling the ball, and avoiding contact with others. (How did you keep the ball under control to avoid others? Were you able to cover all the available space?)

Variation:
a. On the signal stop the ball and on the next

Figure 26-4

Evaluative criteria and teaching points for instep drive.

- Supporting foot is next to ball with both knees bent.
- Eyes are on ball with knee and head over ball.
- Kicking leg is brought back with knee bent and heel close to buttocks.

- Contact is made on laces of shoe with toe down, heel up, and ankle firm.
- Lower leg snaps and leg follows through in direction of kick.

signal begin again. (What did you do to stop the ball quickly?)

  b. On the signal, each child pulls the ball to the left, right, or backward and then continues dribbling. (What did you do to keep the ball under control as you moved through space? How quickly could you change direction and then continue moving forward? Was any direction change easier? Why?)

2. In partners, each child has a ball. One follows the other (the leader) as they dribble in general space. Use all the space available. On the signal the follower spurts ahead and becomes the new leader. (What made this activity more difficult than dribbling in space as an individual? What did you do to keep the ball under control and to follow your partner?)

Passing

Passing is a team skill. It consists of propelling the ball to another player so that the ball can be easily controlled. The pass must be accurate and with just enough force to accomplish the task. In addition, it requires timing and the ability to conceal the intended path of the pass to keep the opponents guessing. The player executing the pass has generally two options: (1) to pass the ball to a space past a defender into which a teammate runs to pick it up or (2) to pass to a teammate who has run into a space behind a defender. To achieve greatest accuracy the passer uses as much of the foot as possible in contacting the ball and a long follow through. The point of contact on the ball will determine the height of the trajectory. Accuracy rather than power should be emphasized. The *inside of the foot pass* (push pass) is used mostly for short, accurate passes along the ground but may be used also for medium-distance passes. Before initiating the pass the player looks up to see where the pass is to be made. Contact is made at the center of the ball with the fleshy part of the inside of the foot between the big toes and the heel bone. The lower leg accelerates on contact, and the leg follows through smoothly and firmly in the direction of the pass.

Common errors:
1. Failing to look up to see where pass should be made.
2. Positioning supporting foot too far forward.
3. Failing to focus on the ball at contact.
4. Contacting ball too low or too high.
5. Kicking with the toe.
6. Not accurately turning the kicking leg in direction of pass.
7. Projecting inappropriate force to the ball.
8. Failing to follow through in direction of pass.
9. Moving down field toward the intended receiver before passing.

The *outside of the foot pass* (flick pass) is used in diagonal passing, forward and backward, for short or medium distance. The pass is executed quickly, and since it does not disrupt natural running it is difficult for opponents to anticipate. The passer looks up to see where the pass is to be made. The kick originates from the knee rather than the hip with a short back swing. On contact the eyes are on the ball and there is a quick snap with the kicking leg. The skill ends with a long follow through in the direction of the pass.

Common errors:
1. Failing to look up to see where the pass is to be made.
2. Positioning oneself too close or too far forward or behind the ball.
3. Not keeping foot firm on contact, with toes pointing inward.
4. Not using sufficient force so that the ball does not reach its destination.
5. Failing to have the eyes focused on the ball at contact.
6. Having a short follow through not in the direction of the pass.

The *instep drive* uses a kick with the instep in which the ball is raised off the ground, enabling it to cover greater distance. The passer looks up to see where the intended pass should go. Contact is made through the lower one half of the ball with the instep, the toes pointing downward and in the direction of the kick. On contact there is a snap of the lower leg to give added force, and the leg follows through in the direction of the kick.

Common errors:
1. Failing to look up to see where the intended pass should be.
2. Placing the supporting foot too far forward or behind the ball.
3. Kicking with the toe rather than the instep.
4. Failing to keep ankle firm on contact.
5. Contacting the ball too high.
6. Failing to follow through in the direction of the pass.

Chipping is used to pass over the head of an opponent and when a long distance pass is required. The passer looks up to see where the pass is to be made. The ball is approached at an angle with the last stride a long one to permit a long swing of the kicking foot to add power. Contact is made with the instep, the leg straightening as the ball is kicked. The kicking knee is behind the ball more than in the low drive. The eyes are focused on the ball as contact is made, and the follow through is in the direction of the pass.

Common errors:
1. Failing to look up to see where the pass should be made.
2. Assuming a position too far forward or too far behind the ball.
3. Failing to bend the knees.
4. Kicking with the toe.
5. Contacting the ball too high.
6. Failing to watch the ball on contact.
7. Failing to follow through in the direction of the pass.

Activities to practice passing:
1. With a partner, practice passing, using the type of pass indicated by the leader. Beginning 5 yards apart, increase the distance each time a child has successfully completed five passes. Vary the type of passes used. (What changes

Figure 26-5

Evaluative criteria and teaching points for chipping.

- The ball is approached at an angle with a long last stride.
- The supporting foot is to the side and slightly behind the lower half of the ball; the knees are bent.

- Contact is made with the instep through the lower half of the ball.
- The kicking knee is slightly behind the ball with the body leaning back.

- Follow-through is in the direction of the kick.

---

were necessary in the passes as the distance increased? Were you able to get the ball accurately to your partner?) Variation: Increase and decrease distance on a signal. (Were you able to adjust your passes easily to the changing distances?)

2. Children are in groups of four with one ball. The player with the ball passes the ball to one of the others and then follows the pass as quickly as possible. (What did you do to get the ball directly to the receiver? Were you able to keep the ball moving?)

3. Children are in groups of three, organized as three corners of a square. A passes to B and moves to the empty corner, B then passes to C and moves to the empty space. C then passes back to A and the drill begins again. (What did you do to get the ball accurately to the receiver? What kind of a pass did you want to receive?)

4. Children are in groups of three. The person with the ball passes it to a space and calls out the name of the receiver, who moves to the space to receive the ball. (What are the characteristics of a good pass? Where do you want to receive the ball?)

Shooting

Although the kick with the instep is the most frequently used shot for goal, any of the kicks described in the previous section may be used. The major difference between their use as a pass or shot on goal lies in the intent of the kicker. In passing the objective is to propel the ball so that it can be easily controlled by the receiver, whereas in shooting for goal the intent is to make the kick impossible to stop by the goalkeeper. Both passing and shooting require accuracy. Power is an added ingredient in the attempt to score. Since few goals are scored in soccer, the attack must take as many shots for goal as possible. The attack must quickly react to scoring opportunities and not hesitate to get the shot away. Shots for goal should be directed toward the sides of the goal and preferably the corner farthest from the goalkeeper. Low shots are generally more difficult for the goalkeeper to handle.

Common errors:
1. Missing opportunities to score.
2. Passing off when they should shoot.
3. Using too much power with not enough accuracy.
4. Failing to follow up the shot.
5. Directing kick at the goalkeeper.
6. Failing to look up to see where the shot should be directed.

Teaching suggestions: Shooting practice should involve receiving a moving ball rather than kicking a ball from a stationary position, since the ball will not be motionless in the game.

Activities to practice shooting:
1. In partners, one, the shooter, approaches the goal as the other rolls the ball into the goal area. The shooter receives the ball and then takes a shot for goal. Begin with a gentle roll and gradually increase the force as skill improves. Begin with shots taken close to the goal and gradually increase the distance. Change the angle at which the shooter approaches the goal. After three attempts change positions. (Were you able to receive the ball and get off an accurate shot at goal? What did you do to be sure the ball was directed into the goal?)
2. Children are in partners, with two to four cones placed within the goal. (The cones should be placed so that the middle of the goal is covered and the sides and corners open.) Repeat activity 1 above. The shooter must now make a shot for goal and must place the ball in the goal without hitting the cones to score. (What must you do to control the accuracy of your shot?)
3. In groups of three, repeat activity 1 but add a goalkeeper. (What changes in your shooting were necessary with a goalkeeper protecting the goal? Where were the open spaces in the goal?)
4. Children are in groups of three: two attack and one goalkeeper. The attack brings the ball into the goal area by dribbling and passing. The person with the ball has the opportunity to take a shot for goal and rush the shot or to draw the goalkeeper and then make a quick pass to the other attack player who attempts a quick shot for a score. (What were you able to do to open a space for the ball in the goal?)

Ball Control (Collecting)

Ball control consists of receiving a ball and bringing it under control. It includes trapping when the intent is to stop the ball. Trapping is an important skill for beginning elementary school players, who are learning to control the ball with body parts other than their hands. In beginning games, emphasis is on keeping the ball low, which is more easily accomplished by kicking a stationary ball. However, as skills improve, trapping the ball becomes less important than other forms of ball control. Ball control is an essential skill in the game of soccer, since the time a player has to dribble, pass, or shoot is determined by efficiency in getting the ball under control on receiving it.

In all ball control skills the player must:
1. Move into the direct line of flight of the ball.
2. Move to meet the ball.
3. Use as large a body surface as possible to control the ball.
4. Make a decision about what will be done with the ball before it is received.
5. Relax the part of the body sufficiently so the ball may be brought under control at the feet or slightly ahead of the body when moving with it.
6. Be in a good balanced position with full attention given to the ball.

Ball control practice requires careful placement of the ball so the ball can be received at precisely the level of the body part to be used. It may be difficult for elementary school children consistently to place the ball appropriately to their partners during practice sessions.

Figure 26-6

Evaluative criteria and teaching points for juggling.

- Assume a well-balanced position, slightly crouched, and weight on the balls of the feet.
- Eyes are focused on the ball, which is contacted in a steady rhythm and rebounds no more than 3′ above part giving impetus.

- With the thigh, upper leg is horizontal to the ground; contact is in the middle of the thigh.

- With instep ball is contacted about knee height, the foot is firm.

- With the outside of the foot, toes are raised. Lean at hip away from the ball to make contact at hip height.

- With the head back, the forehead is parallel to the ground and contact is on the center of the forehead.

Juggling is the skill of keeping the ball in the air in which an individual repeatedly touches the ball with the feet, thigh, or head. It is a skill not used in the game of soccer but one that helps players develop "the feel of the ball," concentration, rhythm, control, and confidence in soccer ball handling skills. While this is a difficult skill for young players it should be introduced during the elementary school years. Juggling provides a very good warm-up activity for everyone.

The ball is contacted with a gentle touch. With contact on the instep, the toes are pointed and the foot firm to avoid backspin, and the ball is touched at knee height. When the thigh is used, the ball is contacted in the middle of the thigh from a position in which the thigh is horizontal to the ground. If the ball is to be juggled with the head, it is contacted with the head tilted back, the forehead parallel to the ground, and the player directly underneath the ball. When the outside of the foot is used, the toes are raised, the knees are bent; a bend at the hip away from the ball enables contact at hip height. In using the inside of the foot, the toes are raised and the ball is played fairly close to the body. The juggler establishes a steady rhythm, with the ball going no more than about 3 feet in the air above the body part giving impetus.

Common errors:
1. Failing to concentrate on the ball.
2. Contacting with too much force so control is lost.
3. Failing to establish a steady rhythm.
4. Not maintaining a balanced position, with weight on the balls of the feet.

Teaching suggestions: When practicing juggling, it is easiest for children to begin with a toss to themselves. Later they may lift the ball by jumping with it between the ankles or getting a lift by getting the instep under the ball. Sitting on the ground, juggling with the instep is an easy way to get started. It is important that children have an object that they can handle while juggling. Socks stuffed with rags, or balls of appropriate size and weight and not too much rebound, work best.

The *sole of the foot control* (trap) is used to control ground balls but may also be used to control balls dropping out of the air. The player moves into position in line with the ball's flight with eyes focused on the ball. The ball is contacted in front of the body with the sole of the foot so that the ball is trapped between the ground and the foot. On impact there is a giving in the ankle, knee, and hip to absorb the

Figure 26-7

Evaluative criteria and teaching points for sole of the foot control.

- In line with ball's flight; eyes on the ball.
- Weight on supporting foot, knees bent and arms out to the sides.
- Sole of foot placed squarely on the ball; "give" at the ankle, knee, and hip joints.
- Ball is controlled in front of the body within immediate playing range.

force of the ball. If the ball is dropping from the air, the sole of the foot must contact it at the precise moment it touches the ground or it will rebound away.

Common errors:
1. Failing to line up with the ball.
2. Not being in a balanced position.
3. Jabbing at the ball rather than placing the foot on top of the ball.
4. Stepping on the ball, resulting in a loss of balance.
5. Failing to watch the ball.

The *inside of the foot control* is used primarily to

Figure 26-8

Evaluative criteria and teaching points for inside of the foot control.

- In line with the ball, knees bent, eyes on the ball.
- The ball is contacted with inside of foot as its center, weight balanced on supporting foot.
- Foot and leg "give" at impact to control the ball close to the body.
- For a ball in the air, the leg is raised with a slight lean backward.
- The ball is controlled in front of the body and within immediate playing range.

control balls moving along the ground although it may also be used to control balls dropping through the air. The player assumes a position in line with the ball's flight. The ball is contacted at its center with the foot giving on impact. The ball is controlled close to the feet in preparation for the next move. A ball being controlled that is in the air is contacted off the ground by raising the controlling leg. A slight backward lean aids in bringing the ball to the ground within playing distance.

Common errors:
1. Failing to line up with the ball.
2. Not contacting the center of the ball.
3. Failing to give with foot and leg at impact, resulting in the ball rebounding too far away.
4. Failing to assume a balanced position.

Figure 26-9

Evaluative criteria and teaching points for instep control.

- In line with the ball, eyes on the ball, weight on supporting foot.
- Leg is raised to meet oncoming ball, ankle flexed.
- Upon impact, ankle is relaxed and foot is brought to the ground with ball following it.
- Ball is controlled close to body.

The *instep control* is used to control balls dropping toward the receiver. The receiver assumes a position in line with the oncoming ball. The bottom of the ball is contacted with the instep, and the leg is lowered immediately on impact so the ball follows the leg to the ground. The foot of the controlling leg must be slightly relaxed on meeting the ball or the ball will rebound up into the air. The ball is controlled slightly in front of the body.

Common errors:
1. Failing to position oneself in the ball's line of flight.
2. Contacting the ball as the leg is being raised, which gives it impetus away from the receiver.
3. Failing to relax ankle so the ball rebounds off the foot.
4. Failing to control the ball close to the body.

The *thigh control* is used to control balls dropping toward the receiver. The thigh, being a large, fleshy

Figure 26-10

Evaluative criteria and teaching points for thigh control.

- In line of flight, weight balanced on supporting leg.
- Eyes are on ball as leg is raised to meet the ball.
- Contact at midthigh, slight body lean, arms out and back.
- Leg is dropped to cushion ball and ball drops to the ground.

Figure 26-11

Evaluative criteria and teaching points for chest control.

- In line with the ball in a forward-backward stride.
- Eyes are on the ball, arms out to the side or crossed (girls) and the body in the ball's path.
- Body gives on impact.
- Ball controlled with the feet to keep it close.

surface, is ideal for controlling the ball. The receiver assumes a position in the direct line of the ball's flight. The controlling leg is raised to meet the oncoming ball. On contact with the ball at midthigh, the upper leg is approximately parallel to the ground. The thigh gives at impact, cushioning the ball as it drops in front of the body. The arms are spread to aid balance and to avoid contact with the ball. The ball will rise slightly at impact before continuing to the ground. Balls received at lower levels may necessitate only partially raising the leg before contact to control it close to the body. Balls dropping from greater heights will need to be controlled by the feet also to put the balls into position to be played.

Common errors:
1. Failing to line up with the oncoming ball.
2. Contacting the ball with the knee, so the ball rebounds away.
3. Contacting the ball with the hands or arms.

4. Failing to drop the leg immediately on contact with the ball.

The *chest control* is one that will be more difficult for children to master, although it involves a much larger surface on which to control the ball. The receiver takes a position in line with the ball's flight, with feet a comfortable distance apart. The arms are out at the sides or crossed at the chest and in tight (for girls). On impact the body relaxes, resulting in a slight lean forward (unless the ball is received high on the chest, where it gives more directly backward). As the body gives, much of the body weight may be shifted to the rear foot. The ball must be further controlled by the feet as it drops to the ground to keep it within the immediate playing range.

Common errors:
1. Failing to line up with the ball.
2. Failing to give on impact to cushion the ball.
3. Girls failing to keep arms in tight, resulting

in illegal handling of the ball with the arms. Activities to practice ball control:

1. Individually juggling, children use one or more body parts. They begin sitting, then move to standing and eventually moving. (How many taps can you give the ball before it touches the ground? How many ways can you juggle the ball at the low, medium, and high levels?)

2. In partners, one throws the ball so it can be received appropriately, for the practice of the ball control skill being developed. Children may need to practice throwing to get it to their partners. If the ball cannot be received at the appropriate level, beginners should not attempt the control. Begin from a stationary position with the balls thrown directly to the controller. Have children practice one type of control at a time to give more opportunity to develop timing. (What must you do to receive the ball and get it under control? What body parts were used to absorb the force?)

3. Repeat activity 2 above, but do not throw the ball directly to your partner. Throw it to the right, left, in front, or behind so they must adjust their position to receive it. This will necessitate control while on the move. (What cues did you use to help you line up with the ball? What did you do differently to control the ball while you were moving?)

4. Children juggle with a partner. Partners juggle to each other. (How well could you control the ball? How many taps did you give it before it touched the ground?)

Heading

Soccer is the only sport in which the head is used to play the ball, and consequently children tend to be very timid and even afraid in the beginning stages of learning. The forehead provides the best hitting surface, since it is large, relatively flat, and allows the ball to be seen on contact. The header moves to a position in line with the ball. As the ball approaches, the weight is shifted to the rear leg and the upper body and head are bent slightly backward. Before contact the weight is shifted to the front leg, and the upper body and head swing forward from the hips to give added power. On contact the neck muscles are tense, the chin is down, and the tongue is behind clenched teeth. The head is projected through the ball as contact is made with the forehead in line with

Figure 26-12

Evaluative criteria and teaching points for heading.

- Assume a forward-backward stride position, knees bent, weight evenly distributed on balls of feet. Weight shifts to rear foot, upper body and head bent back, eyes on ball.
- Weight shifts to front foot; upper body and head swing forward, chin down, neck muscles tense. Keep eyes open and watch ball until contact on forehead. Project head through ball, arms out for balance.

the eyes. If height is an important factor, as when heading the ball away from the goal area, the header assumes a position partially under the ball. Jumping to head a ball requires precise timing of the jump (which should be a one-foot take off) to the ball.

Common errors:

1. The ball is allowed to hit the head, rather than the head hitting the ball.
2. Eyes closed before contact.
3. Poor balance.
4. Jumping too soon or too late.

Teaching suggestions: When introducing heading, soft balls should be used. It may be helpful to have the children hold the ball in both hands and hit the ball to their foreheads lightly at first and then harder to get an idea of where contact should be made and also to realize it will not hurt if done properly. Activities to practice heading:

1. Each child has a ball. The children toss the ball up and then head it to themselves. (Where do you want to be in relation to the ball on contact? How long can you keep your eyes open?)
2. Practice juggling with the head individually. (How many times can you hit the ball before it touches the ground? Try using different parts of your head. Which part works best?)
3. In partners, one puts the ball up into the air, and the other moves to it to head it. (Where did you want to be in relation to the ball? Can you head it back to your partner?)
4. In partners, practice heading the ball. (How many times can you head the ball before it touches the ground? What must you do to direct the ball to your partner?)

Tackling

Tackling is the skill of taking the ball away from an opponent. It requires timing, determination, and strength.

The *block tackle* is the most frequently used tackle in soccer and is most effective against a player who is receiving the ball and who does not have it under full control or when an opponent is dribbling the ball. The tackler moves in close to the opposing player. The knees are bent to help absorb the impact and to improve balance. The tackling foot is raised, with the knee turned out, and the ankle firm. Contact with the ball occurs as the ball comes off the opponent's foot. The tackler plays through the ball with the body weight but must be careful not to put all weight on the tackling foot. If the ball becomes blocked between the two players' feet, the tackler must be able to quickly lower the tackling foot to get under the ball to roll it over the opponent's foot. If the ball is successfully contacted while off the opponent's foot, it may be pushed to the side or between the opponent's feet.

Common errors:

1. Failing to time the tackle when the ball is off the opponent's foot.
2. Contacting the ball too high.

Evaluative criteria and teaching points for block tackle.

- The inside of the foot is placed against the center of the ball, ankle firm. The eyes are on the ball, with head and body over the ball.

- The tackler plays through the ball, rolling it over the opponent's foot.

3. Leaning back on contact with the ball.
4. Putting too much weight on the tackling foot so the tackler cannot move the foot to get under a ball blocked between the opposing player's feet.
5. The tackler lacking determination.
6. Failing to keep a firm ankle.

Activities to practice tackling:

1. In partners, each child begins about two steps from the ball. On the signal, the partners both move in to block the ball between their feet, gently maneuvering the ball to get it away. (What must you do to gain control of the ball? How quickly can you move your foot to get under the ball?)
2. In partners, one loosely dribbles down field, while the tackler times the tackle to contact the ball when it is off the dribbler's foot. The dribbler offers little resistance. (What cues did you use to make contact when the ball was not in contact by the dribbler?)
3. Same as activity 2 above, but this time the dribbler attempts to maintain possession of the ball. (What cues did you use to know when to make your move? Did you fool the dribbler?)

Goalkeeping

Goalkeeping is a specialized position in the game of soccer. A successful goalkeeper must have good hands, agility, patience, sharp reflexes, and courage. The major responsibility of the goalkeeper is to try to prevent the attacker from shooting, and, when that is not possible, to defend the goal. The goalkeeper assumes a ready position with the feet in a side stride position. The hands are up with palms facing out, and the arms are close to the body with elbows bent and fingers spread. The thumbs and index fingers form a W. The eyes are focused on the ball and the players in the immediate area. The goalkeeper always presents as large a target as possible to the attempt at goal, and the body is behind the hands.

The goalkeeper gets into a position where there is the greatest chance to stop the ball. The goalkeeper imagines a triangle, with the goal line as one side and the ball at the apex. By standing directly in front of the goal line the goalkeeper allows the greatest target area to the shooter. By moving out toward the attacker the target area is greatly reduced and the shooter must rely on greater accuracy to score. This is often called narrowing the angle. Figure 24-16 in Chapter 24 depicts the angles at various distances from the goal.

The goalkeeper should challenge lone attackers aggressively. By moving toward the attacker the shooter must look at the goalkeeper as well as the ball. This may result in less concentration on the ball

Figure 26-14

Evaluative criteria and teaching points for goalkeeping.

- Assume a side stride position, knees bent, weight on the balls of the feet.
- The hands are up, fingers form a **W**, the upper body is leaning slightly forward, head up and eyes on the ball.

and therefore a greater chance for error. As the goalkeeper moves forward, a position that permits a move to either side should be assumed.

Common errors:

1. Failing to assume a ready position in which the goalkeeper can move in any direction.
2. Not watching the ball.
3. Putting weight on the entire foot.
4. Not keeping hands up and in front of the body.

Activities to practice goalkeeping:

1. Practice assuming the ready position and moving to meet an imaginary ball. (What body position enabled you to move quickly in any direction?)
2. In partners, one dribbles in and shoots for a goal, while the other defends the goal. (What did you do to keep the ball out of the goal? Did the shooter make it obvious where the shot would go? What position enabled you to move quickly to meet the ball?)

The Throw-In

A *throw-in* is taken when the ball is sent over the side lines by an opposing player. The thrower assumes

Figure 26-15

Evaluative criteria and teaching points for throw-in.

- Assume a side or forward/backward stride position, knees bent, the trunk and head arched slightly backward.
- The ball is held in both hands with fingers spread, thumbs close. Behind the head, arms bent at the elbows.

- The arms are brought forward with ball; release overhead or in front of body.
- Arms and trunk follow through in direction of throw and weight is shifted to the balls of the feet or to the front leg as legs extend.
- Both feet are on the ground as the ball is released.

either a side or forward-backward stride position. The ball is held in both hands and is brought back behind the head, with the arms bent slightly at the elbows and the trunk arched backward for added force. The arms are brought forward, and the ball released when it is overhead or in front of the body, depending on the distance to be thrown. Force is applied equally with both hands. Both feet must be on the ground on release of the ball.

Common errors:
1. Having poor balance.
2. Giving impetus to the ball with one hand, rather than equal force with both hands.
3. Lifting one leg on release.
4. Having little follow through, which reduces the distance and accuracy of the throw.

Teaching suggestions: Throwers should be encouraged to throw the ball as quickly as possible and to find and to throw to an unmarked player.

Activities to practice the throw-in:
1. Practice throwing to a partner, gradually increasing the distance to be thrown. (How did the throw change as the distance became greater? How did you use your body parts to increase the force?)
2. In partners, practice throw-ins, increasing and decreasing the distance. The receiver will control the ball as in soccer. (How did you attempt to control the ball? Where did you want to receive it? Was the throw-in easy to control?)
3. Children are in groups of four: one thrower, two attack, and one defense. The thrower attempts to get the ball to one of the attack players who tries to control it before the defense can intercept or tackle. (Were you able

SOCCER CONCEPTS

BODY AWARENESS

Body awareness is important in the analysis and execution of skills. Soccer is unique in that it requires skillful use of the feet as well as the ability to control the ball with body parts, such as the head, trunk, and legs, that are not legally used in most ball games.

SPACE

Self and general space:
1. To move oneself and the ball within the boundaries of the playing area
2. To move in general space in relation to teammates, opponents, and the ball
3. To use all available space
4. To move to an open space while moving in general space
5. To move with control to avoid personal contact
6. To keep your self space between your opponent and the goal or the ball and the goal while playing defense
7. To recognize one's own area of the general space in which to play
8. To pass the ball to an empty space in front of a teammate
9. To place the ball in an empty space in the opponent's goal
10. To use as much space as possible on offense to keep the defense spread out
11. To close spaces open to opponents and the ball, especially close to the goal area when on defense
12. To create open spaces for self, teammates, and the ball while moving in general space by drawing an opponent

Direction:
13. To change direction quickly to avoid contact with others and get around an opponent
14. To change direction quickly to move into position to play the ball
15. To change direction quickly to cover one's area of the field
16. To change direction quickly to open up spaces
17. To change direction quickly to move the ball toward or away from the goal
18. To change direction quickly to stay with an opponent
19. To anticipate the direction changes of teammates and opponents

to get it to the attack so it could be easily handled? Could you disguise your throw?)

SOCCER CONCEPTS

The movement content important to soccer is outlined in the box above. Suggested activities for the development of these movement concepts in soccer activities follow.

Soccer Concept Activities

Space:
Dribbling in general space, each child has a ball. Each dribbles avoiding others' self space and their balls using as much of the available space as possible. The leader indicates an increase or decrease in the available space. (Was it as easy to control the ball in the small space as in the larger space? What did you do as the space got smaller to keep the ball under control and avoid others? Were you able to cover the large space? The small space? Where did you try to go as you dribbled in both spaces? Could you find the empty space?)

Each child has a ball and dribbles in general space. On a signal from the teacher, they quickly change direction.

Variation: Add feinting to the left or right before moving in another direction.

In groups of three, one child faces the others, who

SOCCER CONCEPTS—cont'd

Level:
20. To control a ball received at the high, medium, or low levels

Pathways:
21. To change pathways while moving in space with and without the ball
22. To recognize available pathways within which to move self and ball
23. To anticipate the pathways of teammates or opponents to intercept or avoid that path
24. To close pathways available to opponents
25. To change the expected pathway of the ball
26. To establish a pathway away from the goal on defense
27. To open pathways to the goal on offense
28. To anticipate the pathway of the ball to intercept that path

QUALITIES OF MOVEMENT

Force:
1. To use an appropriate amount of force when passing, dribbling, and shooting for a goal
2. To absorb force effectively with various body parts when receiving a ball
3. To vary the use of body parts in imparting force to the ball

Time and speed:
4. To anticipate the speed of the ball and teammates to meet a pass or to pass
5. To change speed smoothly and efficiently while moving in space
6. To match the speed of the ball and an opponent to intercept or tackle
7. To alter the tempo of the game by speeding up and slowing down

Flow:
8. To combine skills efficiently, such as dribbling and passing or receiving a ball and shooting, into a smooth, continuous movement

line up one behind the other and several yards apart. The dribbler moves toward the first person who steps (keeping one foot stationary) to the left or right when the dribbler is within 2 or 3 feet. The dribbler moves to the available pathway and forward again toward the next person.

Each person has a ball. Each dribbles and attempts to pass the ball so it hits an opponent's ball. There should be no personal contact.

Variation: Begin with half the class attempting to hit, the other half protecting the balls. (What did you do to avoid your ball being hit? Where did you to direct the ball to make contact with another?)

In groups of three, two attempt to pass the ball while the third attempts to intercept. If successful, the person making the errant pass becomes the new defender. (How did you move to create a space for the ball? What did you do on defense to intercept the pass?)

In groups of three or four, one or two persons are in an area between two end players. The end players attempt to kick the ball to one another through the center space, without touching the center players. The center players do not guard the space but move around trying to cover as much of the space as possible. (Were you able to get the ball through the space to your partner? What cues did you use to help identify the available pathways?)

Children are in groups of two and have a ball. On the signal they run out. The one getting to the

ball first attempts to dribble the ball over the opponent's side line; the other goes on defense and tries to keep the ball and opponent away from the line. (How did you protect the ball to get it over the side line? What did you do to keep the person with the ball away from your side line?)

Four or five children without balls are scattered in general space and try to steal the balls from the remainder of the group, all of whom have a ball and dribble in the space. (Were you able to keep control of the ball and avoid the "stealers?" What did you do to protect the ball?)

Children are in partners. One person attempts to dribble the ball to a spot (the goal), while the other attempts to stay between the dribbler and the spot (goal). (Were you able to get by your partner? How did you move? What cues enabled you to stay between your partner and the goal?)

With a partner, children move in general space and practice passing. (What did you do to keep the passes under control and avoid others? Did you use all the space? Were you available to anticipate the open pathways?)

Qualities of movement:

Each child has a ball and dribbles in general space. On a signal, they increase or decrease their speed. (Were you able to control the ball at all speeds? Which was most difficult? How did your dribble change as you moved at a fast speed? Slow? Medium?)

Children are in partners with one ball. Both move down the field in a zigzag fashion, passing back and forth. (Where did you try to place the ball so your partner could continue moving? How did you change your pass as your partner was farther away? Closer to you?)

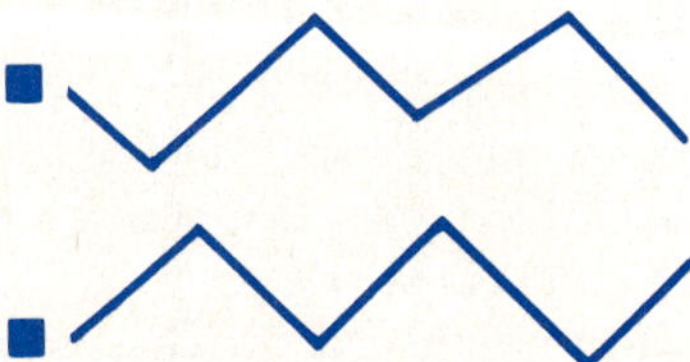

Additional activities that may be adapted for soccer may be found in Chapter 24.

SOCCER LEAD-UP GAMES

The analysis of the games that follow is given in Table 26-1.

LINE SOCCER

Level: II.

Equipment: One soccer ball and pinnies or vests to designate teams.

Area: A field approximately 35 by 50 feet with a line 5 feet from and parallel to each goal line.

Participants: Six members for each team.

Skills: Controlling, dribbling, shooting for goal, tackling.

Description: On the signal, one player from each team runs out from the right end of the team and attempts to kick the ball over the opponents' goal line. One point is scored for each goal. After a point is scored, the players move to the end of their lines and two new players come out on the signal after the ball has been placed in the center of the playing area. A player must control the ball first before shooting for a goal (in other words, they may not simply run out on the signal and immediately kick for goal). Goal line players must control the ball before kicking it to their teammate. Only goal line players may play in the area between the 5-foot lines and goal lines. If the ball is kicked out of bounds, a player from the opposite team's goal line rolls the ball in.

Fouls:
1. Playing the ball with the hands.
2. Kicking for a goal without controlling it first
3. Pushing an opponent
4. Kicking the ball so it rises above waist height.
5. Goal line guards failing to attempt to control the ball first before passing to a teammate.
6. An attack player moving within the five foot restraining line in front of the goal line.

Penalty: A kick for goal to the team fouled against, where the foul occurred. Only goal line players may guard against an offense kick. No kick may be taken closer than 5 yards from the goal line. In case of a defense (goal line guards) foul, a kick is taken 5 yards from the goal line.

Strategy:
1. Keep feet pointing in the direction of opponent's goal.

2. Field players should move to create a space to receive the pass when goal line guards have the ball.

Teaching suggestions:
1. On the opening play pull the ball to the side or backward to control it before shooting for a goal.
2. Encourage controlling the ball on offense and defense.
3. Goal line guards may use the sole of the foot for easy control of the ball.
4. Goal line privileges may be introduced.
5. Opponents should be evenly matched by ability to provide equal opportunity for each pair of opponents.
6. Encourage goal line guards to stand in the area between the goal line and the 5-foot line.

ADVANCED LINE SOCCER

Level: III.

Description: The game is identical to Line Soccer except two or more players from each team come out on the signal. The number of players per team may be increased to eight or ten. The skill of passing is added to those already included in Line Soccer.

Teaching suggestions:
1. See those listed for Line Soccer.
2. Encourage passing. A number of passes may be required before shooting for a goal.

Table 26-1

Soccer games analysis

Name	Game classification	No. of participants	Equipment	Space/organizational pattern	Motor skills	Modifications
Line Soccer	Lead-up	Six per team	One soccerball; pinnies or vests to designate teams	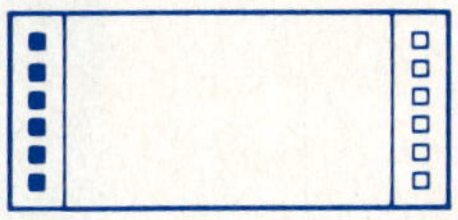	Controlling Dribbling Shooting for goal Tackling	
Advanced Line Soccer	Lead-up	Eight to ten per team	One soccer ball per game; pinnies or vests to designate teams	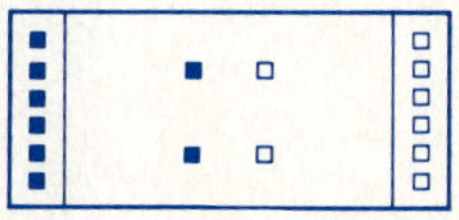	Controlling Dribbling Passing Shooting for goal Tackling	1. Require a specified number of passes before shooting for a goal
Alley Soccer	Lead-up	Six per team	One soccer ball; pinnies or vests to designate teams	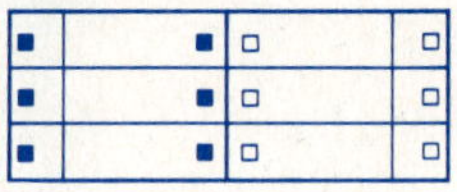	Controlling Dribbling Passing Shooting for goal Tackling	1. Increase number of alleys to five 2. Use extra players as sideline guards to throw the ball in on out of bounds violations
Advanced Alley Soccer	Lead-up	Seven per team	One soccer ball; pinnies or vests to designate team	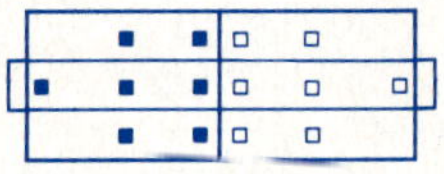	Ball control Dribbling Heading (optional) Passing Shooting for goal Tackling Throw-in Goalkeeping	1. Increase alleys to five
Modified Soccer	Lead-up	Seven per team	One socer ball; pinnies or vests to designate teams	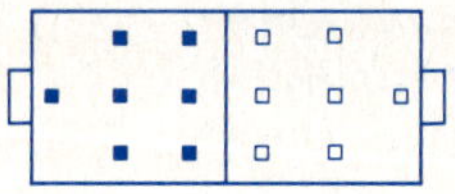	Ball control Dribbling Heading (optional) Passing Shooting for goal Tackling Throw-in Goalkeeping	1. Reduce number of players per team to five

*Numbers refer to the movement concepts in the box on pp. 498-499.

Movement concepts*	Social structure	Strategy	Level
Self/general: 1 to 6, 9, 11 Direction: 1, 4, 7 Pathways: 1 to 4, 8 Force: 1, 2 Time/speed: 2, 3	Social interaction I	1. Keep feet pointing in the direction of the opponent's goal 2. Field players should move to create a space to receive the pass when the goal line guards have the ball	II
Self/general: 1 to 6, 8 to 12 Direction: 1, 2, 5 to 7 Pathways: 1 to 4, 7, 8 Force: 1 to 2 Speed: 1 to 3	Social interaction II	1. Keep feet pointing in the direction of the opponent's goal 2. Field players should move to create space to receive a pass	III
Self general: 1 to 12 Direction: 1 to 7 Level: 1 Pathways: 1 to 8 Force: 1 to 3 Speed: 1 to 4	Social interaction II	1. Encourage passing to a space in front of a teammate 2. Forwards should maintain possession of the ball until the opposing player makes a commitment to them 3. Goal line guards should quickly move the ball away from the goal area 4. Use side alleys to bring ball down toward the goal and center it near the goal	III
Self/general: 1 to 12 Direction: 1 to 7 Level: 1 Pathways: 1 to 8 Force: 1 to 3 Speed: 1 to 4	Social interaction III	1. Encourage passing to a space in front of a teammate 2. Forwards should maintain possession of the ball until the opposing player makes a commitment to them 3. Goalkeeper should quickly move the ball away from the goal area 4. Use side alleys to bring ball down toward the goal and center it near the goal	IV
Self/general: 1 to 12 Direction: 1 to 7 Level: 1 Pathways: 1 to 8 Force: 1 to 3 Speed: 1 to 4	Social interaction III	1. Emphasize using all space available and keeping spaced out 2. Encourage position play	IV

ALLEY SOCCER

Level: III.

Equipment: One soccer ball and pinnies or vests to differentiate teams.

Area: A field 80 by 100 feet long and alleys each 15 feet wide with a line 5 feet from and parallel to the goal line.

Participants: Six per team: a forward and goal line guard for each alley.

Skills: Ball control, dribbling, passing, shooting, tackling, throwing.

Description: One team is designated as the kick-off team. On the signal, the forward in the center alley takes an unguarded kick-off (opposing forwards must be 5 yards away). On the kick-off, the ball must move at least one revolution in a forward direction across the center line. The player executing the kickoff may not play the ball again until another player has touched it. The forwards continue to advance the ball down the field while the opposing forwards try to tackle or intercept their passes. Forwards of either team may not enter the 5-foot area of the goal line players. On a shot for goal, the goal line guards defend only their alley. Goal line guards have goalkeeper privileges and may play the ball with their hands. After stopping an attempt for goal, the goal line guard may throw or kick the ball to a teammate. If a goal is scored, 1 point is awarded and the opposing team will kickoff. To enable each player an opportunity to play all positions, after each goal or designated period of time, players rotate one position clockwise. The ball may be played by the forwards with any body parts except the hands. Balls going out of bounds are thrown into play by the opposing team.

Fouls:

1. Touching the ball with the hands (except goal line guards).
2. Shooting for goal by kicking a ball above the goal line guard's head.
3. Pushing an opponent.
4. Failing to stay in appointed alley.
5. Forwards moving beyond the 5-foot line of the goal area.

Penalty: A free kick is awarded the opponent of the player commiting the foul. All other players must be 5 yards away. A goal may not be scored on a free kick. A hit taken for a foul by a goal line player is taken 5 yards opposite the spot where the foul occurred.

Strategy:

1. Encourage passing to an open space in front of a teammate.
2. Forwards should maintain possession of the ball by dribbling until the opposing players make a commitment to them and before the defenders attempt to tackle.
3. Goal line guards should quickly move the ball out of the goal area.
4. Encourage use of all alleys, using the side alleys to bring the ball down field and centering it as they near the goal.
5. When on defense, forwards should stay between their opponent and the goal.

Teaching suggestions:

1. One or two additional players may be used as side line guards who will put the ball into play when the ball goes over the side line. They would move into field positions when the teams rotate.
2. Control of the ball should be stressed throughout the game.

ADVANCED ALLEY SOCCER

Level: IV.

Description: Similar to Alley Soccer but with the following changes:

1. There is a restricted goal area at the end of the center alley in which one goalkeeper plays.
2. A defense player is added to each alley: right fullback (RF), center halfback (CH), left fullback (LF).
3. Each player now covers approximately three fourths of the field. The forward's area extends to the opponent's goal line. The halfback's and fullback's area begins at their own goal line. One fullback should remain on his or her half of the field.
4. The forward's responsibility is mainly offense. All backs are responsible for taking the ball away from opposing forwards and passing up to the forwards of their team.

Teaching suggestions:

1. See those listed for Alley Soccer.
2. No more than two players should attempt to play the ball at any one time. Other alley players should position themselves in open spaces to receive the ball or in a position to back up the play on defense should the offensive player win the advantage.
3. Increase the number of alleys to five, adding a forward and a defense player (left halfback and right halfback) to each alley.

MODIFIED SOCCER

Level: IV.

Description: Similar to Advanced Alley Soccer, but alley lines are removed. Each team consists of seven players: three forwards, three backs, and a goalkeeper. Children should be encouraged to use all the space available and stay in their positions.

SUMMARY

Soccer provides children with an opportunity to control a ball with most body parts. A variety of skills are used to pass, shoot, and control the ball. Children learn offensive and defensive play in a progression of increasingly complex games in which play requires some differentiation of responsibilities among the players.

Soccer is a large-group activity, although early games provide for a one on one experience until children are ready for more advanced play with larger numbers. In the early stages it is important to develop team play in small-group activities to ensure that all children receive ample opportunities to develop and use their skills.

Application of the movement content is important to success in the game. Considerable time must be spent developing these concepts in individual, partner, and small-group activities.

REFERENCES

1. Beim, G.: Principles of modern soccer, Boston, 1977, Houghton-Mifflin Co.
2. Canadian Soccer Coaches Association: Manual preliminary coaching level, Coach **1**(1):
3. Chyzowch, W.: The official soccer book of the U.S. soccer foundation, Chicago, 1978, Rand McNally and Co.
4. Golfer, G.: A movement approach for teaching soccer in the elementary school, JOPER **50**(5):28, May 1979.
5. Hughes, C.: Soccer tactics and teamwork, South Yorkshire, 1973, E.P. Publishing, Ltd.
6. Kline, L., and Samonisky, M.: The soccer throw-in, JOPERD **52**(5):57, May 1981.
7. Moffat, B.: The basic soccer guide. Mountain View, Calif., 1978, Anderson World Publishing.
8. Vogelsinger, H.: The challenge of soccer: a handbook of skills, techniques and strategy, La Jolla, Calif., 1980, Inswinger.

ADDITIONAL READINGS

Olson, J.: Basic team concepts for beginnnng level soccer players, JOPERD **54**(9):51, November/December 1983.
Eight-player soccer for young soccer players and player responsibilities.

Ramsay, G.: Dribbling for young soccer players, JOPER **50**(7):27, September 1979.
Activities to help children practice dribbling and to help them know when and where to dribble.

Startzell, S.: Soccer teamwork a sport for all, JOPERD **52**(5):55, May 1981.
Helping children with special needs learn soccer.

Sweetland, M.: A soccer unit for primary grades, JOPER **50**(7):67, September 1979.
Developing kicking and body control soccer skills with primary school children.

27

SOFTBALL

CHAPTER OBJECTIVES

1   To discuss the modifications needed in softball for successful play by elementary school children

2   To analyze the skills of softball and describe activities for their development

3   To identify the movement content important for success in softball and to describe activities for its development

4   To provide a series of progressively difficult lead-up games for developing the knowledges and skills of softball at the elementary school level

Softball, a variation of baseball, is a favorite recreational activity of children and adults, whether at family picnics or as simple neighborhood fun. Softball is a difficult game in that the rules are complex and the skills must be performed with pinpoint accuracy. Yet it is a game that is readily modified by groups to meet their recreational needs, at times so much so that children begin to believe the local rules to be official.

Softball is a game where few skills are needed, yet they are skills where control of placement is difficult. It is a game in which a limited number of teammates and opponents are in action at any one time and each player moves into action from a relatively stationary position. It is a game in which the movements of the offensive team are limited to hitting a ball with an implement and running a narrow base path. To be successful in softball, individuals must have speed in running bases and moving to receive balls in the field, agility, strength in the upper body and legs, and accuracy in placing the ball offensively and defensively.

Space concepts are important in softball as the children attempt to cover all the space in the field and to hit to an open space when at bat. On defense players must visually track balls moving through space, make accurate judgments about the ball's flight, and move quickly into position to field the ball. Creating and absorbing force and time (qualities of movement) are important in the game of softball as children project the ball varying distances and in time to beat the base runner to the base. The team at bat must time the run with the pitch and the fielder's attempts to put them out.

SOFTBALL IN THE ELEMENTARY SCHOOL

Softball is a game in which most children will find enjoyment if it is modified to meet their needs.

Equipment: Soft softballs are a must at the elementary school level if the fear of an oncoming ball is to be minimized. When playing or practicing indoors, leather-covered fleece balls should be used to reduce the possibilities of some unsuspecting child getting hit with a poorly thrown or batted ball. When possible, children should be taught to use a glove. Lighter, shorter bats will permit greater control in batting. Base paths should be reduced to 30 feet for intermediate grades and 35 to 40 feet for upper elementary grades.

Skills: Softball requires few, but difficult, skills.

The overhand throwing pattern with a small ball is a difficult skill for children. This not only affects the accuracy of the throw but also the ability of the player to gather it in when it is poorly placed. Batting also poses problems for children, requiring timing the bat to meet an oncoming ball. Most modifications of the game listed below are needed because of the difficulties the skills impose.

The game: For beginning players softball can become a boring, frustrating, and sedentary game unless some modifications are made to keep the game moving and to enable each team to have an equal opportunity for offense (to be at bat). Since few balls are hit out of the infield at this level, teams of six players will help maximize the activity. To maximize the number of innings played in a class period, the batting teams should be changed after each member has had a turn at bat.

Batting is a problem for many beginning players. Striking out is difficult to accept and limits a player's opportunity to learn base running. It is better to allow a player to hit off a batting tee, walk, or throw the ball into the infield after three strikes or five pitches so that each child will have an opportunity to learn all offensive aspects of the game.

One reason for difficulty in batting is the lack of accuracy in pitching. This not only results in batting difficulties but also slows down the game since the catcher must often chase the errant pitches. If possible, the teacher or an aide should pitch; if not, the student with the most accurate underhand throw. It may be helpful to have the batting team supply a back-up to help retrieve balls that pass the catcher.

Children should be encouraged to play a different position each inning. However, only those who can accurately throw the ball over the plate should pitch.

When two or more games are played simultaneously, it may be helpful to play all outs on base as *force outs,* requiring only a step on the base while in possession of the ball to put the runner out. Children are often confused as to when they must tag the runner or merely step on the base. Children have some difficulty with the rule for determining if a ball is fair or *foul.* Since a ball that ends up in foul territory in the infield or a ball that first touches the ground in the outfield is foul, remembering the word SILO may help (*s*ettles in the *i*nfield, *l*ands in the *o*utfield).

The team in the field must strive to cover all the space adequately in the field as it attempts to put the other team out. Position play must be stressed in softball. It is often difficult to get base players to be infielders and to recognize they have a space to cover in addition to the base. Emphasis should be on the area of space to be covered by each player and putting oneself in a position where one can move to a ball coming anywhere in that space. It may be helpful to suggest that infielders move toward the batted ball in covering the infield.

When in the field, players must be thinking about what to do with the ball if it comes to their position. Determining where the ball should go only after one has caught it is usually too late to make a successful play. Encouraging the team to think it through and talk about it will help each player be ready to make the correct play.

The team at bat attempts to remain at bat and to score as many runs as possible. Children need coaching in base running and especially running to first base. They must be encouraged constantly to overrun first base, which is difficult to get many young players to do. The following considerations must be made if the game is to be played safely:

1. Members of the team at bat should stand well away from the playing area and preferably along the first-base side.
2. Batters are responsible for safely putting down the bat after they hit the ball.

3. Fielders should call for balls to avoid collisions.
4. If catcher's equipment is used, its safe use should be taught.
5. Soft softballs or fleece balls should be used indoors.
6. Bases should be secure and, if indoors, not close to walls.
7. Base players and shortstop should be taught to stand where they will not collide with or interfere with the base runners.

SOFTBALL SKILLS

Movement concepts are important in the learning of softball skills. The child must understand how various body parts come into play in sequencing the actions. The accuracy required in throwing skills is a combination of several concepts, including control of force, judging distance, and throwing the ball to an appropriate level. Time is important in judging the speed of a ball when batting, fielding, and running bases. Absorbing force is important in catching and in base running. Flow is essential in the continuous movement when a fielder becomes thrower or a batter becomes a base runner.

Throwing

Points of emphasis for the overhand and underhand throws may be found in Chapter 11.

The *pitch* is the method of putting the ball in play in which the the pitcher, using an underhand motion, throws the ball so it passes over the homeplate within the *strike zone.* The ball is held in the fingers so there is daylight between the palm and the ball. Both feet are on the pitcher's rubber, with the foot opposite the throwing arm slightly forward. The arm swing is smooth, and on release of the ball the arm follows through in the direction of the pitch. The ball crosses the plate at a height between the batter's armpits and knees.

Common errors:
1. Gripping the ball with the palm of the hand.
2. Placing incorrect foot forward.
3. Releasing the ball too soon or too late so that it is not within the strike zone.
4. Pitching arm not extended.
5. Not following through in the direction of the plate.

Pitching is a difficult skill for elementary school children. Few will be successful in consistently getting the ball over the plate within the strike zone. Rules for pitching vary slightly in slow and fast pitch games. Upper grade children should be introduced to the following rules:

1. Both feet should be in contact with the pitching plate.
2. The ball should be held in two hands for at least 1 second and not more than 20 seconds before delivery.
3. Only one step may be taken toward the batter on delivery.
4. Only one motion toward the batter is legal.
5. The strike zone is directly over the plate at a height between the batter's armpits and knees, or the shoulders and knees if slow pitch rules are in use.
6. In slow pitch the ball must be thrown so it arcs 6 to 12 feet above the ground.

Activities to practice throwing and catching:

1. Partners throw and catch, increasing and decreasing the distance after each successful specified number of catches. (What did you do to get the ball to your partner as the distance increased or decreased?)
2. In groups of three or four, two or three field-

Figure 27-1

Evaluative criteria and teaching points for pitching.

- Ball held with three fingers opposite the thumb.
- Face the plate, eyes on target.

- As the underhand swing is taken there is a step on the forward foot with the arm fully extended.

- The follow through is in the direction of the pitch.

ers stand at varying distances away from a thrower, who is facing them. The thrower throws the ball in turn to each of the fielders, varying the force needed to cover the distance. (What adjustments did you make to get the ball to the fielders as they waited at various distances away?)

3. Partners who face away from each other or are facing the same way stand varying distances apart. The lead person throws the ball up, catches it, turns to face a partner who has moved closer or farther away, and then throws the ball to the partner varying the force needed for the distance to be thrown. (What adjustments did you make to get the ball to your partner so that it could be caught?)
4. Children are in partners, throwing and catching as base players. The receiver calls force or tag, and the thrower throws the ball to the appropriate level to make the play, chest high for a force, low for a tag. The ball should be thrown so it would not cross a runner's path

to the base. (How did you adjust your throw to get it to the appropriate level?)

Catching and Fielding

An analysis of *catching* may be found in Chapter 11.

Fielding is an essential skill for all players in the infield and outfield. While waiting for the ball to be pitched, the fielder assumes a *ready position* in a comfortable side stride position, with back straight and approximately at a 45-degree angle to the flexed hips. The fielders are aware of all play options and have tentatively made a decision about what they will do on receipt of the ball.

When fielding the batted ball, the player moves to a position in line with the ball. If the ball is hit directly to the fielder, the fielder immediately shifts to a forward stride position. If the ball is hit to either side, the player steps first with the foot on that side (right foot if to right side) and then uses a cross-over step (that is, left over right if to the right) to reach the ball. If the ball is hit hard and farther to the side, the fielder moves back at a 45-degree angle to the ball. The glove should face the ball. The fielder watches the ball into the glove and the arms are brought in toward the body and up as contact is made to absorb the force and begin to move the ball into position for the throw.

In fielding *fly balls* the thumbs are together with

Figure 27-2

Evaluative criteria and teaching points for fielding.

• Fingers point down for grounders.
• Watch ball into glove, close throwing hand over ball.
• Move quickly to throwing position and throw without hesitation.

• Fingers point up for flies.

the hands up. The fielder judges the speed, direction, height, and wind effect and moves quickly to a catching position to wait to receive the ball. In this way the fielder can make the final adjustments necessary while waiting to catch the ball. The ball should be caught at as high a level as possible to allow more time and space to correct for errors. Before catching the ball, the fielder calls for it to avoid collisions with other fielders in the area.

When fielding *grounders,* the fingers point down with little fingers together. The feet are in a comfortable forward stride position, knees and hips flexed so fingers touch the ground when hanging relaxed. The hands are positioned well out in front of the body. The head is down and the ball is stopped inside the forward foot, allowing the ball to roll into the

glove. The fielder should move forward toward slow-moving balls.

Common errors:

1. Not assuming a ready position before the pitch.
2. Not moving in line with the ball.
3. Failing to bring the arms in and up on contact.
4. Not watching the ball into the glove.
5. Taking the impact of the ball in the nongloved hand.
6. Not preplanning what to do with the ball when it is caught.

Teaching suggestions: Fielding is a difficult skill for elementary school children, since their judgments of speed and ball path tend to be somewhat inaccurate and many children are afraid of a batted ball.

Figure 27-3

Evaluative criteria and teaching points for batting.

- Side faces pitcher in comfortable stride position a step away from home plate.
- Hands grip lower bat handle with hands touching each other.
- Bat is held up and off the shoulder.
- Eyes are on the pitcher and the ball.

- Swing is horizontal.
- Bat contacts ball; weight brought to forward foot on contact.
- Follow through in direction of hit and across body with wrists turning over; batter sets bat down.

Use of the glove must be taught and requires much practice as well as practice in getting the smooth transition from fielder to thrower.

Activities to practice fielding:

1. A leader faces the students, who are spread out in general space and are assuming good fielding positions. The leader fakes a throw to the right, left, in front of, or behind the group. Each moves in the appropriate direction and pretends to field the ball. Players can practice cross-overs and slides to the right and left. (Which ways of moving enabled you to move easily in each direction?)

2. In partners, both with a ball, each quickly rolls a ball to the other, fields, and throws again. (How many pick ups can you do in a row? What positions enabled you to pick up the ball quickly and throw again? What did you do as you fielded the ball to get rid of it quickly?)

3. Children are in partners and practice fielding flies and grounders. Vary the path and force of the ball by throwing to the right, left, in front of, or behind the thrower. (What position enabled you to move in any direction to receive the ball? Where did you want to be as you fielded the ball?)

4. Partners, about 8 to 10 feet apart, have one ball. One throws to the other, who fields the ball and throws again while moving in a clockwise direction. Reverse and move counter-clockwise. Variation: add another ball. (What footwork enabled you to keep moving and successfully field the ball?)

5. In partners, the leader has two balls. Throw one ball to the right of the partner. The partner fields the ball and throws back to the leader, who throws the second ball to the left of the receiver.

6. In partners, one stands in an area 5 by 5 feet. The person outside the square attempts to throw the ball so it touches in the 5-foot area but passes through without contact by the person defending the space. Each successful attempt counts 1 point. After five attempts, change places. (Where did you posi-

tion yourself to be able to defend the court area?)

7. Partners face a wall. One person throws a ball so that it rebounds off the wall. The partner attempts to field on the rebound. (What cues did you use to help you position yourself for the rebound?)

Batting

Batting, the skill used by the offensive team, requires judgments of speed and height, as well as the coordination of swinging the bat to meet the oncoming ball. The batter stands with the side of the body facing the pitcher with the knees slightly bent. The distance from home plate is determined by swinging the bat so the wide part of the hitting surface is over the plate. The hands grip the bat, with the front hand on the bottom and the arms up and away from the body. As the ball is pitched, the batter shifts the body weight to the rear foot and prepares to meet the ball with the bat. The bat is swung smoothly toward the ball. The batter should watch the ball to the bat. The release of the bat is controlled so it lands near home plate as the batter becomes a base runner.

Common errors:
1. Facing the pitcher.
2. Standing too close to the base.
3. Holding bat on the shoulder.
4. Not swinging the bat horizontally.
5. Throwing the bat.

Teaching suggestions: At times young batters may need to "choke up" on the bat by gripping the bat farther up on the handle to allow them better control in swinging the bat to meet the ball. For those having difficulty in batting, beginning with the bat up but in a horizontal plane may help. A batting tee may also be used to practice the swing and in games for children who are not yet ready to hit a moving ball.

Bunting is a modification of batting used in several offensive situations, for example, to advance a base runner. The batter shifts into position by stepping quickly toward the outside of the batter's box with the front foot ad bringing the rear foot up even with it. The toes point toward the pitcher, and the feet are shoulder width apart. As the feet shift the top hand is slid up the bat. The batter watches the

Figure 27-4

Evaluative criteria and teaching points for bunting.

- Face the batter before the ball release; keep knees slightly flexed.
- Slide top hand up toward trademark, fingers underneath, thumb on top.
- Hold bat parallel to ground chest high; elbows slightly away from body.
- Eyes on ball. Adjust body position to keep bat above ball.
- Contact ball out in front of plate, "giving" with hands and arms on contact.
- Ball should hit ground about 4' in front of plate on a sacrifice or 7' for a base hit and directed down the base lines away from pitcher and catcher.

ball and adjusts the body position by flexing the knees and arms to keep the bat above the ball. The hands and arms give on contact (as if catching) to control the ball's force and direction. The ball should be directed down the base lines.

Activities to practice batting:
1. Children are in groups of four: one catcher, one batter, one fielder, and one pitcher. Players switch positions after each batter has five hits. (What did you look for in a good pitch?)
2. Similar to activity 1, but vary size and weight of balls and bats. (What changes did you make to hit a larger or smaller ball? To use a heavier or lighter bat?)

Figure 27-5

Evaluative criteria and teaching points for running to first base.

- Run in a straight line while maintaining speed in reaching the base. (Slow down only after touching the base if stopping at first.)

3. Similar to activity 2, but two cones are placed in the field 5 yards apart. On the pitch, the batter attempts to hit the ball between the cones. Vary the distance between the cones depending on the ability of the players. (How did you modify your batting to hit the space between the cones?)

Base Running

The batter becomes a *base runner* when the ball is hit in fair territory. As the ball is hit, the batter pushes off the forward foot and steps on the rear foot toward first base. The runner runs to a spot beyond first base, maintaining speed until touching the base, in running stride. If stopping at first, the base runner comes back to the base, touching the inside of the base to wait for the next opportunity to run. If running for more than one base, the runner begins the turn by curving slightly outside the baseline and touching the inside corner of the base, as the run to the next base begins.

When waiting on base, with hips, knees, and ankles flexed, the runner leaves the base on the pitch. If the ball is not hit, base runners have the option of returning to the base or stealing if fast pitch rules are being used. On a fly ball, if desiring to proceed to

Figure 27-6

Evaluative criteria and teaching points for running for extra bases.

- Facing next base, forward stride with rear foot touching side of base.
- Flex hips, knees, and ankles for good take-off.
- Run in a straight path.

the next base, the runner must touch the base after the ball is caught, before proceeding to the next base.

Common errors:
1. Failing to run in a straight line.
2. Slowing down before reaching the base, especially failing to over run first base.
3. Failing to assume a ready position while waiting on base.
4. Not watching the play to determine what to do (such as running on a fly ball that is caught).

Activities to practice base running:
1. Groups of three or four are at each base of a softball diamond. On the signal, "go," one person from each group runs the bases, beginning at their base. After completing a trip around the bases, they tag the next person in their line, who then begins the run. The first group finishing wins. (What was the quickest way to round the base? Describe your path. Where did you touch the base?)

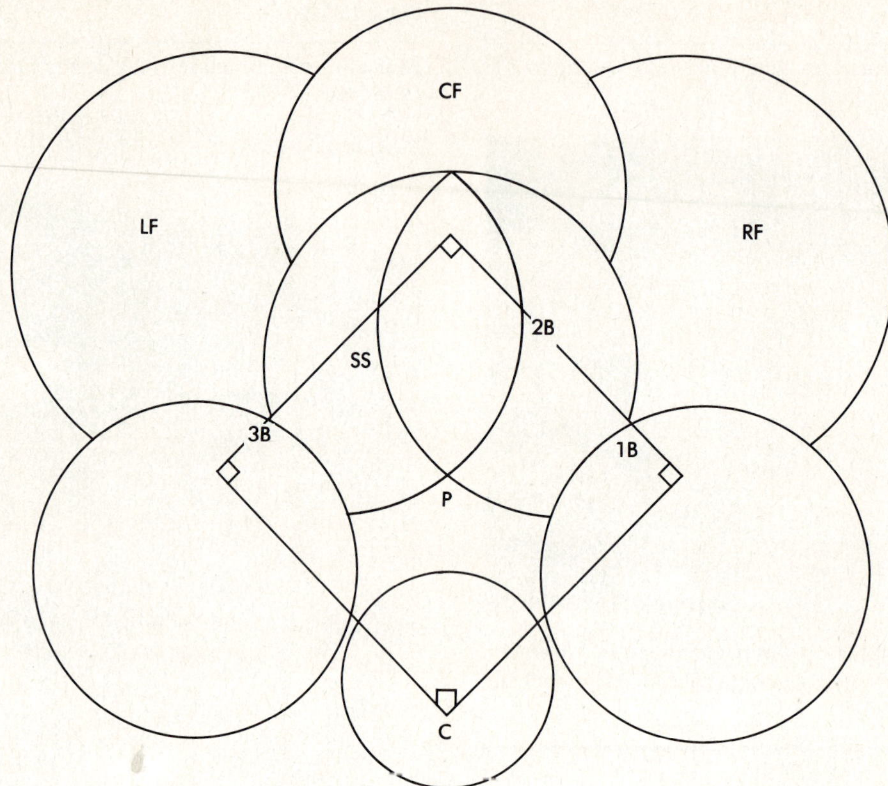

Figure 27-7

Areas covered by positions.

2. Children are in partners, two to each base. On the signal, the first runner attempts to run to the next base before being tagged by the partner. The starting distances between the runners should be two strides if running one base, three strides if running two bases, four strides for three bases, and five strides for a round trip. (What was the quickest path? How did you avoid the tag?)

Position Play

When playing a base and waiting for a throw, the foot should be kept on the side of the base so it will not be stepped on. When executing a force out, touch the base with the foot and move quickly away to avoid a collision with base runner.

Although all fielders have an area of the field for which they are responsible, they must be ready also to assist teammates in situations there they are not directly involved in the play. At times they may be called on to *cover* a base when the base player is involved in fielding a batted ball. In other situations they are needed to *back up* a play by positioning themselves behind a base player in line with a throw to a base or behind a fielder playing the ball so they can receive the ball in case of an error by the intended receiver.

There should be a back up on each play. Outfielders back up balls coming to adjacent areas, as well as the nearest base. Infielders back up balls coming to their adjacent areas. The pitcher will back up throws from the outfield to second and third bases and on throws from second to third. The catcher will back up first unless there are runners in a near scoring position (at second or third base).

Covering is specific to given situations. Generally someone is assigned to cover each base when the base player or catcher have been drawn away to field a ball.

SOFTBALL CONCEPTS

BODY AWARENESS

Body awareness is an important aspect of skill development. The use of body parts and their relationship in the skill sequence should be stressed in the presentation and practice of skills.

SPACE

Self and general space:
1. To cover general space while in the infield and outfield
2. To recognize the area of space to be covered by each position
3. To place the ball into an empty space while at bat
4. To move in the base path while running the bases

Direction:
5. To change direction quickly when covering one's area of the field and when fielding a ball
6. To assume a position that enables one to move in any direction

Level:
7. To throw the ball to an appropriate level when throwing to base players

Pathways:
8. To anticipate the pathway of the ball when fielding
9. To anticipate the path of the ball when backing up a teammate
10. To recognize the quickest pathway when running the bases

QUALITIES OF MOVEMENT

Force:
1. To use an appropriate amount of force in throwing various distances
2. To control and direct force in batting
3. To absorb force in catching and fielding
4. To control force in base running

Time:
5. To time base running with the pitch, the hit, and with other base runners
6. To judge the speed of the base runner to get the ball to the base and make an out

Flow:
7. To combine skills, such as batting and base running or fielding and throwing, into a smooth, continuous movement

Additional activities:
1. Organize a pentathlon in which the events are:
   a. Speed run of the bases.
   b. Distance or accuracy throw.
   c. Place hitting.
   d. Sprint to first.
   e. Pitching.

SOFTBALL CONCEPTS

The movement content important in softball is outlined in the box below. The activities that follow are a few of the possibilities for developing the movement content in softball activities.

Softball Concept Activities

Space:

In groups of four, two base players face each other with a player behind each as a back up. Throwers throw to each other, varying throws to the right, left, in front of, and behind the receiver. Back ups attempt to stay in line with the ball to get to any missed by the receiver. (What position enabled you to move balls quickly to get in line with the ball?)

In groups of three, a leader faces two players. The leader throws to one of the two players. As soon as the receiver is determined the second player moves into position to back up the throw. The back up stays in line with leader, ball, and fielder.

(What cues helped you to stay in line with the ball?)

Modify the game so any ball thrown or hit by the batter that lands in the field and gets through an empty space and is not fielded receives an extra point. (What did you look for to find the empty space?)

In two groups, children are scattered in two halves of a large rectangular playing area. There is at least one soft fleece ball for each two persons. Each team is divided into partners; one is the fielder, the other the back up. On the signal, each team throws the balls to the other team's half of the playing area. Any balls gotten by back ups score a point. (What position helped you move to cover the area and stay in line with the ball?)

Children are in groups of three, one batter and two fielders, with one base 15 feet from either fielder. The batter throws or bats the ball and attempts to run to the base before the ball gets there. One fielder attempts to field the ball while the other covers the base. (Where did you try to place the ball to give you more time to get to the base? Where did the base players want to receive the ball to make the play at the base?)

In groups of three or four, one person, who is in front of the others, throws the ball up. The fielder who will get it calls for it while another backs up the receiver. (How did you determine who would be the back up and the receiver?)

Force:

Children are in groups of five: one thrower, one base runner, one first base player and two infielders. The thrower throws the ball in the area of the infielders, who field the ball and throw it to first before the runner gets there. (What did you do to control the force needed to get the ball to the base so it could be received easily and before the runner arrived? What did you do as base runner to beat the ball to the base?)

Children are in groups of four: one catcher-thrower, two base players and one fielder. The catcher-thrower throws or bats the ball to the fielder, who throws to the base called for by the catcher. (How did you adjust force needed as you threw to the different bases?)

Using home and second and third bases, a thrower at home throws the ball to various places in the shortstop position. The thrower calls the base, and the shortstop throws the ball to the base. (Were the base players able to catch the ball each time? How did you control the force on the throws of varying distances?)

Time:

Children are in groups of eight to ten: one pitcher, one catcher, and the remaining players as base runners evenly distributed at first, second, and third bases. On the pitch, one runner from each base moves to the next base. The first player to the base wins. (What position enabled you to get a good start? Where did you focus your attention on the run?)

Children are in groups of five: one pitcher, one catcher, and three base runners. On the pitch, all three leave the base heading for the next base. The catcher calls fair or foul on receipt of the ball. If fair, runners proceed to the next base; if foul, they must go back. First to the base wins. (What position enabled you to move forward or back on the call? What cues did you use?)

Children are in groups of three: two base players and one runner. The runner attempts to run between the bases without getting tagged as the base players throw back and forth. (When did you time your run to make it safely?)

SOFTBALL LEAD-UP GAMES

An analysis of the games that follow may be found in Table 27-1.

LONG BASE

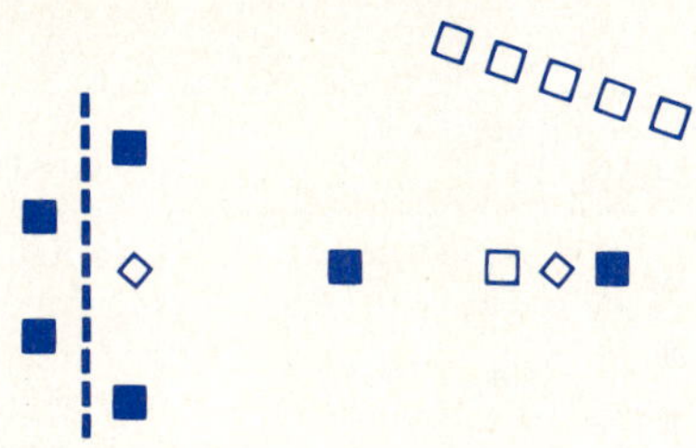

Level: III.

Equipment: Soft softball or leather-covered fleece ball, two bases, and batting tee (optional).

Area: A play area with two bases spaced so batting and fielding teams have an equal opportunity for success.

Participants: Six players per team.

Skills: Overhand throw and catch, fielding flies and grounders, base running.

Description: One team is "at bat," and the other is scattered in the playing area. The first batter throws the ball into the field and attempts to run to the base and back to touch home plate before the fielding team can get the ball to the catcher at home plate. One run is scored if successful. If the catcher gets the ball before the runner makes it home or a fly ball is caught, an out is recorded. After each member of the batting team has a turn, the two teams change positions.

Strategy: Place the ball into an empty space far from home plate. Be sure all areas of the "field" are covered.

Teaching Suggestions:

1. It may be necessary to add the following rule: the ball must touch the ground before the throwing line. This will discourage throwing the ball beyond the fielders and wasting playing time retrieving balls well out of the playing area.

2. This game may be modified to use batting from a batting tee in place of throwing the ball into the field.

BASE ON BALLS

Level: III.

Equipment: A soft softball or leather-covered fleece ball and batting tee (optional).

Area: A softball diamond with bases no more than 30 feet apart.

Participants: Six players per team.

Skills: Overhand throw, catching, fielding flies and grounders, base running, batting from a tee (optional).

Description: One team bats, and the other is scattered within the field, outside the base path. The first batter throws the ball into the field and runs the bases, attempting to get to home plate before the fielding team can get the ball to its catcher. After receiving the ball and stepping on the homeplate, the catcher calls,

"stop." The team counts the number of bases passed before the signal to stop was given, and the base runner then returns to the sidelines with the batting team. After each member of the batting team has a turn, the two teams change positions. A fly ball caught is an out, and no bases are recorded. The team's score is the total number of bases passed by each member.

Strategy: Try to place the ball into an empty space far from home plate. Determine what type of throw will keep the ball away from the fielders longer. Be sure all areas of the playing field are covered on defense.

Teaching Suggestions:

1. It may be necessary to add the rule that balls must touch the ground within the infield to keep the game moving.

2. Batting from a batting tee may be substituted for the throw.

BEAT BALL

Level: III.

Equipment: Soft softball, four bases, bats (optional), gloves (optional), and batting tee (optional).

Area: Softball diamond with bases spaced to provide equal opportunity for batting and fielding teams and not more than 30 feet apart.

Participants: Six players per team.

Skills: Overhand throw, catching, fielding flies and grounders, base running, batting (optional), pitching (optional).

Description: One team bats. The other team assumes the fielding positions of catcher, first-base player, second-base player, shortstop, third-base player, and pitcher. The pitcher throws the ball underhand to the batter. Each member of the batting team throws or bats the ball in turn into the playing area within the base lines. They then run the bases, attempting to get home before the fielding team can throw the ball to first base and then to the catcher at home plate. If the ball beats the player home or a fly ball is caught, an out is recorded. If successful, a run is scored. After each member of the batting team has had a turn at bat, the teams change positions. If the player at bat places the ball outside the base lines, it is a foul ball and the ball is replayed.

Strategy: Place the ball into an empty space away from first base. All players must cover their part of the playing area.

Teaching Suggestions:

1. When batting is used, the teacher, an aide, or the best controlled student should be the pitcher.

2. When batting is used, there are no strike outs. After five pitches, allow the batter to hit from a batting tee or throw the ball into the infield. This will keep the game moving and reduce the frustration of all players.

3. When the fielding team is able to get the base runners out easily, add another base so throws must

Table 27-1
Softball games analysis

Name	Game classification	No. of participants	Equipment	Space/organizational pattern	Motor skills
Long Base	Lead-up	Six per team	Soft softball or leather-covered fleece ball; two bases		Overhand throw Catching Fielding flies and grounders Base running
Base on Balls	Lead-up	Six per team	Soft softball or leather-covered fleece ball; four bases	Softball diamond with 30 feet between bases	Overhand throw Catching Fielding flies and grounders Base running
Beat Ball	Lead-up	Six per team	Soft softball; four bases; bats (optional); gloves (optional)	Softball diamond with 30 feet between bases	Overhand throw Catching Fielding flies and grounders Base running Use of a glove (optional) Batting (optional)
Throw It and Run	Lead-up	Six per team	Soft softball; four bases	Softball diamond with 30 feet between bases	Overhand throw Catching Fielding grounders and flies Base running
Work-up	Lead-up	Eight to 12 per game	Soft softball; four bases, bats; gloves	Softball diamond with two to three at bat and remainder assuming positions in the field	Overhand throw Catching Fielding flies and grounders Base running Batting Pitching
Modified Softball	Lead-up	Six per team	Soft softball; four bases; bat; gloves	Softball diamond with 30 to 35 feet between bases	Overhand throw Catching Fielding flies and grounders Base running Batting Pitching

*Numbers refer to the concepts given in the box on p. 515.

Modifications	Movement concepts*	Social structure	Strategy	Level
1. Add a throwing line beyond the base before which the ball must touch the ground	Self/general: 1, 3, 4 Direction: 5, 6 Level: 7 Pathways: 8, 10 Force: 1, 3, 4 Flow: 8	Social interaction I	1. Look for an empty space in which to put the ball when at bat 2. Be sure all areas of the field are covered on defense	III
1. Ball must touch the ground within baselines as it is thrown by the member at bat	Self/general: 1 to 4 Direction: 5, 6 Level: 7 Pathways: 8, 10 Force: 1, 3, 4 Flow: 8	Social interaction I	1. Look for an empty space in which to put the ball when at bat 2. What type of throw will keep the ball in the air longer and thus away from fielders longer? 3. Be sure all areas of the field are covered on defense	III
1. Since there are no strike outs, when batting is used, the batter should be allowed to throw the ball or hit off batting tee after five pitches 2. Rotate all positions except pitcher each inning	Self/general: 1 to 4 Direction: 5, 6 Level: 7 Pathways: 8, 10 Force: 1 to 4 Flow: 8	Social interaction II	1. Try to place the ball into an empty space 2. Each fielder covers a specific area of the playing field	III
1. Three outs or everyone bats (whichever happens first) constitutes half an inning 2. Ball must touch ground in base path 3. No strike-outs	Self/general: 1 to 4 Direction: 5, 6 Level: 7 Pathways: 8, 10 Force: 1, 3, 4 Time: 5 to 7 Flow: 8	Social interaction II	1. Cover your area on defense 2. Place the ball into an empty space and with greatest time in the air 3. Do not slow down before reaching first base	III
1. No strike outs: walk to first base after five pitches, or throw into in-field, or hit from tee 2. Use force outs only 3. Do not rotate pitchers	Self/general: 1 to 4 Direction: 5, 6 Level: 7 Pathways: 8, 10 Force: 1 to 4 Time: 5 to 7 Flow: 8	Social interaction II	1. Cover your area while in the field	IV
1. Rotate positions each inning 2. Best student or teacher pitches 3. Use extra catcher to help retrieve pitches 4. No strike outs	Self/general: 1 to 4 Direction: 6 Level: 7 Pathways: 8 to 10 Force: 1 to 4 Time: 5 to 7 Flow: 8	Social interaction III	1. Cover your area on defense 2. Back up teammates when fielding or playing the base 3. Run quickly to first base; do not slow down	IV

be made to second, to first, and then to home.

4. If batting is used, gloves should be worn (even with a soft softball), because some children are timid in fielding batted balls.
5. Children should rotate positions each inning, except for the pitcher, who must be the one with the most controlled underhand throw.
6. Emphasize position play, especially for base players who must be responsible for a larger area than just the base.
7. To discourage throwing the bat, make it an out after the first time.

THROW IT AND RUN

Level: III.
Equipment: Soft softball and four bases.
Area: Softball diamond with bases 30 feet apart.
Participants: Six players per team.
Skills: Overhand throw, underhand throw (pitch), catching, fielding flies and grounders, base running.
Description: One team is at bat, and the other team assumes the fielding positions of catcher, pitcher, first-base player, second-base player, shortstop, and third-base player. The pitcher throws the ball to the first "batter," who throws the ball into the field of play. The batter then runs the bases, taking as many as possible before stopping on one of them. The fielding team attempts to put the runner out by getting the ball to the base before the runner gets there (force outs). A runner not making it to home waits on base until the next batter throws the ball. Each time a runner makes it safely to homeplate one run is scored. If the ball gets

to the base ahead of the runner or a fly ball is caught, an out is recorded. After each member of the batting team has had one time at bat, the teams change positions.
Strategy: Be in position to cover your area when on defense. Run quickly, and do not slow down before reaching first base. Place the ball into an empty space and with as much air time as possible.
Teaching Suggestions:
1. Innings may be modified to include three outs or to have everyone bat (whichever happens first.
2. Stress position play, especially for base players, as they tend to stand on the base rather than in a position to cover their area of the field.
3. Have children rotate positions each inning, with the exception of the pitcher.

WORK-UP

Level: IV.
Equipment: Soft softball, four bases, bats, and gloves.
Area: Softball diamond with bases spaced 30 feet apart.
Participants: Eight to twelve players per game.
Skills: Overhand throw, catching, fielding flies and grounders, base running, batting.
Description: Three players are at bat, and the remaining players assume field positions. Softball rules are used. Each batting player takes a turn at bat, hitting the ball into the field and running the bases. When batting, players make an out or after three at bats, they take a position in right field (depending on the number of players), and all other fielders rotate one position as follows: right field to center field to left field to third

base to shortstop to second base to first base to pitcher to catcher to batter.

Strategy: Be sure to cover your area while in the field. Run quickly to first base, and step on the base at full speed.

Teaching suggestions:

1. It may be best to have no strike outs and have the player take first base (walk) after five pitches, hit from the batting tee, or throw the ball so it lands in the infield.
2. You may not want to rotate everyone to pitcher, as this position requires the most control.
3. Have all outs be force outs (ball reaches base before runner).

MODIFIED SOFTBALL

Level: IV.
Equipment: Soft softball, four bases, bats, and gloves.
Area: Softball diamond with bases spaced 30 feet apart.
Participants: Six players per team.
Skills: Overhand throw, catching, fielding flies and grounders, base running, batting, pitching.
Description: Softball rules are used with the following exceptions:

1. Distance between bases is 30 feet.

2. There are six players per team.
3. All outs are force outs.
4. There are no strike outs. After five pitches, the batter walks to first, hits from the batting tee, or throws the ball into the infield.
5. No stealing is allowed.
6. The teacher, an aide, or the best student pitches.
7. After everyone has had a turn at bat, the batting team changes positions with the fielding team, or the teacher sets a time limit for the batting team to provide equal time for both teams to bat.

Strategy:

1. Cover your area on defense.
2. Run quickly to first base. You should touch first base at full speed.
3. Back up teammates when fielding or playing the bases.

Teaching Suggestions:

1. Rotate positions each inning.
2. It may be helpful to have a member of the batting team stand behind the catcher to help retrieve balls, as catching skills may not be well developed yet.
3. Teach backing up throws and fielding for better team defense.

SUMMARY

Softball is a popular game with elementary school children, yet it requires the greatest accuracy in the execution of skills and an understanding of a complex set of rules. Game modifications are necessary to ensure the success of everyone. A smaller diamond and a softer ball are needed. Elimination of the strike out rule and provision for the best possible pitching will help children gain confidence in this team game. The concepts of space, time, and force are very important as children attempt to cover the playing area on defense, to control the force of throws, and to time movements around the bases with other base runners, the pitcher, and the ball. A great variability of ability exists in softball at the elementary school level. Modifications should allow for individual differences as well as keep the game moving.

REFERENCES

1. Jones, B., and Murray, M.: Softball concepts for coaches and teachers, Dubuque, Iowa, 1978, William C. Brown, Publisher.
2. Kneer, M., and McCord, C.: Softball slow and fast pitch, ed. 2, Dubuque, Iowa, 1976, William C. Brown, Publisher.
3. Seidel, B., and others: Sports skills: a conceptual approach to meaningful movement, ed. 2, Dubuque, Iowa, 1980, William C. Brown, Publisher.

ADDITIONAL READINGS

Lopiano, D.: Practice, JOPER **52**(3):28, March 1981.
  Station activities for indoor practice, many of which can be adapted for use with elementary school children.
Arnold, L.: Exercise, JOPER **52**(3):31, March 1981.
  Stretching activities for warming up.
Well, L., and Wright, M.: Pitching, JOPER **52**(3):28, March 1981.
  How to throw various pitches and an analysis of errors and needed corrections.
4. Well, L., and Wright, M.: Offense, JOPER **52**(3):34 March 1981.
  An analysis of batting, including bunting, with an analysis of errors and suggested corrections.
5. Peterson, S.: Softball without strikes, JOPERD **52**(7):72, September 1981.
  A progression for teaching and using batting skills during the elementary school years.

28

NET GAMES AND VOLLEYBALL

CHAPTER OBJECTIVES

1 To identify modifications necessary for teaching net games and volleyball at the elementary school level

2 To analyze the skills used in net games and volleyball and to suggest activities for their development

3 To outline the relationships between the movement content and net games and volleyball and to describe movement activities to help children understand these relationships

4 To describe a series of progressively more difficult lead-up activities for use during the elementary school years

Of all the net games, volleyball is the most popular game played recreationally by adults in the United States from the beaches of California to the gymnasiums and recreation centers of the east coast. Originating in the United States, volleyball is becoming an important international game and an exciting spectator sport as well. Volleyball is unique among team sports. It is a rebound sport rather than a possession sport. It is a game in which the ball is continually moving, being held stationary only prior to the service.

Power volleyball requires a high level of difficult skills, yet with modifications of rules, the novice as well as the highly skilled player is able to enjoy the game. Skilled players must have a variety of striking skills at their disposal, including the serve, overhead volley, forearm pass, spike, and block. Participants in volleyball must assume a ready position that enables them to move in relation to the ball so that the needed skill may be executed accurately. They know not only when to use each skill but also are able to vary the skill in force and placement. The volleyball player executes skills using the full range of level from a few inches above the floor to high overhead and must be able to do so from all positions on the court.

The volleyball participant must be a team player. Although each player has the personal responsibility for coverage of a particular area of the court, each must also accept responsibility for the team effort. The fast-moving game demands assisting teammates in their efforts to win the point or service by coming to their aid when a skill has been poorly executed or ill placed. In volleyball there are few one on one confrontations, but there is truly a team effort as one team goes against the other.

NET GAMES FOR ELEMENTARY SCHOOL CHILDREN

Net games are good for children in that they provide an opportunity for group cooperation and sharing as well as a progression of activities that gradually demands greater use of striking skills.

Equipment: One difficulty in helping children acquire skills involving striking with the hands has been the availability of a ball of an appropriate size and weight. With the introduction of light, plastic or foam balls, some of them specifically designed for volleyball, good striking skills are developed much faster and with fewer injuries to fingers and wrists.

The net height should be adjusted to the level of skill of the children and is usually no higher than fingertip height. Some net games call for a lower net. The court size best suited for elementary school children is approximately 17 feet wide by 44 feet long, or about the size of a badminton court. The size might need to be further reduced for games in which there are four on a team.

Skills: Elementary school children generally lack experience in striking with the hands, especially in an overhand fashion, but this is the most frequently used pattern in volleyball. Volleyball skills are difficult to master. Therefore, a series of net games in which striking skills are gradually introduced is appropriate if children are to be successful. The progression should allow the modification of rules for individual players, since there is a great variation in the children's abilities to execute the skills. Children are usually challenged to attempt the most difficult skill they can master, but they should not be penalized because their skills are under development. It may be necessary to allow some children to catch the ball before setting or forearm passing to themselves to ensure success for all. When serving, having several service lines available, some closer to the net, may aid children in not only getting the ball over the net but also in serve placement. Modifications such as these are acceptable to the group, since each team wants to do its best and have its best chance for success. The return of service is one of the most difficult aspects of the game. As the children begin to master the overhead volley and forearm pass, a modification allowing catching and the set to themselves when receiving the serve may still be needed if the game is to be more than a serving battle.

The game: With the modifications already suggested, elementary school children can find success in net games. Modifications of skills for individuals help create an atmosphere where individual differences find acceptance, each child is successful, and a climate for sharing and teamwork is enhanced. Team work and sharing are not automatic outcomes of games. Children should be encouraged to get the ball to the most advantageous position before sending it over the net by passing to teammates. To ensure team work, at times it may be necessary to require several passes on a side or that only net players may hit the ball over the net.

Since net games are not fast-moving games for beginners, there is often time for poor social behavior especially within the team between points. This is often the result of frustration by the better skilled children for the lack of success of their lesser skilled classmates. Modification of skills for individuals will usually minimize these problems. However, points might also be awarded during or at the end of the game for the team that worked the best together, thus encouraging the development of a helpful, cooperative effort by all children.

The strategies involved in net games take time to develop. Therefore, each unit should be limited to one or two different lead-up games. The children will then have time to experiment with various strategies once the rules are learned.

The offensive team attempts to keep the serve and to score points while the defensive team tries to regain the serve by forcing their opponents into making errors.

The offense attempts to:
1. Serve to an open area of the opponent's court.
2. Move the ball to the most advantageous position on the court before returning it over the net.
3. Change the expected path of the ball.
4. Place the ball in an empty space in the opponent's court on all returns.

The defense attempts to:
1. Cover the area of the court, closing spaces to opponents.
2. Assist each other in controlling the ball as it comes over the net.
3. Move to the offense incorporating the above offensive strategy to force the serving team to make errors.

NET GAMES AND VOLLEYBALL SKILLS

The nature of net games and volleyball lead-ups provides a unique opportunity for participants. Unlike most team games in which players are moving over a large area, the participant is responsible for a relatively small space. This space must be carefully defended, so players assume a ready position from which they are able to move in any direction and to change level if necessary to get into position to play the ball.

Net games and volleyball lead-ups are unique in that there is a more conscientious preparation for the execution of skills, since the ball may not rest even momentarily in the hands. This readiness and preparation are vital to ball control. Volleyball skills require the use of the entire body to control and impart force to the ball, with the legs assuming a more important role than they do in many skills. This requires greater coordination of body parts in the sequencing of the striking movement for efficient and effective performance.

The important concepts involved in skills development are body awareness, including use and relationship of body parts; space, the relationship between striker and the ball; the selection of appropriate skills based on the level at which the ball is received; and the control of force in the reception and propulsion of the ball.

Many injuries to fingers and wrists are the result of failure to prepare those body parts adequately for the skills involved. Even with the lighter weight balls it is a good idea to have children prepare for the activities with a brief period of warm ups. Warm-up activities include the following:

1. Opening and closing the fingers.
2. Squeezing a tennis ball.
3. Shaking the wrists quickly forward and backward and from side to side.
4. Rotating the wrists in a figure eight fashion.
5. With fingers of both hands touching, open and close fingers.

Activities to practice each skill may be found following the explanation and analysis of each. It is assumed that several groups of children may practice on each court since most of the activities require relatively little space.

The Ready Position

The *ready position* is essential to controlled play on the court and is maintained throughout the game in preparation to receive the ball. The player assumes a somewhat crouched position. The feet are in a stride position with one foot forward of the other. As the ball approaches the player is ready to move in any direction into position to play the ball.

Common errors:
1. Carrying weight on the entire foot.
2. Maintaining an upright posture.
3. Not paying attention to the ball.
4. Holding arms straight down or in pockets.

The Pass and Set

Throwing and *Catching* are skills used in early net games. An analysis of these skills is found in Chapter

Figure 28-1

Evaluative criteria and teaching points for ready position.

- Feet in stride position, weight on balls of feet and flexion in hips, knees, and ankles.
- Arms down and to sides, elbows bent.
- Head up and eyes on ball.

11. The *overhead volley* is the best controlled skill in volleyball. It is used in **passing** to the setter and in **setting** to the spiker. The ball is contacted at a point above and in front of the forehead with the fingers of both hands simultaneously.

As the skill is executed there is an increase in knee and hip flexion to allow for full extension of the body as contact is made. The hands are up, elbows flexed and out from the sides. The wrists are bent slightly backward. The head is up and looking up toward the ball. The player assumes this position directly in line with and slightly under the approaching ball. As contact is made with the fingers, the wrists spring forward to help give impetus to the ball. The ball is projected upward several feet above the receiver's head.

Common errors:
1. Not getting in line with the ball.
2. Contacting ball too low in front of the chest

Figure 28-2

Evaluative criteria and teaching points for overhead volley.

- Forward stride, knees bent.
- Fingers spread, elbows bent to sides. Ball contact above and in front of forehead with finger pads.

- Knees and hips extend on contact; wrists spring foward as body extends.
- Follow through up and in direction of flight.

and pushing it forward rather than upward.
3. Contacting with fleshy part of the hands.
4. Not flexing and then extending knees and hips.
5. Stiffening wrists on contact.

Teaching suggestions: The overhead volley is a difficult skill, but modifications can be made for beginning young players. A progression for learning the skill follows. Emphasis should be on getting into a position in line with and under the ball, using the finger pads for a legal contact, flexing and extending the legs in the execution, and putting the ball into the space above the receiver when passing and setting.

1. The individual catches the ball, tosses it up to an appropriate height directly above, gets into position, and then hits the ball. (The biggest difficulties in volleyball are the return of the serve and, for many children, merely hitting a ball coming toward them. In this manner children have more time to execute the skill, to get into an appropriate relationship with the ball, and do not have to deal with the oncoming force.)
2. As the children gain confidence in their ability to hit the ball, net players may hit the ball directly, since balls coming just over the net are probably coming more softly. (Note that

Figure 28-3

Evaluative criteria and teaching points for forearm pass.

- Forward-backward stride; hips, knees, and ankles flexed.
- Contact on flat surface.

- Waist bent (90 degrees).
- Extension of knees, hips, and ankles.
- Follow through in direction of flight.

children should only attempt to hit the balls that are received at an appropriate height for the overhead volley until the forearm pass is learned.)

3. Later, back line players may be given the option of catching first or hitting directly those balls coming to their position.

The *forearm pass* is used to play balls received below chest height. The ball is contacted so that it rebounds off the two forearms simultaneously. This is one of the most difficult skills to control.

The passer assumes a position directly in line with the ball. The body is low, allowing the player to get well under the ball. The hands are held in a manner that presents the forearms evenly to the ball, with attention focused on position of the forearms. This may be accomplished by placing the back of one hand on the palm of the other and rotating the arms so the thumbs are parallel. The arms are held out and away from the body. Ball contact should be at the middle of the forearms. As contact is made the hips, knees, and ankles straighten to give impetus to the ball with the weight moving to the forward foot. On the follow through the body action continues in an upward and outward direction in the line of flight. Emphasize keeping arm surface even throughout contact and follow through.

Common errors:

1. Hitting off an uneven surface.
2. Swinging the arms upward and backward on contact. (The ball should rebound from arms.)
3. Failing to be in line with the ball.
4. Not getting under the ball in preparation for contact.
5. Not using hip, knee, and ankle flexion and extension.

6. Not maintaining a right angle relationship of arms and body.

Teaching suggestions:

1. A progression similar to that for the overhead volley should be used. Allow the children to catch the ball and then toss and hit it first to give them the opportunity to become comfortable with the position and body action. Once this is achieved, they will be ready to get into position for an oncoming ball.
2. This skill should be introduced after the children have experienced some success with the modified overhead volley and the underhand serve.

Activities to practice the pass and set (using a modified or regulation volley or forearm pass):

1. Passing to a partner, vary the distance between partners. (What did you do to get the ball to your partner when the distance increased? Decreased?)
2. In groups of three, two are on one side of the net, and one is on the other. A hits the ball over the net to B, who returns it to A. A then hits the ball to C, who returns it to A. Rotate positions periodically. (What did you do differently to pass the ball the longer distance?) Variation: Have C also vary distance by passing back to A directly on first receipt and to B on the second.

3. Three players are in a line spread across the court. One player on the opposite side of the net using the volley sends the ball over the net, calling the name of the receiver who will receive it at the high level. (How did you move to direct the ball to the named receiver? Were some pathways more difficult? Why?) Variation: Vary the distance receivers are from the net, changing distance after each successful volley.

4. Children are numbered in groups of four. Players 1 and 2 are on one side of the net and parallel to the net, and 3 and 4 are on the other side of the net, positioned in a similar manner. Player 1 sets the ball to 2, who hits it over the net to 3. Player 3 sets to 4, who hits it back over the net to 1. Change positions after a few tries. (Note that as play continues 1 and 3 will have to select either the overhead volley or the forearm pass, depending on the level the ball is received.)

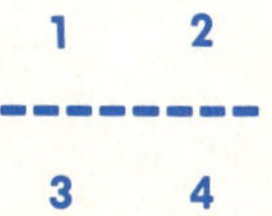

5. Children are in partners scattered in the playing area. Partners pass to a spot to the side of, in front of, or behind their partner. The receiver must move to get into position to receive the ball to pass back. (What ready position enabled you to move easiest to balls to the side of you? In front? Behind? Where did you want to be when you received the ball?)
6. In groups of four, each group has a wall space. Player A volleys the ball to the wall and moves to position D. Other players shift one position clockwise, with B moving to position A to receive the ball. If the ball cannot be received in a high level, catch it and begin again. (Count your consecutive successful hits. What did you have to do to get into position to receive the ball? Where did you attempt to place the ball so the next person could receive it?)

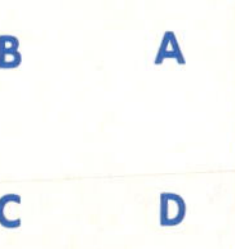

7. Children pass to a partner, varying the level at which the ball will be received. (What did you do to get into position for a high pass? Low pass? Which was easiest to control? How did you vary your hits so they would be received at a low level? High level? What skill did you use for a ball received low? High?)
8. In partners, the receiver calls the level at which the ball is to be received and acts accordingly by moving into the correct position to receive

Figure 28-4

Evaluative criteria and teaching points for underhand serve.

- Opposite foot is forward.
- Ball is held at waist height in front and to the side.
- Contact is made below and behind the ball.

- Weight is transferred to forward foot.
- Follow through in direction of flight.

it. Change receivers after five tries. (How did you control the pass so it could be received at the appropriate level? What position did you assume for balls received in the high level? Low level? Can you keep it going?)

Serve

The serve is used to put the ball in play. Although generally the floater or overhand serving action is used in power volleyball, because of its greater effectiveness the underhand serve is easiest for most elementary school children to master. The *underhand serve* is the easiest serve for both the server and the receiver to control. The ball is contacted by the hand in an underhand swinging motion.

The server assumes a forward-backward stride position behind the service line. The striking arm is brought back and then forward in an underhand swinging motion to contact the ball. Contact with the hand may be made from several hand positions: (1) open hand, contact on the fleshy part of the thumb and hand; (2) with a fist, hand facing upward, contact on fleshy part of the thumb and curled fingers; and (3) a fist, turned sideways so that contact is made on the side of the curled index finger and thumb. The hand and arm continue moving forward and upward in the line of flight.

Common errors:
1. Not planning placement.
2. Placing the incorrect foot forward.
3. Holding or moving the ball to a position that is too high for an effective hit.
4. Failing to transfer weight to forward foot.
5. Not following through.

The *floater serve* uses an overhand hitting position and is difficult to return. The server stands behind the service line with the foot opposite the striking hand forward. The striking hand is raised with the elbow high and arm back so movement is a forward motion only. The controlled ball toss is just high enough so that the ball can be contacted at full extension. The ball is contacted with an open hand, with impetus given by the heel of the hand. The arm

Figure 28-5

Evaluative criteria and teaching points for floater serve.

- Foot in forward-backward stride, weight on rear foot.
- Striking hand raised, elbow high.
- Controlled ball toss.

- Weight transfer to forward foot.
- Contact high and in front of the body.

- Contact with open hand hitting off heel.
- Follow through up and in direction of flight.

continues its motion following through upward and in the direction of flight. The point of contact and the direction of the swing will determine the ball's flight.

Common errors:
1. Not planning placement.
2. Placing the incorrect foot forward.
3. Not making contact at full extension.
4. Not coordinating toss, weight transfer, and contact.
5. Failing to follow through.

Activities to practice the serve:
1. One server faces three players on the opposite side of the net. Opponents call the area, and the server attempts to get the ball into that area. After three to five serves, change positions.

   Variation: Modify the service line if necessary. (What did you do to get the ball into the designated area? Which area was hardest to hit? Why?)

2. One player is on each side of the net with a limited court area. One person moves to a new position, and the server attempts to place the ball in an open space in the court. Change position and server and repeat. (How did you change your movements to get the ball deep in the court? Left or right? Just over the net?)

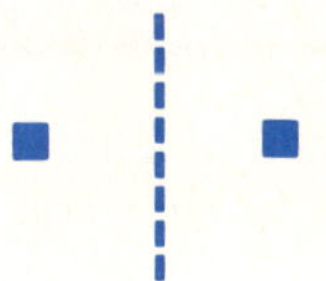

NET GAMES AND VOLLEYBALL CONCEPTS

The concepts to be emphasized in net games and volleyball lead-ups are outlined in the box on p. 530. Activities follow to be selected for inclusion in the daily lessons.

Net Games and Volleyball Concept Activities

Modification of game procedures and scoring may be used to reinforce movement concepts in net

NET GAMES AND VOLLEYBALL CONCEPTS

BODY AWARENESS

Body awareness concepts are important in the analysis of skills in developing an understanding of how body parts are used in the execution of each skill.

SPACE

Self and general space:

1. To move the ball within the boundaries of the court
2. To move on the court in relationship to others, the net, and the boundaries
3. To use all areas of the available space
4. To recognize one's own area of general space to be defended
5. To pass the ball to a space above a teammate
6. To place the ball into an empty space in the opponents' court
7. To close spaces open to opponents
8. To move in relationship to a ball to be contacted, in line with and directly under the ball

Direction:

9. To assume a position that enables one to move in any direction
10. To change direction quickly to cover one's area of the court and to get into position to play the ball

Level:

11. To play the ball with appropriate skills at the low, medium, and high levels
12. To put the ball into the high level when passing to teammates

Pathways:

13. To recognize available pathways within which to move the ball
14. To anticipate the path of the ball coming into one's court
15. To change the expected pathway as the ball is sent into opponents' court

QUALITIES OF MOVEMENT

Force:

1. To impart force to the ball with different body parts
2. To use an appropriate amount of force in passing to teammates and keeping the ball in bounds
3. To vary the force imparted to the ball
4. To absorb force with different body parts

games. A few suggestions follow. Many of the small-group activities may be played on court areas smaller than the size used for lead-up games to maximize the number of children participating at one time. All require controlling force and using space effectively.

The server calls the name of the player to receive the ball. If the server gets it to the player named, a bonus point is earned. The server may not serve it to the same person again until all have had the opportunity to receive the serve. If the serve is received in the appropriate area, it may be returned and play continues with volleyball scoring. (What did you do to get the ball to the desired area?)

Following the serve, the players in the right back court of both teams call the placement of the ball each time it is received across the net. If the ball is accurately placed, 1 bonus point is scored. No player may receive the ball twice in succession. (To what areas of the court was it most difficult to get the ball? What could you do to make it easier?)

Each player plays against an opponent on the other side of the net. Scoring occurs only when a ball lands in bounds, not touched by an opponent. Variations: Doubles with two on each team or three or four on a team. (What did you do to get the ball in the empty space? How did you vary your hits? What position helped you cover your court area?)

Each team, composed of two or three players, creates a new empty space after each hit. The receiving team must look to see where it is for ball placement. One point is awarded each time a hit is made

into the open space. Opponents attempt to get the ball but may not move into the empty space to cover it. (When did you look for the empty space? How did you get the ball to it?)

Play a game in which points are scored only when the ball hits an empty space.

Variation: Award 1 bonus point when the ball hits an empty space. (When did you plan placement of the ball? How did you change placement to hit the empty space?)

NET GAMES AND VOLLEYBALL LEAD-UPS

A games analysis of the games included here may be found in Table 28-1.

BATTLEBALL

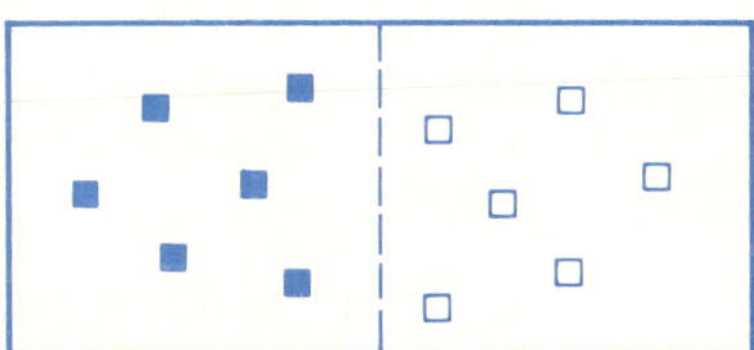

Level: II.

Equipment: Six to eight foam balls, one net, and two net standards.

Area: A rectangular area divided into two courts by a net or rope stretched across the width at a height of about 6 feet.

Participants: Two teams of six to eight players each.

Skills: Throwing, catching.

Description: Each team is in a scattered formation on its own half of the court. The balls are evenly distributed between the two teams. On the signal, each team throws the balls over the net into the opponents' court. The teams continue to catch and throw until the signal to stop is given. The team with the fewest balls on its side wins.

Strategy: Look for empty space. Cover all areas of the

Table 28-1
Net and volleyball games analysis

Name	Game classification	No. of participants	Equipment	Space/organizational pattern	Motor skills
Battleball	Net game	Six to eight per team	Six to eight foam balls; one net 6 feet high; standards		Throwing Catching
Newcomb	Net game	Four to six per team	One volleyball or playground ball; net at fingertip height; badminton sized court		Throwing Catching Passing
Advanced Newcomb	Lead-up	Four to six per team	One foam, plastic or soft volleyball; badminton sized court; net at fingertip height		Catching Modified volley Modified forearm pass (optional)
Deck Tennis	Net game	Two to six per team	One deck tennis ring; 4 foot 8 inch net; deck tennis or badminton sized court		Throwing and catching the deck tennis ring
Modified Volleyball	Lead-up	Four to six per team	Badminton-size court; net at fingertip height; one soft volleyball or foam ball		Catching Modified volley Modified forearm pass Underhand serve Optional: Volley Forearm pass Floater serve

*Numbers refer to those concepts in the box on p. 530.

court. Move the ball quickly to the net.

Teaching Suggestions: The teacher must be alert to balls that are in the air as the signal to stop is given and to see that those balls thrown after the signal are recorded for the appropriate team. Having the children put the balls on the floor when the signal to stop is given may help.

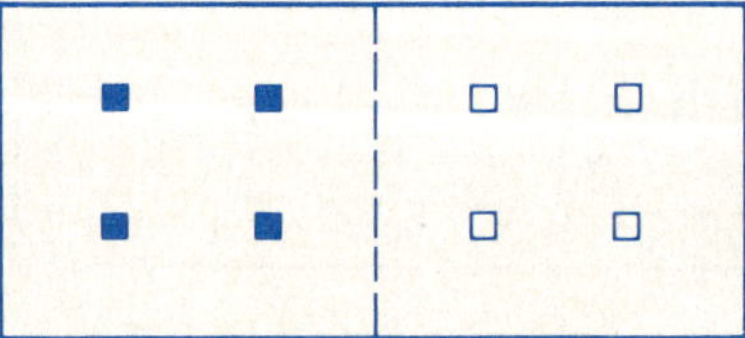

Level: II.
Equipment: One volleyball or playground ball, one net, and two net standards.
Area: A court approximately 20 feet wide by 44 feet deep with a net at fingertip height.

Modifications	Movement concepts*	Social structure	Strategy	Level
1. Use overhand throw for high balls, an underhand throw for low balls	Self/general: 1 to 4, 6, 7 Direction: 9, 10 Pathways: 13 to 15 Force: 3	Social interaction I	1. Get rid of ball quickly 2. Look for empty spaces 3. Cover all areas of the court	II
1. Players in back row may not throw ball over the net, but must pass to net players 2. Require two passes per side	Self/general: 1 to 4, 6, 7 Direction: 9, 10 Pathways: 13 to 15 Force: 2, 3	Social interaction II	1. Pass to teammates 2. Look for empty spaces 3. Change expected path of ball 4. Vary force in returning ball over the net	II
1. Allow several service lines, some closer to net 2. Players in the back row must pass to net players	Self/general: 1 to 8 Direction: 9, 10 Level: 11, 12 Pathways: 13 to 15 Force: 1 to 4	Social interaction II	1. Pass to teammates 2. Look for empty spaces 3. Change expected path of ball 4. Vary force in returning ball over the net	III
	Self/general: 1 to 4, 6, 7 Direction: 9, 10 Pathways: 13 to 15 Force: 2, 3	Social interaction II	1. In team deck tennis use passing to get the ring into a better position 2. Vary types of throws used 3. Look for empty spaces and change expected ring path	III
1. First and second contacts may be caught, third must be hit 2. Move closer to net to serve 3. Three hits per side maximum. 4. Only front line may hit the ball over the net	Self/general: 1 to 8 Direction: 9, 10 Level: 11, 12 Pathways: 13 to 15 Force: 1 to 4	Social interaction III	1. Pass to teammates 2. Look for empty spaces 3. Change expected path of ball 4. Vary force in returning ball over the net	IV

Participants: Two teams of four to six players.

Skills: Throwing, catching.

Description: The ball is put into play by one member of the serving team standing in the right back court. The ball is thrown over the net into the opponents' court. The opposing team catches the ball and returns it to the serving team. Play continues with each team throwing the ball back to the opposing team until one team (1) fails to keep the ball in bounds, (2) fails to throw the ball over the net, or (3) allows the ball to touch the floor in its court. For any of these infractions the opposing team scores. Each team serves three times and then service is given to the opponents. Each team rotates positions in a clockwise manner before beginning the service.

Strategy: Pass to get the ball into the best position before sending it over the net. Look for empty spaces in which to put the ball. Change the expected path of the ball. Vary the force used in placing the ball just over the net or deep into your opponents' court.

Teaching Suggestions: Encourage the children to pass to their teammates and to move the ball quickly. If passing does not occur, introduce a rule to require two passes per side before sending the ball over the net or not to allow the back row players to throw directly over the net.

DECK TENNIS

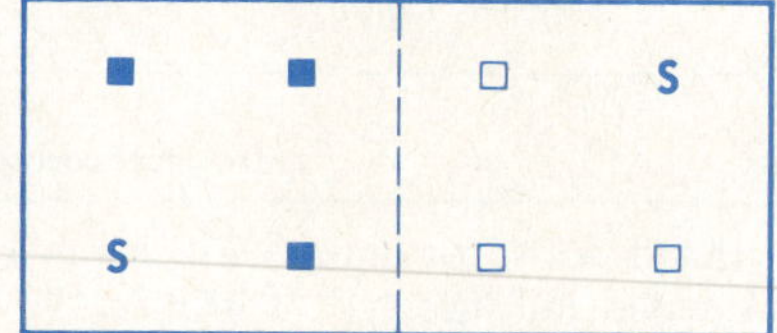

Level: III.

Equipment: One deck tennis ring, one net, and two net standards.

Area: A court 12 feet wide by 40 feet deep. The net is stretched between the courts at a height of 4 feet 8 inches. The width of the court is increased to 17 feet for four players and 22 feet for six players.

Participants: Two teams of two to six players.

Skills: Throwing and catching the deck tennis ring.

Description: The ring may be legally thrown in two ways: (1) with a backhand or forehand motion so that it moves in an arc parallel to the floor or (2) in an end over end manner usually initiated in an underhand motion. It may not be thrown so that it moves perpendicular to the floor. The server begins play by throwing the ring into the opponents' court from a position behind the base line. If the ring hits the net, it may be played by the receiving team if it chooses, or reserved if it falls within the court boundaries. Points are only scored while serving. When the serving team fails to serve the ring within the boundaries of its opponents' court or fails to return the ring legally over the net on the rally, it loses the serve. Rings landing on boundary lines are considered inbounds. The first team to score 15 points wins. A team must win by 2 points.

Strategy: Encourage passing among the teammates, moving the ring to the best position before sending it across the net, looking for empty spaces, and changing the path of the ring. Vary the throws used.

Teaching Suggestions: If played with three or more players to a team, a rotation system should be used in which, on winning the serve, players rotate in a clockwise manner to the next position on the court. If passing does not occur, a rule requiring one or two passes per side may be instituted to ensure more team play. Encourage children to get rid of the ring quickly.

ADVANCED NEWCOMB

Level: III.

Equipment: One volleyball sized foam ball, plastic ball, or soft volleyball; one net.

Area: A court approximately 20 by 44 feet, with a net at fingertip height.

Participants: Two teams of four to six players.

Skills: Catching, modified overhead volley, modified forearm pass (optional).

Description: Similar to Newcomb, with the following exceptions:

1. Score as in volleyball. Points are only scored when serving.
2. Use the modified volley (catch, toss to self, hit) for service and all balls received in the high level.
3. Use the modified forearm pass (catch, toss to self, hit) for balls received in the medium or low levels.

Strategy: Pass to get the ball into the best position before sending it over the net. Look for empty spaces in which to put the ball. Change the expected path of the ball. Vary the force used in placing the ball just over the net or deep into your opponents' court.

Teaching Suggestions: Encourage passing to a space above teammates and not at them. Rules that require passing may have to be introduced as in Newcomb. Emphasize a good toss and getting body in line with and under ball. Several service lines, some closer to the net, may be needed to enable everyone to have success on the service.

MODIFIED VOLLEYBALL

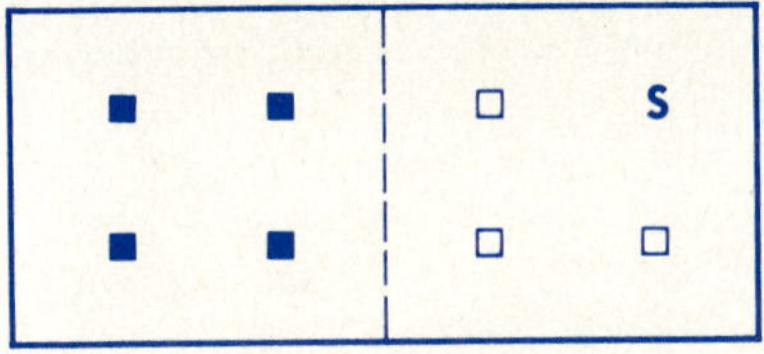

Level: IV.

Equipment: One foam ball, one net, and two net standards.

Area: A court approximately 20 by 44 feet, with a net at fingertip height.

Participants: Two teams of four to six players.

Skills: Underhand serve, modified overhead volley, modified forearm pass. Optional: floater serve, overhead volley, forearm pass.

Description: Similar to Advanced Newcomb, but Modified Volleyball uses volleyball rules, with the following exceptions:

1. Players may catch the ball and then use the modified volley or forearm pass.
2. As skills improve children should be encouraged to use the optional skills, beginning with net players volleying balls received as passes from teammates, and later balls received directly from opponents. The receipt of service is the most difficult to return, with the balls coming to back row players being more difficult than those coming to net players.
3. Several service lines may be used so all can have some success in serving.

Strategy: Encourage passing, varying force and pathways of returns, looking for empty spaces, and planned serve placement.

Teaching Suggestions: Rules requiring passing may be necessary to ensure that team play is developed. Encourage getting the ball to a space above teammates when passing and a good position in relation to the ball in line and directly under it for forearm pass and volley. Encourage children to catch balls not received appropriately.

SUMMARY

Net games and volleyball lead-ups are popular activities with elementary school children if modifications are used. A lighter ball, a smaller court, and preferably fewer players per team offer children a chance for a successful experience. In addition, skills are modified with children selecting skills at a level of difficulty suitable to their ability. Within the game greater variability in skill selection is observed, which serves to help children acquire greater confidence and improves the social environment since all have an opportunity to succeed. Application of the movement content is essential for success, and the beginning games offer children more opportunity to plan the placement of the ball over the net. If encouraged in these beginning games and teaching for transfer is planned, the continued use of the movement content should improve the play throughout the development of volleyball in the elementary school.

REFERENCES

1. Angle, J.: Modern volleyball drills, ed. 2, Huntington Beach, Calif., 1978, Volleyball Publications.
2. Dunphy, M.: Volleyball, New York, 1977, Grossett and Dunlap.
3. Peppler, M.: Inside volleyball for women, Chicago, 1977, Henry Regnery Co.
4. Seidel, B., and others: Sports skills: a conceptual approach to meaningful movement, ed. 2, Dubuque, Iowa, 1980, William C. Brown, Publisher.

ADDITIONAL READINGS

Barker, J.: A simplified volleyball skills test for beginning level instruction, JOPERD 56(5):20, May-June 1985.
Skill tests to use in beginning volleyball, which might be modified as a self-testing activity for children.

Chandler, J.: Modified volleyball play, JOPER 51(5):52, May 1980.
A game using three stations to develop volleyball skills.

Dawson, L., and Polivino, G.: Bridging the gap in volleyball, JOPERD 53(7):25, October 1982.
Using mini games to bridge the gap from instruction to game play.

McBride, M.: Put some bounce into volleyball, JOPERD 52(7):73, September 1981.
Using one-bounce volleyball to develop volleyball skills and game play.

Part Eight

EXTRACURRICULAR OPPORTUNITIES

In addition to the instructional program of physical education offered in the schools, opportunities for participation outside of class are provided. These activities include intramurals, special interest groups, special events, and demonstrations. Teachers may also be asked to help in organizing and conducting youth sport activities for children in community-based programs.

29 School Activities and Youth Sports

29

SCHOOL ACTIVITIES AND YOUTH SPORTS

CHAPTER OBJECTIVES

1 To describe the values and list the guidelines for the extra-class program in the elementary school

2 To identify a variety of possible physical activity experiences for the elementary school child that further the goals of the physical education program

3 To discuss issues surrounding youth sports today and to provide suggestions for physical educators who assume leadership in community-based programs for children

Extra-class programs and special events are an extension of the educational program. As an outgrowth of the regular physical education instructional program, opportunity is provided for further development and use of skills and knowledge introduced in the instructional program, thus supplementing class activities. These activities should provide a positive learning experience for each child through a wide variety of activities aimed to meet the needs of all children and to meet the goals of the school physical education program.

The opportunity for all children, not just the gifted, to participate will not only promote positive attitudes toward participation but also expose children to a variety of recreational or leisure time activities in which they may engage throughout their lifetime. Children need the chance to develop their personal interests in individual as well as in team or group activities.

The conduct of the activities should encourage cooperative behavior and the assumption of responsibility through shared decision-making with other children. The teacher serves as a guide as children are involved in the planning process and the conduct of the activities commensurate with their maturity. The children's responsibility may include selecting the activity, determining whether the activity will be competitive or noncompetitive, formal or informal; establishing the rules to govern the events; setting up tournaments; keeping records and statistics; writing articles for the school paper; publicizing the events; enrolling the participants; and organizing and conducting the event, including officiating when needed. As a result, children should develop the skills needed to be more independent of adult supervision in their leisure activities.

Additional outcomes of these programs that are often cited include a more constructive use of leisure time during the school day and better teacher-pupil relations. Children also have the opportunity to participate with children from other classes and in some activities with children varying in age.

Several different kinds of activities are usually included. Intramurals provide a wide variety of experiences, including tournaments and 1-day or short-term events that may be competitive or noncompetitive and that require individual or group participation. Open gym is another way of organizing activities in a less formal way, which allows the children to check out equipment for activities of their own choosing. Special interest groups may also be organized in which children with similar interests meet on a regular basis to develop skills and knowledge in a particular activity. Special events include field or activity days in which the entire school participates, gym shows for parents, or other classes and demonstrations.

GUIDELINES

The following guidelines should be considered in establishing extra-class activities and special events. They should be implemented with local regulations regarding safety and liability in mind.

All children are free to participate. If the program is to be of interest to all children, an attempt should be made to determine their needs and interests. A student survey conducted by the teacher is one approach to obtaining this information. An interest bulletin board is another. A variety of activities are displayed and the children check those they would like to try as well as list additional activities they would like to see included. Student activity committees might also solicit interests from students in a variety of ways including interviewing individuals, conducting an inquiry on the playground, or leading class discussions.

All participants have parental approval for participation. Many of the activities may be scheduled outside regular school hours. Parent approval is needed, especially if children will be arriving home at some time other than their normal hour or if alternate transportation home will be needed. Since medical approval for participation is recommended for the instructional program, additional medical prescription will probably not be needed.

Equal opportunity is provided for all children to have full participation. All children have not only the right to participate but also the right to participate fully with an equal opportunity guaranteed in the scheduling and conduct of the activities and in the use of equipment. The teacher must carefully monitor the activities to be sure the needs of all interested children are met, including equal participation time and the opportunity to play a variety of positions in games.

The activities are supervised by qualified adults who know children and the activities. The activities selected should meet the physical, social, and cognitive needs

of all participants. Leaders should select activities appropriate to the maturity level of the children and modify activities when necessary to provide a better experience for all.

The activities are conducted with safety as a prime concern. All safety rules are enforced, and the environment is one in which all may participate without fear of injury. Supervisors are trained in standard first-aid procedures in case of injury. Rest periods are provided when necessary to avoid possible injury caused by fatigue. A warm-up period to prepare the students for the activity may be needed before beginning the activity.

The activities are organized to allow children to assume responsibility for the safe and efficient conduct of the activities. Students should assume as much responsibility for the conduct of the activities as their maturity allows. They should be assured of input into the development of the program and its conduct. Many of the activities may be conducted with little direct supervision from adults. The children may be organized informally for play. In other activities student officials may be used.

Noncompetitive as well as competitive activities should be included. Children should be exposed to many different opportunities for use of their leisure time. They should have the chance to do something just for fun, to self-test their own performance, or to compete with one or more children if they desire.

In competitive activities each team has an equal opportunity for success. A contest is more satisfying for all if the competitors are of equal ability. An effort must be made to equalize the teams for competition. Emphasis should be placed on the process of participation rather than on winning. When teams have an equal opportunity for success, cooperative behavior within the team is more likely to occur.

There are coeducational activities as well as some activities organized for girls and boys separately. Children need opportunities to participate with many different children. In some activities and for some events coeducational grouping may be best. In other activities boys may wish to participate with boys and girls with girls. No child should be excluded from an activity because of sex.

Informal grouping of children as well as prearranged grouping of children is used. Children's attendance may be more inconsistent in extra-class activities owing to other commitments and their lack of maturity. Grouping the children as they arrive may facilitate getting activities underway as quickly as possible. Informal grouping also aids in equalizing the teams and may result in a less competitive atmosphere than that which may occur when children are prearranged into teams. Children should, however, have some opportunity for selecting teams and participating with the same group of children on several occasions. This can be of value in helping children learn to play as a team. However, the selection of teams should be accomplished under appropriate teacher supervision.

Some form of recognition for participation is given. Children may receive a certificate for participation or for their individual achievement in a particular event.

A plan for the systematic evaluation of the program is developed. A plan to evaluate the program ensures the program goals are being met. The children should actively be involved in the evaluation process.

EXTRA-CLASS ACTIVITIES

The following suggestions for the conduct of intramurals, open gym, and special interest groups will help the teacher of physical education plan and conduct appropriate extra-class activities for elementary school children.

Intramurals

Intramural sports are the most prevalent extra-class programs in the elementary school. They are usually available to children beginning at the third or fourth grade level. They are most often scheduled at the close of the school day but may be held before school, during the lunch break, or even during recess periods.

A variety of activities may be included in the intramural sports program. Since it is an outgrowth of

the instructional program, the activities scheduled are those in which the skills and knowledge have been introduced in the physical education classes. This extends the opportunity for children to develop and use the skills and knowledge in the less formal atmosphere of intramural play. Obviously if the children are to benefit from the added opportunity for participation, it is best to schedule these activities shortly after they have been introduced in the physical education class and after the children have had some time to work on the skills and develop sufficient knowledge for successful participation. In games where the children will be responsible for their own officiating, rules should be clarified during the physical education class and some instruction in officiating given before it is needed in intramurals.

The availability of intramural activities needs to be well publicized so students and parents can plan accordingly. It is helpful to establish an intramural bulletin board where children can check the schedule of current activities as well as activities to come.

The intramural sports program may also include activities that the time scheduled for the instructional program does not make feasible. Activities such as swimming, bowling, skating, cross-country skiing, and hiking are a few activities in which community facilities may be used and in which a longer period of time may be needed to provide a worthwhile experience.

Nontraditional activities may also be scheduled. Novelty games and events offer a change of pace from the traditional activities and may appeal to some children who are less interested in the traditional activities.

Individual and team sports should be balanced throughout the school year with several options available for students during each season. Competitive and noncompetitive activities should be included as well as coeducational activities for boys and girls.

Activities are usually organized by grade level to provide more easily for the needs of the children varying in age. Activities may be scheduled for 1 day only or for several weeks. The time scheduled for each activity ought to be long enough to maintain enthusiasm but not so long that interest is lost.

Considerations for children with disabilities must be made to allow their participation without jeopardizing the team's effort. Often special modifications may need to be made if disabled children are to participate fully. If they are an active part of the instructional program children will accept them as a part of the intramural group. Children are accepting of any additional modifications that need to be made to make disabled children equal members of the group.

Activities may be organized informally, with the children divided into teams each day or with preorganized teams. Tournaments may be informally organized each day, or a posted schedule of team play may be used.

Several kinds of tournaments may be used. Some, such as the **round robin** or **ladder tournaments,** guarantee the participation of all throughout the tournament. Others eliminate individuals or teams along the way. It is important to plan carefully if elimination tournaments are used to provide for the participation of all children, including those eliminated from the tournament. Scheduled play should be included for teams or individuals who are no longer in the original tournament.

The round robin tournament provides an opportunity for each participant or team to play all other participants or teams. Figure 29-1 explains the procedure for setting up a round robin tournament. The round robin tournament is easily used when teams are selected informally and the number of teams is small. Any number of participants may compete in the round robin tournament. When there is

A Equal number of teams (6)

Round 1	Round 2	Round 3	Round 4	Round 5
1-6	1-2	1-3	1-4	1-5
2-5	3-6	4-2	5-3	6-4
3-4	4-5	5-6	6-2	2-3

B Unequal number of teams (5)

Round 1	Round 2	Round 3	Round 4	Round 5
Bye-5	Bye-1	Bye-2	Bye-3	Bye-4
1-4	2-5	3-1	4-2	5-3
2-3	3-4	4-5	5-1	1-2

Figure 29-1

Round robin tournament. **A.** To determine schedule of rounds, teams are arranged into equal columns. Team in upper left remains stationary while other teams rotate one position clockwise for each round. **B.** This tournament requires that one team have a bye in each round. A procedure similar to that when the number of teams is even is used to determine the schedule.

1. ________	A ________
2. ________	B ________
3. ________	C ________
4. ________	D ________
5. ________	E ________
6. ________	G ________

Figure 29-2

Ladder tournament.

an equal number of teams (N), the number of rounds is equal to one less the number of teams (N − 1). When the team number is unequal the number of rounds equals the number of teams in the tournament.

The ladder tournament is usually used for individual sports but can also be used in team competition. The teams are arranged in a vertical line with the object being to be at the top of the ladder at the end of the tournament. Individuals may challenge players one or two rungs above them on the ladder. When the challenger wins, the two exchange places on the ladder. Some monitoring may be necessary to

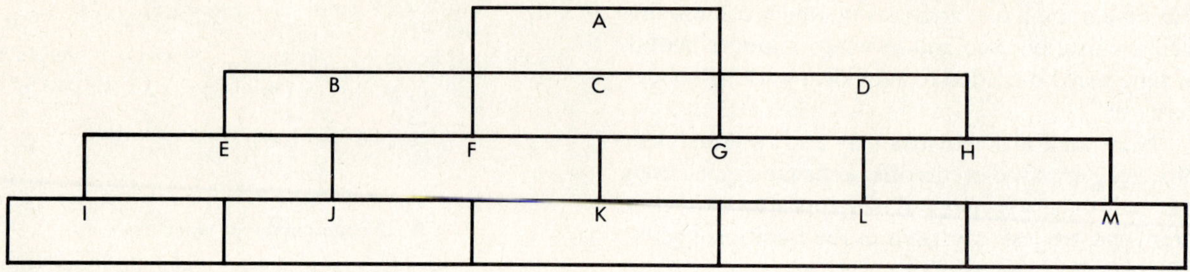

Figure 29-3

Pyramid tournament.

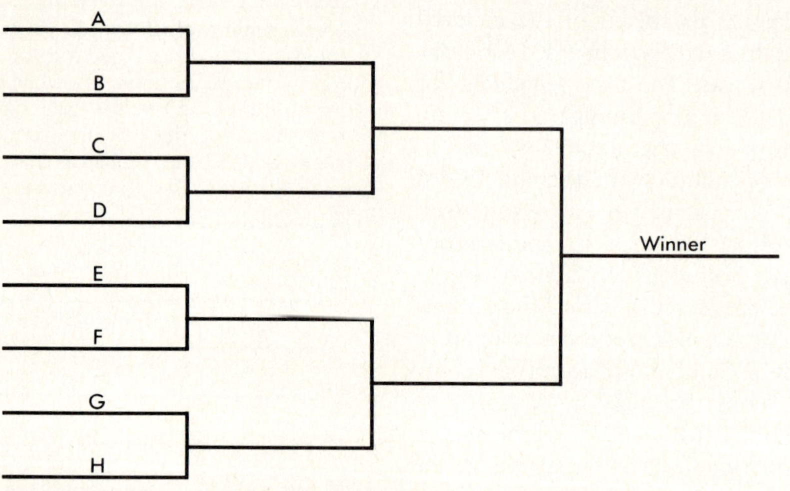

Figure 29-4

Single-elimination tournament.

ensure that all participants have the opportunity to challenge. Figure 29-2 gives an example of a ladder tournament. When many participants are involved, several ladders may be organized.

The *pyramid tournament* is similar to the ladder tournament but permits players more choices in challenging since there are several individuals on the next level of the pyramid. In one variation of this tournament an individual must challenge and win over one player at the same level before challenging a player on the level above. Figure 29-3 gives an example of a pyramid tournament.

In the *single-elimination* tournament each participant remains in the tournament until one match or game is lost. It requires a fewer number of games

to be played to complete the tournament than most tournaments, but consideration should be made to provide continued participation for those players eliminated. The number of participants or teams required is a power of four (4, 8, or 16 teams, and so forth) if the tournament is to be completed without byes. Figure 29-4 gives an example of the single-elimination tournament.

The *double-elimination* tournament enables competitors to remain in the tournament until two matches or games are lost. As in the single-elimination tournament, the beginning brackets require teams in powers of four. Figure 29-5 gives an example of a double-elimination tournament. The winners continue to play in bracket I. In bracket II those

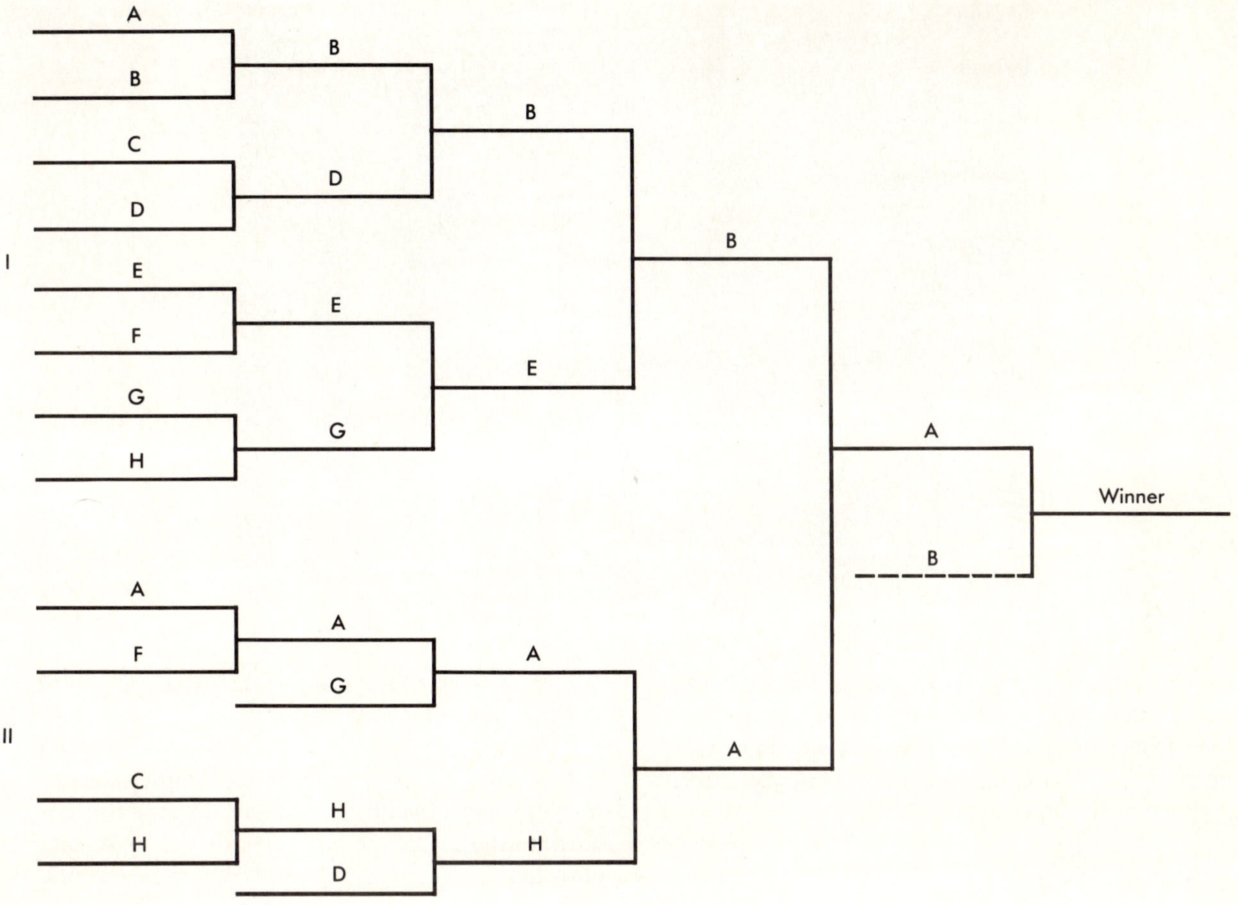

Figure 29-5

Double-elimination tournament.

competitors who have lost once play. If in the final round the competitor with one previous loss wins, resulting in each having lost once, an additional contest is held to determine the winner of the tournament.

Open Gym

Open gym is a regularly scheduled event in which the children are free to check out equipment and to use the facilities for informal play. It may be necessary for the teacher to help organize the available space when several different activities will take place simultaneously. This activity may include children varying in age and interests. Safe play must always be stressed, and at times special considerations for the use of space imposed to ensure the safety of all.

Special Interest Groups

Special interest groups or sports clubs offer an opportunity for children to develop specific interests over a period of time. The goal of these groups is to help children improve their skills for personal enjoyment and/or competition. Each group meets on a regular basis. Special interest groups give children the opportunity to work with others of varying ages who have the same interests. Examples of activities for special interest groups include rope jumping, fitness, gymnastics, and square dancing.

At the elementary school level it may be helpful to schedule special interest groups seasonally. This should encourage children to participate in many different activities throughout the school year rather than specialize in only one.

SPECIAL EVENTS

Special events are usually all-school activities that are held for 1 day or over a short period of time. They may be competitive but more likely are of a self-testing nature in which children strive to see what they can do. For example, a field day might be held in which the entire school participates in a variety of individual, partner, team, or class activities. There might also be a demonstration such as a gym show or a performance for another class or for parents.

One example of a special event is an all-school field day in which children attempt to improve their own performances in various individual events. Another event might be a fitness run in which classes compete in a run to some destination, such as to the state capitol, over a period of a week or two. Laps are completed before school or during their lunch and recess breaks. Individuals record their laps, which are then totalled to determine the class effort. Teacher-student games are an event in which a team of students competes against a faculty team. Another possible event is the super stars. Children compete with other children of their own age and ability in some unusual events, patterned after the television event. These activities may test their courage as well as their skill.

Teachers and students may also plan and conduct a demonstration or gym show for another class or for family and friends. This might take the form of a demonstration of the types of activities, skills, and knowledge taught in the physical education program. It could be a learning project in which the importance of fitness or some other topic is conveyed to a younger group of children. Children may also plan a parents' night in which parents are invited to come and participate with their children in several sports activities or dance.

YOUTH SPORTS

In the past two decades there has been a marked increase in the availability of sports programs for children. It is estimated that approximately 20 million school children participate in these community-based activities annually. The majority of these activities are of a competitive nature, with children following a set schedule of games or matches within the community or with neighboring communities. Participants may be as young as 5 years of age.

The conduct of these programs should closely follow the guidelines listed above for extra-class activities and special events. In 1977 a Youth Sports Task Force was organized by the National Association for Sport and Physical Education of the American Alliance for Health, Physical Education, Recreation, and Dance. This group of dedicated professionals formulated the Bill of Rights for Young Athletes listed in the box above.

Concerns have been raised regarding the actual outcomes of these programs. While the outcomes are positive for some children, there is evidence that they have been negative for others. Teachers of physical education aware of the potential benefits and hazards as children participate in these community programs must assume more leadership in helping communities to plan and conduct programs that are in the best interests of all children. Physical educators may help in the training of volunteer coaches and in helping parents to understand the programs from a child's perspective.

A discussion of specific concerns in the areas of physical development, motor skills, social development, and psychological effects follows, with suggestions for the minimizing of negative outcomes.

Physical Growth

Physical activity stimulates bone and muscle tissue development and increases cardiorespiratory efficiency. Bone size and shape may be altered by external forces, and muscles increase their strength and en-

durance. Therefore, physical activity is essential for normal human development. Youth sports programs have the potential of providing vigorous physical activity during these developing years.

Studies indicate that training at a moderate intensity accelerates growth in stature and body size in youngsters from ages 11 to 14 years.[11] The effects of a heavy training regimen on developing children needs further study. There is some belief that long-distance running as in training for marathons could result in growth plate injury owing to the severe strain placed on the articular cartilage.[3] Children appear to be especially vulnerable to growth plate injury during the pubescent growth spurt.[7]

Orthopedists who rarely saw children with sports-related injuries in the past are beginning to see new types of injuries in children. The elbow, shoulder, knee, and ankle joints are most susceptible to growth plate injury. Stress fractures, tendinitis of the shoulder, bursitis of the hip, and tennis elbow are a few of the injuries that appear to be on the increase for young sports participants. These injuries are believed to be primarily the result of the inappropriate training and overuse of some body segments of young athletes.[7] In the past, when children participated in more spontaneous play, they quit when they were hurt and did not return to the activity until the pain went away. Today, in more organized sports, they are often encouraged to play when hurt. Many children are led to believe only babies refuse to play when hurt or even complain of injuries. Some coaches consider injuries other than fractures of little consequence.

While it is still too soon to tell, some orthopedists[7,11] believe the soft tissue injuries in childhood will result to chronic problems in adulthood if not prevented or not properly treated.

Individuals working with children in youth sports programs need to:

1. Understand the process of physical development and recognize the differences in growth patterns in children.
2. Consider using a combination of chronological age, motor ability, and physical maturation in grouping children for physical activity.
3. Avoid sex stereotyping in working with prepubescent boys and girls.
4. Plan appropriate warm ups and training regimens for the young bodies in their charge.
5. Modify activities to meet the developmental needs of children, such as decreasing the size

of the playing area, shortening the distances to be run, and reducing the number of players active at one time.

6. Establish a reasonable amount of practice time to avoid undue stress and fatigue.
7. Watch for fatigue in young players and adjust play accordingly.
8. Know first-aid procedures, the type of injuries common to the activity, and how to prevent and treat these injuries.
9. Treat injuries promptly and see that injuries are cared for in a reasonable manner, insisting on medical supervision when deemed necessary.
10. See that all players have a physical exam before participation, including an assessment of body parts used excessively in the activity.
11. Prevent injuries by encouraging participation in lifetime and noncontact sports during the developing years.
12. Set a realistic limit on the number of contests to be played in the season and no more than one per week.
13. Limit the distance to be traveled to contests to ensure proper rest for the participants.

Motor Development

Children develop motor skills at varying rates. While most children are exposed to all the fundamental motor patterns before entering school, there is considerable variability in their mastery of these skills. Some of these differences are of a maturational nature, while others are the result of experience with the skills. Sports programs for children must take into account these differences in skill mastery. There is some concern that while the physically more mature children may benefit from these programs, children who do not meet the adult expectations for the skill are discouraged, are not given much opportunity to play, or are dropped from the team.

Individuals working with children in youth sports programs need to:

1. Emphasize the improvement in game skills by teaching correct techniques and helping all children overcome performance errors.
2. Modify games and rules to meet the needs of children at various ages and abilities.
3. Emphasize improvement in individual and group play rather than winning.
4. Recognize when children are ready to try new, more advanced techniques or to combine skills efficiently.
5. Give children the opportunity to play various positions to gain a better understanding of the whole game.
6. Encourage participation in a wide variety of activities resulting in the development of a variety of movement skills.

Social Development

Youth sports greatly influence the social development of children, especially those skills that help individuals behave in socially acceptable ways as they participate. It has often been suggested that youth sports programs further those values we hold dear in our society—to work hard, to play fair, to cooperate with others—when in fact what may really be learned is that winning is everything.

Society recognizes certain behaviors for the true sports person. They include playing by the rules, being a gracious winner, accepting a loss without blaming others, working with others to accomplish a team goal, and showing respect for teammates, opponents, and officials. These behaviors are learned through the modeling of significant others, the reinforcement of appropriate behavior, and the withdrawal of rewards for socially unacceptable behavior.

Spectators often express socially unacceptable behavior at sports events. Professional athletes may be observed behaving in negative ways as well. Children need to be helped to deal with these inappropriate behaviors. They must learn to recognize them as unacceptable for anyone, regardless of the situation, and to minimize the effects of any of these behaviors that may be directed at them as participants.

Individuals working with children in youth sports programs need to:

1. Explain what is appropriate behavior to the children.
2. Be consistent in actions and words not only by expecting children to behave as good sports persons but also by demonstrating those desirable behaviors themselves.
3. Reinforce appropriate behavior through encouragement and praise.
4. Withdraw rewards for inappropriate behavior, for example by removal from the game, for all children, including the star players who behave inappropriately.
5. Emphasize the fun of the activity and the pro-

cess of working together rather than winning.

6. Demonstrate respect by encouraging children to compliment opponents and officials at the close of a match of game.

Psychological Development

The American society values sports participation. Children who engage in sports activities are esteemed by their peers, parents, and neighbors. Feelings of self-worth are affected by one's choice to participate or not and by the participation experience itself.

Not only must children participate but they must also participate successfully. One has only to witness a single event to become aware of the psychological pressures that are brought to children by their parents, coaches, and spectators. Parents live vicariously through their children with their own self-esteem tied up in their children's achievements. Coaches' egos are involved in the team's success or failure. Spectators yell and scream at the players, officials, and coaches. Often the attitudes of these well-meaning adults result in children feeling inadequate about their skills and guilty about their degree of success or even their feelings and commitments to the sports' participation itself.

Children differ in their abilities to handle the pressures of competition. Not only must they please their parents and coaches, but also they must be able to adjust to the crowd and noise, the level of the competition, the reputation of the other team, and their relationships with the individuals on their own team. There may be anxiety over the expectations for winning and the demand for excellence in their endeavors. There may be feelings of apprehension over the role to be played in the game, including whether they will be permitted to participate in the game itself.

Individuals working with children in youth sports need to:

1. Help children set realistic goals for achievement. Help them to challenge themselves but have goals within reach of their efforts.
2. Encourage self evaluation so that children can first assess what they did well and then look at what they might need to improve.
3. Encourage their best efforts and praise them for the things they do well and for trying their best.
4. Recognize that children will make mistakes and help them to be realistic about the errors made.
5. Encourage children to think positively and not to dwell on thoughts of possible failure.
6. Recognize that children differ in their emotional maturity and give them all the support they need when they need it.
7. Always end an activity on a positive note. Be sure they leave the practice or game with positive feelings and are looking forward to the next opportunity for participation.
8. Remember that the activity is for children and not for adults.

In summary, sports participation may result in either positive or negative feelings about participation in motor activities. There is evidence that many children are dropping out of these programs at an early age. While some may drop out because of changing interests, too many quit because they are discouraged and no longer find the activity fun.

Parents play an important role in their children's success. Parents must be willing to allow children to make the decision about whether they will participate. Children should be encouraged to be physically active, but the choice of activity is theirs to make. They may prefer an individual sport over a team sport. They may decide they wish a more or less competitive environment. They may prefer a lifetime activity in which they test their own powers. Parents must learn to respect these choices. They can encourage their children's participation by helping them learn the skills and by giving them positive feedback. Sometimes it may be helpful to show interest, but only observe the activity from some distance away. Whatever children choose to do parents should be able to analyze the situation to be sure it is safe, well supervised, properly equipped, and provides a good learning experience for the child.

Since physical activity is important in maintaining fitness throughout life, it is important that programs for children encourage rather than discourage them from being physically active. It is up to the adults working in these programs to make the programs the best experience for all children by keeping the needs of children in the forefront and the needs of adults in the background.

SUMMARY

Extra-class activities and special events are an outgrowth of the instructional program of physical education. They provide opportunities for children to develop further and to use the motor skills and knowledge introduced in the physical education classes. They also provide opportunities for children to develop the leadership and organizational skills necessary for leisure time participation without adult direction. In addition, special events give children the chance to perform motor activities in front of others to show parents and friends what they are learning.

Opportunities for elementary school children to participate in youth sports programs has expanded rapidly in the past two decades. Teachers of physical education should involve themselves as advocates for children in helping to plan and conduct these activities. They should assist in training coaches and helping adults involved in such programs (coaches, officials, and parents) to view the activity from the children's perspectives.

Extra-class activities, special events, and youth sports can contribute positively to the development of children. All should be conducted under carefully prescribed guidelines to ensure the safe participation of children. Social and psychological as well as physical and motor needs of children must be considered if these programs are to meet the needs of children and to encourage their participation in physical activity for life.

REFERENCES

1. Barber, H.: Teaching attitudes and behaviors through youth sports, JOPERD **53**(3):21, March 1982.
2. Blackwell, D.: Elementary superstars, JOPERD **52**(7):28, September 1981.
3. Caine, D., and Lindner, K.: Growth plate injury: a threat to young distance runners? Physician Sports Med. **12**(4):118, April 1984.
4. Calder, J., and McGregor, I.: How to succeed in intramurals without really trying, JOPER **51**(3):48, March 1980.
5. Feltz, D., and Weiss, M.: Developing self-efficacy through sport, JOPERD **53**(3):24, March 1982.
6. Martens, R., and Seefeldt, V., editors: Guidelines for children's sports, Reston, Va., 1979, AAHPERD.
7. Micheli, L., and others: Sports in childhood: a round table, Physician Sports Med. **11**(8):56, August 1982.
8. Ogilvie, B.: Psychology and the elite young athlete, Physician Sports Med. **11**(4):195, April 1983.
9. Ryan, A.: The very young athlete, Physician Sports Med. **11**(3):45, March 1983.
10. Scanlon, T.: Motivation and stress in competitive youth sports, JOPERD **53**(3):27, March 1982.
11. Seefeldt, V., and Gould, D.: Physical and psychological effects of athletic competition on children and youth, Washington, D.C., 1980, ERIC Clearinghouse in Teacher Education.
12. Tenoschok, M.: Intramurals, above and beyond, JOPERD **52**(7):32, September 1981.
13. Thomas, J., editor: Youth sports guide for coaches and parents, Washington, D.C., 1978, The Manufacturers Life Insurance Co. and NASPE.

ADDITIONAL READINGS

Boulware, C.: Special events: the ultimate Rx, JOPERD **54**(2):27, February 1983.
The use of special events in the physical education program to revitalize intramurals, offer unique nontraditional events, take children away from school, and develop awareness.

Carlton, P., and Stinson, R.: Achieving educational goals through intramurals, JOPERD **54**(2):23, February 1983.
The use of intramurals, clubs, special events, and self-directed activities to meet educational goals.

Devereux, E.: Backyard versus little league baseball: some observations on the impoverishment of children's games in contemporary America. In Yiannakis, A., and others, editors: Sport sociology: contemporary themes, ed. 2, Dubuque, 1979, Kendall/Hunt Publishing Co.
A concern for youth sports and their effect on the spontaneous play of children.

Division of Elementary and Secondary Education: A self-appraisal checklist for intramurals in Ohio's elementary and secondary schools, Columbus, 1978, Ohio Department of Education.
A tool to evaluate an intramural program.

Olsen, E.: Kidd stuff: the expert's view, The Runner **5**(2):36, November 1982.
Concerns for distance running by children.

Orlick, T., and Botterill, C.: Why eliminate kids? In Yiannakis, A., and others, editors: Sport sociology: Contemporary themes, ed. 2, Dubuque, 1979, Kendall/Hunt Publishing Co.
The effects of youth sports on the continued participation of children.

Ralbovsky, M.: Destiny's forgotten darlings. In Yiannakis, A., and others, editors: Sport sociology: contemporary themes, ed. 2, Dubuque, 1979, Kendall/Hunt Publishing Co.
Perceptions of youth sports by former participants.

United States Department of Health and Human Services: Children and youth in action: physical activities and sports, Washington, D.C., 1980, Superintendent of Documents, United States Printing Office.
The age characteristics of children, suggestions for parents to help children develop physical fitness and motor skills and concerns for competitive activities for children and youth.

KEY DEFINITIONS

accent Emphasis put on a beat, usually on the first beat of a measure, but it may occur on any beat. (p. 303)

aerobic efficiency Ability of the body to supply fuel and oxygen to the muscles. (p. 180)

aggression Vigorously pursuing a goal. (p. 171)

American dance Dances of colonial America based on popular tunes of the period. (p. 322)

annual plan A schedule that places all units of instruction in the school calendar for a particular year. (p. 46)

augmented feedback Knowledge of results, information about their performance given by an observer to an individual. (p. 67)

backing up In softball, moving into position behind a fielding player or base man and in line with an oncoming ball to assist if the ball is missed by the player. (p. 514)

blind pass A baton pass in pursuit relays in which the receiver is facing away from the baton as it is passed. (p. 288)

block plan A tentative calendar of objectives and activities developed for a unit. (p. 52)

body awareness Understanding of one's own body potential for movement and a sensitivity to one's physical being. (p. 30)

body composition The relationship in percent of body fat to lean body tissue. (p. 5)

body mechanics Efficient use of the body in maintaining good alignment and in performing daily tasks such as lifting, carrying, pushing, and pulling. (p. 174)

bound flow Control or momentary restraint of movement in which the body may be stopped, such as in changing direction or pathway. (p. 138)

bunch start Crouch start; a starting position used in sprints in which the rear knee is placed next to the forward foot. The thumb and index fingers are spread and parallel to the starting line. (p. 285)

cardiorespiratory endurance The maximal functional capacity of the heart and lungs to continue activity over a period of time. (p. 5)

center of gravity The weight center of the body; the point around which the body weight is equally distributed. (p. 136)

circuit training A training method in which a number of stations for conditioning different parts of the body or different components of fitness are set up and the participants go to each station for a set period of time. (p. 178)

collecting In soccer, the ability to receive a ball and get it under control using body parts other than the hands. (p. 483)

command A teacher-centered approach to teaching in which the teacher presents the material to be learned directly to the students, who are then organized for practice. (p. 71)

competition A contest between individuals or groups. (p. 171)

contingency contract A technique in which the child is offered a reward for behaving in a particular manner: "If you will do this, then you may do that." (p. 101)

cooperation Working together to achieve a goal in which success is dependent on combined effort. (p. 171)

cover In softball, to move into position to make a play at a base by someone other than the usual base player. (p. 514)

criterion-referenced tests Measures of how a person performs; evaluation against a qualitative standard, such as the evaluative criteria considered for the motor skills in this text. (p. 111)

development Changes caused by maturation that lead to more advanced use of particular mechanisms. (p. 11)

direct snap Receiving the football from the center when the quarterback assumes a position over the center with the hands under the center. (p. 473)

direct supervision Supervision in which the teacher is working directly with the students. (p. 85)

direction The six ways the body can move in space with different body surfaces leading: forward, backward, right, left, up, and down. (p. 30)

discipline A process for assisting individuals to adjust to their environment; it is the result of failure to adhere to certain standards of behavior. (p. 100)

distributed practice Practice over a period of time in which the time between the practice periods varies. (p. 66)

double dribble In basketball, dribbling the ball, stopping, and beginning to dribble once again or contacting the ball at anytime during dribbling with two hands. (p. 419)

double-beat jump The rope jumper jumps as the rope passes under the feet and then again as the rope passes overhead. (p. 222)

double-elimination tournament A tournament that ensures the participation of each team or individual until all have lost two matches. (p. 542)

dynamic balance Maintaining balance while moving. (p. 135)

educational game A game with few rules, played by small or large groups, that is selected for the practice and use of previously learned motor skills and movement concepts. (p. 386)

epiphysis The part of the bone where growth occurs, found near the end of long bones. (p. 11)

evaluation The act of making judgments about something. (p. 110)

exploration A child-centered approach to teaching in which the teacher leads the children through a series of very general movement challenges designed to help them learn about their own movement potential or the use of a particular piece of equipment. Many different responses by the children are possible. (p. 28)

feedback Information received while observing one's own performance. (p. 66)

flexibility The range of motion in a joint. (p. 5)

floor exercise A combination of stunts, tumbling skills, balances, dance, and locomotor and other movements in which the performer moves on a square mat, using as much space as possible and traveling in several pathways. (p. 244)

flow The ability to combine movements smoothly. (p. 138)

folk dance A traditional dance of the people handed down from one generation to the next. (p. 322)

force out In softball, an out made by getting the ball to the base before the runner and tagging the base. If the player must run to the base the player may be forced out. (p. 507)

foul ball A batted ball that settles outside the base line or lands outside this extended line in the outfield. (p. 507)

free flow A continuity of movement. (p. 138)

gallop A slide performed in a forward direction. (p. 149)

general space The area that is available for movement, defined by imposed or natural boundaries. (p. 30)

give and go An offensive strategy in which the passer draws an opponent, passes a square pass to a teammate, and then receives a return pass after moving around the opposing player. (p. 450)

growth Change in size. (p. 11)

guided discovery A teaching style in which the teacher leads the children through a series of activities, narrowing their focus at each step of the way until the one or a limited number of solutions to the movement challenges are reached. (p. 73)

health-related physical fitness The ability to perform strenuous activity shown without excessive fatigue and to show evidence of the traits and capacities that limit the risks of developing disease or disorders that limit a person's functional capacity. (p. 5)

hop A locomotor movement in which the performer takes off on one foot and lands on the same foot. (p. 145)

indirect supervision Supervision provided by a teacher being in the area of the activity. (p. 85)

individual education plan (IEP) A plan of long- and short-term goals, activities, and services to meet these goals; it is required for all disabled children by P.L. 94-142. (p. 103)

instruction The activities the teacher uses to move the class toward the lesson objectives. (p. 87)

integrated curriculum model Educational program that includes the study of human movement as an important aspect of each instructional unit. (p. 28)

intensity The loudness or softness of an accompaniment. (p. 303)

interpersonal communication skills Verbal and nonverbal behaviors that stimulate inquiry between two individuals. (p. 97)

intersensory integration The ability to use input from several sensory organs at the same time. (p. 15)

intrasensory discrimination The ability to use various sensory stimuli from a single sense organ. (p. 15)

jump A locomotor movement in which the performer takes off on one or both feet and lands on two feet. (p. 143)

kyphosis A postural deviation characterized by an increased thoracic curve. (p. 197)

ladder tournament A tournament arranged as the rungs of a ladder. Participants may challenge players on one or two rungs above their own position. The winner assumes the higher rung. The individual or team at the top of the ladder at the end of the tournament is the winner. (p. 541)

lead-up game A game with some of the skills, rules, and game elements of a team sport. (p. 336)

lean body weight The weight of the bones, muscles, and internal organs. (p. 182)

leap An extended running step, in which the performer takes off on one foot, travels forward through the air, and lands on the opposite foot. (p. 147)

learning A change in behavior brought about as a result of practice. (p. 60)

legal liability Responsibility for the children in one's care as obligated by law. (p. 85)

level High, medium, and low in relation to the standing position or the location of body parts. (p. 30)

lesson plan The day's plan for meeting unit objectives, including objectives for the day, activities to meet objectives, points of emphasis, and organizational strategies. (p. 54)

line of gravity An imaginary line that passes through the body from head to foot passing through the center of gravity and dividing the body into two equal parts from front to back and from side to side. (p. 136)

line of scrimmage In football, the imaginary line running the width of the field that marks the forward progress of the ball. Teams line up on their side of the line to begin play. (p. 467)

locomotor movement A movement through space from one place to another. (p. 141)

lordosis A postural deviation characterized by an increased lumbar curve. (p. 197)

low intensity exercise An exercise that gets the individual moving but does not increase the heart rate to a fitness-improving level or result in overheating or other discomforts. (p. 181)

mainstreaming The placing of disabled persons in the least restrictive learning environment. (p. 103)

management Operations used to move the class through the lesson from one activity to the next. (p. 87)

marking Being responsible for an opponent while playing defense. (p. 442)

massed practice Practice periods scheduled close together. (p. 66)

maximum heart rate The maximum number of heartbeats per minute attained, dependent on age and physical condition. (p. 180)

measure Underlying beats grouped together into a unit, the number of which depends on the meter. (p. 302)

medium start A start used in sprints in which the feet are a comfortable distance apart and the hand position is as in the bunch start. (p. 286)

meter The number of beats in a measure, such as 2/4, 3/4, 4/4, or 6/8. The upper number represents the number of beats to a measure, the lower number the type of note to receive one beat. (p. 303)

mixed grip In gymnastics, gripping a bar with one hand assuming a regular grip, the other a reverse grip. (p. 268)

mood The character of an accompaniment that depicts feelings, such as sadness, gaiety, or seriousness. (p. 268)

motivation The process of getting an individual to act in ways that satisfy a need or desire. (p. 62)

movement concepts The elements important in the study of human movement: body awareness, space, and qualities of movement, including force, balance, time, and flow. (p. 6)

movement education A child-centered approach to learning in physical education designed to help children develop greater understanding of themselves as movers, the space in which to move, and the factors affecting efficient movement. (p. 27)

muscular endurance The ability of the muscles to sustain effort over time. (p. 5)

muscular strength The amount of force a muscle can exert. (p. 5)

nonlocomotor movement A movement executed while the individual remains in one place. (p. 153)

norm setting Applying reality therapy to a group. (p. 101)

norm-referenced tests Measures of quantitative data that serve as a comparison with scores of other children of the same age and sex tested under like conditions, such as the AAHPERD health-related physical fitness test norms. (p. 111)

obstruction Placing the body between an opponent and the ball. (p. 441)

off-side A play from either team moving across the line of scrimmage before the ball is centered. (p. 480)

ossification The hardening of cartilaginous tissue into bone in the development process. (p. 14)

parallel play The play of young children in which they participate alongside other children but not dependent on the others for success or for meeting their play objective. (p. 386)

pass In volleyball, the skills used on receipt of the ball coming over the net to move the ball to the player who will set to the player (in the official game the spiker) who will send the ball over the net. (p. 524)

pathways Lines of movement in space: straight, curved, or combinations of straight and curved. (p. 30)

perception The ability to use information coming in through the sense organs to make judgments about the environment. (p. 15)

phrase A group of measures that constitutes a musical thought. (p. 303)

physical education specialist A teacher specially trained and certified to teach physical education. (p. 3)

pivot A method of changing pathways by rotating the body around one stationary foot that remains in contact with the floor. (p. 429)

problem solving A teaching style in which the teacher leads the children through a series of activities in which the children find an increasing number of possible responses to a movement challenge. (p. 28)

pursuit relay A relay run on an oval in which each member runs a particular distance of the course. (p. 284)

pyramid tournament Participants are arranged in a pyramid. Players challenge others in the level above. The winner assumes the higher position. At the end of the tournament the player or team at the top is the winner. (p. 542)

qualities of movement Factors affecting efficient movement, such as balance, force, time, and flow. (p. 30)

qualitative objective A statement that identifies the behavior necessary for success, such as the way body parts are used in performing a motor skill. (p. 49)

quantitative objective A statement that measures the result of the behavior, such as the degree of success in a particular situation. (p. 49)

range The relation of the body parts to each other or of the body to objects in space. (p. 30)

rating scale An evaluative technique in which values are arranged on a continuum from high to low; on the basis of observation, children's performance is placed along the continuum. (p. 113)

reality therapy A technique used to help persons be responsible for their behavior by identifying undesirable behavior and the consequences of that behavior and developing a plan to meet desired goals. (p. 101)

regular grip In gymnastics, gripping a bar with the fingers on top, the thumbs underneath, and the palms facing away from the performer. (p. 268)

reinforcement An event that increases the probability of a behavior occurring again. (p. 67)

retention Degree to which learning is remembered over time. (p. 67)

reverse grip In gymnastics, gripping a bar with the thumbs closest to the performer, the fingers behind the bar, and the palms facing the performer. (p. 268)

reverse turn A method of changing pathways from a stride position in which the body turns toward the rear foot as both feet remain in contact with the floor. (p. 420)

rhythmic pattern A combination of notes, even and uneven in time, that constitutes a measure or a phrase. (p. 303)

round robin tournament A tournament in which each participant plays every other participant in the tournament with the winner determined as the one with the best winning record. (p. 541)

scoliosis A postural deviation characterized by one or more lateral curvatures of the spine. (p. 197)

self space The area of space the body occupies and that space within the body's natural extensions. (p. 30)

self-concept Feelings a person has about her or himself, in which the person places value on her or his being.

set The movement of the ball to the player who will send it over the net. (p. 524)

shotgun In football, receiving the ball from the center from a position in which the quarterback stands several yards behind the center. (p. 473)

shuttle relay A relay run back and forth between two lines. (p. 284)

single-beat jump The rope jumper jumps only as the rope passes under the feet. (p. 222)

singing games Activities of young children in which children's poems are put to music and imitative movements are used. (p. 322)

single-elimination tournament A tournament in which players are eliminated after one loss. The player or team winning all matches is the winner. (p. 542)

skill game A game in which the primary purpose is the practice of a motor skill. (p. 386)

skinfold caliper An instrument for measuring percent of body fat. (p. 183)

skip A step-hop combination executed in an uneven rhythm, alternating the lead foot. (p. 149)

slide A locomotor movement executed in uneven rhythm in which the performer steps to the side, closes the trailing foot to the lead foot, transfers the weight back to the trailing foot, and repeats the action again. (p. 148)

sportsmanship Conduct becoming a sportsman, including respect for rules and authority, playing fair, working with others in a group effort, being a good competitor, and accepting winning and losing in a socially acceptable manner. (p. 170)

spotting Giving physical assistance to a person performing a motor skill, especially in gymnastics where the possibility of injury is increased in the learning phase. (p. 234)

sprint A dash or short-distance race of 20 to 50 yards for elementary school children. (p. 284)

square dance Dances of American origin executed in a four-couple set. (p. 322)

square pass In soccer, also called the flat pass. A pass parallel to the end line between two players. (p. 450)

static balance Balance while stationary. (p. 135)

strike zone In softball, the area between the batter's armpits and the knees. (p. 508)

sway A nonlocomotor pendular movement with the axis below the moving part. (p. 154)

swing A nonlocomotor movement characterized by a circular or pendular movement around a stationary center. (p. 153)

task A style of teaching in which learning objectives and activities are selected and organized by the teacher but in which the students assume responsibility for learning by selecting those objectives and activities on which they need to work. (p. 72)

teaching styles Teaching methods and strategies for organizing and presenting learning experiences to children. (p. 71)

tempo The rate of speed from fast to slow. (p. 303)

terminal objectives Statements of the intended final outcomes of the objectives of a unit. (p. 49)

through pass In soccer or hockey, a pass parallel to the side line in which the passer hits the ball straight ahead and the receiver moves forward past an opposing player and cuts for the ball. (p. 450)

time-out Removing a child from activity as a means of controlling inappropriate behavior. (p. 101)

traditional curriculum model An activity-centered curriculum composed of several units of instruction, such as games, dance, and individual activities. (p. 28)

transfer The ability to apply what was learned in one situation to new situations. (p. 64)

traveling In basketball, while in possession of the ball, taking more than two steps before dribbling or passing. (p. 419)

turn Parallel or full rotation of the body while shifting its base of support. (p. 154)

twist A rotation of the body or a body part around a stationary base. (p. 154)

underlying beat The pulse beat; a steady, even beat found in any piece of music. (p. 302)

unit curriculum model Curriculum similar to the traditional curriculum to which a unit in movement content has been added. (p. 2)

unit plan A series of related learning experiences organized around a common theme. (p. 48)

upfield pass In soccer or hockey, a pass on the diagonal, passed at an angle in front of a player who is closer to the goal. (p. 450)

vaulting In gymnastics, a movement in which the performer passes over a piece of equipment to land off the equipment. (p. 280)

visual pass In track events, a pass of the baton in which the receiver watches the baton into the hand. (p. 288)

APPENDIX ONE: SUGGESTED EQUIPMENT AND RECORDS

Suggested equipment for elementary school physical education

Item	Quantity (Class size 20-25)	Can be improvised
GENERAL		
Bags to carry balls	6	
Ball inflator	1	
Ball repair kit	1	
Blackboard	1	
Bulletin board	1	
Cones or jug markers	8	X
First aid kit	1	
Line marker	1	
100-foot measuring tape	1	
Pinnies, sashes, or vests (3 colors)	30	X
Record player (with speed control)	1	
Stopwatch	2	
Whistles and lanyards	3	
SMALL EQUIPMENT		
Balance boards	6	X
Beanbags	25	X
Discs (Frisbees)	8	
Duck or bowling pins	24	X
Elastic ropes		
Long	2	
Short	25	
Fleece balls	25	
Hoops	25	X
Horseshoes (rubber)	2 sets	
Jumping ropes		
Long (10 to 15 feet)	8	X
Short (6, 7, and 8 feet)	25	X
Nerf balls (small)	25	
Paddles	12	X
Rings	25	X
Scooters	6	X
Stilts	6	X
Tennis balls	25	
Wands (dowels or golf tubes)	25	
Wiffle balls	6	
Yarn balls	25	X

Suggested equipment for elementary school physical education—cont'd

Item	Quantity (Class size 20-25)	Can be improvised
DANCE/RHYTHMIC ACTIVITIES		
Dance drum	1	
Lummi sticks	25 pair	X
Records		
Rhythm instruments	12	X
Wood blocks		
Maracas		
Triangle		
Scarves, ribbons, other props		X
Tambourines	4	
Tinikling poles	12	X
LARGE APPARATUS		
All-purpose climber	1	X
Balance beam (4 inch)		
Low	1	X
Adjustable (30 to 36 inches)	1	X
Climbing ropes	2	X
Horizontal bar	1	
Horizontal ladder	1	
Mats (4 by 8 feet)	8	
Parachute	1	
Parallel bars	1	X
Uneven bars	1	
Vaulting bench or box	1	X
GAMES AND SPORTS		
Cage ball	1	
Nerfballs		
7 or 8-inch	24	
Playground balls		
5-inch	24	
7- or 8-inch	24	
Tether balls	2	
Tether ball poles	2	
Basketballs (junior)	12	
Eight foot portable baskets	4	
Goals (portable)	2	X

Continued.

Suggested equipment for elementary school
physical education—cont'd

Item	Quantity (Class size 20-25)	Can be improvised
Goalkeeper's equipment	2	
Hockey balls	12	
Hockey pucks	12	
Hockey sticks (junior or plastic)	25	
Old automobile tires	4	X
Shin guards	25	
Flags	2 sets	
Kicking tee	1	
Footballs (junior or Nerf)	12	
Soccer balls (size 4)	25	
Bases		
Indoor	2 sets	
Outdoor	2 sets	
Batting helmets	3	
Batting tee	2	

Suggested equipment for elementary school
physical education—cont'd

Item	Quantity (Class size 20-25)	Can be improvised
Chest protector	2	
Gloves	12	
Face mask	2	
Softballs (Soft)	12	
Softball bats	6	
Volleyball standards	2 sets	
Volleyball net	2	
Volleyballs		
Leather	4	
Nerf	12	
Batons	4	X
Hurdles	4	X
Shot (4 pound)	2	
High-jump standards	1 set	X
High-jump pit	1	X
Long-jump pit	1	X

SUGGESTED RECORDS
Singing Games, Folk and Square Dance

Young People's Folk Dances: Set of 7 records; single records may be purchased. A series of dances increasing in difficulty for children of all ages. Each record has its own simply worded instructions and drawings of formations and dance positions used.
Source: Educational Record Sales

World of Fun: Set of 7 records; single records may be purchased. A series of records with a variety of dances including singing games, folk and square dances appropriate for children of all ages. An instruction book is included which describes all dances, dance steps, terminology, positions and dance formations.
Source: Discipleship Resources, P.O. Box 840, Nashville, Tn 37202

Folk Dances from "Round the World": A set of five records, also sold singly. A progression of dances for children and adults with simple directions, historical information, and a dictionary of steps and positions.
Source: Educational Record Sales

Folk Dance Fun: An album of dances for children in grades K-6.
Source: Kimbo Educational

Dances in a Line: No partner, easy dances for upper elementary school children.
Source: Kimbo Educational

Everybody's Square Dances: A set of five records, which may be purchased singly. A variety of square dances varying in complexity including singing and patter calls, visiting, and other square figures. Instructions are included with each record with complete descriptions and illustrations of figures. Music includes all calls.
Source: Educational Record Sales

Get Ready to Square Dance: An album of eight movement games to teach beginning square dance patterns. An instruction booklet is included.
Source: Kimbo Educational

Rhythmic Activities

Musical Ball Skills: Use of bouncing, throwing, rolling and catching in rhythmic patterns and simple routines.
Source: Educational Activities, Inc.

Ball Gymnastics: Activities utilizing throwing, bouncing, and catching. Ask for Elementary Manual.
Source: Kimbo Educational

Lummi Sticks for Kids: Simplified lummi stick activities for preschoolers through 3rd grade.
Source: Kimbo Educational

Rhythm Stick Activities: Music, activities and instructions for rhythm sticks.
Source: Educational Activities, Inc.

Synchronized Lummi Sticks: Activities for rhythm sticks complete with illustrated manual.

Source: Educational Activities, Inc.

Clubs and Hoops: Skills and routines using hoops and clubs with instructions and illustrations of skills.
Source: Hoctor Dance Records, Inc.

Rhythmic Rope Jumping: 17 piano tunes. Ask for Elementary Manual.
Source: Kimbo Educational

Jump to the Beat: Aerobic and precision rope jumping routines for beginning and advanced jumpers.
Source: Kimbo Educational

Rope Jumping: Music of various tempos and rhythms for rope jumping. Instruction manual included.
Source: Educational Activities, Inc.

Rhythmic Parachute Play: Using parachute skills while moving to the music.
Source: Kimbo Educational

Fitness

Aerobic Dance for Kids: Aerobic exercises including activities to warm-up for activity and to cool down. Music with voice cues and music alone are included.
Source: Educational Activities, Inc.

Motor Fitness Rhythm Games: Simple activities to enhance fitness and psychomotor coordination.
Source: Educational Activities, Inc.

A Thriller for Kids: A 20-minute work-out including warm-up, stretches, jogging, and cool down activities to contemporary tunes.
Source: Kimbo Educational

Movement Activities

Hap Palmer: Getting to Know Myself: Body awareness and activities to enhance the understanding of space relationships.
Source: Kimbo Educational

Hap Palmer: The Feel of Music: Experiencing the feeling of music—joy, soft and loud, etc.
Source: Kimbo Educational

Hap Palmer: Learning Basic Skills Through Music, vol. 1: Activities to enhance body awareness and awareness of colors, numbers, and the alphabet.
Source: Kimbo Educational

Hap Palmer: Movin': Musical moods to explore and creative movement responses.
Source: Kimbo Educational

Hap Palmer: Walter The Waltzing Worm: Stretching, twisting and other nonlocomotor movements from slow to fast tempos.

Source: Kimbo Educational

Bean Bag Activities: Games, dances and other activities to develop coordination.
Source: Kimbo Educational

Individualization in Movement and Music: Action songs, dances, games, and stories to encourage individual responses.
Source: Educational Activities, Inc.

CARE AND STORAGE OF EQUIPMENT

1. All equipment should be stored according to manufacturer recommendations.
2. Equipment should be stored in a central location so all physical education teachers have easy access to equipment for their classes.
3. Storage should be organized with areas labeled for storage of particular equipment.
4. Bins, racks, and wire baskets make equipment more easily accessible than bags.
5. Children must be taught to take responsibility for the care of equipment. It should be used only for those activities for which it was manufactured. Children should be encouraged not to sit on the balls (it's very hard on the valves) nor to pull apart foam balls.
6. All equipment should be marked with waterproof markings for easy recognition as equipment belonging to the school.
7. The equipment purchased should be the best the school can afford. Buying inexpensive equipment won't save money in the long run.
8. Equipment used for recess should be stored separately from that used in the physical education classes.
9. Balls should be stored partially deflated and when in use inflated to manufacturer's specifications.
10. Ropes may be color coded by length by dipping the ends in paint or using colored tape on the ends to specify various lengths. Storing ropes by folding them and then tying them into a single knot will keep them from being tangled.
11. All equipment should be checked periodically and repairs made before use.
12. Equipment should be kept clean. Children may be recruited for periodic cleaning parties.
13. Empty large ice cream containers provide adequate storage for small items.
14. Equipment should be carefully checked in after use in class, recess, or intramurals.

APPENDIX TWO: VENDORS

EQUIPMENT, APPARATUS, AND SUPPLY VENDORS

BSN Sports
P.O. Box 7726
Dallas, TX 75209
(800) 527-7510

Balls and sports equipment, small equipment, standards, stopwatches, cones.

Flaghouse
18 W 18th St.
New York, NY 10011
(212)989-9700

Large apparatus, mats, balls, small equipment, parachutes, foam.

GSC Athletic Equipment
600 N. Pacific Ave.
San Pedro, CA 90733
(213)831-0131

Large apparatus, rhythmic gymnastics, balls, foam, playground apparatus, standards, mats.

Graves-Humphreys
1948 Franklin Road S.W.
P.O Box 13407
Roanoke, VA 24033
(800)336-5998

Balls, sports equipment, large apparatus, playground equipment, mats, parachutes.

Hammett
Physical Education Division
Hammett Place
Box 545
Braintree, MA 02184
(800)225-546

Balls, mats, foam, small equipment, sports equipment, standards, records.

North American Sports
1175 State St.
New Haven, CT 06511
(800)243-5133

Balls, mats, standards, small equipment, parachutes, stopwatches.

Passon's Sports
1017 Arch St.
Philadelphia, PA 19107
(800)523-1557

Balls, small equipment, large apparatus, mats, standards.

Shield Mfg.
425 Fillmore Ave.
Tonawanda, NY 14150
(800)828-7669

Foam and plastic equipment, goals, training hurdles.

Sportime Division
Select Service and Supply Co., Inc.
2905-E Anwiler Rd.
Atlanta, GA 30360
(800)241-9884

Balls, sports equipment, foam, small equipment, standards, mats, large apparatus.

Sidney Laner and Co.
5315 N. Lincoln Ave.
Chicago, IL 60625
(800)526-1300

Small equipment, balls, parachutes, large apparatus, mats.

Things From Bell, Inc.
4 Lincoln Ave.
P.O. Box 706
Cortland, NY 13045
(607)753-8291

Ball, foam, small equipment, parachutes, large apparatus.

U.S. Games, Inc.
Box 360874
Melbourne, FL 32936
(800)521-2832

Balls, playground equipment, parachutes, small equipment, sports equipment, standards.

Wolverine Sports
745 Circle
Box 1941
Ann Arbor, MI 48106

Balls, small equipment, large apparatus.

SOURCES FOR RECORDS

Educational Activities, Inc.
  P.O. Box 382
  Freeport, NY 11520
  (800)645-3739

Education Record Center
  472 East Paces Ferry Road
  Atlanta, GA 30305
  (404)233-5935

Educational Recordings of America
  P.O. Box 231
  Monroe, CT 06468

Educational Record Sales
  157 Chambers St.
  New York, NY 10007
  (212)276-7437

Folk Dancer Record Service
  P.O. Box 201
  Flushing Long Island, NY
  11520

Hoctor Dance Records Inc.
  159 Franklin Turnpike
  Post Office Box 38
  Waldwick, NJ 07463
  (201)652-7767

Kimbo Educational
  10 North Third Ave.
  Post Office Box 477
  Long Branch, NJ 07740
  (201)229-4949

Appendix Three: Plans For Homemade Equipment

BOUNDARY/GOAL MARKERS

Plastic jugs with handles partially filled with sand and painted or taped in bright colors make adequate boundary markers that can be easily seen and are not easily knocked or blown over.

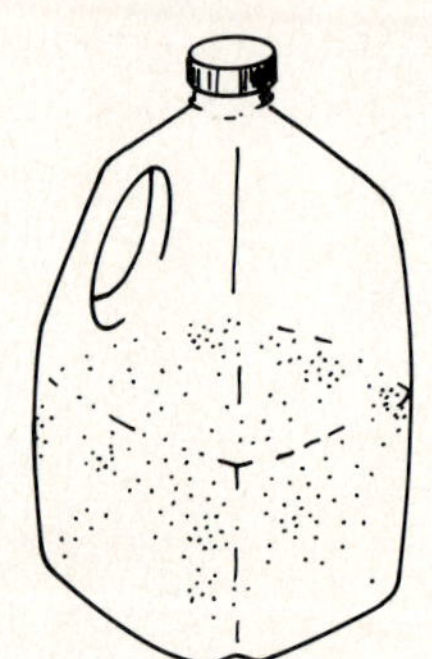

RHYTHM/LUMMI STICKS

1- to 1½-inch dowels cut into 1-foot lengths make good rhythm sticks.

Magazines (*Time* size) or newspapers rolled tightly (1-1½ inches in diameter) and secured with tape make rhythm sticks which are quieter to use.

The sticks may be painted and decorated by the children.

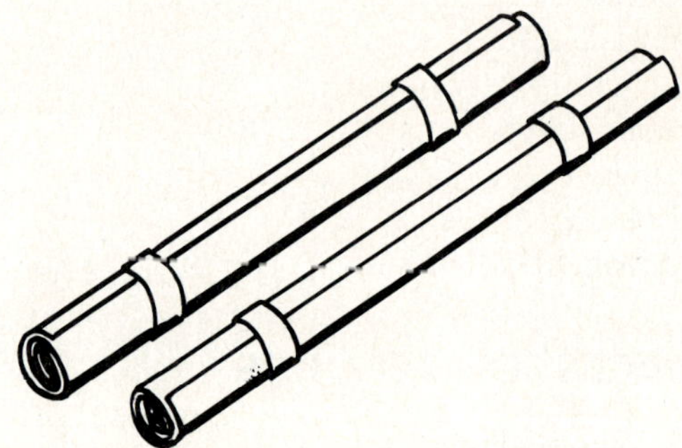

JUMP ROPES

16-pound sash cord or yacht braid (½ inch in diameter) may be cut into 10 to 15-foot lengths for long ropes, and 6, 7, and 8-foot lengths for short ropes. Lengths should be color-coded by taping the ends or dipping the ends in paint, which will also prevent fraying.

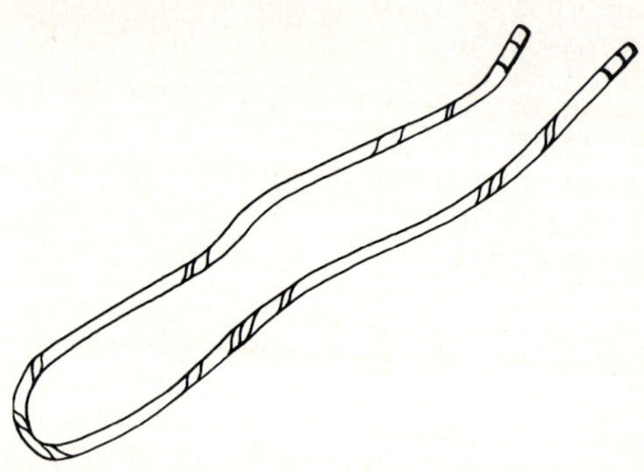

BEANBAGS

Canvas and denim make ideal covers for beanbags 5 by 6 inches in size filled with beans or corn.

YARN BALLS

Using 2 cardboard circles (5 inches in diameter) with the center cut out, wrap at least one skein of yarn as shown until the hole in the center is filled. Inserting a scissors between the two circles, carefully cut the yarn around the outer edge of the circle. Secure the yarn by wrapping a light cord between the two circles and tying it tightly. Remove the circles and trim any long ends.

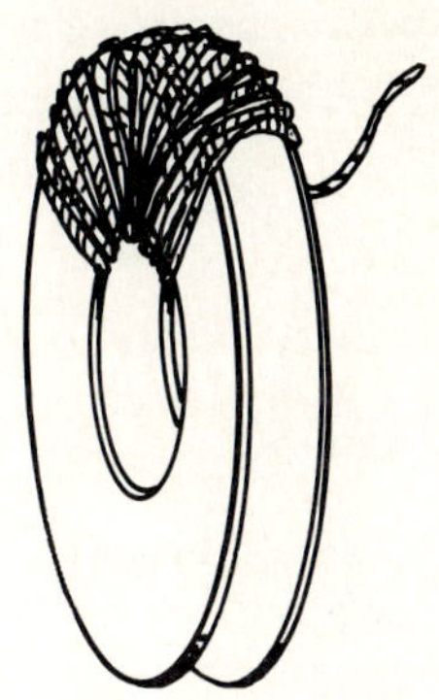

HOOPS/RINGS

Black plastic water pipe (½ inch) can be used to make hoops of varying sizes. Children may decorate the hoops to make them more pleasing in color. A piece 7 foot 10 inches in length makes a hoop approximately 30 inches in diameter. The ends are joined with plastic pipe fittings or a 3-inch piece of ½-inch dowel glued inside the two ends.

One-half inch rubber tubing such as garden hose (18 inches in length) will make a smaller ring. The ends are joined by glueing 2-inch pieces of ½-inch dowel into the two ends and covering the joint with colored tape.

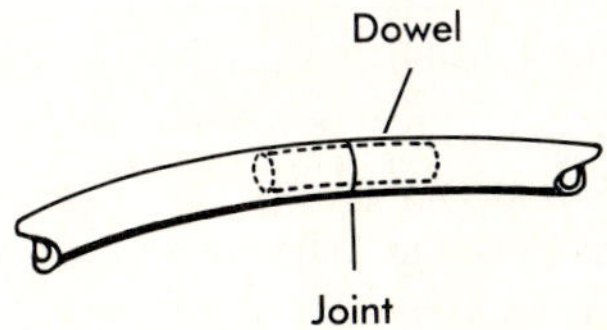

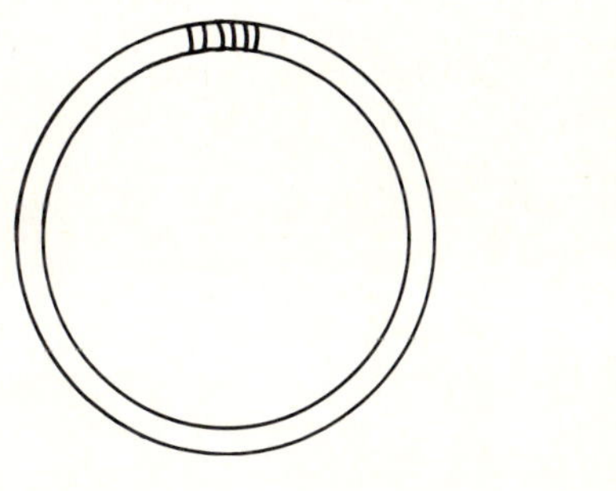

TIN CAN STILTS

Two empty tin cans (#10 preferred) may be used to make stilts. Holes are made on opposite sides of each can with a beer can opener. One end of a piece of rope approximately 60 inches in length is put through the holes and knotted on the outside to form loop which the children hold while walking on the stilts.

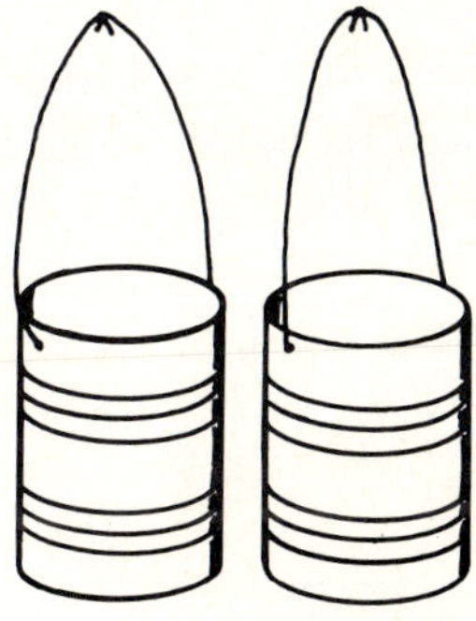

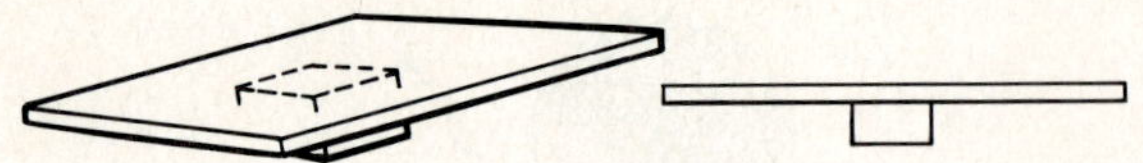

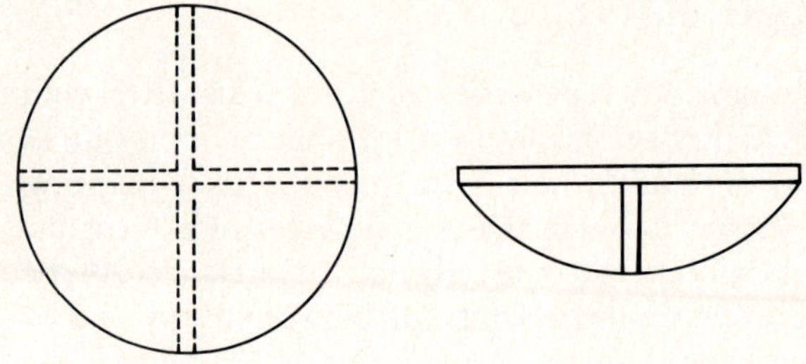

BALANCE BOARDS

Several different styles of balance boards may be made. A piece of rubber matting should be glued to the top of each to prevent slipping. The boards should be used on mats for safety.

An 18-inch square of ¾-inch plywood (**A**) may be used with several interchangeable bases 6 inches or 3 inches square and 3 inches high.

A round balance board 15 inches in diameter (**B**) with a curved base as shown may also be constructed of ¾-inch plywood.

A rectangular balance board (**C**) may be made using a piece of pole 3 inches in diameter as the base. Strips of 1 by 1 inch wood are glued to the bottom of the board close to the outside edges to prevent the roller from moving outside the board.

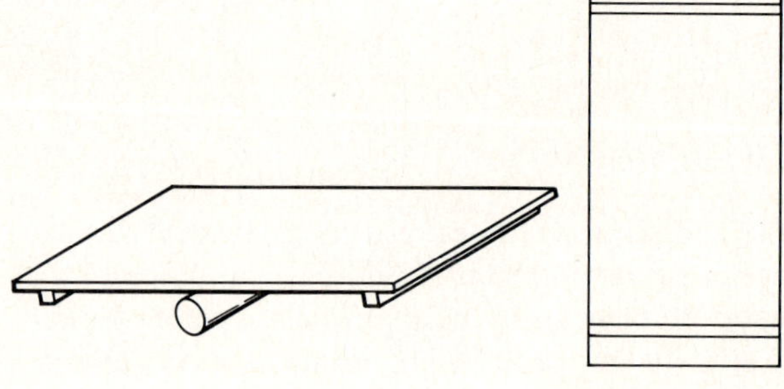

PADDLES

Paddles may be cut from ¼ to ⅜-inch plywood as shown. Each paddle requires a piece of wood 8 × 15 inches in size. The thinner paddle is easiest for young children to handle. The handle should be reinforced by glueing strips ½ inches thick along the handle which are tapered on the paddle end. A hole is drilled at the end of the handle to attach a leather thong.

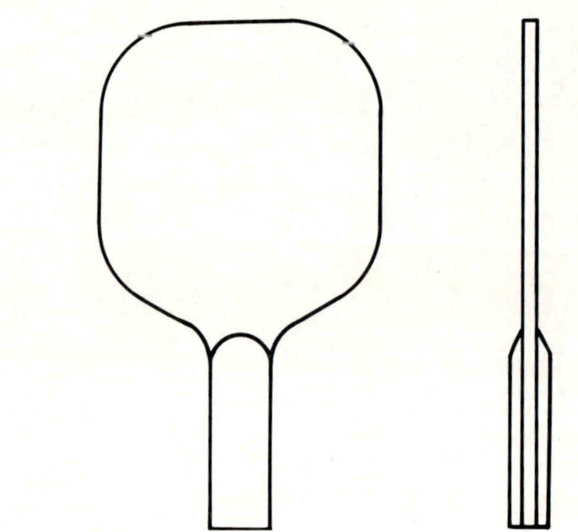

SCOOPS

Plastic jugs cut as shown make scoops for catching and throwing small balls.

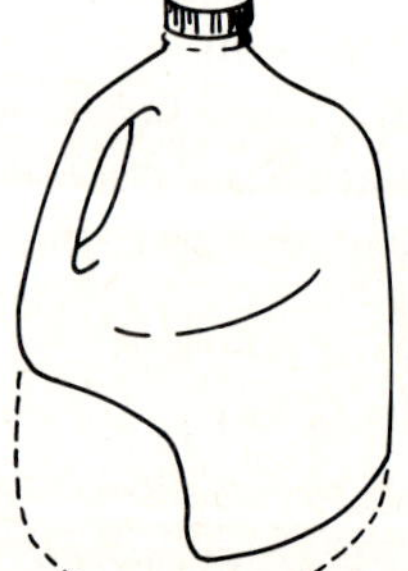

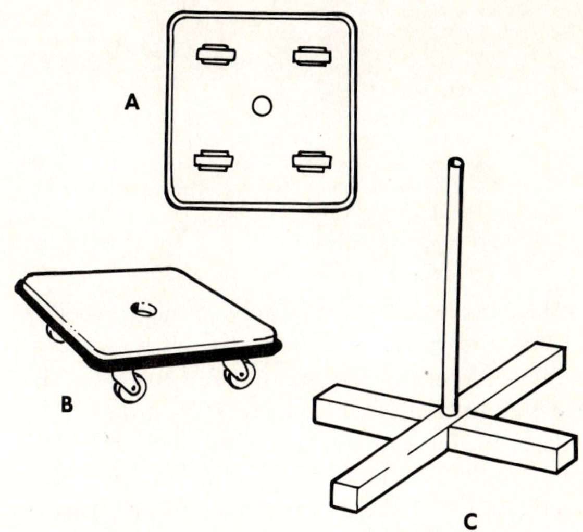

SCOOTERS

Twelve by twelve inch scooters may be made of 1-inch plywood or thicker wood. The edges should be rounded and a rubber strip glued around the edges. Four heavy duty casters (**B**) are screwed to the bottom edges. With a hole drilled in the center they may be stored on a dowel stand (**C**).

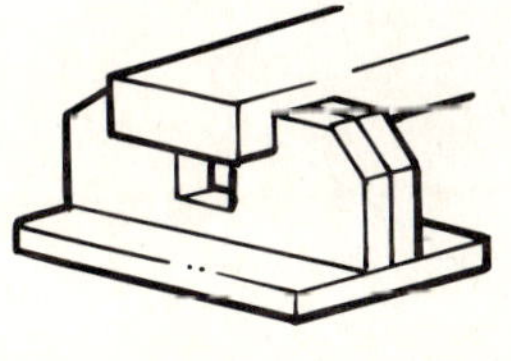

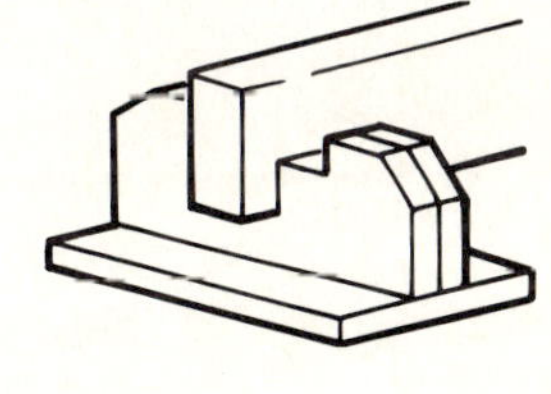

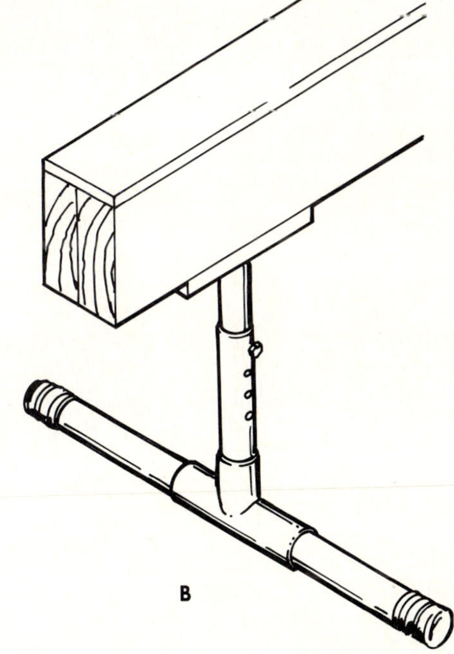

BALANCE BEAM

A low balance beam (**A**) may be made with a hardwood 2 × 4 10 to 12 feet long supported on a base as illustrated either as a 2- or 4-inch beam. The base may be made of 3 pieces of 1-inch plywood glued together as shown.

An adjustable high beam (**B**) may be made using two 2 × 6's 12 to 14 feet long glued together with a 1 × 4 piece of hardwood glued to the top and supported as in the diagram on galvanized pipe. Holes are drilled through each section of the base through which bolts are fastened to regulate the height of the beam. The ends of the base should be taped to prevent scratching the floor.

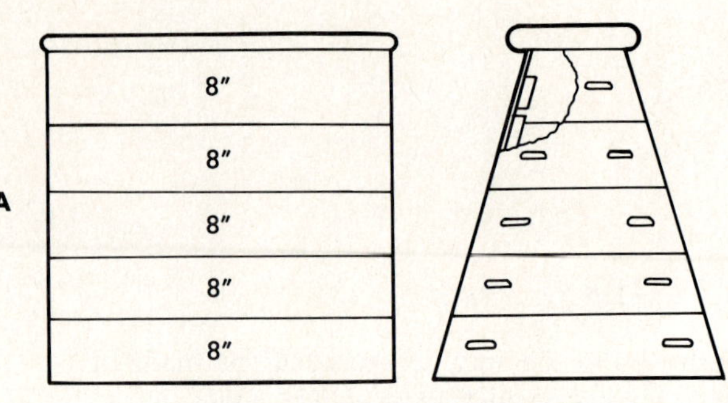

VAULTING BOX

A padded box with 8-inch sections to vary the height as shown provides for children of all sizes. Constructed of ¾-inch plywood, holes in the sides (**B**) make each section easily handled. The top should be padded with foam or sponge rubber with a vinyl or denim cover. Two-by-two's are used on the inside corners and at the center to secure the sections as shown (**C**).

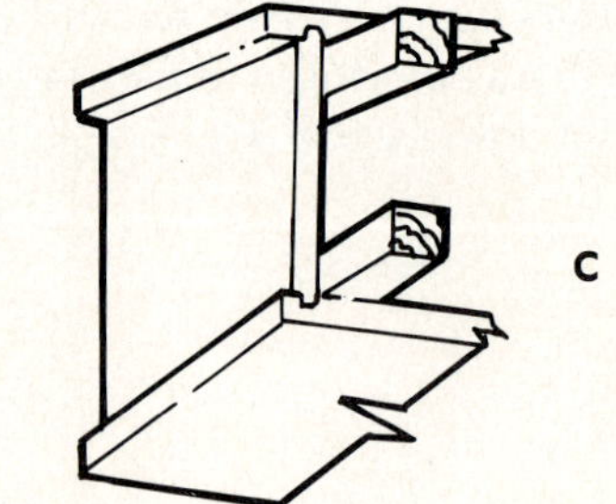

BEAT BOARD

A board to use in vaulting, mounting equipment, or for jumping activities may be made of ¾-inch plywood supported on one end with a 2 x 4 and a 1 x 1 on the other.

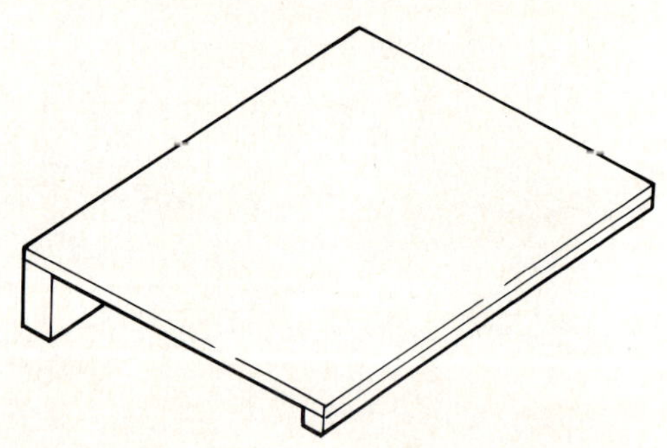

PARALLEL BARS

Parallel bars 4 feet in height may be made of pipe as shown. Adjustments in width between the bars may be made by turning the base, moving one bar slightly forward of the other.

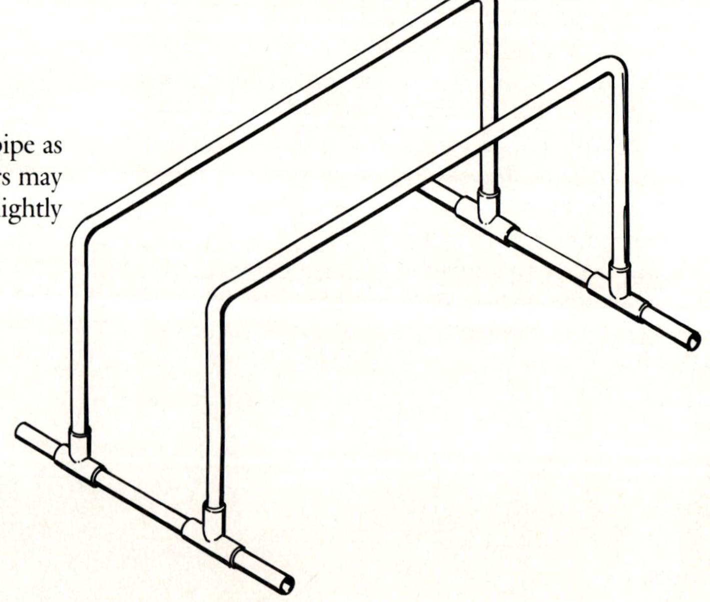

HURDLES

Hurdles constructed of 1-inch plastic pipe with Velcro tear-away cross bars take away the fear of hitting the hurdles. The cross bars should be made of webbing to which Velcro is attached. The height of the hurdles may be easily adjusted for children varying in size and ability.

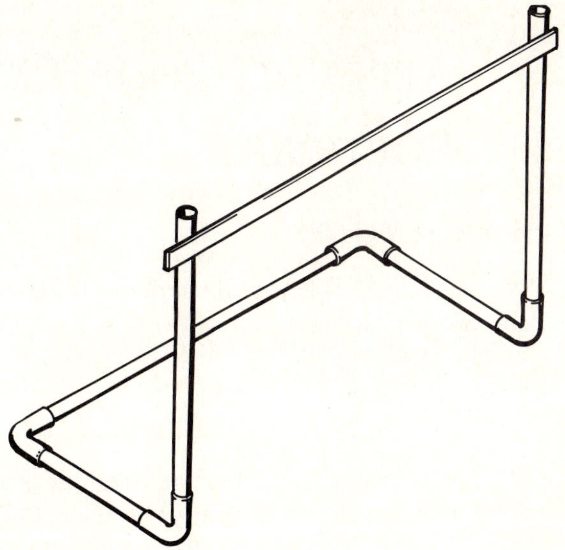

JUMPING PITS

A large net bag filled with foam pieces provides a safe landing surface for the high jump. Several smaller bags laced together may be used to allow for easier storage in the off-season.

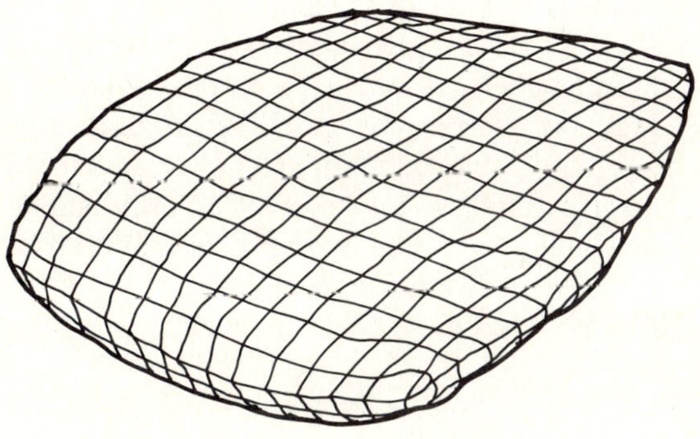

APPENDIX FOUR: COMPUTER SOFTWARE

PHYSICAL FITNESS

Personal Body Profile: Determine desirable weight and calorie intake from entry input of age, height, weight, skinfold measures and activity level.
Grade 6
Apple (48K) and IBM with Quadlink
CompTech Systems Design

AAHPERD Youth Fitness: Data base management system for administration, management, and analysis of youth fitness test. Several reporting options are available.
Grades 5 and 6
Apple (48K)
CompTech Systems Design

AAPHERD II: Program allows school to enter own norms rather than use 1976 AAHPERD norms. Has some features as AAHPERD youth fitness program above. In addition, student data may be compared to both local and 1976 norms and documentation with step-by-step instructions on how to enter predetermined data tables.
Grades 5 and 6
Apple (48K)
CompTech Systems Design

Health Fitness Profile for Children: Reports raw scores and national norms for AAHPERD Health Related Fitness Test with a graphic presentation of individual fitness profiles.
Grades 1 through 6
Apple II
AAHPERD

Computer Applications of Health Related Physical Fitness Test: Class records management, including viewing, storing, and printing data, locating individual records, determining norms, and producing individual fitness profiles.
Grades 1 through 6
Apple II
AAHPERD

Analysis Health-Related Physical Fitness Test Scores: Displays or prints data for up to 100 students per class, computes percentile norms and class averages, compares pre and post test results and produces individual report cards.

Grades 1 through 6
Apple II
AAHPERD

AAHPERD Youth Fitness Data Base Information Processor: A management system for youth fitness scores of up to 900 students for a period of up to 6 years. Provides percentile norms for student test results and includes fall and spring 3-year reports for individuals and class, and class and individual averages.
GRADES 5 AND 6
Apple IIe
Networkers

Parkway School District Wellness Profile of Children: Data base management of AAHPERD health-related fitness scores for up to 960 students over a 6-year period. Can produce fall and spring 3-year reports, and compare scores to national and district norms.
Grades 1 through 6
Apple IIe
Parkway School District

Aerobics: Program allows user to design own exercise program using a variety of exercises and routines. Joystick, Koala Pad or Paddles necessary to operate this program.
Grade 6
APPE (48K), Atari, Commodore 64
CompTech Systems Design

The Heart: A Mighty Pump: Allows child to follow a red blood cell through the heart and circulatory system. Good prerequisite for Heart and Exercise.
Grades 1 through 6
Apple (48K)
CompTech Systems Design

Heart and Exercise: Four programs to teach children the heart; role of veins and arteries and effects of exercise; where to find the pulse, and how to take it; and how the heart is affected by participation in various sport activities. Includes a teacher utility program to generate tests and worksheets.
Grades 6
Apple (48K)
CompTech Systems Design

PHYSICAL EDUCATION ACTIVITIES

Sports Terminology Series: Program for learning and reinforcing sport vocabulary and definitions. Uses Word Find, Word Game, Spell and Mix-Up developed by Minnesota Education Computing Consortium. The series may be purchased as a set or as individual disks. Included are: Individual/dual/team sport; Aquatic sports; Swimming and rescue; and Winter sports.
Grades 4 through 6
AppleII/IIe/IIc
CompTech Systems Design

MOVEMENT

Right of Way: Introduces and reinforces spatial relationships. Rango the monkey shows children how to know right and left. Activities allow children to use right/left concept in steering cars.
Grades K through 4
Apple (48K)
CompTech Systems Design

MISCELLANEOUS

Round Robin Scheduling: Prints complete schedule of teams, dates and time of game, schedule of facilities, etc.
Apple II (64K)
Good Deal Software
Physical Education Record Keeper: Program to keep records of student progress. Includes biographic and class data, tests and objectives, test scores, indication of objectives still to be met, target goal for each objective, and activity prescription to meet goals not yet attained.
Apple IIe-c
Dr. Dick Hurwitz

ADDRESSES OF SOURCES

AAHPERD, 1900 Association Drive, Reston, VA 22091, (703)476-3481
CompTech Systems Design, P.O. Box 516, Hastings, MN 55033, (612)437-1350
Dr. Dick Hurwitz, Cleveland State University, Cleveland, OH 44115, (216)687-4878
Good Deal Software, 1721 Skyline Dr., Wenatohee, WA 98801, (509)663-7827
Networkers, 7542 Oxford, Clayton, MO 63015, (314)724-7868
Parkway School District, 455 N. Woods Mill Rd., Chesterfield, MO 63017, (314)851-8100

APPENDIX FIVE: SCREENING DEVICES, SOURCES, AND IEP FORMS

AAHPERD Health Related Physical Fitness Test:
See Chapter 13.

Bruininks-Oseretsky Motor Development Scale:
Battery of 8 tests to measure gross and fine motor skills including running, speed and agility, balance, bilateral coordination, strength, upper limb co-ordination, visual-motor response speed, and upper limb speed and dexterity. The complete battery or a short form may be used. Scoring is pass/fail. The score is a composite of all items or a single score if the short form is used.
Source: American Guidance Services, Circle Pines, MN 55014

Denver Developmental Screening Test:
Contains 105 tasks to identify developmental delays in children age zero to 6 in fine motor, gross motor, social, and language skills. The test is administered individually and scored pass/fail, refusal, or no opportunity to respond. Norms indicate the age level when 10, 25, 50, 75, and 90 percent of the children can perform the task.
Source: Frankenberg, W., Dodds, J. & Fandel, A.: Denver Developmental Screening Test manual/workbook for nursing and paramedical personnel, Denver, Colorado, University of Colorado Medical Center.

I CAN:
Developed as a program of physical education for the handicapped. The screening tests may be used to determine specific difficulties in technique in a variety of body management, fitness, social, fundamental, and sports skills.
Source: Michigan State University, Lansing, Michigan.

Hyde Motor Development Checklist:
See attached form.
Source: Hyde, B.: A motor development checklist of selected categories for kindergarten children, Unpublished thesis, University of Kansas, 1980.

I Can Physical Education IEP Form

School District/School ____Central-Westside School____

Student Name or Number ______Katie - #B123______

Recommended Total Time
in Physical Education __3__ Days/Week __30__ Minutes/Day

Current Placement _Special Physical Education - TMI_

Date Submitted ______9/20/77______

Date of Planning Meeting______9/1/77______

Date(s) of Review ______(Listed when scheduled)______

Teachers______Ronald Kowalski______

	Program goal areas in physical education	Present level(s) of performance	Annual student goals	Short term objectives	Time required (min/day)	Duration dates Begin	End	Regular education placement	Special designed instruction	Support personnel needed (see back)	Goal attained (date)
Area 1	Body manage-ment	Body planes-2.a,c	3. a,b,c	2.b/3.a,b,c	10	9/20	10/20	✓			
		Forward roll-1.c	3. a,b	1.a,b/2.a,b,c/3.a,b	20	1/4	1/18		✓	✓	
Area 2	Fundamental skills	Gallop-primary	2.	1./2.	10	9/20	11/4		✓		
		Kick-2.a	3. a,b,c	2.b/3.a,b,c	15	4/15	5/15	✓	✓	✓	
		Overhand throw-primary	3. a,b,c	1.a,b/2.a,b/3.a,b,c	15	3/15	4/15				
Area 3	Fitness	Heart/lung endurance-primary	3.	1./2./3.	2	9/20	6/15		✓	✓	
Area 4	Sport/Leisure	Dribbling-primary	2. a,b	1.a,b,c/2.a,b	15	1/18	2/18		✓		
		Batting-2.a,b	3. c,d	3.a,b,c,d	15	5/15	6/15	✓			
Area 5	Social skills	Take turns-2.c,d	3. a,b	3.a,b	5	9/20	6/15	✓			

From I CAN Physical Education, Janet A. Wessel, Director. Copyright © 1976, Michigan State University.
Reprinted with permission of publisher, Hubbard Scientific Co., Northbrook, IL.

Continued.

Short Term Instructional Objectives	Personnel Responsible Including Related Support Personnel Needed (name and title)	Date Services Begin	Date Services End
Forward roll	Physical Therapist	10/5	To be determined at review meeting
Overhand throw	Occupational Therapist	1/4	3/15
Heart/lung endurance	Physical Therapist Regular Physical Education-- Intramurals	9/20	6/15

____
Date of parental acceptance/rejection

____
Signature

DETROIT PUBLIC SCHOOLS
Individualized Educational Program
Phase II
Local School Planning and Implementation

DATE:_______________________________________

TO BE COMPLETED: • Determination of Educational Goals/Instructional Objectives/School Services
• Referrals for Related Services, as Appropriate
• Educational Provisions in the Least Restrictive Environment
• Program Monitoring and Review Provisions

I. Pupil Information

Name _________________________ Birthdate__________

Student Height ____________________ Weight__________

D.P.S. Student Membership Number ________________

Parent/Guardian/Parent Surrogate _______________

Address, Zip Code _______________________________

Telephone (Home) ________________ (Work)__________

School____

Grade/Program_________________________________

II. Phase II IEP Implementation Team

Position	Name	Signature
Chairperson		
Parent/Guardian		
Parent Surrogate		
Instructional		
Administration		
Student (as Appropriate)		
Other		
Other		

Program Monitoring and Review Provisions					Annual Program Review Meeting (see attached rec.)
	Date	Date	Date	Date	Date:________________
Local School Administrator					**Review Team Member:**
Special Education Supervisor					Name Position
Parent					
General Education Teacher					
Other					

Used with permission of Detroit Public Schools.

Continued.

III.	Referral Recommendations for Related Services Referral for Evaluation only					To Be Completed by Person Responsible for Delivering Requested Service		
√	Requested Program or Service	Projected Duration of Service From / To		Person Responsible for Initiating Referral	Date Referral Initiated	Date Service Initiated	Person Responsible for Delivering Service	Comments
	Speech Pathology							
	Bilingual Instruction							
	Occ./Phys. Therapy							
	Audiology							
	School Social Work							
	School Psychology							
	Vocational							
	Diagnostic/Remedial/ Tutorial Services Available In Region or Local School Type of Service Requested							
	Other:							

IV.	As required in P.L. 94-142 statutes, handicapped children must be provided with a physical education program. John Smith, Adaptive Physical Education Specialist, Special Education Department is available to provide supportive assistance to local school personnel in developing, modifying, adapting or improving physical education programs to meet the needs of handicapped students. Mr. Smith may be reached at 555-5555.

√	Physical Education Program	Projected Duration of Service From / To		Person Responsible for Physical Education Program	Comments
	Regular Physical Education Program				
	• Selected Activities in Physical Education Program				
	• Self Contained Physical Education Program				
	• Supportive reports and documentation must be available to support the decision for the selected physical education program option.				

MOTOR DEVELOPMENT CHECKLIST

Name _________________________   Examiner _________________________

Birthdate __________ Sex ______   Date _________________________

Category   Special Notes and Remarks

Category			
Static balance	__does not attempt tasks	__heel-toe stand, 5 secs balance on preferred foot, arms hung relaxed at sides __ __ __ __ __5 secs	__heel-toe stand, eyes closed, 5 secs balance on preferred foot, arms hung relaxed at sides, eyes closed __ __ __ __ __10 secs __5 secs __ __ __ __ __10 secs
Hopping reflex	__no response __no righting of head, __trunk no step in direction of push __right __left __forward __backward	__head and body right themselves __step or hop in direction of push, __right __left __forward __backward	
Running pattern	__loses balance __almost __twists trunk __leans excessively __jerky, uneven rhythm	__elbows away from body in arm swing __limited arm swing __short strides	__full arm swing in opposition with legs __elbows near body in swing __even flow and rhythm
Jumping pattern	__loses balance on landing __no use of arms __twists or bends sideways	__arms at side for balance __legs bent throughout jump	__arms back as legs bend __arms swing up as legs extend __lands softly with control
Throwing pattern	__pushing or shoving object __loss of balance __almost	__body shifts weight from back to front without stepping	__steps forward with same foot as throwing arm __steps forward with foot opposite throwing arm
Catching pattern	__loses balance __almost __shies away __traps or scoops	__arms stiff in front of body	__arms bent at sides of body __arms "give" as catch __uses hands
Kicking pattern	__misses __off center	__arms at sides or out to sides __uses from knee down to kick	__kicks "through" ball __arm opposition __uses full leg to kick __can kick with either foot

Courtesy Beverly Hyde.

APPENDIX SIX: VIDEO MATERIALS FOR PHYSICAL EDUCATION/HEALTH

SUGGESTED VIDEOS FOR CHILDREN IN GRADES K THROUGH 3

A Visit To The Doctor: To help allay fears, this program takes students through a physician's office and a typical physical examination. It shows actual surroundings and the instruments used and people involved.
VS-446 Videocassette, guide $59.00
Source: Educational Activities, Inc.

Bearobics: An imaginative and fun game and exercise program based on the music of the BeeGees.
7 SQ 5007V VHS ½-inch Videocassette $16.00
Source: Education Record Center

Drugs, Poisons, and Little Children: Introduces children to place of medicine and drugs in their lives. This program emphasizes that drugs make children sick if they mistake them for candy and poisons lurk in many places and containers.
VS-418 Videocassette, Guide $49.00
Source: Educational Activities, Inc.

Eye and Ear Care: Two whimsical and exciting stories impress young people with the importance of proper care of their eyes and ears. Each story can be shown separately. "Princess Ocula" (eyes) runs 16 min and "Gullible Jeb" (ears) runs 15 min.
VS-445 Videocassette (31 min), Guide $69.00
Source: Educational Activities, Inc.

Nutrition For Little Children: Helps students develop positive attitudes toward food, accept a variety of foods, and understand the difference between nutritious foods and "junk" foods.
VS-436 Videocassette, Guide $49.00
Source: Educational Activities, Inc.

SUGGESTED VIDEOS FOR CHILDREN IN GRADES 6 AND ABOVE

Enemies of the Body I: Helps demystify cancer, hypertension, heart attack, and diabetes by explaining the known causes and giving recommendations for prevention and treatment.
VS-487 Videocassette (49 min) $99.00
Source: Educational Activities, Inc.

Enemies of the Body II: This fascinating history of communicable diseases takes students from ancient times to the present; this program provides an in-depth study of each disease-causing organism and includes prevention and treatment.
VS-224 Videocassette (53 min) $99.00
Source: Educational Activities, Inc.

SOURCES FOR VIDEOS

Educational Activities, Inc.
P.O. Box 392
Freeport, NY 11520
(800) 645-3739

Education Record Center
472 East Paces Ferry Road
Atlanta, GA 30305
(404) 233-5935

APPENDIX SEVEN: INDOOR CLASSROOM ACTIVITIES

All too often teachers find they are forced to hold their physical education classes in the regular classroom. This is necessitated because of the size of the school, inclement weather, or a variety of other reasons. Many of the activities described in this book can be performed in the classroom under close supervision. Listed below are activities recommended and the page references.

DANCE ACTIVITIES
American and International Folk Dance

Creative Dance

Rhythmic Activities

Singing Games

INDEX

DANCE ACTIVITIES

American and International Folk Dance

Creative Dance

Dance Figures

Dance Steps

Rhythmic Activities

GAME ACTIVITIES

INDIVIDUAL ACTIVITIES

CREDITS AND ACKNOWLEDGMENTS

Chapter 1 Physical Education in the Elementary School
p. 3   From the Superintendent's Office, South Burlington, Vermont, School District.

Chapter 2 The Elementary School Child
pp. 12-13   Courtesy Ross Laboratories. Adapted from Hamill, P.V.V., Drizd, T.A., Johnson, C.L., Reed, R.B., Roche, A.F., and Moore, W.M.: Physical Growth: National Center for Health Statistics percentiles. Am. J. Clin. Nutr. **32:**607-629, 1979. Data from the National Center for Health Statistics (NCHS) Hyattsville, Maryland. p. 15 Used with permission from Tuddenham, R., and Snyder, M.: Physical growth of California boys and girls from birth to eighteen, Berkeley, 1954, University of California Press.

Chapter 3 The Elementary School Physical Education Program
p. 27   From Logsden, B., and others: Physical education for children: a focus on the teaching process, Philadelphia, 1984, Lea & Febiger. p. 33 From Jewett, A., and Mullan, M.: Curriculum design: purposes and processes in physical education teaching-learning, Washington, D.C., 1977, AAHPER. Reprinted by permission of the American Alliance for Health, Physical Education, Recreation, and Dance, 1900 Association Drive, Reston, Virginia, 22091. pp. 34 & 35 From Singer, R., and Dick, W.: Teaching physical education, ed. 2, Boston, 1980, Houghton Mifflin Co.

Chapter 7 Safety, Organizational Strategies, and Classroom Management
p. 89   From Cooper, J., and others: Classroom teaching skills: a handbook, ed. 2, Lexington, Mass., 1982, D.C. Heath & Co.: Adapted from Classroom management: theory and skill training, Lois Johnson and Mary Bany, New York, 1970, MacMillan Publishing Co., Inc.

Chapter 10 Understanding Human Movement
pp. 136, 137   From Broer, M., and Zernicke, R.: Efficiency of human movement, ed. 4, New York, 1973, Holt, Rinehart, & Winston.

Chapter 13 Fitness and Movement Efficiency
p. 180   From the Greatest College Football Marches, VSD 29/30, Vanguard Record Society, Inc. 171 West 23rd St. New York, N.Y. 10010. p. 184, 185, 186, 187, 191, & 192 AAHPERD: Health-related physical fitness test manual, Reston, Va., 1980, AAHPERD. Reprinted by permission of the American Alliance for Health, Physical Education, Recreation, and Dance, 1900 Association Drive, Reston, Virginia, 22091. p. 186 From Seltzer, C., and Mayer, J.: A simple criterion of obesity, Postgraduate Medicine **38:**101A, 1965. p. 188, 196, & 197 Adapted from Kendall, H., and others: Posture and pain, Huntington, N.Y., 1975, Robert E. Krieger Publishing Co., Inc. p. 194 Hunsicker, P., and Reiff, G.: AAHPERD youth fitness test manual, rev. ed., Reston, Va., 1976, AAHPERD. Reprinted by permission of the American Alliance for Health, Physical Education, Recreation,

and Dance, 1900 Association Drive, Reston, Virginia, 22091. p. 195 Ross, J., and others: New standards for fitness measurement, JOPERD **56**(1):62, January 1985. Reprinted by permission of the American Alliance for Health, Physical Education, Recreation, and Dance, 1900 Association Drive, Reston, Virginia, 22091.

Chapter 16 Track and Field
pp. 286, 290   From AAHPERD youth fitness test manual, rev. ed., Reston, Va., 1976, AAHPERD. Reprinted by permission of the American Alliance for Health, Physical Education, Recreation, and Dance, 1900 Association Drive, Reston, Virginia, 22091. p. 294 From AAHPER youth fitness test manual, 1965, Washington, D.C., AAHPER. Reprinted by permission of the American Alliance for Health, Physical Education, Recreation, and Dance, 1900 Association Drive, Reston, Virginia, 22091.

Chapter 29 School Activities and Youth Sports
p. 545   From Martens, R., and Seefeldt, V., editors: Guidelines for children's sports, Reston, Va., 1979, AAHPERD. Reprinted by permission of the American Alliance for Health, Physical Education, Recreation, and Dance, 1900 Association Drive, Reston, Virginia, 22091.

Appendixes
pp. A15-A16   From I CAN Physical Education, Janet A. Wessel, Director, copyright 1976 Michigan State University. Reprinted with permission of publisher, Hubbard Scientific Publishing Co., Northbrook, Illinois. pp. A17-A18 Used with permission from Detroit Public Schools. p. A19 Courtesy Beverly Hyde.